Infantrymen of the Air

An Operational History of the Royal Italian Airborne Forces in the Second World War, 1936-1943

Jeffrey W.S. Leser

Helion & Company

Helion & Company Limited
Unit 8 Amherst Business Centre
Budbrooke Road
Warwick
CV34 5WE
England
Tel. 01926 499 619
Email: info@helion.co.uk
Website: www.helion.co.uk
Twitter: @helionbooks
Visit our blog at blog.helion.co.uk

Published by Helion & Company 2023
Designed and typeset by Mach 3 Solutions (www.mach3solutions.co.uk)
Cover designed by Paul Hewitt, Battlefield Design (www.battlefield-design.co.uk)

ISBN 978-1-915113-70-2

British Library Cataloguing-in-Publication Data.
A catalogue record for this book is available from the British Library.

For details of other military history titles published by Helion & Company Limited contact the above address or visit our website: http://www.helion.co.uk.

We always welcome receipt of book proposals from prospective authors.

Contents

List of Images

List of Armoury and Uniforms Images

List of Colour Maps

Acknowledgements

I would like to gratefully acknowledge the following individuals who assisted in making this book a reality: Andreas Biermann (The Crusader Project website, research materials from KEW), Massimo Di Martino (*Paracadutisti d'Italia 1938–1969* and rare manuals), Professor John Gooch (his own research materials), Guido Abate (many Italian books), Slawomir Walencykowski (research materials from NARA), and the Military and Civilian Staff at the *Ufficio Storico dello Stato Maggiore dell'Esercito* (ten. col. Emilio Tirone, magg. Emanuele Di Muro, CMCS Claudio Piddini, CMCS Marro Presta, and especially Dottore Alessandro Gionfrida). The members of both the Comando Supremo and WW2 Talk websites generously assisted with many files and documents from their personal research.

I must especially acknowledge the assistance of two individuals that were critical to the completion of this book: Maurizio Bragaglia who helped shepherd this book from the very beginning and caught my egregious assaults against the Italian language, and my brother Steve Smith who did the same for my English and drew all the wonderful maps for the book.

This book could never have been written without the loving support of my spouse Marje, who encouraged me to research and write, and who closed her eyes so my office could be as messy as I needed it to be for my writing.

Abbreviations & Translations

A.A.r.n. – Arma Aeronautica ruolo naviganti – Air Force navigator speciality
A.C.I.T – Armata Corazzato Italo-tedesca – Italian-German Armoured Army
abiar – well, cistern
alam – cairn, rock
Arditi – Italian assault troops
Armata – army
art. – artiglieria – artillery
A.S. – Africa settentrionale = North Africa
Ascari – the native born Berber or Arab soldiers that served in the Libyan colonial army units
autoportato – truck transported
autotrasportabile – semi-motorized unit
aviotrasportata – air transport, air landing
Bers. – Bersaglieri – Italian motorized light infantry units
Bir – water well, cistern
brg. – brigata – brigade
btg. – battaglione – battalion
btr. – batteria – artillery battery
c.a. – controaerei – anti-aircraft
Cantonina, Cantoniera – road inspector/control house
Carabinieri – military police – gendarmerie
carri/carristi – tank/tankers
c.c. – controcarro – anti-tank
CC.NN. – Camicie Nere – "Blackshirts" – Paramilitary units of the Italian Fascist Party – See M.V.S.N. below
CC.RR – Reale Carabinieri – Royal Carabinieri
Cd'A – corpo d'armata – army corps
C.S. FF.AA. A.S. – Comando Superiore Forze Armata Africa settentrionale – High command Armed Forces North Africa
Comando Supremo – Wartime name for the Italian Military General Staff. See STAMAGE
cp. – compagnia
Det. – Detachment
Deir – Depression

d. at. – divisione autotrasportabile – semi-motorized division
d. aviot. – divisione aviotrasportabile – air landing divisions
d. cor. – divisione corazzata – armoured division
d. f. – divisione fanteria – infantry division
d. para. – divisone *paracadutisti* – parachute division
eluet – hill
fatt. – fattoria – farm
Gebel – mountains/mountain chain
guastatori – assault engineers
Heer – German Army
Hus. – Hussars – British armoured unit
K.D.G. – Kings Dragoon Guards (British)
K.R.R.C. – Kings Royal Rifle Corp (British)
ministerio – ministry
moto. – motorizzata – motorized
motociclisti – motrociclists
motomitraglieri – motorcycle machine gun unit
M.V.S.N. – Milizia Volontaria per la Sicurezza Nazionale – Voluntary Militia for National Security – "Blackshirts"
Naqb – pass or cutting
nucl. nucleo – detachment
pista – track, trail
pl. – plotone – platoon
qarat – low Hill
quota – hill, height (Italian)
R.A. – Regia Aeronautica = Royal Air Force (Italian)
RAF – Royal Air Force (British)
R.C.T.C. – Royal Corps of Colonial Troops
R.D.L. – Regio Decreto Legge – Royal Legislative Decree
R.H.A. – Royal Horse Artillery (British)
R.E. – Regio Esercito – Italian Army
R.M. – Regina Marina – Royal Navy (Italian)
reparto/reparti – unit/units
RN – Royal Navy (British)
RTR – Royal Tank Regiment (British)
ragg. – raggruppamento – regimental ad hoc formation – kampfgruppe
rgt. – reggimento – regiment
Rid. – Ridotta – Redoubt
sahel – region
sem. – semoventi – self-propelled artillery
Settore – sector/area
Sidi – tomb
Siret – ruins
S.M.G. – Stato Maggiore Generale – Italian Military General Staff (Joint)
S.M.R.A. – Stato Maggiore Regia Aeronautica – Italian Air Force General Staff

S.M.R.E. – Stato Maggiore Regio Esercito – Italian Army General Staff
S.M.R.M. – Stato Maggiore Regina Marina – Italian Navy General Staff
STAMAGE – Comando Supremo until April 1941
Superalba – Comando Superiore Forze Armata Albania – High Command Armed Forces in Albania
Superaereo – Wartime name for the Italian Air Force High Command. See S.M.R.A.
Supercomando – Comando Supremo after April 1941
Superesercito – Wartime name for the Italian Army High Command. See S.M.R.E.
Superlibia – Wartime name for the High Command Armed Forces in Libya
Supermarina – Wartime name for the Italian Navy High Command. See S.M.R.M.
sz. – sezione – section
sotosettore – subsector
sq. – squadra – squad
tattico – tactical
Uff. S.P.E. – Ufficiali servizio permanente effettivo – career officers
Uff. di compl. – Ufficiali di complemento – reserve officers
Wadi – Valley, ravine or drainage channel, usually dry for most of the year.

Ranks (Italian – UK/USA – German)

Soldato – soldier/private – schutze
Soldato scelto – senior private/private 1st Class – oberschutze
Caporale – corporal (not an NCO rank in the Italian Military) – Gefreiter
Caporale maggiore – obergefreiter
Sergente – sergeant – unteroffizer
Sergente maggiore – senior sergeant – Oberfeldwebel
Maresciallo ordinario – Lowest senior NCO normally in technical specialities
Maresciallo capo – Middle-grade senior NCO normally in technical specialities
Maresciallo maggiore – Highest senior NCO normally in technical specialities
Aiutante di battaglia – Senior NCO rank awarded solely through war merits
Aspirante d'ufficale – officer cadet
Sottotenente – 2nd lieutenant – leutnant
Tenente – lieutenant – oberleutant
Primo tenente – senior lieutenant – na
Capitano – captain – hauptmann
Primo capitano – senior captain – na
Maggiore – major – major
Tenente colonnello – lieutenant colonel – oberstleutnant
Colonnello – colonel – oberst
Generale di brigata – brigadier/brigadier general – generalmajor
Generale di divisione – major general – generalleutnant
Generale di corpo d'armata – lieutenant general – general
Generale d'Armata – general – generaloberst
Maresciallo d'Italia – field marshal/general of the armies – generalfeldmarchal

Preface

My interest in the Italian military during the *Seconda Guerra Mondiale* (Second World War) started many years ago out of curiosity. When reading about the battles in *Africa Settentrionale* (North Africa), one often came away with the understanding that the battles were mainly between the United Kingdom (UK) and Commonwealth (CW) against the Germans with a large number of Italians somewhere in the background. The portrayal of the Italian participation during that fighting was usually brief and dismissive, with negative stereotypes substituting for serious research. Many reader's are more likely to recall the apocryphal Churchill story with the future German Foreign Minister Ribbentrop at a dinner party to illustrate their understanding of Italy's role in the war than having read any books addressing how the Italian war machine had been shaped in the years before the war.[1] It was the lack of detailed English-language discussions of the Italian participation the war that fueled my research into the Italian military.

This was clearly not the reality of the fighting in North Africa, yet few English readers have access to accounts that detail the Italian involvement in that theater of the war. Not surprisingly, I had to delve into Italian accounts and research to seek what I was looking for. What I discovered was a complex reality that combined original thinking, budgetary constraints, entrenched conservative viewpoints, political maneuvering, personal grudges, etc. that were present in every military that fought during the war. Fascist Italy struggled with the same issues of predicting what future war would require as did all nations and how best to prepare their military to successfully meet its challenges. For various reasons Italy was unable to effectively prepare for the coming war, and then again failed to successfully adapt to the reality that had presented itself. Much of this narrative is beginning to be offered in English language accounts but that information remains unconnected to the presentation of the battles and campaigns as an integral part of those narratives. Of interest is that I found that Italian accounts often shared the same disconnect.

1 The story begins on 12 March 1938 during the farewell events held when then Ambassador Ribbentrop was set to return to Germany. Ribbentrop reportedly stated that in a future war against Britain, Germany would have Italy on its side. Churchill reportedly responded with 'That's only fair – we had them last time', an inaccurate negative reference to Italy's performance during the First World War.

This viewpoint and approach should not be construed to argue that the Italian military was uniformly effective during the war; it had many flaws that ultimately caused its failure to successfully defend the Italian nation. What it does offer is that there is often a line of reasoning that is highly nation-centric that is not considered when assessing why decisions were made.

This work is meant to be an introduction into the employment of the Italian airborne force during the war and a discussion of its effectiveness for the English reader. The story begins in 1936 and presents the thinking and decisions that led to the creation and preparation of the *paracadutisti* that fought during the war. By examining these prewar decisions, the reader is better prepared to analyze and understand the reasons behind the successes and failures of the speciality in the years of combat.

This book presents details of the individuals battles in which the parachute force was a participant. While the history of the *«Folgore»* at El Alamein has been reasonably documented in Italian and English works, the smaller actions in 1940, 1941 and 1943 have only been presented with any detail in Italian. Even in those Italian works, the story of the *paracadutisti* is often incomplete. Few of those books and articles fully incorporate the Allied side of the actions and battles described and tend to focus on the glories of individuals rather than the effectiveness of these units as a whole. The result is that the reader is often left with an incomplete understanding of the events that shaped the outcome of those battles.

The reader will not find a complete retelling of the various battles and campaigns during which the *paracadutisti* were involved. There are many English titles that present these events in greater detail and completeness and this book is not attempting to duplicate those works. What is presented within these pages is a detailed account of those parts of the battles and campaigns in which the *paracadutisti* fought or were otherwise involved. This account is meant to read along with those other works to gain a fuller understanding of the participation of the *paracadutisti* in those specific actions.

This is not the definitive history of the *paracadutisti italiani*. There is more material in the archives of the Italian Army, Navy, and Air Force that needs to be fully explored. There are several events chronicled within these pages where the various accounts disagreed and no definitive answer could be determined. I have attempted to reconcile those events to the best of my ability and the discrepancies are noted in the footnotes. It is likely that the correct answer lies in the Italian archives and requires only time and dedicated research to be discovered. The hope is that this work becomes a starting point and resource for further study and discussion on the Italy military during this period.

One will encounter within these pages the use of Italian military ranks, unit names, and military terms. This is intentional as this is a history of the Italian military during the Second World War. The *Regio Esercito*, *Regia Marina* and *Regia Aeronautica* had developed several unique military concepts and units in their attempt to solve the operational problems of modern warfare. Rendering these in English is often awkward and unnatural to the English reader. Using terms such as *celere* (fast troops) or camionette (commandos that used vehicles to reach their targets) flow better in written

English. Once a new term is explained, the Italian word is used. For those words/terms that have direct English translations, Italian is still used to maintain consistency. If Fallschirmjäger, Luftwaffe, or Panzer Division are acceptable in English accounts on the German military, then *paracadutisti, Regia Aeronautica,* or *divisione corazzata* are valid usage in an account on the Italian military.

The maps in this work use the Italian military symbology that was taught/used before and during the Second World War. I found that it clearly communicates both the type and the size of the unit depicted while presenting less clutter on the maps than the use of the NATO symbology would require. A guide is presented at the beginning of the map section and I feel that readers will find the system easy to master. Like the use of Italian language, the use of the map symbols is an intentional reinforcement that this is a history of the Italian military.

Ranks are given in the named individual's language. This hopefully will assist the reader to know whether the individual is Italian, German, British (or Commonwealth), or American. To the best of my ability, the given rank was the one held by the individual at the time of the event.

All translations within this volume are done by the author. Any errors are mine alone. Words in brackets [ ] are added to clarify quoted passages and allow the sentence to flow smoother in English.

Introduction

When the Wehrmacht crossed the Polish border on 1 September 1939, only three nations possessed a significant airborne capability: Soviet Russia, Nazi Germany, and Fascist Italy. In the following four years until Italy's surrender in September 1943, the Fallschirmjägers would execute airborne operations in Poland, Denmark, Norway, Belgium, The Netherlands, and Greece. The Soviets would deploy their Vozdushno-desantnye voyska (Airborne Troops) in Bessarabia in 1940 and then conduct airborne operations of increasing size throughout the war. During the same period the United Kingdom, the United States, and Japan would create and employ their own airborne forces in various campaigns. Only Italy, a leader in airborne capability in 1939, would never conduct a major airborne operation. The pages that follow seek to examine why the *paracadutisti*, lauded in the fascist press were never doctrinally employed during the war.

The need for airborne units must be examined within the framework of a nation's strategic, operational, and tactical understanding of war. Strategy shapes the why, the reasoning behind a nation's decision to opt for war. Strategy must identify what a nation intends to gain from the conflict; in better words it defines the goals of the war. As part of that process, strategy should examine the means available to fight the war and determine whether those means are sufficient to achieve the goals. In addition, strategy must allocate the means to support the multiple efforts national strategy often require.

Operations (or operational art) takes those goals and means and develops/implements how the war will be fought. Operations define the time, place, and forces that structure the campaigns and battles used to achieve the nation's strategic goals. The concept of operations as a separate level of war was relatively new in the 1930s–40s and was mainly ushered in by Soviet military thinkers. For the militaries of the 1940s, operational art is something that was done but not fully understood as a separate level of war. When reading period military works and manuals, the word strategy is often used when it is actually discussing what is now known as operations.

The tactical level of war describes how those battles are fought. It is the mechanics of war, the way commanders/leaders put the tools of combat together to achieve battlefield success. The tools must be able to implement the operational plan. If the operational plan requires fighting a war in mountainous terrain, there is an operational requirement for units organized, trained, and equipped to fight in the mountains. This type of unit has a different organization and requires different training and equipment than those units needed to fight a war in a desert. If a nation plans to seize an island, there is an operational need for a navy, transports, landing craft, etc.

These examples are oversimplifications but illustrate that not all militaries require the same capabilities based on their strategic goals. When a nation's strategic goals require a capability that the military doesn't possess, an operational capability gap is created.

The history of warfare is filled with nations developing the means to close an operational capability gap. The Romans required a navy to fight Carthage and developed a method to overcome superior Carthaginian seamanship. Cannons were developed to overcome the evolving technology of castles. The development of the submarine was seeking a means to overcome the lack of a powerful navy when fighting against a naval power. Tanks were designed to overcome the capability gap created by the problem of increased firepower that manifested as trench warfare.

Airborne forces were developed to solve two different operational capability gaps. The first problem was how to sustain an offense. The strength and mobility of the defense made achieving decisive results difficult. It was Soviet theorists that first viewed airborne forces as a means of preventing the defender from easily massing forces to stop a Soviet breakthrough of its defense. Called the Deep Battle, the Soviet operational planners saw that battle plans need to consider enemy forces and their possible actions to a distance of over 100 kilometres behind the frontline. Friendly operations must flow seamlessly from penetration, breakthrough, and into pursuit so to reduce the time available to the defender to affect the operation. The enemy must be attacked simultaneously throughout the depth of this larger battlefield to prevent them concentrating their efforts against the friendly main effort.

The Soviet concept of the Deep Attack as part of the Deep Battle incorporated the use of large parachute units with coordinated air attacks and deep artillery strikes to delay, block, or destroy enemy forces behind the frontlines. Parachute units could secure vital chokepoints and key locations to aid a rapid advance or hinder enemy movements. The Russians demonstrated these concepts in a series of exercises that grew progressively larger and more complex over a span of years during the 1930s.

The second operational problem was to attack an enemy that was protected by a geographical barrier. Normally this was seen as crossing a water barrier such as a major river, a channel, or a sea. These force entry operations required the friendly force to approach the battle area by means unsuitable for sustained combat. Naval transports launching landing craft was one traditional method to force an entry under these circumstances. Paratroops could be used to disrupt or unhinge a defence of these barriers, allowing easier access by the main force. In some cases, paratroopers would be the sole means used to secure an objective such as an island.

The common thread in both of these concepts was they involved offensive operations. The friendly force was using paratroops to create an advantage that would be leveraged into operational success. The inherent understanding was that any advantage gained would be fleeting as their isolated position couldn't be maintained without additional forces. The fragility of airborne force significantly limited their value as part of a defence. Once these units began to be used on the defence, they quickly acquired additional weapons and equipment that rendered them unsuitable for airborne missions.

Italy was the first military to embrace the use of the parachute in an offensive role. The insertion of three officers behind enemy lines in 1918 was the first use of paratroopers for a combat mission. Their mission was to provide intelligence in preparation of an Italian offensive effort in 1918. This was not a tactical mission but one to fulfill an operational requirement.

The concept of parachute operations languished in the post-First World War period. Most nations saw their security needs in terms of the defence and parachute units didn't satisfy a defensive requirement. Parachuting was relegated to aircrew safety and demonstrations of daring at fairs and circuses. The military application of airborne units was understood either as raids or sabotage. This limited understanding relegated the parachute as something that didn't require specialized training or large standing units.

Once Soviet Russia introduced an operational role for airborne forces in the early 1930's, other countries took notice. Germany recognized the possibilities that airborne forces offered to its own ideas on rapid offensive war and began forming its first unit in 1935. By 1940 Germany possessed a parachute division and an air landing division suitable for offensive operations. These forces would be instrumental in the conquest of Denmark, Norway, The Netherlands, and the island of Crete.

The German achievements using paratroopers inspired Japan to create its own airborne force in late 1940. These forces were used with some success during their offensive campaign against the Dutch East Indies in early 1942. The United States and Great Britain also noted the German success and began their own efforts to create major airborne formations in 1940. These forces would be employed to conduct major offensive operations in 1943 and 1944. The Soviets would also employ significant airborne forces in offensive operations during the war with mixed success. In all of these cases, the use of parachute units was in support of an offensive objective.

Italy too would begin to create its own airborne capability after observing the Russian manoeuvres. Starting with the actions of *maresciallo dell'aria* (Air Marshal) Italo Bablo in 1938, Italy would go on to create two complete parachute divisions with a third planned, along with an air landing division, all by 1943. Yet at the time of the Italian surrender on 8 September 1943, the largest airborne operations carried out by the *paracadutisti italiani* were limited to a number of squad-size raid missions of little operational consequence. The airdrop of seventy-two parachutists on the Greek island of Kefalonia, the largest actual Italian airborne mission during the war, happened days after the Greek surrender. The unit's operational mission wasn't to defeat Greek forces but to deny Kefalonia and two other Greek islands from occupation by Italy's German ally.

This lack of any major airborne operations by the *Regio Esercito* (Royal Army) in World War 2 is not surprising when examining their wartime employment against

Italy's strategic and operational requirements. The lack of an offensive plan at the outbreak of the war meant the *paracadutisti* had no role to fill that would guide and boost its development. The series of hasty offensive efforts that followed Italy's entry into the war gave too little time to prepare the airborne force to support those efforts. It wasn't until late 1941 that an operational requirement was identified that finally gave purpose to the *paracadutisti* and guided its development. By the time the capability was ready, the conditions had changed and Italy was no longer on the offense.

When Italo Balbo created the first Italian parachute unit, he gave the unit the grand title of *I Fanti d'aria*; Infantrymen of the Air. While it is evident that Balbo had a grand vision of the future use of the *paracadutisti*, one must ask, 'Did Italy have an operational requirement for airborne forces?' This question goes beyond whether Italy had the capacity and ability to create and employ such a force. It frames the question as whether such a force was needed given Italy's strategic situation in 1940. This is the question that this book will seek to explore.

To address that question, this work explores how the airborne speciality was perceived by the Italian military leadership and the manner of its actual employment. It examines the genesis of the speciality from 1936 through an arc that reaches its maximum potential in 1942 and finally to its demise in 1943. Did the development and employment of these units follow any discernible logic that was linked to an operation requirement that achieved a strategic goal? The following pages are a start to answering that question.

Maresciallo dell'aria Italo Balbo. (AUSSMA)

1

Castel Benito

If one wished to identify the single individual responsible for creating the airborne force of fascist Italy, that name would be Italo Balbo, *Maresciallo dell'Aria* and *Governatore Generale della Libia*. Balbo, the dashing Alpini lieutenant who earned three medals for bravery during the First World War and was one of the *quadrumviri* during the March on Rome.[1] Appointed the Undersecretary of Aviation 1926 and then the Minister in 1929, he began to rebuild the Regia Aeronautica (R.A., Royal Airforce). In a series of mass-transoceanic training flights and other prestige events, the handsome young flier was internationally recognized as representing the vigor and determination of the fascist efforts to modernize Italy. By 1938 he was seen by many as second in succession after Count Ciano to replace Mussolini as head of the Fascist Party and leader of the Italian nation.[2]

Balbo's personal interest in military parachuting was likely sparked in 1927. On 6 November at the Cinisello Balsamo airport, he watched as nine paratroopers simultaneously jumped from a single airplane during a large air show. Previous demonstrations only showcased individual jumpers and highlighted the safety of the parachute and the high altitude of the aircraft at the time the parachutists jumped. The parachute drops executed on this date demonstrated the ability to rapidly insert a patrol behind enemy lines. The jumpers were using the new Salvator B parachute developed by Prospero Freri, the leading expert on parachuting in Italy. The nine parachutists jumped from an altitude of 500m as a unit and safely reached the ground. Among the paratroopers was a World War I veteran, *tenente pilota* Giuseppe Baudoin de Gillette. Both Freri and Baudoin would be intimately involved in the development of Italy's airborne force before and during the war.[3]

1 Monte S. Finkelstein, 'Quadrumvirs', in Philip V. Cannistraro (ed.), *Historical Dictionary of Fascist Italy* (Westport: Greenwood Press, 1982), p.444. The quadrumvirs were the four Fascist Party members appointed by Mussolini to plan and execute the March on Rome in October 1922. They held seats on the Fascist Grand Council.

2 Claudio G. Segrè, 'Balbo, Italo', in Cannistraro (ed.), *Historical Dictionary*, pp.57–58.

3 Anon, 'Storia del paracadutismo Militare Italiano', Sezione di Monza dell'Associazione nazionale *paracadutisti* d'Italia (2019) <http://www.*paracadutisti*monza.it/storia-

During this period, the use of airborne units was seen as a capability for executing raids and sabotage missions behind enemy lines. This was partly due to the lack of suitable aircraft to carry a large number of paratroopers en masse, but mainly it was because no country had developed a military doctrine that provided a role for large airborne operations. The missions discussed for paratrooper units were tactical in nature: seizing a key bridge or terrain feature to facilitate the rapid movement of ground units, or the destruction/delay of enemy forces that could affect the friendly plan. These missions did not require large units and used surprise and speed to compensate for the lack of mass. These types of actions were supportive in nature to the main effort and were not often decisive in their own right. The future assaults on Eben-Emael and the Netherlands by the Germans in 1940, or the 1945 attack on Corregidor by the Americans in 1945 were examples of the tactical use of small airborne forces. Even if such operations ended in failure, the success of the overall operation was not seriously jeopardized. One could argue that the role of paratroopers in the 1920s and early 1930s was to create a distraction and generally be a nuisance to the enemy.

No country had yet to develop a role for airborne forces at the operational level of war. The pre-war Russian strategist Georgii Isserson discussed the challenge of the operational art as … *how to link separate, tactically independent combat efforts in space along a front and in time, i.e. throughout the depths, in order to achieve a general aim.*[4] Employment of airborne forces at this level of warfare required that the force have a mission that is independent and complementary to the plan, not simply supportive of a tactical objective. The impact of the mission on the enemy had to be significant, causing either a major relocation of resources and consumption of time by the enemy, or they are the decisive act of the operation. Examples of such missions include the German assault and seizure of Crete or the planned Italian assault against Malta. These operations would require large forces that could sustain themselves for longer than a day or two and withstand serious enemy attacks to achieve that operational effect.

It was the Russian concept of deep operations to solve Isserson's challenge that provided the role and spurred the development of large airborne forces. Debated and refined in the late 1920s and early 1930s and then codified in the 1936 Field Regulations, the Soviet doctrine was aimed at sustaining the offensive past the breakthrough stage. Besides integrating the use of motorized and mechanized units, the Soviets saw the need for timed sequential combat operations throughout the depth of the enemy's defense. They divided the defensive into three areas, the tactical zone (up to 6 kms deep), the operational zone (from 6 kms to 60 kms from the front line), and the strategic zone (greater than 60 kms from the front lines). The Soviets predicted that the operational zone would contain the bulk of the enemy's reserves, supply

del-paracadutismo-militare-italiano/> (accessed on 12 Feb. 2021); Nino Arena, *I PARACADUTISTI Cinquanta' anni di storia, cronaca e immagini del paracadutisti italiano* (Modena: Società Tipografica Editrice Modenese Mucchi, 1972), 43–44.

4 Georgii Isserson, *The Evolution of Operational Art* (Fort Leavenworth: Combat Studies Institute Press, 2013), tr by Brice Menning, p.26.

depots, and rail heads. Large airborne forces could be used to seize operationally critical locations 40–100 kms behind the enemy's front line, drawing the enemy reserves towards those locations and away from reinforcing the front lines.[5]

The Soviet Army's maneuvers in 1934, 1935, and 1936 helped spur Italian (and international) interest in airborne operations. In each of these three years, Soviet airborne units executed a range of military missions based on their new doctrine while increasing the number of troops employed. The 1935 maneuver saw a mass jump of 1,200 paratroopers to seize an airfield, followed by the air landing of an infantry brigade complete with artillery and light armored vehicles. The 1936 maneuver was even larger, dropping a full division of paratroopers and then supplying it by air during subsequent operations.[6] By the end of 1936, the Soviet Army possessed three airborne brigades and three airborne regiments, all trained to support their new operational doctrine.

The *Regio Esercito* (R.E., Royal Italian Army) had sent *generale di corpo d'armata* Francesco Grazioli to observe these maneuvers. *Generale* Grazioli had served during the First World War and was a veteran of both Caporetto and Vittorio Veneto. He had commanded both regular units and units of *Arditi*, the specialized assault troops of the R.E. The latter provided him a background when reviewing developments in specialized units. Now a Senator in the Italian government, he was occasionally employed by the R.E. for various foreign tasks, including acting as a military observer. His comments on the possibilities of employing were positive and recommended further study.

His report was followed by that of *generale di corpo d'armata* Edoardo Monti, commander of the military forces on Sardinia. Monti's report on the Soviet maneuvers was more forceful on the role of the airborne units. He highlighted the combined use of paratroopers and air transported infantry that were demonstrated during the maneuvers, the latter increasing the self-sufficiency and enhanced independent role for the airborne force. A movie crew accompanied his mission and filmed the Russian paratroopers during the exercise. Monti called on Benito Mussolini after his return to Italy to discuss his observations and showed him the films. Thus inspired, Mussolini then pressed the *Stato Maggiore dell'Esercito* (S.M.R.E., Italian Army General Staff) to study whether to create an Italian airborne capability.[7]

There is an undated document in the archives of the *Esercito Italiano* (the Italian Army) entitled *Studio per l'impiego di unità paracadutisti* (Study on the employment of parachute units).[8] The document lacked a cover page or a signature block to help

5 Isserson, *Operational Art*, pp.46–47, 52, 68.
6 Lt. Col. Oleksiy Nozdrachov *Application of the Soviet Theory of "Deep Operation" During the 1939 Soviet-Japanese Military Conflict in Mongolia* (master's thesis, CGSC, 2010), 24–25; David M. Glantz, *Soviet Operational Art and Tactics in the 1930's* (Fort Leavenworth, Kansas: Soviet Army Studies Office, 1990), 18; David M. Glantz *The Soviet Airborne Experience* (Fort Leavenworth, Kansas: Combat Studies Institute, 1984), 11–13.
7 Nino Arena, *La Regia Aeronautica 1939-1943* (Rome: USSMA, 1981-86) vol 1, p.118.
8 AUSSME, no date, *Studio per l'impiego di unità paracadutisti,* I-4, b.17,f.4.

identify when it was written and who were the authors. The study itself is only five pages long and originally included multiple diagrams as stated in Part III, but those were not found in the file. The study was likely written prior to June 1940 as the first sentence in Part I (Purpose of the Study) states 'To determine the purpose of using paratroopers, especially in the initial phase of hostilities." Whether this is the study ordered by Mussolini in 1936 would require further research, but the discussion itself is general in nature and reads as if it was written before the parachute units were raised. Whether it was written in 1936 or a year or two later, it does provide insight on the prewar doctrinal thinking of the Regio Esercito on the use of airborne units.

The study identifies a requirement for two types of *reparti paracadutisti* (parachute units): units (identified as battalion-size) and *nuclei* or *elementi* (detachments). Detachments are used to destroy important resources (magazines, depots, and other point targets) by sabotage, while units are used to deny avenues of movement by occupying choke points and securing key terrain. An unusual mission type was to secure the flank of an advancing friendly force as it moved deep into the enemy's rear area. This concept of dropping parachutists in support of moving forces instead of them occupying a key location and the moving forces then link-up is unique to R.E. The idea does mesh well with the Italian doctrinal concepts of *I celere* (1935–1938) and the later *guerra di corso rapido* (1938). In those doctrines, the speed of the Italian *celere* (fast) and *motorizzata* (motorized) divisions' advance would create vulnerable flanks that an enemy counter attack could exploit. The study stated that airborne forces could be quickly dropped to protect those vulnerable flanks and guard against any enemy interference as the friendly operation was unfolding. This mission of flank protection is highly suspect as the armament of these units as stated in Part IV of the study appears too light to handle any threat greater than a raid.

Much of what the study presented mirrored the understanding held by many of the militaries of other countries. It placed the use of paratroops as a tactical tool to solve tactical problems. There is no discussion of their employment at the operational level of war as the Soviet Union was currently discussing or that Germany would demonstrate in 1940.

Based on the results of the study, official interest in creating a parachute unit was formally expressed by the army in a memorandum on 1 May 1936 by *generale d'armata* Federico Baistrocchi, the Chief of the S.M.R.E. The memorandum was then sent to Mussolini for his approval of the concept. Mussolini favored the idea of the *paracadutisti* as it would again demonstrate that fascist Italy was on the cutting edge of military thinking and he gave his authorization to proceed. *Generale* Baistrocchi conceived that a battalion of paratroopers would provide a capability to raid behind enemy lines to interrupt movement by attacking roads, railways and infrastructure of value in support of ongoing operations.[9] At this point no greater vision for the use of airborne forces was under consideration.

9 Arena, *La Regia Aeronautica*, vol 1, p.118.

The *Stato Maggiore dell'Aeronautica* (S.M.R.A, the General Staff of the Regia Aeronautica) responded to the S.M.R.E.'s proposal on 31 July 1936 with a proposal of its own for the establishment and operation of a parachuting school.[10] The dueling proposals initiated discussions between the R.E. and the R.A. over which arm of the military would be responsible for establishing and controlling this new branch. The R.A. position was that it was responsible for providing, supporting, and employment of all aircraft. The R.E. argued that parachute units were essentially ground combat units and the organization, equipping, training, and employment should be under its jurisdiction.

The issue was finally resolved when the Regio Decreto Legge (R.D.L.) 220 was published on 22 February 1937. In it, the R.A. was given the requirement to create, staff, and operate a parachute school. The R.E. was given responsibility for the training and operational use of the new units. In this, the Italian military differed from the Russian and German counterparts. The Russians placed responsibility for all aspects of airborne operations under the army. The Fallschirmjäger of Germany began under the control of the army, but responsibility was transferred in total to the Air Force. Later the US and the UK would see their airborne forces under their respective armies. Only Italy had the responsibility split between two services. The Japanese experience was different, with the army and navy each having their own parachute schools and forces. At this point it appeared that the groundwork had been completed and the Italian parachute school and first operational units could be organized. That this did notimmediately happen was due to bureaucracy and more inter-service fighting.

Bureaucracy became an issue due to the issue of hazard pay and injury/death benefits for those who volunteered for parachute duty. None of these points had been proposed, discussed, or undergone approval in the budgetary process. Until this was done, the two services could not begin to recruit volunteers for the new parachute specialty.[11]

A lesser, but still important bureaucratic issue was where to build the school. The location of a school for parachute training required several critical features: it must house a large number of trainees and trainers; it must have large buildings for packing, maintaining, and repairing the parachutes; large open spaces for ground and tower training, a nearby airfield to load the trainees in to aircraft for practice jumps, good weather for most of the year, and it must have a large open area for use as a drop zone. All these features should be in close proximity to each other to reduce the time between training events. When the weather is favorable for jumping and the aircraft are available (two things that do not always coincide), the proximity of these training areas can allow for multiple training jumps in a single day.

The R.A. established a commission to research and make a recommendation for the location of the new school. The military airfields at Aviano, Viterbo, Tarquinia,

10 Marco Di Giovanni, *I paracadutisti italiani* (Gorizia: Editrice Goriziano, 1991), p.30.
11 Di Giovanni, *I paracadutisti*, p.30.

Brindisi, L'Aquila, and Siena were identified as candidates. A significant complementary issue was the cost to develop the required infrastructure needed to support the training. Who would pay for the development of new capabilities was a common debate during the 1930's between the various branches of the Italian military. A similar battle was underway between the R.A. and the R.M. (*Regia Marina*, the Italian Royal Navy) over development of torpedo bombers. These financial fights would delay the maturing of emerging military concepts in fascist Italy and allow foreign militaries to gain leads in fields previously held by Italy.

Whilst the commission was working, the head of the S.M.R.A., *generale d'armata aerea* Giuseppe Valle, gave a personal endorsement in support of the new airborne arm by making his first parachute jump at Viterbo on 14 September 1937. *Maggiore* Prospero Frei gave him a quick session of parachute training and then jumped with the general from Valle's personal Ca.133 aircraft.[12]

The inter-service fighting and posturing between the R.E. and the R.A. continued throughout 1937. Budget concerns and defining each services' authority in the matter were the main problems, with both sides attempting to achieve some sort of political gain in the process. While the school itself was to be operated by the R.A., various aspects such as tactical training and physical/mental assessment and preparation was seen by the R.E. as their responsibility.[13] Continuing research and testing of associated airborne equipment was also seen as an area that did not solely reside with the R.A. Personal assignments by service within the school could not be discussed and finalized until all these areas of responsibilities were decided. None of these smaller issues were resolved by the language in R.D.L. 220.

While Mussolini had pressed for the creation of an airborne capability, he did not actively press on the execution of the requirement. There was apathy on the part of the senior R.E. leadership about the usefulness of airborne forces. Marco di Giovanni noted that there was little discussion of parachute units in Italian or intentional professional journals by Italian military officers. What little there was tended to focus on minor or secondary roles.[14] The conservative senior leadership of the R.E. remained unconvinced of the value of the new specialty. *Generale* Baistrocchi, an innovator who had initiated the discussion on an airborne force, was replaced just six months after he presented his memorandum (October 1936). No other senior army leader came forward as the champion of the *paracadutisti*. The result was nothing had been accomplished by the end of 1937.

12 Nino Arena, *50ª di Tarquinia, 1939-1989, Scuole Militare paracadutismo* (Comitato Promotore ex Istruttori delle Scuole Militari di Paracadutismo, 1989), p.11.

13 Nino Arena *I Fanti dell'Aria da Castel Benito ad Azizia (Libia) 1938-1941* (Bologna: Edizione Eurographis, 1989), 15.

14 Di Giovanni, *I paracadutisti*, pp.29–30.

Castel Benito

Maresciallo Balbo in Libya had followed the activity that swirled around the creation of the new specialty. He was a believer in the use of paratroopers and had become increasingly frustrated at the bureaucratic inertia that was preventing the creation of an Italian airborne force. In late 1937 he decided to act. As Governor General of Libya and in his position within the Fascist Party structure, he had a degree of autonomy from the service General Staffs. The bureaucratic issues that were blocking further development of the airborne forces also applied to the R.E. forces in Libya. He did, however, have greater control over the *Regio Corpo Truppe Coloniali* (R.C.T.C.; the Royal Corps of Colonial Troops), the indigenous forces raised in Libya. It was within the R.C.T.C. structure where Balbo formed the first Italian parachute units.[15]

The R.C.T.C. units were organized under different laws than the Italian metropolitan units and came under the budget for Libya and not the Army. Still compromises and agreements were needed to move the creation of a *reparto paracadutisti* (parachute unit) from a desire to a reality. The final compromise was to institute a provisional command structure that was joint in nature between the services and organizations involved. The school with its associated administration and physical infrastructure, parachute and flight equipment would be under the responsibility of the R.A.'s *Comando Aeronautica della Libia* (Air Force Command Libya); physical and military training, and school disciplinary responsibilities would be under the R.C.T.C.; Pre-jump and jump training responsibilities under the R.A. with joint instructors from the R.E. and R.C.T.C. Funding would be divided between the *Ministero della Guerra* (Ministry of War), *Ministero dell'Aeronautica* (Air Ministry), and the *Ministero dell'Africa italiana* (Ministry of Italian Africa), with costs to be managed and accounted for by each entity's common expenditure lines. Oversight of everything would fall under the R.E. General Inspector, supported by S.M.R.E. In the words of historian Nino Arena, a typically intricate "Italian" compromise.[16]

Where to locate the school was not an issue. The large military airfield at Castel Benito met all the requirements. Located twelve kilometers south of Tripoli, the airfield possessed plenty of space to develop the new training center. Administration buildings and barracks would need to be built, but large hangers to maintain and prepare the parachutes were available and there were storage facilities for the parachute equipment. It offered easy access to senior government officials located in Tripoli and the port that was the main entry for supplies and materials for Africa settentrionale (A.S.).

15 Filippo Cappellano and Paolo, 'Italo Balbo e le grandi manovre in Libia del 1938 in Libia', *Storia Militare*, 218 (2011), pp.4–5; John Gooch, *Mussolini and his Generals* (New York: Cambridge University Press, 2007), p.371; Basilio Di Martino, 'Il controllo a lungo raggio del deserto. Le esperienze italiane in Libia negli anni Trenta' *Antologia Militare* 1:4 (2020), pp.40–41.

16 Arena *I Fanti*, 16.

In early January 1938, Balbo requested that *tenente colonnello* Prospero Freri be assigned to Libya. Freri was still the leading expert on paratrooper training and parachute design in Italy and had previously developed a proposed training program for a parachute school in 1930.[17] That program had languished somewhere inside the Italian military bureaucracy so Freri did not hesitate in accepting Balbo's request to establish a school in the colony. He asked that a few key individuals be assigned to work with him which Balbo then arranged. Soon afterwards, three experienced parachutists, *capitani* Nicholai, *tenente* Remorino, and *maresciallo* Casioli joined the airborne school staff. Always with an eye toward publicity, Balbo also recruited the noted aerial cinematographer, *capitano* Ponzi, to document the activities at the school for public consumption.[18]

To cut costs and avoid the long development times for new equipment, existing equipment was to be used wherever possible by the school. The R.A.'s Salvator (Savior) D.37 parachute was selected for use by the airborne forces as it was readily available. This parachute had been developed for flight crews and was not especially suitable for repeated use by combat troops. This would create problems for the school in the months ahead, but given the number of parachutes required for training, it was the only real option at the time.

The Salvator D.37 was a compact, light-weight parachute developed to be worn by air crews during flight. The harness consisted of a wide waist belt, one shoulder strap over the left shoulder, and one leg loop around the right leg. The canopy was folded and carried in the pack tray fastened to the harness. The parachute could be activated by a static line or by using the manual release located on the waist belt. When activated, a strong spring pushed a pilot chute out into the air-stream of the falling jumper, which then inflated and pulled the main canopy out of the pack tray. The main canopy would fully inflate before the suspension lines had completely deployed, delivering a very strong shock when the lines were pulled taut. This could injure the jumper and occasionally rendered him unconscious. The canopy was forty-nine square meters of silk and provided a descent rate of seven meters per second (7m/s) for an unladen man. The 16 suspension lines that secured the canopy were connected to a ring on the rear of the waist belt. The entire pack weighed 8 kgs. and the system was reliable and simple.[19]

The air detachment to support the training initially consisted of two Ca.101 and one Ca.133 transports, aircraft types that Freri had used before. For the aerial photography, a SM.81 was selected as it offered greater interior space for the camera crew. Before training began, two additional SM.81s were assigned to the school. Aircraft

17 Propero Freri, 'Arditismo Aero', *Rivista Aeronautica*, XIII: 7 (1937), pp.18-24
18 Arena *I Fanti*, 15.
19 Guy Richards, *World War II Troop Type Parachutes: Axis* (Atglen: Pennsylvania: Schiffer Military History, 2000), pp.13–14.

Maresciallo dell'aria Italo Balbo reviews members of the *I btg.* «*Fanti dell'aria*» at Castel Benito. The *Ascari del cielo* are equipped with the D.37 parachutes, the leather jump cap and the unit waist stash. (AUSSME)

A 1.2 A pack-tray deployed parachute. A US parachute T4 or T5 during a training jump. Note that the suspension lines are only beginning to deploy when the canopy is already inflating. (US Army Signal Corps Photograph)

from the *15° Stormo da Bombardamento Terrestre* (SM.81 bomber squadron) would supplement the school for mass jumps when required by the training schedule.

Always the showman, *Maresciallo dell'Aria* Balbo recognized that creating a new capability did not mean it would be adopted. Balbo knew he needed some demonstration that would impress and excite Mussolini and the Italian senior military leadership on the possibilities of the new speciality. The method he selected was to leverage the annual grand military maneuvers to showcase his new units. The Italian military normally executed a series of military maneuvers each year in various locations around Italy. Balbo had been preparing to execute a grand military training maneuver in Libya in April 1938 that King Vittorio Emanuele III and other senior officials were scheduled to attend.

The fact that a Grand Maneuver was scheduled to be held at all in Libya in 1938 was another victory for Balbo. The cost of the war in Ethiopia that had just concluded and the ongoing support to the Nationalists in Spain had drained the budgets of the three services. Mussolini had canceled the planned maneuver in Libya, only to have the intervention of the King and the Capo (head) of the S.M.R.E., *generale d'armata* Alberto Pariani, to approve the event. Mussolini was swayed by the promise to reduce the scope of the similar maneuvers planned in Italy during that year. With this formal approval, Balbo continued to prepare his Grand Maneuver.[20]

Balbo planned to incorporate his new parachute unit into the exercise as it would be an excellent way to demonstrate the capability of this new specialty. It would also showcase Balbo's ability to quickly create and integrate a new military system, a task that the Regio Esercito was still trying to accomplish in Italy.

Such was his confidence in his ability to achieve this milestone that he sent a letter to the *Ministero dell'Aeronautica* on 23 February 1938 observed:

> Having said this, it is deemed necessary to [...] establish a special school that should begin its operation as soon as possible in order to promptly prepare the first group of paratroopers to be employed during the Grand Maneuvers at Gefara on the occasion of the arrival of His Majesty the King Emperor."[21]

At the time he wrote the letter, not a single Libyan soldier had been trained and the Grand Maneuver was scheduled to start in May.

Recruiting officially began in February 1938. The bulk of the enlisted men would be taken from the R.C.T.C. to circumvent the unresolved benefits issues, while the senior noncommissioned officers and commissioned officers would be volunteers recruited from Italians serving in Libya. Initially only those officers in *servizio permanente effettivo* (S.P.E.) were authorized to apply. Officers in S.P.E. were the R.E. career officers,

20 Filippo Cappellano and Paolo Formiconi, 'Italo Balbo e le grandi manovre in Libia del 1938 in Libia', *Storia Militare*, 218 (2011), p.16.

21 Di Giovanni, *I paracadutisti italiani*, pp.32–33.

having entered service through the various military academies and managed under a specific set of regulations. Response from this group was disappointing, with many not willing to risk their careers in a new specialty that could quickly disappear and negatively affect chances for promotion. The unresolved benefits issue likely played a part in their reluctance. After a short period of time, the call for volunteers was opened to officers *di complemento* (reserve officers) that served for only two-three years and then either applied to remain on military duty or returned to civil life. With this change, enough officers *di complemento* volunteered so the project could move ahead.

The response from the indigenous servicemen was excellent. There was an initial concern that the Libyan *ascari* would be unresponsive or afraid to fly in an airplane, let alone parachute from one. An additional concern was whether they could accept and adapt to the highly disciplined training and associated hard work involved in parachute training. There was the unstated prejudicial belief held by many colonial powers about the ability of 'natives' to function in the modern world and become elite soldiers. This concern alone made Balbo's experiment more dangerous and could affect Italian colonial rule. Regardless of the concerns, the Libyan *ascari* proved to be excellent soldiers and quickly mastered the new skills.[22]

The *Scuola Paracadutisti della Libia* was formally established by Order n.64 published on 24 March 1938 (Comando Superiore FF.AA.AS. Ord. nº 64, 24 March 1938, *Oggetto: direttive circa il funzionamento della Scuole paracadutisti costituita presso l'Aeroporto di Castel Benito*). The order outlined the roles and responsibilities of the school itself, as well as the training program that was to be implemented. The order merely codified the reality as training for the school instructors and the battalion cadre had already begun prior to its publication.[23]

The school was tasked to "instruct groups of soldiers of the various armed forces, chosen from among volunteer personnel, equipped with particular physical aptitudes, endowed with very lively enthusiasm and above all animated by the highest spirit of sacrifice, in individual and collective jumps with parachutes from aircraft, in various atmospheric and environmental conditions, in order to organize units for special wartime missions." The school was to be "a purely aeronautical institution, having the primary purpose of training excellent paratroopers." The R.E., not the school or the R.A., was responsible for recruiting, organizing, and training parachute units for wartime activities. The program itself was to last one month and focus on two areas: the majority of the training was to be ground and air parachute instruction; as time allowed, the secondary area would be initial ground tactical training that would be expanded upon after the graduates joined their units.[24]

22 Arena *I Fanti*, p.18.

23 Arena *I Fanti*, pp.146–151; Massimo Di Martino, *Paracadutisti d'Italia – Uniformi distintivi equipaggiamenti.* (Milan, Edizioni Libreria Militare, 2019), vol I, p.9. Arena on p.18 states 20 March 1938, but the copy of the actual order starting on p.146 states 24 March 1938.

24 Arena *I Fanti*, pp.146–151.

Order n.64 also established that the commander of the Castel Benito airfield would also be the director of the school. The school thus was placed under the command of *colonnello* Stefano Cagna, the commander of the military airfield. Cagna was a long-time trusted subordinate of Italo Balbo, having been one of the pilots who flew with Balbo during his trans-Atlantic flights. While the politicians in Italy in 1928 were debating whether to aid in the Arctic search and rescue efforts to find Umberto Nobile and the missing airship *Italia*, Balbo sent then *maggiore* Cagna and *tenente colonnello* Umberto Maddalena in a Savoia-Marchetti SM.55 to Norway. They were the first to find the explorer and other survivors, dropping supplies and guiding other rescuers to their location.[25] Cagna was 37 years old at the time the school was established and brought a youthful aggressiveness to the organization and operation of the new program.[26]

Parachute training itself was divided into two phases. The preliminary ground training phase would consist of individual physical training, the use and maintenance of the parachute, and mastering jump positions and exit drills. The flight phase would consist of orientation flights in the jump aircraft, dropping cargo parachutes, individual jumps without equipment (Hollywood jumps in modern slang), and individual jumps with combat equipment. These would be followed, given available time, by jumps onto varied terrain types, night jumps, and collective (mass) jumps.

The ground tactical training would consist of gymnastic-sporting exercises, topography and map reading instructions (initially for officers only), shooting exercises with automatic weapons, hand grenade practice, basic defensive skills, and other real war training in no particular order if time was available. While it is not clear in the available information, the tactical training was not evaluated to determine successful completion of the course and award of the parachutist certification.

When examined in hindsight, this parachute training program is very similar to the parachute instruction in use today by many countries. The main focus is on the technical skill of parachuting, with the tactical training left to the units once the students graduated from the course. The tactical training offered at the school appeared to be more a plan to use the available time when the students were not engaged in actual parachute training, when weather or aircraft availability created a pause. This differs from the German approach in which the parachute schools trained both individuals and units.

25 Gary Hogg *Airship over the Pole* (London: Abeland-Schuman, 1969), pp.106–107.
26 Stefano Cagna (25 December 1901–1 August 1940). Later the youngest aviator promoted to *generale di brigata* (Brigadier General), Cagna would be killed leading his Stormo in an attack against a Malta bound convoy in 1940 and awarded a posthumous *Medaglia d'oro al valor militare* (Gold Medal of Military Valor).

Battaglione Paracadutisti

Order n. 64 also established the organization of *battaglione paracadutisti* (parachute battalions). The battalion was organized based on the ideas put forth by Balbo in a letter to the *Stato Maggiore dell'Aeronautica* dated 23 February 1938 where he observed:

> In consideration of the great possibilities that, in the vast colonial theater, [one] can have detachments of men carefully chosen, powerfully armed and above all decisive, especially if their action can lead to the rear of the main adversary lines, s.e. the Air Marshal [...] came with the determination to create special "paratrooper units" in both the indigenous and the metropolitan forces.
>
> These units, perfectly trained since peacetime, would be promptly launched in case of hostility by large aircraft behind the enemy troops and in areas of particular sensitivity to the effects of their resistance, so that their disruptive action could be successful and as effective as possible. Having said this, it is considered necessary to [...] establish a special school which should begin its operation as soon as possible in order to promptly prepare a first group of paratroopers to be activated during the great maneuvers in Gefara on the occasion of the coming of His Majesty the King Emperor.[27]

Later Balbo reinforced this thinking in another letter sent in 1939 stating '*above all, the expected use of the battalion was in small detachments, with the purpose, we can assume, of sabotage*'.[28]

The planned structure, in accordance with Order n.64, consisted of a command group and three line companies. Each line company would have four squads. The squads would have a junior officer, an NCO, a graduato, and five soldiers.[29] Total for a company was 33 men (one commanding officer, with four squads of eight men each); for the battalion was 100 men (one commanding officer and three companies). No weapons larger than rifles or carbines were authorized.[30]

This was a very small battalion by any nation's standard. The World War One infantry companies of all the combatants, including Italy, were normally 200 to 250 men in size. A World War Two Italian regular infantry company was 158 men and included 12 light machine guns and a supply section. Such a small unit clearly was not meant for sustained combat or possess the ability to attack strongly defended enemy positions. The unit lacked a command and control element; the single battalion level

27 Di Giovanni 32–33.

28 Stefano Ales, Piero Crociani, and Andrea Viotti *Struttura, Uniformi, distintivi ed insegne delle truppe libiche 1912-1943* (Rome: USSME, 2012), p.66: "si prevedeva l'impiego del battaglione soprattutto in piccoli nuclei, con finalità, possiamo presumere, di sabotaggio."

29 A graduato was a caporale (corporal) or caporale maggiore (corporal major). These ranks were considered senior privates in the RE rather than non-commissioned officers.

30 Arena *I Fanti*, pp.146–151; Ales, Crociani, Viotti *Struttura*, p.66.

officer was more of a garrison administration official as he lacked any means to plan or issue orders during combat. The unit also lacked any capacity to resupply itself or to recover and treat casualties. The sabotage/raid role of these units was evident in their structure, reflecting a capability that allowed for multiple squads to execute independent missions. Most of the prewar discussion indicated that these squads were expendable.

The order went on to address the weapons and equipment for the battalion. It is interesting that the order stated, "In principle, the main armament of the paratroopers will be a semi-automatic carbine and hand grenades." It is unclear to which weapon this passage identifies. It could be the newly developed *Moschetto Automatico Beretta* (MAB) 38A. Chambered in 9mm parabellum, the MAB 38 would later be considered one of the best submachine guns of the war. The issue is that while the MAB 38A was called a carbine, it was a fully automatic weapon. A second trigger did allow for semi-automatic fire, but the MAB was never referred to as a semi-automatic carbine. The other possibility is the Armaguerra Mod. 39 semi-automatic rifle (sometimes referred to as the Revelli semi-automatic rifle) that was being developed for the R.E. While this rifle would be authorized in later *reparti paracadutisti* organization documents, the rifle itself was untested and not accepted by the R.E. until 1939, a year after Order n.64 was issued. Nor was the rifle referred to as a carbine; it is always listed as a *fucili semiautomatici* in the documents. With the *Polizia dell'Africa Italiana* (Police of Italian Africa) receiving the MAB in 1938, the Beretta is likely the weapon Order n.64 was addressing.[31]

A unit completely armed with this weapon would have excellent firepower in close combat, the type of combat envisioned by all proponents of airborne units. For various reasons the R.E. was very reluctant to purchase and issue this weapon to army units. At the start of the war, only the *carabinieri* and the *Polizia dell'Africa Italiana* (P.A.I.) would have these weapons in any significant numbers, and those numbers were still very small. Nor would the Armaguerra Mod. 39 be available for use by the *paracadutisti*. As the semi-automatic rifle used the new 7.35mm cartridge that Italy had decided to abandon when it entered the war, the production of the rifle was stopped in June 1940 after only 2,000 rifles had been produced.

The *paracadutisti* main weapon for most of the war would be the moschetto per cavalleria (cavalry carbine) M91 Carcano. This was a 6.5mm bolt action carbine that used the Mannlicher magazine system. The rounds were held in a six-round clip that was inserted into the top of the rifle and pushed down until it locked into place. Once all six rounds had been fired, a fresh clip was inserted and it pushed the empty clip out the bottom of the carbine. Many individuals claim that this design created a weakness by allowing dirt and other debris into the system causing jams. The Mannlicher system was widely used by many other military rifles without this criticism being as forcefully applied to those weapons, and there is no evidence that the system was any

31 Arena *I Fanti*, pp.150.

better or worse than other magazine systems. The carbine had a fixed spike bayonet that was folded under the barrel when not in use. The carbine was light, easy to handle, and very reliable. The ammunition was packaged in boxes containing three clips (18 rounds) that fit into the standard leather ammunition pouch.[32]

Finally, Order n.64 stipulated that "In principle, a sufficient number of students will be admitted to each course to form a paratrooper battalion". How often a course would be offered is not stated, nor is there any discussion of maintaining the strength of existing parachute units addressed. One must remember that this order was the first in establishing a new speciality in the R.E. and further orders would be needed as the army gained experience in the use and support of the parachute units.

First Units

Recruiting had already begun in late 1937 and the first course for the battalion leadership and the school instructors started on 17 March 1938. One hundred and thirty students were in the course, which included twenty-four officers and NCOs from the R.A. that would be instructors at the school. Notable was the one senior officer in the course, *maggiore del genio* Gofferdo Tonini. He enlisted in the R.E. at the age of 18 in 1917 as a *bersaglieri* but transferred to the engineers. Assigned to a flamethrower company, his excellent wartime performance was recognized and he was sent to the reserve officers course at the *Regia Accademia di Artiglieria e Genio* (Royal Academy for Artillery and Engineers). Promoted to *tenente* in 1919, he earned a *Medaglia d'oro al Valor Militare* (Gold Medal for Military Valor) in Libya in 1923, and a combat promotion to major in 1936. He is the only senior (field grade) officer that volunteered to serve in the new parachute units and was appointed commander of the first battalion.[33]

The *I battaglione paracadutisti libici* was formally authorized on 20 March 1938 at Castel Benito.[34] The ground training was completed on 28 March and the first qualifying parachute jumps were made beginning on the 29th. *Maggorie* Tonini and 26 instructors made the first jumps. Joining them was *colonnello* Cagna, the Castel Benito commander and director of the parachute school. Qualifying jumps continued to be made on 31 March and 1 April.

The first course for the Libyan *ascari* began on 1 April with over 100 students. 1 April was also the first time the larger SM.81 aircraft was used; the previous drops were flown using the three Caproni. It was on this day that the school experienced its first fatality. The parachute of a Libyan *ascari*, Bu Ali Ugashi, failed to fully open

32 Russ Arendell & Steve Wooddrum, *Italy's Battle Rifle: The Story of the Mannlicher-Carcano Series of Rifles* (Arditi Press, 2012), p.29.

33 Goffredo Tonini (12 September 1898–19 April 1970). Captured during the war, he continued to serve in the post war Italian Army, reaching the rank of *generale di divisione* (Major General).

34 Arena *I Fanti*, p.18; Ales, Crociani, Viotti *Struttura*, p.328.

Maggiore Goffredo Tonini with the *I btg. «Fanti dell'aria»*. They are wearing D.39 parachutes and standing in front of SM.81 aircraft, likely from the *15° Stormo da bombardamento*. Tonini is the tall officer in the front left of the photograph. (AUSSME)

during a parachute drop from an altitude of 500 meters during the morning training. He was also seen to be unstable during his fall, which likely contributed to the parachute failure. He survived the fall but died shortly afterwards. After a pause, the parachute drops were continued, with an additional 79 successful jumps completed on that day.[35]

The training proceeded with few problems, and both classes together completed a mass parachute drop on 16 April in the presence of Air Marshal Balbo. Over 200 *paracadutisti* were dropped near the Castel Benito airfield starting at 1700. The *15° Stormo da Bombardamento* supported the mission, providing the transport aircraft for the exercise. In all, 24 SM.81 flew in formation to execute the drop. While the exercise was considered successful, problems with the parachutes began to surface, with three fatalities and 12 injuries attributed to its use.[36]

The experts at the school immediately began to analyze the problem. Several issues were subsequently identified. One was the positioning of the individual

35 Arena *I Fanti*, pp.20.
36 Arena *I Fanti*, p.22.

A Libyan parachutist jumping with a D.37 parachute. Note the leather cap, fascia di battaglione (waist sash), and the exercise shoes the jumper is wearing. (AUSSME)

A company of *paracadutisti libici* at Castel Benito. The picture was likely taken during the training of the *I btg. libici* in March–April 1938 as the company is organized in accordance with Order n.64, with four squads of eight men each. (AUSSME)

aircraft in the three-ship formation used for the drop. The three aircraft flew at the same altitude which allowed the turbulence from the propellers to affect the opening and deployment of the parachute canopy. Another issue was the shock of the parachute deployment causing the jumper to slide in the harness, with the possibility of inducing a spin or tumbling. The Salvator D.37 only had one shoulder strap over the left shoulder, and one leg strap around the right leg, an arrangement that did not fully secure the jumper in the harness. A final issue was that twisting in the harness could cause the parachutist to prematurely open the parachute too close to the aircraft. The jumper exited the aircraft with his right hand on the manual release and the twisting movement could cause the parachutist to unintentionally pull the release with that hand. Procedures were added to the training to minimize these problems, but the Salvator D.37 was proving to be unsuitable as paratrooper equipment.[37]

The mass parachute drop on 16 April completed the training of the first airborne unit in the R.E. The unit itself was given the name «*Fanti dell'aria*» (Infantrymen of the air) and included both the Italian officers and non-commissioned officers and the Libyan soldiers. The name itself was selected by Balbo to partially desensitize the senior military leaders to the fact that he had formed a paratrooper unit at a time when issues remained unresolved between the services. The name «*Ascari del cielo*» (Ascari of the sky) was the name for only the Libyan paratroopers. Often the two names are used interchangeably which is incorrect.[38]

The organization of the battalion at this time differed from that outlined in Order n.64, being twice again as large (300 men). The battalion was organized with a command platoon and four instead of three line companies. The companies themselves were larger and organized similar to the alpini companies of the R.E. These changes enabled the unit to operate as a battalion, with the command platoon providing a limited offensive capability and a degree of logistical support.[39]

This undocumented change now added a new weapon for the *paracadutisti*, the Breda 30 *fucile mitragliatori* (f.m., light machine-gun). Whereas Order n.64 stated the main weapons would be the semi-automatic carbine and the hand grenade, the addition of two f.m. provided the nine-man *squadra paracadutisti* with considerable firepower. A regular Italian infantry squad of seventeen men also only had two f.m. The Breda 30 itself has been generally condemned as the worst light machine-gun of the war and there is a degree of truth in that statement. It was an awkward weapon to handle and the reloading system prevented sustained fire. Initially infantry squads in the 1930s were only authorized one f.m. but this was changed to two f.m. working

37 Arena *I Fanti*, p.22–24.

38 Di Martino, *Paracadutisti d'Italia*, vol 1, p.9.

39 Arena *I Fanti*, p.36 states that four companies were formed. Photographs of the parachute units taken during *Operazione «Gefara»* and Herman Göring's visit in April 1939 showing a nine-man squad equipped with two Breda 30 fucile mitragliatori, see Arena *I fanti*, pp.53 and 76.

together to provide sustained fire. The Breda 30 proved to be a serviceable, if less than ideal weapon that continued to be used throughout the war.[40]

The *II battaglione paracadutisti libici «Fanti dell'aria»* was authorized on 20 April 1938. Training began shortly afterwards and was completed with a mass parachute drop on 10 May. This battalion would never reach its full authorized strength of three hundred men, possibly indicating that the reported deaths and injuries were beginning to impact recruiting. Command was given to an infantry officer, *maggiore* Virgilio Corrente.[41]

With the training of the *II battaglione* complete, Balbo now officially created the *1° reggimento libici «Fanti dell'aria»*. Command was given to *Console della Milizia* Giovanni Rocca, an officer of the Milizia Volontaria per la Sicurezza Nazionale (M.V.S.N., known as the Black Shirts). This was more of an honorary command, as operational command of the regiment would be exercised by *maggorie* Tonini. Command of Tonini's *I btg.* was passed to *maggiore* Ermete Dondini.

On 18 May 1938, the entire regiment executed a parachute drop in the presence of the Air Marshal and those senior officers of the *Stato Maggiore Italiano* that had arrived early for the grand maneuvers scheduled to be held later in the month. Five hundred parachutists took part in a drop near the Castel Benito airfield supported by the 15° *Stormo*. The latter was reinforced by the *14° Stormo da Bombardamento* which had flown to Libya from Sicily to participate in the exercise. Again death and injuries marred the event, with seven deaths and 42 men injured. The large number of deaths shook the morale of the Libyan *ascari* and it took all the leadership skills and enthusiasm of the officers to keep the unit from breaking up. Practice jumps were executed on 19–21 May with no additional injuries and the confidence of the *ascari* was restored. The lessons from 16 April were further refined which included using a higher jump altitude and the remaining time was focused on training the new procedures.[42]

Maresciallo dell'Aria Balbo had accomplished in four months what the Regio Esercito had failed to do since May 1936; create and train a regimental size airborne unit. The question now was how well would the regiment perform during the Grand Maneuver.

Operazione «Gefara» (Map 1.1)

Such was the focus of the maneuver on the *paracadutisti* that the grand maneuver was given the name *Operazione «Gefara»*. Gefara was a plain in the desert south of Tripoli that was the objective of the *divisione aviotrasportabile* during the exercise. Planning

40 *Fucile mitragliatori* would normally be translated as submachine-gun, but the Breda 30 is actually a light machine-gun. It was called a *mitragliatrice leggera* (light machine-gun) until 1936.

41 Arena *I Fanti*, p.36.

42 Dante Pariset, *Storica del paracadutismo* (Roma-Milano, Vito Bianco Editore, 1962), p.69; Arena *I Fanti*, p.36.

for the upcoming maneuver had already been completed that included the new regiment, an indication of Balbo's intent to showcase the new capability.

Large scale military maneuvers had been a staple for many countries for the past decades as a means to train both senior leaders and major units and to test new concepts and equipment. For Balbo in Africa settentrionale, the 1938 maneuver would examine the Italian defensive plan against a French invasion of Libya. War planning under generale Pariani had transitioned from a passive defense to options for offensive action on either the Tunisian or Egyptian fronts. Pariani also recognized the need to motorize the army and was considering the creation of two motorized divisions for Libya.[43] With this in mind, the stated goals of the exercise were: 1) test the movement by road of an army corps from the Cirenaica to Tripoltania to reinforce the western border, 2) to train divisions in maneuver warfare, and 3) to train colonial units to operate with national (metropolitan) units. To the testing of these concepts Balbo now added a fourth, "experiment with new forms of aerial force intervention in battle".[44]

The maneuver structure was envisioned as an Italian defense against an attack by France from Tunisia.[45] The Red team (France) consisted of the XX Corpo d'Armata, with three *divisioni autotrasportabili*, the *60ª d. at. «Sabratha»*, the *61ª d. at. «Sirte»*, and one notional division called the *59ª*; the *58ª divisione di fanteria aviotrasportata di formazione* (experimental aero-transport division);[46] a *gruppo tattico libico*; and a colonial aviation group. The Red Force was supported by a bomber stormo (SM.81) and the *50º Stormo d'Assalto* (ground support with Ba.65s) from the R.A. The Blue forces (Italy) consisted of the *XXI Corpo d'Armata* with three divisioni autotrasportabili, the *62ª d. at. «Marmarica»*, the *63ª d. at. «Cirene»*, and a notional division; a *gruppo tattico libico*; and a colonial aviation group. The Blue was supported by a bomber stormo (SM.81) and a fighter group from the R.A.

The experimental *divisione aviotrasportata* was organized with a headquarters unit, the *1º reggimento «Fanti dell'aria»*, the *70º reggimento fanteria* from the *d. at.* «Sirte», the *10º reggimento libici*, a gruppo artiglieria libici da 65/17 with three batteries, a

43 John Gooch, *Mussolini and his Generals* (New York: Cambridge University Press, 2007), pp.361–362.

44 AUSMM Governor Generale della Libia, Comando Superiore Forze Armata Africa Settentrionale, *Esercitazione anno XVI in libra (XI–XXIV maggio 1938)* (Cartelle Numerate b.2726/f.2), p.6.

45 The main sources for the discussion of the 1938 maneuver are: Filippo Cappellano and Paolo Formiconi, 'Italo Balbo e le grandi manovre del 1938 in Libia', *Storia Militare*, 218 (2011), pp.4–16; Basilio Di Martino, 'Il controllo a lungo raggio del deserto. Le esperienze italiane in Libia negli anni Trenta' *Antologia Militare* vol 1, n. 4 (2020), pp.3–60; John Gooch, *Generals*, pp.416–417; Arena, *I Fanti*, pp.36–40; AUSMM Governor Generale della Libia, *Esercitazione anno XVI in libra (XI–XXIV maggio 1938)*, cart. b.2726/f.2.

46 A *divisione autotrasportabile* is a regular infantry division with vehicles replacing animal transport for the artillery and services. Formazione is normally translated as training or to indicate a unit in the process of being raised, formed, or created. Experimental better defines this unit.

plotone motomitraglieri with twenty motorcycles,[47] an engineer company, and various support services (supply, medical, and chemical). Balbo understood the need for close coordination between the R.E. and the R.A. given the method used to transport such units in combat. To aid this coordination, Balbo directed that the division's deputy commander and the senior transportation officers be assigned from the Regia Aeronautica.

It was decided that only select units would be fully mobilized to test the mobilization plans for Libya. The majority of the units would be at peacetime strength, between approximately 30–50 percent of their wartime authorization. The entire event would consist of 21,000 national (Italian) soldiers, 4,000 Libyans, 2,400 animals (horse and camels), 3,000 vehicles, and 180 aircraft. Included in these numbers were the 500 men of the *1º reggimento «Fanti dell'aria»*.

The maneuver plan for the exercise was broken down into three phases. The first phase was the movement of the *XXI Corpo d'Armata* from Cirenaica to Azizia, just south of Tripoli. 8,100 men with 1,150 vehicles traveled the 1,550 kilometers in three serials representing the three divisions in seven stages. At the same time, Red was planning an attack along the coastal road in the north and along a track in the south towards Jefren. This phase was executed between 11 and 18 May. The second phase brought the opposing forces into contact. Blue decided to attack south-west against the Red's southern group. Red attacked in Blue's center to try to break through to Aziza. This phase ended in a stalemate on 22 May.

Operazione «Gefara», the airborne operation, was the third phase. The *58ª divisione aviotrasporta* had been moving as the reserve for the Red Force until 22 May. On that day the unit moved to Castel Benito. At the airport the unit linked up with the four bomber *stormo* designated to support the airborne operation. The *15º Stormo Bombardamento Terrestre* (B.T.) was permanently assigned to Libya and had previously supported parachute training. The *14º Stormo B.T.* had arrived from Sicily in April to support the parachute training leading up the operation. The *33º* and *34º Stormo B.T.* had arrived from Italy on 19 May to support the second and third phases of the maneuver. One hundred aircraft were available to support the airborne portion of the event. The parachute drop and air movement had to be organized at Castel Benito as it was the only air field capable of handling the large number of aircraft. To simulate flying from an airfield behind friendly lines, the aircraft would make a wide detour over the Gulf of Sirte before heading inland to the drop zone. The drop zone itself was the Plains of Sidi Belgasen located just east of Bir el-Ghnem. It was 40 kms behind the enemy lines.

The SM.81 bomber had been designed to be capable of both the bombing and transport missions. Testing in April had determined that little needed to be done to prepare the aircraft for parachute operations. To airlift the 65/17 guns and the

47 *Motomitraglieri* are motorcycle-mounted machine-gun units. They use a combination of two-wheeled and three-wheel motorcycles.

motorcycles, the aircraft require a quick modification which included removing the bomb racks and laying planks over the open bay to make that space useable for cargo. As the 65/17 gun was designed to be broken down for transport by mule in five loads, loading the guns onto the aircraft was greatly simplified. After testing, the aircraft were rated to carry 2,000 kilograms. This translated into 20–25 fully equipped infantry, or a single 65/17 gun with its ten man crew and eight ammunition boxes, or a motorcycle mounted machine gun and fifteen soldiers. With any of these loads, the SM.81 still had a round-trip range of 500 kms with a crew of four men.[48]

On the morning of 23 May, the fighters and ground support aircraft took off at 0800 and began to attack targets in the plain by 0850. At 0900, the *15° Stormo* carried the *1° btg. libico «Fanti dell'Aria»* arrived over the drop zone and the *paracadutisti* began to exit the aircraft. Implementing the lessons learned from the parachute jump exercises of 16 April and 18 May, the 200 men all landed safely with only a few minor injuries amongst the unit. The battalion quickly established a perimeter and a radio station, the latter allowing them to contact the aircraft supporting the operation. At this point on, the *paracadutisti* on the ground controlled the operation by radio. Flight and weather information was passed to the arriving aircraft while controlling the flow of the SM.81s in landing and discharging their cargo at the air strip.

The *34° Stormo* was the first to land at 0915, discharging the division command, the *plotone motomitraglieri*, and the service elements. The *33° Stormo* landed the *10° rgt. libici* at 0925, followed by the *15° Stormo* that was returning with the artillery at 0935. The *14° Stormo* then landed with the *70° rgt. fanteria* at 0945. By 1000 hours, the division was ready to move towards its objective at Bir el-Ghnem.

The Grand Maneuver ended later that same day. The parachute drop and the air landings had been observed by the King and senior members of the military. On 24 May a review of the units involved was held and honors were conferred on the participants by the King. *Maggiore* Tonini received the *Cavaliere dell'Ordine dei Santi Maurizio e Lazzaro*, while Console Rocca received the *Grande Ufficiale dell'Ordine della Corona d'Italia*. Other officers were presented with lesser awards.

Many had been impressed, but it is unclear how many saw the airborne unit as a capability worth developing. The actual parachute drop of the exercise went well with no deaths and only 17 injuries.[49] In a report given to Mussolini after the Grand Maneuver:

> … the launch of the reggimento «Fanti dell'aria» (200 men) and the air transport of an infantry division (3,200 men with twelve 65/17 guns), carried out without special preparation, with Salvator parachutes and using normal bombing aircraft (a hundred SM.81s), have shown that this new form of maneuver is practically feasible in war: all skepticism is now overcome; the vertical envelopment

48 Di Martino, 'Il controllo', p.49.
49 Arena, *I Fanti*, p.38.

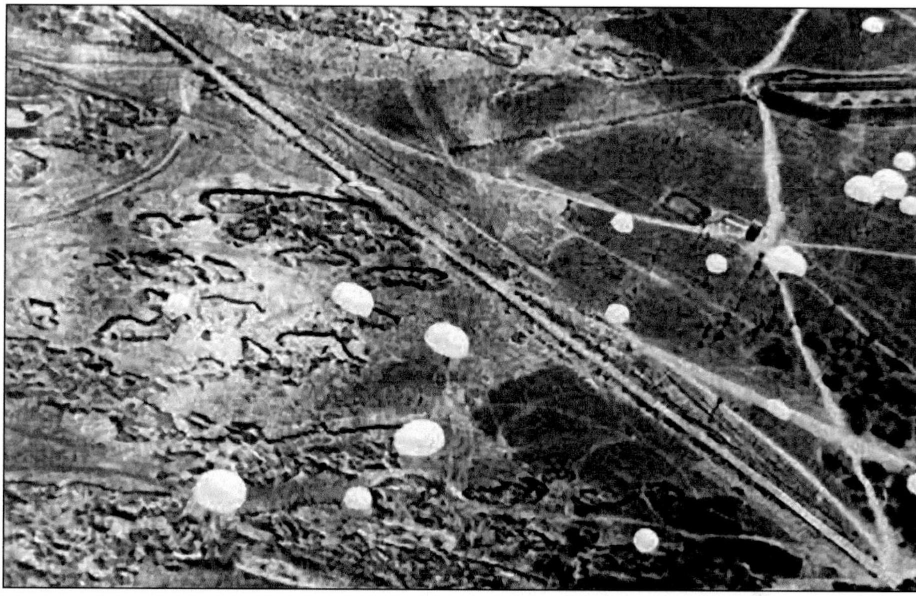

The mass parachute drop on 16 April 1938 attended by Maresciallo Balbo. The 15° Stormo da Bombardamento provided the aircraft for the exercise. (AUSSME)

A *squadra paracadutisti libici* during *Operazione «Gefara»*. Note the two Breda 30 fucili mitragliatori that are not authorized under Order. n.64 or under the 1939 authorization. (AUSSME)

> maneuver, very possible in North Africa, based on speed and surprise that is a vital essence of offensive strategy, can have grandiose decisive effects and opens new horizons in the doctrine of war of rapid decision.[50]

One important statement in this report is the phrase 'very possible in North Africa'. This again touches on the theoretical discussion of whether large-scale airborne operations were possible in continental Europe. North Africa, with its wide open spaces and most of its small population confined to a limited number of cities and towns, offered operational solutions that many did not see as valid options in Europe. The additional points on the use of the D.37 and normal bombing aircraft hold the hint that development of a better parachute and dedicated aircraft could enhance the effectiveness of vertical envelopment as an operational maneuver option. Now that Balbo had demonstrated the possibilities, how were the lessons absorbed by the Italian senior military leadership?

50 Cappellano and Formiconi, 'Italo Balbo', pp.13-14.

2

Paracadutisti libici

The immediate impact of *Operazione «Gefara»* was demonstrated by what was not done or changed. Whilst Balbo had established the first parachute regiment in the Italian military, it was still very much an experimental unit. The S.M.R.E. still did not recognize the parachute school at Castel Benito or the *1º reggimento «Fanti dell'aria»* and treated both as uniquely colonial. Nor was the issue of indemnity for families of *paracadutisti* injured or killed fully resolved. Due to these factors and the concerns about the Salvator D.37, parachute training at Castel Benito was immediately suspended after the maneuvers by the *Comando Superiore FF.AA. in A.S.* The school itself would be maintained and continue to experiment and test new equipment and launch procedures, but no new parachute courses would start until the issues with the Salvator parachute had been identified and corrected. This in itself was a costly decision by Balbo, as the S.M.R.E. would only allow the school to continue if the entire budget was funded by the colonial administration.[1]

The other casualty due to the lack of any formal support from the S.M.R.E. was the disbanding of the *II btg. paracadutisti libico «Fanti dell'aria»* and the *1º rgt. «Fanti dell'aria»*. Recruiting had slowed and the second battalion had never reached its authorized strength. Especially lacking were officers and senior NCOs to volunteer to fill the leadership positions. In the three months that the two battalions had been actively jumping, there had been twenty-three deaths and over one hundred serious injuries. The large number of casualties incurred during the jumps on 16 April and 18 May (10 deaths and 54 injuries) was seen as a major factor in this problem. *Maggiore* Tonini and the other battalion officers worked hard to maintain morale and discipline within the unit. Even though additional demonstration jumps on 19, 20 and 21 May were executed without incident, morale had taken a severe blow and some *ascari* would

1 Marco Di Giovanni, *I paracadutisti italiani Volontari, miti e memoria della seconda guerra mondiale* (Gorizia: Editrice Goriziana, 1991), pp.33–34.

leave the unit after the completion of the Grand Maneuver.[2] The *ascari* from the now disbanded *II btg.* were either assigned to the *1° btg.*, transferred back to other R.C.T.C. units, or released from service. The regiment headquarters itself was always ad hoc with no formal authorization, so was disbanded at the same time.[3]

With parachute training halted, the battalion focused on enhanced unit training and improving individual skills. The rapid creation of the two battalions and the need to complete parachute training in time for the Grand Maneuver left little time for unit training. For the remainder of 1938, the men of the *I btg.* practiced a wide range of infantry and raiding tasks. Standard infantry instruction on marksmanship and tactical movement were interwoven with demolition training, survival skills, use of radio and telephone systems, land navigation, and the use of air recognition panels to coordinate air support. *Ascari* learned to drive and maintain vehicles as raids and sabotage missions behind enemy lines could require the use of captured vehicles. The wide scope and duration of the training was significantly better than that given to the average Italian soldier, crafting a unit that was tactically competent from the squad through to battalion level. The comprehensive nature and intensity of the training would be a hallmark of the Italian *paracadutisti*.[4]

The lack of parachute training did not cause the work at the school to stop. The priority task was reducing or eliminating casualties during parachute jumps. Freri looked at both the material (the D.37 parachute) and the training aspects to resolve the problem.

The problem with the D.37 was that the parachute was not designed to support the increased weight of a fully equipped parachutist. The smallish canopy size was meant to fit inside the confined space of an aircraft cockpit and to handle only the weight of a pilot without any equipment. The opening shock was quite hard and the single shoulder and leg straps allowed the jumper to shift in the harness. This shifting affected the stability of the parachutist during the fall, inducing spin. The buckle system was not designed for the speedy release and removal of the harness once on the ground. Designed for single use by air crew, the parachute itself was too lightly made to handle the repeated use required for training.[5]

The resolution of these problems required that a new parachute be developed. The new parachute was a modified version of the D.37 and was called the Salvator D.39 and was developed and tested during the latter part of 1938. The main changes were the addition of a second shoulder and leg strap to better secure the jumper in the harness,

2 Nino Arena, *I Fanti dell'Aria da Castel Benito ad Azizia (libia) (1938-1941)* (Bologna : Edition Eurographis, 1989), p.36

3 Sources intermix the use of *I btg.* and *1° btg.* when identifying the Libyan battalion. *1° btg.* instead of *I btg.* is used here to indicate that the battalion was no longer associated with a regiment.

4 Arena, *I Fanti*, p.40.

5 Arena *I Fanti*, 20; Guy Richards, *World War II Troop Type Parachutes: Axis,* (Atglen, Pennsylvania: Schiffer Military History, 2000), p.14.

modifying the canopy pack tray, and increasing the size of the canopy to handle the weight of a fully equipped soldier. The new canopy was 54 sq.m. of silk and reduced the descent rate to 6 m/s. The complete pack weighed 12 kgs. The location of the manual handle and the suspension lines remained unchanged, and the canopy was still pack tray deployed.[6]

The D.39 parachute. The harness has two shoulder and two leg straps, a single buckle and the static line pouch on the right side of the waist belt. (R.E. parachute manual) (AUSSME)

Reevaluation of the training was done at the same time the D.39 was being tested. One problem that had been identified was the premature opening of the canopy by the accidental activation of the manual release. The initial procedure taught to the *paracadutisti* was to grip the manual release handle with the right hand while the left hand guided the static line carabiner along the static line cable when approaching the aircraft door. The reason behind this procedure was so the paratrooper could quickly activate the parachute if something was wrong. The combination of the diving jump position and the impact of the air striking the parachutist as he exited the aircraft caused jumpers to jerk the manual handle, opening the parachute. This often happened before the jumper had fully cleared the aircraft. This could result in the prop wash preventing the canopy from fully inflating or it being struck by the aircraft, causing damage to the canopy. The procedure was changed so that the right hand gripped the left shoulder strap above the manual release.[7]

Another issue was how the left hand gripped the static line as the parachutist moved towards the door inside the aircraft. The parachutist had to move/guide the static line hook/carabiner along the overhead static line cable inside the aircraft as he moved towards the exit door. As he reached the door, he released the carabiner and assumed the jump exit position. Grabbing the static line the natural way to guide the

6 Richards, *World War II Troop Type Parachutes*, p.14.
7 Arena, *I Fanti*, p.40.

carabiner in the palm with the fingers wrapped around with the static line hanging straight down from the static line cable made it possible for the static line to get caught under the parachutist's left arm. The parachutist had to remember to release the carabiner and bring his left hand over the line to grab the right shoulder strap. The change adopted was to create a loop in the static line that was held between the thumb and index finger such that the static line to the parachute laid on-top of the left hand. When released, the left arm was under the static line and could grab the right shoulder strap without trapping the static line under the arm.[8]

The method of exiting the aircraft was also changed. Previously the *paracadutisti* were taught to dive out of the door and assume the angel position (arms and legs extended out in an X position). This placed the jumper in a nearly horizontal position when the parachute opened, jerking the body skyward by the waist belt. This could introduce a violent shock injuring the parachutist. The exit was changed to a standing position with the parachutist jumping straight out from the aircraft instead of downward, opening his body to the angel position as the parachute deployed. This helped to stabilize the parachutist and reduce any violent twisting motion while the canopy opened.[9]

As previously mentioned, the three aircraft vee formation was modified, reducing the turbulence through which the parachutists were traveling. All together these changes reduced the deaths during parachute drops from 3 percent to 0.3 percent and injuries from 18 percent down to 2 percent.[10] With other minor adjustments, the rate became even lower. Between January 1939 to the start of the British offensive in December 1940 which ended airborne training in A.S., over 6,000 parachute jumps were completed. The casualty rate (deaths and injuries) for these jumps was only 0.1 percent of the total.[11]

The issue of funding the parachute school and the payment of indemnities for injury or death were finally resolved in November 1938. The decree that finally addressed the issue was sent to the King on 24 November 1938 and placed the financial burden on the Ministry for Italian Africa, with compensation to the RA for costs incurred to that point. Funding to support the continued operation would be shared between the War Ministry, the Air Force Ministry, the Ministry for Italian Africa, and the Governo Generale for Libya. In all, a complicated arrangement that gave official approval to the school at Castel Benito and the «*Fanti dell'aria*».[12]

It was not until January 1939 that the *1º battaglione libico «Fanti dell'aria»* was able to resume parachute training. At the same time, the battalion was reorganized,

8 Arena, *I Fanti*, pp.40–41.
9 Arena, *I Fanti*, p.41.
10 Arena, *I Fanti*, p.41.
11 Arena, *I Fanti*, p.61; Nino Arena *50ª di Tarquinia, 1939-1989, Scuole Militare paracadutismo* (Comitato Promotore ex Istruttori delle Scuole Militari di Paracadutismo, 1989), p.106.
12 Arena, *I Fanti*, p.41.

A hanger at Castel Benito. Training jumps were executed in the area of the airfield. (AUSSME)

increasing its authorized size to 175 men. This organization was documented in March 1939 and included an enlarged headquarters company and three line companies. The headquarter's company now consisted of a command group, a command platoon, a communication/liaison platoon, and a service platoon. Each parachute company had a *guastatori* platoon and five rifle platoons.[13] Total authorized strength of the battalion was 24 officers, 1 NCO, and 150 soldiers. The unit equipment included 17 f.m., 134 carbines, staff car, truck, and 2 bicycles.[14]

The new structure provided a command and control element that was previously lacking. The service platoon gave the battalion some capability to sustain itself during combat operations. The two changes together (command and control and sustainment) would allow the unit to operate in a limited fashion as a ground maneuver unit for longer periods. The restructured parachute companies were now able to assault

13 The guastatori were a specialized type of sapper, often referred to as assault engineers. They specialized in breaching/destroying structures and defensives. They did not build bridges, structures, or defenses, unlike sappers in other armies.

14 Stefano Ales, Piero Crociani, and Andrea Viotti *Struttura, Uniformi, distintivi ed insegne delle truppe libiche 1912–1943* (Rome: USSME, 2012), pp.66–67.

defended locations, with five f.m. and a *guastatori* platoon to breach the defenses. The battalion's small size (175 men) meant it required fewer aircraft for transport, but limited the use of the unit to a single mission as the unit lacked any staying power once it took casualties.

There is little evidence that the battalion was fully reorganized under this structure. The unit maintained its current four company structure and pictures of the unit during this timeframe continue to show two f.m. in the squad, not one. The few existing company rosters only reflect three platoons without any assault engineers. As all the soldiers underwent the *guastatori* type training, it is likely that the need for a separate platoon was perceived as unnecessary.[15]

Other changes were happening in 1939, the most noticeable being the uniform. From the creation of the *reparti paracadutisti*, the officers and men executed their parachute jumps in the same uniform they wore in their original units. For officers, it was the khaki sahariana style tunic and riding breeches, tall leather officer boots, and bustina (the bustina was rapidly replaced by a pilot's leather helmet). The *ascari* wore their regular khaki tunic and breeches, puttees and sandals, and the red tachia (a fez style cap) with tassel of the Libyan troops. The *fanti dell'aria* also wore the *fascia di battaglione* (battalion waist sash) that was part of the R.C.T.C. uniform. These fascia were colored patterned sashes wrapped around the waist that denoted the various units in the R.C.T.C. The *fanti dell'aria* originally had a solid celestial blue fascia in 1938, which was changed to a white fascia with azure blue vertical stripes in 1939.[16]

Such uniforms were not very practical for parachuting and reflected the haste in the creation of the new speciality. The lack of a tall boot to support the ankles and a functional helmet for head protection were the root cause for many of the earlier landing injuries. The tunics had many features that could snag parachute lines and harness straps, and did not secure small items in pockets against the force of the air. The fascia and puttees, the latter a functional uniform item in many ways, were exceedingly dangerous during jumps. One must be impressed with the bravery of the *ascari* when parachuting wearing such a uniform. Combined with the issues with the Salvator D.37, the high injury rate is more understandable.

The regular uniforms were replaced by a khaki overall with four zipper pockets for parachuting. The leg cuffs and wrists were closed by buttoned straps and the physical training canvas shoe replaced the sandals. The *ascari* wore a red or maroon leather cap, similar to a leather flight helmet during jumps, while officers wore the R.A. standard maroon leather flight helmet. Shortly afterwards the officers' khaki overalls were replaced by the Marus flight suit as worn by R.A. pilots. Foot wear remained unchanged, an element that would not be corrected until 1941.

15 Arena, *I Fanti*, p.145

16 Arena, *I Fanti*, p.60; Ales, Crociani, and Viotti *Struttura*, pp.185–186; Massimo Di Martino, *Paracadutisti d'Italia – Uniformi distintivi equipaggiamenti. Vol 1, 1938–1943* (Milan: Edizioni Libreria Militare, 2019), p.13..

Using the hangar at Castel Benito for parachute training. Note the jumping *ascari* is wearing the single piece overalls and the leather helmet. (AUSSME)

New insignia was introduced for the specialty. The paratroopers wore the Libyan infantry fregio (hat badge), but a distinctive *paracadutisti* badge was authorized for wear on the right breast of the tunic. The badge in red indicated three parachute jumps; and a silver badge denoted 20 jumps.

At the same time as the jump training resumed for the battalion, the school began to conduct training for new *paracadutisti*. Recruitment had improved due to the resolution of indemnities and additional pay for the members of the R.C.T.C. and 12 classes were completed during the course of 1939. In total 360 Italian officers, NCOs, and enlisted men were trained, along with an unspecified number of Libyans which were to maintain the *I battaglione* at its authorized strength. A new parachute was also under development and testing, the Salvator D.40. This parachute design for the first time incorporated twin risers that suspended the parachutist from the shoulders instead of the waist. New quick release buckles were introduced and the manual release handle was moved from the waist belt to the left shoulder strap. The D.40 was tested and could be safely jumped from an altitude as low as 70 meters. The testing also included the parachutists jumping with their weapons attached to the harness instead of using the resupply containers.[17]

New Doctrine

While the technical work of creating an airborne force was ongoing, the conceptual and doctrinal work of how these units would be employed was also evolving. The *Ministero della Guerra* released the first formal document that presented how the *reparti paracadutisti* would be used during wartime. The *Addestramento e impiego dei reparti paracadutisti* was dated 19 January 1939 and was written mainly by the R.A. The introduction indicated the tentative nature of the manual:

> These regulations are for guidance; the practical application of them may suggest the variants and modifications of the [various] cases.
>
> Within the scope of these regulations:
>
> - the directives and instructions for physical training and for the use of the paratroopers on the ground are the responsibility of the Ministry of War, Headquarters of the General Staff;
> - the directives and instructions for training in parachuting and for air transport are the responsibility of the Ministry of Aeronautics, Office of the General Staff.
>
> The instruction and training materials described herein, already existing at Royal Army units and already subject to initial tests, are to be considered entirely experimental and therefore susceptible to improvements and replacement based on the results of definitive practical tests to which they will be subjected at the parachute school.[18]

The first paragraph of the manual then states, "The paratrooper units, arranged in squads, platoons, companies and battalions, are the arditi units of heaven and earth."[19] This focus on small unit actions, the raison d'être of the arditi, continues

17 Arena, *I Fanti*, p.60; Richards, *World War II Troop Type Parachutes*, p.14.
18 Anon, *Addestramento e impiego dei reparti paracadutisti* (Rome: Ministero dell'Aeronautica, 1939), p.5.
19 Anon, *Addestramento e impiego dei reparti paracadutisti*, p.11.

throughout the manual. Paragraph 4 states that it would be something exceptional to employ an entire battalion.[20]

It is Paragraph 8 that gives one an understanding of how the Italian senior military leadership perceived the use of the parachute force.

> The use of the paratrooper unit is the responsibility of the supreme command, which, in principle, decentralizes them, for effective action, to the commands of army and army groups.
>
> It is up to these last commands to specify the purposes to be achieved and to set the time limits within which they must be achieved, the forces and vehicles to be used, the drop zones (after consulting with the commander of the paratroop unit), and the modalities for action on the ground.[21]

The assignment of these units to the theater commander places their employment at the tactical level. The Italian military did not assign joint commands at the theater level (a single commander in control of the three services in a theater) but maintained separate service commands that were coordinated by *Stato Maggiore Generale* (S.M.G., *Comando Supremo*). A theater commander lacked the resources needed to employ these units as paratroops without going back to *Comando Supremo* for the required assets. The German use of the fallschirmjägers in Denmark, The Netherlands, and Crete were operations initiated by either the Oberkommando der Wehrmacht (High Command of the Military Forces) or the Oberkommando des Heeres (High Command of the Armies), both headquarters functioning at the national/strategic level. The assignment of the *reparti paracadutisti* to the various theaters without a specific operational goal relegated their employment to traditional infantry roles as future events will show.

Planning for War

With the school and the parachute battalion now a reality, did Italy actually identify a need for the capability? Well, yes and no. Balbo had worked hard to create the new speciality, but there was some question at that time whether he had a vision for these units beyond their propaganda value. Balbo and his staff never wrote a complete offensive plan for the Italian forces in Libya. In response to a routine request from the S.M.R.E. to update the current plans, Balbo submitted his Piano di Radunata D (P.R.D.) on 26 October 1938.[22] The P.R.D. was mainly a mobilization plan that outlined the required forces, the location of those forces by front, and some broad

20 Anon, *Addestramento e impiego dei reparti paracadutisti*, p.12.
21 Anon, *Addestramento e impiego dei reparti paracadutisti*, p.13.
22 Anon, *In Africa settentrionale: La preparazione al conflitto l'avanzata su Sidi Barran*i (Rome: USSME, 1955), pp.47-48.

objectives and scheme of maneuver. The D in the identifier indicated that the plan was provisional and required additional forces provided from Italy. It presented an operational scheme of defense in the west facing the French and an offense in the east against the United Kingdom. The plan called for an Italian offensive into Egypt by the *10ª Armata* while the *5ª Armata* defended against the French in Tunisia. This plan, developed months after *Operazione «Gefara»*, did not include any proposed use of parachute troops as part of the operation. Given Balbo's support for the development and use of paratroopers and his successful demonstration, this omission was surprising.[23] The proposed P.R.D. ran counter to *maresciallo* Badoglio position of a defense on both fronts and was not approved.[24]

Apparently the possibilities demonstrated by *Operazione «Gefara»* did not go unnoticed by the army staff. An initial discussion and study on *truppi aviotrasportabili* took place in March 1939. In the 8 May 1939 Army Council meeting called by Mussolini, the S.M.R.E. presented its assessment on the R.E. requirements to meet the national strategy. In it, the R.E. proposed a *corpo aviotrasportabile* that would consist of two divisions. What was not included was the rationale for its likely deployment to justify its creation.[25]

The concept for the corps is interesting and indicates the army's thoughts on airborne operations. Each division consisted of an air echelon and a ground echelon. While not stated, the divisions likely would have followed the organization used in *Operazione «Gefara»*: a parachute regiment and an infantry regiment with supporting arms. The proposal specifically stated that none of the support services would be parachute capable, limiting what the air echelon could accomplish on its own. It is not known whether the infantry regiment would be air transportable, but the proposal specifically states that it would be moved by vehicles and used to complete the unit as a normal divisione fanteria (infantry division). The air landing of a conventional regiment during the grand maneuver did demonstrate that no special organizational changes were required, leaving the option of air transport as a possibility. When the two echelons operated together on the ground, the unit was intended to function as a regular infantry division. The proposal did identify the two divisions recommended to form this corps, the *23ª divisione fanteria «Ferrara»* and the *53ª divisione fanteria «Arezzo»*.[26]

Like several of the R.E. initiatives in the 1930s, this proposal favored a design that made the units multifunctional. As the R.E. was in reality a light infantry army, most of the company and battalion weaponry was already man portable and suitable for use in airborne operations. The disadvantage to this approach was that units

23 Lucio Ceva, 'Balbo e la preparazione della guerra in Africa Settentrionale', *Italia Contemporanea*, 243 (2006), p.215; Mario Montanari, *L'esercito italiano alla vigilia della 2ª guerra mondiale* (Rome: USSME, 1982), pp.62–65.
24 Gooch, *Generals*, pp.466–467.
25 Gooch, *Generals*, p.470.
26 AUSSME Consiglio dell'esercito, 8 maggio 1939 I: Nuovo ordinamento dell'esercito e principali provvedimenti nel campo organico, pp.5–7. Rep F-9 racc. 6/f.3.

lacked heavier weapons that would be required for sustained combat against conventional forces. What is unknown from the proposal is whether the ground detachment contained additional heavy support weapons that would be used by the air element when the two are operating as a regular infantry division. Because half the unit is lighter than a normal infantry regiment, it is less capable of fulfilling the traditional role of regular infantry without augmentation.

The split nature of the divisions limited what this corps could achieve. It is assumed that the ground echelon was the main element to create a link-up with the dropped parachutists. Two parachute regiments, without support weapons and services, were likely too weak to survive for an extended length of time. Two regimental sized ground units (assuming both divisions were used together) were likely insufficient to create a breakthrough of enemy lines to reach the deployed paratroopers.

The multifunctional design is an indication that no specific strategic or operational requirement had been identified. Instead this proposal appears to be more of a half-hearted attempt to create a capability with as little effort as possible and without a validated requirement. Balbo's division was a fully air landing unit, with a parachute regiment to secure a landing zone and the remainder of the division arriving by air. It possessed its own supporting weapons and services also delivered by air. It was capable of putting mass behind enemy lines to achieve an operational objective. The 1939 proposal fell far short of creating that type of capability by limiting half the division to ground movement only.

The discussion on creating a *corpo d'armata aviotrasportabile* was continued within the S.M.R.E. on 8 May 1939. The *sottocapo di S.M. per il reparto operazione* (Deputy of the Operations Section of the Stato Maggiore), *generale di brigata* Paride Negri wrote a memorandum on 12 June 1939 addressing the possibility of testing the concept. While brief, the memorandum stated that the requirements of the Albania and Mediterranean Theaters of operations warranted consideration of this type of unit. The Operations Section would proceed with the development of the concept and felt that testing with the existing aircraft (SM.81s and CA.133s) was possible. [27]

The results of the study on the airborne corps was documented in a 12 November 1939 memorandum. The study identified a 20,000 man corps, of which 7,000 men were paratrooper qualified. The corps would have 317 vehicles (129 airborne), 563 (129 airborne), 228 light machine guns (146 airborne), 102 mortars (84 airborne), and 84 artillery pieces (48 airborne). While the memorandum states airborne *(aviotrasportabili)* for many of these items, it is unclear whether the intent is that they would be truly parachute capable only or merely air transportable.[28]

27 Filippo Cappellano and Nicola Pignato *Gli autoveicoli da combattimento dell'Esercito Italiano* (Rome: USSME, 2002) volume secondo, pp. 723–726.

28 Cappellano and Pignato *Gli autoveicoli*, pp. 724–725. Aviotrasportabili can be translated as both airborne or air transportable.

The document then discusses how actual testing can be conducted. Of interest is that two divisions already identified to form the corps, the «*Ferrara*» and the «*Arezzo*» would not be used, but two other divisions substituted for them during the testing. As SM.82 transports were not yet available, the number of substitute aircraft needed to replace the larger aircraft was also addressed. Restrictions on the length of the test are presented, limited by the need to minimize the removal of aircraft from operational roles.

The problem of removing air units from operational roles for the experiment was again highlighted by *generale d'armata* Ubaldo Soddu (undersecretary in the Ministry of War) in a 29 November memorandum. Here Soddu stated that the conversion of the two divisions should be postponed and testing should be delayed until the actual number of required transport aircraft are available. *Generale di corpo d'armata* Mario Roatta (Deputy of the S.M.R.E.) responded, stating that 90 transport planes were available and could be used. As he stated in his reply:

> In these conditions the transport [requirement] does not exceed an ordinary tourist air rally [show]. And therefore it does not require special studies and special units.[29]

Graziani's (who had replaced Pariani by this date) reply to Roatta's statement was terse:

> It takes more![30]

The reality was that little work was done on creating a *corpo d'armata aviotrasportabile* after 1939. The concept languished due to the lack of resources, the lack of will in the senior leadership, and the lack of any identifiable employment of this type of unit in the war plans. Without an operational requirement that this new capacity could satisfy, there was no forcing function to drive the capability to maturity. It remained a 'great idea' that could be brushed off at will in the moment, but the necessary components needed to employ the capability would not be available if the capability was called upon.

Approach of War

Whilst the discussion of the airborne corps was ongoing, the issue of where to locate the parachute school appeared to be resolved. The fourth class airfield at Tarquinia was selected in the summer of 1939, but the cost to develop it into a training facility and who would pay for that effort began a new round of discussions. Nothing had been started at that new location when Balbo wrote to the *Ministero dell'Aeronautica* on 1 December 1939. In his memorandum, Balbo recommended that Castel Benito

29 Cappellano and Pignato *Gli autoveicoli*, pp. 726.
30 Cappellano and Pignato *Gli autoveicoli*, pp. 726.

be designated as the parachute school for the Italian military, thereby offering a way to avoid the cost to refurbish Tarquinia. *Generale d'armata aerea* Francesco Pricolo, the new Chief of the S.M.R.A. saw merit in Balbo's proposal and suspended work at Tarquinia on 10 December. Work would not restart at Tarquinia until February 1940.[31]

During all this activity, Italy's strategic situation changed overnight: war had begun in Europe. Germany attacked Poland on 1 September 1939, with France and the UK declaring war on 3 September. Italy had declared its neutrality on 2 September, but now the Italian military faced a very real possibility of executing the plans it had been working on over the past decade.

The war had started at least two years too early for Fascist Italy. None of the three services, the R.E., the R.M., and the R.A., were ready for the conflict. All the rearmament programs for the services were scheduled to be completed in 1942-1943. For the military, the announcement of non-belligerence declared by Mussolini on 2 September provided hope that Italy's involvement would be delayed until the nation was ready.[32]

This did not mean that Italy would stand on the sidelines and do nothing. Some army units were already mobilizing prior to September in accordance with P.R.12. These units were those identified in the plan to operate either against Yugoslavia (*Armata del Po*) or as reinforcements scheduled for Africa settentrionale (A.S.). Two of the divisions earmarked for A.S. were already embarking on ships for transport in the last weeks of August. Two more divisions would follow in September. Other forces in Italy would begin to mobilize in September including units assigned to face France in the west across the Alps. Italy was slowly putting itself onto a full wartime footing.

In the A.S., the Italian units were mobilizing and moving to their deployment areas. For the *I btg. paracadutisti libico*, it was more training. The battalion would be expanded from the 168 men in January 1939 to 320 men by the end of the year.

Almost immediately after the invasion of Poland, both Pariani and Balbo sent letters that crossed each other addressing the changing situation. Balbo's letter, written on 10 September, again returned to the need for an offense against Egypt while establishing a defense against Tunisia. Pariani's letter, written on 11 September, requested that Balbo update the existing plan based on the current strategic and operational situation.[33]

This initiated an exchange of ideas and concepts between September 1939 and January 1940, Balbo wrote to Pariani and later his successor *Maresciallo* Rodolfo Graziani, with those two individuals sharing the correspondence with Badoglio. In these letters, Balbo argued for an offensive against Egypt based on Italy's strategic

31 Arena, *I Fanti*, p.61; Di Giovanni, *I paracadutisti*, pp.37; Arena, *Tarquinia*, pp.16–17.
32 John Gooch, *Mussolini and his Generals* (New York: Cambridge University Press, 2007), pp.494–495; John Gooch, *Mussolini's War* (Allen Lane 2020), p.64; Montanari *L'esercito italiano*, p.135.
33 Dorello Ferrari, 'Il piano segreto di Balbo', *Studi Storia-Militari 1984* (Rome: USSME, 1985), pp.81.

situation. Pariani basically agreed but countered that the means Balbo required were not available.[34] Graziani was absolutely against an offensive in North Africa mainly because of the equipment problems. The updates to P.R.12 during this period continued to state that Italy would maintain a strategic defense on all fronts. Any offensive action would be based on whether any exceptionally favorable circumstances arose. None of the Italian plans that were developed based on P.R.12 offered a mechanism to create such circumstances.[35]

Balbo did outline his thinking for an offensive in Africa settentrionale in his correspondence with the S.M.R.E. In his letters, Balbo identified Egypt as the primary target as he felt that an attack against the French in Tunisia would fail to achieve any strategic success. Even if the Italians gained an operational victory, the French could retreat into Algeria or even Morocco. The major ports in these two colonies would allow the French to build forces that could successfully counterattack the Italian thrust. The French would thereby remain a threat and the western front of Libya could never be militarily secured. An attack eastward into Egypt, once the Suez Canal was seized, would leave the British without the port infrastructure to mount any major threat to Italian control.

His concept of an attack against Egypt would unfold in three phases. The first phase was a surprise attack into Egypt with Marsa Matruh as its objective. The second phase was a build-up of the additional forces from Italy and securing the El Alamein area. The third phase was the drive to Cairo and the Suez Canal. Balbo did not present a scheme of maneuver or any other operational level detail on how his forces would maneuver to gain these objectives.

Balbo did list the means required for such an offensive in these exchanges. The first phase would use the existing forces in Libya that have been suitably modernized. The significant parts of this modernization was motorizing the units in Libya and equipping the armour units with cannon-armed tanks. Along with the need to modernize the army was the creation of a *divisione aviotrasportabile libica*. No details were provided, but the likely organization would have been similar to the *58ª divisione* structure used during *Operazione «Gefara»*, namely a parachute regiment and an air-transportable regiment.

For the second and third phases, a second *divisione aviotrasportabile* would be provided from Italy directly into Egypt to join the existing Libyan unit.[36] Balbo did not provide any statements or even clues on how these two units would be employed during the attack, but the size of the force implied something more than raids and sabotage. Given the mission executed in *Operazione «Gefara»* was a vertical envelopment rather than a series of raids, it is quite possible that Balbo was thinking of the use of two airborne divisions as an operational maneuver element.

34 Ferrari, 'Il piano segreto di Balbo', pp.81; Gooch, *Mussolini's War*, pp.65–66.
35 Ferrari, 'Il piano segreto di Balbo', pp.81–82; Gooch, *Generals*, pp.452,460.
36 Di Giovanni, *I paracadutisti*, pp.34; Ferrari, 'Il piano segreto di Balbo', pp.83.

While the proposal was not presented as a definitive plan, it does make clear that Balbo had considered some type of role for the fledgling airborne force that was missing in his P.R.D. in 1938. The requirement for two divisions implied a mission at the operational level, but the lack of any details leaves little except speculation. Balbo was in a position to create the Libyan division, but as will be seen, it is questionable whether the metropolitan division could be organized in the near future. But Balbo might have known that a metropolitan airborne division could be available. As previously discussed, Balbo was likely aware of the May 1939 memorandum to create a two-division '*corpo di aviotrasportabile*'. The question remained whether there were any plans by the S.M.G. to employ this capability?

Balbo's 1940 concept could have become the raison d'être for the fledging *corpo aviotrasportabile* if it had been approved and transitioned into an operational plan. With a specific method of employment, the force structure, equipment, and training could have been refined and used to drive the necessary doctrinal development and material procurement. But the military leadership instead saw the airborne force as an experiment without a purpose. It was tolerated but not given the resources for rapid development to create a functional capability.

The first months of 1940 for the parachute battalion involved training the new personnel and organizing a new battalion formed from Italian nationals living in Libya. Like the «*Fanti dell'aria*» in 1938, Balbo had not waited for approval to begin raising the unit. Experienced men were taken from the Libyan battalion to supplement the training cadre at the parachute school to better handle the increased training load. The school also received nine SM.75 aircraft detached from the *604ª Squadra* that were quickly modified for parachute drops. This gave the school access to a total of 15 aircraft for school operations.[37]

Maresciallo dell'Aria Balbo was continuing his effort to build up the airborne forces. After reading about the success of the German Fallschirmjäger in the Netherlands and Belgium, he sent a telegram to Mussolini on 24 May 1940 formally requesting permission to create a new battalion.

> May 24, XVIII, given the situation and unless otherwise ordered, I will establish a 300 man national paratrooper battalion using volunteer personnel already available in AS.[38]

Mussolini replied on 25 May:

> I approve of the increase in the number of parachutists. You can form two battalions of which one is made up of nationals. Germans have not invented anything

37 Nino Arena, *Aquile senza Ali: I paracadutisti italiani nella seconda guerra mondiale* (Milan: Mursia 1970), p.17.

38 Di Giovanni, *I paracadutisti*, p.35; NARA, Ministero dell'Africa Italiana telegramma 24 maggio 1940, 32884, T821, roll.130.

> absolutely secretly new or similar. They just applied on a large scale, with seriousness, some of our principles.[39]

As noted above, the Libyan battalion was already in existence while Balbo had already started training Italian nationals that had volunteered beginning in September 1939. From those national volunteers, Balbo ordered the creation of the *1° btg. paracadutisti nazionale* early in 1940. The battalion was organized using the same structure as the Libyan battalion with four companies. Mussolini's approval gave the unit official authorization. The new battalion began its unit qualification jumps during the last week of May using the new Salvator D40.[40]

With the recruitment and training of a second parachute battalion, it would appear that Italy would have a viable airborne capability in 1940. Yet a critical component for the employment of this force was missing: an air transport fleet that could deliver the *paracadutisti* to their objective. The lack of an operational vision to employ this force allowed the Italian senior leadership to avoid creating the necessary means to deploy it.

Air Transport units

With the creation of its first parachute units, Germany had simultaneously created a transport unit dedicated to supporting its Fallschirmjägers. The initial transport unit in May 1936 was the IV Gruppe/Kampfgeschwader 152 Hindenburg equipped with two squadrons of twelve Ju 52 transports each. In 1937 the Gruppe was expanded to four squadrons with a total of 48 JU 52s and five staff support Ju 52s.[41] When Germany initiated the opening of the Second World War in September 1939, IV/KG 152 had grown into the Kampfgeschwader zur besonderen Verwendung 1 (KGvb1), a full transport wing of five gruppe with 265 Ju 52 transport aircraft. The unit was directly subordinated to the German parachute division, Flieger Division 7 (Fl.Div.7) which ensured availability of the aircraft when needed. Additional transport aircraft would be assigned as needed.[42] In 1939 Germany possessed a total of 552 dedicated transport aircraft (Ju 52) organized in separate transport units.[43]

With Italy's planned expansion of its own airborne force, what transport capability did Italy possess in May 1940 to deploy these units? The Regia Aeronautica did not maintain a separate aerial transport organization prior to 1940. Each *stormo* and

39 Di Giovanni, *I paracadutisti*, p.35
40 Di Giovanni, *I paracadutisti*, p.35; Arena, *I Fanti*, pp.61-61; Arena, *Aquile pp.16-17.*
41 Karl-Heinz Golla, *The German Fallschirmtruppe 1939-41* (Milton-Keyes: Association of the United States Army and Helion & Company, 2013), pp.33–34, 37–38.
42 Golla, *The German Fallschirmtruppe*, pp.41 fn 8, 46, 48.
43 Dancy, Peter and Vajda, Fernec A., *German Aircraft Industry and Production 1933–45* (Bath: SAE International, 1998), p.49.

gruppo had several support aircraft assigned, normally either Ca.101s or Ca.133 to support all transport requirements. If a mission required more and/or larger aircraft, a bomber *stormo* would be tasked to support the requirement. The R.A. had a limited number of passenger aircraft assigned to the *Stato Maggiore Generale* and the *Zona Aerea Territoriale* (Z.A.T., Aerial Territorial Zones). These aircraft were militarized civil airliners (SM.75, 79, 81, and 83s) and generally used for VIP transportation or other high level missions.[44]

This approach worked to a degree as the bomber fleet was developed using dual purpose aircraft design; the planes were built primarily as bombers that could be employed as transports as needed.[45] The use of bombers to drop supplies during the Ethiopian War is one example of this methodology, with *Operazione «Gefara»* as another example. The SM.81 and the SM.82, the main transports used during the war, both reflected this design philosophy. The SM.81 was initially designed as a bomber that could be employed as a transport, while the SM.82 was a transport that could (and was) used as a bomber. The R.A. also planned to mobilize the aircraft of the three Italian airlines, Ala Littoria, Società Linee Aeree Transcontinentali Italiane (L.A.T.I.), and Società Avio Linee Italiane (A.L.I.) to support the transport mission. The result was that Italy's transport capability was fragmented and formed by a collection of multiple aircraft types. This would complicate any planning for a large airborne operation.

This approach could work to a degree if the bomber force was not fully tasked during the conflict and the types of mission were limited to passengers and transporting cargo and not paratroops. Specialized crew training is needed to support airborne operations as formation flying, precise navigation, and ability to read the weather are needed to accurately drop the paratroopers onto the drop zone. No serving R.A. officers were trained as *ufficiali osservatori per paracadutisti* (navigators for parachute operations) and training had not begun for any *direttori di lanico* (aircraft jumpmasters) beyond those stationed at the schools. Shortages of trained personnel for both roles would become an issue in 1942.

The occupation of Albania in April 1939 demonstrated the need for a dedicated transport capability within the R.A. For the first time the R.A. had to manage a daily flow of aircraft over an extended period carrying men and materials. The R.A. formed a temporary transport unit, *28° Stormo T*, by requisitioning all the Ca.133 aircraft assigned to the fighter and assault squadrons to support this mission.[46] The type of scheduling and synchronization requirement to operate an air line of communications was different from what the bomber squadrons were accustomed to executing. The R.A. officially approved the organization for a *Stormo T* (transport wing) of two gruppi with three squadriglie (squadrons) each for a total of thirty-six transports in

44 Nino Arena, *La Regia Aeronautica* (Rome: USSMA, 1981–1986), vol 1, pp.95–96.
45 Arena, *La Regia Aeronautica*, vol 1, p.639.
46 Arena, *La Regia Aeronautica*, vol 1, p.639.

the spring of 1940. This was followed by the creation of the *Comando Servizi Aerei Speciali* (C.S.A.S., Special Air Services Command) on 4 June 1940 to manage/control all aerial transport requirements for the R.A.[47]

At the same time as the S.A.S. was officially formed, the first four *gruppi da trasporto* (transport groups) were organized. Each gruppo would have two/three squadriglie of nine aircraft each. Lacking a dedicated transport aircraft, most of the aircraft required were mobilized from the commercial airlines.

145° Gruppo T – 604ª, 610ª Squadriglie with a total of 11 SM.75.
147° Gruppo T – 601ª, 602ª, 603ª Squadriglie with a total of 13 SM.75.
148° Gruppo T – 605ª, 606ª Squadriglie with a total of 13 SM.73.
149° Gruppo T – 607ª, 608ª, 609ª Squadriglie with a total of 12 SM.82.
Autonoma Squadriglie – 615ª, 616ª Squadriglie with a total of 8 SM.83, 1 SM.79, and 3 SM.74.[48]

Thus Italy had 61 transport aircraft in general support of the R.A. All these aircraft would be needed if both the existing parachute battalions were to be employed for an airborne operation. In June 1940 all the SM.81 aircraft were still in frontline bomber units, so any additional aircraft would need to be pulled from those units to be used as transports. Even if the R.E. decided to rapidly expand the parachute force in 1940, the R.A. lacked the ability to transport more than two battalions simultaneously to their objectives without using additional aircraft taken from the bomber units.[49]

Better equipment for the *gruppi T* was on its way. *Maresciallo d'aria* Balbo had recognized the need for a transport aircraft capable of transporting large numbers of troops and cargo over long distances to support requirements in Italy's oversea possessions. During the King's visit during *Operazione «Gefara»* Balbo had the opportunity to pilot Savoia-Marchetti's new passenger aircraft, the SM.75. Impressed by the plane's capability and handling, Balbo pressed the R.A. and the Savoia-Marchetti company to develop a military version that could be used for cargo and parachute operations. A development contract was let on 15 July 1938 and the initial prototype was delivered for testing in February 1939.[50] Initially called the SM.82 *«coloniale»* for its Africa origins, it later took the name *«Marsupial»*. Not only did Balbo establish

47 Arena, *La Regia Aeronautica*, vol 1, p.95; Civoli, Massimo, *S.A.S. I Servizi Aerei Speciali della Regia Aeronautica 1940-1943* (Cavallermaggiore, Gribaudo, 2000), p.15. Initially the squadriglie would only have two sezione of three aircraft each.

48 Giuseppe Santoro, *L'aeronautica italiana nella seconda guerra mondiale* (Rome, Edizioni ESSE di A. Silvestri, 1957), p.90; Arena, *La Regia Aeronautica*, vol 1, p.96; Chris Dunning, *Courage Alone The Italian Air Force 1940-1943* (London: Hikoki Publication Ltd.,1998), pp.110–118. There are a few differences between the accounts.

49 Arena, *La Regia Aeronautica*, vol 1, p.664.

50 Emilio Brotzu and Gherardo Cosolo, *Dimensione Cielo, Aerei Italiani nella 2ª Guerra Mondiale Trasporto 9* (Rome: Edizioni Bizzarri, 1976), pp.7–8; Arena, *La Regia Aeronautica*, vol 1, p.638.

the requirements for the aircraft's range and cargo capacity, but he specified that the transport be able to carry and drop a *compagnia paracadutisti* (33 men) or transport a standard infantry platoon.[51] Production of this excellent transport had barely commenced in 1940 and only fifty aircraft were on order for that year (twenty more were ordered after the outbreak of war). Balbo had created the first airborne units and now ensured the procurement of the necessary aircraft to employ them.

During 1938-39, Italy's military strategy was based on remaining on the defense. No strategic interest was identified by the leadership beyond securing Italy and its possessions from enemy threats. No preemptive requirement was perceived as meaningful or possible, as the given threats were greater than what the Italian military could handle. Without a national interest which required offensive operations, were the resources to develop a unique offensive capably justified? In a defensive fight, airborne forces had limited utility as their light structure and weapons provided little sustained capability. One can ask whether the slow development of the new speciality might be a subconscious recognition of this fact. Only Balbo in A.S. had identified the offensive as an operational solution to the strategic problem created by France and the United Kingdom against Libya. The lack of other critical capabilities necessary to secure Libya, mainly tanks and trucks precluded the development of any detailed offensive planning and thereby likely hindered the transition of his *fanti dell'aria* from being perceived as only an experiment to a valid and valued battlefield capability.

Buried within all these discussions in the plans and discussions about operations in Africa settentrionale there is one omission. This omission, given the events of the next three years in the Mediterranean, was surprising. Its consideration would have fully justified the creation of a large airborne capability to achieve an operational goal. The omission was the operational challenge presented by Malta.

51 Brotzu and Cosolo, *Dimensione Cielo 9*, p.7. This was a parachute company organized under Order N.64. Each man would carry 120 rounds, 20 grenades, and a pack with two days of food and water.

3

Tarquinia

The selection of the aeroporto «Americo Sostegni» outside Tarquinia in 1939 to be the home of the *Regia Scuola Paracadutisti dell'Aeronautica* was unexpected in many ways.[1] It was an unmanned 4ª class airfield with only one runway, two buildings, and possessing none of the associated infrastructure needed for operating a large number of aircraft and the specialized equipment used by airborne units. Yet it would be the airfield most associated with the *reparti paracadutisti* and remained the schoolhouse for the specialty until 1943.

The airfield at Tarquinia had been originally established in the area during the 1920s as the Corneto-Tarquinia Airfield. It was listed in 1926 as an emergency landing facility for aircraft in trouble and had no permanent staff beyond caretakers.[2] The *Regia Aeronautica* decided in 1936 to construct a true airfield along the road between Tarquinia and Civitavecchia near the Saline di Tarquinia. The new airfield was officially opened on 27 March 1938, the occasion of the Festa dell'Arma Azzurra (celebration of the founding of the Regia Aeronautica in 1922). The airfield was named after *capitano* Americo Sostegni from Montalto di Castro, a pilot who died in an aircraft accident in 1937. The airfield had one small, paved runway, a brick operations/caretaker building, and a steel hangar. There was nothing else.

While the Regio Decreto Legge (Royal Law Decree) of 22 February 1937 decided that the Regia Aeronautica would be responsible for establishing and operating the parachute training school, little was done by the R.A. at that time. No strategic consideration appeared to drive the need for parachute units so budget fights and modernizing the services were the focus of the senior leadership of the two services rather than quickly establishing the school. What was accomplished was establishing a commission in late 1937 to identify a suitable location for the new parachute school.

1 Giuseppe Lundari, *I paracadutisti italiani 1937/45* (Milan, Editrice Militare Italiana di Ivo Fossati, 1989), p. 6; Nino Arena, *50ª di Tarquinia, 1939-1989, Scuole Militare paracadutismo* (Comitato Promotore ex Istruttori delle Scuole Militari di Paracadutismo, 1989), p.14–15.

2 Associazione Arma Aeronautica Sezione di Tarquinia <https://assoaerotarquinia.weebly.com/la-storia.html> (accessed 10 March 2021).

The requirements for the location were: proximity to Rome; ease of logistical support to the school staff; optimal conditions that supported airborne training to include meteorological and environmental; and offering space for future development and expanded capabilities.[3]

Lacking any pressing priority, the commission worked through 1937 and 1938. It was this delay that drove the frustrated *Maresciallo dell'Aria* Balbo to take matters into his own hands and created the school at Castel Benito in 1938. Yet this development did not spur the commission into greater effort and it was not until February 1939 that the commission finally offered its findings to the S.M.G.

The commission examined six locations for the school: Aviano, Brindisi, L'Aquila, Siena, Tarquinia, and Viterbo. Aviano was determined to be too far from Rome, a challenge for logistical support, and experienced significant fog affecting visibility. Brindisi was too far from Rome and likely would be focused on supporting operations in the Balkans. L'Aquila was too remote, still under construction, and the mountains presented challenging weather conditions and limited expansion. Siena was also too far and the environment limited expansion. Tarquinia was suitable but had a small airfield, required significant infrastructure improvements, and possessed only modest potential for expansion. Viterbo was considered excellent with good weather, expansion possibilities, but it too was under construction.[4] The initial recommendation was Aviano, with its well-developed airfield and large open areas suitable for use as drop zones. However the distance from Rome was considered too much of an issue by the senior leadership and the final decision fell on Tarquinia. Viterbo was stated as an alternative if issues with Tarquinia later manifested.[5] The memorandum also outlined the proposed program of training for the new speciality. This decision was passed to the *Stati Maggiori* of the two services for concurrence.

The S.M.R.E. took four months assessing the committee's work before it finally concurred with Tarquinia as the site for the new school. This decision was transmitted to the S.M.R.A. on 23 June 1939 in a memorandum signed by *generale* Pariani, the current Chief of Staff of the S.M.R.E. The S.M.R.A. then delayed and it was not until 29 August 1939 that the S.M.R.A. issued a final decree that identified Tarquinia as the location for the new parachute school in the *madrepatria* (Italian homeland).[6]

When one looked at a map of the area, there were valid reasons for choosing this location. The airbase was near major rail and road networks needed to move a large number of trainees and units, with the base being only 70 kilometers north of the capital city of Rome. It was set on a flat, open plain between the city of Tarquinia and the sea which offered areas suitable for drop-zones and tactical maneuver training.

3 Arena, *Tarquinia, 1*, p.14
4 Arena, *Tarquinia* pp.14–15.
5 Arena, *La Regia Aeronautica* I:119.
6 Arena, *Tarquinia* pp.15.

The map, however, did not inform the viewer of the potential issues with the site that would later became apparent.

In the same 23 June 1939 memorandum, the R.E. accepted all the plans for the training with one exception. The plan in the S.M.G. memorandum established that the instructor training would begin in September 1939, and the first student training would start in January 1940. Student training would be carried out in battalion courses, with a course set at 250 men. The S.M.R.A., in coordination with the S.M.R.E. had issued the first manual addressing the training and employment of the *reparti paracadutisti*. The manual focused on the raid and sabotage missions with squad and platoon size elements and stated, "The use of the combined battalion must be reserved for exceptional cases, for example such as preventing the occupation of an area of land by the landing of large airborne forces."[7] This manual would be a major consideration in the development of the final training program.

The exception to the plan was the length of the training. The training program was overseen by *tenente colonnello* Freri who had previously been assigned to Castel Benito under Italo Balbo. The program used at Castel Benito was only focused on parachute training and even that was limited given Balbo's requirements to have the «*Fanti dell'aria*» ready for the Grand Maneuver.[8] Freri was now in a position to fully implement his concept of paratrooper training set out in his proposals written in the early 1930s and his article from 1937.[9] The original consideration identified an eight-month long course for the instructors and students. The program would encompass both the parachute training and the unit training to create combat-ready airborne battalions. This was now shortened to a three-four month long course, with the battalions requiring additional training after the course was completed. The shortened course would allow the school to train several battalions in a year.

On 15 October 1939, the *Regia Scuola Paracadutisti dell'Aeronautica* was officially established. The R.A. was tasked with the technical and administrative operation of the school; The R.E. was responsible for the actual training and tactical employment of the airborne units. Selected to build and command the school was *colonnello pilota dell'Aeronautica* Giuseppe Baudoin. Originally an officer in the *bersaglieri*, the 43 year old *colonnello* had a distinguished military career prior to being selected to command the new school. Joining the *bersaglieri* in January 1916 as an enlisted soldier, he was quickly promoted to corporal. Given his battlefield performance, he was nominated to be an officer cadet in September 1917, but was captured a month later during the Caporetto battles before he could attend the officer's course. Promoted to *tenente* in 1921, he learned to fly in 1921 and later, after receiving his military pilot qualification he transferred to the Regia Aeronautica. After his promotion to *colonnello* in 1938,

7 Anon, *Addestramento e impiego dei reparti paracadutisti* (Rome: Ministero dell'Aeronautica, 1939), p.12.

8 It should be noted that modern airborne instruction at Fort Benning is only 15 days long while the training at Castel Benito was 45 days long.

9 Prospero Freri, 'Arditismo aereo', *Rivista Aeronautica*, XIII:7 (1937), pp.18–24

he was assigned as the commander of the *Scuola di Osservazione Aeroplani Terrestri* (Scuola O.A.; School for Aerial Reconnaissance and Observation). On 1 November 1939, Baudoin was officially appointed as the commander of the parachute school.

Opening the New School (Map 3.1)

Building a school is an accurate description of the task laying ahead for *colonnello* Baudoin. Before accepting the position, Baudoin traveled to inspect the aeroporto «Americo Sostegni» in August 1939 to assess the new command. What he found was initially disappointing: a small make-shift landing field that was only 300x700 meters, a grassy track, a small metal hangar, and a small airfield building used by the caretaker, all affected by strong sea winds from the Tyrrhenian Sea. Barracks, and mess buildings, classrooms, parachute rigging buildings, physical training facilities, tactical training areas, airfield operations structures and maintenance hangars, storage, and of course the all-important jump training facilities all needed to be constructed. Simultaneously, the actual training course needed to be created, both for preparing the necessary cadre to run the school as well as the training course that students would undergo during their time at Tarquinia. It is not surprising that Baudoin required a week to consider the offer before he finally decided to accept the command and give up his position at the Scuola O.A.[10]

The commission had identified the requirements needed to prepare Tarquinia for its new role. Construction included a building for the packing and maintaining of the parachutes and other unique airborne equipment; photo laboratory; adjusting the perimeter fence for the expanded base; extending the buried electrical service to accommodate the new facilities; buildings for the security force, headquarters, administrative offices, classrooms, and barracks; hangars and maintenance buildings for the Flight Detachment; and all the office/classroom furnishings need to make the building functional. The first step was obtaining a modular modello Saporiti hangar for use as the parachute packing and storage building.[11]

The work recommended by the commission and pressed by *colonnello* Baudoin had begun a few days after the outbreak of the war on 1 September 1939. With Italy's decision to remain neutral, there appeared to be little energy to complete the school and begin training. The memorandum detailing how the school would function was not signed until 11 November 1939. Part of the delay was due to Mussolini's changes to the Italian senior leadership. *Generale* Pariani was fired on 31 October as head of the S.M.R.E. and replaced by *generale* Graziani. while *generale di squadra aerea* Francesco Pricolo replaced *generale* Valle as the head of the S.M.R.A. With the now signed memorandum, Baudoin was released from his assignment at the Scuola O.A.

10 Arena, *Tarquinia* p.16.
11 Arena, *Tarquinia* p.16.

The main airport building at Tarquinia. In the foreground are the wooden barracks being built to accommodate the school. (AUSSME)

An aerial view of the temporary barracks area. Tarquinia lacked permanent facilities, so everything for the school needed to be constructed. Tents are used by the students and the mobile hangers on the right are for storage and training. (AUSSME)

and assigned to the *Ministerio dell'Aeronautica* until he could assume his position at Tarquinia.[12]

For training, the school would receive 300 parachutes for R.A. stocks that consisted of a mixture of Salvator D.37 and D.39 parachutes. The Flight Detachment was authorized six Ca.133 for use as jump aircraft and two Ca.100 for liaison and support requirements.

Active work at Tarquinia only lasted until the end of November. A letter from *Maresciallo dell'Aria* Italo Balbo was received by the S.M.G. in Rome proposing that Castel Benito (or Barce as previously discussed) be the sole Italian school for parachuting. For Balbo, having this proposal approved would render permanent his work to create an airborne force and the school's official recognition would resolve many of the budget issues. His proposal fell on receptive ears as noted in the S.M.R.A. assessment of the proposal:

> This provision, in addition to determining the uniqueness of direction in the organization and functioning of the School, will make it possible to achieve a significant economy by eliminating the splitting of means; finally, it will allow the RA to use the Tarquinia Airport for its own needs.[13]

Work at Tarquinia would not restart until February 1940 after an intervention by Baudoin and Freri with Mussolini and *generale* Pricolo, reversing the decision. Not only did this delay completion of the training facilities at the school, but volunteers arriving for the first training course by 15 February 1940 had to be returned to their units until 28 March as billets and other garrison structure had not been finished.

While the drama over the location of the school in Rome was unfolding, *colonnello* Baudoin needed to select a staff to provide the administration for the operation of the school. What is surprising is that none of the cadre/instructors that had established and operated the school at Castel Benito were brought back to Italy to help with the new school. The school in A.S. had been operating for nearly two years, trained over 1,200 *paracadutisti*, and executed over 10,000 parachute jumps.[14] The only indication of why this was the case was written by *maggiore* Giovanni Vernando who was the officer responsible for the tactical training of the units at Tarquinia:

> Colonel Baudoin preferred to work alone with "new people" in order to train without interference a group of "sui generis" instructors, with preparation and skills that it was believed the Libyans did not have. I do not remember ever

12 Arena, *Tarquinia* p.16.

13 Marco Di Giovanni, *I paracadutisti italiani Volontari, miti e memoria della seconda guerra mondiale* (Gorizia: Editrice Goriziana, 1991), p.35 and fn.56.

14 Arena, *Tarquinia*, p.18.

> complaining about the absence of collaboration from colleagues on the other side [of the sea], nor that the need for such collaboration was ever felt. [...] I myself, who was later in charge of preparing a regulation for the training and the tactical use of paratroopers, since the existing booklet did not seem very satisfactory, in terms of content and completeness, I did not feel any need to seek the concurrence of thought of those who had begun to deal with the problem long before me.[15]

From the cadre volunteers that were arriving, he selected the officers that would lead the various departments within the school. *Tenente colonnello di fanteria* Augosto Saltalamacchia was selected as the vice comandante (deputy) and *maggiore del genio* (engineer) Alberto Bettica was in-charge of the Studies and Experimental Department. *Capitano da bersaglieri* Giovanni Vernando was transferred from the army's Scuola di Guerra (War College) to head the Tactical Training Department. *Capitano degli alpino* Paolo Cosso was an equipment designer and *capitano degli alpino* Vincenzo Caratti di Lanzacco, an osservatore d'aeroplano (aircraft navigator) were both destined for the Flight Detachment. *Tenente del genio* Felice Loffredo was in charge of the explosives training and communications; medical *tenente* Leporace "for the study of the psycho-physical problems of parachuting". Other assignments included:

> Reparti di Volo (Flight Detachment) – *Capitano pilota* Dante Salvetat (R.A.).
> Servizio Sanitario – *Tenente med.* CSA Gaetano Polistena (R.A.).
> Nucleo ripiegatori (parachute packing section) – *Maresciallo 3ª Classe* Giuseppe Francesoni (R.A.).
> Ufficiale di collegamento (liaison officer) S.M.R.A. and S.M.R.E. – *Maggiore* Giorgio Lo Blanco (R.E.).[16]

The men selected as the garrison cadre at the school began arriving at Tarquinia in January 1940. With no accommodations or facilities at the airfield for anyone other than the airfield maintenance and caretaker staff, the newly arriving cadre were billeted in Tarquinia. Breakfast was provided free in Tarquinia, after which a R.A. bus would transport everyone to the airfield. Lunch was provided by a small canteen at the aeroporto «Americo Sostegni». At the end of the duty day, the personnel would return to Tarquinia for dinner and relaxation.[17]

The volunteers to form the instructors and the leadership cadre for the training battalions began to arrive in March 1940. These men had to undergo an admission test

15 Di Giovanni, *I paracadutisti*, p.35–36 and undated account, fn.59.

16 Di Giovanni, *I paracadutisti*, p. 37; Arena, *Tarquinia* pp.19–20; Nino Arena, *I PARACADUTISTI Cinquant'anni di storia, cronaca e immagini del paracadutisti italiano* (Modena: Società Tipografica Editrice Modenese Mucchi, 1972), pp.74, 266.

17 Anon 'Settant'anni fa ci lanciavamo così: Scuola militare di Paracadutismo, Aeroporto di Tarquinia', <https://folgore.it/storia_e_tecnica/tarquinia.htm> (accessed 10 March 2021).

before entering the course. Testing began shortly after the volunteers began arriving and consisted of various athletic events including high and long jumping; timed runs of 100, 1000, and 10,000 meters; push-ups, rope and pole climbing.

Volunteers also had to pass a battery of medical and psychological tests. These tests were administered based on the concepts and goals set by Freri and Baudoin.

1. age not to exceed 35 years
2. height not less than 1.63 m (optimum between 1.65 m/1.70 m).
3. eurythmy movement excluding those with short or long limbs.
4. strength and muscle agility for weights to be supported before and after the jump.
5. absence of skeletal injuries of any kind (especially lower limbs).
6. absence of flat feet, equinus, valgus, any alterations to the ankles.
7. absence of labyrinth reaction (hearing issues).
8. normal vision with at least 7/10 in each eye, sense of depth, normal stereoscopic vision.
9. ready and sharp intelligence with the exclusion of the illiterate and intellectually slow or lazy. The C.N.R.and the Scuola di Psicologia had collaborated in developing this program, integrating the methods of Father Agostino Gemelli. Prof. Barisone and a team of 12 volunteer paratroopers tested the program before it was adopted.[18]

Part of the psychological assessment included a tower jump test to ensure the volunteers were mentally able to handle jumping out of an airplane.[19] These standards were significantly higher than the army's regular induction testing and ensured a very physically fit and mentally ready volunteer for training. By the time the cadre course had begun on 1 April 1940, 57 volunteers had qualified for the training.[20]

Parachute Training

The original concept for the cadre course curriculum was an 8 month course. It was an extensive program covering more than learning how to jump from a moving airplane. The cadre would learn how to pack and unpack the parachutes, how to organize and load aircraft for a jump, the actual parachute training, and aerial resupply packaging

18 Arena, *Tarquinia*, p.31. Agostino Gemelli was a Franciscan friar and noted psychologist and founder of the Università Cattolica del Sacro Cuore.

19 Anon 'Settant'anni fa ci lanciavamo così: Scuola militare di Paracadutismo, Aeroporto di Tarquinia', <https://folgore.it/storia_e_tecnica/tarquinia.htm> (accessed 10 Mar. 2021).

20 Anon,'La Regie Scuole Paracadutisti: Tarquinia e Viterbo', Associazione Nazionale "Nembo", <http://www.nembo.info/Paracadutismo/le_regie_scuole.htm> (accessed 11 March 2021). The number of cadres that started this training vary depending on the source.

and aircraft loading. Parachute instruction included both individual and mass parachute drops. Physiological instruction focused on the effects of parachuting on the human body was included. Finally the tactical training completed the course. The cadre learned unit actions on the drop zone which was considered a critical event and when the paratroopers were most vulnerable. Actions practiced included assembling the men and recovering the weapons containers, and then organizing a defensive perimeter. The main mission that was practiced was airfield seizure, indicating a possible use of the *paracadutisti italiani* in future operations.

This was an aggressive training program, but it would create a cadre of well trained and conditioned instructors that could impart a sense of pride and elitism into the new airborne arm. The first instructor/trainer course started on 28 March 1940. The 57 officers and NCOs selected for training consisted of three *capitani*, 13 *tenenti*, one *sottotenente*, two *marescialli*, and 34 *sergenti maggiori*. Only 36 of these men will graduate on 30 June and they would need to quickly transition from being students into their new role of instructor.

The early graduation of the instructor class was due to outside factors. The events of April and May 1940 changed the attitude of the Italian senior leadership towards airborne forces. The successes of the Fallschirmjäger in Denmark, Norway, Belgium and France demonstrated a wider use of paratroopers beyond small unit sabotage and disruption. Now there was a push to create a larger airborne force better able to execute traditional infantry missions. New orders were issued to *colonnello* Baudoin to speed up the opening of the school.

Colonnello A.A.r.n. Pericle Ravagli was sent in May from the S.M.G. to inspect and report on the status of the school and its ability to rapidly increase its training capacity. He noted in his report (28 May) that barracks for officers and men had been built and the 59 meter tower had been erected, the latter donated by the *Vigili del Fuoco del Genio Militare* (Fire Brigade of the Military Engineers) at Villa Glori in Rome.[21] The cadre course had already begun in April with 57 students and that the school had scheduled the first training battalion to begin their course in July.[22]

Italy's declaration of war on 10 June 1940 initiated several changes. One of the first changes was the activation of the wartime headquarters. The *Stato Maggiore dell'Esercito* (S.M.R.E.) was now *Superesercito*, with the general staffs of the Regia Marina and the Regia Aeronautica as *Supermarina* and *Superaereo* respectively. The *Stato Maggiore Generale* (S.M.G.) would be known as STAMGE until May 1941 when it became officially known as *Comando Supremo*.

21 Lundari, *I paracadutisti*, p. 7, di Giovanni, *I paracadutisti*, p.38.
22 di Giovanni, *I paracadutisti*, p. 38.

Training Begins

The declaration of war also gave more emphasis to creating an operational airborne capability. There was not much time as the first student course was to begin on 10 July 1940. Recruitment was open for all members of the R.E. regardless of their branch of service. Starting on 1 July, over 2,000 volunteers began arriving at Tarquinia. The newly trained cadre was organized into three training battalions: *1º btg.* commanded by *tenente colonnello (fanteria)* Camille Benzi; *2º btg.* commanded by *maggoire (Carabinieri)* Bruto Bixio Bersanetti; *3º btg.* commanded by *tenente colonnello (carristi)* Valerio Pignatelli di Cerchiara). More equipment was required as well to meet the higher demand. The number of D.39 parachutes was increased to 600 and the Flight Detachment was increased to 19 Ca.133 transports. The length of the final training course was again reduced from three/four months to no more than 60 training days.[23]

The training curriculum for students was different from that used for preparing the cadre. The actual student curriculum was designed for 50 training days, followed by a variable number of days for tactical training as a unit. This altered the original concept for creating battalions of 250 men ready for combat operations to a concept that would create partially trained units.[24] This was a different approach from that developed by the Allied nations and Germany. The airborne schools created by the Allies were strictly for the technical parachute training and all tactical unit training was performed at a different location under the control of the unit commanders.

The training program was divided into two phases: The 1st Phase consisted of two parts. The first part is what would today be called ground training. It focused on physical training which included running, jumping, stretches, harness suspension, and bicycling using the collapsible bicycles developed for the *bersaglieri*. These bicycles could be employed by the *paracadutisti* because of their compact size once folded. The second part would today be called tower training. Here the students learned the various techniques to safely parachute from a plane. These included jumping from a height into a canvas slide to practice the proper body position (heights from 5m increasing to 20 m), free jumping from the tower using breaking ropes (similar to bungee jumping today except upright) and how to handle the parachute by dropping from a 52m tall tower, both tethered and free. Finally the students took familiarization rides in the school's aircraft to practice loading and to overcome any fear of flying.[25]

The most visual aspect of the 1st Phase of training was the Parachute Tower. The tower was of metal construction topping out at 59 meters. Eighteen platforms were

23 Arena, *Tarquinia* p.31.
24 di Giovanni, *I paracadutisti*, p. 36.
25 This information is distilled from several sources: Arena, *Tarquinia* pp.34–35; Arnoldo Ferrara, *I carabinieri dell'Aria* (Rome: Ente Editoriale per l'Arma dei Carabinieri, 1983), pp.31–34; Aldo Giorleo, *Palestra Azzurra L'aeronautica militare e il paracadutismo cronistoria dalle origini ad oggi* (Roma, USSMA, 1975), pp.39–40.

built into the structure that were three meters apart. The top platform had an airplane engine with a propeller with shortened blades that was mounted on a movable base, allowing the assembly to rotate 360°. The base of the tower was anchored by huge concrete blocks. Four types of jump training could be executed off the tower:

- With a braked parachute: the man in a regular harness, was suspended by his parachute which was held partially open by a circular ring. The ring was held by a metal arm that extended horizontally from the tower. A cable was affixed to the apex of the parachute that ran along the arm to a winch inside the tower. The parachute would be released from the ring, allowing the jumper to float to the ground with the cable controlling the speed of the descent. As the student gained confidence with landing, the speed could be increased until the student was allowed to float down without the braking effect of the cable.
- Jumping into a canvas slide: a canvas slide was attached just below the fifth platform. Trainees would jump from the fifth platform falling several meters before landing onto the canvas, then sliding down the remaining distance. As the trainees become comfortable with the jump, they would jump from the next higher platform. In all, the trainees would jump from distances between five and twenty meters above the slide. This exercise was designed to get the trainees comfortable with jumping from a height. This exercise was supervised by the NCOs from the Fire Brigade.
- Harness slide: The trainee would don a parachute harness to which, instead of risers connected to a parachute, the risers had a large carabiner attached. Two ropes connected to the tower were routed through the carabiner and then to two groups of men on the ground. Each group held a single rope and the groups stood side-by-side in parallel so the ropes were together as one. The trainee would jump from the tower and assume the correct falling position, the ropes being held slack so the trainee would fall a distance. On signal, the two groups of men holding the rope would quickly separate, pulling the ropes apart in-front of the carabiner and slowing the trainee's descent. The speed of the fall could be controlled by opening and closing the ropes
- Parachute jump: the trainees would climb to the top platform in harness and parachute. Here the aircraft engine would be running, turning the propeller and creating an airflow. Once correctly positioned, the parachute was deployed, catching the airstream and pulling the trainee off the tower with a fully inflated parachute. The trainee would float down and land, completing a jump. During testing using a mannequin, it was determined that inexperienced jumpers could easily drift back into the tower and be injured, especially with the wind from the wrong direction. After discussion, it was decided not to continue the use of this training method.[26]

26 Settant'anni fa ci lanciavamo così: Scuola militare di Paracadutismo, Aeroporto di Tarquinia retrieved 10 March 2021

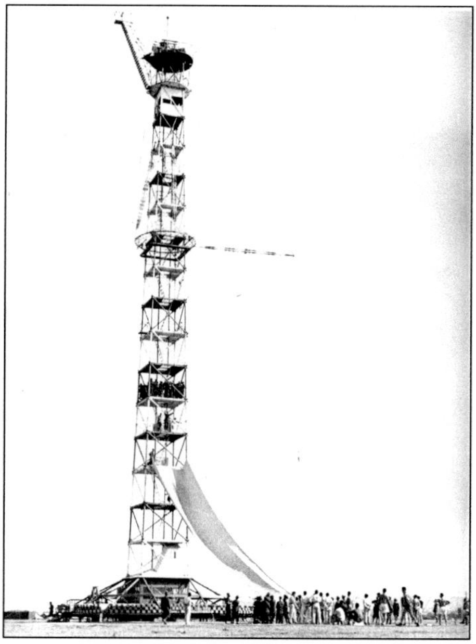

The parachute training tower at Tarquinia. The students are jumping into the cloth slide from the sixth platform. (AUSSME)

The parachute training tower at Tarquinia. The student jumping off the tower is on the Harness Slide with the students on the ground controlling the two ropes. Note the arms that are used for the braked parachute drops. (AUSSME)

Next to the tower was the harness swing training equipment which was used to practice landing falls. These were wooden frames from which the students were suspended in the parachute harness. The student in the harness could be raised and lowered and swung forwards and backwards like a child's swing. The student would climb a set of stairs that were offset from being directly under the frame cross bar and ended in a platform that was about 5–7 meters hight. The student would jump forward which started a swinging motion while remaining suspended at a set height. As the student began to either swing forward or backwards, the instructors would quickly lower the harness to simulate the parachutist dropping to the ground, requiring the student to execute a landing fall.

Once the students had successfully completed this training, they would begin their qualification jumps. Each student was required to executing three parachute jumps; one from 250 m, then 200 m, and finally at 150 m. However successful completion of the three jumps did not qualify the students as *paracadutisti* but certified them to begin the 2nd Phase.

The 2nd Phase was the tactical training. Here the students were turned over to the R.E. and were taught those skills needed to operate as a unit. This training included

An aerial view of the tower and training area. The harness swing training is to the left of the tower. The students on the left side of the tower are using the canvas slide. The students on the right are using the harness slide. (AUSSME)

A group of students awaiting their first parachute jump in 1940. Note the mix of uniforms worn by the students as an official airborne jump uniform had yet to be adopted.

Students boarding a CA.133 for a training jump at Tarquinia. They are wearing D.39 parachutes. Note the puttees, ankle boots, and the lack of helmets. (AUSSME)

three mass parachute jumps (one at night), followed by a live fire exercise. Only after this phase was completed were the students graduates of the training and awarded the *paracadutisti* insignia and certification.

Integrated into the training at various times were theoretical lessons in anatomy, physiology and hygiene: topography; transmissions: driving school for trucks, cars, motorcycles, armored vehicles and tracked vehicles. A specialized course on explosives was also carried out at the school of the Engineers at Civitavecchia, commanded by *colonnello* Cazzaniga: the lessons were taught by *maggiore* Boschetti.

Student training began on 10 July. Seventeen-hundred men had volunteered for the training to form the first three battalions. Ten days earlier the first *battaglione paracadutisti* was formally authorized on 1 July and would be the first unit to train at Tarquinia. The *I battaglione paracadutisti* was formed by volunteers from all branches of the R.E. The second battalion, *II Battaglione Carabinieri Paracadutisti*, authorized on 12 July, would be raised exclusively from the *carabinieri* and would begin training on 15 July. Plans were made for a third battalion to follow. Shortly afterwards the first two battalions were renumbered as the *Reale Carabinieri* were the senior military corps in the Regio Esercito. Due to this seniority within the army, the *I battaglione* would now become the *II battaglione*, and *II battaglione* would now become the *I battaglione*.

As the facilities at the aeroporto «A. Sostegni» were still incomplete, the training would be conducted at various locations:

- at the «A. Sostegni», decision testing, various practice jumps off the tower, landing technique, and acclimatization flights on the Caproni 133;

- at the sports field of Tarquinia, physical preparation/exercise;
- in the countryside around Tarquinia, tactical training and marches;
- at the mouth of the Marta River, marksmanship training;
- in Porto Clementino, live-fire maneuver;
- on the beach of Tarquinia, swimming training;
- in the Engineer School at Civitavecchia, explosives and sabotage training;
- in the cantonment area, theoretical lessons in topography, regulations and various subjects, as well as weapons practice, first aid, parachute folding, refueling loading, etc. The students were immediately engaged in decision tests or psychophysical tests, with the purpose of ascertaining their ability to successfully complete the type of activity they intended to undertake.[27]

Continuing Parachute Problems

After the problems with the Salvator D.37 parachute and the transition to the newer D.39 at Castel Benito, the decision was to use both types of parachutes in the school at Tarquinia. Unfortunately problems arose during the first course when between July 25 and 27, four deaths occurred during the first training jumps. One of the deaths was *tenente* Adolfo Angeloni, an officer from the *II btg. libici paracadutisti* with six previous parachute jumps to his credit. The use of both types of parachutes was suspended and all parachute training halted until the cause and a solution had been identified.

The school's *Reparto Studi ed Esperienza* under *tenente colonnello* Bettica immediately investigated the problem. All four deaths were due to the problem of extracting the canopy from the pack. The D.40 was developed as a replacement for the D.39 but made only a few improvements. The main changes were moving the risers from the waist belt to the shoulders and replacing the buckles used on the previous parachutes with quick-release versions. This parachute could be jumped as low as 70 meters AGL. However the canopy deployment problem remained unresolved and this parachute was only used for a brief period of time.[28]

All parachutes were based on the initial Salvator design and had been developed for use by aircrew to escape damaged aircraft. These earlier parachutes needed to be compact to fit into a pilot's seat or quickly donned inside the aircraft. Given they were worn at all times by the flight crews as they worked, they were made as light and less bulky as possible. This meant that these parachutes were designed to meet the minimum safety requirements and not manufactured for repeated heavy use. The pack tray deployment of the canopy also was a significant factor as aircrew parachutes required to be manually activated. Many of the parachute accidents were due to these

27 Ferrara, *I carabinieri*, pp.30–31.
28 Guy Richards, *World War II Troop Type Parachutes: Axis* (Atglen, Schiffer Military History, 2000), p.14.

design parameters. The *Reparto Studi ed Esperienza* would continue to work on solving the parachute problems into 1941.

It was during the summer of 1940 that the *Ministero della Guerra* released their manual on airborne battalion organization and tactics and the associated circolore for the organization of the units. The earlier 1939 manual was mainly written by the Regia Aeronautica and focused on the technical aspects of military parachuting. The new manual was also a joint effort by the R.E. and the R.A., but now with the R.E. writing the majority of the work. The *Organizzazione e impiego tattico dei reparti paracadutisti*, along with the 12 June 1940 *Formazioni provvisorie di guerra del battaglione paracadutisti* fully defined the scope, missions, and organization of the parachute units.[29] Signed by *generale di corpo d'armata* Ubaldo Soddu, the Undersecretary of War on 27 July 1940, this new manual did not replace the earlier manual authorized in 1939.

> These present regulations, taking into account the experiences known so far from the war in progress, complete those contained in the publication «*Addestramento e impiego dei reparti paracadutisti*» [Training and use of paratrooper units], ed. 1939-XVII which continues to be in force.
>
> These [regulations] essentially concern the ground action of paratroopers and airborne troops;
>
> Criteria and methods of use are not mandatory, they must therefore be adapted to the variable, contingent, and particular factors of each operation.[30]

The organization of the battalion reflected the tactical missions detailed in the manual. The battalion had a *plotone minatori* (sapper platoon) as part of the battalion headquarters to support the sabotage mission. The parachute companies were organized similar to the regular infantry, but half the size (nine men instead of seventeen in the infantry). The enlarged unit command platoon with its communication systems would allow the commander to control battalion-level maneuver. The new battaglione *paracadutisti* was only 313 men strong and lacked heavy weapons, a limitation when compared to most other infantry battalions. In all, the battalion structure is better suited to execute traditional combat missions than the earlier organizations focused on small-unit raids and sabotage.[31]

What was highly unusual was the number of officers authorized within the battalion. Whereas an infantry, bersaglieri, or alpini company had four officers (a company commander and three platoon commanders/leaders) and were fortunate if all were present, the *compagnia paracadutisti* had eight officers (a commander, vice commander, and a commander/vice commander for each platoon). Given the shortage

29 Anon, *Organizzazione e impiego tattico dei reparti paracadutisti* (Rome: Ministero di Guerra Stato Maggiore Regio Esercito, 1940); AUSSME, Stato Maggiore R.E. circolare, *Formazioni provvisorie di guerra del battaglione paracadutisti*, M7, racc.404, cart.1.

30 Anon, *Organizzazione e impiego tattico*, p.5.

31 Anon. *Formazioni provvisorie di guerra del battaglione paracadutisti*, pp.3, 5–6.

of NCOs and their limited leadership role in the R.E., the large number of authorized officers helped alleviate the leadership shortages that were experienced in the army as a whole.[32]

The *I* and *II battaglioni paracadutisti* continued their training for the remainder of the year. During training, *maggiore* Bersanetti who commanded the *battaglione carabinieri paracadutisti* was injured and had to be removed from command. He was replaced by *maggiore* Edoardo Alessi on 28 August. The *III battaglione paracadutisti* was officially authorized but was still being formed. One reason for the delay was that 58 percent of the men volunteering for parachute training had failed to pass the acceptance test. The standards for the *paracadutisti* were significantly higher than for the R.E. in general and the specialty was an all-volunteer force.[33] With the Italian invasion of Egypt on 13 September and followed by that of Greece on 28 October 1940, there were now two theaters where the *reparti paracadutisti* could be employed to support offensive operations. The question is how would the units be used now that Italy was at war?

32 Anon, *Organizzazione e impiego tattico*, p.45; US Military Intelligence Service, *Handbook on the Italian Armed Forces 2 August 1943* (Nashville, Tennessee: Battery Press, 2004), pp.62,65,69.

33 Arena, *Tarquinia* p.23.

4

Gruppo Mobile *«Tonini»*

With Italy's entry into the war on 10 June 1940, *Maresciallo dell'Aria* Balbo was eager to put the units to use. *Tenente colonnello* Freri briefed Balbo on what was needed to prepare the two battalions for offensive operations.. Freri's list included the need for a larger number of suitable aircraft, cargo parachutes, radio equipment, improved small arms and special explosives, as well as the need to develop a logistical support structure.

Balbo concurred and directed Freri to fly to Rome with the list and he was successful in obtaining much of the needed equipment. Eighteen SM.75 aircraft from the *Servizi Aerei Speciali (S.A.S.)*, including their flight and maintenance personnel were transferred to Africa. He also obtained large cargo parachutes capable of handling the 47/32 anti-tank guns, several RF2 radio stations, and was able to get thirty of the MAB 38A submachine guns from the *Polizia dell'Africa Italiana* (P.A.I.). The *1º btg. paracadutisti libico* was the first army unit to receive these new automatic weapons.[1]

After the armistice was signed with France (24 June), the main Italian forces began to reposition eastward towards the Egyptian border. With the nation at war, Castel Benito became the major airfield in Libya and its expansion was urgently required. It was clear that the increased air activity along with the required infrastructure improvements would interfere with the parachute training so the decision was made to move the battalions to the Benina airport outside Bengasi. The *1º btg. paracadutisti libico* moved by air while the *1º btg. paracadutisti nazionale* made the 1,000 km move by truck.[2]

This move was only a temporary one for the *paracadutisti*. There had already been discussions to move the school and parachute battalions to the airfield at Barce prior to Italy entering the war. With less air traffic at Barce, there would be fewer scheduling issues that could impact training and the location provided easy access to larger training areas.

1 Arena, *I Fanti*, p.64. Why the army limited authorization/issue of the MAB during the war is an area requiring more research.
2 Arena, *I Fanti*, p.69.

The SM.75s and equipment that Freri had obtained during his trip to Italy arrived at Benina shortly after the move. Here the SM.75s were modified for paradrops, allowing them to carry 20 paratroopers and 1200kg of supplies. Training was immediately restarted and the activity included testing of parachuting the 47/32 anti-tank gun. The results were that a single 47/32 gun, its crew, and 25 rounds of ammunition could be carried and dropped by parachute from a single SM.75 aircraft. This gave the *paracadutisti* a new capability that would increase their combat effectiveness once on the ground.[3]

The parachute battalions had lacked an anti-tank and infantry support weapon if they were to be used as a ground combat unit. The Breda 47/32 controcarro (c.c., anti-tank) gun had been adopted in 1935 by the R.E. and was replacing First World War vintage 65/17 gun throughout the army. At the time it was adopted and up into 1941, it remained an effective weapon against most tanks. It could also fire a useful high explosive round that could be used against infantry and hasty field fortifications. It was designed to be man-handled, so it was light and could be pulled by a team of men. The gun could also be broken down into four loads for animal transport or carried into mountainous terrain. It was a good weapon for the *paracadutisti* but it would become increasingly ineffective as the better British and American tanks appeared on the battlefield. The problem for the Regio Esercito was it could not replace the 47/32 c.c. with anything better. The Breda gun would remain the standard anti-tank weapon until the Italian surrender in 1943.[4]

It was during the time at Benina that the word of the death of Italo Balbo reached the units. His plane had been shot down on 28 June by friendly fire as it was landing at Tobruk. The bodies of the *maresciallo dell'aria* and the others on the plane were flown from Tobruk to Tripoli on 29 June. The plane stopped at Benina and the *reparti paracadutisti* presented military honors to the fallen. Immediately afterwards the ceremony, the *I btg. paracadutisti libico* boarded their SM.75s and flew up to Barce.[5]

With *Maresciallo* Balbo's death, the airborne units lost their champion. No other military leader of his stature had his passion for the airborne speciality and a desire to take his place. *Maresciallo* Graziani, who was a strong advocate for remaining on the defense in Libya, was appointed as his replacement. Graziani observed a parachute drop on 25 July at Barce but this did not appear to have made much of an impression.[6] Instead, the two battalions were issued trucks and released to the operational control of *Comando Superiore FF.AA. dell'A.S.* (*Superasi*) as conventional infantry units. It is rather ironic that the two airborne battalions became one of the few fully motorized units in the Italian Army in North Africa in 1940.[7]

3 Arena, *I Fanti*, p.66.
4 Filippo Cappellano, *Le artiglierie del Regio Esercito nella seconda guerra mondiale* (Parma: Alberti Edizione Speciali s.r.l., 1998), pp.248–255.
5 Arena, *I Fanti*, p.66.
6 Di Giovanni, *I paracadutisti*, p.89 and fn.3.
7 Arena, *I Fanti*, p.68.

The Italian Offensive

In early September the *10ª Armata* began to reposition its forces along the Egyptian border in preparation for the long awaited offensive. The Italian Army began to cross the border on 13 September, advancing as a frontal assault with no attempt at maneuver. Four days and 130 kilometers later the attack was over with the *10ª Armata* consolidating its position around Sidi el Barrani on 16 September.[8] There was no heavy combat as the UK forces used delaying tactics to harass the advance while the Italians never attempted to cut off any portion of the defending force. The actual execution of the unimaginative offensive demonstrated that the Italian plan of maneuver did notoffer any possibility of successful employment of the *paracadutisti.*

The two battalions remained in the Barce area through the end of September. In early October 1940, both battalions were moved from Barce to Martuda (just south of Derna) along the via Balbia. Operating from Martuda, the battalions organized auto-columns to patrol sections of the desert south and east of Martuba to protect the area from any Long Range Desert Group patrols. While this finally offered a chance at combat, the reality was a lot of driving with little action. Cleaning weapons and maintaining the vehicles occupied most of the paratrooper's time, with rarely any contact with British patrols. The battalions returned to the Barce at the end of the month.[9]

During the battalion's movement back to Barce, the news of the Italian invasion of Greece arrived on the morning of 28 October. A report on 7 November gave the strength of the Libyan battalion at 410 parachutists fully trained and the national battalion at 312 parachutists, of which 200 of the latter were fully trained.[10] That report and another parachuting demonstration by the *1º btg. nazionale* on 12 November appeared to offer the possibility of employment in their primary role.[11] A meeting within the S.M.R.E. held on 15 November examined whether to transfer one of the battalions currently being trained at Tarquinia to A.S. The discussion examined the possible use of airborne units as part of an advance against Alexandria. With the current offensive in Greece underway, the focus on their use in A.S. and not Greece indicated a lack of any operational concept for their employment. Graziani had not requested an additional battalion and lacked any plans to employ the two he did have. No decisions were made at this time by the S.M.R.E., but the issue of deploying airborne units to A.S. would be raised again in 1941.[12]

The impact of the fighting in Greece on the *paracadutisti* was felt in the following two weeks. As the fortunes of the Italian forces in Greece deteriorated, more resources were pulled from other theaters in attempts to stem the defeats. The SM.75s dedicated

8 Mario Montanari, *Le operazioni in Africa settentrionale*, vol I, Sid el Barrani (Rome: USSME, 1985), pp.104-112.
9 Arena, *I fanti*, pp.85-86.
10 Di Giovanni, *I paracadutisti*, p.90.
11 Arena, *I Fanti*, p.68.
12 Di Giovanni, *I paracadutisti*, p.90.

to the school were pulled from A.S. to reinforce the aerial supply line operating between Italy and Albania. By the end of November all parachuting activity at the school in Barce had ground to a halt due to the lack of aircraft.

Because of this, the training staff with all the associated equipment and parachutes were transferred back to Castel Benito and the school at Barce was closed. Also returned to Castel Benito were the parachute riggers and the two technicians from the Società Aerostatica Avorio, the company that produced parachutes for the military. The invasion of Greece had ended the last hope that the airborne units would see combat as paratroopers in North Africa.[13]

Both battalions were sent to the Wadi al Bakur area located six kilometers east of Tocra at the end of November. Here the wadi crossed the via Balbia and the *paracadutisti* now were ordered to become engineers. Their mission was to build an anti-tank trench on either side of the via Balbia. Serious work for the *paracadutisti* who lacked any type of heavy equipment for digging into the rocky ground. The battalions continued to be garrisoned at Barce while performing the work at the Wadi al Bakur.

Operation Compass (Maps 4.1 and 4.2)

The British offensive, codenamed Operation Compass, opened on 9 December. The skillful use of their mobile force, and judicious employment of the Mk II Matilda tanks allowed the British to overwhelm the *10ª Armata* defenses at Sidi Barrani. By the time Bardia was captured on 6 January 1941, eight Italian divisions had been destroyed and the *10ª Armata* rendered incapable of launching offensive operations.[14] With these initial successes, the British had immediately pressed on towards Tobruk.

The first British mobile formations occupied the terrain west of Tobruk on 7 January 1941, cutting communications with the remaining Italian forces further west. The *10ª Armata* found itself with few units outside the fortress that could support its defense. Reinforcements were arriving, but in numbers too small and were disembarking too far away from the fighting to seriously affect the approaching British assault. Holding Tobruk with the current forces was unlikely: Bardia, with a shorter defensive perimeter and significantly larger force than those now holding Tobruk, had fallen in a few days. The question for the Italian leadership was how much of the Cirenaica could be saved rather than whether Tobruk could be held.

Plans for creating additional defenses west of Tobruk had already been initiated in late December 1940. The best route from Tobruk to Bengasi follows the via Balbia which runs through the Gebel Akhdar, the mountainous plateau region that occupies the Cirenacia bulge that juts into the Mediterranean Sea. By holding both Derna and Giovanni Berta along the via Balbia, the Italians could deny the British access

13 Arena, *I Fanti*, p.86.
14 Playfair, I.S.O., *The Mediterranean and Middle East*, vol 1 (London: HMSO, 1954), p.287.

to this route. The operational problem for the defense is that the gebel itself can be bypassed to the south. Starting at Martuba, southeast of Derna, a force can travel west to Mechili and then on to Msus and finally to Antelat near the coast south of Bengasi. Such a move would trap any Italian forces in the gebel.

Both Graziani and *generale di corpo d'armata* Giuseppe Tellera, the recently appointed commander of the *10ª Armata*, knew that the current forces were unlikely to stop the British advance.[15] Available for the defense against the British were the *60ª divisione fanteria «Sabratha»* (*generale* Della Bona) that was newly transferred from the *5ª Armata*, the *brigata corazzata speciale «Babini»*, the *10º reggimento bersaglieri*, and various garrison units of the *Guardia alla frontiera* (GaF). To this force, *Superasi* in the Cirenaica could only add a *raggruppamento motorizzato* with two machine gun battalions, an artillery gruppo, the *VI btg. carri M* (a M13/40 tank battalion) and the two paratrooper battalions.

Previously several artillery and machine-gun units had been stripped from the infantry divisions in the *5ª Armata* to reinforce the *10ª Armata*. Those units were the motorized components of the divisions and could be quickly redeployed unlike the foot-bound infantry units. Those units were collected as they traveled along the via Balbia and assigned to the various defensive sectors as needed. The defenses thus created in this manner were ad hoc in nature without a functional command and control system, unbalanced in composition, and lacking experience in operating together as a team.[16]

Generale di divisione Giudo Della Bona, commander of the *d.f «Sabratha»*, was placed in command of the defenses in the Derna-Berta area which controlled access to the Gebel Akhdar from the east and south. The terrain of the gebel did not offer any insurmountable natural obstacles that could not be bypassed by a determined attacker, however the numerous wadis and narrow valleys could be effectively used to delay an enemy advance through the hilly terrain. *Generale* Della Bona's challenge was to defend three widely separate locations with inadequate forces.

On 15 January 1941, *Superasi* ordered the *1º btg. paracadutisti libico* to move from Barce to Derna. To the 430 *ascari* of the battalion were added 50 men from the parachute school and two platoons of 47/32 c.c. guns. The battalion was placed under the command of *generale di corpo d'armata* Annibale Bergonzoli. Bergonzoli (later known as 'Electric Whiskers' in the western press) had commanded the *XXII Corpo d'Armata* which had defended Bardia. Avoiding capture, he escaped to Tobruk and having no active command in that fortress, was able to leave before the fortress fell.

Generale Tellera recognized that the span of control was too large for one headquarters and reorganized the defense. With *generale* Bergonzoli now available, Tellera assigned the defense of the settore Derna to him. That sector extended from Derna

15 Montanari, *Le operazioni*, vol I, pp.248 and 315. Tellera replaced *generale* Mario Berti as commander of the *10ª Armata* on 22 December 1941.

16 Anon, *La prima offensiva britannica*, p.209

on the coast to just south of Martuba. Bergonzoli's mission in Settore Derna was to prevent the British from gaining access to the Gebel Akhdar from the east.

Southwest of this sector was the settore Berta-Mechili which Tellera placed under the command of *generale di corpo d'armata* Ferdinando Cona, commander of the *XX Corpo d'Armata*. The key to this sector was the crossroad junction at Mechili, the control of which would block any attempt to gain access to the gebel from the south through Giovanni Berta or to block any attempt to bypass the gebel to the south using the Mechili-Msus route.

Battle of Derna (Map 4.3) [17]

The key to defending the eastern approaches into the gebel was the coastal city of Derna. Unlike Bardia and Tobruk, it did not possess a fortified perimeter as the town is dominated by a 250 meter high escarpment which rises abruptly from the coastal plain just one kilometer south of the city limits. Whomever dominated these heights would control the city and the via Balbia that passed through it. The road represented the only way down the escarpment and onto the coastal plain for vehicles, allowing them to continue westward into the gebel. As such, Derna was a choke point and it was on the escarpment that the Italian defenses were concentrated.

What made Derna an effective choke point was the Wadi Derna, an imposing .5–1.5 kilometer wide by 200m deep canyon which bisects the coastal escarpment and extends inland for a distance of more than 30km. Derna sits on the Mediterranean Sea astride the north-end of the wadi. The wadi itself offered few locations for dismounted infantry to cross, but more importantly it blocked any vehicle traffic from moving east to west. Not until one nears Mechili can vehicles once again enter the gebel.

Defending the wadi prevented any enemy advance against Derna from the south. Italian troops situated on the west side of the wadi had a natural moat to protect them. As long as the wadi line is held, any attack against Derna must come from the east.

On the crest of the escarpment above Derna were four old forts; "Rudero" and "Piemonte" on the eastern ridge of the Wadi Derna, and "Lombardia" and "Segnale" on the western ridge. These were old-style colonial masonry forts dating back to the Barbary Wars (1805) and the Italo-Turkish war (1911-12) and offered little protection against modern weapons. At the start of the British offensive, the speed of the attack, and the lack of materials and labor for construction had only allowed for hasty battlefield positions to be prepared. The army engineers corps had focused more on

17 Matching dates between the various accounts has been a challenge. The Australian official account has differences from the Australian unit war diaries. The Italian accounts tend to be dated one/two days earlier. The dates given are a best attempt to reconcile the differences.

road interruptions on the Via Balbia and mining limited areas of the escarpment and various cross roads south of the Derna defenses.

Derna itself was held by *II btg., 86° rgt. f.* «*Sabratha*», the *btg. di formazione* (depot battalion) of the *115° rgt. f.* «*Marmarica*» (the regiment itself had been destroyed at Bardia), and the *XVII btg. mitraglieri* (machine gun battalion) from the *d. f.* «*Pavia*».[18] The available artillery was a collection of batteries and gruppi from various units: *I gruppo da 75/27* (a total of 20 guns); *VII gruppo da 75/46 c.a.* (seven anti-aircraft guns); a battery of 75/27 guns from the *II gruppo del 10° reggimento artiglieria* from the *d.f.* «*Bologna*», a battery of 76/40 (four guns); two R.M. coastal batteries of 102/45 guns in fixed positions; a R.M. battery of 152/45 guns in fixed positions; and a mobile R.M. battery of 120/45 guns. Fort Piemonte and Ridotta (redoubt) Rudero each had two 75/27 guns and one 47/32 c.c. Five other 47/32 c.c. were available to the defense.

Only the *II btg., 86° rgt. f.* and the *1° btg. paracadutisti libico* were organized infantry battalions. The *btg. di formazione* was a collection of replacements without formal organization and lacked heavy weapons. The machine-gun battalions had significant firepower but no ability to hold terrain against ground assault. Also lacking for the defense were mortars (only the *II/86° f.* had mortars), a higher artillery headquarters to coordinate fires, and communication equipment to connect the batteries with the combat troops for indirect fire support. Bergonzoli had less than 3,000 infantry and only four tanks to hold a position approximately 25 kilometers long.

Arriving on 15 January from Barce, *tenente colonnello* Tonini decided to initially position his battalion on several of the key heights to the south that overlooked the town and the main routes.

While the *1° btg. Paracadutisti libico* was moving into positions above Derna, British units were already approaching the town. C Squadron, 3rd Hussars, had been ordered towards Derna as a reconnaissance force. The squadron occupied the abandoned Italian seaplane base at Bomba on that same day and continued to push westward a few additional miles along the via Balbia.

On 17 January Tonini was ordered to concentrate his battalion to protect the eastern approaches to the town. The position Tonini occupied were the hills on the east side

18 Arena, *I Fanti*, p.92. Arena errs in the identification of the two machine gun battalions on p.92, stating they are the *17°* and *50° battaglioni* from the «*Brescia*» and «*Savona*» divisions. Machine gun battalions were numbered after their parent divisions' number, hence «*Brescia*» battalion would be the *XXVII* and «*Savona*» would be the *LV*. Anon, *La prima offensiva britannica*, p.209, identifies the battalions as the *XVII* «*Brescia*» and *LV* «*Savona*». While the latter is correct, the former (*XVII*) should be from «*Pavia*». *Prima offensiva* consistently identifies the unit as the *XVII* in the text and on all the maps. Ibid *Schizzo 20* placed the «*Brescia*» machine-gun battalion near Bengasi on 25 January (named *Brescia* but incorrectly labeled *XVII*) while placing «*Pavia*» at Derna (correctly labeled *XVII*). Montanari *Le operazioni* vol I, p.320 states that both «*Brescia*» and «*Bologna*» machine-gun battalions were assigned to *raggruppamento Bignami* on 22 January and still part of that unit on 5 February (p.343). That raggruppamento remained near Bengasi during this time period. The *XVII btg. mtr.* «*Pavia*» is placed at Derna in this account.

of the Wadi Derna overlooking the Plain of El Fteiah. The Plain of El Ftieah was a plateau which has its highest elevations along the Wadi Derna and then slopes downward for approximately 10 kilometers going south and east towards Gazala. The Derna airfield was located on this plain with its metal hangar and several support buildings. The Fattoria (Farm) le Grotte was located just north of the airfield. There were several shrines (sidi) and abandoned farm buildings to the front that could be used as forward positions. To the north the plateau drops abruptly down into the coastal strip which cannot be observed from the main position. To the south was a wide-open desert that would allow the enemy to approach the eastern side of Wadi Derna and then attack northward. The *II/86° fanteria* defended the Wadi Derna in this area, but they were stretched thin along the west side of wadi. The battalion lacked vehicles and artillery support so was holding fixed positions.[19]

The main defense of Derna itself was reorganized, with the previously mentioned *II/86°*, along with the *XVII btg. mitraglieri* moved south to protect the west side of the wadi. The town itself was now held by the *btg. di formazione/115° rgt.* and the recently arrived *XVIII btg. libico*, the *LV btg. mitraglieri* from the *d.f.* «*Savona*», and the *7ª btr. libica da 20/65.*[20] All the artillery was concentrated to the south-west of the town using the broken terrain of the escarpment to conceal the batteries. Four fixed coastal batteries of the Regia Marina were available and capable of firing landward as well as out to sea.

Since the arrival of the parachute battalion on 15 January, several miscellaneous units had been added to Tonini's command. To the men of the *1° btg. «fanti dell'aria»* had been added six 20mm anti-aircraft guns, two bersaglieri anti-tank platoons (four 47/32 c.c.), three additional anti-tank guns (47/32 c.c.), and the btr. of 75/27 from the *II/10° rgt. art. «Bologna»*. With these forces, Tonini organized his main position along the line of Quota (Height) 263, the Fattoria Le Grotte, Casa Aronne, and Quota 260. This oriented his defense to the south across the plain. He employed mobile patrols to cover the coastal area known as the Sahel es Sneibat between his position and the sea. He created strongpoints at several forward positions in the plain at Sidi Aziz, Umm el Ghemen, Sidi Sultan, and Quota 237. Small detachments were placed in the airfield hanger and other buildings in the area.

19 The Libyan parachute company identifications/locations on Maps 4.3–4.10 are best estimates using mainly secondary sources. Additional research is required.

20 Arena, *I Fanti* p.92, states the Libyan battalion is the *XVII*. This is incorrect as the *XVII btg. Libico* was with the *raggruppamento libico «Maletti»* at Nibeua and destroyed during the fight (Montanari, *Le operazioni* vol I, pp.202 and 597). Anon, *La prima offensiva britannica* p.205 has the *XVIII btg. libico* south at Martuba on 23 January. The *7ª btr.* is assumed to be Libyan as the numbering matches that used for Libyan 20/65 batteries and was likely with the *gruppo btg. libici* on 23 January (Anon, *La prima offensiva britannica* p.205; Stefano Ales, Piero Crociani, Andrea Viotti, *Struttura, uniformi, distintivi, ed insegne delle truppe libiche 1912-1943* (Rome: USSME, 2012), pp.91–92, 333.

To the front of Tonini's position was the *Gruppo «Pancano»* which held a forward position at Cantontina (roadhouse) 17/Siret el Chreiba. The *gruppo* had deployed a forward element over-watching the bridge at the Wadi Bagr between Martuba and Derna that was approximately 10 kilometers from the main position.[21] The *gruppo* was entirely motorized with all the 20mm c.a. and the 47/32 c.c. being carried in trucks.

Tonini had to cover nearly 16 kilometers with this force, which would contract to the eight-kilometer long main position once the forward positions were pulled back. The lack of sufficient infantry for such a long front and the dearth of indirect-fire weapons created several problems for the defenders. Most of the *gruppo* weapons were direct-fire and unable to engage an enemy that hid behind hills and in folds in the ground. Combined with the *gruppo* lack of mortars, the broken terrain provided an attacker with multiple places to advance against the defense. The only artillery support for the entire defensive area were the four 75/27 guns in the attached battery; most of the artillery positioned around Derna could not range the forward positions. Limited means of communication (the paratroopers only had four radios and no field telephones) would negatively impact rapid maneuver and artillery support fire. Nighttime afforded additional opportunities for an enemy advance as it limited the usefulness of the Italian heavy weapons and the widely spaced infantry positions offered many gaps in the defense. At eight kilometers, the approximately 650 infantry was covering 10-12 meters per individual soldier. Being an airborne battalion, the unit lacked engineering tools to dig formal fighting positions into the rocky ground, The soldiers were limited to scrapping shallow holes and building rock sangars. The lack of tools also meant that the truck-mounted heavy weapons could not be dug-in at all, leaving hull down positions the only option whenever possible to utilize cover. This type of positioning limited where those weapons could be placed with good fields of fire. The inability to entrench meant that both men and vehicles were very vulnerable to any type of indirect-fire and air attack. The *paracadutisti* would find themselves hard pressed to hold back the impending enemy attack.

While protecting the British envelopment of Tobruk, some forward elements of the 7th British Armoured Division were probing westward towards the Italian positions covering Derna and Mechili between 17 and 23 January. Along with C Squadron, 3rd Hussars, the 1/Royal Tank Regiment (RTR) supported by elements of the 60th King's Royal Rifle Corps (KRRC) had moved westward as well and were operating in

21 Anon, *La prima offensiva britannica*, schizzo 19; Anon, 'Reggimento *paracadutisti* "Fanti dell'aria", <https://it.wikipedia.org/wiki/Reggimento_*paracadutisti*_%22Fanti_dell%27aria%22cite_ref-10> (no date) accessed on 3 October 2021. There is very little information on the *Gruppo «Pancano»*. It was likely it was the planned reconnaissance unit for the *brigata speciale corazzata* under gen. Babini. Formed on 9 January at Gazala, it consisted of *60° cp. bersaglieri motociclisti* (two platoons); *14ª batteria contraerea* (six 20mm AA guns); and *Plotone di formazione, I Battaglione, 4° Reggimento Carri Medi* (four M11/39 tanks). See Anon, *La prima offensiva britannica in Africa settentrionale (ottobre 1940-febbraio 1941)* (Rome: USSME, 1964), pp.162, 209.

Libyan *paracadutisti* with a Breda 30 f.m. at Derna. Note the hasty defensive positions and the open nature of the terrain. (AUSSME)

the area southeast of Derna at this time. The fighting was mainly between opposing patrols running into each other, pitting the truck mounted paratroopers and bersaglieri motorcycle troops against the reconnaissance and light armoured forces of the enemy.

The RAF was also very active, making attacks on various positions around Derna during this period, with one attack on the Fattoria Le Grotte on 19 January causing 32 casualties.[22] The RN was active as well, bombarding various defensive locations with destroyers. Against these the Italian had little recourse except to suffer under those attacks. The R.A. could provide little protection as the rapid retreat and combat losses had crippled the air arm. The R.M. was focused on protecting the convoys bringing reinforcements, a critical role if Italy was to retain Libya

British armour activity was threatening the bersaglieri motorcyclists covering the bridge over the Wadi Bgar. The MK VI light tanks and armored cars were finding routes across the wadi and pushing their reconnaissance towards Derna. On 18 January Bergonzoli ordered the *Gruppo «Pacano»* to destroy the bridge and pull back about two kilometers from the Wadi Bagr to the high ground around Siret el Chreiba

22 Arena, *I Fanti*, p.97.

and Blockhouse 17. This pulled the exposed *gruppo* closer towards the *1° btg. paracadutisti libico* forward positions, thereby protecting the smaller unit's flanks.

The elements of the British 7th Armoured Brigade continued to develop the tactical situation against the Italian defenders at Siret el Chreiba on 21 January. Light skirmishing took place on 22 January between the 1/RTR and *Gruppo «Pancano»* with neither side gaining an advantage.

On 23 January, Tonini was ordered to release a parachute company to occupy a position on the Wadi Mbacch covering the western approaches of Derna. This was also the day when the tanks of the 1/R.T.R., supported by men of the KRRC pushed forward and forced *Gruppo «Pancano»* to withdraw from their positions around Siret el-Cheriba. With the retreat of *«Pancano»* into the lines of the *I btg. paracadutisti libico*, Bergonzoli disbanded the *gruppo* and added those units to Tonini's command. The combined forces defending the eastern approach were renamed *Gruppo mobile «Tonini»* and *tenente colonnello* Tonini was formally given command of the eastern defenses. Tonini now had a total of 850 paratroopers, infantry, bersaglieri, and artillerymen. The *gruppo* consisted of:

- *1° btg. «fanti dell'aria»* (430 *paracadutisti libici*, 50 *paracadutisti nazionali*), four 47/32 c.c.[23]
- Two bersaglieri anti-tank platoons (four 47/32 c.c., 83 men)
- *60ª compagnia bersaglieri motociclisti* (only two platoons), 129 infantry and bersaglieri.
- *14ª batteria contraerea* with six 20/65 c.a. guns.
- four M11/39 tanks and a captured Herrington armored car.
- One btr. da 75/27 from the *II/10° rgt. art. «Bologna»*.
- 175 men with various weapons, six 20/65 c.a. guns, and three 47/32 guns.[24]

As the Italian defenders were being reorganized, the Tobruk fortress fell to the Australians on 22 January. The Australian 6th Division was ordered to assemble an advance guard and move from Tobruk towards Derna. The reinforced 19th Australian Brigade would follow and would be in overall command of the attack against Derna. The advance guard departed the Tobruk area on 23 January and consisted of:

A Squadron, 6th Australian Cavalry (Major MacArthur-Onslow)
- battery of the 2/1 Field Artillery (FA) Regiment (twelve 25 pdr guns);
- troop from 'J' Battery, Royal Horse Artillery (RHA) (four 2 pdr AT guns);

23 Both Anon, *La prima offensiva britannica*, p.209 and Arena, *I Fanti*, p.92 give the *gruppo* a total of eleven 47/32. cc. The actual breakdown of sub-units only lists seven of these guns. It is likely that the *btg. paracadutisti* itself had four guns (two platoons) assigned to it while at Barce.

24 Anon, *La prima offensiva britannica*, p.209; Arena, *I Fanti*, p.92. It is assumed that the elements of *«Pancano»* were integrated into Tonini's defense as support weapons and not sa separate maneuver elements.

- troop from 37 Light Anti-Aircraft (LAA) Regiment (four 40mm Bofors);
- MG company from 1/Royal Northumberland Fusiliers (RNF) Regiment (Machine Gun battalion);
- various support services.[25]

This force arrived behind the units of the 7th Armoured Brigade on 24 January. The armour had advanced a few kilometers past the wadi and was shelling Italian units holding the Siret el Chreiba area and the blockhouse that protected the southern side of the Derna airfield. The British armour, supported by artillery, pressed the action against Cantoniera 17, forcing Tonini to reinforce the position. Fighting between the British tanks and artillery on one side, and the 40 paratroopers, two 47/32 c.c. guns, and four heavy machine-gun continued throughout the day. In the evening, sensing the growing pressure on his line, Tonini ordered the unit to fall back during the night on the Fattoria Le Grotte. This move abandoned the Fattoria El Fteiah and the southern end of the airfield to better consolidate his limited forces.[26]

25 January (Maps 4.4 and 4.5)

The Australians relieved the British armour on the morning of 25 January, the latter which had occupied the abandoned Italian positions around Siret el Chreiba. Major Onslow, the squadron commander of A/6 Aust. Cav., decided to probe forward to test the Italian defenses. He sent a section of Bren carriers north to the escarpment overlooking the eastern end of the Sahel el Chenisa and the coast, while another group of carriers was sent around and across the airfield. Both groups were fired upon by elements of *gruppo mobile «Tonini»*. Onslow decided that his squadron could not rush Derna by itself but would need to wait for the infantry. He did note that while his reconnaissance elements had been fired on, the fire was not heavy and consisted of a mix of a few artillery pieces, and some anti-tank and heavy machine guns. This information would be passed on to the 19th Aust. Bde as they arrived in the area.[27]

Onslow did not need to wait very long as the lead elements of the 19th Aust. Bde had begun to arrive while the cavalry were moving forward. The brigade consisted of:

19th Australian Brigade
2/4 Aust. Infantry Battalion
2/8 Aust. Infantry Battalion
2/11 Aust. Infantry Battalion

25 Gavin Long, *To Benghazi* (Canberra: Australian War Memorial, 1961), p.242 fn.
26 Arena, *I Fanti*, p.101.
27 AWM, *War Diary 6 Australian Division Cavalry Regiment January 1941*, AWM52 2/2/7/10, p.39.

1/Royal Northumberland Fusiliers (2 coys)
the reminder of the 2/1 Field Artillery Regiment

The Australian commander, Brigadier Robertson, ordered the 2/11 Australian Infantry Battalion to move along the via Balbia towards the airfield and Derna. The infantry disembarked from its trucks at 1230 south of Siret el Chreiba and began to move northwest. D Coy was ordered to move north to reach the escarpment overlooking the coast while C Coy was ordered to cross the airfield towards the Fattoria Le Grotte. A Coy would cover the left (south-east) flank of the battalion's advance and B Coy was held in reserve.

D Coy, moving east of the Italian defenses, reached the escarpment without any loss. C Coy marched up to the southern edge of the air field and linked-up with the cavalry patrol posted there. The patrol informed the company commander, Captain Honner, that only light resistance had been encountered and one of its patrols had reached the hangars at the north end of the field and returned. With this information, the company began to advance across the airfield. They overran a small position held by some of the *bersaglieri* motorcyclists, but then the *paracadutisti* with machine guns and 20mm c.a. opened fire from the Fattoria le Grotte, the hangar buildings, and Quota 263. The Australian infantry continued to move forward until they were about 3,000 meters from their objective, when the sweeping fire pinned them in place. The supporting machine-gun company and the anti-tank section, caught by the same fires, were unable to move close enough to provide any effective support to the pinned infantry.[28]

Assessing the situation, Captain Honner decided to wait until dark to continue the attack. As dusk settled in, the Italians could not see the Australians in the gloom but the Australians could still see the outline of the Italian positions. Using the cover of the night and the fire from their mortars, the Australians were able to reach the hangars and the buildings. The *paracadutisti* and *bersaglieri* fought as best they could, but they were too few and the main Italian positions were on the ridge about 400 meters beyond the airfield. Lacking mortars of their own, the paratroopers could only pin down the Australians as they tried to move, but could not place direct fire into the folds they were using for cover. A few small Italian positions were captured, but once past the airfield buildings the Australians could not advance any further that night.

The second Australian battalion to arrive at Martuba, the 2/4 Aust, was ordered to move directly west and occupy the eastern bank of the Wadi Derna. This battalion drove to Gahr el Carmusa and dismounted, moved northwest to the wadi, arriving as night was falling. Rather than waiting for morning, the 2/4 Aust. pushed two platoons across to the west side during the early hours of 26 January. The third battalion, the 2/8 Aust. arrived late in the afternoon and moved forward to occupy Siret Medaanat between the 2/11 in the north and the 2/4 in the south.

28 Long, *To Benghazi*, p.245–246.

A bersaglieri 47/32 c.c. deployed at Derna. (AUSSME)

By the fall of night of 25 January the 700 men of *Gruppo Mobile «Tonini»* now faced over 2,000 Australians, supported by an artillery regiment with twenty-four 25 pdr. and a cavalry squadron. The southern flank of the position was in danger of being turned and the enemy was pressing along its entire front. The unit had lost 35 dead and 56 wounded during that day. Assessing the situation, *generale* Bergonzoli ordered Tonini to withdraw from the forward positions back closer to the town. Tonini pulled his companies back to the Ridotta Rudero and the flanking wadis and laid a hasty minefield across the via Balbia.

26 January (Maps 4.6, 4.7)

As the British armor had been stopped by the *brigata corazzata speciale* under *generale di brigata* Valentino Babini at Mechili, the British plan for 26 January was to have the Australians push on through Derna to flank the Italian force holding Mechili. The British 7th Armoured Division would pin the Italian armored brigade in place around Mechili, giving time for the 6th Australian Division to dash to Bengasi. Based on this plan, Brigadier Robertson issued his orders for the morning of 26 January. The 2/11 Aust. was ordered to clear the Italians from the escarpment on the eastern side of the wadi; the 2/4 Aust. would hold the bridgehead on the western bank of the wadi created during the night; and the 2/8 Aust. would advance west from Siret Medaanat between the two other battalions and secure that section of the wadi. Those movements would position the brigade for a concentric attack against the town on 27 January.

During the early morning hours, the 2/4 Aust. had sent more troops to the western side of the wadi. Part of C Coy had crossed the wadi and established itself during the hours of darkness on the morning of 26 January. Detecting this unit, the *II/86° fanteria* sent a patrol to investigate. This patrol attacked the Australians but was beaten off. The Italians then sent a larger force of over 100 men. Simultaneously the remainder of C Coy crossed over, followed by A and D Coys. B Coy established itself on the eastern side of the wadi. It was this much larger force that met the second Italian attack, with the Italians being easily defeated. The Australians continued to improve their hold on the wadi during the day.[29]

As 2/4 Aust. was solidifying its hold across the wadi, 19th Brigade headquarters informed the 2/11 Aust. that the enemy had abandoned their forward positions and the battalion should now advance on Derna itself. The commander of the 2/11 Aust. sent D Coy down the escarpment and into the Sahel es-Sneibat to approach the town from the eastern side along the coast. B Coy would move through C Coy and continue the attack along the main road, while A Coy would move generally westward to clear the eastern end of the wadi. C Coy would rest and act as the battalion reserve.[30]

For the men of 2/11 Aust., it quickly became evident that the *paracadutisti* had not retreated. Covering the withdrawal of *1ª cp. paracadutisti*, Tonini launched a limited attack with the tanks and the captured Herrington armoured car, supported with machine gun and artillery fire. The attack was not pressed very hard and C Coy was able to fend it off, but *1ª cp.* successfully disengaged. B Coy was shelled as it crossed the airfield and passed through C Coy. Leaving the cover of the buildings at the northern end of the airfield, the company advanced towards the Ridotta Rudero. *3ª cp. paracadutisti* defending that point, provided suppressing fire against the attackers. Stopped by the hasty minefield, heavy machine gun fire and artillery, B Coy was pinned in-place. Unable to move further, the company took shelter late in the afternoon in the wadi just south of the road. C Coy consolidated their positions and moved the wounded to the rear.[31]

D Coy also found the way into Derna well blocked. Climbing down the nearly precipitous escarpment onto the coastal plain, they moved west along the coast until pinned by nearly point-blank artillery and machine-gun fire as they neared the Ridotta Rudero. Opting to remain in place until nightfall to attempt a night attack, that plan was abandoned once it was determined that the company could not be supplied with water and ammunition. Ordered to withdraw, D Coy used the night to climb back up the escarpment. A Coy held its position during the day, unable to advance due to the machine gun fire from the *XVII battaglione mitragliatrici* on the western side of the wadi.

The 2/8 Aust. advanced to the eastern wall of the wadi but could not move any further. Machine gun fire from the *XVII btg. mitragliatrici* hindered any effort to thoroughly recon for a route down and across wadi. The wadi was too steep and deep to climb down, so the battalion had to seek cover and hold in-place.

29 Long, *To Benghazi*, p.248; War Diary of the 2/4 Australian Infantry Battalion, January 1941, AWM52 8/3/4/7, pp.63-64.

30 Long, *To Benghazi*, pp.247–248.

31 Arena, *I Fanti*, p.102; War Diary of the 2/11 Australian Infantry Battalion, January 1941, AWM52 8/3/11/7, p.42.

While these actions were occurring, Robertson received reports late on 26 January of a large enemy force to his south. His concern was the brigade lacked sufficient forces to counter a possible enemy counterattack against his southern flank if he continued against Derna. Only the A/6 Australian Cavalry and two infantry companies remained uncommitted. He decided to halt the attack against the town until the situation to the south was clarified. Issuing the order at 2337 hours, it would take time to reach the battalions.[32]

At *10ª Armata* headquarters, *generale* Tellera was considering a counterattack against the enemy penetrations of the Wadi Derna in the Mechili-Berta sector. *Maresciallo* Graziani had released the *VI battaglione carri M* (M13 tanks) to *10ª Armata* for such an attack and Tellera had the *10º reggimento bersaglieri* available. With these forces, Tellera issued orders at 1500 for the counterattack to happen that evening or the next morning. These orders were then countermanded that evening based on new reports of new enemy activity and the *brigata corazzata speciale* was ordered to withdraw northwest into the gebel.[33]

For the Italians, *generale* Bergonzoli could be pleased with the fighting over the past several days. Overall, *gruppo mobile «Tonini»* had held its positions and halted the Australian's advance. The *paracadutisti* had taken many casualties due to the Australian artillery and the daily RAF attacks. The lack of indirect fire support meant that the *paracadutisti* had to use local counterattacks to push the Australians out of some of their gains, exposing themselves to greater losses. The Italians had become concerned about the Australian activity at the southern end of the Wadi Derna line, so it was decided that some action was required.

That evening Bergonzoli instructed *tenente colonnello* Tonini to conduct a sweep in the Wadi Derna on the morning of 27 January. Bergonzoli had received reports that enemy units had entered the wadi and could be advancing towards Derna from the south. The *gruppo*, as the only mobile unit available to Bergonzoli, was to provide a rapid reaction force to secure the southern flank. Tonini selected *capitano* Sartini's *1ª cp.* to execute the mission, and added instructions that he should link-up with the Enver Bey strongpoint held by elements of the *II/86º fanteria*. Sartini would have his company, two truck mounted 20mm guns, and a detachment of motorcycle bersaglieri; in all approximately 100 men.[34]

27 January (Maps 4.8 and 4.9)

On the morning of 27 January, the *1ª cp.* moved out to execute its task of a reconnaissance towards the southwest. *Capitano* Sartini decided to follow the road on the

32 War Diary of the 19 Australian Infantry Brigade, January 1941, AWM52 8/2/19/3, p.13.
33 Anon, *La prima offensiva britannica*, p.220.
34 Arena, *Fanti*, p.104; Anon, *La prima offensiva britannica*, p.219 and fn. 2.

western bank of the wadi that connected Enver Bey with Derna, checking the wadi as they traveled south. Ahead of them were the two Australian infantry companies, reinforced by a platoon of heavy machine-guns from the 1/Royal Northumberland Fusiliers. The Australians had established a kill zone and caught the paratroopers by surprise as the Italians moved south. A running fight ensued, with the *paracadutisti* attempting to break out of the trap. Unable to break free and finally out of ammunition, the survivors surrendered. The *1ª cp.* was completely destroyed with a loss of 40 dead and 56 men captured. According to the Italian accounts, only one of the *bersaglieri* motorcycle soldiers managed to escape and report back on the fight.[35]

The 19th Bde order to stop its advance did not reach the 2/4 Aust. until late in the morning. The battalion was moving more men to the western side of wadi. The battalion commander, Lt Col. Ian Dougherty, stopped the movement of his companies until he could learn the reasons for the canceled attack. Informed of the large enemy formation to the southwest, he decided to pull his companies back to the eastern side of wadi and establish a defense position to protect the brigade's southern flank. These Italian forces did attack during the day but were repulsed by the battalion.[36]

The 2/11 Aust. also did not initially receive the order until after it began to advance. B Coy worked itself forward and was able to capture the Ridotto Rudero but was forced back by artillery fire after a few hours attempting to hold its gains. Stopping their operations during the day, the Australians used aggressive patrols during the night to infiltrate and finally clear most of the *paracadutisti* from the eastern escarpment. These were small, squad/platoon level unit fights which often resulted in combat at close quarters given the broken terrain. The *paracadutisti* were spread very thin to cover all the areas in the sector and Tonini was constantly moving forces to counter the Australian's actions. In order to preserve his unit's strength, Tonini finally ordered a withdrawal to the western side of the wadi. He was able to fully disengage his units prior to daylight on 28 January. Positioning his companies on the western edge of the wadi, the unit was able to cover the roads and paths leading down into Derna from their new positions.

While these combats were unfolding, the British plans changed yet again on 27 January. The «*brigata corazzata speciale*» under *generale di brigata* Valentino Babini had retreated from Mechili after stopping the British advance on 24 January. The British now discovered that Babini had retired during the night, leaving the desert route running south of the gebel open to the British. Lacking fuel and operational tanks, it was decided that the 6th Australian Division would push through Derna while the armored division quickly refitted. The plan was to convince the Italians that the main British threat was through Giovanni Berta along the via Balbia. Once replenished,

35 Arena, *Fanti*, p.104; There is some confusion on the date of this action. The Italian sources and Long, *To Benghazi*, p.248, place this action on the morning of 27 January. The 2/4 War Diary appears to place it on 26 January, but also has several actions happening on 27 January which are also discussed in Long p.250.

36 Long, *To Benghazi*, p.250; 2/4 War Diary, pp.64.

the 7th Armored Division would push along the southern route in an effort to cut off the Italian retreat to Tripolitania.[37]

28–29 January (Map 4.10)

28 January found the *paracadutisti* committed in a series of local counterattacks. The Australians of the 2/11 Battalion were working to clear the few remaining Italian holdouts on the eastern side of the wadi. Reoccupying the Ridotto Rudero, the Australians could clearly observe into the town of Derna itself. The small actions on that day continued to wear down the *paracadutisti*. The Australians had finally gained a firm hold on the eastern ridge of the wadi/escarpment while Tonini continued to reinforce the positions on the western side of the wadi.

At the headquarters of the Italian Army, *Maresciallo* Graziani received intelligence on 28 January that the British were planning to hold in front of Derna while encircling the defending forces by driving from Mechili to Bengasi. Aerial reconnaissance and reports from the *XX Cd'A* holding Chaulan and Eluet el Asel indicated that large numbers of British vehicles were moving westward. Meeting with *generali* Tellera, Cona, and Bergonzoli on 29 January, Graziani ordered the units in Derna to withdraw that evening to an intermediate position approximately 15-20 kilometers west of the town.[38]

Whilst this discussion of their fate was happening in Berta, 29 January was a quiet day for the *gruppo mobile «Tonini»*. The enemy activity was mainly limited to artillery shelling while completing their occupation of the eastern ridge. The Italian artillery continued to fire upon any Australian movement, impacting what the enemy could do during the day. When the order to retreat was received at Derna that afternoon, the Italian artillery redoubled its fire as any ammunition not expended would be destroyed or abandoned. The Australian artillery, hampered by limited ammunition stocks, could do little to affect the Italian fires. This gave the defenders a breathing space to prepare for the withdrawal.

Under the cover of the Italian artillery, the defenders prepared to abandon the town and destroy any material they could not withdraw. The Australian units reported an increase in artillery fire that evening. Sensing that the Italians were withdrawing, they sent a patrol towards the town on the evening of 29 January. The *paracadutisti* quickly stopped this probe and it was not until early morning on 30 January that the Australians observed fires starting inside the town. Another patrol was dispatched which was again stopped by the paratroopers in the rearguard. It was only after daylight that the Australians learned from local Libyans that the Italians were gone.[39]

37 Playfair, *Mediterranean and Middle East*, vol 1, pp.353–355; Long *To Benghazi*, p.249.
38 Anon, *La prima offensiva britannica*, p.225; Long *To Benghazi*, p.253.
39 Anon, *La prima offensiva britannica*, p.228; Long *To Benghazi*, p.253; Montanari, *Le operazioni*, vol I, pp.329–330; Arena, *Fanti*, p.109.

Tonini had skillfully blocked the Australian patrols and quietly withdrew his units westward toward Bir es Sibil, ending the action at Derna. The Italian rearguard had held the British advance for six days. *Gruppo mobile «Tonini»* had lost 114 men dead, 207 men wounded, and 56 men taken prisoner, nearly 50 percent of its total force. Australian losses were not as high, with approximately 100 casualties during the same time period. While the casualties appear very one-sided, the native-born *paracadutisti* had fought a battle-experienced Australian brigade and forced it to fight for every meter of ground.[40]

The *paracadutisti* fought under several handicaps. The British had command of the air and sea, allowing daily attacks by the RAF against Italian positions. When formed, the *gruppo* was an ad hoc mixture of small units that had never operated together as a team. The *gruppo* lacked balance in weapons, training, and communication equipment. A serious issue was lack of heavy weapons capable of sustained suppressive fire. The Breda 30 f.m., with its fixed 20-round magazine was inadequate for this role. The 20mm anti-aircraft guns were too large to effectively engage deployed infantry units. The reality that *battaglioni paracadutisti* was not authorized any unit level mortars meant that the *paracadutisti* lacked an immediate indirect fire capability, and poor communications hampered the timely use of the available Italian artillery.

These challenges allowed the dispersed Australian infantry to work-up close to the Italian positions. It was a slow process, but the Australian artillery and mortars could effectively suppress Italian positions as their infantry advanced. When finally forced to ground, the Australian waited until dark to continue the attack. The widely spread Italians found themselves fighting in small groups against a larger Australian force, allowing the defenders to be infiltrated and eliminated. The Italian O.T.O. and S.R.C.M. grenades lacked explosive power in these close combats, forcing the *paracadutisti* into costly counterattacks. These were usually successful, but increased the number of casualties reduced the available manpower to continue the defense. The *reparti paracadutisti* were an offensive weapon, and their employment in the defense committed them to an attritional battle that the unit was not designed to sustain. *Gruppo mobile «Tonini»* was worn down as manpower was substituted for firepower.

Retreat to Bengasi

As the *gruppo* retreated westward along the via Balbia, the engineers cratered the road and destroyed bridges and culverts behind them until they reached Bir es Sibil, 8 km west of Derna. It is here that the road leaves the coast and climbs up the coastal

40 The losses were totaled from what was provided in *I Fanti*. Approximately 200 of the killed and wounded were from the *I btg. paracadutisti libico*. Arena, *Fanti*, p.104. The Australian losses are based on the limited information provided in the war diaries (only the 2/11 provided a complete list of casualties, the remainder only an occasional mention of specific losses).

escarpment and into the high terrain of the gebel. Tonini took some time to reorganize the *gruppo*, placing some troops and a machine gun company at the top of the escarpment to delay any pursuing Australians. With that force in-place, he hastened the withdrawal of the men, equipment, and supplies not needed by the rearguard to Giovanni Berta 30 kilometers to the west

The Australians used 30 and 31 January to clear and repair the roads leading down into Derna from the east and back up out of the town going west for vehicles. The lead battalion, the 2/8 Aust. reached the new Italian delaying position at Bir el Sibil on the afternoon of 31 January. Italian artillery and machine-gun fire prevented any attempt to scale the escarpment until after dark. During that night, D Coy was able to move up the escarpment and capture the machine-gunners defending the ridge line. Tonini had to turn and move his *paracadutisti* back towards the east to block any further enemy advance along the road, forcing the Australians back to the crest of the escarpment. Tonini then quickly disengaged and moved his unit back down the via Balbia towards Berta. Because the road up the escarpment had been badly cratered, the Australian infantry at the top of the escarpment were separated from their trucks and artillery below. The Australians could not pursue until the road was once again made passable for vehicles.[41]

Gruppo mobile «Tonini» moved through Ain Mara on 2 February, stopping briefly to destroy part of the road behind them. Reaching Giovanni Berta later that same day, the *gruppo* stopped to destroy the bridge over the wadi and establish a blocking position outside the town. Here *generale* Bergonzoli met with *tenente colonnello* Tonini and thanked the unit for the excellent defense of Derna. He then ordered the *gruppo* to continue its retreat to D'Annunzio where they could collect the men and equipment that had been sent ahead, and then proceeded to Barce to link-up with the *1° btg. nazionale paracadutisti*. The reassembled parachute battalions would then continue to Agedabia for reorganization and preparation for future operations. This order held a promise for the unit to conduct actual airborne missions as part of an Italian effort to reconquer what had just been lost.[42]

Shortly afterwards Tonini received new orders placing the gruppo under the control of the *XX Corps d'Armata* commanded by *generale* Cona. Cona reorganized his force into three mobile groups under Bergonzoli, Della Bona, and *generale di brigata* Virginio Villanis (artillery commander of the *XXI Corpo d'Armata*). Reaching Berta, *generale* Della Bona met with *tenente colonnello* Tonini and canceled the previous order of *generale* Bergonzoli and now assigned the *gruppo* as part of the corps rearguard under *colonnello* Colpani. Prior to the change in orders, Tonini had sent off the first group of *paracadutisti* and other infantry of the *gruppo* towards Agedabia, including the 75/27 battery and the M11/39 tanks. Once the last units of the corps had cleared Berta (2 February), the *gruppo* was next ordered to occupy the crossroad at Lamluda.

41 Long *To Benghazi*, p.257.
42 Arena, *Fanti*, p.110.

The Australian cavalry squadron pressed the parachutists on 3 February between Berta and Lamluda, with the Italian losing seven dead and ten wounded but keeping the pursuit at arm's length. Following the northern route of the Balbia, the *gruppo* found itself without adequate fuel for its vehicles. Sending out the *bersaglieri* motorcycle patrols in a search for fuel, one patrol found three drums of fuel in Cirene, allowing the *gruppo* to refuel and continue its retreat.[43]

Another one of the motorcycle patrols returned from Beda Littoria with a message from *generale* Bergonzoli. His order was for the *gruppo* to move a few kilometers west of the town to the Wadi el Cüf to protect the engineers while they destroyed the bridge located there. Once the destruction was completed, Tonini was to move his unit back to the crossroad that covered any possible enemy movement from Mameli and Slonta to the south against the via Balbia. *Gruppo mobile «Tonini»* remained at that position through the night of 3 February.

At 2300 hours on 4 February, yet another order from Bergonzoli sent the gruppo *mobile «Tonini»* in retreat back to Barce, stopping at La Maddalena to destroy that bridge. Once that had been accomplished, the *gruppo* was ordered to continue its retreat to Agebadia. *«Tonini»* reached the town of Coefia just north of Bengasi at about 0600 on 5 February.[44]

At this point it is best to quickly touch upon the activities of the *1º btg. nazionale paracadutisti* before moving into the confusing period of the Battle of Beda Fomm. During the fighting at Derna, the *1º btg. paracadutisti nazionale* had remained at the Wadi al Barkur continuing the defensive work. On 4 February the battalion was attached to the *raggruppamento «Pasquali»*, which was part of *colonna «Villanis»*. Holding the wadi position until 5 February, the *raggruppamento* was ordered to retreat and reached the Ghemines area south of Bengasi during the night of 5-6 February.[45]

Battle of Beda Fomm (Maps 4.11–4.13)

From Benghazi to el-Agheila there are 280 kilometers of open road that the Italian *10ª Armata* needed to travel to the relative safety of el-Agheila. Not only were the pursuing Australians behind them, but the mobile British forces from the 7th Armoured Division could threaten the retreat from the east. The campaign was now a race to see whether the Italian forces could reach el-Agheilia before the British forces could cut the road in front of them. *Generale* Tellera now organized his army to provide for both a strong rearguard and a blocking force to protect the eastern flank of the march to the south.

43 Nino Arena, *FOLGORE Storia del paracadutismo militare italiano* (Rome: Centro Editoriale Nazione, 1965), pp.58-60; Arena, *I fanti*, p.112.

44 Arena, *Fanti*, p.110; Arena, *FOLGORE*, pp.60-61; War Diary 6 Australian Division Cavalry Regiment February-March 1941, AWM52 2/2/7/11, p.4.

45 Anon., *La prima offensiva britannica*, p.249.

By 4 February, the remaining Italian forces had been organized into several *raggruppamenti* for the retreat. *Generale* Cona had once again reorganized the forces within his three mobile *colonne* (columns). Della Bona now commanded the *raggruppamenti «Moech»* and *«Colpani»*, along with the *nucleo motorizzato «Allergi»*. Della Bona's mission was to clear the way south for the retreating army. Bergonzoli's new force consisted of the *brigata corazzata speciale*, *raggruppamento motorizzato «Piana»*, and the *nucleo «Crucillà»*. His mission was to protect the army's eastern flank facing the desert. Villanis was given the *raggruppamento «Pasquali»*, the *VI battaglione carri M*, the *10° reggimento bersaglieri*, and the *VII gruppo contraerei da 75/46* to form the army's rearguard. Its role was to protect the retreat from the pursuit along the via Balbia.[46]

Both *battaglioni paracadutisti* now found themselves as part of *colonna Villanis* but were not operating together. While *«Tonini»* was apparently attached to *raggruppamento «Colpani»*, Bergonzoli's multiple direct orders made it clear that the *gruppo* was now an independent unit. On the evening of 5 February, Tonini with the remains of the *1° btg. «fanti dell'aria»* was at Coefia north of Bengasi. At that same time, *Raggruppamento «Colpani»* was south of Bengasi and nearing kilometer marker (km) 50. The strength of the *1° btg. libico* was likely no more than 150 men with seven 47/32 c.c. and a number of 20/65 c.a. guns. The *1° btg. nazionale* under *maggiore* Arturo Calascibetta was at Ghemines as part of *raggruppamento «Pasquali»*. That *raggruppamento* had a machine gun company, an artillery gruppo of 75/27 (twelve pieces), a platoon of 47/32 c.c. (four pieces), and two sections of 20/65 c.a. (four pieces). The *1° btg. nazionale* likely had about 250 men, a platoon of 47/32 c.c. (three guns), and a section of 20/35 c.a. (two guns).[47]

There are few accounts detailing the actions of the two parachute battalions during the battle of Beda Fomm. None of the existing accounts agree on all the main points. The following account of the actions on 5-7 February 1941 follow the locations and activities described by Arena.[48] Accepting the understanding that *«Tonini»* maneuvered separately from the remainder of *Raggruppamento «Colpani»*, Arena's accounts successfully meshes the movements of two parachute units to the known locations of the various *raggruppamenti* as provided in the Italian histories.[49]

46 Montanari, *Le operazioni*, vol I, p.338; Anon, *La prima offensiva britannica*, pp.252-256.
47 Raffaele Girlando, *I Paracadutisti Libici* (Foggia: Italia Editrice new di Giancarlo Arcano, 2006), p.99; Arena, *I fanti*, p.112, 114; Anon, *La prima offensiva britannica*, schizzi 20 and 22.
48 Arena, *I fanti*, pp.112-118; Arena, *Aquile senza Ali*, pp.13-14; Arena, *FOLGORE*, pp.56-61. Arena reproduces the *gruppo mobile «Tonini»* war diary in *FOLGORE*.
49 Montanari, *Le operazioni*, vol I, p.340-372; Anon, *La prima offensiva britannica*, pp.263-281.

5 February

The *colonna Della Bona* had been ambushed by Combeforce at 1230 near km40, just east of Sidi Saleh. The *10° rgt. bersaglieri* had rushed south to attempt a counterattack and break through the roadblock. Attacking without tanks and artillery in support, the effort failed against the combined arms defense of the British. Due to the lack of radios in most Italian units, it was hours before the *10ª Armata* leadership began to understand the dire situation that was developing at the head of the column. By 1730 hours the British 4th Armoured Brigade had arrived on the scene further north near km50 and deployed on Rus ben Hagen – a modest ridge to the east of the via Balbia which has since been referred to as The Pimple – and began attacking the flank of the retreating column. The Italians, under the perception that the main enemy threat was to their rear, had placed all their tanks in their rearguard near Bengasi and were unable to quickly respond to this new threat. The reports received from the fighting were unclear, but the decision was made to push the available tank battalions south to attack through the British positions early the next morning.

6 February

Tenente colonnello Tonini received orders on the evening of 5 February to continue the march to the south. After refueling, the *gruppo* began moving through Bengasi, leaving the city at 0145 on 6 February. Its movement was stopped at 0400 after passing Ghemines due to the congestion in front of them on the Balbia. At this time Tonini received orders to support the action of the *VI btg. carri M* that was moving south from Bengasi to attack the British blocking position.[50] Tonini, with 150 *paracadutisti* in seven trucks, three 47/32 c.c., and four 20/65 c.a., moved to link-up with the thirty-six M13/40 tanks of the *VI btg.* At 0700 the combined force began its movement south to clear the via Balbia of any enemy forces for the *10ª Armata*.

The battlefield that awaited the two battalions as they drove south was at first a massive traffic jam. Vehicles and equipment of all types were stopped on the road and parked along side of it on both sides. Soldiers were milling about awaiting orders and hoping to continue their journey south to safety. Due to the line of vehicles, the two battalions were forced off the via Balbia to bypass the jam and drove in desert paralleling the road; the *VI btg. carri M* to the east and «*Tonini*» to the west.[51]

50 Arena, *I fanti*, p.114 states it was the *V btg. carri M*, but the timing and target of the attack matches that of the *VI btg. carri M*. The movements presented in the war diary of the *V btg. carri M* also supports that «*Tonini*» fought with the *VI* and not the *V btg*. Ten. col. Emilio Iezzi, *V° battaglione Carri M.13/40 costituito il 5-11-1940* (Associazione Nazionale Carristi d'Italia, n.d.), pp.12-13.

51 Arena, *I fanti*, p.114; Anon, *La prima offensiva britannica*, pp.273–274.

Once passed the traffic, a chaotic scene of burning destroyed vehicles blocking the road lay to their front. As the combined force approached The Pimple, the *VI btg. M* began to veer to the southeast towards the hill and deploy into company vee formations, with one company leading and two companies echeloned behind to the left and right. The *paracadutisti* turned to the east and crossed the road in their trucks, falling in behind the tanks to support them as best they could.

Maneuvering to the northeast side of "The Pimple", the *VI btg. M* and *«Tonini»* approached the enemy blocking force. Facing them were the 19 cruiser tanks of A Squadron, 2/Royal Tank Regiment (A/2 RTR) which was defending the hill using hull down positions. While the 36 tanks of the *VI btg. M* were fully exposed in the open, the cruiser tanks of A Sqdn were hidden behind the crest of the hill. Moving forward so only their turrets were above the crest, the cruisers began firing at the advancing Italian force. The British tanks were more accurate in their shooting as they were firing while stationary, then reversing back down behind the top of the hill to avoid the Italian return fire. The advancing Italian tanks either had to fire while moving with the associated decrease in accuracy or make a brief halt which made them an easier target to hit by the British gunners.

The Italians pressed their attack while their tank losses began to mount, but their maneuver to the northeast of The Pimple began to expose the hidden British tanks. Though *«Tonini»* was following, the *paracadutisti* were not safe from the British shooting and several trucks were hit. The Italian artillery was now supporting the attack, destroying or damaging several British cruiser tanks. Running low on ammunition and being flanked to the northeast, A Squadron was forced off The Pimple and back towards Mosque Ridge. The *VI btg. M* gained the height while *«Tonini»* followed up and set a hasty defense.

This first attack had finally been a success but the cost had been high. At least 21 M13/40 tanks were lost, while the paratroopers lost 25 dead and 24 wounded. Two of the 47/32 c.c., two 20/65 c.a. were lost when their trucks were destroyed during the attack.[52]

With the 2/RTR pushed back off The Pimple, the road was once again open to the south. The *XXXIV btg. libico* and several Italian artillery batteries occupied the newly won position, covering the eastern flank of the retreating Italian army. Released from that task, the *VI btg. M* and *«Tonini»* again turned to the south.[53] While The Pimple was being secured by the *carristi* and *paracadutisti*, the trucks of *«Colpani»*, *«Pasquali»*, and *«Moech»* pushed once again to the south, passing the slower moving *VI btg. M* and *«Tonini»* in their dash to reach safety.[54]

52 Arena, *I fanti*, p.114; John Latimer, *Operation Compass 1940* (London: Praeger, 2004), pp.80–81; Playfair, *Mediterranean and Middle East*, vol 1, p.360.

53 Montanari, *Le operazioni*, vol I, p.361 identifies the unit as the *XXXIV btg. libico.*

54 Arena, *I fanti*, p.114.

Italian infantry advancing under artillery fire. The photograph displays the challenge of an infantry force attacking in the open desert. (AUSSME)

The rush south by the three *raggruppamenti* did not last for long. Stopped by Combeforce between km50 and km40, these groups once again found themselves waiting for the tanks of the *VI btg. M* to arrive. The approximately 15 remaining tanks and «*Tonini*» immediately launched another attack at about 1030 against Combeforce. The four companies of the 2/Rifle Brigade, along with eight 37mm anti-tank guns were dug-in around the road and along the sandy high ground along the east side of the via Balbia. A hasty minefield blocked the road and the immediate terrain on either side. The ground was too sandy further away from the road to allow easy maneuvering, forcing the *VI btg. M and «Tonini»* to make a frontal attack against the Rifle Brigade. All the remaining tanks were quickly destroyed by anti-tank gun fire and the *paracadutisti* of «*Tonini*» then attempted to deploy to set a defensive screen. The hope was that additional Italian forces would arrive and continue the attack, but further efforts failed to make any headway. The parachutists found themselves pinned by the fire of the 2/Rifle Brigade and were unable to disengage. By the afternoon the British infantry were pressing forward and the remains of *mobile gruppo «Tonini»* were finally forced to surrender. In all, 101 *paracadutisti* were captured, including *tenente colonnello* Tonini who had led his unit so effectively in combat over the past two months.[55]

The *1° btg. paracadutisti nazionale* was with *raggruppamento «Pasquali»* during the *I btg. paracadutisti libico* movements on 6 February. After the attack that temporally cleared The Pimple, the *raggruppamento* moved south with the other units until stopped by the fire of Combeforce. *Maggiore* Calascibetta, hearing of the failed attack of the Italian tanks and the *ascari* of *«Tonini»*, led his men westwards towards the sea to try and escape the trap. By this means, about 150 men were able to bypass Combeforce and reach Agheila. The remainder of the battalion, like the men of *«Tonini»* were captured by the British.[56]

Fate of the *Paracadutisti*

Whilst the Battle of Beda Fomm marked the final combat of the two *btg. paracadutisti* raised in A.S., it was not the end of their story. The 150 Italians from the *1° btg. nazionale paracadutisti* that managed to escape the defeat were reassembled in Tripoli. During the Axis offensive in April that reconquered much of the Cirenica, more Italians *paracadutisti* were freed from captivity. The question debated in Rome was what to do with these men? Initially the decision was that they would remain in Libya to form the nucleus of a rebuilt national airborne battalion, the *battaglione nazionale paracadutisti «Cirenaica»*.[57] The conditions that unfolded over the next several months were such that a reborn battalion was unlikely, so the S.M.R.E. decided it would be better to transfer these men to Tarquinia. This would allow them to complete their training and be assigned to the new airborne units currently being formed. The S.M.R.E. sent the formal request to STAMGE asking for their return to Tarquinia on 16 May. While the majority would return, the request included a plan to retain a small cadre in Tripoli to train a new Libyan battalion.[58] STAMGE agreed to the request and on 27 May authorized the return of the men to Italy.[59]

The final fate of the Libyans was a bit different. Those Libyans of the *1° btg. «Fanti dell'aria»* as prisoners were moved to Barce where they were held in a British

55 Latimer, *Operation Compass*, pp.75–76; Arena, *Aquile senza Ali*, p.33. Ten col Tonini would be transferred to a POW camp in Palestine, then on to India. After the war, he would return to the Corps of Engineers and reach the rank of *generale di brigata*, Arena, *I fanti*, p.134.

56 Arena, *I fanti*, p.114; Arena, *Aquile senza Ali*, p.33.

57 Antonello Biagini and Fernando Frattolillo (eds.) *Diario Storico del Comando Supremo* (Rome: USSME, 1992) vol IV book I, pp.256

58 Biagini and Frattolillo *Diario Storico del Comando Supremo* (Rome, USSME, 1992), vol IV, book I, pp.126-127; Di Giovanni, p.90.

59 Biagini and Frattolillo *Diario Storico*, vol IV book I, p.200.

POW camp. Many of these men escaped over the next few months and hid in the gebel or with the local population until Bengasi was re-occupied by the Axis in April. The *btg. «Fanti dell'aria»* was then reconstituted using these men and new recruits from the R.C.T.C. The battalion first moved to Suani ben Aden and finally to Azizia. At Azizia, a new school was established and parachute training was restarted. Unable to access aircraft for training due to their demand for transporting reinforcements and supplies from Italy to A.S., an engineer unit with a captive balloon was assigned to the new school. Only a few training jumps were made as the balloon was quickly determined to be unsuitable for the training. With no other options and an overall lack of resources, the school was closed and the unit disbanded in September 1941. The remaining Libyan *paracadutisti* were ordered to rejoin various units in the R.C.T.C., while the Italian cadre were reassigned to Tarquinia.[60] This decision marked the end of the story of the Libyan parachute units but not the end of Libyan parachutists.

The closing of the school at Azizia did mark the end of Italo Balbo's experiment in building a colonial airborne force. No other major Second World War combatant raised or trained an airborne force composed of indigenous colonial troops with the exception of Great Britain, which formed the 50th Indian Parachute Brigade in October 1941 – the very time that the Libyan *paracadutisti* were disbanded.

While never given the opportunity to execute their primary mission of parachuting behind enemy lines, the «*Fanti dell'aria*» did demonstrate that Balbo had been successful in creating a well-trained and effective military force. What was missing was the operational plan for their employment. No clear vision had emerged on how these units would enable Italian success against their enemies in North Africa. None of the offensive planning written during 1939 and 1940 established a role for these units. Whilst it is possible that a defined role existed at a point in time, it was lost with the death of Italo Balbo.

Without an offensive mission, these units were committed into combat in a defensive role. Intended to leverage speed and surprise, there is nothing fast when fighting a defensive fight and little opportunity to achieve surprise. The two battalions demonstrated the inherent limitations of airborne forces in sustained combat. Designed to be transported into battle by aircraft, the battalions were small in numbers when compared with a normal infantry battalion and lacked the heavy support weapons in the latter. The «*Fanti dell'aria*» needed to be transformed into the *gruppo mobile «Tonini»* with the addition of heavy weapons and transport to successfully operate against the British and Commonwealth forces. Without the addition of men and heavy weapons provided by the integration of *gruppo «Pancano»*, the daily attrition during the battle for Derna would have destroyed the battalion.

Balbo's death removed the daring vision needed for the employment of airborne forces in the war in North Africa. But while *gruppo mobile «Tonini»* was fighting in

60 Di Giovanni, *I Paracadutisti*, p.90; Arena, *I fanti*, p.118; Arena, *Aquile senza Ali*, p.33

A.S., the Italians had planned and initiated another offensive campaign: the attack against Greece. Was there another senior Italian military leader who possessed the daring vision to consider the use of parachute forces in that operation? To answer that question, one needs to step back to 1939 and examine the planning leading up to 28 October 1940 and the subsequent prosecution of that campaign.

5

Esigenza «G»

Military professionals and historians have stated that the Italian invasion of Greece in late October 1940 was hastily planned and poorly executed. While this is true to an extent, there were several systemic issues that had a greater effect on the outcome of the campaign other than the planning. Issues of training, outdated equipment, and lack-luster battlefield leadership all played a considerable role in the overall failure of the Italian military in Greece. Greece, however, is the first offensive operation directed from its inception by Rome and therefore had access to all the military tools available to the fascist state. It is within the providence of the campaign planning that one can examine whether the use of airborne forces was seen as a capability worth leveraging in support of this strategic decision.

As previously discussed with war planning for Africa settentrionale, there had not been any long-term planning for offensive operations against Greece prior to the occupation of Albania in April 1939. *Piano di Radunata 12* (P.R. Mobilization Plan) discussed the possibility of an attack against Yugoslavia, subject to the availability of forces and the occurrence of particularly favorable circumstances.[1] Beyond that discussion, all the existing directives based on P.R.12 reflected an initial defensive stance against Yugoslavia or if Yugoslavia and Greece allied together.[2] What is important is that Greece alone was never discussed as a target of Italian aggression until after April 1939.

Planning

The occupation of Albania in April of 1939 positioned Italy on the north-west border of Greece, making an invasion of Greece possible without a simultaneous invasion

1 John Gooch, *Mussolini and his Generals* (Cambridge University Press, 2007), pp.413-414; John Gooch, *Mussolini's War* (London: Allen Lane 2020), p.64.

2 Mario Montanari, *L'esercito italiano alla vigilia della 2ª guerra mondiale* (Rome: USSME, 1982), pp.138, 185.

of Yugoslavia.[3] Planning for an invasion of Greece started on 22 August 1939 with a directive issued by Mussolini stating twin strategic objectives; the conquest of both Greece and Yugoslavia.[4] The planning for operations against Greece was documented as *Esigenza G* (*Contingency G*), while that against Yugoslavia was *Esigenza E*. Airborne operations were never considered during the planning for *Esigenza E*.[5] What followed for *Esigenza G* was an evolving series of four different plans that reflected the changing political situation and the associated military objectives. The four plans in order were: Piano Guzzoni-Pariani, Aug. 1939; Piano Gelso, July 1940 (two variations); and *Emergenza G* (September 1940).

The four plans differed in the ultimate end state of the campaign and the allocation of forces. The Guzzoni-Pariani plan was to overrun all of Greece (Salonica and Athens were the operational objectives) and required 20 divisions. The other three plans only considered capturing the Epirus region of northwest Greece, with Korçe and either Arta or Missolungi as the operational objectives. The number of divisions fluctuated from ten, to eleven, and finally to nine.[6] It was not until 14 October 1940 that Mussolini again expanded the requirement to include all of Greece.

None of these plans considered the use of unorthodox maneuvers or special forces in a unique manner to create an operational advantage. They were all very conventional, force heavy, direct assaults on Greece. Italian masses and their bravery would triumph over the weaker Greek nation.[7] The use of an amphibious assault against Corfù was planned, but it would be executed after the initial success on the mainland. No plans were made to use the Italian naval superiority to turn any potential Greek defensive line. There is no evidence that the use of airborne forces were discussed during the months of planning until September 1940.

A letter dated 6 September 1940 (received on 7 September) was written by Zenone Benini, the Undersecretary for Albania under the Italian Foreign Office, to *generale* Francesco Pricolo, the Chief of Staff of the Regia Aeronautica (*Superaereo*).

> Caro Pricolo,
> In the program that is being quickly prepared, in any eventuality, to carry out the well-known action towards the Albanian regions subject to Greece (Ciamuria and adjacent territories), the following points have been included:

3 John Gooch, *Generals*, p.468.
4 Mario Montanari, *La campagna di grecia* (Rome: USSME, 1980), vol 1, p.45.
5 Teodoro Zurlo, 'Emergenza «E». Studi e Predisposizioni Militare alla Frontiera Giulia nel periodo Luglio-Ottobre 1940', *Memorie Storiche Militari 1979* (Rome: USSME, 1980), pp.369-426.
6 Montanari, *Grecia*, vol 1, p.57. A detailed discussion of Italian planning can be found in Vol. I, Chapter IV.
7 MacGregor Knox, *Hitler's Italian Allies* (New York, Cambridge University Press, 2000), p.152.

a) [to] prepare parachutes to drop weapons and ammunition in Ciamuria, at convenient locations;
b) have the Royal Ministry of Aeronautics study the possibility of preparing a parachute unit for possible operations in Ciamuria. In this regard, the idea of setting up a quick training course for Albanians who wish to join this action is also suggested.

In principle, His Ecc. Ciano has approved these proposals, as long as they are considered feasible by the Ministry of Aeronautics. I therefore take care to inform you and I will be grateful if you would like to let me know your thoughts about it "

Affez.mo Berini[8]

Why the Undersecretary for Albania wrote this letter is unknown. It is very unusual that an outside agency would offer such a unique military proposal.

This letter apparently did surprise *generale* Pricolo as it was from a Foreign Office undersecretary and not a military staff officer.[9] Pricolo had only learned about the plan to invade Greece on the same day the letter was received. Now he was being asked to consider an airborne operation for a plan he had not fully read.[10] *Generale* Pricolo responded on 9 September:

Caro Bellini,
The question that you raise to me with your letter of September 6, u.s. was known to me only indirectly: only yesterday, in fact, a short time after your letter, did I receive the study from the S.M. di Regio Esercito, relating to an action towards the Albanian regions subject to Greece.

From a technical and operational point of view, the operations you mention does not present serious difficulties. The Air Force is equipped with aerial supply systems for weapons and ammunition in quantities that I believe are sufficient for the purpose.

With regard to the paratroopers, however, I have to advance some particular reservations, due to the fact that the few existing units are still in their training phase and are under the authority, in effect, of the Ministry of War.

As for the idea of establishing a rapid training course for Albanian volunteers, I have no facts about their need for special employment and therefore cannot

8 Montanari, *Grecia*, vol I, p.58.

9 Giuseppe Santoro, *L'Aeronautica italiana nella seconda guerra mondiale* (Rome: Edition ESSE di A. Silvestri, 1957), vol 1, p.126.

10 This was the R.E.'s *Emergenza «G»* plan dated 4 September 1940. This plan was only transmitted to *Comando Supremo* on 7 September 1940. Montanari, *Grecia,* vol II, pp.85-93 (documents 26 and 27).

> express myself with adequate knowledge of the facts on the duration and results of the course itself.
>
> However, should the project be implemented, it seems appropriate that it be submitted to the S.M. Generale, to issue the necessary general directives to order the establishment and conduct of the operation and coordinating the activities of the various Armed Forces.
>
> As regards to the R. Aeronautica it will be important and indispensable to have precise information on the ground on the defensive organization, on the feelings of the population and on what references to the local situation, in order to be able to define with certainty the points of greatest vulnerability and the points of support, both for the dropping of weapons and ammunition and for the use of paratroop troops.
>
> For my part, while I assure you of all the assistance of the R. Aeronautica, I would like to receive timely warning, in order to prepare the operation, for the area of my responsibility, in order to ensure rapid and full success "
>
> Pricolo[11]

At the same time that *generale* Pricolo responded to Benini's letter, he forwarded copies of both the original request and his response to the *STAMAGE*. *Generale di divisione* Quirino Armellini, (vice chief of staff of *STAMAGE*) responded back on 10 September to *generale di squadra aerea* Giuseppe Santoro, Deputy to Pricolo under *Superaereo*.

> Caro Santoro
>
> I have submitted to His Ecc. Badoglio the letters of His Ecc. Benini and your answer that you sent me yesterday. His Ecc. Badoglio spoke to the Duce about it and returned the letters to me with this note: "do nothing about it, Greece is going down"
>
> Tanto per tua norme — Devoti saluti — Q Armellini[12]

The first part of Badoglio's note, "do nothing about it", can be interpreted several different ways. The first possibility is that the use of paratroopers was unnecessary given the scheme of maneuver developed for the operation. This could be due to the lack of a suitable objective or an acceptance that conventional means met all the invasion's requirements. A second possibility could reflect that the proposal came with no recommended course of action for their use and/or it was offered too late in the planning process. Without a defined role as part of the proposal, a complete mission analysis would be needed to determine a viable role for such forces. The proposal would

11 Montanari, *Grecia*, vol 1, p.59 contains an edited version of this letter. Santoro, *L'Aeronautica italiana*, vol.1, p.126 has the complete letter.

12 Montanari, *Grecia* vol 1, p.59; Santoro, *L'Aeronautica*, vol 1, p.127.

require additional time to study and assess, a resource that was currently lacking. A third possibility is that the suggestion, as it came from outside the military, could be seen as meddling or interfering and therefore not worth the trouble to examine. In better words, it is easier to simply ignore it. None of these possibilities give any insight to the R.E. thinking on an Italian perspective of the doctrinal use of paratroopers in 1940. What can be inferred from the lack of any discussion is that the role of airborne units in modern war was not yet a capability worth considering.

It is difficult to discern the thinking behind the second part of Badoglio's note. He had passively opposed the attack against Greece, considering a diplomatic solution or an operation limited to Epirus as likely. It was not until his meeting on 18 October with Mussolini that Badoglio appeared to finally support the full scope of the invasion to secure all of Greece. So a statement implying the total defeat of Greece on 10 September appears out of sync with his opinion at the time it was written.[13]

Examining this issue from hindsight, there were multiple valid reasons why the employment of airborne forces would be problematic during the Greek campaign. The first issue was the timely availability of the airborne units. The *I btg. paracadutisti* had begun training at Tarquinia on 10 July 1940 and should have completed training by the end of October. However, issues with the Salvator D.39 parachute previously discussed forced the school to halt parachute training at the end of July. The only airborne units in existence in 1939-1940 were the two battalions in Libya raised by Italo Balbo. These were colonial units under the control of the Libyan Governor General, not the *Superesercito*.[14] As such, they were not seen as units generally available for operations outside North Africa. The reality of a European military establishment and a colonial military establishment, separate from each other, was not uncommon at the start of the war.[15] Only the *1° btg. libico* was considered fully ready, the *1° btg. paracadutisti nazionali* had not completed its parachute training due to the lack of aircraft.[16]

Another issue was the question of the suitability of the personnel and equipment in these battalions for operations in Greece. Recruited from the Libyan population, it is unclear how well these troops would have handled the terrain and weather conditions of northwest Greece. This concern is focused more on the *1° btg. paracadutisti libico*, recruited from ingenious Libyans than the European settlers that formed the *1° btg. paracadutisti nazionali*. Clothing would be another problem. Their uniforms were better suited to the arid and generally warm conditions of North Africa and not the wet and cold conditions that existed in October 1940 Greece. These battalions would need to be reequipped with proper continental clothing to operate effectively during

13 Richard Carrier, *Mussolini's Army against Greece* (NewYork: Routledge, 2021), pp.37-39

14 *L'esercito italiano tra la 1ª e la 2ª guerra mondiale* (Rome: USSME, 1954), p.160.

15 Marco di Giovanni, *I paracadutisti italiani* (Gorizia: Editrice Goriziana, 1991), p. 90. The British Indian Army of the United Kingdom or the Dutch Koninklijk Nederlands Indisch Legeris are two such examples.

16 Di Giovanni, *I paracadutisti*, pp.89-90.

the campaign. The lack of heavy weapons would also limit their employment to raids against lightly defended objectives.

Weather and terrain were other considerations. The actual date of the attack placed the operation during some of the worst weather of the year.[17] Any airborne operation would certainly have to be flown out of southern Italy, but the close air support needed to sustain the paratroopers on the ground would need to come out of Albania. Navigation and the challenge of successfully identifying the planned drop zones are both greatly weather dependent. The generally mountainous terrain of Epirus limited where airborne forces could be inserted and would impact the viability of any planned missions.

A critical problem was the lack of any suitable missions for an airborne operation as part of the invasion. The number of available airborne units limited what could be reasonably accomplished with such a small force. The only operationally sensitive location for the Greeks would be the Metsovo area as it controlled the main line of communications (LOC) between Epirus and Greece proper.[18] Closing this route would prevent the Greeks from supplying and reinforcing the forces that faced the Italian invasion. Metsovo was also the final operational objective for the *3ª d. alpina «Julia»*. The plan, expecting a rapid collapse of any Greek defense, had *«Julia»* moving through the Pindos Mountains to seize the pass at Metsovo to trap any retreating Greek forces.

If used together, the two parachute battalions were not strong enough to hold this critical location against an expected Greek reaction for any length of time. Metsovo was too far away for the *«Julia»* to rapidly reinforce the paratroopers. The Greeks could quickly assemble units, likely using reinforcements moving along the LOC, to counter-attack to clear the route. Finally as previously mentioned, a lack of suitable terrain for use as drop zones would prevent the Italian paratroopers from landing close to their objective, forcing them to march a significant distance to block the LOC.

Without a viable operational target, what tactical possibilities existed? The Italian invasion plan itself prevented the identification of any worthwhile targets for the airborne units to act in support of a tactical action. The invasion was a broad offensive crossing the Albanian-Greek border in multiple locations. None were identified as the main effort.[19] Possible objectives like the bridge at Perati were close to the starting locations of Italian ground units and were to be captured on the first day. As a result, there was not a single location where the use of the paratroopers would significantly assist any of the planned ground operations. Given that the operation was to be

17 It rained during the first two days of the offensive and grounded all R.A. flying operations in Albania and Greece. Southern Italy was clear and some Italian bombing missions did fly against Greek targets.

18 Hellenic Army General Staff (HAGS), *An Abridged History of the Greek-Italian and Greek-German War 1940-1941* (Athens: Army History Directive, 1997), pp.41-42 and Sketch Map 4.

19 Montanari, *Grecia,* 'II Direttive per le Operazioni ipotesi Offensiva «G»', vol 2, pp.237-245.

rapidly executed and the ground commanders had discretion in wide zones of attack, no location offered a target which allowed for the tight mission planning required when employing airborne forces.

There was one mission that offered the potential to use airborne forces. Occupation of the island of Corfù was an on-again/off-again aspect during the planning for the invasion. The concern was that the British would use the island as a base for light naval forces and aircraft to support the Greek defense in Epirus. Seizure of the island was not seen as a critical task or one needed to support the main operation on the mainland. Occupying the island was part of the follow-on phase in all the various plans developed prior to the invasion. Generally one division (*47ª d.f. «Bari»*) was earmarked for the occupation of the island and one can speculate whether the use of airborne troops to support the landing would have been beneficial. On 27 October 1940 a message from Rome confirmed the date of the attack on Greece (28 Oct), but stated that the date for the landing on Corfù would depend on the sea conditions.[20] On 29 October the landing was postponed.[21] The actual landing was canceled on 30 October and Mussolini ordered that those forces be redirected to Valona.[22] Not immediately being informed of Mussolini's decision, on that same day *STAMAGE* established a date of 2 November for the landing with a caveat that the issue would be examined at a meeting with the vice chiefs of the three services.[23] Once informed of the decision, Badoglio met with the vice chiefs on 1 November where the decision to send the *«Bari»* to Valona was reaffirmed.

In all, there is not any evidence that those involved in the planning for *Esigenza «G»* gave any thought to the use of airborne forces. From this review, the use of airborne forces was addressed only once during the period of planning and that was initiated by an outside agency. The start of the planning co-existed with the long-awaited creation of the parachute school at Tarquinia. As no date for the invasion was set until late September 1940, planners could have considered possible use of a new capability with the assumption it would be ready. Such an approach helps drive the actualization of new capabilities by providing the priority needed to move it to fruition. The rapid expansion of Germany's Fallschirmjäger in 1938-1940 is an example of how such a capability benefited when it was understood to solve an operational problem.

Esigenza «G»

Within a week after the Italian forces crossed the border on 28 October, the possible use of airborne forces was raised by Mussolini himself. The invasion of Epirus was slowing to a halt and it was clear that additional forces would need to be sent to

20 Montanari, *Grecia* vol 1, p.132.
21 Antonello Biagini and Fernando Frattolillo (eds) *Diario Storico del Comando Supremo* (Rome: USSME, 1986-2002), vol II, book I, p.302.
22 Montanari, *Grecia* vol 1, p.212.
23 Biagini and Frattolillo, *Diario Storico*, vol II, book I, pp. 312, 315.

Albania. On 3 November, *STAMAGE* began considering landing up to three divisions behind Greek lines at Arta and/or Prevesa. This discussion was being driven by the lack of decisive success in northern Epirus and as a way to overcome the shipping bottleneck at the ports of Valona and Durazzo.[24] The capture of Arta and Prevesa would allow Italian reinforcements to land in the Gulf of Arta and threaten both the Greek defense and their main LOC through Ioannina. Two bersaglieri regiments would be employed (*2° and 4° rgt. bersaglieri*) for the operation.

In that meeting, *maresciallo* Badoglio communicated the comments made by Mussolini about the use of airborne forces. Rather than seeing the use of the paratroopers as a way of gaining an initial advantage in the operation to secure the Arta-Prevesa area, Mussolini instead saw then as a follow-on force that would be deployed after the beachhead was secured by the *bersaglieri* regiments.

> [Badoglio quoting Mussolini]
> The influx of other forces, including airborne forces, immediately afterwards will make it possible to deploy on the Preveza-Arta line, which will make the fate of the Greek troops stationed in Ciamuria problematic.
>
> Once the beachhead operation has been completed and the existence of airfields in the vicinity has been ascertained, the use of the paratrooper battalion that is ready and willing to be tested will be examined.
>
> The repercussions of the descent of a paratrooper battalion could be considerable in Greece and elsewhere.[25]

The remainder of the meeting focused on the issues surrounding the seaborne operation and the use of the paratroopers was not further mentioned.

This exchange indicated that the Italian military leadership had not yet to develop a concept for airborne operations. This could be a recognition of the reality given the incomplete training of the units and the lack of transport aircraft. It also can be seen as an abandonment of the sabotage and disruption role originally given as the main airborne mission. While fully trained battalions might not be available, squad and platoon size raiding units could be rapidly created and used to support the upcoming offensive. Such units would require only a single aircraft for each objective area. In all, an assessment can be made that the Italian higher leadership still lacked an acceptance of the viability of airborne operations, even when considered at its lowest level.

What is notable is that this discussion was five months after the German employment of paratroopers in Norway, the Netherlands, and Belgium. Where Germany saw the use of airborne forces to create opportunity and exploit weakness, the Italians were

24 Montanari, *Grecia* vol 1, pp.217-219.

25 Antonello Biagini and Carlo Mazzaccara, eds., *Verbali delle riunioni tenute dal Capo di SM Generale* (Roma, USSME, 1983-19), vol I, pp.114-115; Pier Paolo Battistelli, *The Balkans 1940–41* (1), p.30.

looking at their use in Greece as nothing more than a demonstration of capability. The employment of the paratroops after the seaborne landing lacked any military value. Fear of their possible use would negatively impact Greek operations appears to be the implied goal of their employment. Such was the thinking of the Italian senior military leadership in 1940.

After the decision to send the *47ª d.f. «Bari»* to Albania, there was still ongoing discussion and planning on the intent to occupy Corfù. Events on the Albanian front, especially the defeat of the *3ª d. alp. «Julia»* which had been stopped by the Greeks on 8 November and forced to retreat on 10 November, focused the senior Italian leadership away from the operation against Corfù. This setback in the Italian plan was followed by the initiation of the Greek operational level counterattack across the entire Albanian front on 14 November.

Employment of the *Paracadutisti*? (Map 5.1)

The current status of the paratroop units was discussed in a memorandum written by the Operations Office of the *Comando Superiore Aviazione* under *Supereservito* and transmitted to *STAMAGE*.[26] The memorandum outlined that while two of the three battalions (*I* and *II*) had completed their tactical ground training, weather conditions at Tarquinia had prevented the conduct of the parachute training. If weather conditions improved to allow the resumption of parachute training, all three battalions would be ready by the end of December.

It is the second paragraph of the memorandum that is of greater interest. Here *Supersercito* is asking whether the battalions will be sent to Africa or was there is a greater need to maintain them in Italy. Italy had ongoing offensives in both Greece and A.S., but this memorandum makes clear that there was no comprehensive planning supporting the development of the parachute speciality. One would believe that as a new capability was being readied, there would be a discussion of its future employment. *Supersercito*, as the headquarters responsible for ground operations, should be offering recommendations for the employment of the *paracadutisti*. Instead all that is stated is that a decision to deploy the battalions to A.S. would require that headquarters (*Superasi*) provide the necessary transports. The memorandum notes that the R.E. lacked the necessary aircraft and that the R.A. had requirements to support missions other than airborne operations.

On 16 November, *STAMAGE* was informed that Mussolini wanted the study of the Corfù operation to resume and the results would be used as a basis for a decision to implement the plan.[27] This was followed by two additional communications from

26 NARA, Stato Maggiore R. Esercito memorandum 15 novembre 1940, *Oggetto: Battaglioni paracadutisti*, T821, roll 130.
27 Biagini and Frattolillo, *Diario Storico*, vol II, book I, p.387, book II, p.153.

Mussolini on 17 November that were transmitted by Badoglio to the staff. The first expanded the study to include a possible operation against Corsica and provided some general guidance for the Corfù operation which included the following statement:

> As there are suitable airfields for maneuvering on the island of Corfù, the use of a paratrooper battalion which can be followed by air landing must also be studied.[28]

The second communication was specific to the use of the paratroopers.

> Badoglio, chief of the General Staff, Army General Staff, and, for information, the Air Force General Staff
>
> Record n. 3896 Operations — Roma, 17 November 1940
>
> Subject: Parachute Battalion.
>
> As stated in my message of 3895 dated today, it is the Duce's understanding that in a possible and perhaps even imminent landing on Corfù for the occupation of the island, that a paratrooper battalion be employed.
>
> This General Staff, in agreement with the Regia Aeronautica General Staff, will therefore have to complete the preparation of this battalion as a matter of urgency.
>
> The other two battalions – whose training will have to be accelerated – could be kept at home, in locations that this General Staff will want to define, pending the opportunity to employ them.[29]

After two deaths during training on 10 and 27 November, parachute training was once again suspended on 27 November. On the same day, the intent to rapidly complete the training of the parachute force was reinforced by a 27 November memorandum from *Superesercito*. This memorandum stressed that the battalions must complete their parachute training prior to any commitment to combat. It then outlined a program focused on ground training to better prepare the units for parachute training when it would resume. The final paragraph implied that only one qualification jump would be needed to certify a unit for deployment.[30]

It was not until 22 November that the Italian leadership finally understood the gravity of the situation in Albania. In a communication on that day to the various service staffs, Badoglio informed them:

28 Biagini and Frattolillo, *Diario Storico*, vol II, book II, p.154.
29 Biagini and Frattolillo, *Diario Storico*, vol II, book II, p.155.
30 NARA, Stato maggiore R. Esercito memorandum 27 novembre 1940, *Oggetto: Esercitazione di paracadutisti*, T821, roll 130.

> It is the Duce's understanding that the landing in Corfù will take place when the Greek attack currently underway is completely exhausted and our positions are consolidated.
>
> Please keep me informed of the progress of the preparations.[31]

The study requested by Mussolini on 17 November was submitted on 26 November. In it, the idea of using the paratroopers to seize the airfield at Garitsa, followed by air landed troops was rejected. A landing near Garitsa was also rejected. The reasoning behind both recommendations was that the Greeks forces and defenses were too strong for a single airborne battalion to overcome. At the time, the Greek garrison of the island consisted of the 10th Infantry Regiment, a battery of 105mm guns, and a platoon of 105/19 howitzers. The operation proposed by *STAMAGE* was for the battalion to land in the open fields of either Megan Livadi or Barusi that are located west of the town of Corfù. From there, the battalion would move southeast to occupy a line of hills between Vutelatica and Kastri, thereby protecting the Italian landing beaches planned for the southern part of the island.[32]

Unlike the concept for the parachute operation against Prevesa that was more of a demonstration, the Corfù operation placed the *paracadutisti* as a means to enable a successful seaborne landing. The rapid deployment and movement of the unit to block any Greek counterattack against the beaches is a classic mission for airborne forces. The Allies would use their airborne forces in a similar manner during Operations Husky and Overlord.

On 18 November, Badoglio communicated Mussolini's decision to land the *Corpo d'Armata Celere* at Prevesa after it had been captured. The corps would then form a reserve for the Italian Army advancing in Greece. On 3 December Mussolini finally decided to postpone, for now, the operations against both Prevesa and Corfù.[33] Both of these operations would be discussed over the next several months, but not until April 1941 would there be any serious consideration given to actually carry out these operations. By then, Greece had surrendered and the mission would change to one to deny the occupation of strategic locations by the Germans.

A new battalion manning document was approved on 10 November 1940. This document made a small increase in the size of the battalion, mainly in the support structure. Added were a small medical section, cooks for the both the headquarters and companies, and trumpeters to act as runners. Each parachute rifle platoon gained a second officer to act as a deputy commander, further enhancing the leadership

31 Biagini and Frattolillo, *Diario Storico*, vol II, book II, p.181; NARA, Stato Maggiore R. Esercito memorandum dated 26 novembre 1940, *Promemoria N° 316 segreto per l'Ecc. il Capo di S.M. Generale Occupazione di Corfù*, T821, roll 128.

32 Biagini and Frattolillo, *Diario Storico*, vol II, book II, pp.219–220.

33 Biagini and Frattolillo, *Diario Storico*, vol II, book II, pp.399 and 485. Montanari, *Grecia* vol 1, pp.337, fn.167. The C.A. Celere consisted of the three *divisioni celere* (fast divisions) and would be supplemented by 15 battalions of *Camicia Nere* (Blackshirts).

structure of the unit. Two drivers were also included, although no vehicles were authorized. Armament remained the same with no addition of heavy weapons. These changes increased the strength of the battalion from 313 to 338 men.[34]

Superesercito updated the status of parachute training on 10 December 1940. In this memorandum written by the *Comando Superiore Aviazione*, the combined problems of weather and parachute malfunctions were again highlighted. This was followed by a discussion of the development of a new parachute that had successfully passed testing using dummies. Once final testing and production was started, the training of the *I* and *II battaglioni* would be completed as quickly as possible. During this time, a fourth battalion would be created and its training completed by spring. The uncertainty of how the units would be employed was still present, with the statement "… making employment possible in the various theaters of operations as necessary, where the necessary favorable conditions would arise."[35]

It was in March 1941 that the use of the airborne force in Albania and Greece was again discussed by *STAMAGE*. One must remember that at this time the two colonial battalions had already been destroyed during the British pursuit during Operation Compass in early February. The only existing airborne units were those units undergoing training at Tarquinia.

At the time their employment was once again raised, the Italians had managed to stop the Greek February offensive and had stabilized the front. Their own offensive, the *Offensiva in val Deshinizza* (popularly and unofficially known as the *Offensiva Primavera/Spring Offensive*) was scheduled to begin on 9 March. This operation was planned as a decisive breakthrough of the Greek defenses. At a meeting held by the Deputy *Comando Supremo*, *generale* Guzzoni, on 3 March the following is recorded:

> 1° Paratroopers
> The question relating to their degree of training is raised and His Excellency Guzzoni orders that it be accelerated and completed – with the collaboration of all – not so much for immediate use as for foreseeable future needs. In any case, if ready, given that the Germans would provide the means of transport, they will be used for the occupation of Janina [Ioannina].[36]

Two important observations are seen in this discussion. First, the training of the initial battalion of *paracadutisti* was not completed. Accelerating the training for the first three battalions was discussed back in November 1940, yet three months later the training of any of the battalions had not been completed. The safety issues with the

34 AUSSME *Formazioni provvisorie di guerra del battaglione paracadutisti*, 12 giugno 1940, with change Circolare 7720 dated 20 November 1940.

35 NARA, Stato Maggiore R. Esercito memorandum 10 dicembre 1940, *Oggetto: Paracadutisti*, T821, roll 130.

36 Antonello Biagini and Fernando Frattolillo, (eds) *Verbali delle riunioni tenute dal Capo di SM Generale* (Rome: USSME, 1983-19), vol II, p.22.

The target of *Operzione «P2»*, the bridge over the Corinth Canal. The Gulf of Corinth is at the top of the picture, the Saronic Gulf is at the bottom. The bridge itself is near the center by the white area along the right side of the canal. (AUSSMA)

parachutes, the shortage of suitable aircraft, the issues with Tarquinia itself, and the increased training requirements had impacted the rate of training at the school. The second point is that the R.A. did not possess the required number of transport aircraft needed to support large-scale airborne operations. An 18 February 1941 memorandum from the *Ministero dell'Aeronautica* listed twenty-eight operational SM.82 transport aircraft, the aircraft best suited for airborne operations. Of these 28, two were operating in Africa Orientale Italiana (Italian East Africa), seven were configured to transport vehicles, two were configured to transport engines and other large assemblies, three to transport armoured vehicles, one at the experimental workshops at Guidonia, and two provided logistical support for the Linee Aeree Transcontinentali Italiane (L.A.T.I.). The remaining eleven SM.82 transports could transport 330 paratroopers if redirected from their current missions for a period of time. That was enough aircraft to lift one battalion with supplies, so a second lift would be needed for two battalions. This does not account for any losses during the operation or follow-on resupply.[37]

37 Filippo Cappellano, Nicola Pignato, Nicola *Gli autoveicoli da combattimento dell'Esercito Italiano* (Rome, USSME, 2002) volume secondo, p.732; Massimo Civoli *S.A.S. I Servizi*

This exchange was followed by a shift in thinking between 6 and 10 March. On the 6th, Badoglio held a meeting of the *STAMAGE* that discussed both the occupation of Kefalonia and Zakynthos (still seen as a seaborne operation) and to discuss the employment of the airborne forces.[38] On the 10th, at the next meeting of *STAMAGE*, it was stated that the *Comandante di Superiore Albania* (Overall Commander in Albania), *generale* Cavallero:

> … is preparing, by order of the Duce: a landing operation on Preveza using a Black Shirt battalion; [and] a possible jump of paratroopers in the area of the Corinth Canal to prevent any damage by the Greeks.[39]

The planning for a landing at Prevesa had actually begun in January 1941. The initial guidance was issued by *generale di armata* Alfredo Guzzoni, the Sottocapo di Stato Maggiore Generale (Deputy Chief of *STAMGE*) on 26 January to the S.M.R.E, S.M.R.M., and the S.M. della M.V.S.N.[40] During the planning for this operation that culminated with the issuance of *Direttive per Esigenza 4 B (Prevesa)* on 8 March 1941, the use of paratroops was never considered.[41]

The use of the paratroopers to seize the isthmus is the first time a proactive operational-level employment of the units was discussed. The plan for the occupation of Corfù back in November saw the *reparti paracadutisti* used in a tactical role to better enable the success of the seaborne invasion. The mission to seize the Corinth bridge is operational in scope, ensuring Italian ground units access to the Peloponnese. *Superesercito* responded to this requirement for *STAMAGE* with a study on the operation on 6 March.

> Due to its complexity, the action requires at least two paratrooper battalions (as is well known, one battalion has now completed its training; the other is nearing completion, but can be considered usable in cases of absolute necessity).
>
> An indispensable condition for the action – essentially based on the effect of surprise – to have a probability of success is:
>
> - that it is carried out when the Greek collapse has clearly manifested itself with the consequent disintegration of the armed forces;
> - that the action of the paratroopers does not precede the arrival at the isthmus of the first elements of our troops by more than 24 hours. […]

Aerei Speciali della Regia Aeronautica 1940-1943 (Cavallermaggiore, Gribaudo, 2000), p.17.

38 Antonello Biagini and Fernando Frattolillo (eds) *Diario Storico del Comando Supremo* (Roma, USSME, 1986-2002), vol III, book I, p.447.

39 Biagini and Frattolillo, *Diario Storico*, vol III, book I, p.472.

40 NARA, Comando Supremo message 5852 dated 26 gennaio 1941, *Oggetto: Preparazione di quattro btg. cc.nn. per operazione di sbarco,* T821, roll 128.

41 NARA, Comando Supremo directive dated 8 marzo1941, *Oggetto: Preparazione di quattro btg. cc.nn. per operazione di sbarco,* T821, roll 128.

> With regard to aircraft, it is necessary to prepare in good time, and therefore as soon as possible, the transport aircraft for paratroopers, with 26 aircraft, plus 4 in reserve, if type JU 52, or 13, plus 2, if of type S.82, for each battalion and detachment of marines."[42]

Here the issue of aircraft availability is once again raised. Availability of aircraft will be a continuing concern whenever Italian airborne operations are discussed. The option of using either Italian or German aircraft demonstrates that *Supereseercito* was well aware of this issue. The two allies had established an understanding in the previous month that Germany was willing to support Italian operations with German aircraft.[43] Such an agreement would be situational, with Germany making the decision whether the aircraft could be spared at the time of the Italian operation. This would complicate any future Italian planning for an airborne operation.

A key point is the requirement that the ground force be able to reach the paratroopers within 24 hours. This was a major consideration in the prewar discussions on the role of airborne units. Its inclusion in *Supereseercito's* operational guidance demonstrates that the army leadership did have some understanding of the limitations of airborne units.

What appears to be missing is a lack of any use of the *paracadutisti* in support of the *Offensiva Primavera*. Why limit a landing at Preveza to one battalion of CC.NN.? A landing to seize both Preveza and Arta was considered back in December 1940 as a way to break the Greek defenses and to open new ports to supply the Italian armies. Such a landing now, at the same time a major offense was opened in Albania could generate an overwhelming synergistic force on the Greeks. Discussion of the employment of the R.M. had been notably absent during the campaign against Greece, being limited to convoy protection. Landing at Preveza would allow Italy to introduce additional forces without overburdening the already stretched logistical system in Albania. Of course, such a discussion needed to happen back during the genesis of the offensive, not in early March when the attack was about to launch. Once again, conservative thinking limited any considerations for bold planning to transform an unfavorable situation.

The exchange on 10 March was followed by a discussion of airborne training on 18 March, by which time the failure of the *Offensiva Primavera* was known. On 20 March, an order was issued to …

> …the Regina Marina and the Regia Aeronautica Staffs to study together with the Royal Army Staff, a plan for the means to contribute to the action of two

42 Di Giovanni, *I paracadutisti*, p.91.
43 Di Giovanni, *I paracadutisti*, p.92

> paratrooper battalions on the Corinth Canal, whose action is currently being studied by the Royal Army Staff;[44]

Superaereo responded to the order on 31 March. They provided their observations about the preparation of aircraft and which actions had been completed to support an operation of the paratroopers on the Isthmus of Corinth.[45] Included in that assessment was this section.

> «The R. Aeronautica does not have the units or adequate aircraft particularly intended for the transport of paratroopers and landing troops.
>
> Only aircraft of the S.82 type are suitable for such a service but, if you want to use them, you should suspend transport for the A.O.I.; it would appear that, at the initiative of the Regio Esercito, agreements have been made between Comando Supremo and the German Supreme Command regarding the temporary transfer, by the Reich Air Force, of air transport units for the implementation of operations of the kind of the one in question and in my case the R. Aeronautica will make one or two airports available and will provide all the necessary assistance. [...]
>
> If, for contingent reasons, the planned use of paratroopers should take place during the day and require the intervention of the escort, it is necessary to bear in mind that – given the limited range of fighter aircraft – the operation should be delayed until the bases of our fighters are moved to Epirus.[46]

The statement that only SM82 aircraft are suitable is surprising, given the successful use of the SM.81s in the prewar operations conducted in Libya. The SM.81 was already identified as inadequate for use as a frontline bomber and it was seeing greater use as transport aircraft. As demonstrated by *Operazione «Gefara»*, a number of aircraft could be quickly released and prepared for airborne operations. The lessons of the Libyan experiences apparently remain forgotten.

With this assessment, *Superesercito* submitted their directive for *Esigenza «2P»* (the operation against the Corinth Canal) to *STAMAGE* on 4 April.[47] On 8 April, *STAMAGE* gave the authorization for the *«2P»* project. An information copy of the directive that was issued by the *Superesercito* was sent to *STAMAGE* on 11 April.[48]

Esigenza «2P» provided for the landing of two battalions of paratroopers and a platoon from the *reggimento San Marco* (Regia Marina marines that were currently undergoing parachute training at Tarquinia) on either side of the canal. The paratroopers would seize the bridge over the canal as well as the banks on both sides. The

44 Biagini and Frattolillo, *Diario Storico,* vol III, book I, p.540
45 Biagini and Frattolillo, *Diario Storico,* vol III, book I, p.614.
46 Di Giovanni, *I paracadutisti*, p.92.
47 Biagini and Frattolillo, *Diario Storico,* vol. 3, book I, p.641.
48 Biagini and Frattolillo, *Diario Storico*, vol 3, book I, p.696.

«San Marco» marines were charged to clear any barriers at the western entrance of the canal for a squadron of MAS boats to support the capture of Posidonia.[49] The force would have 740 paratroopers from the newly formed *1° reggimento paracadutisti* and approximately forty marines. The force would be armed with 108 light machine guns (the Breda 30 f.m.), six heavy machine guns (the Breda 37), and 12 lanciafiamme (flame throwers).[50] While the Italians had perfected parachuting the 47/32 anti-tank gun in 1940, none of these dual-purpose weapons were included in the plan.

Events overtook any possibility of an airborne operation to capture Ioannina or on the isthmus. The Italian spring offensive failed to break the Greek defense and was ended on 25 March. Yugoslavia joined the Tripartite Pact on that same day which triggered a coup on 27 March, placing the Italian forces in Albania in greater danger than before. The situation was then completely transformed by the German assault on Greece and Yugoslavia that began on 6 April, the German occupation of Salonica on 9 April, and forced the surrender of Yugoslavia on 17 April. The Greek Army in Albania began to retreat on 12 April and the Italian Army was finally able to advance back into Epirus. Trapped, the Greek Army in Epirus surrendered on 20 April. The German invasion now turned into a pursuit of the British forces and to rapidly occupy as much of Greece as possible.

Finally a Mission (Map 5.2)

With the retreat and surrender of the Greek Army, the *STAMAGE* began to consider what locations would need to be secured with an eye towards limiting German control. The Corinth Canal was already being considered, but the islands of Corfù, Kefalonia, and Zakynthos were always in the plan to be secured by Italy. Corfù controlled the Straits of Otranto, while Kefalonia, and Zakynthos controlled access to the Gulf of Corinth and the western end of the Corinth Canal. Planning for the occupation of the islands had been initiated in January but had been suspended given the lack of any Greek or UK use of the harbors and the size of the Greek garrisons. When planning was resumed in March, the plan had the occupation troops carried by naval assets and were to land on beaches to secure the islands. It was decided to place the operation on hold until such time as the occupation could be achieved peacefully.[51] At least that was the plan until 27 April.

The change was triggered by the rapid advance of the German units and the issues created when German and Italians units came in contact. The Balkans were considered as within the Italian sphere of influence, yet Germany was seen encroaching

49 Luigi Emilio Longo, *I «reparti speciali» italiani nella seconda guerra mondiale* (Milan, Mursia 1991), p.281. Longo states the town's name is Poseidonia, but it is actually Posidonia.

50 Di Giovanni, *I paracadutisti*, p.137 and fn.18.

51 Di Giovanni, *I paracadutisti*, p.95.

in the region. *STAMAGE* needed to ensure strategic locations within Greece were controlled by Italy and not Germany. Problems arose in Epirus where Italian units were being blocked by German units when moving towards Prevesa. The Germans preempted «*2P*» by launching their own airborne assault on the Corinth Canal bridge on 26 April. After the German failure to seize the bridge, the Italians looked towards the island of Kefalonia as a possible airborne objective.

STAMAGE took up the issue at a meeting on 27 April.

> ... He [Guzzoni] then goes on to examine the question of Corfù which keeps maturing and which is becoming — for political reasons — as the occupation of Kefalonia is becoming a necessity and to also compensate for the loss of Dessie.
>
> His Excellency Riccardi agrees, but to guarantee the use of the sea lanes, he deems it essential to carry out the necessary dredging and ensures that it is not possible to start it before the current month.
>
> This of course is assuming that there is no reaction!
>
> His Excellency Guzzoni acknowledges and adds that immediately after Corfù it is necessary to proceed with the occupation of Kefalonia. He refers to the fact that the Adolf Hitler regiment has arrived in Patras and that their allies, using motorboats, have already been able to proceed with the occupation of numerous islands of the Greek archipelago.
>
> He [Guzzoni] orders flights to be made over Cephalonia to observe whether or not a reaction develops.
>
> He [Guzzoni] therefore arranged for General Magli to inform His Excellency Cavallero of what is being prepared for Corfù and Kefalonia ... [52]

Rather than a military mission, the use of the *paracadutisti* are now being examined in the light of political need. Their use was being considered because of the speed in which they could execute the mission. Delaying until the operation could be carried out peacefully reduced any military risk. Touted as the first combat use of the Italian airborne force, it is difficult to categorize the actual operation as a combat mission. It is certainly the first operational employment for these units and offered both a demonstration of their capabilities and limitations.

The many accounts of this operation vary in the details, especially the dates of the common events. In most sources, no dates are provided. In others, the given dates do not support the flow of the narration or present internal inconsistencies. The following has been reconstructed using as much of the common information as possible, but there is still some uncertainty in the flow of events.[53]

52 Lucio Ceva, *La condotta italiana della guerra* (Milan, Feltrinelli Editore, 1975), meeting notes p.142

53 The main sources used for the operations on Cefalonia and Zante are: Nino Arena *Aquile senza Ali* 48-54; Nino Arena *FOLGORE Storia del paracadutismo militare italiano* (Rome: Centro Editoriale Nazione, 1965), pp.87-94; Nino Arena, *I paracadutisti, Cinquant'anni*

On the morning of 28 April, *STAMAGE* issued a verbal order for the occupation of Kefalonia to *Superesecito*, *Supermarina*, and *Superaereo*. *Superesercito* followed by issuing their verbal order to the *II battaglione paracadutisti* at 1235 hours to prepare for the mission. The plan specified by *Superesercito* was for a parachute drop of two companies (150 men), timed with a simultaneous landing of a command group by seaplane in the harbor of Argostoli, the capital city of the island. The battalion was currently stationed at Civitavecchia on the Tirrenian coast outside of Rome. The battalion commander, *maggiore* Mario Zanninovich, quickly drove to the *1º reggimento paracadutisti* headquarters where he spoke to *generale di brigata* Enrico Frattini by telephone. The general instructed Zanninovich to prepare two of his companies with full jump equipment and aerial resupply canisters for movement by train at 2230 hours that night. The unit was augmented with a radio section equipped with a RF2A radio, and with an additional long range TXO transceiver modello SIM. A corporal of Albanian descent was attached to act as a Greek interpreter.[54]

Returning to his battalion area, *maggiore* Zanninovich had a difficult task: deciding which of his three companies would not participate in the upcoming mission. Like any elite unit of volunteers that had spent months in specialized training, all the men were eager to finally get into action. Zanninovich called together his three company commanders, *capitaini* Pescuma (*4ª compagnia*), Avogadro (*5ª cp.*), and Macchiato (*6ª cp.*), and outlined the new orders. Turning to *capitano* Pescuma, he was told to stand down his company; they would remain in Civitavecchia with the regimental headquarters.

The two companies selected for the mission loaded the train and departed Civitavecchia that night. By midday the next day (29 April) they reached Lecce in the Salento region (the 'heel' of the Italian peninsula) and after transferring to trucks, arrived at the Galatina airfield outside the city. It was a warm, clear blue sky with a light breeze. Excellent flying weather and good for jumping if the same weather held over their objective.

As with any military operation, friction could not be avoided. The issue that manifested was a lack of aircraft. The requested transports had not yet arrived at Lecce and time was running short. *Maggiore* Zanninovich was able to reach the commandant of the Parachute School at Tarquinia, *colonnello* Baudoin, and explained the

di storia, cronaca e immagini del paracadutismo italiano (Modena: Società Tipografica Editrice Modenese Mucchi, 1972), pp.99-100; Nino Arena, *La Regia Aeronautica 1940–1943* (Rome: USSMA, 1982), vol. 2, pp.133-335; di Giovanni, *I paracadutisti*, pp.94-100; Giulliano Manzari and Marina Pagano, *La Regina Marina nelle Isole Ionie*, pp.37-43; Santoro, *L'Aeronautica*, vol 1, pp.220-222.

54 Arena, *La Regia Aeronautica*, vol. 2, pp.334-335. Dante Pariset, *Storica del paracadutismo* (Rome-Milan:Vito Bianco Editore, 1962), pp.126–127 states the plan was a parachute drop on Cefalonia on 30 April by the *5ª cp.*, followed by simultaneous drops on Itaca and Zakynthos by the other two companies on 1 May. No other source mentions this version of the plan.

situation. *Colonnello* Baudoin stated he would assist and ordered the school's Caproni CA.133 flight detachment to support the companies. The commander of the detachment, *maggiore* Dante Salvetat and his personnel worked to prepare both the school's detachment of three CA.133s as well as an additional nine CA.133s scheduled to support the school for the training jumps on 30 April. Twelve of this type of aircraft could carry the two companies for the mission.

All 12 of the CA.133s from Tarquinia arrived at Lecce on the morning of 30 April ready to fly the mission. In the meantime, the Regia Aeronautica's *4a Squadra Aerea* originally tasked to support the mission finally was able to provide three of the six required SM.82 transports that were outfitted for parachute drops. These aircraft came from one of the *Servizi Aerei Speciali gruppo.*[55] This meant only half of the intended 150 paratroopers could be transported. *Maggiore* Zanninovich had to tell *capitano* Macchiato that his *6a cp.* would remain behind. Only *capitano* Avogadro's *5a cp.* would fly the mission to Kefalonia. While the efforts of *maggiore* Salvetat's aircrew were recognized, they too would remain at Lecce and could only watch when the *paracadutisti* departed.

Colonnello Baudoin had flown down with the school flight detachment to Lecce. In recognition that this was the first operational jump of the Italian airborne forces, he gave *maggiore* Zanninovich the school's flag and asked that it be flown over the island during the mission.[56] Zanninovich accepted the flag, and after a brief hug, he and his *paracadutisti* boarded the three SM.82s; 24 paratroopers per aircraft for a total of 72 paratroopers.

The *paracadutisti* presented a transitional appearance as they climbed into the aircraft. They were still wearing the wool M40 grigio-verde uniform that was standard for all Italian troops. Instead of the M33 helmet, they had the new M40 *elmetto per paracadutisti* that had been adopted in December 1940. Covered underneath the waist harness of the parachutes, each paratrooper carried a M34 Beretta pistol and M38 *pugnale da combattimento* (combat knife) attached to the M1909 g-v leather waist belt. The tall black leather *scarpe per reparti paracadutisti* (paratrooper boots) had replaced the earlier leather ankle boots and would become standard authorization in October 1941.[57]

It is unclear how the individual *paracadutisti* were equipped for the jump. The known pictures of the men as they boarded the aircraft are not clear enough to discern equipment details. It is likely that the *5a cp.* used the Salvator D.40 parachute for the jump.[58] The design of the IF41/SP was not finalized until the first months of 1941 and

55 Arena, *La Regia Aeronautica,* vol. 2, p.334.
56 Arena, *FOLGORE*, p.90.
57 Di Martino, *Paracadutisti*, vol. I, p., vol. II, p.323; Anon. `30 aprile 1941 – La Folgore si lancia a Celefona'
58 Guy Richards, *World War II Troop Type Parachutes: Axis,* (Atglen: Pennsylvania: Schiffer Military History, 2000), p.14. Pariset, *Storica del paracadutismo*, p.126 states the IF41/SP was used.

Capitano Dante Salvetat demonstrates the Salvator D.40 parachute to students at Tarquinia in 1941. Some versions of this photograph mis-identifies the parachute as a D.39. (AUSSMA)

an order placed for their production with SNIPA (Societa' nazionale industria paracaduti e affini).[59] Jumping with the D.40 meant that their cavalry carbines were likely dropped using resupply containers and not carried by the paratroopers.

Photographs of the men on Kefalonia after the drop show them wearing white cloth or canvas bandoleers with ten pouches for 6.5mm Carcano ammunition clips.[60] These replaced the leather M1936 ammunition pouches normally issued as none are seen in the photographs. Several men have one bandoleer wrapped around their waist with a second bandoleer worn over their right shoulder. The bandoleers are similar in design to those used by other armies to package ammunition in ammunition containers for easy distribution. The R.E. did not use such packaging for their small arms ammunition, so these bandoleers reflect something developed for the *paracadutisti*. It is not known whether the men parachuted wearing the bandoleers or if they were packed with the carbines, the latter being most likely. These bandoleers were not employed in any other operation.

Packs consisted of only the M29 tascapane (haversack) without the mess kit as none are seen strapped to the outside of the haversack. Beside the two large compartments

59 Nino Arena, *50º di Tarquinia 1939/1989* (Comitato Promotore ex Istruttori delle Scuole Militari di Paracadutismo, 1989), p.41

60 Massimo di Martino, *Paracadutisti d'Italia – Uniformi distintivi equipaggiamenti*, Volume 2°, 1943-1969, (Milan: Edizioni Libreria Militare, 2019), p.323; Anon. `30 aprile 1941'

The *paracadutisti* of the *5ª compagnia* loading their SM.82 at the Galatina airfield on 30 April 1941. (AUSSMA)

for rations, spare clothing, and other items, the haversack had two inside pockets for either two boxes (36 rounds) of 6.5mm Carcano or two grenades. Several canteens can be seen and appear to be the larger two liter alpini type. Several men are carrying cassetta per caricatori (ammunition boxes) for the Breda 30 f.m. Each box held 300 rounds on fifteen stripper clips for the Breda. No cassetta per accessori e parti di ricambio (accessories and spare parts boxes) are present. The spare barrels for the Breda, normally carried on the spare parts box were instead carried in their individual storage tubes and strapped to the haversack. The guaina per serbatoio (magazine case) for the Breda that is normally worn on the gunner's belt is also strapped to the haversack. All these items would have been dropped separately using the resupply containers and not carried by the individual paratroopers during the actual jump.

The likely ammunition load for each man was 120 rounds of 6.5mm (two bandoleers), 14 rounds of 9mm (two clips) for the Beretta pistol and two grenades carried in the haversack. Three men with ammunition cases can be seen with the fourth man carrying the Breda 30, so likely 900 rounds of ammunition was carried per f.m. in the squad. This was a heavier ammunition load than the typical Italian infantry squad which was 72 rounds of 6.5mm per man and 600 rounds for each f.m. The

The drop over Kefalonia. (AUSSME)

infantry squads did have an additional 36 rounds per man and 2400 per each f.m. in the battalion trains, something the *paracadutisti* lacked.[61]

The aircraft took off at 1230 into a clear, bright sky and after forming up headed southeast from Lecce towards Kefalonia. Argostoli, the capital of Kefalonia, was approximately 310 kilometers from Lecce, a two-hour flight at the SM.82's cruising speed of 160 kph. Simultaneously, two Cant Z 506 seaplanes transporting R.A. *colonnello* Renzo dalle Mole, *colonnello di S.M.* Arena (designated commander for the operation), *CC.NN. Consulo* Pesce, *sottotenente di vascello* Andrea Pirandello (R.M.), an unnamed *capitano* and *tenente* from the R.E., and three CC.NN soldiers departed from Brindisi. These individuals would handle the political and civilian affairs for the occupation. While Brindisi is further from Kefalonia than Lecce, the higher cruising speed of the Cant Z 506 aircraft allowed them to arrive at the same time as the slower SM.82s.

Arriving over the island a little before 1430 hours, the aircraft did a quick circle to check their location and to inspect the terrain below. The jump master, *maggiore* Giovanni Verando, looked out the door and verified the drop zone. The zone itself was located in the Krancia region three kilometers south-east of Argostoli. The zone consisted of a large open field set between stone walls. It was stony, hard ground that is typical for the Greek Ionian islands. He then ordered the *paracadutisti* to get ready.

61 Anon., *La Squadra della fanteria* (Parma: Scuola di Applicazione di Fanteria, 1943), p.12.

The first jumper positioned himself in the door while the remaining members of the stick closed in behind him.

It was around 1430 when the aircraft passed over the drop zone for the actual jump. The *paracadutisti* rapidly cleared the aircraft and floated down, landing in and around the drop zone. The drop itself was scattered, with fifteen injuries of which eight were serious. The issue was later identified as the use of flight crews without training on parachute drops and no flight testing had been conducted with the new SM.82 transports to develop techniques for airborne operations.[62] The remaining men under Zanninovich and Avogadro quickly formed up and secured the area. A status report was transmitted to the circling Cant Z.506 observer aircraft and the company set out toward Argostoli. The Cants headed back over to Argostoli and prepared to land in the port.

The city was secured without any fighting as the Greek battalion which previously garrisoned the island had already been disbanded. The only armed forces that remained were the gendarmerie and 8 Greek sailors that served under the control of the Port Captain. *Colonnello* Arena and the other members of his party had by that time landed and moved to join up with the *paracadutisti*. The civilian authorities met the Italian delegation at the Government building and the surrender documents were presented and signed. Afterward a flag raising ceremony was held. The Greek Civilian Prefect informed the Italians of the food shortage on the island and *maggiore* Zanninovich made arrangements for 20 quintals (two tons) of grain to be flown to the island by the SM.82s.

Plans had been made to send a detachment of *paracadutisti* to secure the nearby islands of Itaca and Zakynthos using boats seized at Argostoli. The time used to secure the town and port had delayed the possible start of that part of the mission until late on the 30th, so it was decided to wait until the next morning. On 1 May, two officers and 13 *paracadutisti* were sent to Itaca, while four officers and 35 *paracadutisti* were sent to Zakynthos; both groups using Greek motorboats that had been seized in the port.

On 2 May, the Italian minesweeper R160 *Intrepido* arrived from Prevesa and checked the harbor approaches for mines. On 3 May, the process was repeated, this time using the minelayer *Azio* and the minesweepers R130 and R140 (converted from fishing vessels). This precaution prepared the way for the arrival of the light cruiser *Bari* and three torpedo boats escorting three cargo ships transporting four *battaglioni CC.NN. di sbarco* (*Camicia Nere* landing battalions) to garrison the island.[63] These

62 Di Giovanni, *I paracadutisti*, p.96 and p.138 fn. 29; Arena, *Tarquinia*, p.42. Arena states that two lieutenants from the school were sent to jump from a SM.82 the day prior on 29 April to learn its characteristics. This single jump by two individuals from a new type of aircraft, flown by a crew inexperienced in parachute drops was unlikely to reveal all the procedural changes needed.

63 Biagini and Frattolillo, *Diario Storico,* vol 4, book I, p.33.

The *5/II btg. paracadutisti* raising the Italian flag in the main city square in Argostoli, Corfù on 30 April 1941. Note the white ammunition bandoleers; one worn over the shoulder and one around the waist. (Museo Storico delle Aviotruppe)

The detachment of the *5ª cp. paracadutisti* landing on the island of Zante on 1 May 1941. (Museo Storico delle Aviotruppe)

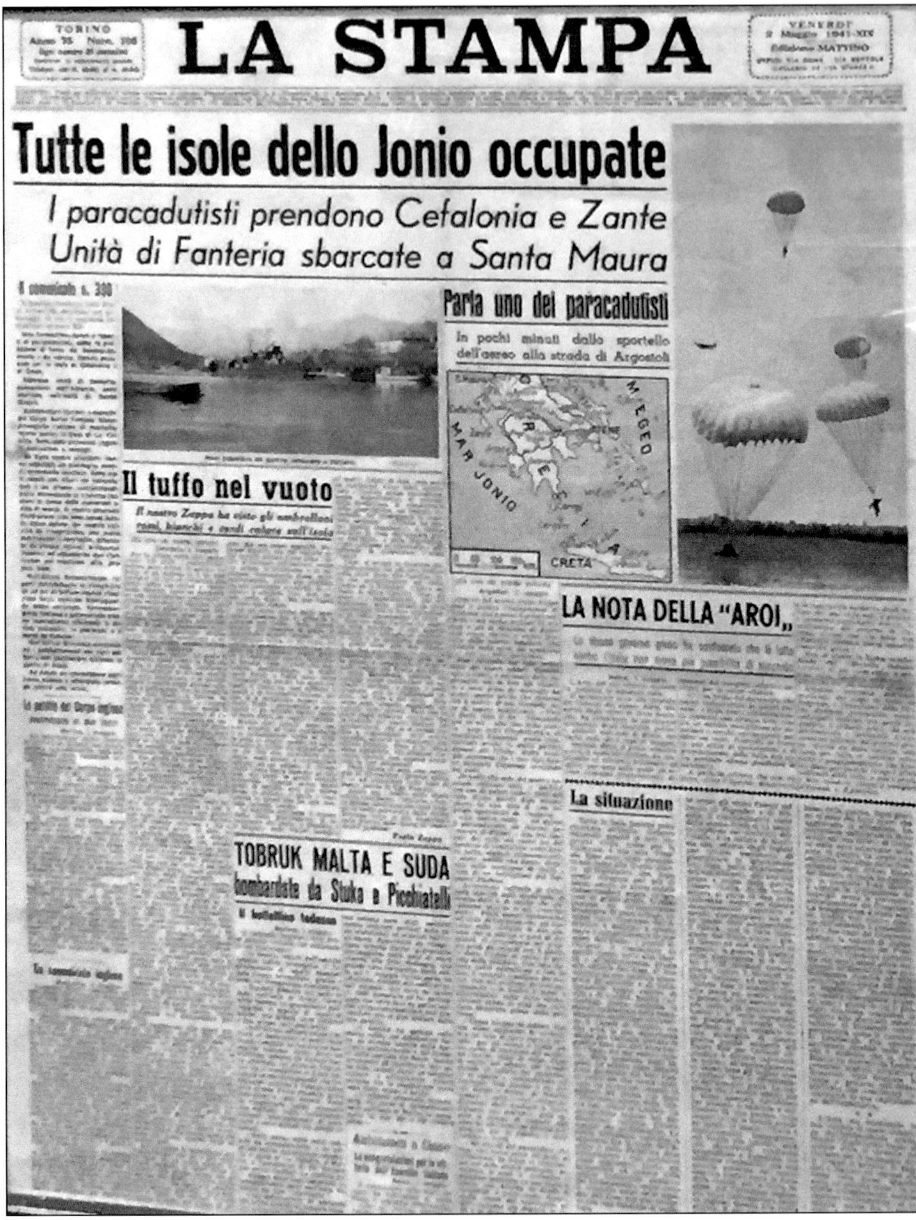

LA STAMPA

Tutte le isole dello Jonio occupate

I paracadutisti prendono Cefalonia e Zante
Unità di Fanteria sbarcate a Santa Maura

Il comunicato n. 330

Parla uno dei paracadutisti

In pochi minuti dallo sportello dell'aereo alla strada di Argostoli

MAR JONIO
MAR EGEO
CRETA

Il tuffo nel vuoto

LA NOTA DELLA "AROI"

La situazione

TOBRUK MALTA E SUDA
bombardate da Stuka e Picchiatelli

The front page of the newspaper *La Stampa* (The Press) on 2 May 1941.
(Museo Storico delle Aviotruppe)

garrison troops arrived on 4 May. On 6 May, one of these battalions was transported to Zakynthos and a part of another battalion to Ithaca as garrisons.

At some point during the *II btg. paracadutisti* time on the island a Greek ship with 700 returning Greek soldiers sailed into Argostoli's port. The story recounted in some sources is that *maggiore* Zanninovich feared that if the ship docked at the quay, the Greek soldiers could overpower his small force. To prevent this, he ordered the Port Captain to have the ship anchor out in the bay and transfer the soldiers ashore by boat 20 men at a time. This would allow the *paracadutisti* to disarm the Greek soldiers and maintain control of the situation. The date given for this event by Arena is 1 May; Manzari and Pagano state the event happened on 14 May. As the later date is after the arrival of the four *btg. di sbarco,* the concern about the number of Greek soldiers does not support the 14 May date.[64]

It is unclear when the *paracadutisti* departed the islands and returned to Civitavecchia. A meeting of the *Comando Supremo* (the renamed *STAMAGE*) on the evening of 5 May stated the need to recover those units that were currently deployed.[65] *Capitano di fregata* Salvatore Pesce assumed responsibility for Kefalonia on 7 May, so the men of the *5ª compagnia* likely returned shortly after that date.

There were three remaining opportunities for the use of the airborne force during this campaign. After learning of the German plans for the assault on Crete, *STAMAGE* stated on 29 April that they had eight parachute companies ready for operations. However there is no indication that this information was passed on to the Germans.[66] During the meeting on 5 May, the use of paratroopers is mentioned in reference to the occupation of the islands of the Cicladi and of Kythera.[67] No employment orders followed and the occupation was completed using shipping. The final opportunity was in support of the Italian landing on the eastern shore of Crete during *Unternehmen Merkur* (Operation Mercury). *Comando Superiore AA.FF. Egeo* (Headquarters Aegean Forces) was given a warning order on 22 May to begin planning for a possible operation against Crete by a regiment or larger force.[68] There is no record that the use of the paratrooper units was discussed. The actual landing was executed on 28 May in the Bay of Sitia using elements of the *50ª d.f «Re»*.[69]

Considerations

And so ended the Greek Campaign for the *paracadutisti*. Three observations stand out from the events of the previous six months. One is that any consideration for the use of

64 Arena, *FOLGORE*, p.93, Manzari and Pagano, *Regina Marina,* p.45.
65 Biagini and Frattolillo, *Verbali*, vol II, p.58
66 di Giovanni, *I paracadutisti*, p.93.
67 Biagini and Frattolillo, *Verbali*, vol II, p.58
68 Biagini and Frattolillo, *Diario Storico* vol IV, book I, p.161.
69 Biagini and Frattolillo, *Diario Storico,* vol 4, book I, p.205

the *paracadutisti* was generated by outside agencies (Mussolini and the Foreign Office) and not from within the R.E. internal planning process. A second was that the army leadership failed to consider their employment as an offensive tool, passively accepting Mussolini's concept of their secondary role at Prevesa. The third observation was the issue of aircraft availability to support airborne operations. This later point is less understandable as Italy possessed a number of suitable aircraft. The *149º Gruppo T (transport)* possessed up to 80 aircraft at various times during the campaign.[70] The SM.81 aircraft of the bomber units could be rapidly prepared for paratrooper launches if needed as previously demonstrated in Libya in 1938. Using these aircraft for such an operation would require removing them from their current duties, but that time could be quite brief. Given that the military leadership did not view the use of the *paracadutisti* in terms of generating decisive results, any cost benefit analysis would likely not support the diversion of the aircraft.

As an offensive campaign, the invasion of Greece should have offered possibilities for the use of the airborne force in support of operational or tactical objectives. A combination of hasty planning, a lack of parachute units and aircraft, weather, and terrain made any use of these units a difficult proposition. However, these issues appear to be less of a factor to the lack of an understanding and desire to employ unconventional capabilities. The campaign offered excellent possibilities for the use of seaborne landings to turn the Greek defense, yet it was the Greeks who executed the only seaborne operation of the campaign.[71] The planned amphibious landing on Corfù was an ancillary task to secure the island after the victory was secured, not a plan to help gain that victory. It too was never executed. With the Italian leadership unwilling to consider the use of a capability such as amphibious assault that they had previously employed, it is not surprising that the potential of parachute operations was always an afterthought, if considered at all.

This did not mean that the development of an airborne force was at its end, the question remained whether it would be seen as a valuable asset. A decision on 6 May would open the path for the use of the *paracadutisti* in future operations.

70 Chris Dunning, *Courage Alone* (Aldershot: Hiki Publications, 1998), pp.117,189; Nino Arena, *Regia Aeronautica*, vol 2, pp.319-325;

71 HAGS, *Abridged History*, p.94; Montanari, *Grecia*, vol I, p.311.

6

Btg. carabinieri *paracadutisti*

As highlighted in the previous chapter, one of the factors curtailing any use of the *paracadutisti* during the Greek Campaign was the incomplete training of the units. None of the first three *battaglioni paracadutisti* had been able to fully complete its parachute training prior to the attack on Greece. The delay due to the inability to identify and correct the issues with the D.39 and D.40 parachutes threatened the future of the speciality.

Fearing that this problem would prematurely end the development of airborne forces in the Italian military, *colonnello* Baudoin personally communicated with Mussolini. In the communication, Baudoin urged Mussolini to allow training to continue. The fighting in Albania was not going well for Italy and Baudoin wished to have the paratrooper units ready for employment when needed. Mussolini told Baudoin to be patient and allow the investigation to continue until a solution was identified. At the same time, Mussolini promised that he would ensure the use of the *reparti paracadutisti* at the first favorable opportunity.[1]

During the summer of 1940 a number of academics had joined the staff at Tarquinia on a rotational basis. These men were professors/instructors of physical conditioning and health from the Accademia Militare di Modena and the Accademia della Gioventù Italiana del Littorio. One of these individuals, *tenente* Ruggero Martinotti, became interested in the problems with the Salvator parachutes. He began to study the films of the parachute jumps and was able to identify several issues with the training. The first was the positioning of the right hand on the manual opening handle while the left hand had to move from the static line to the right shoulder strap. Here the lesson learned from the school at Castel Benito had not been adopted by Tarquinia and

1 Nino Arena, *50ª di Tarquinia, 1939-1989, Scuole Militari paracadutismo* (Comitato Promotore ex Istruttori delle Scuole Militari di Paracadutismo, 1989), pp.39-40. It is uncertain the date and format of the communication. It likely happened between 27 November and 12 December as the S.M.R.E. notified *Comando Supremo* of the problems at Tarquinia on 12 December. See Antonello Biagini and Fernando Frattolillo (eds.), *Diario Storico del Comando Supremo* (Rome: USSME, 1988), vol II book I, p.533.

needed to be relearned; the right hand should hold the left shoulder strap and not the manual release handle. Martinotti also noticed that should the jumper not quickly position his left hand on the opposite shoulder strap, the aerodynamics of the asymmetrical body position could induce spin. These problems could be corrected through training and with that assurance training could be resumed.[2]

With these changes approved, the halt on parachute training was lifted in late October but was again curtailed after two more fatal accidents on 10 and 27 November as previously mentioned. Taken together, eight students had died during the sixty days of active parachute jumping from the start of training on 10 July until 27 November. Morale within the parachute units had dropped to a dangerously low level due to the deaths. Parachute training was again stopped by order of *Superesercito* on 27 November 1940 and all three battalions began another period of intensive tactical training until the parachute problems could be corrected.[3]

A New Parachute

While members of the faculty and staff were studying ways to improve the current D.39 and D.40 designs, the Studies/Experiences Department under *tenente colonnello* Bettica were completing a detailed report on the Salvator series of parachutes. Its conclusion was that the Salvator design was unsuitable for military airborne units and that Italy should begin development of a parachute specifically designed for airborne operations. Bettica felt that at least six months were needed to develop and test a new design. The senior leadership felt that length of time was excessive given the current strategic situation facing Italy. Noting the success of the German airborne operations, it was agreed that examining the current German parachute designs offered the quickest path to an improved parachute.[4]

Superaereo arranged for an Italian mission to the German parachute school at Stendal and the factory making the Ruckenpackung Zwangauslosung (RZ) series of parachutes. Initially approved by the Germans, the trip was later canceled. *Colonnello* Carlo Teucci, the Regia Aeronautica liaison in Berlin, was able to obtain several RZ.16 parachutes and send them to Tarquinia. The German parachutes were tested along with possible modifications to the Italian designs.

While working this issue, *tenente colonnello* Bettica sent two letters through *Superesercito* to *Comando Supremo* in January 1941. These letters addressed a range of problems specifically facing the parachute training and the reparti *paracadutisti* in general. On the issue of the parachutes, Bettica wrote:

2 Arena, *Tarquinia,* pp.26-27, 39.
3 Arena, *Tarquinia,* p.39.
4 Arena, *Tarquinia,* pp.40–41; Nino Arena, *La Regia Aeronautica* (Rome: USSMA, 1981-1986) vol I, p.121

> The jump material consists of the Salvator D. 39 parachute and the German parachute, still under testing. Several fatal accidents have occurred with the Salvator parachute, [while] with the German one it has not yet been possible to eliminate the drawback of the bridle tearing. Consequently, the battalions that should have stayed at the School for only three or four months cannot leave because they have not yet been able to complete their training.
>
> Given this situation, it is logical that the paratroopers do not show excessive confidence in the material, all the more so because the memories of the misfortunes that occurred are too recent.[5]

There has been an ongoing historical debate on whose parachute design influenced whom, as the RZ series itself was loosely based on the early Salvator design. There was a degree of information exchange and visits between the airborne personnel of all the militaries before the war, so ideas were likely exchanged. This question is unlikely to be resolved but while the final design of the Italian parachute was similar to the German, it incorporated improved features the RZ series lacked.

The new parachute developed by the team at Tarquinia was the *Imbracatura da Fanteria 41/Scuola Paracadutisti* (Infantry harness 41/Parachute School, IF41/SP). As it was not meant to replace the Salvator series as used by aircrew, this parachute could be larger with increased canopy size and a harness designed for repeated use. The new design focused more on safety than reduced weight/bulk and the ease of wearing. Unlike the Salvator parachutes, the IF41/SP used a deployment bag for the canopy rather than a pilot chute/pack tray. No manual system for deploying the canopy was provided. The static line pulled the deployment bag from the pack and allowed the suspension lines to fully extend while the canopy remained folded in the deployment bag. Once the lines were fully taut, the static line then pulled the bag off the canopy, allowing it to inflate. This provided a softer opening and thereby reduced opening shock to the jumper. This was the system used by the German RZ and the British X type series of parachutes.[6]

Testing of the new design began in December 1940.[7] *Captaino* Leonida Turrini wanted to ensure that the IP41/SP was strenuously tested using 'Sigismondo', a parachutist mannequin before proceeding with human jumps. Once he was satisfied, further refinement continued with test jumps executed by *colonnello* Baudoin, *tenente* (istruttori) Ruggero Martinotti, and *capitano* Turrini before the new parachute was approved for use in early 1941. An immediate order for 2,500 of the new parachutes was placed with the Società nazionale industria parachute affini (SNIPA). The IF 41/

5 Biagini and Frattolillo, *Diario Storico*, vol III book II, p.137.

6 Guy Richards, *World War II Troop Type Parachutes: Axis,* (Atglen, Pennsylvania: Schiffer Military History, 2000), p.14; Guy Richards, *World War II Troop Type Parachutes: Allies* (Atglen: Pennsylvania: Schiffer Military History, 2003), pp.24, 27.

7 NARA, Stato Maggiore R. Esercito memorandum 10 dicembre 1940, *Oggetto: Paracadutisti*, T821, roll 130.

Tenente colonnello Alberto Bettica. Bettica was responsible for many of the improvements in equipment and training. He would be killed by the Germans after September 1943.

'Sigismondo', the jump dummy that was used to test the various design changes before a *paracadutisti* would jump with any new parachute or equipment. (AUSSME)

The IF41/SP parachute. Note the two quick release buckles across the chest that allow the parachutist to quickly remove the harness. (Ministero della Guerra manual)

Bag-deployed parachute. Italian IF41/SP.. The suspension lines are nearly fully deployed while the canopy is still in the deployment bag. Note the static line connected to the bag. (USSME)

SP was a very successful design and nearly eliminated all parachute initiated accidents. It would remain in use with modifications until 1954.[8]

In the same letters, Bettica identified other factors besides the Salvator parachutes that impacted the training program at Tarquinia and delayed certification of the first two battalions. A major factor was Tarquinia itself. Viewing the site of the school in January 1941, Bettica had this to say in his 22 January 1941 letter:

> The airport consists of a small makeshift emergency airfield adaptable to fit the needs of the School. It is located almost at sea level and is swampy: if it rains, the camp remains impassable for weeks and months, and then it is not possible to fly or provide parachute training.
>
> The airport is constantly beaten by winds which always have considerable speed, such as to hinder the use of the parachute or make it dangerous when landing.
>
> Everyone agrees that the airport is not suitable for a parachute school and I personally have been able to see that from December 31 to today there has been only one day with almost no wind.[9]

In the same letter he discussed other factors impacting morale:

> The paratrooper units, the instructors, and the commanders have a special mentality dependent on the difficult environmental conditions and on the continuous struggle between the technical requirements of training and the practical possibilities, much lower than the logically indispensable minimum. The painful experience of the jump tests carried out, and the memory of the accidents that took place greatly influenced this mentality [...]
>
> The staff, locked in the very restricted environment of Tarquinia and its accommodations, continuously in contact with the same individuals with almost no possibility of distraction, ends up being obsessed with this situation and it becomes a fixed idea. The officers' mess is not jovial like all military canteens, it is wearying and hollow. The unstoppable nightmare of the parachute looms over it.[10]

Bettica's correspondence then moved on to discuss other factors and ideas of military parachuting. The problems of weapons and the need for other equipment specifically designed to meet the requirements of the airborne force were raised in his discussion. He foresaw that the element of surprise was no longer something that could be

8 Arena, *Tarquinia,* p.41.
9 Antonello Biagini and Fernando Frattolillo (eds.), *Diario Storico del Comando Supremo* (Rome: USSME, 1989) vol III book II, p.136; Marco di Giovanni *I paracadutisti italiani Volontari, miti e memoria della seconda guerra mondiale* (Gorizia: Editrice Goriziana, 1991), p.37-38
10 Biagini and Frattolillo, *Diario Storico,* vol III book II, pp.136–137.

assumed when planning parachute operations. Rapidity of action, immediate access to weapons other than pistols and grenades, and tactical training that reflected landing in a contested drop zone rather than parachuting into fields devoid of enemy fire were some of the issues he identified. Many of the concerns foreseen by Bettica in January would play out during the German invasion of Crete in May 1941.[11]

While *colonnello* Baudoin and the staff at Tarquinia were working through these issues, *Supereservito* was pressing to expand the airborne force. The new parachute allowed training to be restarted at Tarquinia. The *III btg. paracadutisti* had been officially authorized in early 1941 and the *IV btg. paracadutisti* in April. At the same time, the *1° reggimento paracadutisti* was officially organized on 1 April 1941. The regiment was initially formed using the *I btg. paracadutisti CC.RR.* and the *II* and *III battaglione paracadutisti*.[12]

This assignment of battalions to the *1° rgt. paracadutisti* would not survive for long. On 4 June 1941, *Comando Supremo* took up a proposal to send the *I btg. paracadutisti carabinieri* to North Africa.[13] On 14 May *Superasi* informed *Supereservito* on the plan to create two new parachute battalions in Libya. There were 41 officers and NCOs, 134 national and 281 Libyan paratroopers that had been gathered at Castel Benito by May 1941. The Libyan command was requesting one major or lieutenant colonel, three captains and 21 lieutenants to complete the two proposed units.[14]

Supereservito responded on 16 May in a memorandum that was signed by Roatta stating that it would be better if the survivors were returned to Tarquinia. The logic was that the survivors no longer formed a homogeneous unit and had lost all their equipment. The following sentence is instructive. "In Tripolitania, if it is deemed appropriate to maintain a formed parachute unit and a training department, the *CC.RR. btg.* of the *1° rgt.* can be sent [to Libya]." The fact that the decision to maintain a parachute battalion is at the discretion of *Superasi* and not a decision made by *Comando Supremo* is another indicator that fascist Italy lacked a strategic concept for the use of the speciality.[15]

The following paragraphs in the memorandum then outlines the rationale for offering the *I btg. CC.RR.* and not one of the other battalions. The issues presented did not outline an argument of training or one addressing either operational or tactical considerations. Instead the reasons indicate that *Supereservito* was getting rid of a unit that did not 'fit' with the other battalions. The reasons listed included the different

11 Biagini and Frattolillo, *Diario Storico,* vol III book II, pp.131-151.
12 Di Giovanni, *I paracadutisti italiani*, p.130; AUSSME, Ministro della Guerra letter 26 marzo 1941, *Oggetto: Costituzione del 1° reggimento paracadutisti*, racc.404, cart.5.
13 Antonello Biagini and Fernando Frattolillo (eds), *Diario Storico del Comando Supremo* (Rome: USSME, 1992), vol IV book I, p.263.
14 AUSSME, Comando Superiore AA.FF. in A.S memorandum 14 maggio 1941, *Argomento: Paracadutisti in A.S.*, fondo I, busta 135-5.
15 Stato Maggiore R.E. memorandum 16 maggio 1941, *Oggetto: Paracadutisti in A.S.*, fondo I, busta 135-5.

uniform, insignia, and rank structure of the *CC.RR.*; officer seniority; the command of companies by junior officers unlike their army brethren, and the fact the battalion was controlled by the Carabinieri Reali and not the Regio Esercito. In all, the appearance is one of the army removing a problem rather than supporting a valid operational requirement.

While Rome was discussing the various options, *Superasi* issued a memorandum dated 28 May 1941 ordering the creation of the two battalions.[16] The *btg. nazionale* would be structured the same as the battalions at Tarquinia. The *btg. libico* would be organized under the mobilization structure of the *Regio Corpo Truppe Libiche* and would consist of only two companies.

This decision was quickly modified on 3 June. A telephone conversation between *generale d'armata* Italo Gariboldi at *Comando Supremo* and *Superasi* informed the staff in Libya that the transfer of the *I btg. para. CC.RR.* had been approved. It was also decided that the national paratroopers currently in Africa would return to Italy. In a 5 June 1941 memorandum to *Comando Supremo*, *Supereservito* stated there was a lack of trained parachute officers to complete the national battalion being raised in Africa. It recommended that the *I btg. para. CC.RR.* be sent to A.S. and a mixed Italian national/Libyan parachute battalion be raised by the *Superasi*.[17] Regardless of the reasons, the decision was made and the battalion commander, *maggiore* Eduardo Alessi, was given his new orders on 17 June.

The *Ministero della Guerra* authorized additional equipment for the battalion for operations in Africa. Three SPA 38R trucks were provided for various support requirements, two bicycles were assigned to the battalion headquarters, while *maggiore* Alessi was allowed a Spider staff car. All the battalion's individual and the unit's parachute equipment was packed and shipped with the battalion, raising hopes that the battalion would be parachuted behind enemy lines.[18]

The battalion departed Tarquinia on 8 July and traveled to Napoli. The *carabinieri* remained there for several days until enemy activity forced a change. Rather than loading and departing from Napoli to Tripoli, the ships were diverted to Taranto. The *carabinieri* moved by train from Napoli to that city. While awaiting the transports, they were met at Taranto on 14 July by *comandante generale* Remo Gambelli, the commanding general of the *Carabinieri* to inspect the unit before it left. At that time *maggiore* Alessi requested three two-seat motorcycles for liaison between the companies and the battalion headquarters before the convoy departed Italy. The general promised to do his best to fulfill the request. The convoy arrived on 15 July and loading immediately commenced. The convoy departed Taranto destined for Africa on 16 July.

16 AUSSME, Comando Regio Corpo Truppe Libiche memorandum 28 maggio 1941, *Oggetto: Costituzione battaglioni paracadutisti (nazionale e libico)*, fondo I, busta 135-5.

17 Biagini and Frattolillo (eds), *Diario Storico,* vol IV book I, p.271; Stato Maggiore R.E. memorandum 5 giugno 1941, *Oggetto: Paracadutisti in A.S.*, fondo I, busta 135-5.

18 Luigi Emilio Longo, *I «reparti speciali» italiani nella seconda guerra mondiale* (Milan: Mursia 1991), p.265.

Africa Settentrionale

The Axis situation in North Africa had changed dramatically between February 1941 and the arrival of the *I btg. paracadutisti CC.RR.* in Tripoli on 18 July 1941.[19] After Beda Fomm, the British were poised to complete their conquest of Libya. Several events conspired against them to prevent that from happening. The British first needed to reposition their logistics forward to support an advance further west towards Tripoli. Simultaneously the Germans had decided on 17 January to send an armoured corps under Generalleutnant Erwin Rommel to support the Italians in Libya. The first of these units arrived in early February and had established a forward position at Sirte by 16 February. Italy had begun reinforcing the Regia Aeronautica and was shipping additional armoured and motorized divisions to Libya. After all the failures that led up to the Battle of Beda Fomm, *Maresciallo* Graziani was replaced by *generale di armata* Italo Gariboldi.[20]

On the Allied side the Greeks had accepted the British offer of assistance against the Italians on 24 February and British reinforcements earmarked for North Africa were now being redirected to Greece. The Greek decision meant that Wavell was required to pull additional units from the Western Desert Force to meet the force level demands for Greece. The British adopted a defensive stance in the western Cirenaica at Marsa el Brega and the whirlwind offensive that started on 9 December 1940 had come to a close.[21]

When *maggiore* Edoardo Alessi landed in Tripoli, the Italo-German force had already launched its counter-offensive on 31 March. The German units quickly captured Marsa el Brega and continued on to el Agedabia which fell on 2 April. From there, the Italo-German forces split into various combat groups and took multiple routes through the desert and north to Bengasi. That city fell on 4 April, freeing many Libyan paratroopers held by the British since their capture at Beda Fomm. The Axis units reached Tobruk on 11 April but were unable to seize the town and its port. Isolating Tobruk, Italian and German units bypass the port and reach the Libyan-Egyptian border on 11 April.

April–June 1941 saw a series of battles to capture Tobruk by the Axis or to relieve it by the British (Operations Brevity and Battleaxe).[22] Halfaya Pass was lost, recaptured,

19 Arnoldo Ferrara, *I carabinieri dell'Aria* (Rome: Ente Editoriale per l'Arma dei Carabinieri, 1983), p.40; Enrico Cursi, *I Leoni del Deserto* (Rome, edizioni Chillemi, 2014), p.57.

20 Gariboldi was the *5ª Armata* commander and replaced Graziani in February 1941. He would be replaced by generale Ettore Bastico in July 1941. Brian Sullivan, 'Bastico, Ettore' and 'Gariboldi, Italo', in Phillip V. Cannistraro, (ed.), *Historical Dictionary of Fascist Italy* (Westport: Connecticut: Greenwood Press, 1982). pp.63 and 240.

21 I.S.O. Playfair, I.S.O., *The Mediterranean and Middle East* (London: HMSO, 1954-1968) vol 1, pp.367–368; Mario Montanari, *Le operazione in Africa settentrionale* (Rome, USSME, 1985), vol I, pp.392–404.

22 Tobruk was attacked on 13–14, 16–17, and 29–30 April. Brevity was 16-17 May. Battleaxe was 15–17 June.

and again lost again by the British. By July both sides required a pause, having exhausted their units, material, and supplies. The Western Desert Force had been renamed the 8th Army, while the *Deutsche Afrika Korps* had been renamed *Panzergruppe Afrika* and now included several Italian units. The next several months would be used to receive replacements and reinforcements, replace equipment, and build up supplies in preparation for the next major battle.

Although they were part of the initial German-Italian build-up of forces, the *I btg. paracadutisti CC.RR.* did not participate in these initial offensive moves. Disembarking from the transport ships Oceania and Marco Polo on 19 July, the *carabinieri* were moved that evening by train to the town of Zavia (Zauia) approximately 47 kilometers west of Tripoli. Here *Superasi* had established a reception camp to allow units and replacements to acclimatize to the conditions in Africa settentrionale. The unit arrived at the camp with 28 officers, 39 non-commissioned officers, and 271 carabinieri *paracadutisti*. The battalion also had 4 additional noncommissioned officers and 31 men who were not airborne qualified but assigned to fill support and logistical roles.[23] While at Zavia, the battalion was placed under the command of the *5ª Armata* (5ª Army) responsible for the defense of Tripolitania.[24] *5ª Armata* was given several specific tasks for the battalion by *Superasi*, to include refresher parachute training, testing combat footwear, and a new reserve combat ration.[25]

The battalion was organized in accordance to the February 1941 *Formazione ed organici del reggimento paracadutisti, 17 febbraio 1941* document but with several new changes.[26] It appeared from the units and weapons assigned to the *carabinieri* that the battalion had started the transition to the organization specified by the *Formazione provvisorie guerra dei reparti di ftr. paracadutisti, 18 luglio 1941*. This transition was apparently was incomplete at the time the battalion was deployed to A.S. The battalion still possessed the plotone minatori of the February document but now possessed the machine guns and anti-tank weapons authorized under the new document. Still missing were the 81mm mortars and the flamethrowers that were also authorized in the July organization. Manning had increased to a small degree, but not enough to compensate for the increase in weapons.

The battalion consisted of a *comando di battaglione*, a *plotone minatori* (engineer platoon), and three *compagnie paracadutisti*. The engineer platoon was attached to the *1ª cp.* and was not under the *comando di battaglione*. A service/support platoon (*plotone*

23 Cursi, *I Leoni*, p.58.
24 Cursi, *I Leoni*, p.58. Cursi states the battalion was assigned to the *V Corpo d'Armata* but that is an error. The *V Cd'A* never served in Africa and he likely meant the *5ª Armata* which was responsible for Tripolitania at this time. Rodolfo Puletti and Franco Dell'Uomo, *L'Esercito e i suoi corpi – Sintesi storica* (Rome: USSME, 1971) vol 2, book 1, pp.32–33.
25 Cursi, *I Leoni*, p.58.
26 AUSSME, *Formazione ed organici del reggimento paracadutisti, 17 febbraio 1941*, M7, racc. 405, cart. 5.

servizi) was added to the battalion to provide a level of logistical sustainability not provided in the normal parachute battalion organization. The authorized *battaglione paracadutisti* structure relied on the use of *aerorifornimenti* (aerial resupply containers) for logistical support. As resupply would now be handled through the regular ground supply system, a portion of the 35 non-airborne qualified soldiers were likely assigned to support this logistical requirement. The service platoon provided limited medical support (five personnel including a doctor) and cooks (nine personnel), with the remaining 21 personnel handling logistics or supplementing the manning of the additional weapons (Fiat machine guns and anti-tank rifles).[27] This platoon was also attached to the *1ª cp.* It is likely that the engineer and support platoons were attached to a line company for administration, allowing the limited battalion staff to focus on operational concerns.

The battalion was equipped with the same weapons as that available to the previous parachute units. The basic weapon was the M91 *moschetto per cavalleria* (cavalry carbine) M91 Carcano for the individual *carabinieri*, with the Beretta M34 pistol as the standard side arm. The light machine gun was still the Breda 30 *fucile mitragliatore* (f.m.), of which the battalion had 27 (one per squad for a total of nine in each company). It is unknown why the battalion only had 27 f.m. when the 1940-1941 parachutist battalion authorization provided two f.m. per squad (for a total of fifty-four f.m.).[28] While the *paracadutisti* documents authorized the MAB 38A submachine guns as a preferred replacement for the Carcano for officers and non-commissioned officers, none of these weapons were issued to the battalion.[29]

All the sources state the battalion possessed twelve Fiat mod. 35 heavy machine-guns, two Solothurn 20mm A/T rifles, and ten 47/32 c.c. guns when it arrived in Tripoli.[30] It is unlikely that the battalion arrived in A.S. with the anti-tank guns. Ten 47/32 c.c. guns are more than what an Italian infantry regiment was authorized and the manpower needed to man these weapons is not included in the battalion total given by the same sources. During the various moves of the battalion in A.S., the number of trucks used to move the battalion would be insufficient for the men and the

27 These support personnel numbers are based on information found in Adoldo Naldi, *I servizi della fanteria* (Rome, Istituto Poligrafico dello Stato, 1931), Allegato A, p.37, and may not be 100% accurate.

28 Longo, *I «reparti speciali»*, p.265 fn.31 has a brief discussion on the discrepancy in the number of weapons given in various accounts. Nino Arena, *I PARACADUTISTI Cinquant'anni di storia, cronaca e immagini del paracadutismo italiano* (Modena: Società Tipografica Editrice Modenese Mucchi, 1972), p.102 states twelve f.m. Arena's number provides only four f.m. in a company which is far below the standard R.E. level of authorization. The number present here is from Cursi, *I Leoni*, p.86.

29 Anon, *Organizzazione e impiego*, p.14.

30 Ferrara, *I carabinieri*, p.49; Cursi, *I Leoni*, p.86. In Longo, *I «reparti speciali»*, pp.265 states that the battalion had the twelve Fiat mod. 35, four Solothurn 20mm A/T rifles, and ten 47/32 c.c. when it arrived in Tripoli. All sources agree on the Fiat mod. 14/35.

additional heavy weapons.[31] What is possible is that the 47/32 c.c. weapons were part of the Tripoli defenses when the battalion occupied their assigned sector. When the battalion was reassigned to the corps in Cirenaica, these weapons were left behind.

The issue of whether the battalion was issued the Solothurn anti-tank rifle posed an interesting problem. This was the Swiss S18-1000 anti-tank rifle known as the *Fucile controcarro tipo S* in Italian service. This weapon is never mentioned in the conduct of the fighting in November. In the list of weapons and ammunition recovered by the battalion after the fighting at Eluet el Asel was a Polish anti-tank rifle and ammunition.[32] Whereas the Solothurn was never authorized for issue to a jump-capable parachute battalion until 1943, the Polish Model 35 anti-tank rifle was authorized and issued. Called the *fucile controcarro 35(P)*, 800 of these weapons were captured by Germany and sold to Italy with many issued to the paratrooper units. It is possible that these rifles are mentioned only as *fucile controcarro* in the primary accounts and assumed to be the better known Solothurn.[33]

The twelve Fiat 14/35 machine-guns presented a final challenge. Heavy machine guns were not authorized weapons for a parachute battalion in February 1941 but ten were authorized under the July document. As previously stated, a possible explanation is that the battalion had begun to reorganize under the new document and this action was incomplete. The two additional machine guns were likely in reserve as spares, a common authorization in the R.E. These machine-guns are included in the list of surviving weapons after Eluet el Asel.

How these machine guns were organized and employed during the battalion's time in A.S. is unclear. None of the accounts mention their placement or role during the fighting on 19 December. If these machine guns were in fact issued just prior to the battalion's departure for Africa, there might not have been time to integrate these weapons into the battalion as authorized by the documents. One clue is the mention of a fourth platoon in the 3ª cp. in one source during the battle of Eluet el Asel. Parachute

31 Anon., *Manuale di Regolamenti per i corso allievi ufficiali di complemento* (Rome: Comando di Stato Maggiore, 1940), Tavola H, shows thirty-nine men for a machine gun platoon of four guns. Twelve guns would require 117 men. Anon., *La Squadra della fanteria* (Parma: Scuola di Applicazione di Fanteria, 1943), p.72 list indicates eighteen men for a platoon of two 47/32 c.c. guns without the animal transport. A 47/32 c.c. gun required one truck to carry it as the gun cannot be mechanically towed.

32 Cursi, *I Leoni*, p.113.

33 The (P) stood for *paracadutisti*. In Battista G. Trovero, *Ritorno a el Alamein* (Milan: Mursia, 1999), p.90 fn.6, he calls both the Swiss and Polish weapons 'Solothurn', an indicator that the smaller Polish weapon might be misidentified as the larger 20mm weapon. There are no pictures of *paracadutisti* with the *fucile controcarro tipo S*. One can see the *fucile controcarro 35(P)* in several photographs of Italian paratroopers: Giuseppe Lundari, *I paracadutisti italiani 1937/45* (Milan: Editrice Militare Italiana di Ivo Fossati, 1989), p.95; Arena, *I PARACADUTISTI*, p.119; Massimo Di Martino, *Paracadutisti d'Italia – Uniformi distintivi equipaggiamenti* (Milan, Edizioni Libreria Militare, 2019), vol. 2, p.330; Piero Crociani, Piero and Pier Battistelli, *Italian Army Elite Units & Special Forces 1940–43* (Oxford: Osprey, 2011), p.26.

A carabinieri student at Tarquinia in 1940. He is wearing a D.40 parachute. A CA.133 used for training is behind him. (Museo Storico delle Aviotruppe)

A *carabinieri paracadutisti* with the *fucili controcarro 35(P)*. This anti-tank rifle was authorized for all the parachute battalions until 1943. (Museo Storico delle Aviotruppe)

companies only had three platoons so it is possible that each company received four Fiat 14/35 machine-guns that were organized as a fourth platoon in the companies. This even distribution of the weapons would make detailing their employment less important as each company possessed the same capability. Until further research becomes available, this organization is assumed to be the case in the following account.[34]

The provision of communications equipment was both better and worse than a standard Italian infantry unit. It was better as each company was authorized a R.F.1(P) radio, while the *comando di battaglione* had a R.F.1 and a R.A.1 radio. This authorization allowed the R.F.1 radio net to be used for internal battalion communications, while the R.A.1 connected the battalion to its assigned higher headquarters. It was worse in the sense that no field telephone equipment was authorized or issued, limiting communication to runners between companies and platoons. Before leaving Italy, *maggiore* Alessi had requested an authorization for three motorcycles to be used for liaison duties while the unit was in Africa. S.M.R.E. finally responded on 4 August denying the request. The reasoning used in the denial was that the training and doctrinal employment of the airborne speciality did not provide for the use of those vehicles. This obviously ignored the non-doctrinal conditions of the missions the battalion would be assigned while serving in Africa settentrionale.[35]

The battalion did not remain long at Zavia. At the end of July, the battalion marched from Zavia to the Suani Ben Adem area, 25 kms from Tripoli. The unit occupied the military barracks at Raghed el Duera and Ras el Goz near the Castel Benito airfield. On 2 August, the *comando di battaglione* and the *2ª* and *3ª cp.* moved and occupied the defensive post of Casa Fortunato, while the *1ª cp.* occupied the Casa Russo defensive post on 3 August. These defensive posts protected a section of the Tripoli-Suani railway and the Castel Benito airfield. *Generale d'armata* Ettore Bastico, the commander of *Superasi* reviewed the battalion on 13 August at Suani Ben Adem. On 16 August, the battalion was reassigned to the command of the *XX Corpo d'Armata* which had replaced the *5ª Armata* as the operational headquarters responsible for the defense of Tripolitania. During this entire period, the battalion was executing reconnaissance patrols and continuing training exercises south and east of Tripoli.[36]

The battalion was transferred to the control of the *Corpo d'Armata di Manovra* (*C.A.M.*, Army Corps of Maneuver) on 10 September 1941.[37] The logic for this reassignment is unclear. The airborne doctrine published in 1940 states:

> Therefore, [such] a complex unit which is slow to create should be used exclusively for tasks fitted to their characteristics and only in cases where their intervention is indispensable with a good probability of success.[38]

34 Cursi, *I Leoni*, pp.98 and 103.
35 Cursi, *I Leoni*, p.61.
36 Cursi, *I Leoni*, pp.61 and 68.
37 Cursi, *I Leoni*, p.68.
38 Anon, *Organizzazione e impiego*, paragraph 3, p.10.

Colour Map Section

List of Maps

Unit Symbology
comando armata - army command
comando C. d'A - army corp command or group of Libyan Div.
comando divisione fanteria - infantry division command (regular / motorized)
comando brigata fanteria - infantry brigade command
comando reggimento fanteria - infantry regiment command
comando battaglione / grouppo - infantry battalion / group command
comando compagnia fanteria - infantry company command
battaglione / compania / plotone fanteria - infantry battalion / company / platoon
paracadutisti / guastatori paracadutisti - parachute infantry / engineers
bersaglieri / bersaglieri motorciclisti - bersaglieri / motocycle unit
battaglione Granatieri - Grenadier Battalion
Camicie Nere - Black Shirt Battalion
Libico - Libyan unit
compania / plotone controcarro - anti-tank artillery company / platoon
genio - engineers
avieri - Regina Aeronautica troops
mitraglieri - heavy / light machine gun unit
mortai da 81 - 81 mm mortar
compania / squadra / batteria controaerei da 20 - 20mm anti-aircraft battery
batteria cannoni - artillery battery
batteria contraerei - anti-aircraft battery
batteria da posizione Regina Marina - naval coastal battery medium, heavy
batteria da controaerei Regina Marina - naval anti-aircraft battery
carri M - medium tanks
compagnia carri L - light tank
semoventi - self-propelled artillery - assault guns
autoblindo - armored car
autogruppo - motorized transport unit
Italian
German
British/Allied

Map Legend

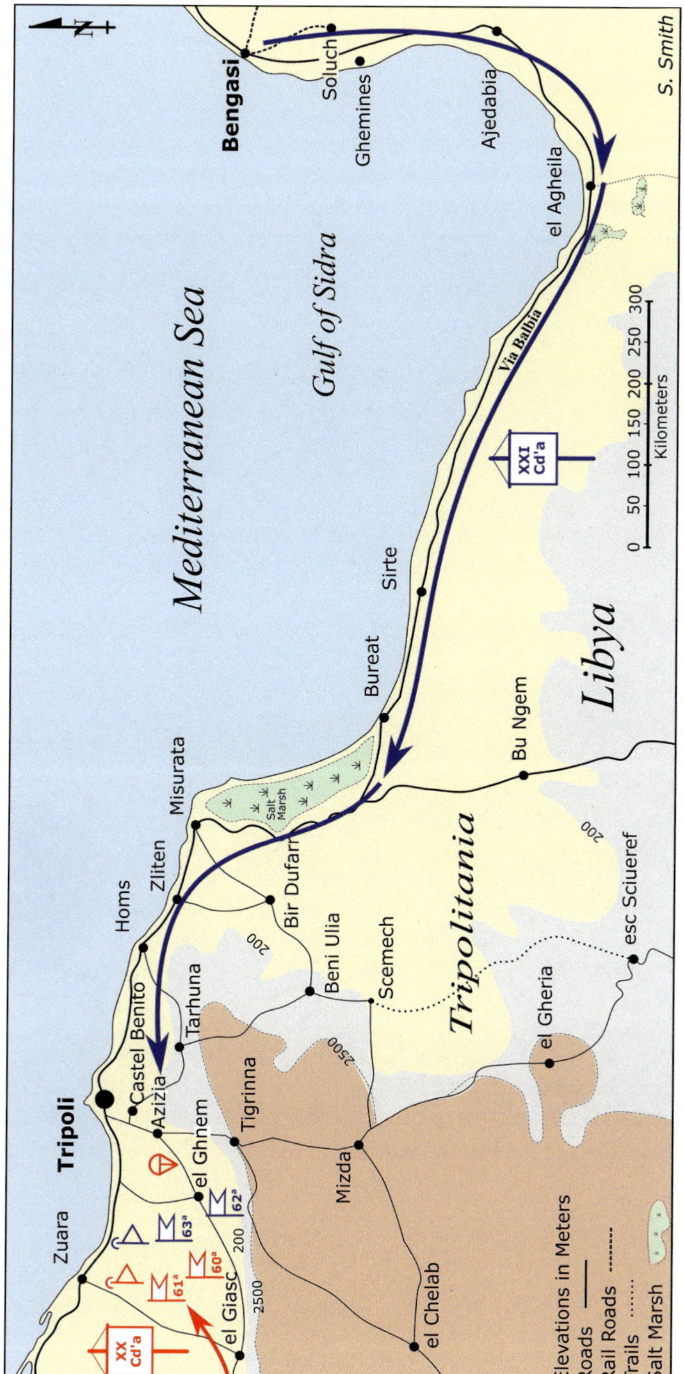

Map 1.1 Movements of Italian units during Operation Gefara 11–23 Apr 1938. (Map by Steven C. Smith)

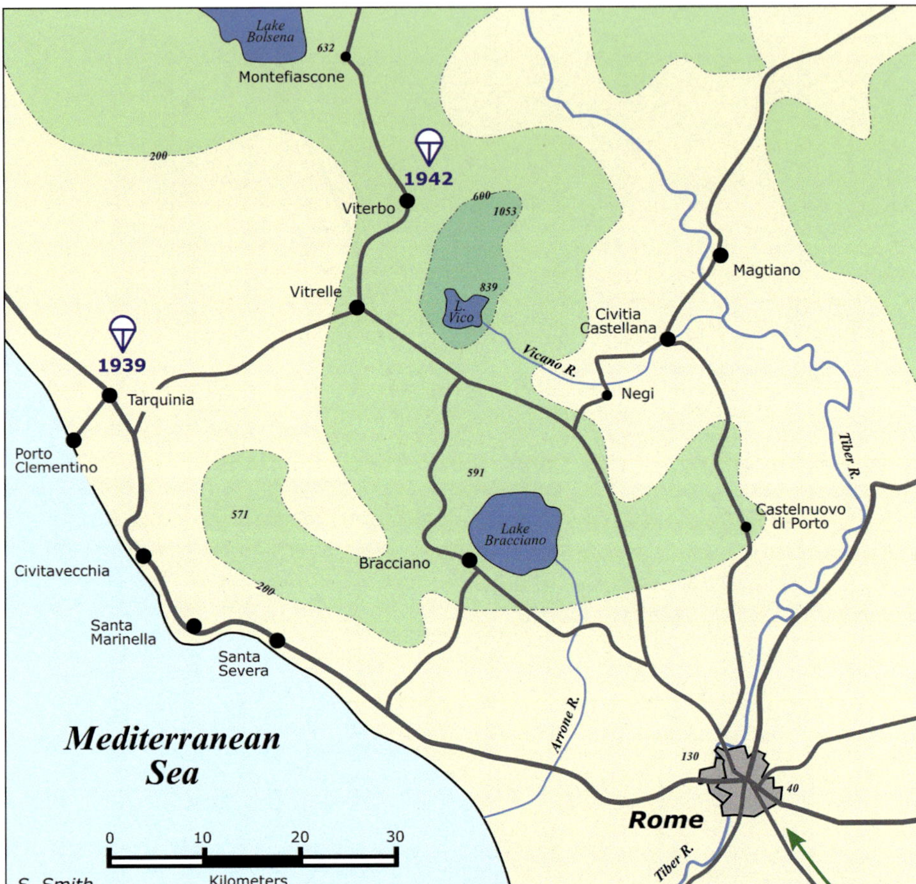

Map 3.1 Locations of the Parachute Schools 1939–1943. (Map by Steven C. Smith)

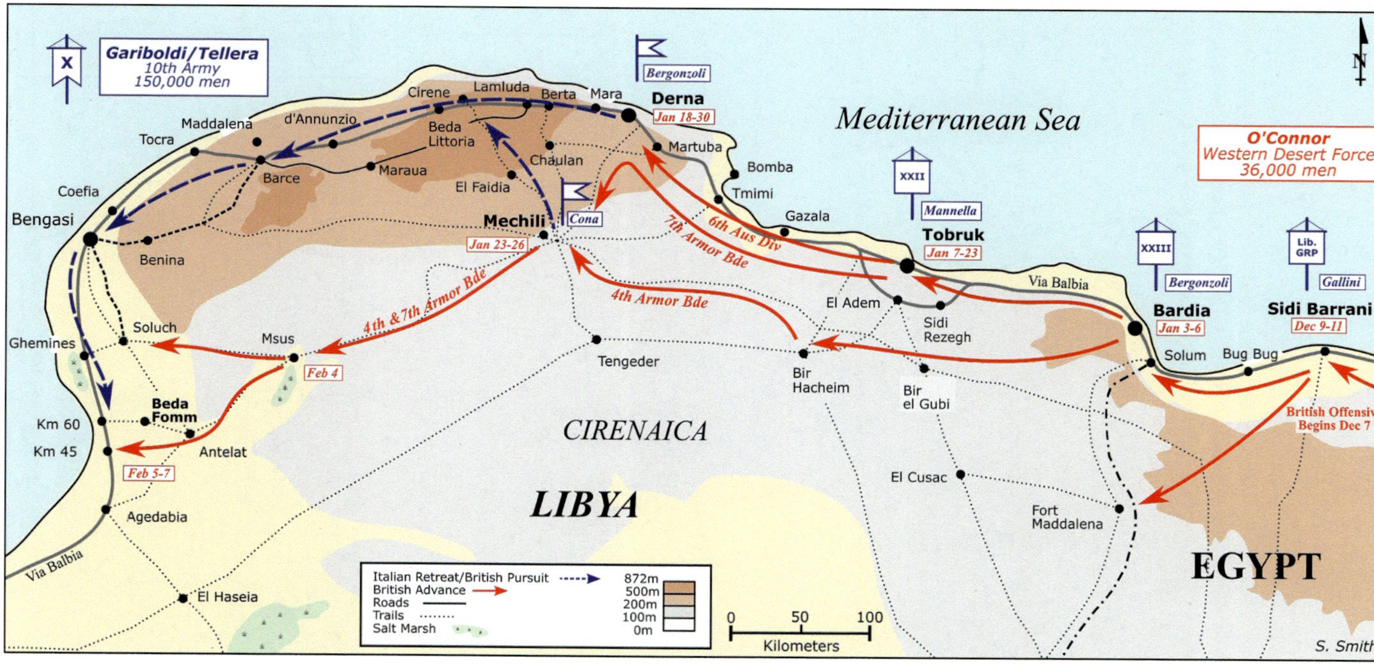

Map 4.1 Overview of Operation Compass Dec 1940–Feb 1941. (Map by Steven C. Smith)

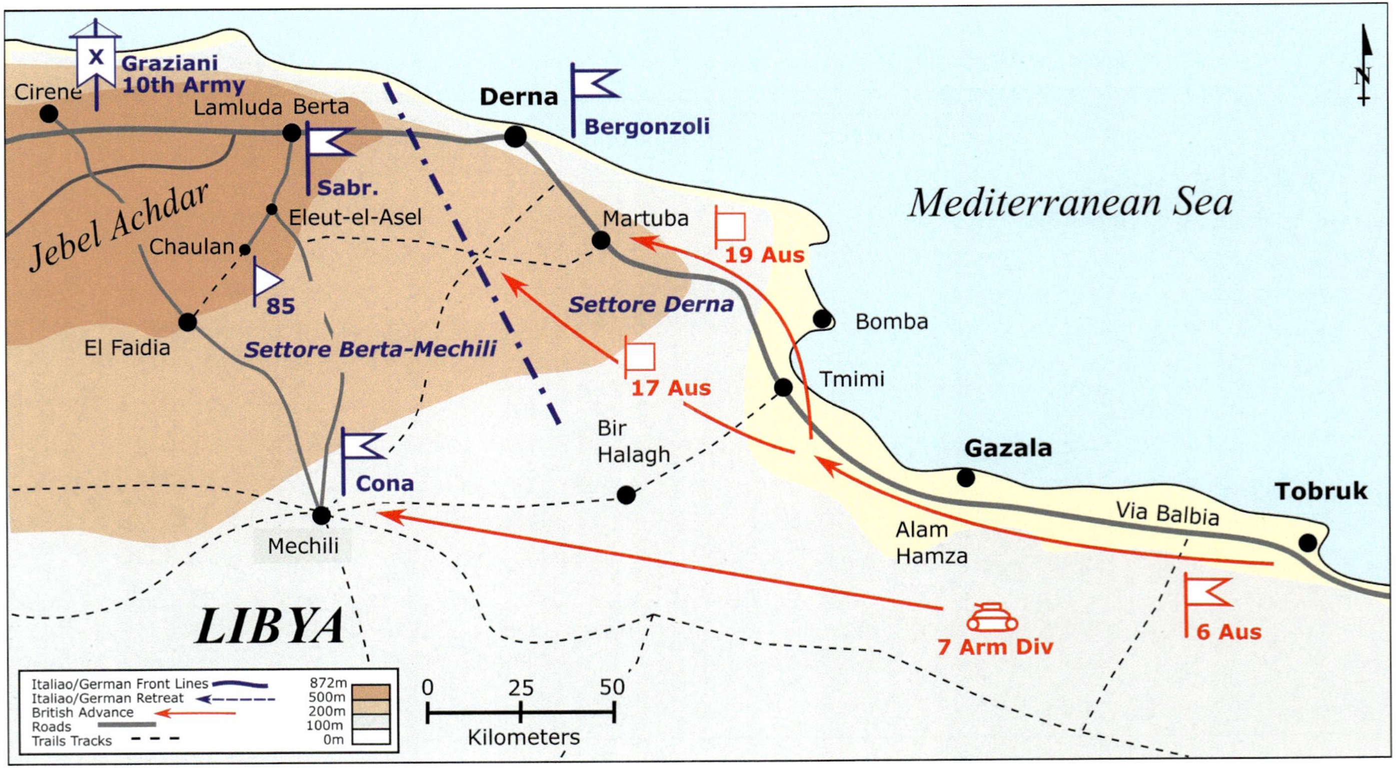

Map 4.2 Italian Defense and British Movements after the fall of Tobruk Jan 1941. (Map by Steven C. Smith)

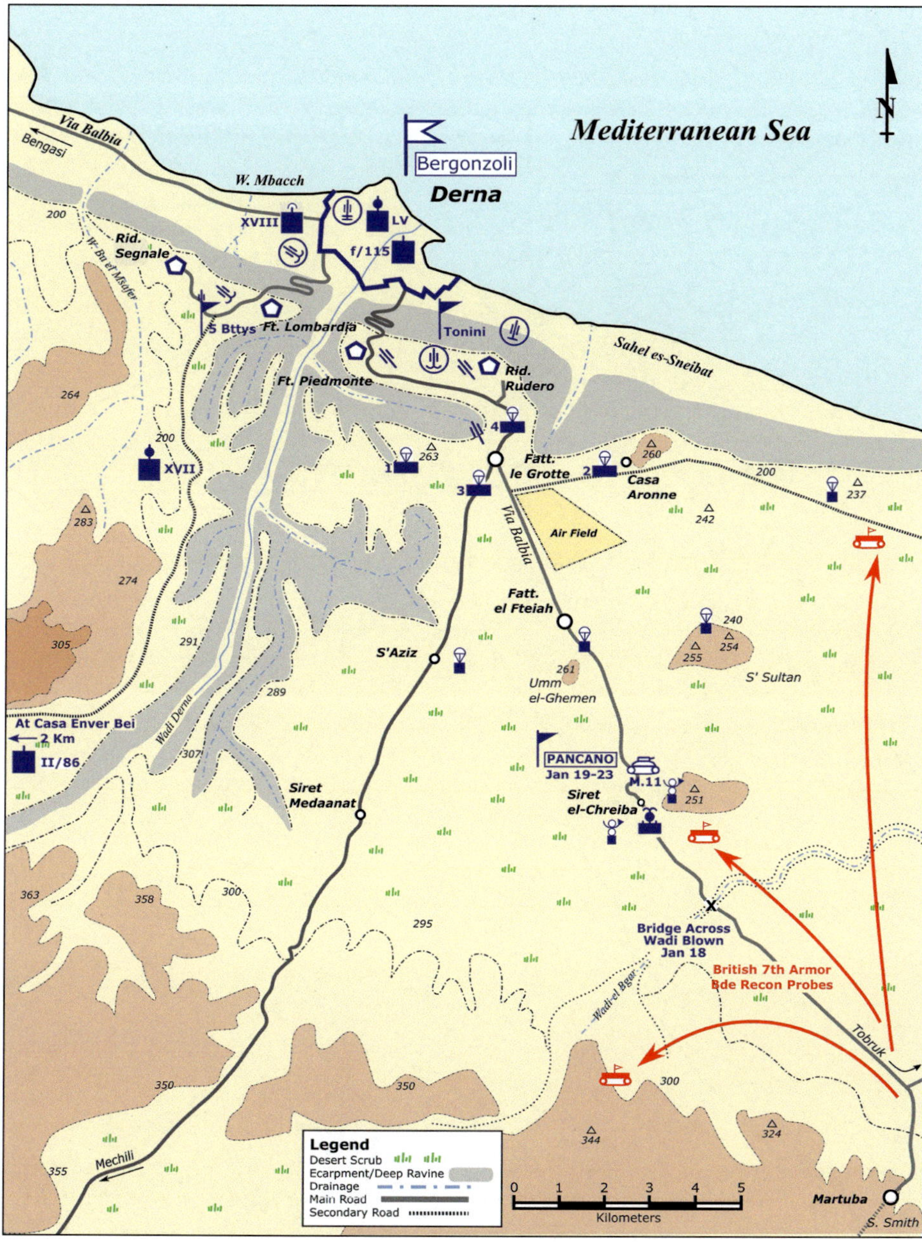

Map 4.3 Battle of Derna 18-24 Jan 1941. (Map by Steven C. Smith)

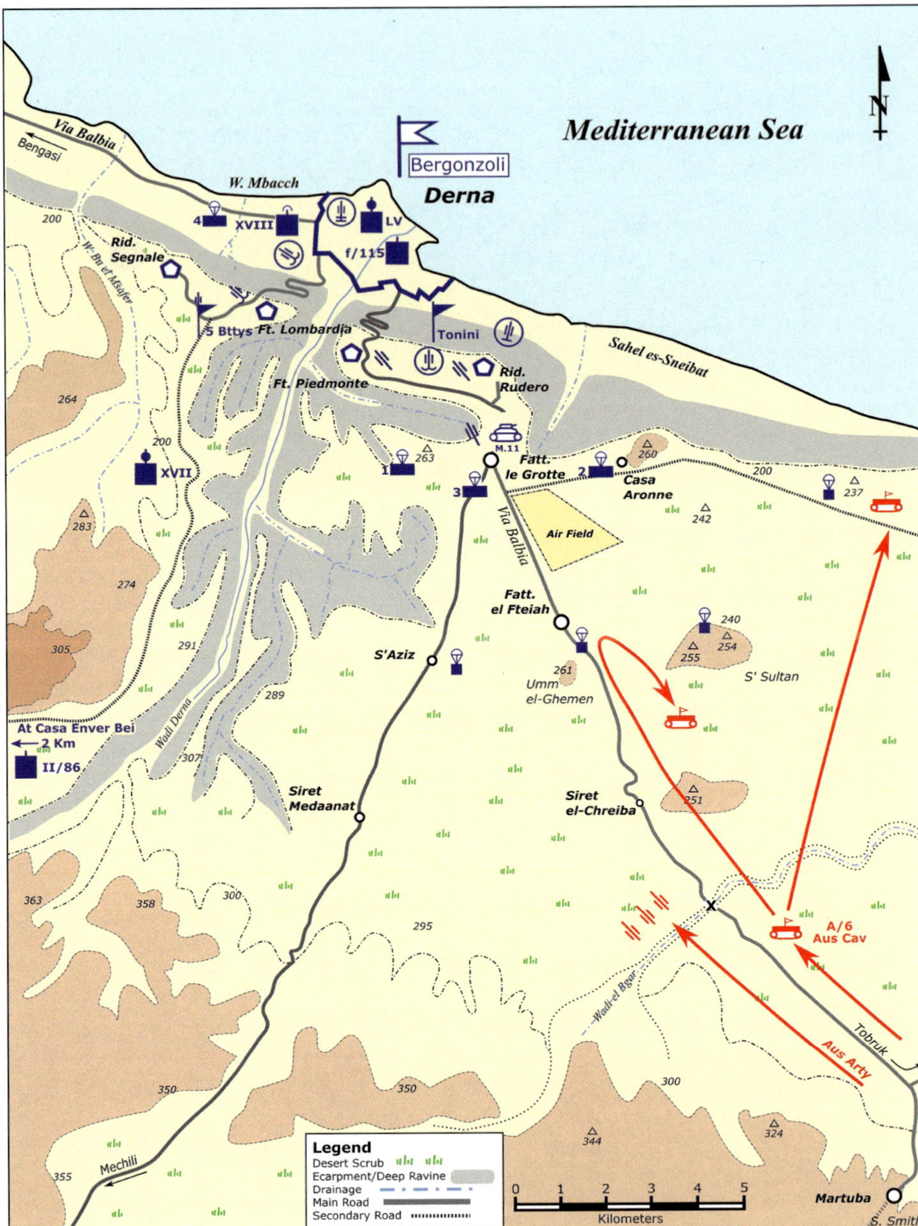

Map 4.4 Battle of Derna 25 Jan (AM) 1941. (Map by Steven C. Smith)

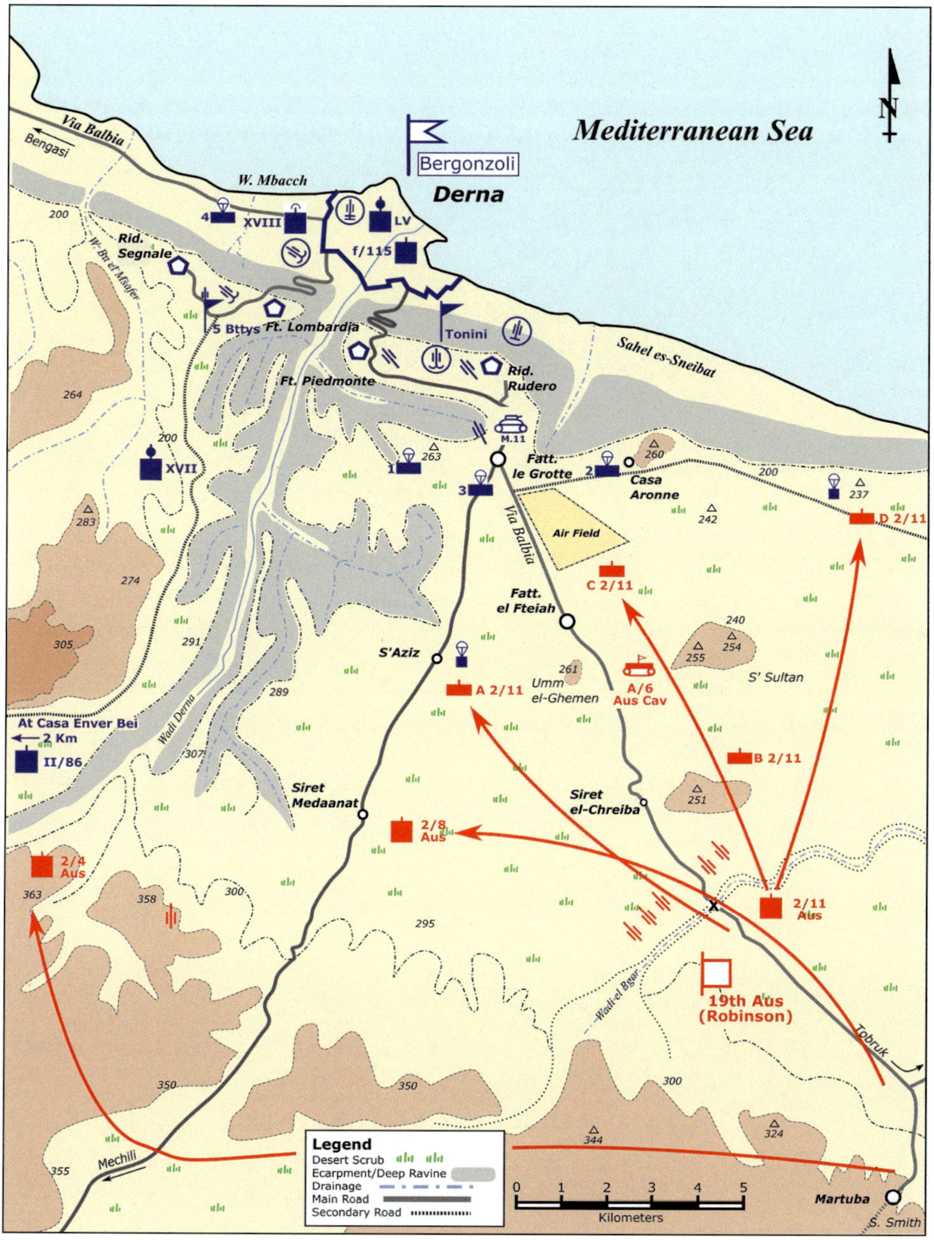

Map 4.5 Battle of Derna 25 Jan (PM) 1941. (Map by Steven C. Smith)

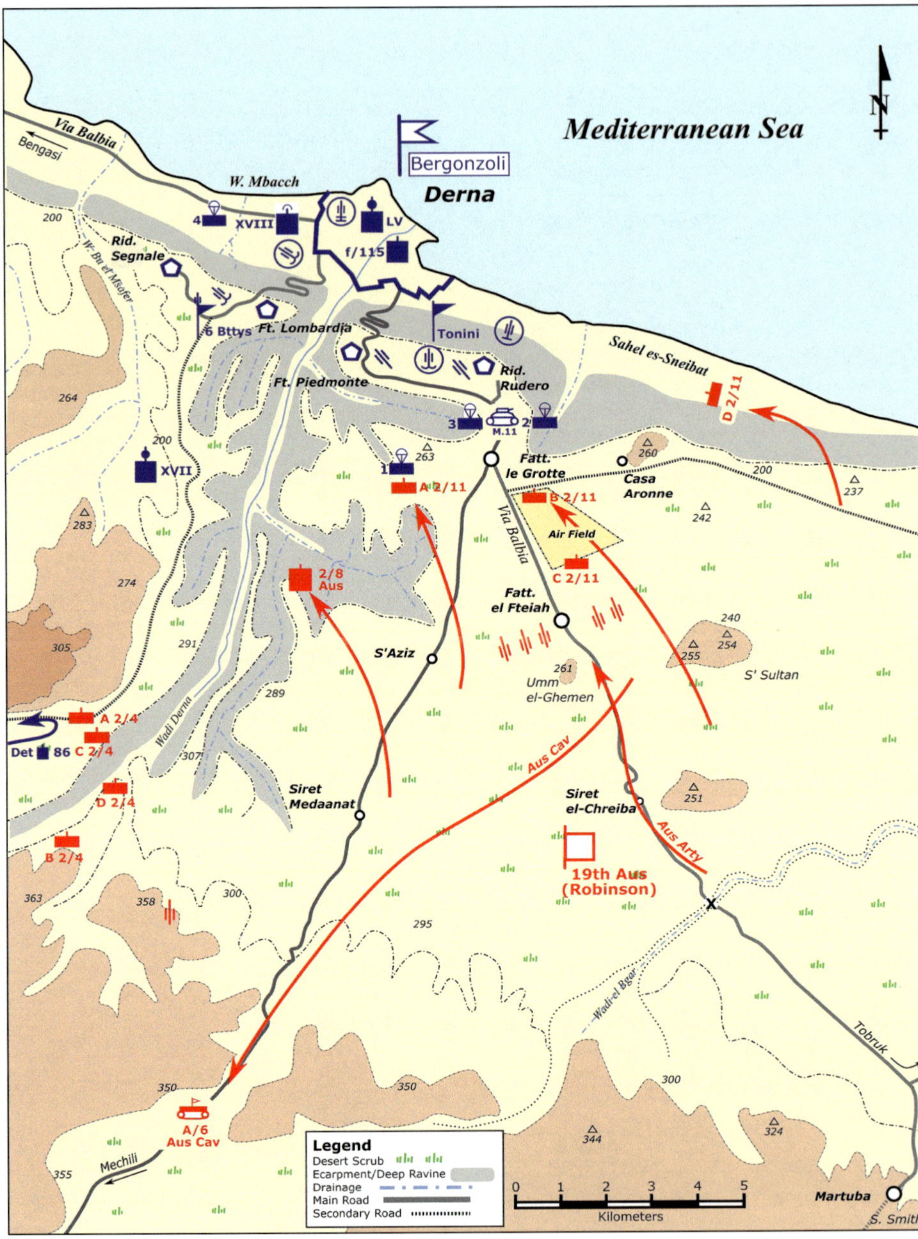

Map 4.6 Battle of Derna 26 Jan (AM) 1941. (Map by Steven C. Smith)

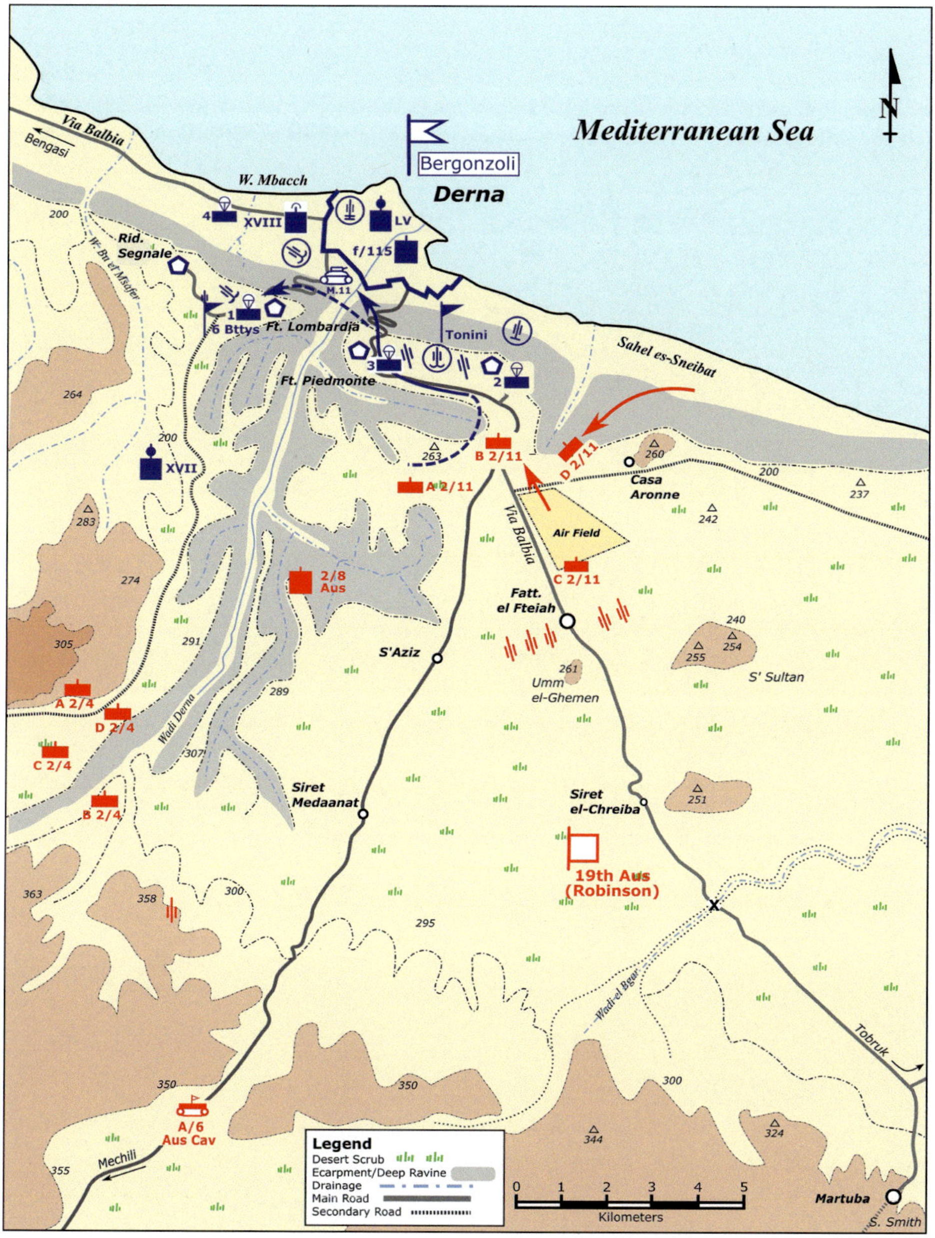

Map 4.7 Battle of Derna 26 Jan (PM) 1941. (Map by Steven C. Smith)

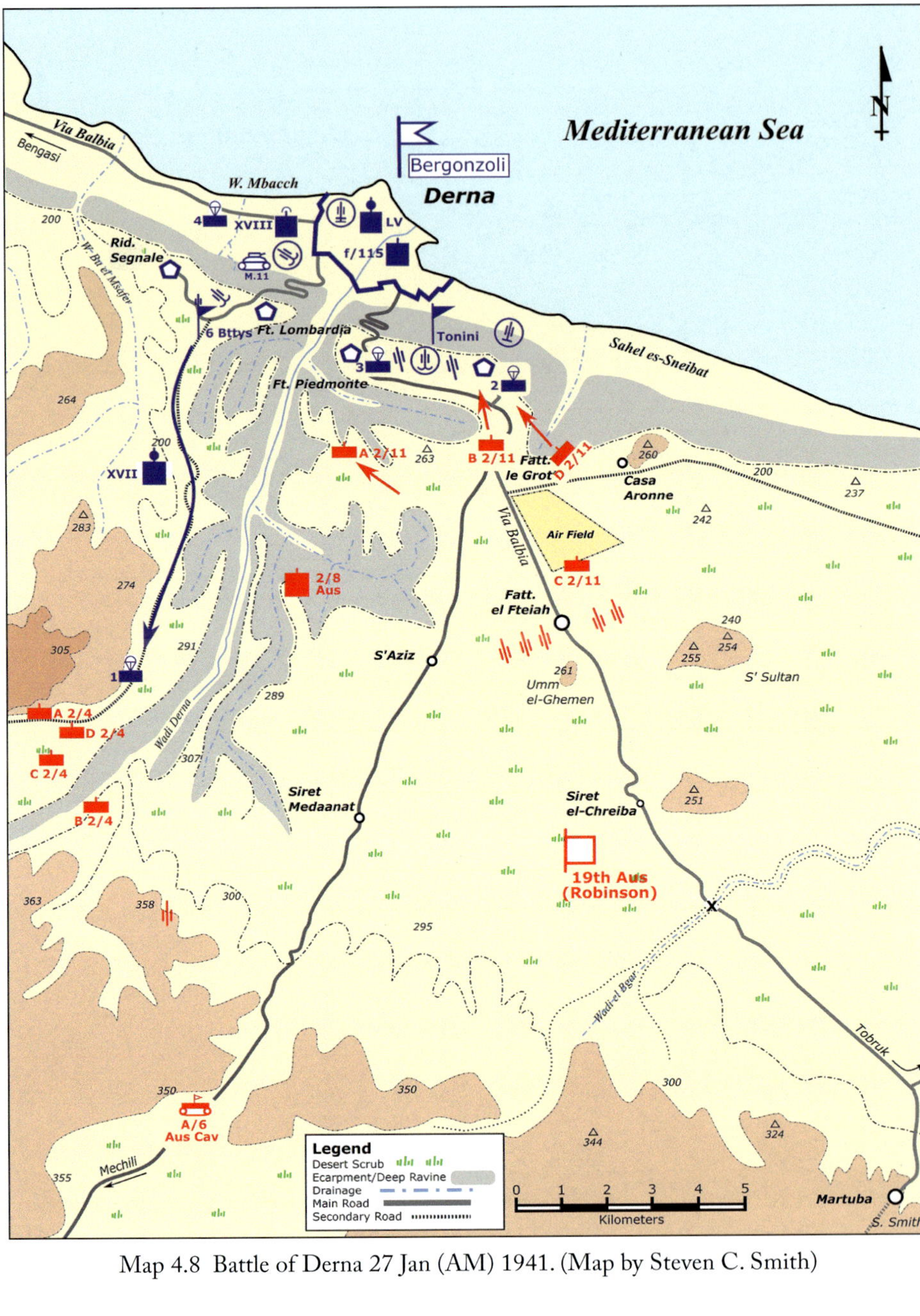

Map 4.8 Battle of Derna 27 Jan (AM) 1941. (Map by Steven C. Smith)

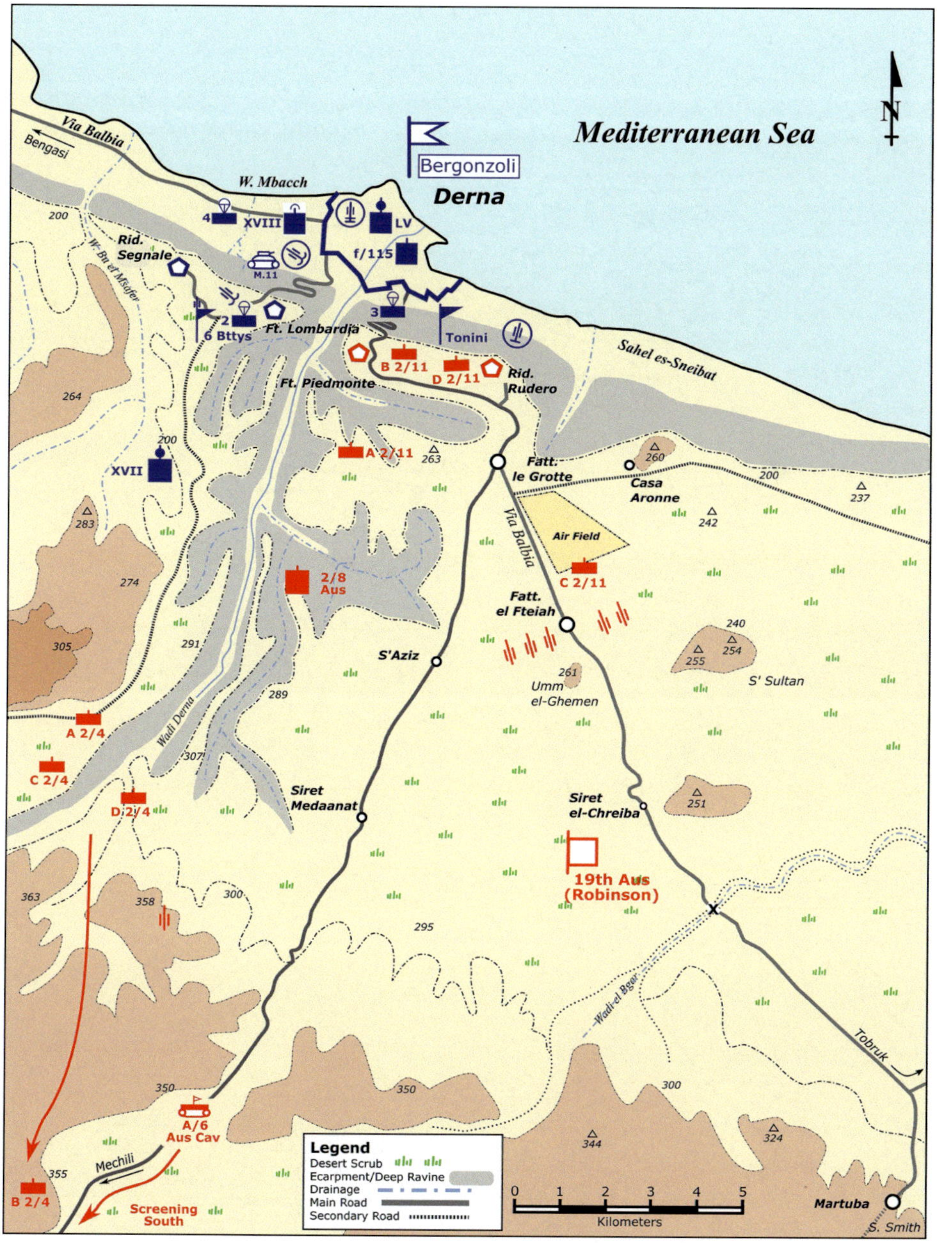

Map 4.9 Battle of Derna 27 Jan (PM) 1941. (Map by Steven C. Smith)

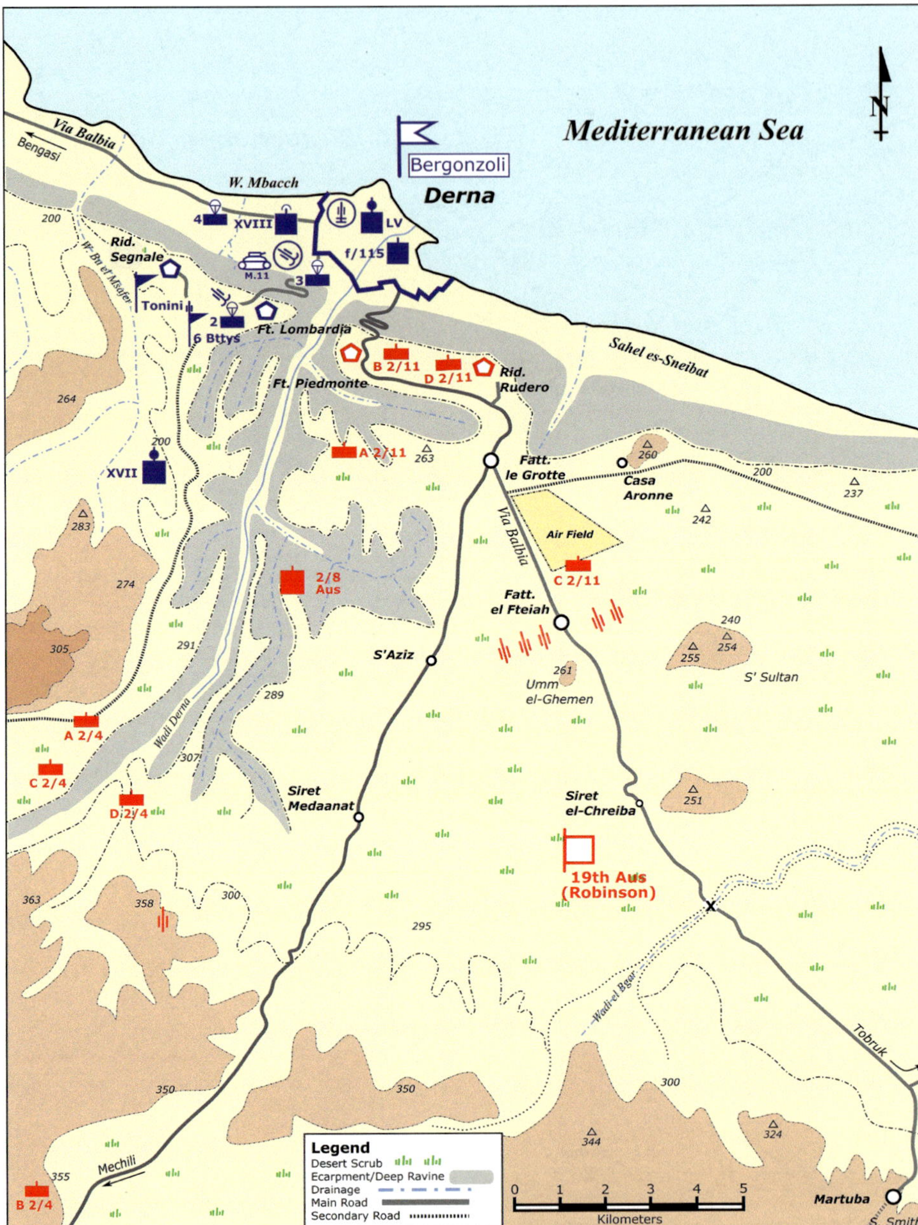

Map 4.10 Battle of Derna Situation 28-29 Jan 1941. (Map by Steven C. Smith)

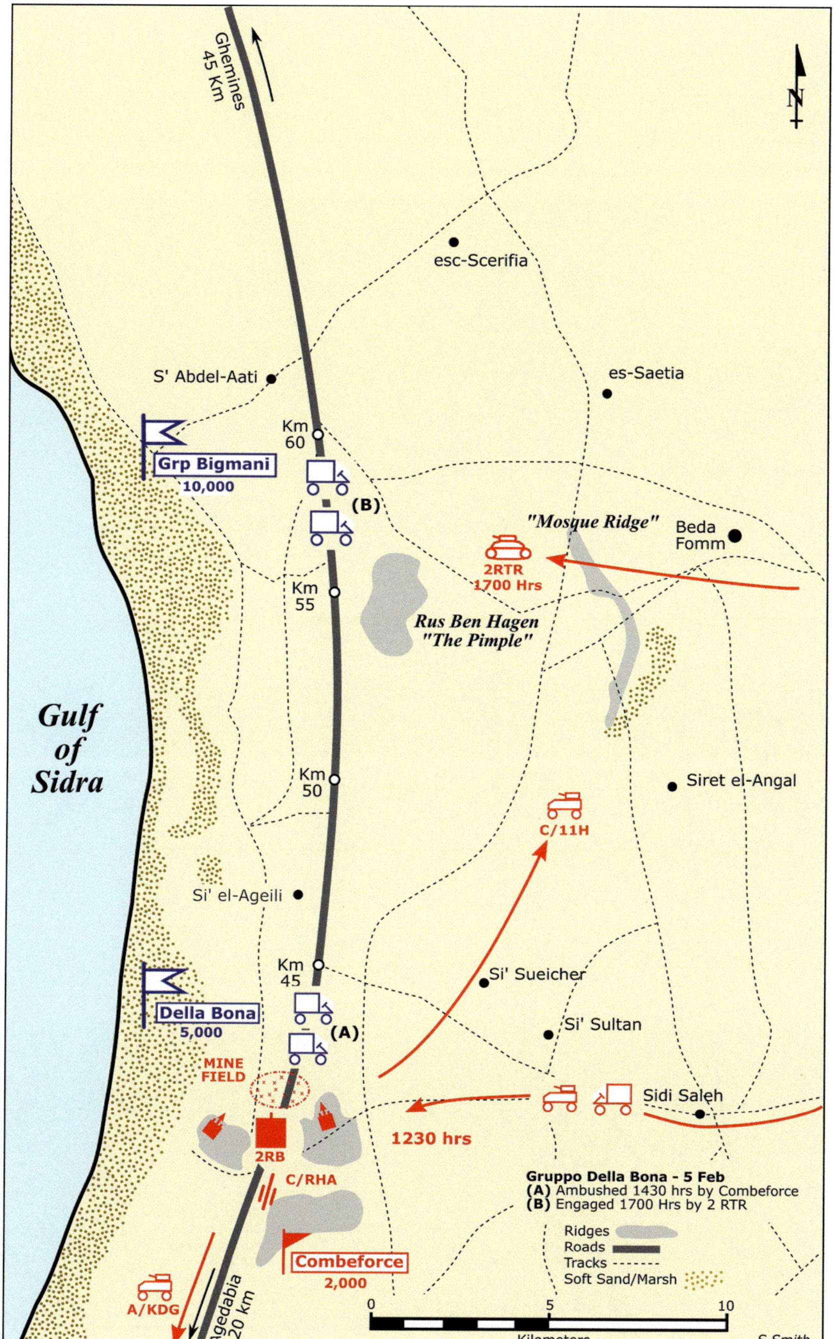

Map 4.11 Battle of Beda Fomm Overview First Day 5 Feb 1941. (Map by Steven C. Smith)

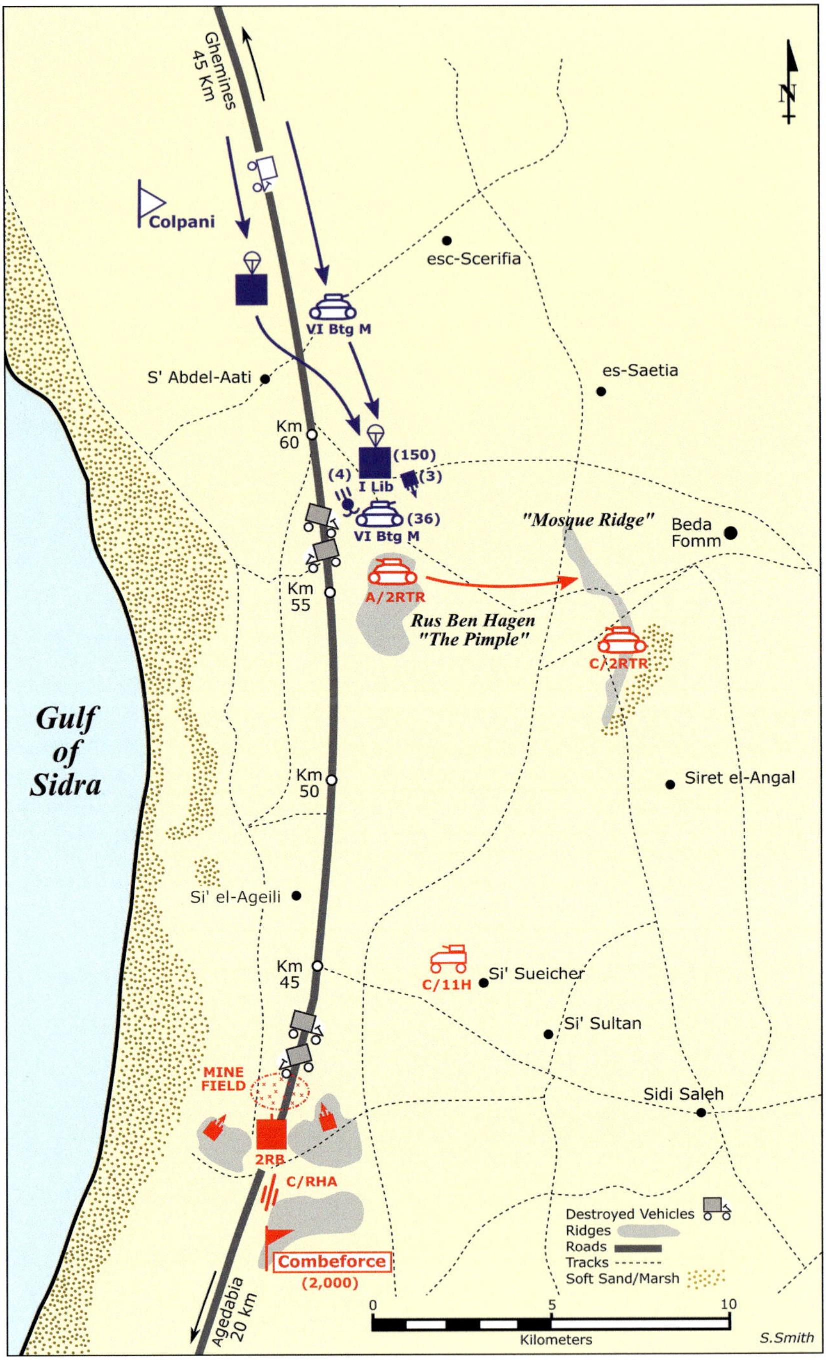

Map 4.12 Battle of Beda Fomm 0830 hrs 6 Feb 1941. (Map by Steven C. Smith)

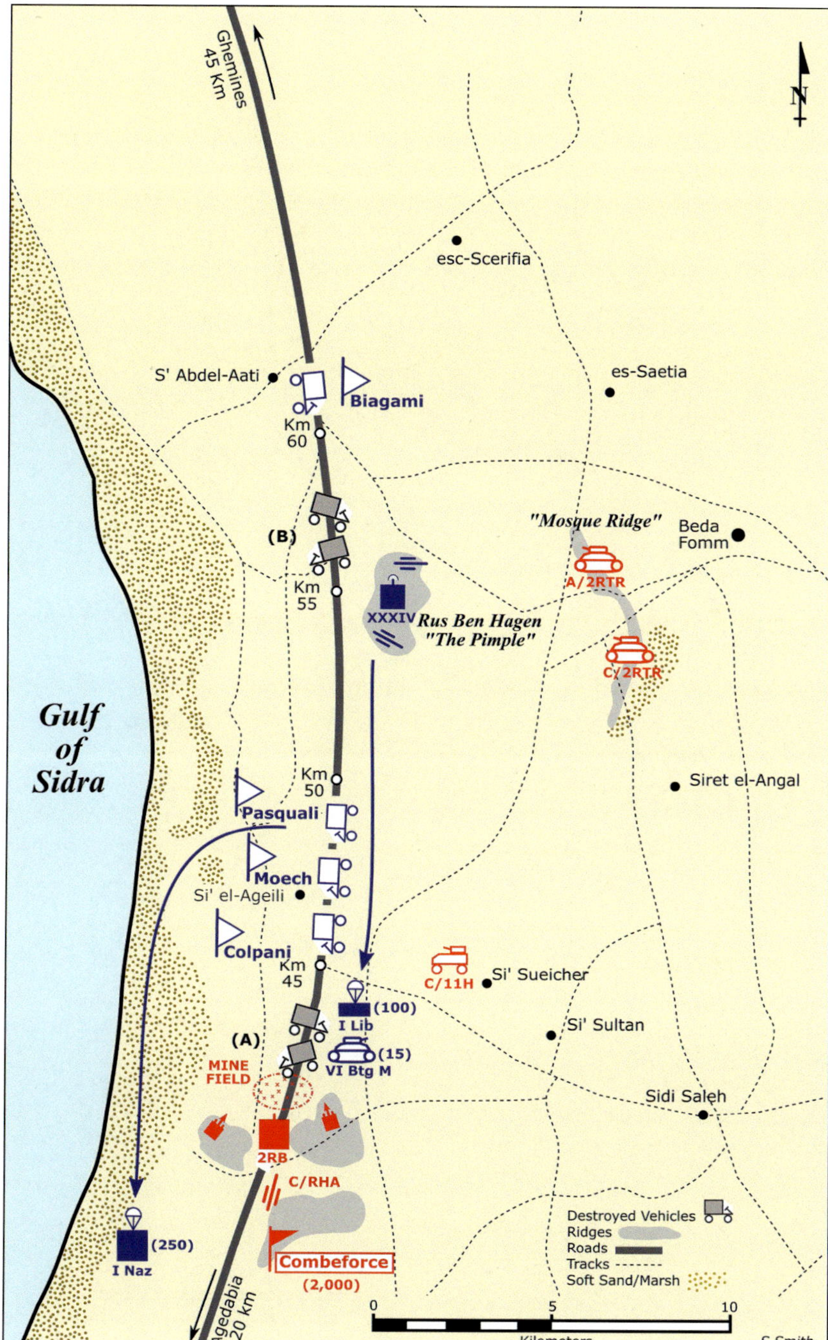

Map 4.13 Battle of Beda Fomm 1030 hrs 6 Feb 1941. (Map by Steven C. Smith)

Map 5.1 Planned Invasion of Corfu 1940. (Map by Steven C. Smith)

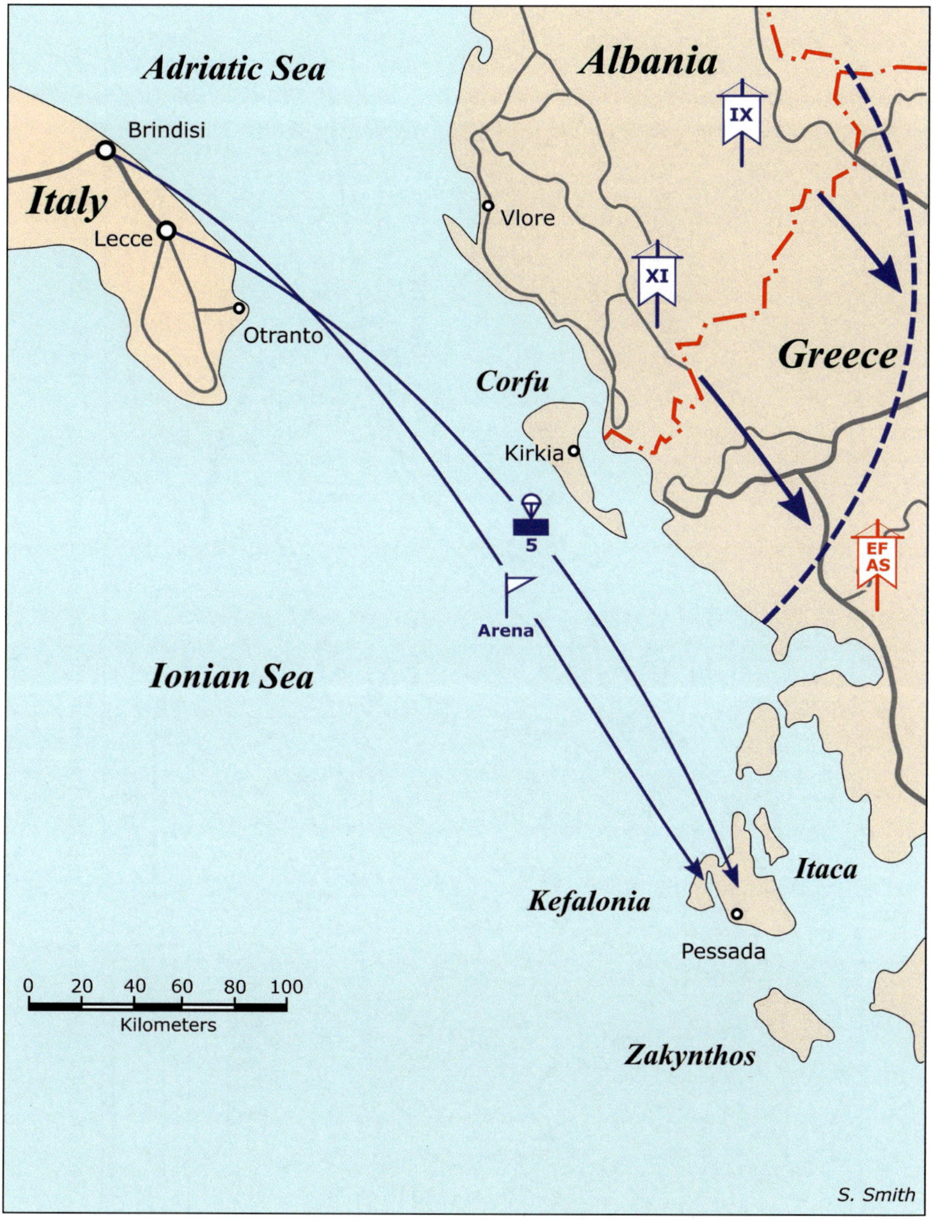

Map 5.2 Parachute Drop of the 5ª cp. Kefalonia 30 Apr 1941. (Map by Steven C. Smith)

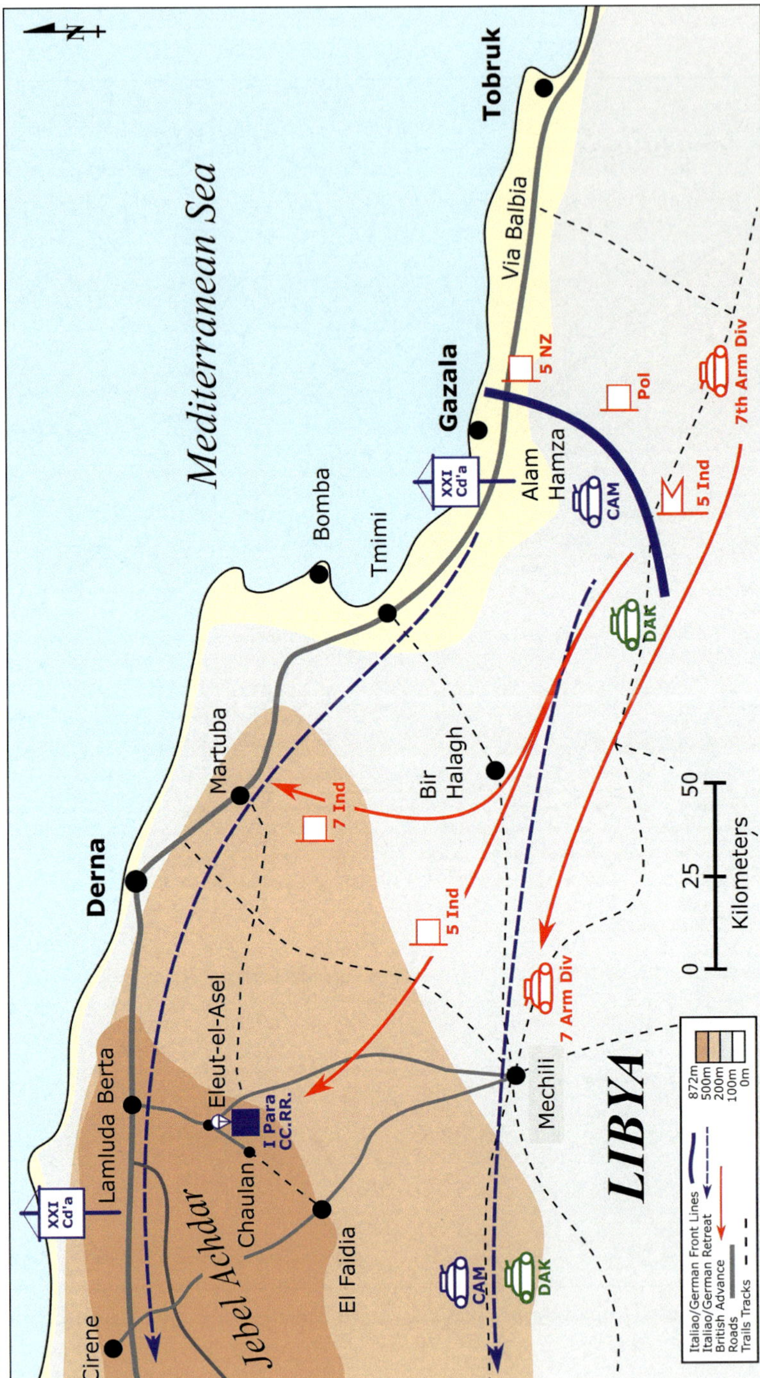

Map 6.1 Italian Defense and British Movements after Operation Crusader Dec 17–19 1941. (Map by Steven C. Smith)

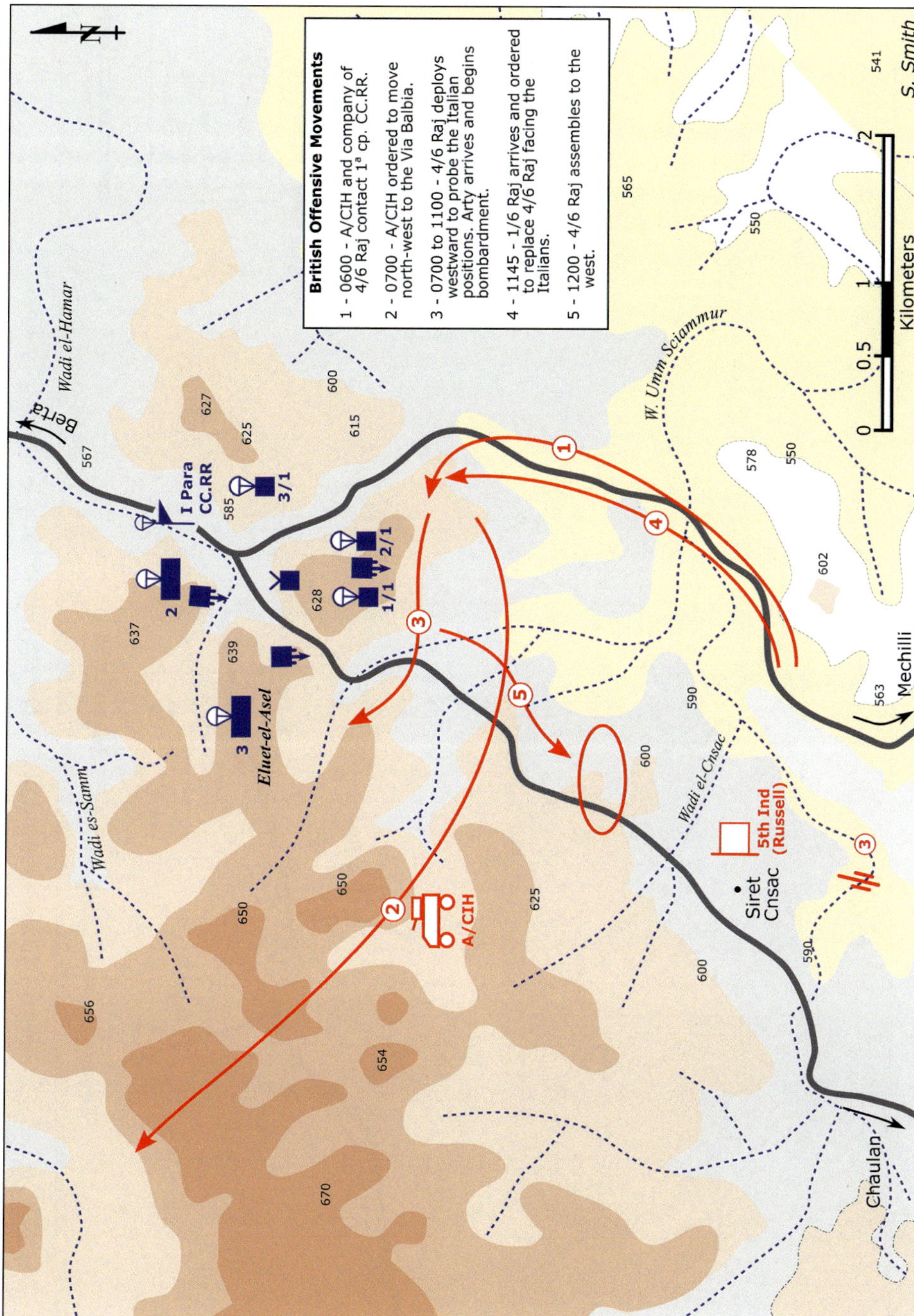

Map 6.2 Battle of Eluet el Asel 19 Dec (AM) 1941. (Map by Steven C. Smith)

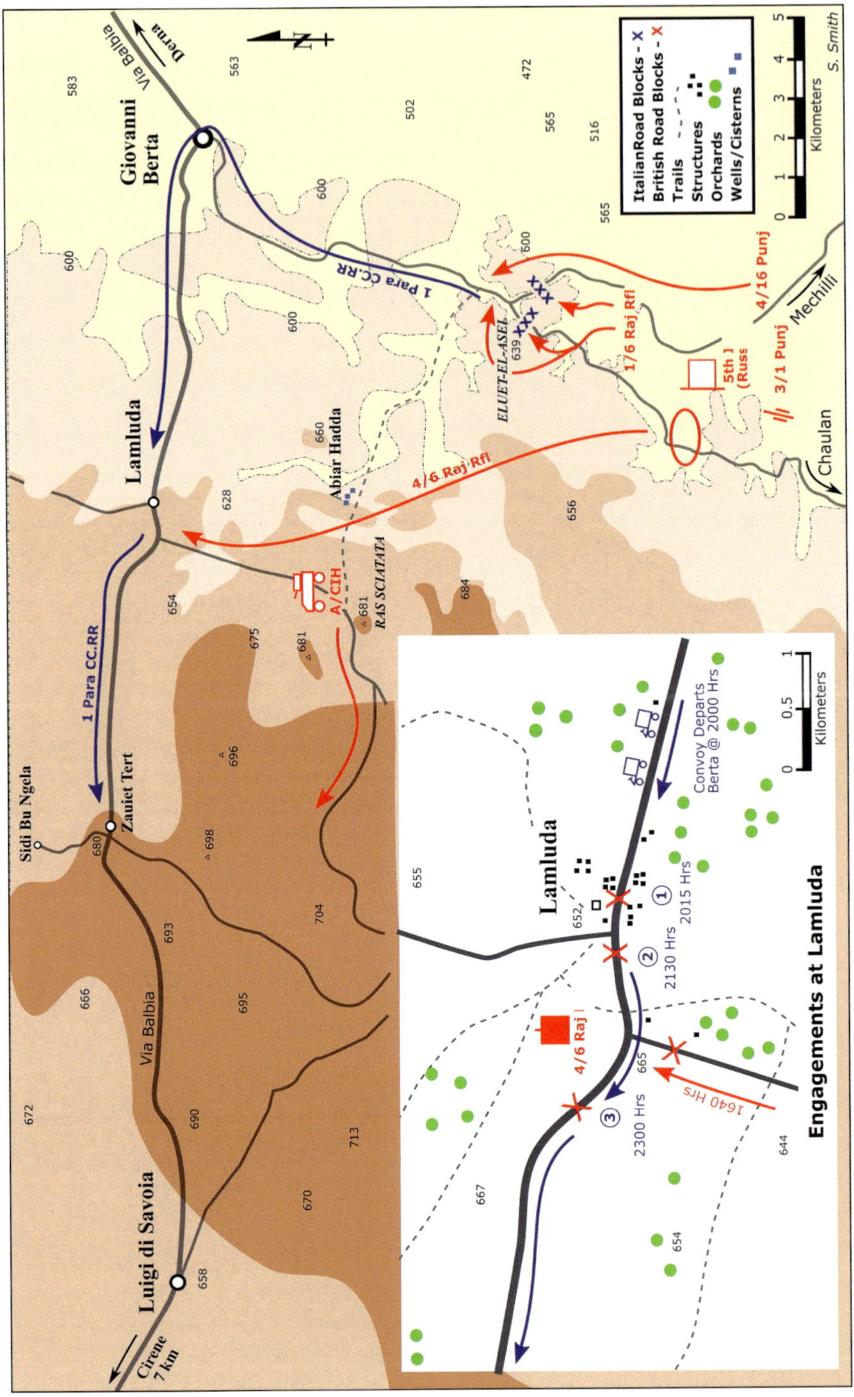

Map 6.3 Battle of Eluet el Asel 19 Dec (PM) 1941. (Map by Steven C. Smith)

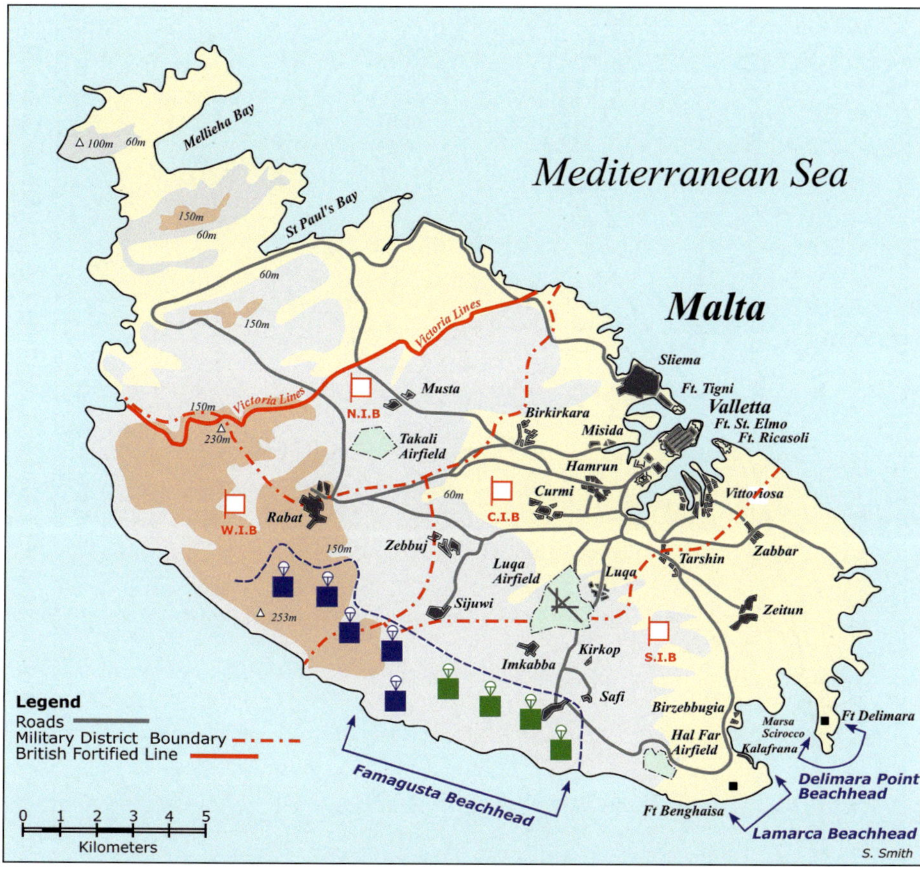

Map 9.1 Planned Invasion of Malta (Operazione «C3») Summer 1942. (Map by Steven C. Smith)

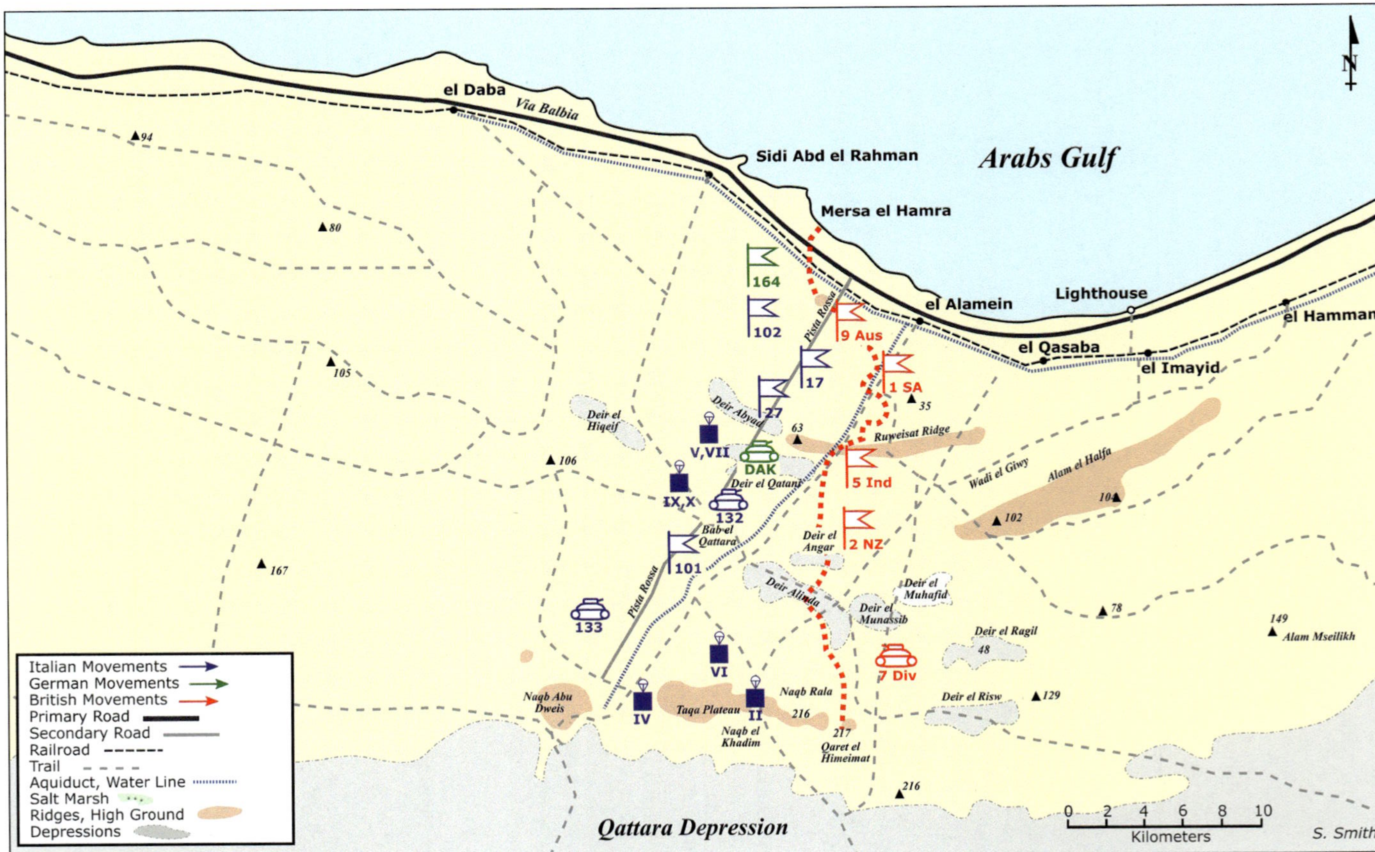

Map 10.1 Overview of Situation at El Alamein 1 Aug 1942. (Map by Steven C. Smith)

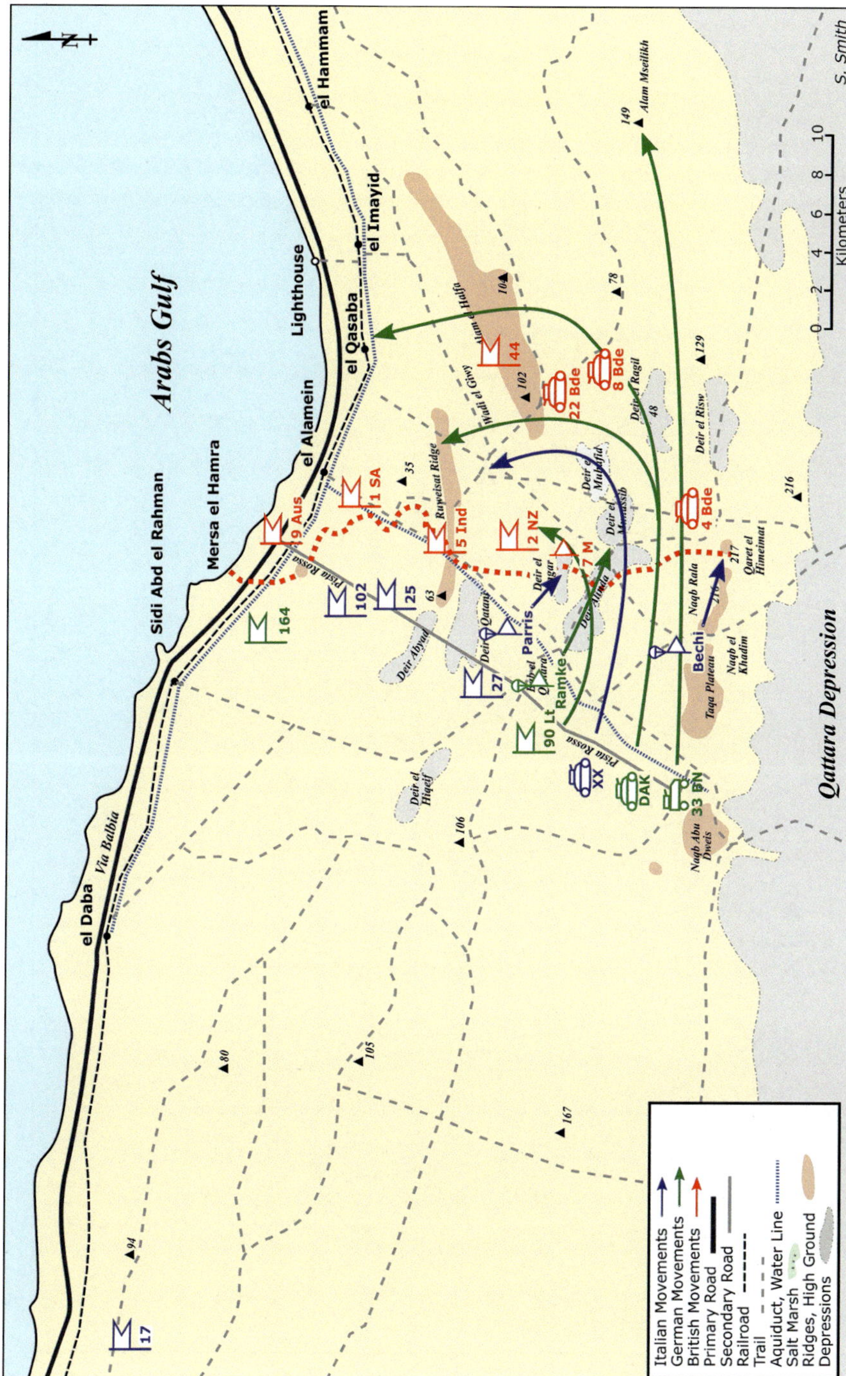

Map 10.2 Planned Italo-German Attack 30 Aug 1942. (Map by Steven C. Smith)

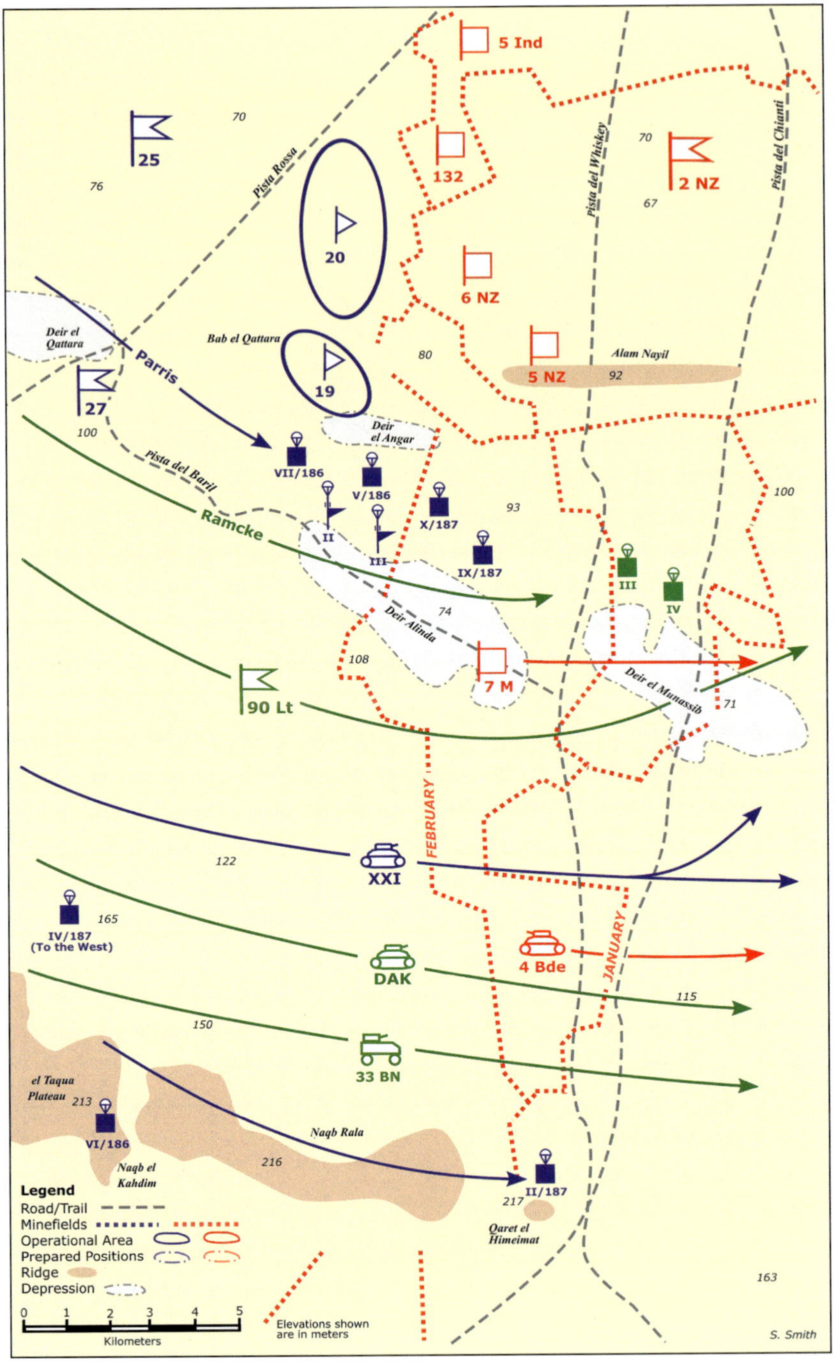

Map 10.3 Battle of 2nd Alamein 31 Aug PM 1942. (Map by Steven C. Smith)

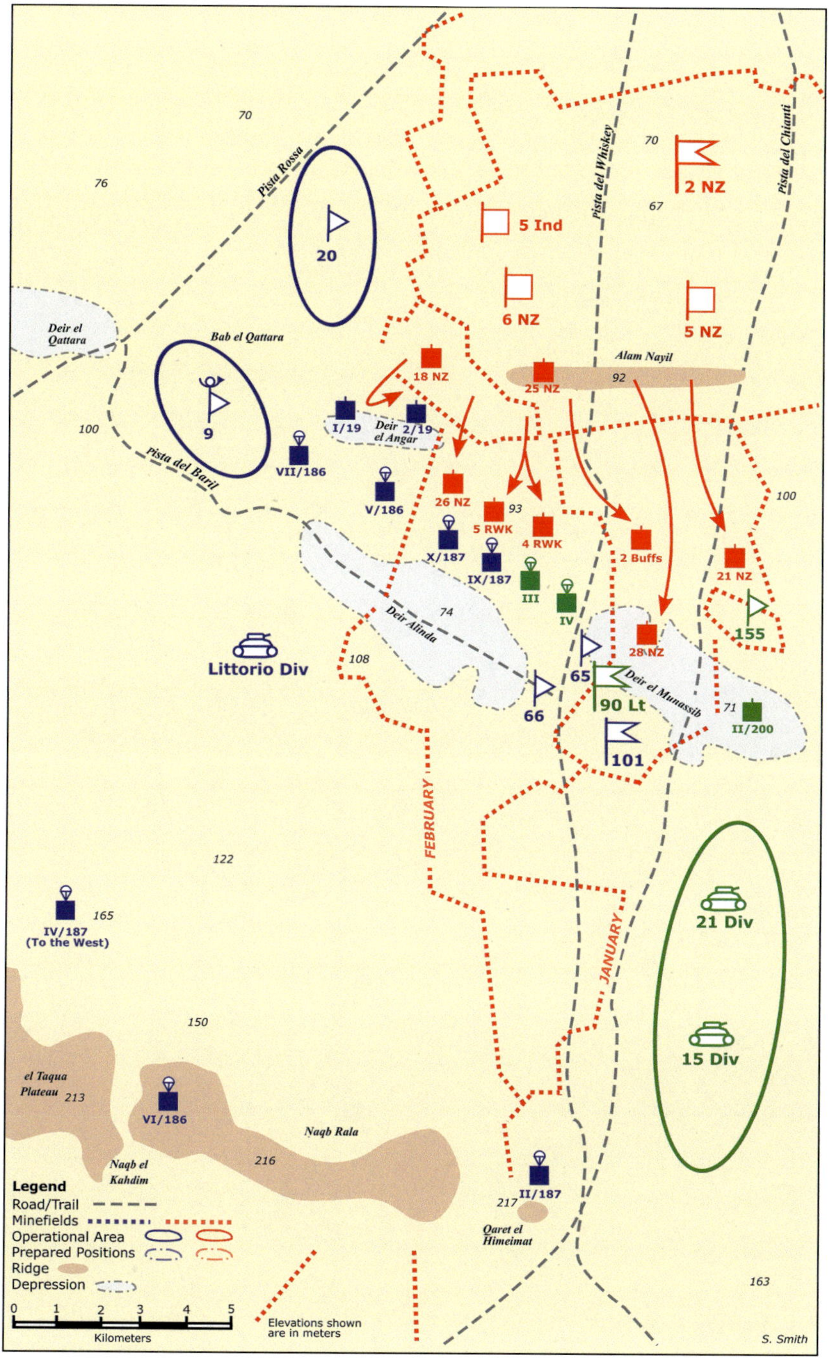

Map 10.4 Battle of 2nd Alamein 3 Sep 1942. (Map by Steven C. Smith)

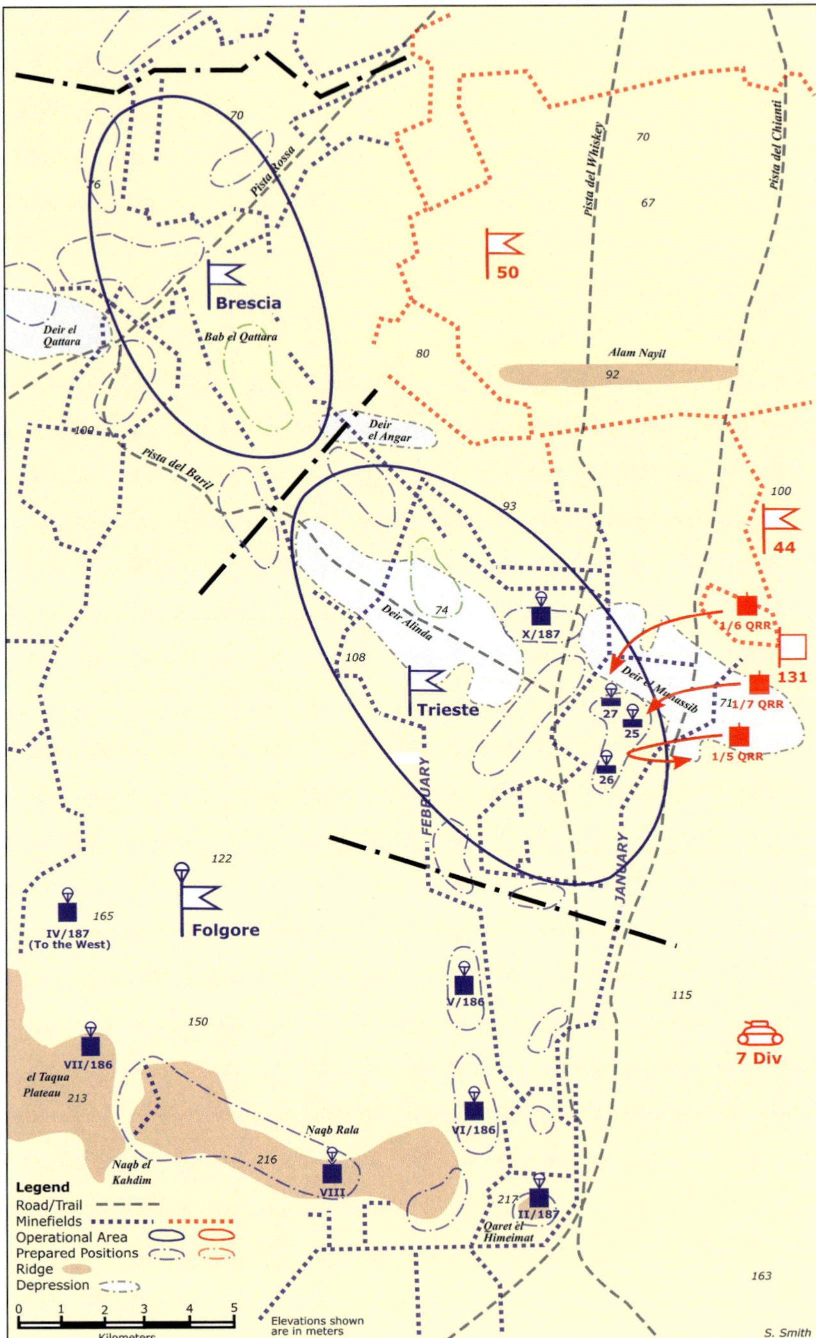

Map 10.5 Operation Braganza 30 Sep 1942. (Map by Steven C. Smith)

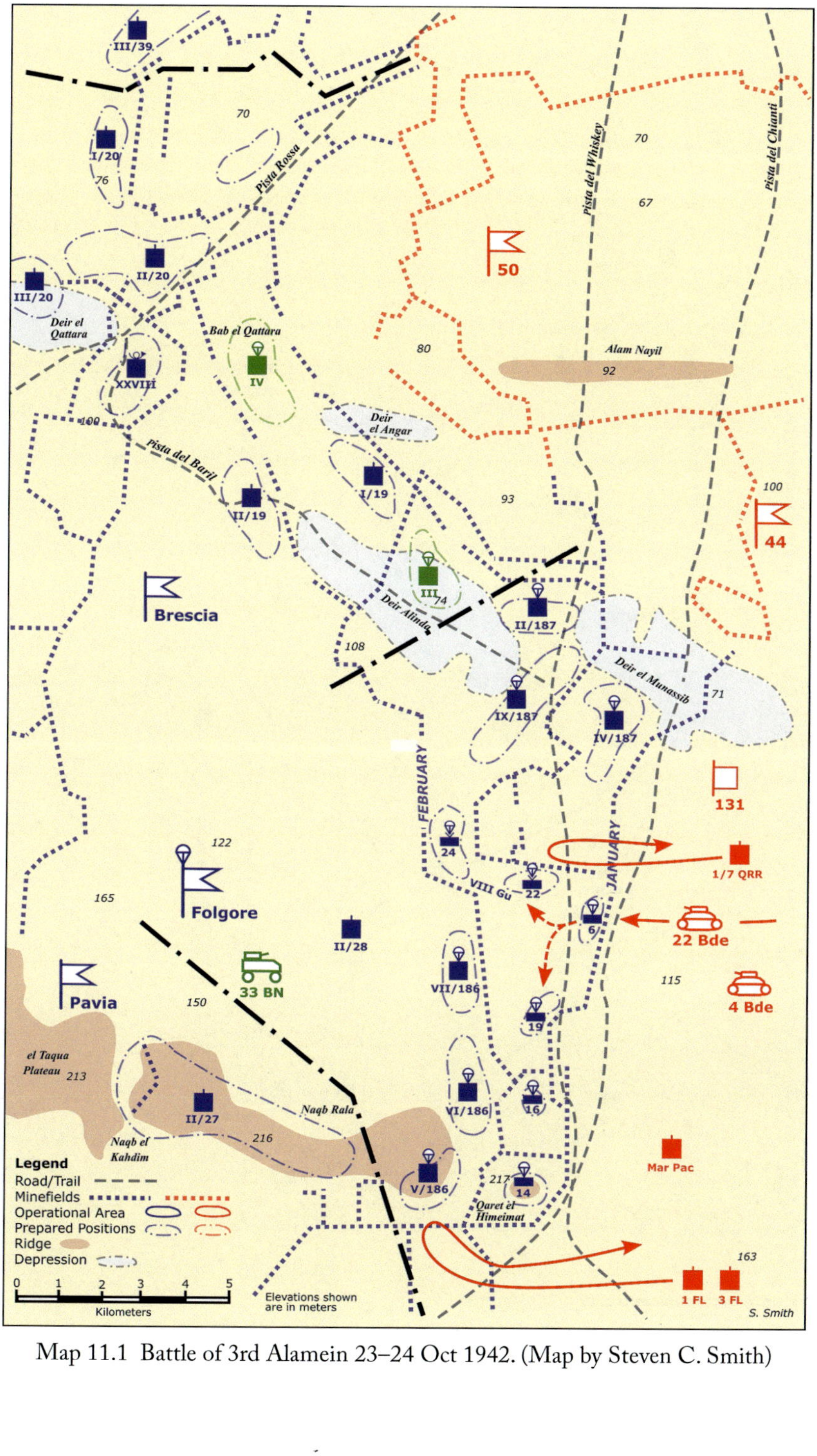

Map 11.1 Battle of 3rd Alamein 23–24 Oct 1942. (Map by Steven C. Smith)

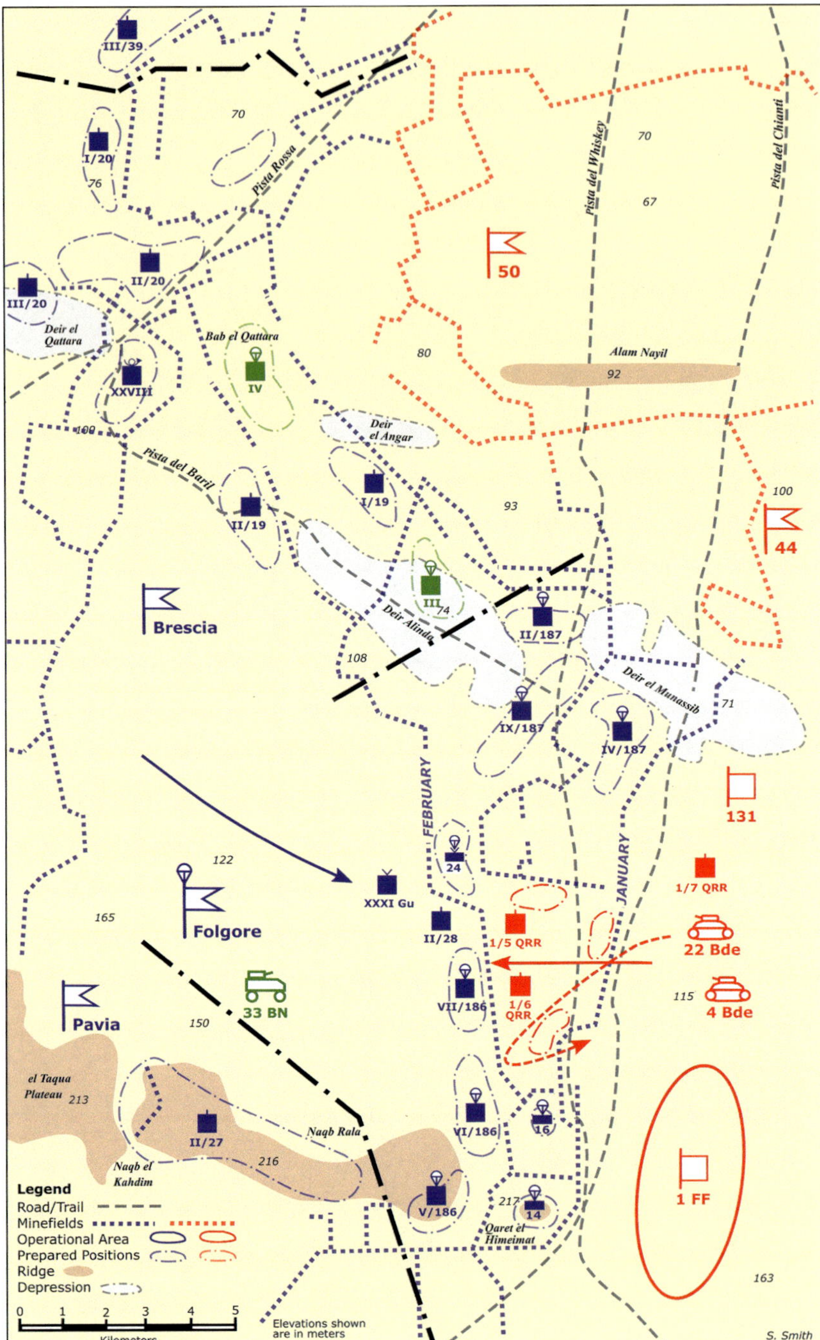

Map 11.2 Battle of 3rd Alamein 24–25 Oct 1942. (Map by Steven C. Smith)

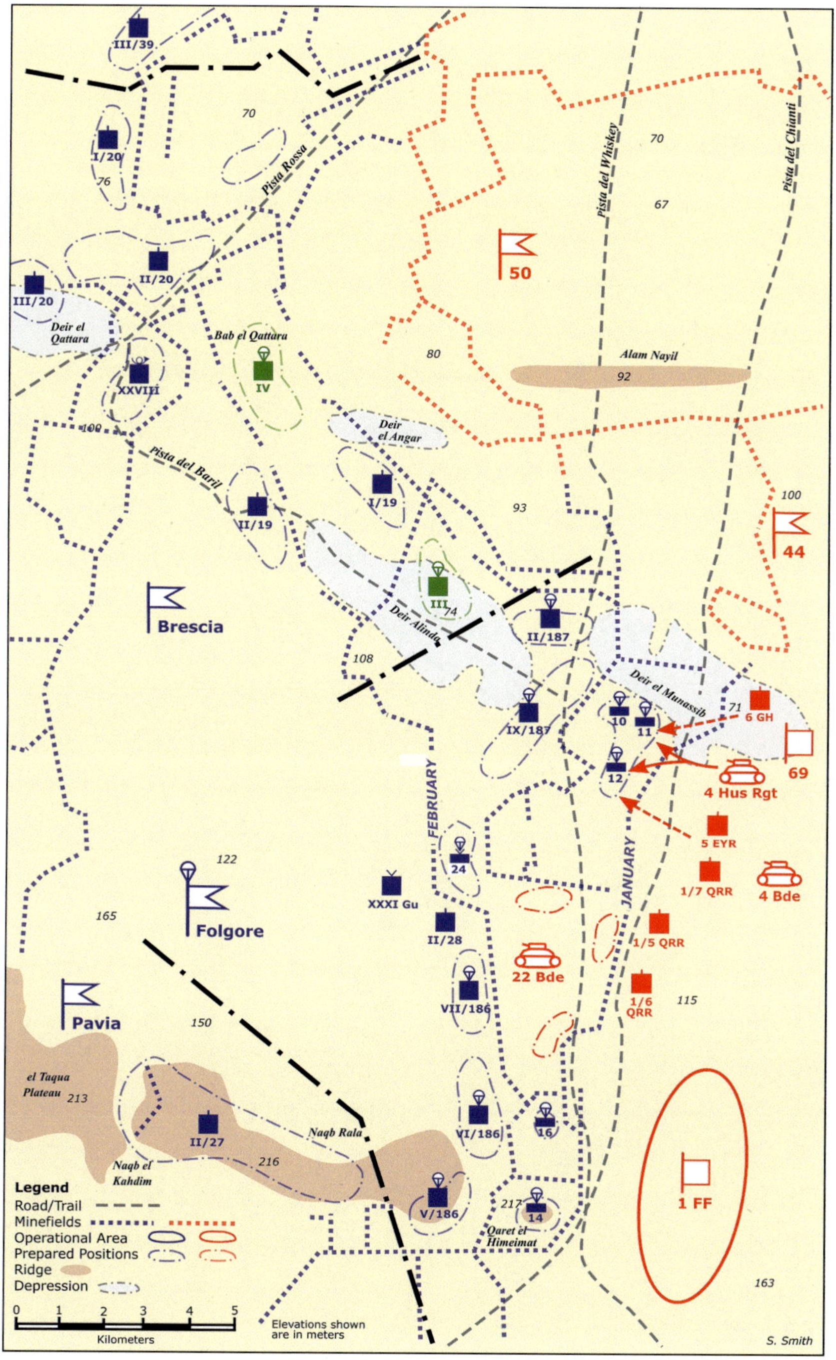

Map 11.3 Battle of 3rd Alamein 25–26 Oct 1942. (Map by Steven C. Smith)

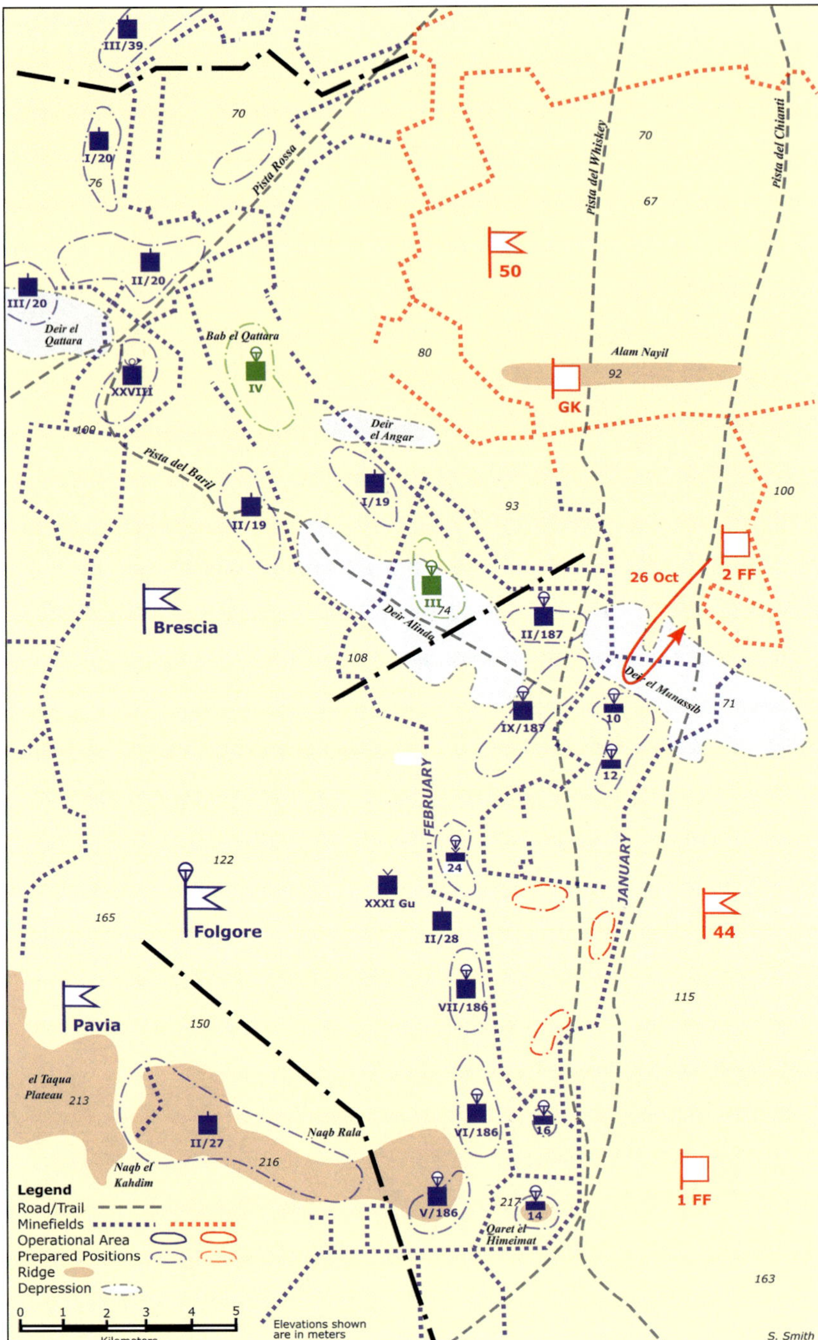

Map 11.4 Battle of 3rd Alamein 26–30 Oct 1942. (Map by Steven C. Smith)

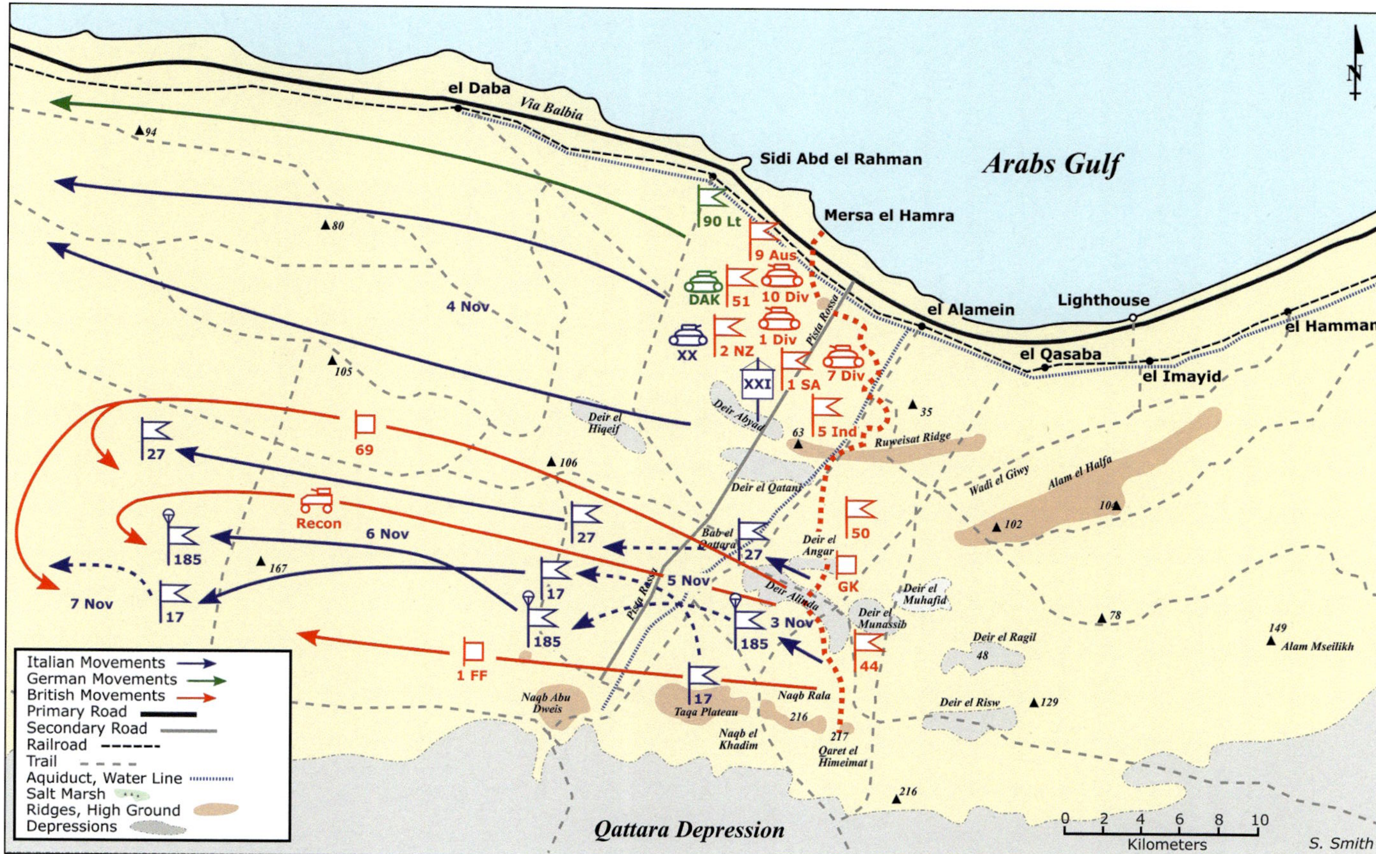

Map 11.5 Battle of 3rd Alamein Italo-German Retreat 4–7 Nov 1942. (Map by Steven C. Smith)

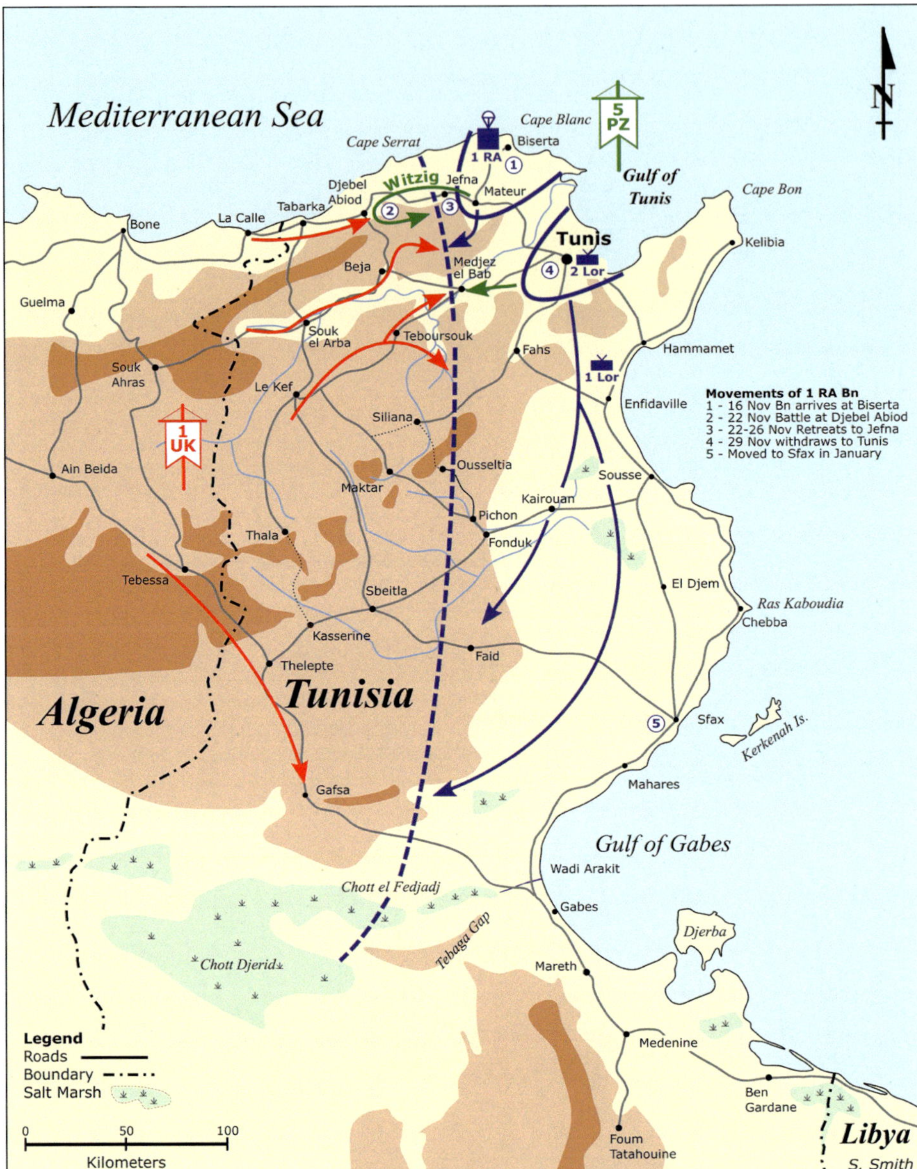

Map 12.1 Overview of the Situation in Tunisia 10 Nov 1942–12 Jan 1943.
(Map by Steven C. Smith)

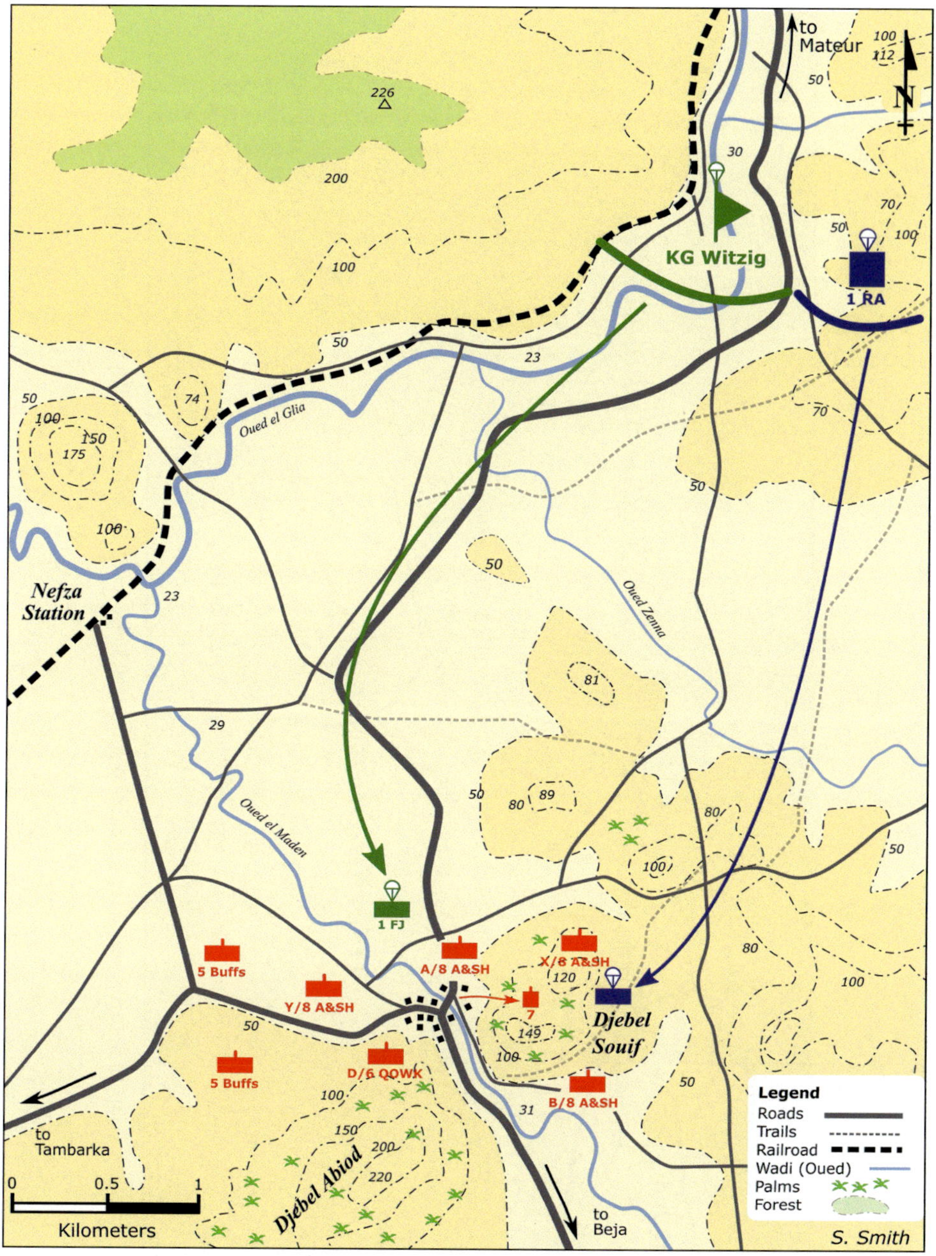

Map 12.2 Battle of Djebel Abiod 22 Nov 1942. (Map by Steven C. Smith)

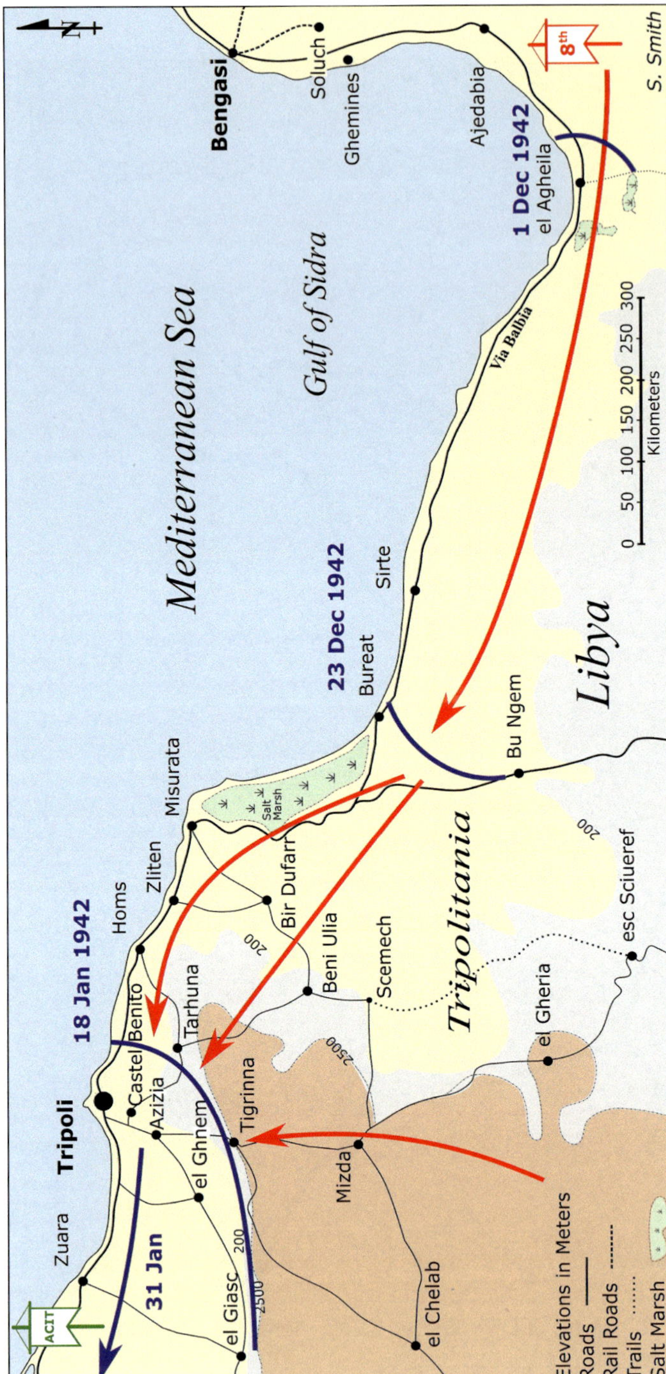

Map 12.3 Overview of the Panzerarmee Retreat 1 Dec 1942–31 Jan 1943. (Map by Steven C. Smith)

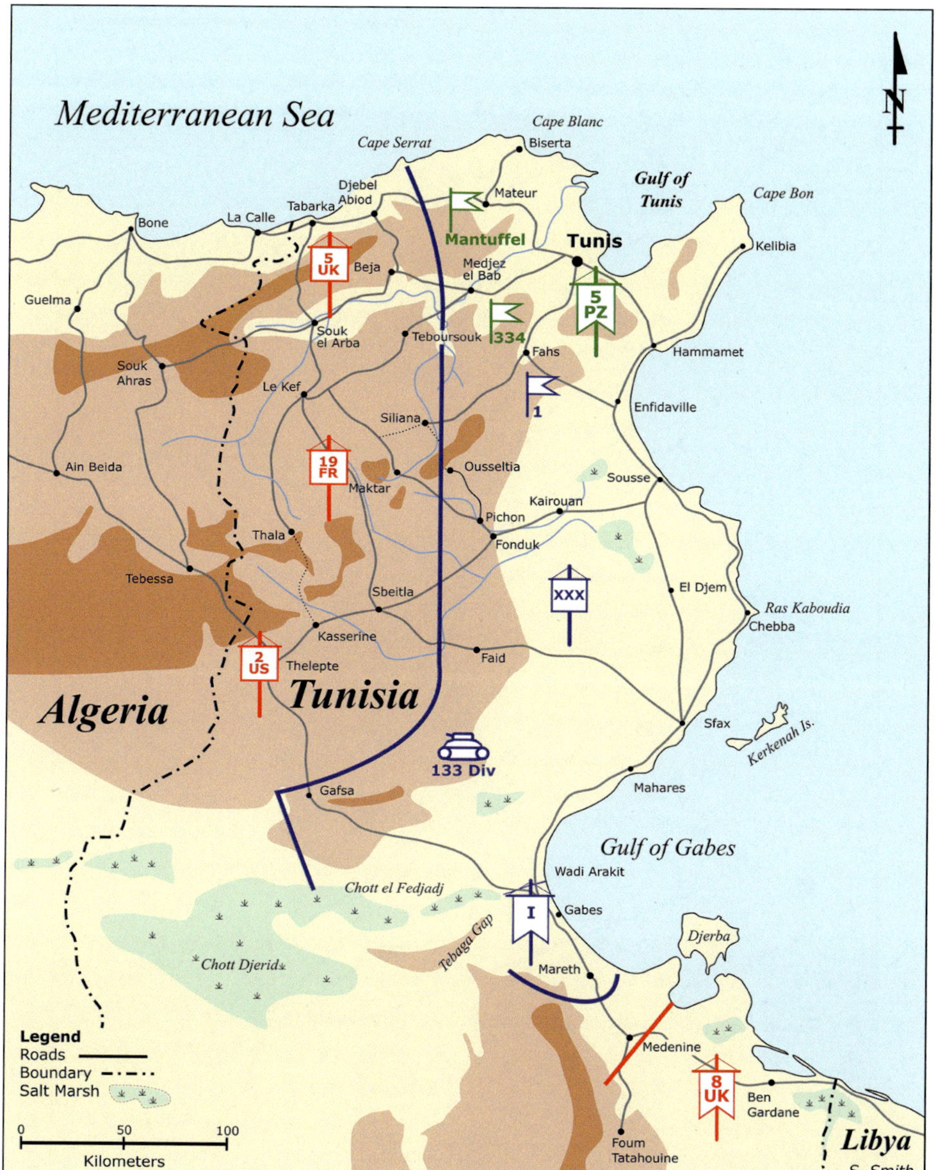

Map 12.4 Overview of the Situation in Tunisia 1 March 1943. (Map by Steven C. Smith)

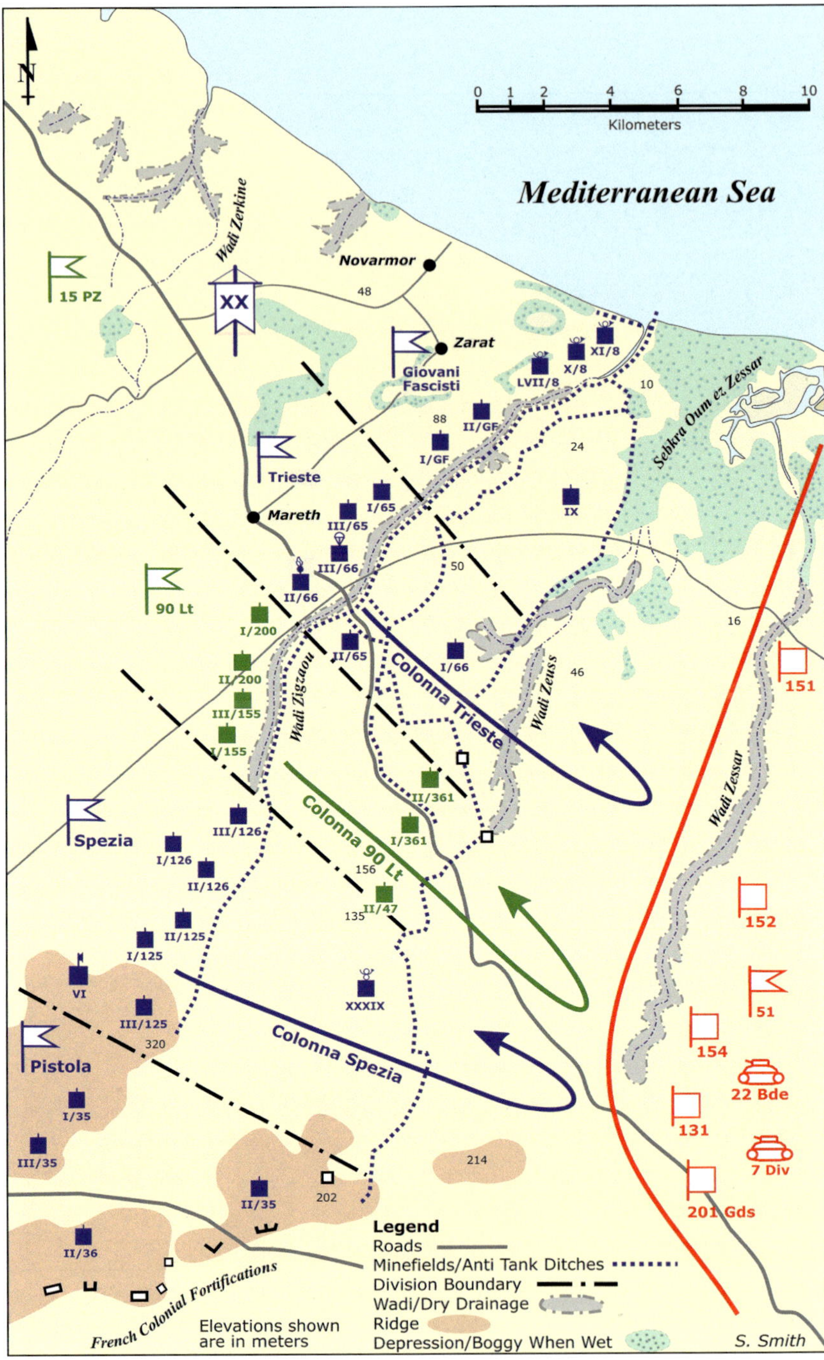

Map 12.5 Operation Capri 6 March 1943. (Map by Steven C. Smith)

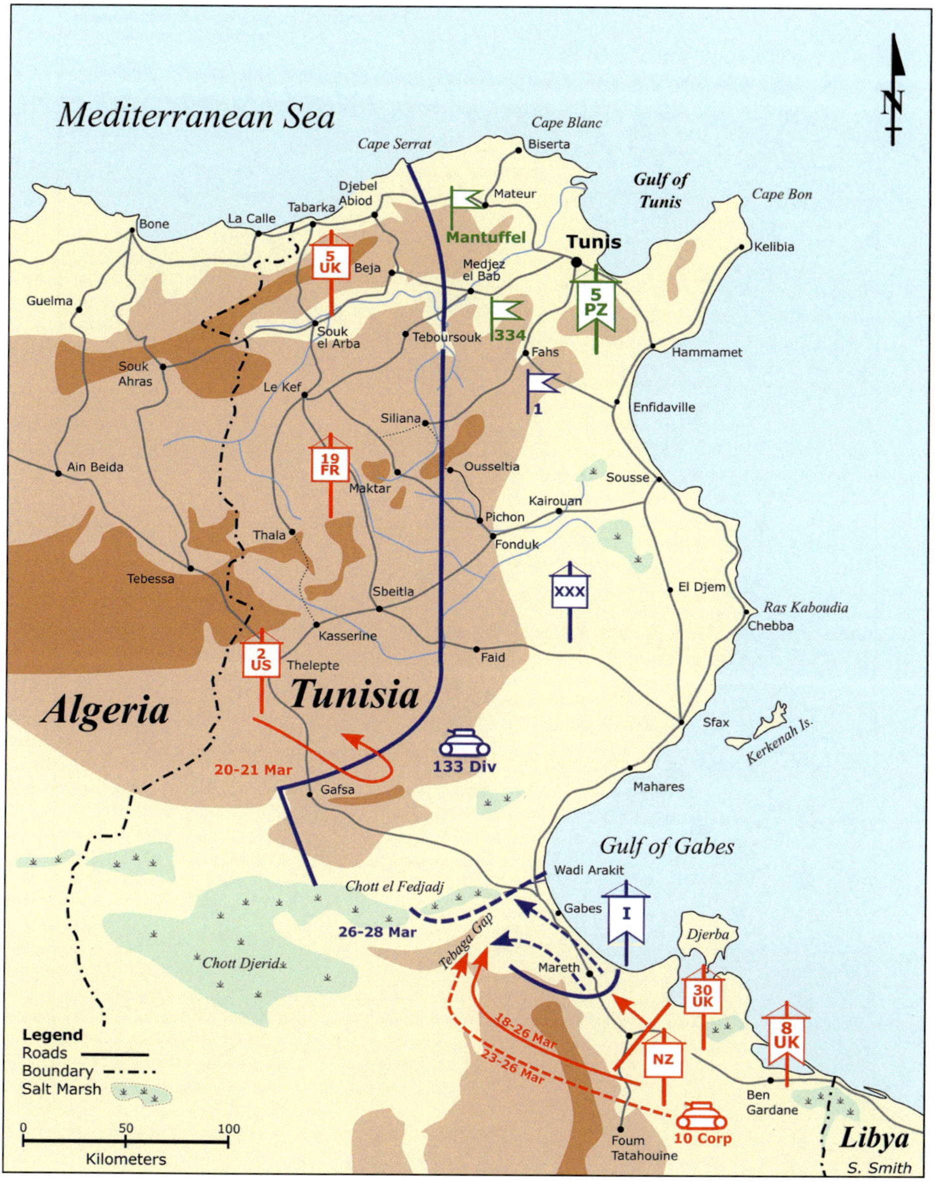

Map 12.6 Battle of Mareth 16–28 March 1943. (Map by Steven C. Smith)

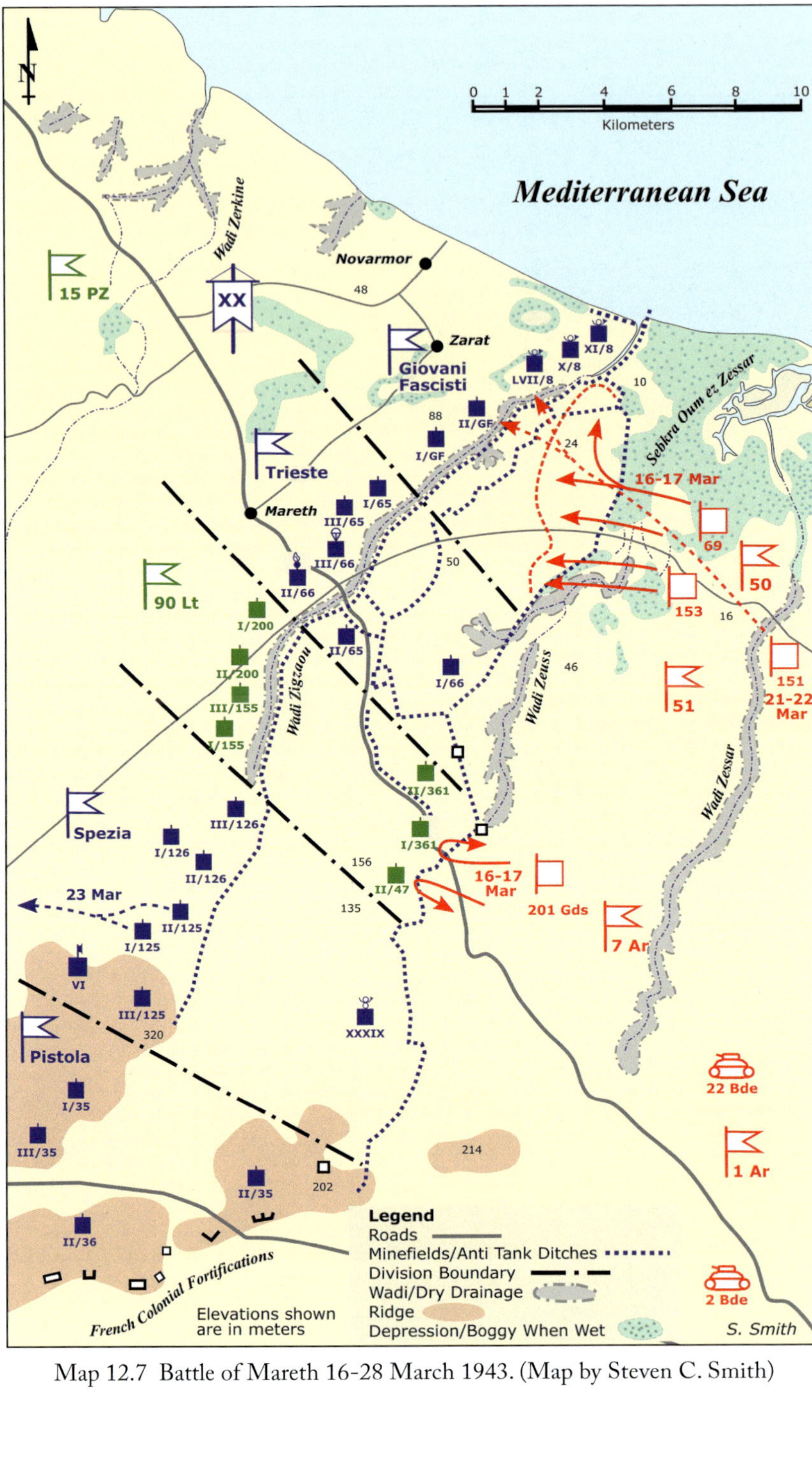

Map 12.7 Battle of Mareth 16-28 March 1943. (Map by Steven C. Smith)

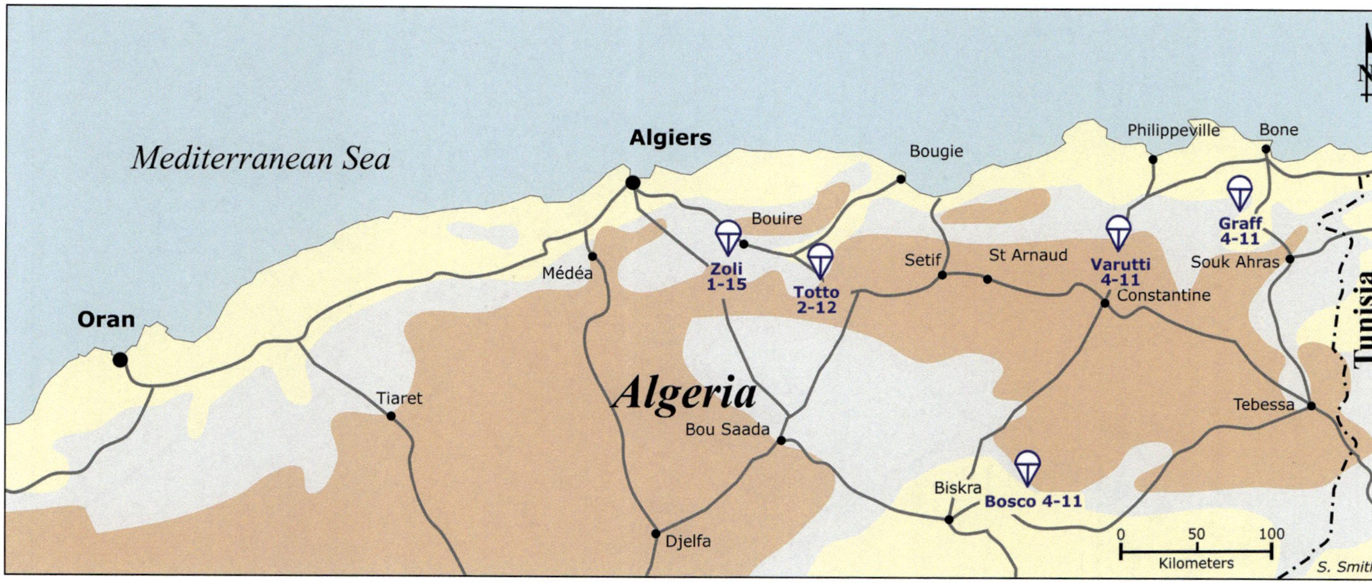

Map 12.8 Overview of Arditi Raids Jan–Apr 1943. (Map by Steven C. Smith)

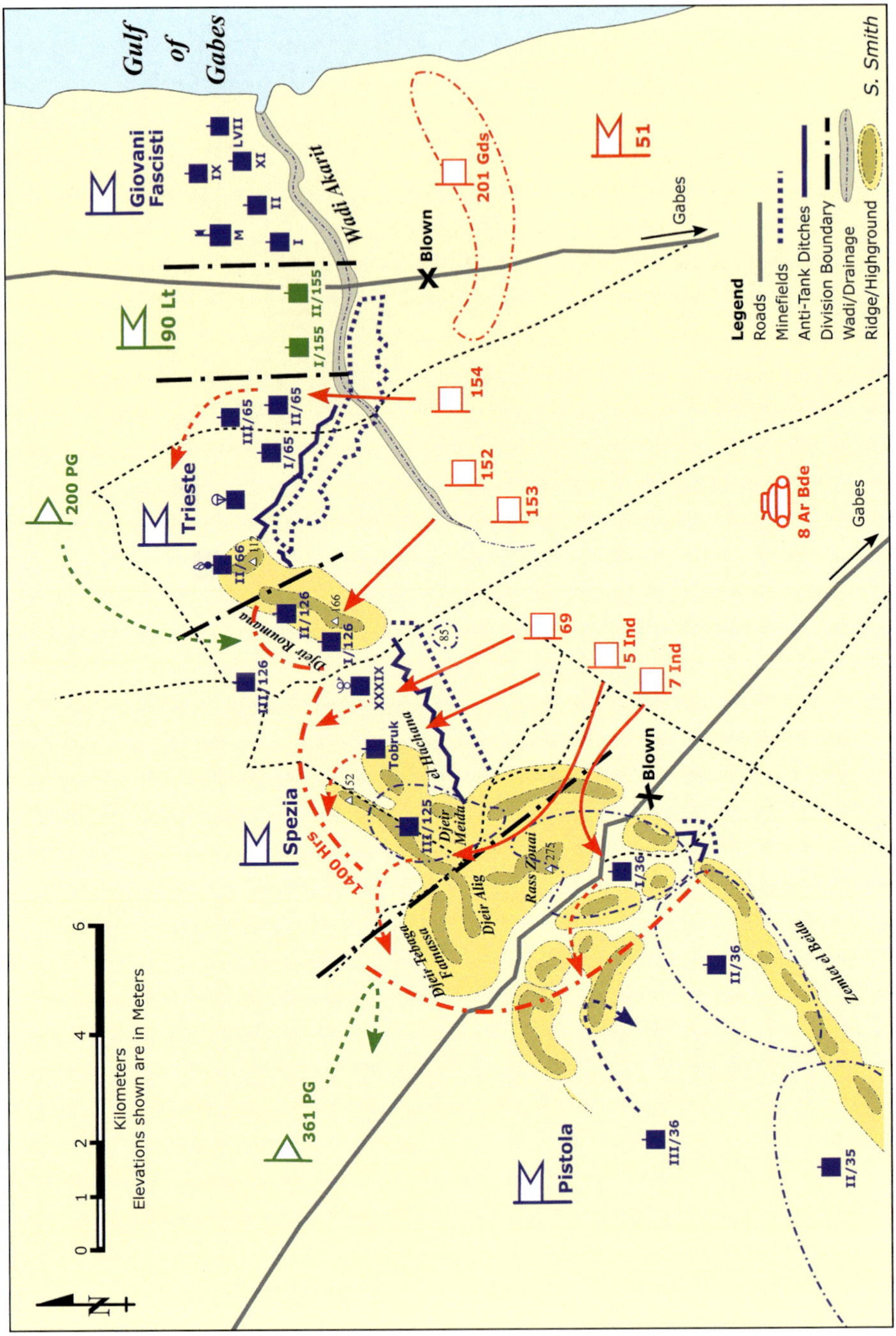

Map 12.9 Battle of Wadi Akarit 5–7 Apr 1943. (Map by Steven C. Smith)

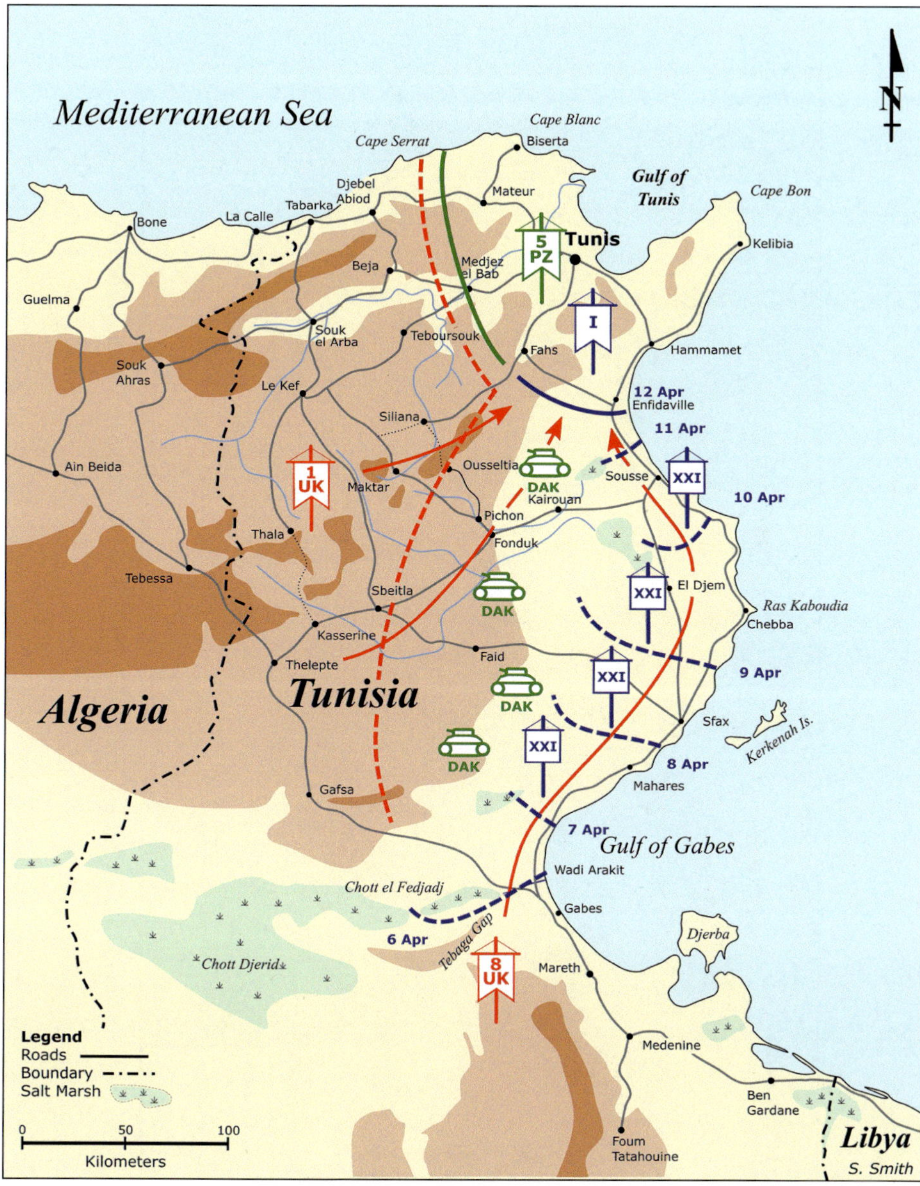

Map 12.10 Overview of the Retreat after Battle of Wadi Akarit 6–12 Apr 1943.
(Map by Steven C. Smith)

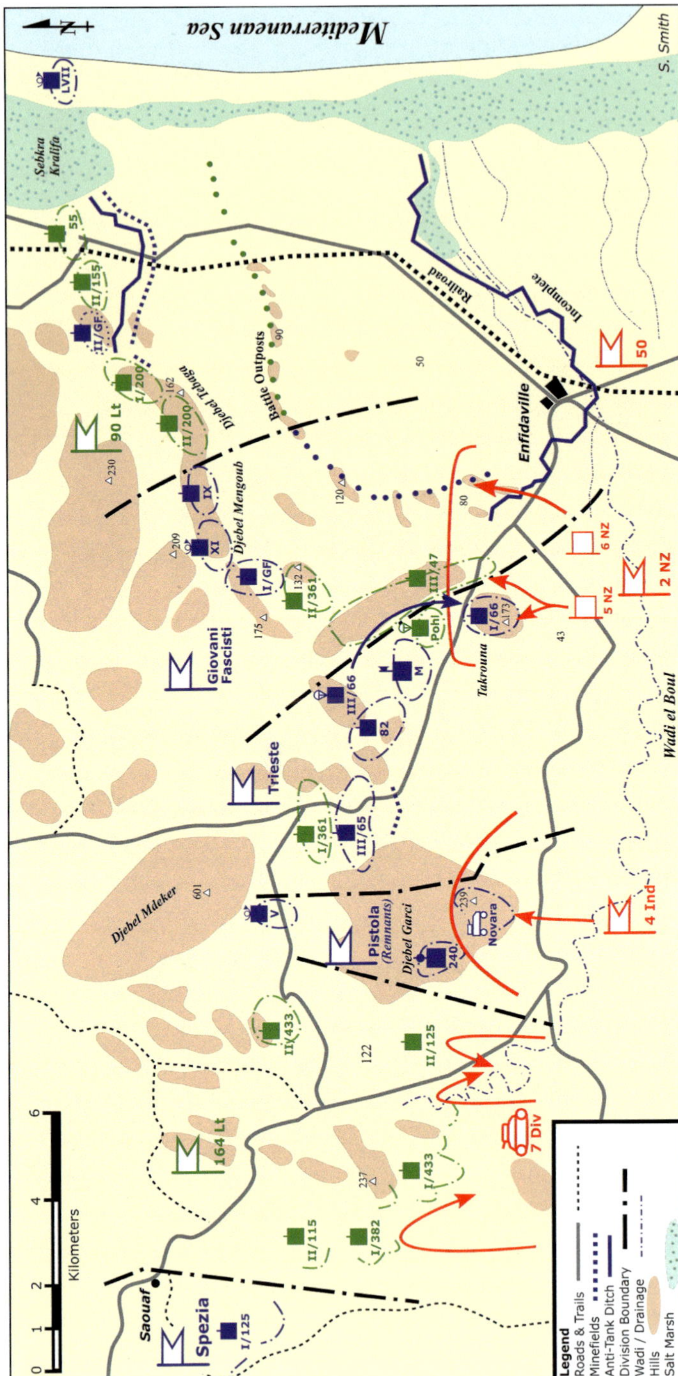

Map 12.11 1st Battle of Enfidaville 19–20 Apr 1943. (Map by Steven C. Smith)

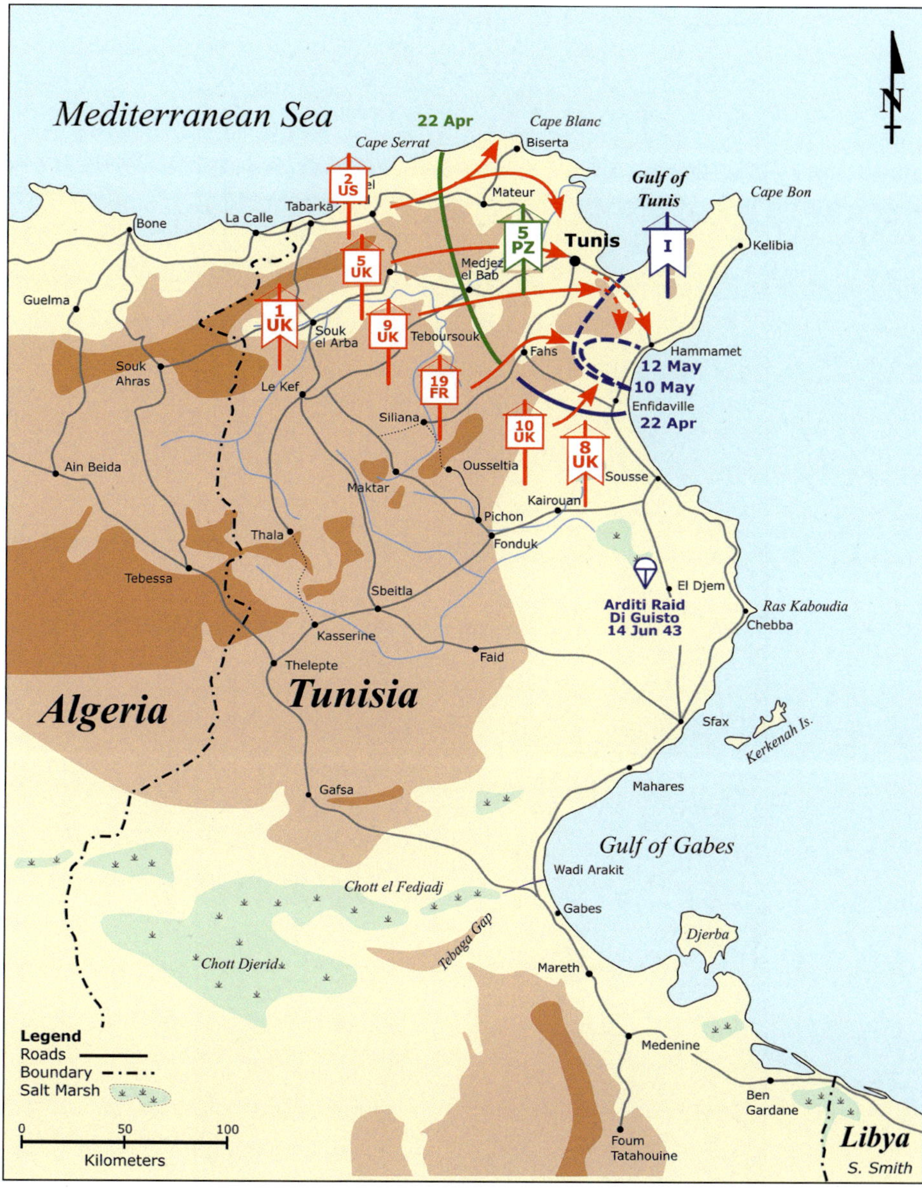

Map 12.12 Overview of the final battles 22 Apr–13 May 1943. (Map by Steven C. Smith)

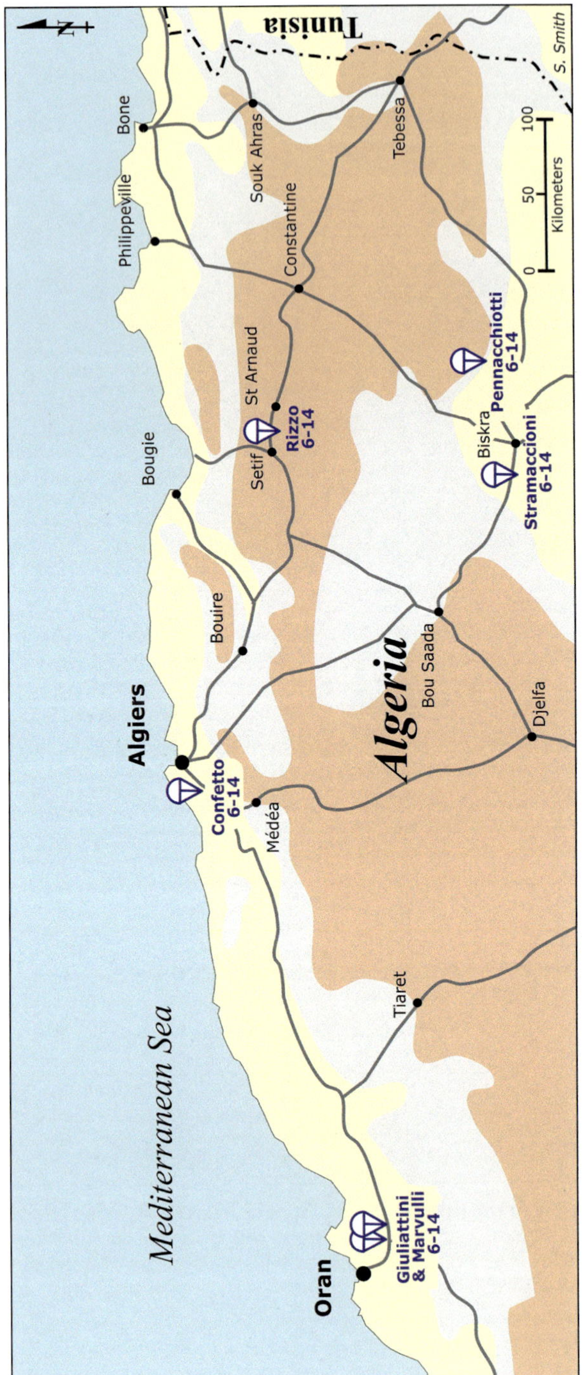

Map 13.1 Nembo in Sardinia Jun-Sep 1943. (Map by Steven C. Smith)

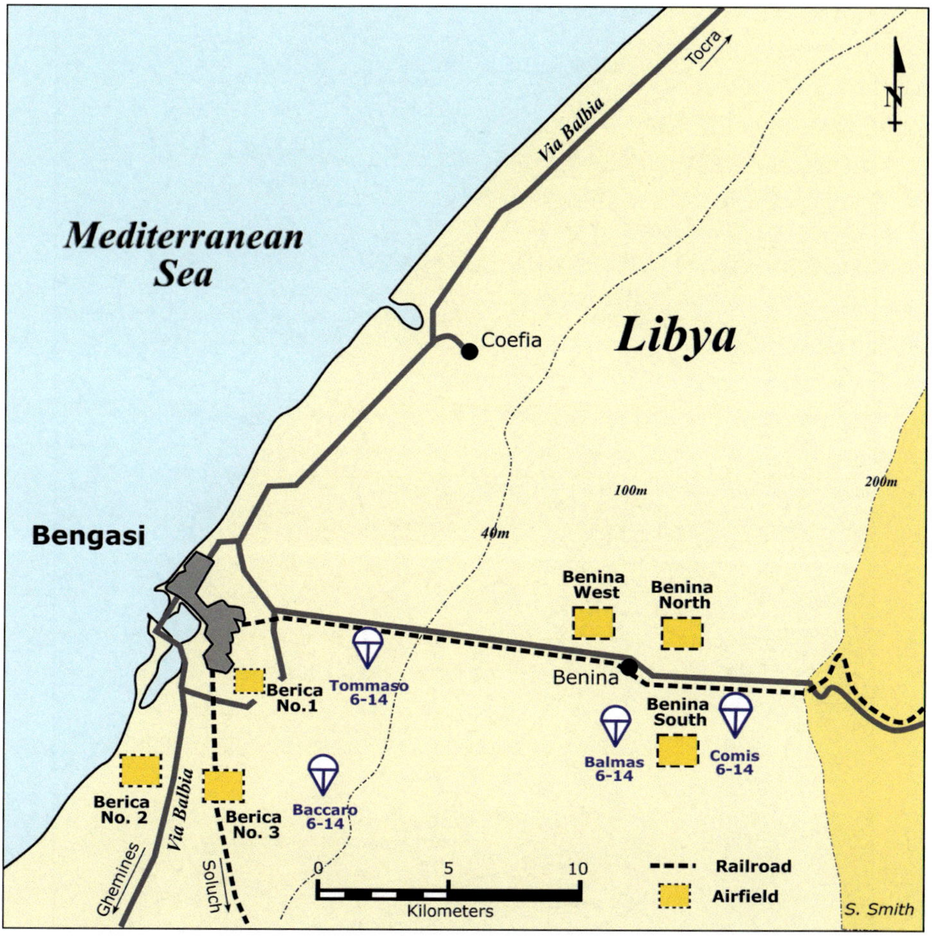

Map 13.2 Overview of Arditi Raids Algeria Jun 1943. (Map by Steven C. Smith)

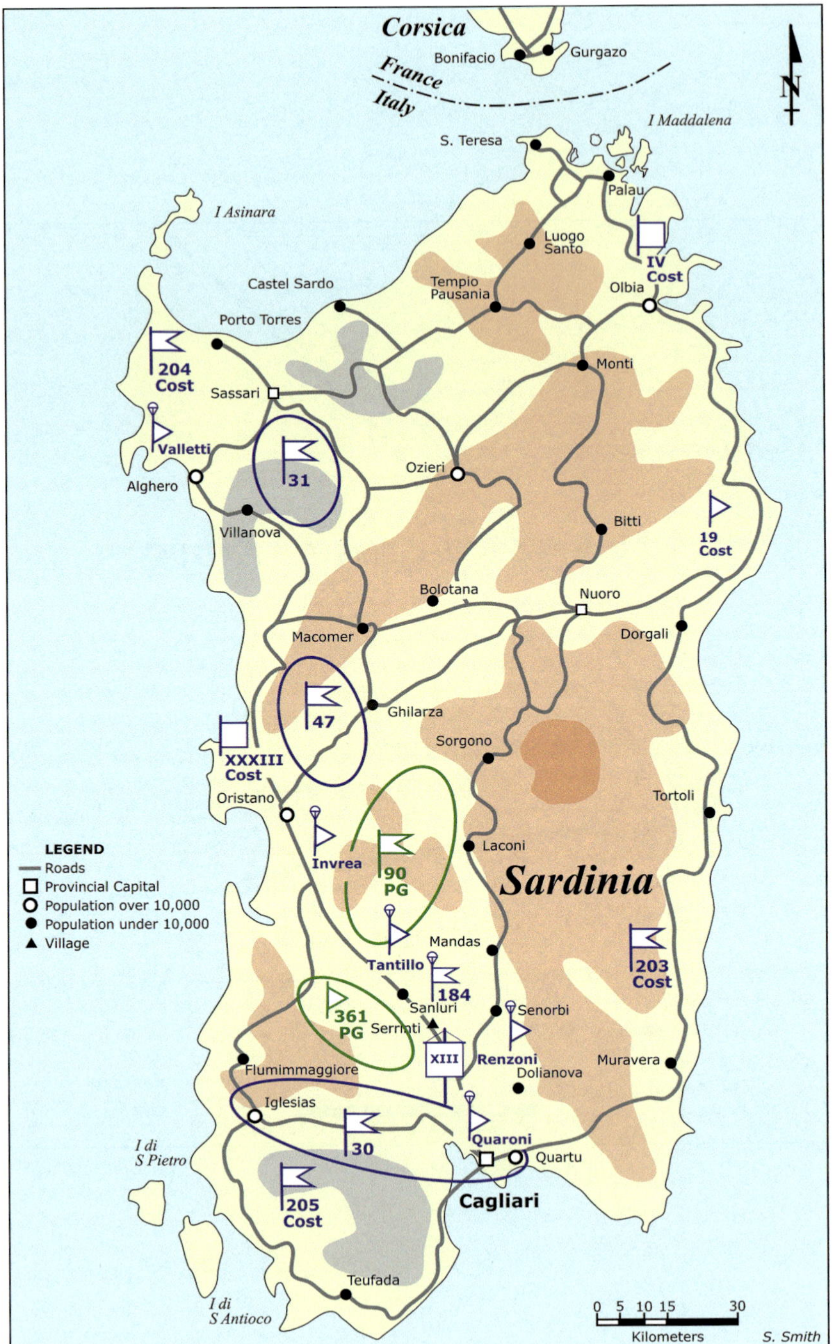

Map 13.3 Overview of Arditi Raids Libya Jun 1943. (Map by Steven C. Smith)

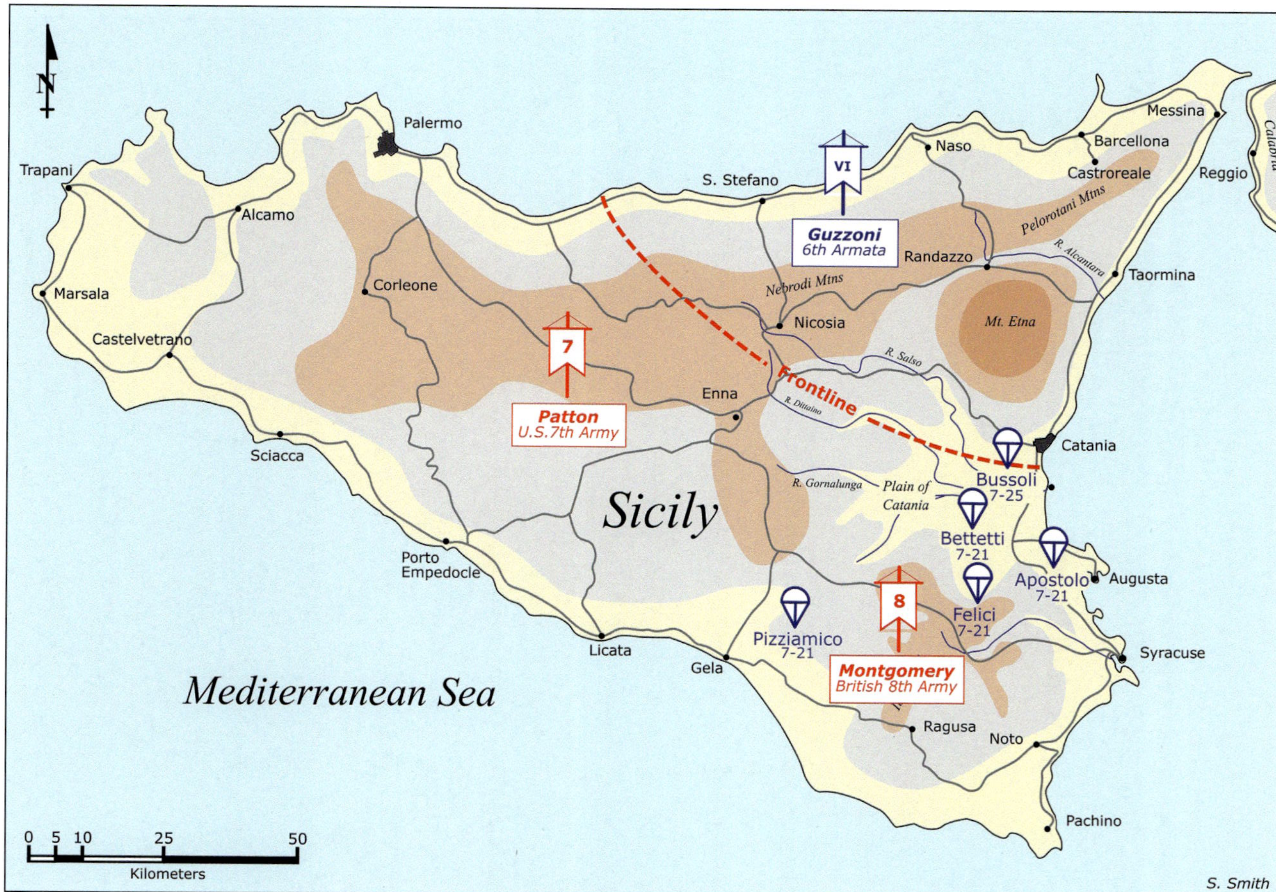

Map 13.4 Overview of Arditi Raids, Sicily Jul 1943. (Map by Steven C. Smith)

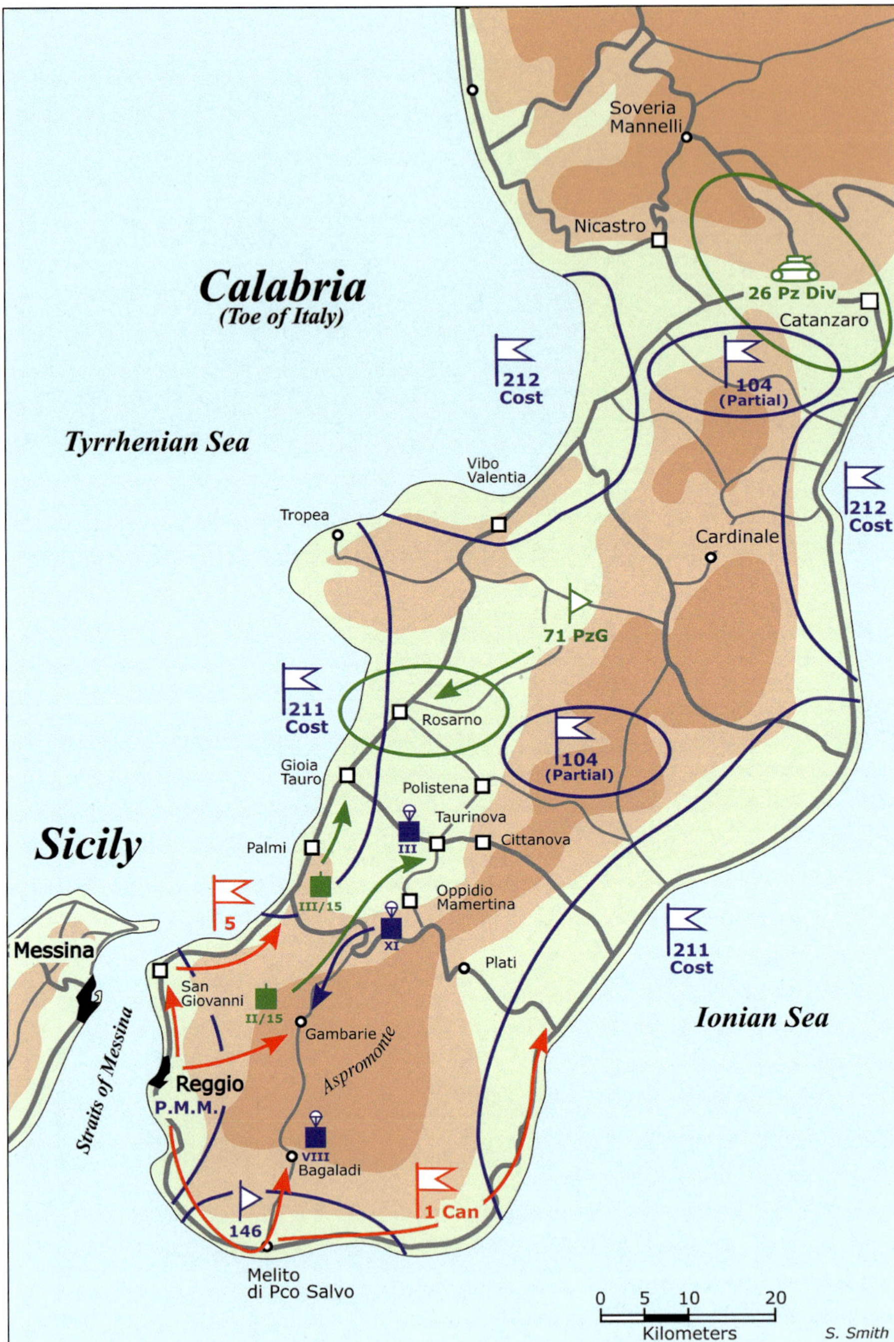

Map 13.5 Operation Baytown, Calabria 3–4 Sep 1943. (Map by Steven C. Smith)

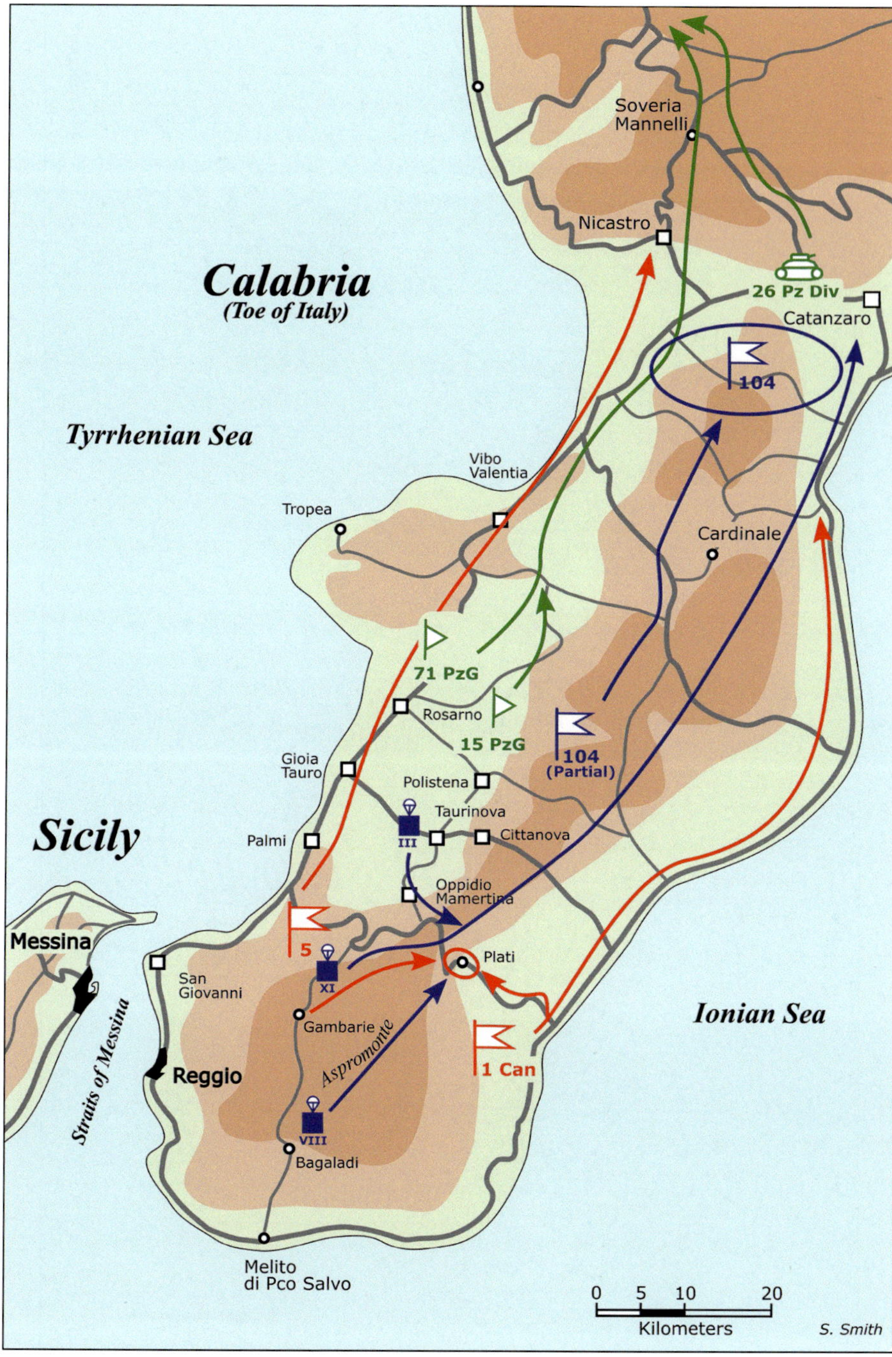

Map 13.6 Operation Baytown, Calabria 5–8 Sep 1943

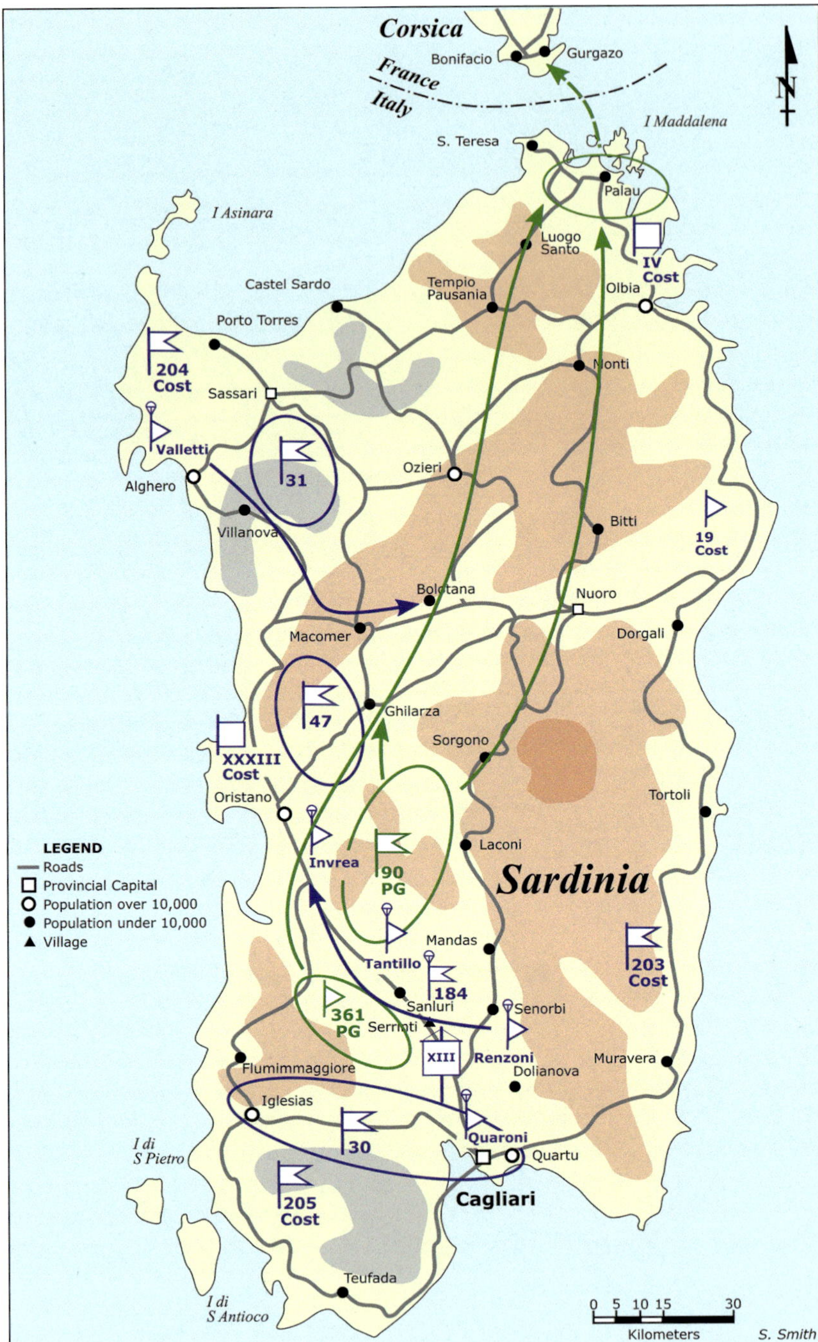

Map 14.1 Nembo in Sardinia Sep 1943. (Map by Steven C. Smith)

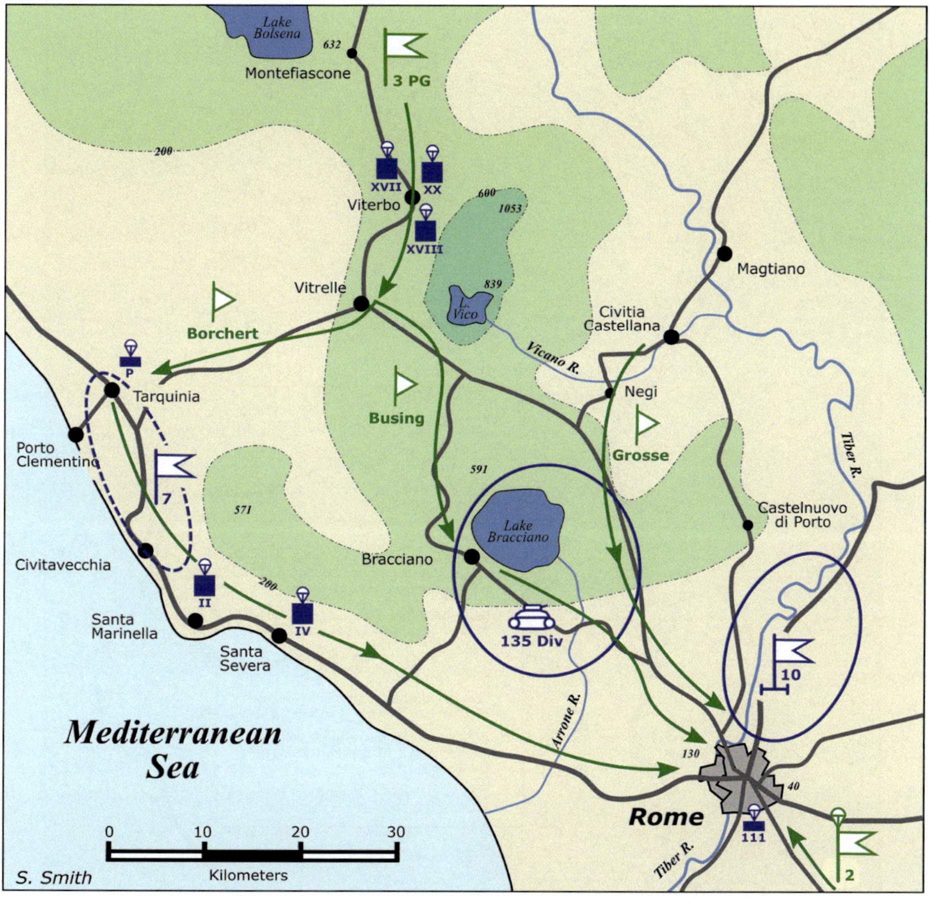

Map 14.2 The German Advance 8 Sep 1943. (Map by Steven C. Smith)

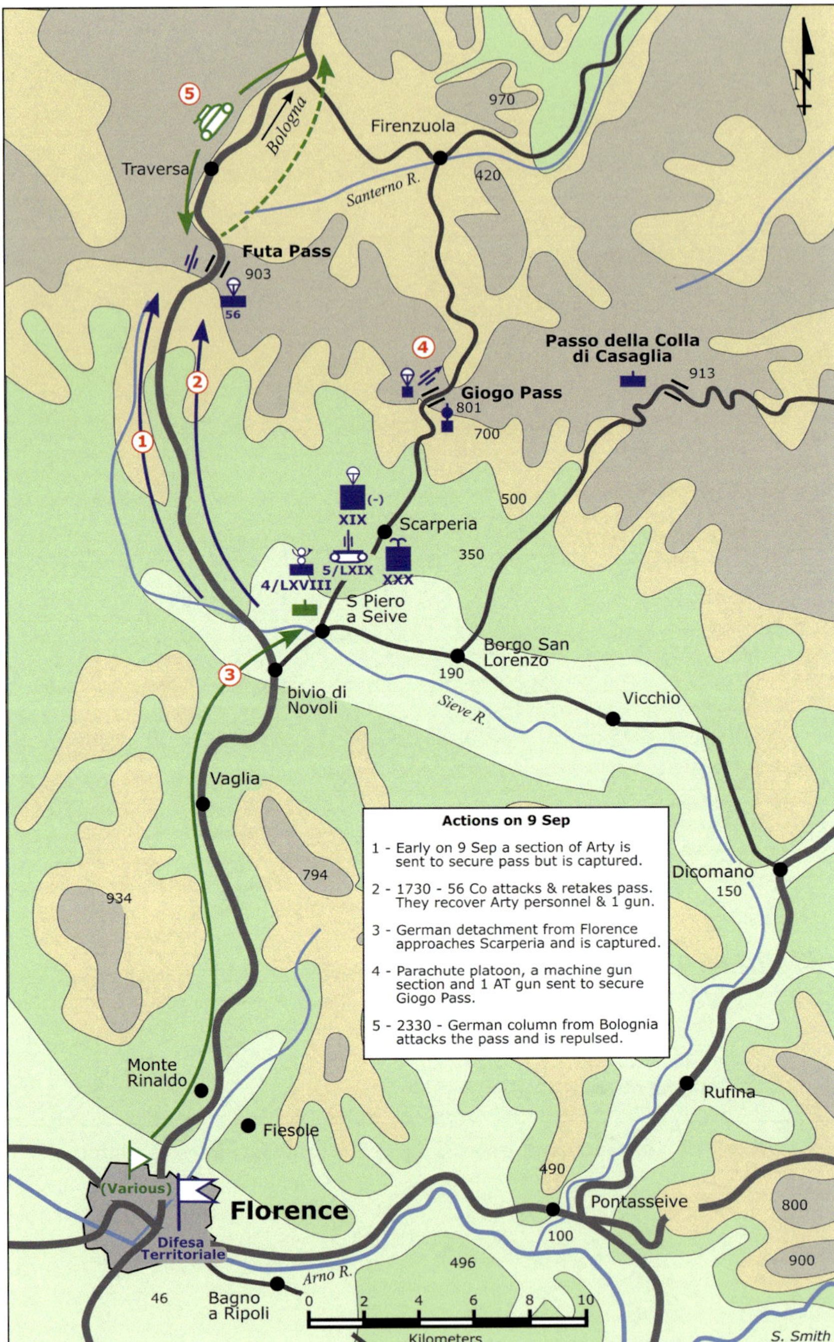

Map 14.3 Actions for the Apennine Passes 9 Sep 1943. (Map by Steven C. Smith)

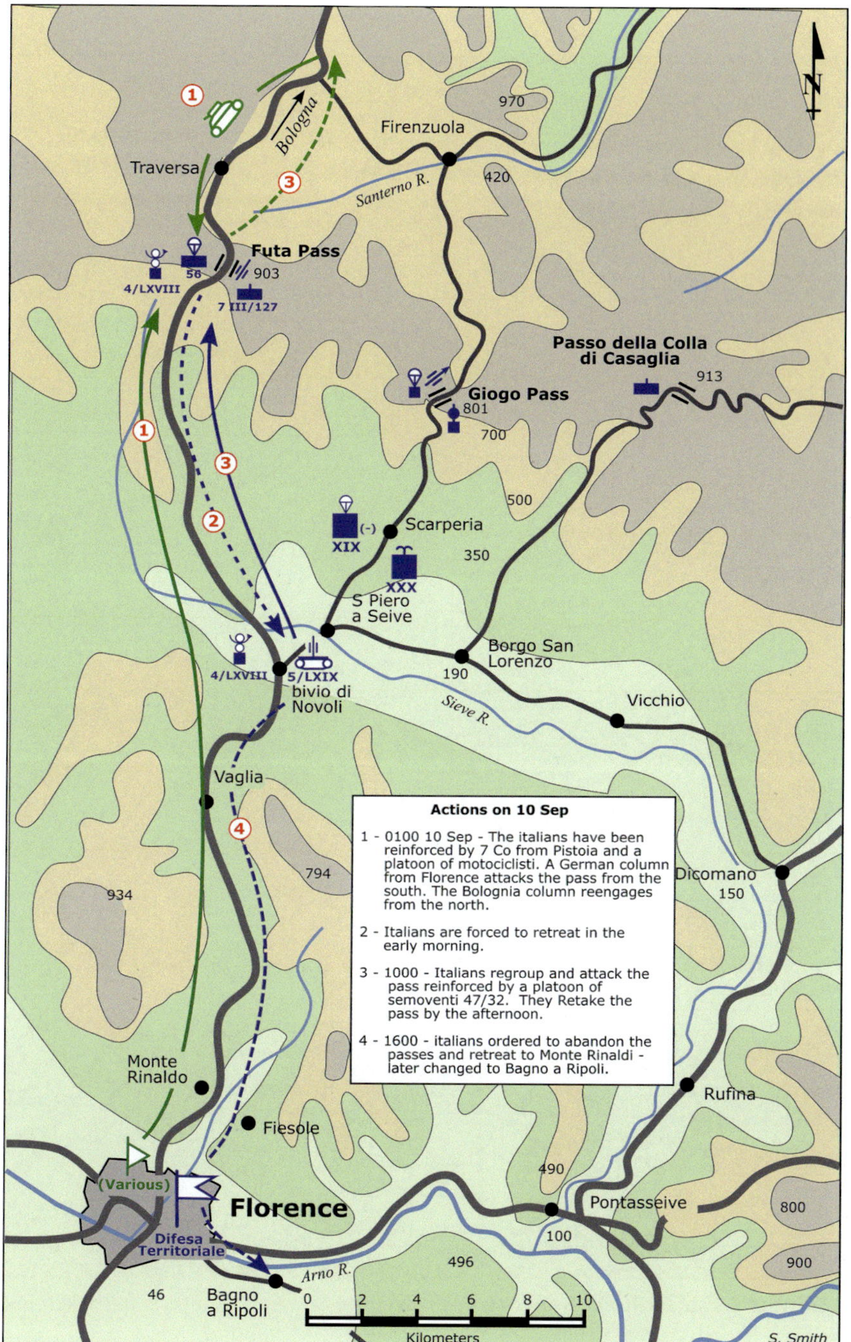

Map 14.4 Actions for the Apennine Passes 10 Sep 1943. (Map by Steven C. Smith)

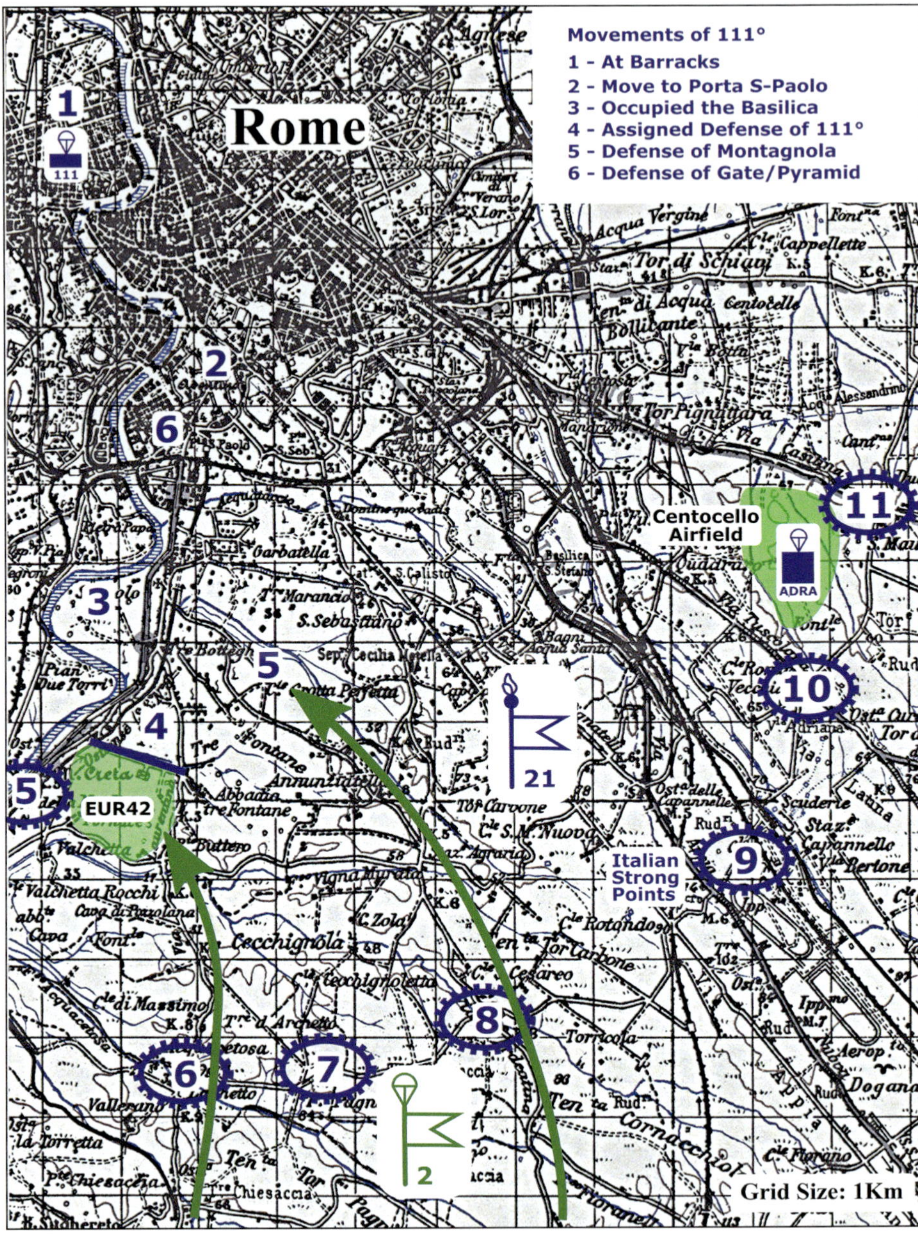

Map 14.5 Battle for Rome 8–10 Sep 1943. (Map by Steven C. Smith, map background courtesy of the University of Texas Libraries)

An army corps lacked the capability and resources to employ the battalion as paratroopers. If the *C.A.M.* desired to use them in an airborne operation, the commander would need to request the necessary assets for such an operation from the army/theater. Transport, fighter protection, and ground attack aircraft would all need to be approved by *Superasi* for use. The link-up and relief by ground forces would need to be integrated into ongoing operations if the mission was to seize and/or secure a deep objective. If the mission was sabotage/disruption of an enemy capability, the effects of such a raid would need to be synchronized with other operations designed to leverage such an event. The necessary planning, resourcing, and coordination for any of these employment options are decided/executed at the army/theater level. Diversion of the required resources from ongoing operations must be justified by an objective/effect that has an operational impact. If such an objective were identified, placing the parachute battalion at the corps level only complicates the planning and execution. The reassignment can only be seen as a strong indicator that the *Superasi.* lacked the vision and desire necessary to employ this unique resource. If this was not the case, *Superasi* could have retained the battalion in Tripolitania for future use as the current situation did not require the commitment of the *paracadutisti* as ordinary infantry.

Although the battalion had been assigned to the *C.A.M.*, the unit remained in the vicinity of Tripoli. The *carabinieri* continued to man the defense positions and execute reconnaissance patrols south into the desert. This period of training and patrolling the rear areas of the Italo-German Army ended on 6 November 1941. *Superasi* ordered the *I btg. paracadutisti CC.RR.* and the *XIX btg. Carabinieri Reali* to Cirenaica to reinforce the coastal defenses. Before the move, twenty Libyan *paracadutisti* from the now disbanded *I btg. paracadutisti libico* were assigned to the battalion.[39] Departing by truck on 10 November, the *carabinieri* traveled over the next several days and arrived at Tert late on 13 November. The battalion was placed under the command of the *Comando Carabinieri Reali della Libia* (*Cdo CC.RR. della Libia*, Royal Carabinieri Command of Libya) and was moved to Lamluda.[40]

Under the *Cdo CC.RR. della Libia*, the battalion was given assignments better fitting the *carabinieri* mission than those performed as an airborne battalion. The battalion was split to perform garrison and security duties at several locations. The *3ª cp.* was sent to reinforce the units protecting the headquarters of the *Superasi* at Cirene. The *comando di battaglione*, *1ª cp.*, and *2ª cp.* remained at Lamluda to protect the crossroads.[41]

39 Cursi, *I Leoni*, p.79; Ferrara, *I carabinieri*, p.50. It is unclear when these Libyan paratroopers joined the battalion. Cursi states two were killed on 19 or 20 November. Ferrara states on 16 December that the Libyans are 'recently arrived.' As the Libyan parachute battalion had been disbanded in late September 1941 at Tripoli, it is logical that they would have had the opportunity to join the *I btg. paracadutisti carabinieri* at Tripoli before they were assigned to other units.

40 Cursi, *I Leoni*, pp.75.

41 Ferrara, *I carabinieri*, pp.43–44; Longo, *I «reparti speciali»*, p.266.

On 16 November, the battalion was instructed to position a platoon on the coast near Cirene as an anti-commando force. The *3º plotone* of the *2ª cp.* was selected and moved to their new location. On that same day, the remainder of the *2ª cp.* was ordered to Derna to protect the port, the fresh water systems, and the airfield.[42] The headquarters and *1ª cp.* remained at Lamluda.

Operation Flipper (Map 6.1)

Unknown to the battalion, the British were preparing to launch their new offensive to relieve Tobruk and defeat the Italo-German forces in Cirenaica. Named Operation Crusader, it was set to begin on 18 November. As part of the initial moves, a commando raid was included to disrupt the Italo-German command by attacking various rearward locations on the night of 17–18 November. Code named Operation Flipper, the original targets were the assumed headquarters of Panzergruppe Afrika at Beda Littoria, the communication and intelligence center of the *Superasi* at Cirene, a radio station at Apollonia, and the headquarters of the *divisione motorizzata «Trieste»* near Slonta.

The *I btg. paracadutisti CC.RR.* was not involved in the initial action against the commandos.[43] Landing on the night of 14–15 November near Apollona, the commandos experienced a series of problems that resulted in only half the force making the shore. Bad weather continued to beset the group and the leaders decided to only attack the headquarters at Beda Littoria and the communication/intelligence center at Cirene. They executed the attacks on the night of 17–18 November without success.

Alerted to the attacks early on 18 November, the *3º pl.* was ordered to sweep the area west of the Apollona – Cirene road. *S. Tenente* Alfredo Mercuro,[44] the *3º pl.* commander, was given two local Libyan *carabinieri* who knew the area as guides. With his 32 *paracadutisti carabinieri*, *s. tenente* Mercuro began his sweep at 0530 on the morning of 19 November. At 1030 hours, the platoon spotted several Arabs on a hill that appeared to be acting suspiciously. Deploying his platoon, Mercuro had one of the local *carabinieri* call out to the men. The Arabs ducked behind some cover as the paratroopers advanced. Calling out again, the Arabs open fire on the platoon. Returning fire, the Arabs fled into a wooded area, followed by the paratroopers. After

42 Ferrara, *I carabinieri*, pp.43–44.

43 A detailed account of the raid can be found in many sources. This account will only focus on the participation of the *paracadutisti* carabinieri. Sources are Cursi, *I Leoni*, pp.73–81; Ferrara, *I carabinieri*, p.46; Longo, *I «reparti speciali»*, pp.266–267.

44 *S. ten.* Mercuro later commanded the *27ª sezione carabinieri* in the *d.f. «Acqui»* stationed on Cefalonia in September 1943. He will be executed along with the other officers in the division for resisting the Germans after the Italian surrender. Longo, *I «reparti speciali»*, p.266 fn.12.

a chase of several hundred meters, the lead paratroopers began to receive automatic weapons fire.

Throwing themselves to the ground, the platoon deployed to both the right and left of the enemy which now could be seen as including British soldiers. *s. tenente* Mercuro set his three Breda 30 f.m. to provide covering fire as the *paracadutisti* used fire and maneuver as practiced for so many months to encircle the enemy. The combination of the flanking maneuver and covering fire forced the British and Arabs back into a nearby cave. Suppressing the entrance with small-arms fire, the *paracadutisti* threw a number of grenades into the cave. When the enemy still refused to surrender, Mercuro, speaking French, threatened to use a flamethrower (which he did not have) to burn them out. Trapped with no way out and the threat of a flamethrower, the enemy finally gave up. An officer and four soldiers were captured, all wounded during the fight. A further sweep in the area resulted in capturing four Arabs that were assisting the commandos. Two *paracadutisti* were wounded during the firefight, one of them seriously. The platoon returned to Cirene with their prisoners on 20 November.

During the fight against the commando raid, the British launched Operation Crusader on the early morning of 18 November. As the *paracadutisti carabinieri* were not involved in the major actions of the battle, only a brief summarization will be provided.

The initial British movement was undetected due to the bad weather grounding the aircraft on both sides. Because the *Panzergruppe* was unaware of the British advance, it did not react in the manner predicted by the British 8th Army. Changing their plan, the British were rebuffed by the *d. cor. «Ariete»* at Bir el Gobi (19 November), defeated in the 1st Battle for Sidi Rezegh (19–24 November), ignored Rommel's Dash to the Wire (24-26 November), linked-up with the Tobruk garrison (27 November), won the 2nd Battle for Sidi Rezegh (27 November–1 December), forced the Italo-German force away from the Tobruk perimeter (2–10 December), and finally forced the Italo-German army back to Gazala (10–14 December). With Tobruk relieved, the British could now plan how to trap the *Panzergruppe* before it could escape back to Tripolitania.

The *I btg. paracadutisti carabinieri* continued to protect Derna and Cirene while awaiting the results of the great clash of forces in the east. With the withdrawal of the *Panzergruppe* away from Tobruk to Gazala, *maggiore* Alessi made preparations for the likely retreat westward. On 11 December, he ordered *s. tenente* Armando Ragnini to collect all the parachute equipment stored at Luigi Savoia and transport it back to Tripoli. The *2ª cp.* was ordered to rejoin the battalion at Cirene, leaving Derna on 13 December. On the same day, Alessi was informed that his battalion had been placed under the command of the *Panzergruppe*. He was ordered to report to the *Panzergruppe* headquarters to receive his new orders.[45]

45 Cursi, *I Leoni*, p.83; Longo, *I «reparti speciali»*, p.267.

Arriving at the headquarters on 14 December, *maggiore* Alessi was ushered in to meet with *General der Panzertruppe* Rommel, commander of *Panzergruppe Afrika*. Rommel explained the operational situation and instructed him to move his battalion to Eluet el Asel and establish a blocking position facing to the south. His battalion was to prevent any enemy pursuit moving north from the Martuba-Mechili area using the road from Chaulan to Giovanni Berta. If the decision was made to have the Italo-German Army abandon Cirenaica, the Italian infantry divisions would be retreating along the via Balbia. Those divisions would need time to get clear and holding Eluet el Asel would prevent the British from blocking that escape route. The Italo-German mobile forces would be used to block the desert route south of the gebel, preventing the British from repeating their movement that ended at Beda Fomm earlier that year.

Battle of Eluet el Asel (Maps 6.2, 6.3)

Returning to the battalion at Cirene, *maggiore* Alessi found a detachment of the *9ª cp.* of the *8º rgt, bersaglieri* from the *divisione corazzata «Ariete»* awaiting his orders. The detachment was commanded by *s. tenente* Alberto Coglitore and consisted of a truck column with 59 men, thirty trucks, and six 47/32 c.c. guns.[46] After speaking with Coglitore and ordering his *paracadutisti* to begin loading equipment and supplies, Alessi went to the *Comando Superiore del Genio* (Superior Headquarters of the Engineers) at Battisti to meet with *generale di divisione* Luigi Grossi.[47] Alessi requested engineer support to build fighting positions at Eluet el Asel. During the meeting he was told about a new anti-armor bomb that had been recently developed by a member of their staff.

Earlier that same day, *s. tenente* Renato Mattei, the commander of the *I btg. paracadutisti carabinieri* engineer platoon, arrived with *ten. (genio)* Passaglia, the developer of the bomb. The *bombe anticarro tipo Passaglia* was a rudimentary hand thrown anti-armor grenade constructed using a Chiarizia soup can filled with approximately 1-2 kilograms of explosive. The can was attached to a wooden handle that had a standard O.T.O. hand grenade attached to its base to act as the igniter/fuse for the can of explosive. A soldier would simply pull the firing pin from the grenade and toss the *bomba* at

46 Longo, *I «reparti speciali»*, p.268 states "The battalion was reinforced, as we have seen, by 10 47/32 light anti-tank guns with personnel from the 9th company of the 8th Bersaglieri Regiment [from the] *Ariete* ..." This is referring to Longo's statement when the battalion arrived in Tripoli (p.265). It is highly unlikely that the *8º rgt. bersaglieri* from the *«Ariete»* would have left a complete anti-tank company at Tripoli in July–August 1941 at a time when the Italo-German forces were rebuilding strength along the Libyan-Egyptian border. Ten is an unusual number of guns as eight guns is the authorized strength of a *cp. controcarro*.

47 Cursi, *I Leoni*, p.84. Cursi mis-identified this officer as *generale* D. Grossi.

the target. While crude, the amount of high explosive could damage a tank if it hit the target. After a quick demonstration and training session, *tenente* Passaglia returned to his unit with a promise to deliver 400 of the new grenades.[48]

The column left Cirene at 1200 hours on 14 December and reached Eluet el Asel at 2200 hours that night. Early the next morning (15 December), *maggiore* Alessi walked the terrain and planned his defense. One must wonder if Alessi understood that he was there to execute a rearguard mission for a retreating army at a location near where *tenente colonnello* Tonini was ordered to execute the very same mission with his *paracadutisti libici* less than a year ago. Whereas Tonini defended the eastern entrance into the gebel at the northern end of the Wadi Derna, Alessi was now defending the southern entrance at the far end of the Wadi Derna.

Eluet (Hill) el Asel was a crossroad where the roads from Mechili and Chaulan joined together before continuing northeast to Giovanni Berta. The crossroad itself was about 560 meters in elevation, surrounded by hills reaching 630-640 meters high. The ground was very broken and rocky with a lot of scrub and trees, making cross-country travel by vehicles challenging.

Finishing his reconnaissance, Alessi decided to defend the cross road with all three companies in line due to the length of the position. The battalion strength was 320 *paracadutisti carabinieri*, a platoon (20 men) of *paracadutisti libici* released from the disbanded Libyan airborne battalion, the *9ª cp. bersaglieri controcarri* (56 men), and the 35 men in the *plotone servizi*; a total of 431 effectives. The battalion possessed 27 f.m, six 47/32 c.c., 12 Fiat 14/35, two *fucili controcarro 35(P)*, and the 400 *bombe Passaglia*.[49]

The *1ª cp.* with the engineer platoon, twenty Libyan paratroopers from the previously disbanded battalion, and one platoon of anti-tank guns (two 47/32 c.c.) would hold the center position just south of the road junction on the forward slope of Quota (height) 628. From this position, the company could fire on both roads. The *2º cp.* would hold the left (east) flank on Quota 585 with one platoon of anti-tank guns (two 47/32 c.c.). The *3ª cp.* would hold the right (west) flank with one anti-tank platoon (two 47/32 c.c.) on Quota 639. The battalion headquarters and the first aid station was positioned between Quotas 585 and 567 north of the crossroad. While not stated, each company likely had four Fiat mod. 35 machine guns (one platoon). The positioning of the *fucili controcarro 35(P)*s are not stated by any source, but likely held in reserve by the battalion headquarters.

48 Cursi, *I Leoni*, p.84; Ferrara, *I carabinieri*, p.49.

49 Cursi, *I Leoni*, pp.86 states six 47/32 c.c. but discusses the positioning of ten 47/32 c.c. on p.85, followed by the positioning of only six guns on p.86. Ferrara, *I carabinieri*, p.50 states only six 47/32 c.c. Longo, *I «reparti speciali»*, pp.266 and fn.12 states ten 47/32 and four Solothurns and positions all ten but states all ten came from the *9ª cp. bersaglieri*. All the other sources state only six guns with the bersaglieri. The two *fucile controcarro 35(P)* are based on the list of surviving weapons and the lack of any mention of Solothurns in the accounts of the battle.

The next morning (16 December), *colonnello* Gherardo Vaiarini from the *d.f. «Bologna»* arrived with additional troops. He informed *maggiore* Alessi that Alessi's battalion was now under his command and Eluet el Asel would now be a *sottosettore* (subsector) in the *«Bologna»* defensive sector of responsibility. *Colonnello* Vaiarini was given two companies from the *65º rgt. f. «Valtellina»* and the *btg. del Centro di Istruzione fanteria di Barce* (the training battalion of the Center for Infantry Instruction at Barce) in addition to *maggiore* Alessi's troops for the defense.

Colonnello Vaiarini decided that the additional units would be deployed to extend the flanks of Alessi's blocking position, with the *btg. del Centro di Istruzione* extended to the left (east) flank of the position adjoining the paratroopers with an c.c. platoon (two 47/32 c.c.). The two infantry companies of the *65º rgt.* would form the right (west) flank of the defense. These companies were currently at Chaulan (about twelve kilometers south) and would remain there to block the Chaulan/Eluet el Asel road. By leaving the two companies forward, the right flank of the *I btg. paracadutisti carabinieri* was effectively 'up in the air' without support.

With this new disposition Alessi needed to rearrange his battalion. The ridgeline east of the crossroads formed by Quota 585–625–627 and hills further east would now be held by the *btg. del Centro di Istruzione*. The c.c. platoon attached to that battalion was positioned to cover the road. The *1ª cp.* remained on Quota 628 and *3ª cp.* remained at Quota 639. *2ª cp.* was ordered to Quota 654 to extend the battalion's defense to the west, covering the open flank.

The *XX Cd'A* commander, *generale di divisione* Benvenuto Gioda, arrived at Eluet el Asel on the morning of 17 December to inspect the position. With him was engineer *maggiore* Zecchi from the corps engineer command. The engineer major reviewed the defense position selected by the *paracadutisti* and made some small adjustments. The schematic of the position was sent back to the engineer command for the allocation of engineer sources.

That afternoon a *compagnia genio d'arresto* (engineer barrier company) and the *17ª cp. lavoratori* (labor) arrived and set up camp in the Wadi Hamar behind the *paracadutisti* position. Both units were from the *III btg., 2º raggruppamento Lavoratori* (Labor grouping) of the *1º raggruppamento speciale genio A.S.* (special engineer group for North Africa). *Maggiore* Alessi once again walked the ground with the engineer commander and the planned locations for the minefields and the positions were marked. They quickly began work, but only a few positions had been dug in the rocky ground and a few small minefields laid before the engineers were recalled on the afternoon of December 18. The army's new engineering priority was to repair the damage inflicted by the British air attacks against the roads and bridges along the Via Balbia to support the retreat of the army.

As little work on the planned defenses had been completed by the engineers, it was up to the paratroopers to complete what they could. Similar to the infantry defenses of Derna eleven months earlier, the *paracadutisti* found themselves building a defensive position with only the limited tools and materials at hand: rock walls and sangars would replace properly dug-in fighting positions. Stacks of mines remained in the wadi to rear of the position as the British attack started before the *paracadutisti carabinieri* were able to emplace them as part of the defense.[50]

While the *paracadutisti* were working at the cross road, the senior leadership of the Axis forces participated in a series of meetings between 16–18 December at Cirene and Giovanni Berta. Generalfeldmarschall Kesselring, *Comando Armate Sud* (Southern Army Command) argued for a rapid retreat before the British could cut off the Italo-German forces. General Rommel supported Kesselring but the timing of the movements became a point of contention between the Germans and *Generali di Corpo d'Armata* Ettore Bastico (*Superasi*) and Gastone Gambara (*Corpo d'Armata di Manovra*). The Italian generals were concerned that the Italian infantry would be left behind due to the lack of transport. The issue was not resolved until the morning of 18 December, when a rapid withdrawal was agreed upon.[51]

The Italo-German forces were defending a position from the coast at Gazala south into the desert. The Italian *XXI Cd'A* (*divisioni «Trento», «Brescia» and «Pavia»*) held the northern part of the line. The *C.A.M.* (*divisioni «Ariete»* and *«Trieste»*) held the center and were echelon back to the west. The *Deutsches Afrika Korps* (DAK) with the *21.* and *15.Panzerdivisonie* held the open southern flank. The *XXI Cd'A* would retreat along the via Balbia through Derna and through Bengasi to el Agedabia, while the *C.A.M.* and DAK would retreat along the desert trails through Mechili. This would create a gap between the two forces that the *I btg. para. CC.RR.* would fill by holding Eleut es Asel, protecting the *XXI Cd'A* from any UK force trying to cut their retreat. The future of the battalion had been decided.[52]

Maggiore Alessi had dispatched reconnaissance and security patrols to the south on the night of 17 December to provide intelligence and early warning of any approaching enemy activity. They returned and reported that no enemy activity was observed. On the morning of 18 December the result of the meeting at Giovanni Berta could be heard and seen from the crossroad. Artillery fire could be heard from the east and southeast near Derna, along with tall columns of flame and smoke from the burning depots. Numerous columns of Italian vehicles were now moving through the crossroad to escape the advancing enemy, slowing down to a trickle in the afternoon.[53]

New orders arrived for *colonnello* Vaiarini that afternoon at 1500 hours. The *btg. del Centro di Istruzione* and the two companies from the *65º rgt. f. «Valtellina»* were immediately withdrawn towards Bengasi. The *I btg. paracadutisti carabinieri* remained under orders from *Superasi* to hold Eluet el Asel. The battalion would cover the retreat until the evening of 19 December then withdraw towards Bengasi along the via Balbia. Alessi called a meeting with his company commanders to discuss the new tactical situation. Both flanks of the battalion will now be uncovered. Recognizing that a

50 TNA WO 169/3H32: 1/6 Rajputana Rifles I.A. War Diary, 20 Dec. 1941.

51 Cursi, *I Leoni*, p.88; Mario Montanari, *Le operazioni in Africa settentrionale* (Rome: USSME, 1985), vol II: Tobruk, pp.687–697.

52 Montanari, *Le operazioni*, vol. 2, p.687

53 Cursi, *I Leoni*, p.95.

successful withdrawal was now in jeopardy, the *maggiore* ordered the destruction of all correspondence and unnecessary materials. At 1815 hours, he ordered the *2ª cp.* from Quota 654 to a reserve position behind the *1ª cp.* and near the battalion headquarters. The *1ª cp.* was ordered to position one platoon on Quota 585 on the east side of the Eluet el Asel-Mechili road to better cover the crossroad.[54] Alessi also dispatched two trucks to a supply depot at San Saf that was located between Cirene and Luigi Savona. The men were to draw five days of dried foods to support the battalion during its retreat from Eluet el Asel to Bengasi and beyond. This team under *tenente* Enrico Ferrari would never return as it was captured by the advancing British forces along the via Balbia.[55]

Maggiore Alessi dispatched two more reconnaissance patrols on the evening of 18 December. A small team under *tenente* Grilli from the *3º plotone* of the *1ª cp.* moved down the Mechili road. They did not find any enemy and returned before dawn on the 19 December. The second group, the *1º plt* from the *2ª cp.* under *tenente* Fanelli moved down the Chaulan road. Traveling south, they contact the advance elements of an Indian brigade about two kilometers from the advanced posts of the *paracadutisti*. While the main body of the patrol escaped detection, two *paracadutisti* were captured. When questioned, the two claimed to be lost and managed to escape a few hours later and return to the Italian lines. The platoon would remain with the *3ª cp.* to support that company's defense. With this warning, the battalion braced for the expected enemy attack.[56]

The battle was initiated by several shots fired by the 47/32 c.c. guns of *1ª cp.* covering the Mechili road at 0500 hours. Several enemy vehicles tried to pass up to the crossroad in the predawn darkness and were quickly stopped by anti-tank and machine gun fire. This was the 1 Platoon of the 3rd South Africa Reconnaissance Battalion (3/SAAC) and an infantry section from the 4th/6th Rajputana Rifles (4/6 Raj) who had been ordered to move to Giovanni Berta. The enemy backed off and took positions on the hills south of the crossroad and began firing upon the Italian positions. *Maggiore* Alessi moved to Quota 585 to observe the enemy movements and informed *colonnello* Vaiarini of the enemy's activity. Querying Alessi if he could hold or whether he should retreat the battalion, Alessi decided to hold.

The enemy was the 5th Indian Infantry Brigade under Brigadier Dudley Russell. The brigade was part of the 4th Indian Division, which included the 7th and 11th

54 There are two maps of the battalion's positions during the battle that do not agree. Ferrara, *I carabinieri*, pp.54-55 shows what is described above with the addition of Quota 615 to the east in the battalion's position. The same map is in Longo, *I «reparti speciali»*, pp.274. The map in Cursi, *Carabinieri Paracadutisti*, color section between p. 20 and 21, depicts the battalion's defense as further south along the line of (east to west) 594–590–west of Siret Cnasc on the west side of the road to Chaulan. This forward position does not match with the battle descriptions.

55 Cursi, *I Leoni*, pp.88; Longo, *I «reparti speciali»*, pp.270–271

56 Ferrara, *I carabinieri*, p.51; Cursi, *Carabinieri Paracadutisti*, p.;

Indian Brigades and other attachments. The 4th Indian Division was pressing two lines of pursuit as the Italo-German Army abandoned the Gazala line; the 7th Indian Brigade was moving against Derna and westward along the via Balbia, while the 5th Indian Brigade would move south of the jebel and then advance north through Chaulan/Eluet el Asel to Giovani Berta. The plan was for the 5th Brigade to reach Giovanni Berta before the retreating Axis forces and trap them between the two brigades. To achieve this, 4th Indian Division had ordered the two brigades to begin their movement the night of 18 December.[57]

The 5th Brigade had two of its infantry battalions, the 1/6 and 4/6 Rajputana Rifles (Raj) advancing northward. The 3/1 Punjab Battalion was protecting the rear of the brigade advance. Attached to the brigade were the 1st Coy. of the 3/SAAC, A Sqdn of the Central Indian Horse (CIH), and the 1st Field Regiment, Royal Artillery. Attached to A/CIH was a battery from the 31st Field Regiment, RA (four 25 pdrs). The CIH was equipped with Indian Pattern Carriers, while the 3/SAAC was equipped with Marmon Harrington armoured cars. These latter vehicles were likely Marmon Harrington Mk. III vehicles. Weeks of combat during Crusader had reduced the rifle companies to approximately 40-50 men, but they still retained all their heavy weapons.[58]

Towards 0700 hours, the 25 pdrs begin to beat upon the *paracadutisti* positions on Quota 628 and 639. The *carabinieri* had nothing to throw back at the enemy guns; they could only press themselves against the ground in their makeshift positions and await the next attack. What they could not see were the companies of the 4/6 Raj. maneuvering to their right (west) while keeping suppressive fire on the Italian positions. The Indians used the terrain to mask their movement and launch probing attacks as needed. Alessi ordered a platoon from the *2ª cp.* forward to support a counterattack by the *1ª cp.* to clear the Indians in front of the position. Using maneuver and fire, the *paracadutisti* forced the Indians to fall back. This action lasted about an hour.

As the exchange of fire and probes were happening around Quotas 628 and 538, Brigadier Russell understood he could not allow the Italian defense to delay his advance towards Giovanni Berta. He ordered patrols out to discover a way around the western flank of the Italian positions that was suitable for armoured cars and motorized infantry. A Sqdn of the CIH had already been ordered by the 4th Indian Division to press further west then north to gain the via Balbia at a point west of Giovanni Berta. Initial reports from the squadron indicated that there was a possible route, rough but passable. With this information, Russell ordered the 4/6 Raj. and

57 TNA Operations – 4th Ind. Div. 18 Nov. 41 – 28 Feb. 42, TNA WO 221/559, 18–20 December 1941; Secret War Diary of the 5th Indian Brigade, May–December 1941, TNA WO 169/3342 PAIF Box 15, 15-20 December 1941.

58 5th Indian Brigade War Diary, 18–20 December 1941; Central Indian Horse War Diary, March–December 1941, TNA WO 169/3409, 15-20 December 1941 and TNA WO 169/3434: 3rd South African Armored Reconnaissance Battalion War Diary, Box 384, Appendix A, pp.8-9.

the SA armoured cars westwards to position themselves for an advance north around the Italian right flank. He then ordered the artillery to begin fires against Quotas 628 and 639 to prepare those objectives for an attack by the 1/6 Raj. to envelop the Italian position from the west and south. The attack would cover the movement of the flanking force and possibly turn the Italian position and open the direct route to Giovanni Berta.

Maggiore Alessi noted the shift in the enemy's artillery fires and sensed that Indians might possibly attack the western flank of the *3ª cp.* to turn the position. At 0900 hours he received orders that instructed him to hold until 1900, then retreat back to Giovanni Berta. At 1000 hours, he ordered the 47/32 c.c. platoon that was in reserve with the *2ª cp.* to move to a position slightly behind the extreme western flank of *3ª cp.* where it could fire on any enemy attack against the west or northwest of Quota 639. Once near their selected position, the gunners were unable to occupy it as the artillery fire made the final movement too dangerous. As he was making these adjustments, he was unaware of the enemy forces preparing to bypass his position and travel north to the via Balbia. The *paracadutis*ti had too much terrain to cover and the broken ground allowed plenty of concealment for the Indian's movement. Alessi believed that the terrain to the west would prove too difficult for the rapid movement of motorized forces. Dismounted infantry could possibly slowly traverse the terrain, but the Eluet el Asel crossroad blocked the route the enemy trucks and armoured cars would need to travel to interdict the Italo-German retreat.

Casualties mounted from the enemy artillery and suppressive machine gun fire during the morning hours. The shallow firing positions and rock sangars provided little protection against the high-explosive rounds of the British 25 pdrs and mortars. Only the smaller high-explosive rounds of the 47/32 c.c. could return fire, but the flat trajectory of the anti-tank guns could not reach the enemy guns behind the hills.

During the time the artillery had been firing on the defensive positions, the Indian infantry had been working forward against the right (western) flank of the *1ª cp.* on Quota 628. Using the cover of the numerous spurs from the hills, they attempt to infiltrate to get close to the Italian positions to prepare for a rush. The movement was noticed by the *1ª cp.* and small arms fires were directed to suppress their movement.

At approximately 1300 hours the enemy fire intensified starting in the east against the *1ª cp* holding Quotas 585 and 628 and then across the front. All the *paracadutisti* could do was press closer against the ground and await the Indian attack. Any movement up the roads was blocked by high-explosive rounds fired by the 47/32 c.c., rifle fire and hand grenades. The *bombe Passagli* were particularly effective with their large explosive content, much better than the smaller standard issue O.T.O and S.R.C.M. hand grenades.

The 4/6 Raj. started its cross-country move at 1330 hours. The battalion had the South Africa armored cars leading, with the four companies of the battalion traveling in a diamond formation. Their line of advance was well west of the *carabinieri* positions and went unobserved. The two Italian infantry companies of the *65º rgt.* that had withdrawn the day before would have provided some warning if they had remained.[59]

The 1/6 Raj. began its attacks against the Italian positions at 1400 hours. A and D Coys had shifted west to maneuver around the *paracadutisti*'s open flank. B Coy moved north to continue to put pressure on Quota 628 while C Coy remained in reserve. During this time, A and C Coys, 4/16 Punjab arrived behind the 1/6 Raj. and were fed into the fight. The 4/16 Punjab had been ordered by 7th Ind. Bde. to also advance to Giovanni Berta to cut off any possible enemy retreat. The route selected now found it on the same road the 5th Ind. Bde was attempting to clear.[60] The *paracadutisti* had stopped the advance of four infantry battalions, two armoured car squadrons, and their supporting artillery.

The fighting against the *3ª cp.* saw the Indian troops use the broken ground to maneuver close to and around the defenses while the *paracadutisti* used rifle and machine gun fire, along with heavy use of grenades to repel the attacks. Once the Indians were pinned down by fire, the *paracadutisti* began to use two/three-man teams to maneuver around their positions to trap them into a cross fire. Seeing the danger of their exposed positions, the Indians fell back to their concealed positions south of the hill line. By 1500 hours the battle had quieted down, with only the continual artillery fire informing everyone that the battle was not over.

During this lull in the fighting *maggiore* Alessi sent the commander of the *2ª cp.*, *tenente* Casini, to report on the situation with *3ª cp.* and recalled the *1º pl* of the *2ª cp.* to rejoin its company. At the same time, the 47/32 c.c. platoon was finally able to reach its position on the exposed right flank of *3ª cp.* Once there, the *bersaglieri* gunners built a bit of protection for the two guns using rocks while other *bersaglieri* hauled ammunition to the position.

This was also a time for the *paracadutisti* to move their wounded to the aid station near the battalion headquarters. Only basic first aid treatment could be performed as the battalion possessed only basic medical supplies. *Tenente med.* Giuseppe Leporace did what he could for the men and then the wounded were moved to the trucks in the Wadi el-Hamar in preparation for the battalion's eventual withdrawal.

The Indians had also used the lull to continue their envelopment. At 1600 hours the *3ª cp.* reported a large number of infantry west and north of their position. The recently repositioned 47/32 c.c. guns now had targets and began a slow fire with high explosive shells to harass and slow down the movement of the Indian troops. It became clear to *maggiore* Alessi that the enemy planned to attack the *3ª cp.* from the northwest and turn the battalion's defense. He committed two platoons from the *2ª cp.* to counter the enemy movement while keeping the third platoon of the company in reserve.

59 TNA WO 169-3434: 4/6 Rajputana Rifles I.A. War Diary, Dec. 1941, 18-20 Dec. 1941.
60 TNA WO 169-3344: 4/16 Punjab I.A. War Diary, 18-20 Dec. 1941.

The two platoons moved north from Quota 585 to the rear of Quota 637 and then used the hill to mask their approach to a point where they could overlook the Wadi es-Samm. Once they arrived on the western slope of Quota 637, they should have been able to see the 47/32 c.c. platoon covering the western flank of *3ª cp.* They could not spot the anti-tank position, so continued to move forward. Suddenly the lead platoon began to receive enemy fire. Two Indian infantry companies from the 1/6 Raj. had moved around Quota 654 and onto the high ground on the south side of the Wadi es-Samm. This placed the enemy directly west from Quota 639 and able to threaten the right flank of the battalion.

The two platoons from *2ª cp.* initially attacked with the lead platoon establishing a base of fire while the trailing platoon maneuvered to flank the enemy from the north. The westernmost platoon of *3ª cp.* was able to add its fires to the attack, increasing the pressure on the Indians. The Indian troops soon recognized the danger of being flanked in turn from the north, and quickly fell back behind Quota 654.

The enemy's turning movement had exposed the anti-tank platoon's position and they came under intense fire. Ordered to withdraw, the *bersaglieri* gunners were unable to prepare the guns for movement. With no other options, the guns were disabled and the crews withdrew back towards the battalion headquarters. The *3ª cp.* was able to move their wounded back to the aid station during this time frame. During this action, some of the *paracadutisti* had observed a number of enemy vehicles to the west that were traveling north through the broken terrain.

With darkness rapidly descending over the battlefield, *maggiore* Alessi ordered the companies to begin to disengage at 1800 hours. A rear guard of 40 men was tasked to remain behind to cover the retreat of the battalion. *Tenente* Lino Grilli and his platoon from *1ª cp.* would hold Quota 628, while *tenente* Enrico Mollo and his platoon from the *3ª cp.* would hold Quota 639. Both had orders to hold their positions until 2200 hours and then disengage to rejoin the battalion.

Reviewing his resources, *maggiore* Alessi initially feared that there were not enough trucks to move the entire battalion. A search of the area found an Italian truck that was likely abandoned by one of the retreating units the previous day. With all the *paracadutisti* loaded and led by Alessi's command car, the ten trucks set out for Giovanni Berta at 1840 hours. Two trucks were left in the Wadi el-Hamar for the rearguard. As the small convoy drove north, Alessi was unaware of the significant change in the operational situation along the via Balbia.

Retreat to Bengasi

As previously discussed, Brigadier Russell had ordered the twenty armoured cars of the 3/SAAC, along with the 4/6 Raj., and the battery of the 31st RA to follow the route identified earlier by A Sqdn/CIH. Their orders were to make a dash to the via Balbia to secure the crossroad just west of Lamluda to block any retreating enemy. Traveling cross-country, the movement was initially quite slow due to the broken and rocky nature of the ground. At 1500 hours near Abir Hadda the commander of A/CIH met with the battalion commander of the 4/6 Raj., Lieutenant Colonel Laurenson, and briefed him on the situation. Patrols of the CIH had traveled several kilometers west from Ras Sciatata along the southern road and had been fired upon but no large organized enemy forces were in the area. Laurenson explained his battalion's orders and instructed the CIH squadron to screen his battalion's west flank.

Moving north, the column reached the southern route of the via Balbia approximately halfway between Ras Sciatata and the Lamluda crossroad shortly after 1600 hours. The armoured cars and infantry lorries of the lead company were able to quickly drive to the crossroad and the lead elements occupied the area at 1630 hours. This move took the retreating Italians and Germans by surprise as some small Axis elements were quickly captured. As the other companies arrived, Laurenson established roadblocks to the east, west and south of the crossroad. Each position was manned by one company with his fourth company held in reserve.[61]

The British and Indian troops began to capture more men, equipment and supplies as the Italian and German forces literally retreated blindly into the roadblocks as no alarm had yet been sounded about the danger. As darkness fell, A/CIH closed up with the battalion while 1 Coy, 3/SAAC worked independently driving westwards along the via Balbia.

Simultaneously, elements of the 7th Indian Brigade had entered Derna on 18 December. While the 5th Indian Brigade had been delayed by the *paracadutisti* at Eluet el Asel, the majority of the 7th Indian Brigade had been stopped and its trucks taken from it to support the movement of the armoured forces in the south. Only small patrols were working towards Giovanni Berta. Italian rearguard units were holding Giovanni Berta but were collapsing westwards to escape. *Maggiore* Alessi and the *paracadutisti carabinieri* were driving north in the belief that their escape route was still open.[62]

The *paracadutisti* column arrived at Giovanni Berta at 1930 hours. Here *maggiore* Alessi met with *colonnello* Vaiarini. Word that the enemy was approaching from the east had arrived, so the column was organized such that the *paracadutisti* provided security for both the front and rear of the column. One truck with a platoon of *paracadutisti* from the *2ª cp.* would depart to clear the way forward, followed in 30 minutes by the main column. The main column was led by two *bersaglieri* motorcycle soldiers, followed by five trucks with the two remaining platoons of the *2ª cp.* the engineers and the *comando di battaglione*, and then *maggiore* Alessi in his staff car. The center section was a mixed collection of various fleeing units led by *colonnello* Vaiarini's staff car. The

61 TNA 5th Indian Brigade, 19 Dec 41, WO169/3342 PAIF Box 15; TNA WO 169: 3434: 4/6 Rajputana Rifles I.A. War Diary, Dec. 1941; TNA WO 169/3409: 3rd South African Armored Reconnaissance Battalion War Diary, Appendix A; TNA WO 169/3409: Central Indian Horse War Diary, March–December 1941.

62 P.C. Bharucha, The North African Campaign 1940–43 (Delhi: Ministry of Defence Government of India, 2012), pp.283–284.

third section contained the remaining two platoons from the *1ª cp.* and two platoons of the *3ª cp.* in five trucks.[63]

The lead truck departed at 2000 hours with the main body following at 2030 hours. The main body only had driven about six kilometers before they saw the lead truck stopped on the side of the road just short of a hilltop. *Tenente* Fanelli informed *maggiore* Alessi that an Italian column of artillery technical troops with fifteen trucks was in front of them and had been brought to a halt by an enemy roadblock near Lamluda. The roadblock consisted of damaged trucks, barrels of rocks and dirt, and any other material that was readily found in the area. The roadblock was covered by mortar and machine gun fire. With the enemy's attention focused on the artillery column to their front, the arrival of *paracadutisti* went unnoticed.

After conversing with *colonnello* Vaiarini, Alessi ordered two platoons from the *2ª cp.* to dismount, placing one platoon on each side of the road. Once in position, they were to flank and attack the enemy positions. The third platoon would rush the roadblock in their truck and clear the obstacles. The plan depended on surprise and speed. One advantage used by the *paracadutisti* was their extensive knowledge of the terrain gained during their time garrisoning the area.

The two flanking platoons advanced quietly while the enemy's attention was focused on the roadblock, firing at any movement or noise. Once in position, the *paracadutisti* opened fire and surprised the enemy. Pressing the attack, the platoons forced the enemy to retreat as the third platoon moved up the road and opened a path through the obstacles. While the *2ª cp.* was securing the area, *maggiore* Alessi reorganized the column as the *paracadutisti* were the only organized combat unit in it. With the most dangerous threat now likely to be in front of them, the two platoons from the *1ª cp.* and the two platoons of the *3ª cp.* from the rear of the convoy were moved forward in the column.

While the obstacles were being removed, loud firing and flares could be seen ahead of them. It was evident that the enemy was establishing another roadblock several hundred meters further west. Speed was now more important to deal with this new threat before the enemy became too strong to defeat. *2ª cp.* was already moving forward to deal with the new problem. A message from the company requested that several Breda 30 f.m. be set-up to provide covering fires as the company advanced. *1ª cp.* dismounted their f.m. and positioned them to support *2ª cp.*

This new roadblock was built on a small bridge using damaged German and Italian trucks. A small stone wall had been hastily erected to cover the road. It was now close to 2130 hours and the *2ª cp.* pushed ahead to again flank the enemy. When the time was right, *maggiore* Alessi committed the *3ª cp.* frontally as the enemy was dealing with the flanking movement. The enemy was using flares to illuminate the area, exposing the Italians to rifle and machine-gun fire. *Tenente* Perrone and *brigadier* Romano were able to identify the enemy's location and suppressed the enemy launching of the flares,

63 Cursi, *I Leoni*, p.105; Ferrara, *I carabinieri*, pp.58–59.

allowing the *paracadutisti* to use the darkness to rapidly advance. The enemy retreated as the *paracadutisti* cleared the area and opened a gap in the roadblock.

While the fight at the second roadblock unfolded, twenty *paracadutisti* from the rear guard left at Eluet El Asel under *tenenti* Solito and Grilli joined the rear of the column. They had been holding Quota 628 and were able to follow their orders and disengage from the enemy at 2200 hrs. They had no information on the status of *tenente* Mollo's men on Quota 639.[64]

Passing through the gap made in the second roadblock, the fourth vehicle in line was hit by machine gun fire. The firing had wounded the driver, but *tenente* Perrone was able to control the truck and keep it moving. The dismounted *paracadutisti* continued to move and clear the area, allowing the column to continue its westward movement.

Disorganization was beginning to set in and the *carabinieri* were getting tired. Gaps began forming in the long line of trucks as they moved down the road in the darkness. Four of the battalion's trucks got separated from the main body and became entangled with other Italo-German units attempting to flee. The head of the column moved through Lamluda and then the crossroad to the west, only to find another roadblock. It was 2300 hours and the battalion had only traveled eleven kilometers in three hours. The *2ª cp.* again dismounted and attacked, forcing the Indians away from the roadblock. The *paracadutisti* reached the roadblock and cleared a gap through the wreckage. Only four of the battalion's eight trucks were together in the lead. *Maggiore* Alessi could not wait for the remaining four trucks and ordered the column to move ahead.

The lead four trucks drove through the gap and headed west. A short time later the four trucks of the rear section approached the third roadblock. As the lead vehicle entered the gap, it hit a mine and overturned, blocking the gap. The Indian soldiers had been reinforced and now a second fight for the third roadblock began. Close combat ensued in the dark, but the *carabinieri* were running low on ammunition and were exhausted. As the lead section with the *2ª cp.* continued to drive down the via Balbia, the *1ª cp.* and part of the *3ª cp.* had run out of options. Some surrendered to the Indian troops while others avoided capture and used the darkness to slip into the countryside. Organized resistance by the column collapsed and the four trucks that previously passed the last roadblock were all that was left of the battalion.[65]

The remaining *paracadutisti carabinieri* now traded security for speed. Three kilometers further down the road, the column crossed that of an enemy column. Darkness, speed, and surprise allowed both sides to pass before anyone could think about firing. A few kilometers further down the road at a bend, the lead truck driving without its lights hit a rock and was stopped. It was the fourth roadblock. The *paracadutisti* quickly dismounted and established security. There was no firing and *maggiore* Alessi realized that the roadblock was unmanned. Clearing the blockage, the column then sped off, passing through Luigi Di Savoia before reaching the crossroad that led to Cirene. Here they stopped and

64 Ferrara, *I carabinieri*, p.61.
65 Ferrara, *I carabinieri*, p.62.

awaited the trucks of the second group, not knowing the fate of the column. After ten minutes two trucks appeared in the dark. The trucks were under the command of *tenente* Perrone was carrying a mix of *paracadutisti* and other Italian soldiers. They had managed to escape in the confusion of the night and now rejoined *maggiore* Alessi.[66]

After waiting a few more minutes, more vehicle sounds were heard. These were certainly those of an enemy column. The *paracadutisti* loaded their trucks and continued the journey to Bengasi.

Arriving at Bengasi, they found there was no plan to defend the town. The *paracadutisti* located a fuel depot before the officer in-charge ordered its destruction. The *paracadutisti* were able to refuel their trucks and then take their dead and wounded to the Bengasi hospital, leaving them to the care of the hospital staff. Two hours later they were on the road driving south and arrived at Agedabia on the evening of 20 December. There they found the two companies of the *65° rgt. fanteria* that had previously held Chaulan. The *paracadutisti carabinieri* were finally able to rest. *Maggiore* Alessi could count a total of 44 *paracadutisti carabinieri,* and ten men from the engineer platoon.[67]

While the main body of the battalion were attempting to escape the trap that the British and Indians had set, the two rearguard platoons continued to fight at Eluet el Asel. The Indians maintained their pressure on Quota 628 and 639 and tried to maneuver around the Italian positions. As the 1/6 Raj. was focused on enveloping Quota 639, the platoon on Quota 628 was able to disengage and move back to the Wadi es-Samm and the trucks. Mounting up, they drove north at 2200 and rejoined the battalion as previously stated.

The platoon under *tenente* Mollo on Quota 639 was unable to break free of the enemy. After the retreat of *tenente* Grilli's platoon, A and C Coys of the 4/16 Punjab had been able to push forward four kilometers north of the crossroad and block the road to Giovanni Berta. A few hours later D Coy, 3/1 Punjab then relieved the two 4/16 Punjab companies so they could rejoin their battalion. *Tenente* Mollo's platoon was now effectively surrounded. Their ammunition was now running low and no reserve ammunition was left in the Wadi es-Samm where the battalion's *plotone servizi* had maintained the battalion trains. Mollo was faced with the fact that there were no remaining positive options for the *paracadutisti* defending the hill.[68]

Sensing a lull in the firing at 2300, *tenente* Mollo ordered his men to infiltrate the enemy lines to the west of the position and escape to Luigi Savoia. They managed to break free and reach Acquaviva near El-Chegab, just ten kilometers southeast of Luigi Savoia at 0900 hours on 20 December. Here they learned from the villagers that the British had occupied the entire area and motorized columns had continued further

66 Cursi, *I Leoni*, pp.112–113.
67 Ferrara, *I carabinieri*, pp.62–63; Longo, *I «reparti speciali»*, p.279.
68 This account of tenente Mollo and his men in the following paragraphs is from Cursi, *I Leoni*, pp.115-123 and briefly mentioned in Ferrara, *I carabinieri*, p.62.

west. Realizing that further escape was impossible, the *paracadutisti* accepted the offer to remain in the village.

Hearing that a *tenente* of the *carabinieri* was at Acquaviva, the head of the Luigi Savoia district Mr. Giuseppe Gagliotti, invited the *tenente* to his house. The Arab population had begun attacking Italian settlements, so Gagliotti was instructing the people to move to Luigi Savoia for safety. Most of the Italian settlers were women and children, so having the *carabinieri* at Luigi Savoia would provide protection to the settlers. Steps needed to be implemented to hide the *paracadutisti carabinieri* from the British, but that could be done.

Over the next two months until the Italo-German forces recaptured the area, *tenente* Mollo and his men secured the area to protect the settlers and collected other Italian soldiers who had escaped the British. They eventually numbered over 150 men, including 60 *paracadutisti*. The British executed several sweeps in January 1942 to find escaped Italian soldiers, recapturing 60 of them which included twenty *paracadutisti*. After the Axis reoccupied the area in February 1942, Mollo and 72 men were able to rejoin with the other survivors of the battalion at Aziza.

With the final count of losses, the *I btg. paracadutisti carabinieri* had present at Aziza on 5 March 1942 a total of 112 men: 14 officers, eight non-commissioned officers, two engineer non-commissioned officers, 72 *carabinieri*, and two engineers of the parachute battalion, along with one regular *carabinieri* and twelve soldiers of other various branches.[69] The battalion itself had been formally disbanded on 28 December 1941, leaving the question of how to employ the surviving personnel?

On 10 January the *Comando Superiore Aviazione R.E.* decided the battalion would not be rebuilt. On 7 March, the S.M.R.E. ordered the survivors of the *paracadutisti carabinieri* transferred back to Tarquinia. It would be in August of 1942 before any *reparti paracadutisti* returned to Africa.[70]

It is difficult to avoid a comparison between the fates of the *I btg. paracadutisti libico* and the *I btg. paracadutisti carabinieri* in Africa settentrionale. Both units fought in a theater of operations that lacked any plans for their employment as parachutists. Both were held back during the major operation that decided the fate of the Italian forces in 1940–1941 and Italo-German forces in late 1941. Both were committed as rearguards to protect the retreat of their defeated armies against a fully mobile enemy, and both lacked a balanced combined arms structure when they fought.

These battalions demonstrated a high degree of small-unit combat efficiency. The majority of the units in the Italian army were manned by conscripts with only simple and basic combat training before they joined their units. The majority of officers in those units were *ufficiali di complemento* (reserve officers) whose education and experience was lacking as well. There was a shortage of officers and noncommissioned officers, leaving many platoons and companies short of experienced leaders. Most

69 Cursi, *I Leoni*, p.123.
70 Cursi, *I Leoni*, pp.119, 125.

Italian units often lacked any company and battalion maneuver and live-fire training before entering combat. These factors often negatively affected the performance of the R.E. on many battlefields during the war.[71]

The two parachute battalions were formed with volunteers whose officers and men tended to remain with the units for an extended length of time. Those *di complemento* officers who volunteered saw the speciality as a way of advancement in a service where *ufficiali in S.P.E.* had the advantage.[72] The dynamic of officers spending all their time with their men implemented by *colonnello* Baudoin at Tarquinia created the type of camaraderie and strong leadership seen in only a few units in the Italian army.[73] Due to the problems with the Salvator series of parachutes, all the early airborne units had profited from extensive tactical training during the times jump training had been suspended. The units were fully manned and the officer and NCO authorizations themselves were greater than other units in the army. This combination of factors made the *reparti paracadutisti* formidable opponents on the battlefield.

The question remains of why were airborne units dispatched to Africa settentrionale? None of the documents offer a compelling rationalization for the employment of paratroopers in North Africa. The *battaglioni libico* and *nazionale* were formed in A.S., so their presence was the natural outcome when Italy declared war. Sending the *carabinieri* appeared to lack any identified requirement necessitating their transfer. The deployment of the battalion must also be examined with the understanding that the R.E. was forming a *divisione paracadutisti* at Tarquinia. Why send a fully trained battalion at a time when Italy was experiencing difficulty in training the number of units required by the new division?

Three parachute battalions had now been lost in Africa fighting as regular infantry. Would the formation of a division-sized parachute unit change the perception of how these units should be employed? Was there a role for such a unit in any future offensive planning by *Comando Supremo*? 1942 would provide opportunities that had not previously existed to observe whether the Italian senior leadership possessed an understanding, a capability, and a desire to execute large-scale airborne operations.

71 Brian R. Sullivan, 'The Italian Armed Forces, 1918-40' in Allan R. Millett and Williamson Murray (eds.), *Military Effectiveness* vol III (Boston, Allen & Unwin, 1988), pp.200–204; Richard Carrier, 'Some Reflections on the Fighting Power of the Italian Army in North Africa, 1940-1943', *War in History,* vol 22, no 4 (2015), 516–523; Macgregor Knox, 'The Italian Armed Forces, 1940-43' in Allan R. Millett and Williamson Murray (eds.), *Military Effectiveness* vol III (Boston: Massachusetts: Allen & Unwin, 1988), pp.160–166.

72 *Ufficiali in servizio permanente effettivo* (S.P.E.). These were the regular officers in the RE. As the promotion system in the RE was very rigid, S.P.E. officers held a significant advantage for advancement.

73 The *alpini* and *carristi* (tankers) were also known for their strong officer-enlisted relationship. This characteristic of leadership is often cited in the success of many armies during the war.

7

Grande Unità Aviotrasporta

The work initiated in 1939 to study and possibly create a *corpo d'armata aviotrasportabile* (airborne corps) had basically been curtailed by the recommendation in the 26 November 1939 paper.[1] The final paragraph paper stated:

> Towards the end of the next year, when the air transport aircraft will become available, it will be possible to talk about the airborne unit which this office would however [prefer] to see reduced to more modest proportions than those previously estimated (at most one division).

The earlier designs had conceived of a corps consisting of two mixed divisions, each with both airborne and air-transportable combat elements. This vision would now be downscaled to a single parachute division. The call to delay any further work did not completely stop all on-going studies and experimentation. One project initiated in 1940 had its origin based on the corps discussion was to create an armor component that could be air transported and landed.[2]

An Armor Component

The vehicle selected was the *carro leggere L3 lanciafiamme* (lf, flame thrower). This was a CV35/L3 tankette that had been converted by replacing one of the two machine-guns with a flamethrower. Lacking adequate internal storage, an armored trailer was developed which was towed behind the vehicle to carry the liquid fuel. The trailer held 500 liters (110 imperial gallons), enough for approximately 20 seconds of continuous firing by the system. Range for the flamethrower was approximately 40 meters. An

1 Filippo Cappellano and Nicola Pignato *Gli autoveicoli da combattimento dell'Esercito Italiano* (Rome: USSME, 2002) vol. 2, p.724.
2 Cappellano and Pignato *Gli autoveicoli da combattimento*, vol. 2, p.727.

offensive weapon, this system was seen as a valuable addition to the airmobile corps. The study was to determine whether the L3 lf could be carried by a SM.82 transport aircraft.

After discussions with the Savoia-Marchetti company, it was determined that the current system exceeded the weight that could be safely carried by the aircraft. To reduce weight, the modification that had been developed during the combat in Spain would be used. As the trailer seriously affected the mobility of the L3, the liquid fuel trailer had been removed and a smaller 306 liter tank was mounted on top of the engine compartment. The large tank increased the height of the L3 lf, complicating the aircraft connecting mechanism needed for the project.

Even this configuration was deemed too heavy, so the *Centro Studi della Motorizzazione* (Study Center for Motorization) in Rome was instructed to develop a solution. The center had a production version of the L3 lf vehicle available and proceeded to design a smaller container that held 125 liters of liquid fuel. This not only reduced the weight to within the aircraft's limits, but the flat shape of the fuel tank resulted in retaining the original height of an unmodified L3. The major disadvantage of the new fuel tank was that the amount of fuel reduced the flamethrower's continuous firing time to approximately 5 seconds, making the final compromise of dubious combat value. A wooden mock-up of the fuel tank was built and installed for testing. The specifications for the modified lf fuel tank were also sent to Savoia-Marchetti for their approval and development of the aircraft coupling system. The final modifications were approved on 12 July 1940. Ansaldo was instructed to build ten armored versions of the 125 liter fuel tank and the *Centro Studi della Motorizzazione* was to prepare 10 vehicles for conversion. The L3 lf mock-up was shipped to the Savoia-Marchetti factory in Vergiate for full-scale design and testing of the coupling system.[3]

On 21 August 1940, *Superesercito* ordered that one of the modified L3 lf be sent to the Ansaldo factory for final testing of the aircraft connecting mechanism using a fully modified vehicle. This testing was satisfactorily completed and the remaining nine modified lf tanks were ordered to the depot of the *4º reggimento carristi* near Rome on 10 October.

A 10 October 1940 memorandum from *Superesercito* established the *compagnia carri L 3 lf Aviotrasportabile.* The company consisted of the company command (one L3 lf for the commander and one reserve L3 lf), and two platoons of four L3 lf each. The attached table of organization to the memorandum only lists the essential combat elements of the company (thirty-one officers and men and ten L3 lf vehicles). Other components of the company would be the same as a normal *compagnia carri L* (light tank company).[4]

3 Filippo Cappellano and Nicola Pignato *Gli autoveicoli da combattimento dell'Esercito Italiano* (Rome: USSME, 2002), vol. 1, 538; Cappellano and Pignato *Gli autoveicoli,* vol. 2, p.727.

4 Cappellano and Pignato *Gli autoveicoli,* vol. 2, pp.730–731.

The L3 lanciafiamme modified for transport by SM.82. Note the very small fuel tank for the component flamethrower mounted above the rear deck. (AUSSME)

Developing the method to carry the L3 lf under a SM.82. (AUSSME)

The final system fully achieved the design intent, even if the vehicle itself was marginally useful in combat. A SM.82 could carry a single L3 lf under its belly with the coupling mechanism installed in the bomb bay of the aircraft. The flame thrower tank could be quickly released and driven away from the aircraft in minutes. No provision of resupply of the fuel/oil mixture by air drop was developed, limiting resupply to using additional air landing sorties. Thirty-six tank crewmen from the *4° reggimento carristi* were selected and sent to Tarquinia for parachute training.

Whilst an interesting concept, the airborne armor company was never employed. The L3 flamethrower tanks were not a successful design and rarely saw combat even in its unmodified form. There was a number of the unmodified L3 lf in North Africa at the start of the war and twenty-four more arrived with the *divisione corazzato «Ariete»* in 1941. No known use of these vehicles has been documented.[5] The modified vehicles remained at the depot near Rome until October 1941.[6]

There was apparently another initiative to provide the airborne force with armour support. The Caproni aircraft company had begun working on a concept for an aircraft that could transport a M13 tank. The concept drawing shows a four engine transport identified as a Ca 180 that would carry the tank internally inside the fuselage. It is not known whether this work was initiated by the R.E. or whether Caproni was developing an independent proposal. No date for the concept is known and the work appears not to have advanced beyond this basic concept stage.[7] The idea of an airborne armor component would not be raised again until 1943.

Movements towards a Large Formation

The success of the German airborne operations in 1940 reignited interest in creating a *grande unità paracadutisti* (a large parachute unit) within the R.E. A significant step was taken on 26 March 1941 when *Superesercito* authorized the formation of the *1° reggimento paracadutisti*.[8] Up until this time, the focus was on separate battalions that would likely be employed individually or broken into smaller units for specific missions. Raids and sabotage were the most likely tactical operations the battalions would undertake. A regimental size unit implied the possibility of being used for a single mission and a mass airborne drop as demonstrated by the *1° rgt. paracadutisti «Fanti dell'aria»* during *Operazione «Gefara»* in 1938. The regiment would be based at Viterbo, the large military air field approximately 20 kms northeast of Tarquinia.[9]

5 Cappellano and Pignato *Gli autoveicoli,* vol. 1, p.538–539.
6 Cappellano and Pignato *Gli autoveicoli,* vol. 1, p.538.
7 Cappellano and Pignato *Gli autoveicoli,* vol. 2, p.242, 281.
8 Di Giovanni, *I paracadutisti*, p.130; AUSSME, *Costituzione dei 1° reggimento paracadutisti, 26 marzo 1941*, M7 405, cart. 6.
9 Puletti, Rodolfo, and Dell'Uomo, Franco *L'Esercito e i suoi corpo – Sintesi storica* (Rome: USSME, 1979) vol 2 book 1, pp.439–441; AUSSME, Ministero della Guerra

The possibility of a regimental-sized operation was reinforced by the planned structure of the regiment. The initial organization of the regiment was documented on 17 February 1941 and maintained the current battalion structure.[10] The regimental headquarters added a command and control capability that would allow the tactical handling of the three battalions. The headquarters now also contained a small *plotone servizi* (services platoon) that added a logistical support element that had been previously lacking. Still undecided was the addition of a support weapons company. The document listed a *compagnia d'armi d'impiego eventuali (paracadutisti)* (weapons company for eventual employment) but listed a range of options for its structure similar to a modern day modular unit. The company could include heavy machine guns, both 45mm and 81 mm mortars, 47/32 c.c.guns, and flamethrowers depending on the specific mission requirements. The document defined the squad organization for each of these weapons, with the number and mix of squads to be likely determined by mission requirements. A regimental depot completed the planned organization of the unit.

With this start, the major challenge facing the S.M.R.E. was to design a divisional structure that was capable of successfully achieving its assigned missions while able to be transported by the existing aircraft. This problem resulted in two different approaches in the design of the proposed division. These two solutions were debated within the S.M.R.E. in a series of memorandums in May and June of 1941.

The Ufficio Operazioni (Reparto I) sezione IIª of the S.M.R.E. presented the challenges in its 6 May 1941 memorandum.[11] The main identified issue was:

> However, the paratrooper formation – due to the limitations imposed by the jump – will need to have sufficient means to carry out a decisive mission even if alone: that is, it will have to have means suitable for the offense to normally ensure the possession of one or two airfields in order to achieve certain preliminary objectives. However, it will also need to have means of defense to be able to react to enemy counter-offensives and, if necessary, last until the arrival of the air landing [elements].

The main threat identified in the memorandum were enemy tanks and aircraft. The parachute units need to have substantial blocking (anti-armor) and anti-aircraft units. It was recognized that anti-armor capability was limited to the 47/32 c.c. guns or smaller, while the anti-aircraft weapons were limited to the 20/65 c.a. guns and smaller. The R.E. understood that the 47/32 c.c. was reaching the limit of its effectiveness against the latest Allied tanks, but there was no replacement under preparation to replace it.

memorandum 26 marzo 1941, *Costituzione del 1° reggimento paracadutisti*, M7 racc. 404 2ª, cart. 9.

10 AUSSME, *Formazione ed organici del reggimento paracadutisti, 17 febbraio 1941,* M7, racc. 405, cart. 5.

11 AUSSME Stato Maggiore R. Esercito paper 6 maggio 1941, *Oggetto: Note sulla costituzione di una divisione paracadutisti,* F7, racc.426, cart.5.

In partial compensation, the staff recommended that flamethrower detachments and *guastatori* units be added to the divisional organization. The flamethrowers were seen as both an offensive and defensive weapon, while the *guastatori* could be employed for assaults and sabotage while providing limited field engineering capabilities.

A key recommendation was that those weapons which were normally used in all types of operations (i.e,. mortars and machine guns) be decentralized and assigned to lower echelons than what was common in the R.E. For those more specialized weapons and units that were used only under certain situations (i.e. anti-tank and blocking units) be centralized higher under division control.

Mobility was also seen as a challenge for a division-sized parachute unit. It was desirable that the division be assigned a *battaglione motociclisti* (motorcycle battalion) and a *reparto motocarrelli* (small, motorized cargo truck unit). The former would give the division an ability to rapidly move a forward detachment to seize key terrain or location; the latter would provide logistical support and offer some capability to move a detachment of *paracadutisti* by vehicle once on the ground. Motocarrelli had originally been developed for use in mountainous terrain and had proven to be a successful small transport vehicle.

No successful techniques had so far been developed to parachute these vehicles. The recommendation was that the motorcycles be replaced by a *battaglione ciclisti* (bicycle battalion) which offered the additional advantage of not requiring fuel to operate. There was not a good replacement for the motocarrelli other than authorizing carrettini (hand carts) for the movement of supplies.

Artillery support was another consideration addressed in the memorandum. The 47/32 could fire a useful high-explosive (HE) shell that could provide limited artillery support but lacked range and the capability for indirect fire. Techniques for parachuting the 47/32 c.c. had already been developed at Benina in 1940 and so these guns were available to be used as part of the division. The cannoni 65/17 infantry support gun had been air-transported during *Operazione «Gefara»* and was now being tested to see if it could be parachuted as well. If used as the artillery piece in the *gruppi artiglieria paracadutisti*, not only would it provide a larger HE shell and a longer range than the 47/32 c.c. gun, but it would provide an indirect fire capability that the smaller gun lacked. The 65/17 gun did weigh nearly twice as much as the 47/32 c.c., but the gun could be broken down into five loads which could be dropped individually. Because of future decisions, the work on parachuting the 65/17 gun was not pursued.

The proposed unit structure in the 6 May document to meet these challenges was a parachute division with two components: a fully parachute-capable organization that would comprise the bulk of the division, and an air landing component that would quickly follow and comprised the heavier artillery and sustainment parts of the division. This structure differed from the earlier design with two equal components that effectively limited the combat power of the division that could be parachuted onto an objective.

An attached list of units and an organization table detailed the proposed design. The parachute capable part of the division would consist of:

- *Comando divisione.*
- Two *reggimenti paracadutisti* (each with two parachute battalions, one paracadute bicycle battalion, and one parachute 81mm mortar company).
- A *battaglione divisionale d'arresto* (blocking battalion) with a flamethrower company, two 47/32 c.c. companies, and a blocking/barrier engineer company.
- A *gruppo artiglieria* with three 65/17 gun batteries.
- A *sezione sanità* (medical section) with three medical units.
- A *compagnia divisionale trasmissioni* (divisional communications company).

The air landing part of the division would consist of:

- A *battaglione motociclisti* (motorcycle battalion) with two companies (each with two motorcycle platoons and one motorcycle machine gun platoon).
- A *battaglione carri L* (light tank battalion) with two tank companies.
- A *gruppo artiglieria* with three 75/13 howitzer batteries and light prime-mover tractors.
- A *gruppo contraerei* (anti-aircraft group) with two 20/65 batteries.
- A *reparto motocarrelli* (motocarrelli unit) with two motocarreli sections, each with 20 motocarrelli.

In the notes, it was recommended that once a method was developed to parachute the motorcycles, two motorcycle battalions should replace the two bicycle battalions in the parachute regiments. The motorcycle battalions should then be formed into a third regiment, leaving the two parachute regiments with only two parachute battalions.

This division would have a total of 4,740 personnel, 348 light machine guns, 42 heavy machine guns, 36 81mm mortars, 18 47/32 c.c., 24 flamethrowers, 30 light tanks, 12 65/17 guns, eight 75/13 howitzers, 16 20/65 c.a., 40 motocarrelli, and 80 motorcycles.

This structure created a robust airborne division. The equipment and technique for moving the L3/35 series of tanks using the SM.82 had already been developed for the L3 lanciafiamme. A similar system could quickly be developed to carry the smaller artillery tractors and motocarrelli. The 75/13 howitzer was a mountain howitzer and could be broken down for air transport. In all, there was nothing in the design that was difficult to implement if the decision was made to do so.

The chief of the S.M.R.E., *generale* Roatta responded to the proposal in his 16 May 1941 memorandum that was sent to the two operation sections of the S.M.R.E. and to S.M.G. on 20 May.[12] His main position was that the *divisione paracadutisti* should be designed to operate solely as a parachute unit. If any additional capabilities are required, it is better to have them organized as a separate *divisione aviotrasporto* and not be part of the *divisione paracadutisti*. As Roatta stated:

12 AUSSME Stato Maggiore R. Esercito memorandum n.589, 16 maggio 1941, *Oggetto: divisione paracadutisti*, F7, racc.426, cart.5.

> If this proposal is accepted, the units of artillery, light tanks, or armored cars should not form an integral part of the parachute division in order to maintain this unit's strong aggressive character; but they would be given to the air landing division: this [however] prevents in case you simply wanted to reinforce the parachute division, to have it followed only by units with these weapons.

It is difficult to comprehend the intent behind the last part of Roatta's statement. He appears to be arguing against his own position that these elements should be part of an airmobile division.[13] He is implying that these artillery and armour units cannot be separated from the air landing division, thereby requiring the involvement of that division in the operation. Why then have these units as part of the air landing division instead as part of the parachute division? Would it not also be better to reinforce the parachute division with its own heavy weapons so it could fully function in combat without requiring it to share likely scarce assets with the air landing division?

The 16 May memorandum then continued to address three areas: a revised regimental structure, obtaining sufficient aircraft, and the lack of suitable small arms. The memorandum outlined changes in Paragraph II to the *reggimento paracadutisti* organization that had been initially documented in February 1941 and is discussed in a later chapter.

The discussion of transport aircraft in Paragraph III addressed both production and suitability of the SM.82 transport for parachute operations. The S.M.R.E. calculated that 160 aircraft sorties were required to transport the entire division. At the time of the memorandum, only 60 SM.82 aircraft were in the R.A. inventory. Current production was six aircraft a month, with production increasing to ten aircraft a month later that year. A loss of three aircraft a month was anticipated through various circumstances.

Complicating the issue was that two basic types of SM.82 aircraft were being built: one outfitted with complete military equipment (bomb racks and other features), and one as a pure transport without the military equipment. The R.A. considered that airborne operations required aircraft that were fully fitted with the military equipment as the supply containers were carried and dropped using the bombing mechanisms. Half the current monthly production was built fitted with that equipment, the other half was not. Use of those aircraft built solely as transports for an airborne operation would require that the additional equipment be on-hand and fitted prior to their employment for the mission. This would require a decision to produce and store the necessary items for the conversions prior to any planned airborne mission.

13 The statement is: "Se si accoglie questa proposta, le unità di artiglieria e carri armati leggeri, o autoblindo, non dovrebbero fare parte integrante della divisione *paracadutisti*, per mantenere a questa unità uno spiccato carattere aggressivo; ma verrebbero dati alle divisione aviotrasportabile: ciò impedisce, nel caso si volesse semplicemente rinforzare la divisione *paracadutisti*, di farla seguire soltanto da reparti con queste armi."

This *paracadutisti* is equipped with an IF41/SP parachute, *elmetto per paracadutisti* M41, the *combinazione di tela per reparti paracadutisti* (gray jump smock) that was modeled after the German style, and the *scarpi per reparti paracadutisti* (jump boots). (AUSSME)

Training jump over Tarquinia. (Museo Storico delle Aviotruppe)

Even by this measure, the S.M.R.E. anticipated that multiple lifts (3 to 4) would be required to drop the entire division during an operation. As it was infeasible to maintain the entire transport fleet in readiness for parachute operations, Roatta recommended that the R.E. either purchase 16 SM.82 aircraft for exclusive use by the *divisione paracadutisti* or the R.A. dedicate that same number of aircraft to the division. Sixteen aircraft would adequately support the parachute training at Tarquinia and would allow the rapid deployment of a full *battaglione paracadutisti* for an operational mission.

Paragraph IV then discussed small arms for the *paracadutisti*. Development of a paratrooper version of the M38 moschetto per cavalleria that could be broken down or collapsed for jumps had been initiated. This work was stopped once the R.E. stated that an automatic weapon was preferred. Previously the R.E. had approached Germany to buy the same automatic weapons used by the fallschirmjägers. Germany agreed and offered 2,000 machine pistols, which Italy purchased sight unseen. This number of weapons was sufficient to equip the limited number of parachute battalions planned in 1940.

The reality was that the machine pistols Germany had actually offered were the MP.18 and not the MP.40. The MP.18 was considered unsuitable for use by the paratroops as its side-mounted magazine made the weapon unbalanced. Once the R.E. became aware of this fact, they instructed the Italian military attaché in Berlin to request that the 2,000 MP.18s be returned, or at least be exchanged for the MP.40. If the weapons could not be returned, they would need to be used and a further purchase of 2,000 more weapons (preferably MP.40s) would be required to meet the now larger requirement.

Here again one reads another puzzling statement by Roatta. He stated that the Italian made Beretta MAB 38A was the better weapon, yet its use was only presented as a back-up plan. Regardless of whether adequate numbers of German weapons could be secured, he proposed that the R.E. should immediately order 4,000 MAB 38As. If Italy was unable to obtain enough German machine pistols to equip the division, then the Berettas would be available for issue to the units. More troubling is his following statement that if sufficient German weapons were obtained, the now redundant Berettas could be given to the *Polizia Africa Italiana* (P.A.I.). Why these excellent submachine guns should not be retained and issued to R.E. units is another question that highlights the need for further research on the authorization of submachine guns first noted in Chapter 4.

STAMAGE then wrote what was likely an internal paper that lacked routing addresses and a signature on 21 May assessing the S.M.R.E. proposal.[14] The first section of the paper recapped the S.M.R.E. position from the 16 May document.

14 AUSSME Comando Superiore Stato Maggiore Generale OP/1ª, 21 maggio 1941, *Divisione Paracadutisti*, F7, racc.426, cart.5. The style of the paper itself and that it recommends what should be written indicates that this was an internal working paper. The paper also indicates that some coordination between STAMAGE and the Ministero dell'Guerra had occurred.

Of interest in this section is that the statement "For training and to always allow for immediate use of 1 battalion, it is essential that at least 16 aircraft are always available to the division" was added later as indicated by the different type and its insertion in a blank space at the end of the section. Whether the initial omission of this point was accidental or intentional is unknown.

The second section of the paper is headed Note and here *STAMAGE* offered comments on the four major points of the concept. The first point addressed was the lack of artillery organically assigned to the division. While *STAMAGE* acknowledged the inability to parachute the artillery, that headquarters felt that if an airport was seized, the artillery could be part of the division and air landed. The authors then noted the increased command challenges with two different units of the same echelon involved in operations against the same objective. The idea of creating an air landing division was considered acceptable but commented that aircraft production would likely determine whether a second division was supportable.

The second point was that organic artillery and tank units should be created as part of the division. The writers then agreed with the assessment of the transport aircraft situation in the third comment. The fourth comment was that the use of domestic weapons was preferred over using ones purchased from Germany.

The final section of the paper identified the guidance the writers felt should be provided to the S.M.R.E. and the S.M.R.A. from *STAMAGE*. To the S.M.R.E. the following guidance was recommended:

- That it was appropriate that the *divisione paracadutisti* have its own, albeit limited, artillery and armor units.
- That a study for an air landing division be prepared.
- Agreement on the issue of a lack of transport aircraft.
- That *STAMAGE* agreed with Ministero dell'Guerra that domestic weapons were preferred as there was no guarantee that Germany would continue to support the Italian requirements.

The recommended guidance to the S.M.R.A. was to maintain at least 80 SM.82 aircraft fully equipped for parachute operations and to increase the production of that version of the aircraft whenever possible.

In response to the S.M.R.E. 16 May memorandum, the S.M.R.A. stated on 25 May that it could not dedicate a fixed number of aircraft to the division. The R.A. stated that it could provide SM.82 or other types of aircraft from time to time that were equipped for parachute operations. To do so, the R.A. would require timely notice of the requirement and could not guarantee a fixed number of aircraft in advance. The issue of aircraft availability for training would remain unresolved.[15]

15 Antonello Biagini and Fernando Frattolillo *Diario Storico del Comando Supremo* (Rome: USSME, 1992), vol IV, book I, p.185.

Using the input from *STAMAGE* and Roatta, the Ufficio Operazioni II office again prepared what was apparently another internal working paper lacking routing addresses and a signature.[16] Dated 27 May 1941, the paper provides a side-by-side comparison of the implemented (it is assumed approved) divisional organization and the original staff recommendation from 6 May without the air landing component.

	Implemented	**6 May**
Light machine guns	336	324
Heavy machine guns	36	36
Anti-tank rifles	36	—
Flame-throwers	36	24
81mm mortars	12	36
47/32 c.c.	24	18
65/17 guns	—	12
Personnel	3,300	3,820

The divisional structures were very similar, with the implemented design having 500 less men than the 6 May proposal. While the implemented division appeared to have more anti-tank weapons, the *fucili controcarri* (anti-tank rifles) were the Polish tipo 35/P which offer little effective anti-tank capability. The significant difference between the two designs was the indirect fire systems; the 6 May design possessed forty-eight 81mm mortars and 65/17 guns while the actual design had only twelve 81mm mortars. The lack of indirect fire systems in an infantry fight was problematic as demonstrated by the actions of the *I btg. libico paracadutisti* and the *I btg. carabinieri paracadutisti* during the fighting at Derna and Eluet el-Aset.

The inability to provide heavier artillery that provided indirect fire capability joins the list of questionable decisions as Germany had already demonstrated the answer: the use of cargo gliders. Nowhere during the discussions of the structure of the division were gliders addressed, especially when Germany had formed glider regiments for various types of units within both its own parachute and air landing divisions. The Allies would also embrace the use of gliders in their airborne operations for both troop units and the transport of heavy equipment.

Alianti d'assalto (Assault Gliders)

Like many other European countries, gliders were flown in Italy in the 1920 and 1930s as a civilian hobby. The first school was established in 1927 by Italian aviation

16 AUSSME Stato Maggiore R. Esercito paper 27 maggio 1941, *Oggetto: Divisione paracadutisti*, F7, racc.426, cart.5.

Visit of Umberto di Savoia, Prince of Piedmont, to Tarquinia on 20 June 1941. *Col.* Baudoin is to the left in the picture wearing the bustina (overseas cap). On the right is *gen. di brigata* Frattini who will take command of the «*Folgore*» in 1942. (AUSSMA)

enthusiasts after observing the German sport. The Fascist government saw this as a method to encourage Italians to learn to fly and 35 schools were in operation by 1935 under a program managed by the Gioventù Italiana del Littorio (G.I.L., Italian Youth of the Lictor, the fascist youth organization). These schools were focused more on preparing their students for training in power flight and service in the R.A. and not for any military application of gliders. The number of schools was reduced to ten in 1940.

Gliders had demonstrated their value during the Germans operations in 1940 and recently during the Battle of Crete which unfolded during the time period of these discussions. Providing the *paracadutisti* with heavier artillery and other equipment to support their capture of an airfield could be done using gliders without involving the *divisione aviotrasportabile.* On 27 May 1941, the S.M.G. asked the S.M.R.A. whether there were any Italian gliders suitable for military use. The answer was no. A request send to Germany in June for details on their glider operations on Crete went basically unanswered. It was not until October that the R.A. issued a solicitation to build a military glider.[17]

Gliders offered several positive advantages with few disadvantages. The positive advantages were the lack of special training or equipment for the transported units (no parachute training); the towing aircraft did not need to expose itself to enemy fire

17 Emilio Brotzu and Gherardo Cosolo, *Dimensione Cielo: Trasporto 9* (Rome: Edizioni Bizzarri, 1976), p.75

while flying over a drop zone but could release their tows a distance away; gliders were more accurate in landing as they were piloted; and the men/equipment in the gliders landed as a unit with no dispersal due to weather or other variables. The men and weapons delivered by glider were ready for immediate action with no need to remove parachutes and harnesses, to assemble weapons, or collect supply containers.

There were some disadvantages. Gliders did require to be built, but normally did not require the use of strategic materials; wood and fabric were often used for construction. Glider and tow aircraft pilots required training for the unique skills needed to fly the combination.[18] Overall gliders were a resource that required much up-front investment that then could only be used under very specific circumstances. As such they are a sunk cost to the military that might never be recouped through use.

It was not until the summer of 1942 during the planning against Malta that the R.A. established the *Scuola Piloti Alianti da Sbarco* (School for Assault Glider pilots). The school employed R.A. instructors from the prewar G.I.L. glider program, but few of these pilots had experience in military gliders. Only commercial gliders were available for training in 1942 which allowed for basic flight instruction, but flying these aircraft was significantly different from flying the larger and heavier military gliders. Lacking an Italian military glider, Italy had ordered 110 DS.230s and 10 Go.242s from Germany. The DS.230 order was later reduced to 50, but only 10 DS.230s and four Go.242s would eventually be delivered in 1943.[19]

Without an operational objective and burdened by an overly comprehensive training curricula, nothing became of the Italian glider program. A prototype of an Italian designed and built glider, the AL.12/P was delivered to the school in 1943, as well as the aforementioned German gliders. Renamed the *Nucleo Volo Senza Motore* (N.V.S.M.), only 11 students from a training group of 250 attendees at the school had fully qualified as glider pilots by September 1943.[20]

There would be additional changes to the structure of the *divisione paracadutisti* between the time it was mobilized in September 1941 to its deployment to El Alamein in July 1942, but many of the design concepts had been set during these discussions. The resulting division would be mainly a light infantry force with little heavy firepower and mobility. The R.E. had discussed these limitations and had identified solutions. How well these solutions were implemented would impact the performance of these *grande unità* in combat.

18 Nino Arena, Nino, *La Regia Aeronautica* (Rome: USSMA, 1986), vol.4, p.703.
19 Nino Arena *La Regia Aeronautica* (Rome: USSMA, 1984), p.702.
20 Arena, *La Regia Aeronautica*, vol.4, pp.703–704.

8

1ª divisione *paracadutisti*

1941 was a busy year for the parachute school at Tarquinia. Besides the deployment of the *carabinieri* to A.S., changes were occurring With the parachute problems resolved with the introduction of the IF.41/SP, parachute training at the school could resume in mid-March.[1] The first three battalions completed their qualification jumps by 8 June, but new requirements for training had begun to be placed on the school. Besides the need to meet the Regio Esercito's requirements, the Regina Marina (R.M.) was now requesting training for new units. The school was facing a significantly expanding training requirement with limited resources to achieve it.[2]

Naval Parachutists

The participation of a detachment from the *reggimento «San Marco»* of the R.M. during *«Esigenza 2P»* was briefly discussed in a previous chapter. Their role in the operation was to remove any water obstacles or vessels that could impede the movement of the M.A.S. boats through the Corinth Canal. The volunteers for this new unit of the R.M. were sent to the *«San Marco»* depot barracks in Pola to be evaluated and processed. The detachment, now named *sezione «P»*, consisted of 20 men (two NCOs, two junior NCOs, and sixteen sailors) and arrived at Tarquinia on 10 March. *Sezione «P»* was joined by *tenente di vascello* Mario Biasutti who had been placed in command of the unit.[3] *Capitano del genio navale* (naval engineer Lieutenant) Giovanni (Nino) Buttazzoni was assigned as the technical expert. The men were integrated into

1 Marco Di Giovanni, *I paracadutisti italiani Volontari, miti e memoria della seconda guerra mondiale* (Gorizia: Editrice Goriziana, 1991), p.91.
2 Di Giovanni, *I paracadutisti*, p.130.
3 Nino Buttazzoni, *Solo per la Bandiera: I nuotatori Paracadutisti della Marina* (Milan: Gruppo Mursia Editore S.p.A., 2002), p.55. Massimo Di Martino, *Paracadutisti d'Italia – Uniformi distintivi equipaggiamenti* 1938-1969 (Milan: Edizioni Libreria Militare, 2019), vol. 1, p.213.

the *III btg. paracadutisti* for their parachute training as that battalion was beginning its pre-parachuting instruction. Shortly afterwards, the section was joined by *tenente di vascello osservatore* (naval observer Lieutenant) Giulio Conti who took command of the sailors.[4]

Conti was an experienced naval flight observer with twelve combat missions against Royal Navy ships and bombing raids over Alexandria. He had been awarded one Silver and two Bronze Medaglia al valor militare, as well as one Silver Medaglia al valore di Marina. He remained with the *San Marco paracadutisti* throughout the war.[5]

With the limited amount of time for training, it was hoped that the men of the *San Marco* needed only to participate in actual parachute training. This was quickly proven wrong, as medical issues alone rejected 40 percent of the volunteers. Without participating in the pre-jump physical training and other preparatory aspects of the program, many of the sailors were unable to complete the athletic requirements of the parachute school. *Tenente* Conti found himself requesting replacements for those men that had been eliminated from the program.[6]

By 22 April, 78 additional men had arrived for training at Tarquinia. At the school the sailors were integrated in the intensive program of combat training, including hand to hand combat with the combat knife, shooting the M34 Beretta semi-automatic pistol, M91 Carcano carbine, and the use of grenades. However the future of the detachment was suddenly in question as they received word of the German attack on the Corinth Bridge on 26 April. With the German operation preempting *Esigenza «2P»*, the mission the sailors were training for was no longer required. With uncertainty surrounding the unit, the detachment completed the last of its qualified parachute jumps by the end of May.

Throughout the training in April, *capitano* Buttazzoni had been developing new methods to insert raiding parties into enemy territory. Working closely with *sottotenente di vascello* Eugenio Wolk, an experienced navy diver, he started to experiment with parachuting into the water as an insertion technique. Wolk provided the navy dive suits and water-tight rubber containers for weapons and explosives the *San Marco* sailors would need. Using two rescue rafts issued by the R.A. for aircraft, he conducted an initial test at the end of April. The parachute jump and subsequent paddling of the raft to shore was successful and began to generate interest in the senior leadership in the possible use of this method.[7]

The cancellation of *Esigenza «2P»* left the unit without a role or a mission. Rather than await the likely disbandment of the unit, Conti believed that «*San Marco*»

4 Luigi Emilio Longo, *I «reparti speciali» italiani nella seconda guerra mondiale* (Milan: Mursia 1991), pp.281–282. Nino Arena, *50ª di Tarquinia, 1939-1989, Scuole Militare paracadutismo* (Comitato Promotore ex Istruttori delle Scuole Militari di Paracadutismo, 1989), p.46.

5 Longo, *I «reparti speciali»*, p.282.

6 Longo, *I «reparti speciali»*, p.282.

7 Buttazzoni, *Solo per la Bandiera,* p.50–51.

Paracadutisti preparing for a jump. They are wearing the *combinazione di tela per reparti paracadutisti* (gray jump smock), the improved *elmetto per paracadutisti M42*, and the *scarpi per reparti paracadutisti* (jump boots). (AUSSME)

paracadutisti offered an unconventional warfare capability to that provided by the *Decima Flottiglia Motoscafi Armati Siluranti* (*Xª MAS*).[8] Conti submitted a memorandum on 5 June proposing a *battaglione paracadutisti* as part of the *rgt. «San Marco»*. A 13 June memorandum written by *capitano* Buttazzoni outlined the possible mission set for the unit:

> Various sabotage actions against works located in or near water bodies (destruction of water basins, dams, bridge locks, power plants, etc.);
>
> - landing actions in areas that, due to the conformity of the terrain, do not allow the landing and disembarkation of Navy vehicles or the landing of common paratroopers (establishment of bridgeheads, landing heads, various actions on the ground, etc.);
> - actions to eliminate obstructions or other port defenses, opening the way to special means of the Navy and the Air Force;
> - direct actions on enemy ships, possibly combined with the cooperation of the Navy;

8 The *X MAS* were trained to use small, fast speed boats to penetrate enemy harbors and sink shipping with torpedoes or use explosive boats.

- finally unlisted actions, in cooperation with the Navy, with the Air Force or with the Army paratrooper regiments.[9]

In June, *tenente* Conti and *capitano* Buttazzoni continued to experiment with the concepts first piloted in April. On 12 June, a squad of eight men jumped from a height of 150 meters into the ocean off Tarquinia with two inflatable boats in bad weather conditions. The inflatable boats were a special design, lightweight and easy to handle in the water. They also tested a backpack for explosives that was carried by the parachutists but would separate from the jumper when his canopy deployed. The separation would trigger the opening of a smaller parachute on the backpack, carrying it and its contents safely to the water.

Sezione «P» was suddenly recalled back to Pola on 22 June, interrupting the sailors current training. This change was initially understood to be the beginning of actions to disband the unit. When the men arrived at the *«San Marco»* depot, rumors of reassignment orders for the men were heard to exist. Conti submitted a memorandum on 28 June arguing for the creation of a naval parachute battalion. The document also included a list of the weapons and equipment for the current 50-man detachment.[10] Both Conti and Buttazzoni discussed the possibilities that the unit offered the R.M. to *capitano di fregata* Biagini, the new commander of the *«San Marco»* depot. With his assistance, the two officers were able to convince *Supermarina* (the Naval General Staff) that not only should the unit be maintained, but it should be expanded. On 16 August, the *Supermarina* requested that the R.E. train enough additional sailors to complete a company size unit.[11] While awaiting a final decision on the expanded training, the unit returned to Tarquinia on 22 August 1941.

The expansion of the unit required more space than what was available at Tarquinia. The R.E. was also expanding its parachute force and barracks space was limited at the airfield. The R.M. also had concerns about maintaining secrecy of this new capability under development. The large number of men arriving at Tarquinia for training offered too many opportunities for the word about the unit to spread beyond the school. The R.M. decided to house the detachment at the naval barracks at Porto Clementino on the coast, a few kilometers from the airfield. This provided training areas away from the ones the R.E. used, but still provided easy access to parachute school.

While the detachment was training and experimenting with combat techniques, volunteers were being selected and screened at Pola to form the *compagnia «P»* of the *reggimento «San Marco»*. The company would have 155 sailors in the combat element of the company, and 147 sailors in the support element. There were 45 sailors in the detachment at Porto Clementino, so only 70 additional sailors were required to fill out

9 Longo, *I «reparti speciali»*, p.286.

10 Longo, *I «reparti speciali»*, pp.287–288. The request included 50 MAB 38A submachine guns and 50 Beretta M34 pistols.

11 Antonello Biagini and Fernando Frattolillo (eds) *Diario Storico del Comando Supremo* (Rome: USSME, 1992) vol IV book I, p.592.

the combat element. It was not until the end of November of 1941 that the manning of the company was completed, but the number of total students currently at the school delayed their training until 1942.[12]

Neither Conti or Buttazzoni were satisfied with the weapons and equipment available to the unit. The sailors were issued the same items as issued to the *reparti paracadutisti*. While visiting the Engineer School at Pavia, Buttazzoni was shown the MAB 38A submachine gun currently being manufactured for the *Polizia dell'Africa Italiana* (*P.A.I.*). After testing two examples of the MAB, Buttazzoni persuaded the R.M. to order 5,000 copies of the weapon for the «*San Marco*» regiment. The men of the San Marco were the first *paracadutisti* to be issued the MAB 38A submachine gun, which greatly increased the squad's firepower. It was a weapon the army parachutists had been promised but not yet received.[13]

Buttazzoni also visited Trieste where he spotted a Walter P-38 pistol in a shop. He bought the pistol and after testing it, again persuaded the R.M. to purchase 500 copies of the hand gun. Both the pistol and the MAB used the 9mm Parabellum cartridge, thereby simplifying battlefield resupply.[14]

The new weapons required new individual equipment. The *P.A.I.* carried a single magazine for the MAB (or only magazines that held ten rounds), the former requiring reloading the magazine using stripper clips.[15] This method for reloading was slower than changing the magazine. The «*San Marco*» sailors would use 40-round magazines and needed to carry a number of them in combat. A vest was designed that could carry twelve magazines vertically across the body (five across the front, seven across the back), allowing a man to carry 480 rounds. Because of its usual appearance, it was quickly nicknamed the 'Samurai' vest. The vest included six pouches along the bottom, each containing a hand grenade. It was a very practical item and could be worn while parachuting. It would be modified and adopted by the *guastatori* (assault engineers), the MAS units, and the R.A. parachute units during the war.

Always looking for better armament for the unit, Buttazzoni discovered a design for a lightweight rocket launcher similar to a bazooka or panzerfaust while at the Engineer school. The designer, Claudio Beimondo, worked in Turin and Buttazzoni visited him at his factory. The design was a lightweight, small caliber anti-tank with a rotary magazine. The designer was an engineer and had sent the plans and documentation to the engineer school at Pavia but never received a reply. Buttazzoni took the plans with him to Tarquinia and built several prototypes. The prototypes were

12 Longo, *I «reparti speciali»*, p.289.

13 Longo, *I «reparti speciali»*, p.284. The *I btg. paracadutisti libico* was the first parachute unit to use the weapon. The thirty MABs the Libyans possessed were not issued but received from the P.A.I. stocks.

14 Buttazzoni, *Solo per la Bandiera,* p.52–53; Longo, I *«reparti speciali»*, p.286.

15 A stripper clip is a thin strip of metal holding five or ten rounds of ammunition. The strip is placed in slots on the weapon and then the thumb is used to push the rounds into the magazine. The metal strip is then discarded.

demonstrated but the concept was not further developed. Buttazoni also experimented with silencers for both the pistol and the MAB, recognizing its usefulness for covert entry.[16]

The detachment was organized the same as an R.E. *paracadutisti* unit during the training for *Esignza «2P»*: the squad of eight men led by an officer or NCO. With the firepower of the MAB 38A, Conti decided the basic unit would now be a smaller unit of four men led by an officer or NCO. After the cancellation of *Esigenza «2P»*, the officers reassessed the unit's weapon requirement. Recognizing that the unit could be employed in a more conventional manner, Conti requested that two Breda 37 heavy machine guns be added to the unit's authorized weapons.

The Navy would increase their requirement for parachute training in August 1941 by initiating the formation of two new special assault units, *«G»uastatori* (assault engineers) and *«N»uotatori* (assault divers). Both units would require parachute training in 1942.[17]

Large Units

The authorization of the *1° reggimento paracadutisti* in March was the first step in forming a parachute division but the actual organization of the unit continued to be debated. The 27 May working paper didn't end the discussion on the armament and manning of the division. It was therefore not a surprise that the *1° rgt. paracadutisti* would be mobilized using a new document and not the 17 February 1941 document previously discussed.

Based on the on-going debates, significant modifications were made to the regimental organization in the 18 July 1941 authorization document.[18] The regiment would now consist of the three battalions and the *1a compagnia cannoni paracadutisti* with six 47/32 c.c. guns.[19] The 81 mm mortars, heavy machine guns and flamethrowers planned for the *compagnia d'armi* were added to the battalion *compagnia commando* (command company) and the separate company eliminated. The 47/32 c.c. guns would remained under regimental control as a separate unit. The 45mm Brixia mortars were removed from the regiment and would later be found in the *battaglione*

16 Buttazzoni, *Solo per la Bandiera,* p.53–54; Longo, I «reparti speciali», p.287.
17 Longo, *I «reparti speciali»*, pp.289–290.
18 AUSSME, *Formazione provvisorie guerra dei reparti di ftr. paracadutisti, 18 luglio 1941*, M7 racc. 405, cart. 6.
19 Di Martino, *Paracadutisti*, vol. 1, p.29; Arena, *Tarquinia,* p.33; AUSSME, *Formazione provvisorie guerra dei reparti di ftr. paracadutisti, 18 luglio 1941*, M7 racc.405, cart.6. Arena also stated that the parachute battalions would have 650 men, and include four Breda 37 heavy machine-guns, cp. mortai da 81 (mortar company) with six 81mm mortars and six Brixia 45mm light mortars. Arena implies that his information is from Anon, *Organizzazione e impiego tattico dei reparti paracadutisti* (Rome, Ministero di Guerra Stato Maggiore Regio Esercito, 1940), Arena's information is not found in that manual.

guastatori under divisional control. A new weapon, the *fucile controcarro* (anti-tank rifle) was added to the companies to provide some level of anti-armour capability. These weapons were the Polish-made *fucile controcarri 35(P)*, of which two were authorized to each company. The btg. paracadutisti were now authorized a total of 456 men, while the complete regiment had 1822 men. This was still a small unit compared to the parachute units in other armies. The provision of heavy weapons finally addressed the problems identified in the earlier combats and gave the units greater capabilities.[20]

Two significant changes were made in the July document. Whereas the February 41 document retained the plotone minatori in the battalions, the July 41 document deleted that platoon. No longer was sabotage a part of the battalion mission set. The second change was an increase in the logistical support for the regiment and its battalions. A *compagnia servizi* replaced the earlier platoon and contained a *plotini servizi* for each battalion, with a separate platoon for the remaining regimental assets. This company was not jump-capable as it contained vehicles and would need to be air-landed.[21]

These changes completed the transition of the parachute battalions from the light force for sabotage and raids into ones capable of seizing and holding critical terrain in support of operational level missions. The demolition capability previously provided by the *plotone minatori* was shifted to the new *compagnia minatori-artieri* at the divisional level.[22]

The requirement to organize, train, and equip a large combined arms force expanded the school's current mission. There had been previous work on preparing and parachute dropping the 47/32 c.c. gun, but now the school would need to design and test parachute harnesses and canopy configurations for an increasing number of different pieces of equipment. Resupply containers for ammunition would need to be modified from existing equipment or designed from scratch to support these additional weapons by aerial resupply. Equipment drop canisters for radios, medical supplies, engineer materials, etc. would need to be designed and tested. This work competed against the expanding training of the volunteers coming to Tarquinia to form the new units. *Comando Supremo* was aware of the limitations of the school to meet the expanding requirements, as it was discussed on 5 June between *generale d'armata* Ugo Cavallero, Chief *Comando Supremo*, and *generale di corpo d'armata* Mario Roatta, Chief of *Superesercito*. No new steps were taken to resolve the problem.[23]

The *IV btg. paracadutisti* was officially authorized in early April. Discussions about forming a parachute division followed on 1 May 41. *Generale d'armata* Alfredo Guzzoni, the Deputy of the *Comando Supremo*, held a meeting with the *Ispettore*

20 Antonello Biagini and Fernando Frattolillo (eds) *Diario Storico del Comando Supremo* (Rome, USSME, 1989) vol III book I, pp.221–222.
21 AUSSME, *Formazione provvisorie, 18 luglio 1941*, pp.4–5bis, 10bis.
22 AUSSME Stato maggiore R.E. memorandum 29 settembre 1941, *Oggetto: Mobilitazione di taluni elementi della divisione paracadutisti*, p.14.
23 Biagini and Frattolillo *Diario Storico*, vol IV book I, p.273.

dell'Arma di Artiglieria and *Ispettore dei Servizi Tecnici* on a range of topics. One topic was a discussion on the possibility of organizing a *divisione paracadutisti*.[24] More discussions followed on 6 May which included the integration of artillery and vehicles as part of a division and a proposed draft structure.[25] On 17 May and again on 28 May further discussions were held on forming a parachute division and its composition.[26]

Germany's invasion of the Soviet Union on 22 June 1941 introduced new requirements for the R.E. Mussolini's decision to send the *Corpo di Spedizione Italiano in Russia* (C.S.I.R.) now meant that Italy was fighting in three separate theaters of operation. The need for *Comando Supremo* to maintain a strategic reserve was now of greater importance as reinforcements and supplies now had to be prioritized between the three active theaters (A.S., Russia, and the Balkan theaters). The *1º rgt.. paracadutisti* now could be employed in places other than in North Africa.

During this time the *V* and *VI btg. paracadutisti* were created and began their training. The *1º rgt. para.*, now that its parachute training was complete, was moved to the Trentino for a tactical training cycle. The *IV* and *V btg.* completed their qualification parachute jumps by the end of August; the *VI btg.* completed theirs by the beginning of October. While the *VII btg.* was authorized and had begun its training cycle, the *2º reggimento paracadutisti* was stood up on 1 August 1941. The departure of the *I btg. paracadutisti CC.RR.* for North Africa in July meant a rearranging of the units forming the *1º rgt. paracadutisti*. The *1º rgt.* would now consist of the *II, III,* and *IV btg.* while the new *2º rgt.* would now consist of the *V, VI* and *VII btg.*, along with the new *2ª cp. cannoni para.* Tarquinia was required to train a full battalion every 45 days when the weather was favorable and aircraft were available.[27]

On 17 August 41 *Comando Supremo* notified *Supereserсito* about the planned decision to establish a parachute regiment in A.S. that would consist of two parachute battalions: the *I btg. paracadutisti CC.RR.* that was currently in A.S. and a new battalion to be raised in Libya. The new battalion would be mobilized from the trained *paracadutisti* remaining in Libya and from Libyan volunteers. For the parachute school, that decision meant that a new regimental headquarters and the supporting elements were added to the training load.[28]

24 Biagini and Frattolillo *Diario Storico,* vol IV book I, pp.10.

25 Biagini and Frattolillo *Diario Storico,* vol IV book I, p.44; AUSSME, Comando Supremo, 6 maggio 1941, *Oggetto: Nota sulla costituzione di una divisione paracadutisti*, M7 racc.404 2ª, cart.1.

26 Biagini and Frattolillo *Diario Storico*, vol IV book I, pp.127, 209; AUSSME, Stato Maggiore R.E., 16 maggio 1941, *Oggetto: divisione paracadutisti*, M7 racc.404 2ª, cart.1; AUSSME, Stato Maggiore R.E., 27 maggio 1941, *Oggetto: divisione paracadutisti*, M7 racc.404 2ª, cart.1.

27 Di Giovanni, *I paracadutisti*, p.131.

28 Biagini and Frattolillo *Diario Storico,* vol IV book I, pp.600–601; AUSSME, Commando Supremo, luglio 1941, *Oggetto: Ricostituzione battaglione paracadutisti libico*, M7 racc.405, cart.6;

A *paracadutisti* preparing to land during training. (AUSSME)

The *1ª divisione paracadutisti* was officially formed on 1 September 1941. The *Comando Supremo* was creating a significant strategic asset that could be deployed to any of the combat theaters to achieve an operational goal. If deployed, it would also be *Comando Supremo* that would need to provide the necessary resources and support to execute any airborne operation in North Africa or Russia. Command of the new division was given to *generale di brigata* Francesco Sapienza, an infantry officer. Sapienza had previously commanded the *48º reggimento fanteria «Ferrara»* in Greece as part of the *23ª divisone f. «Ferrara»* where he had performed well during the campaign. The new division would be headquartered in Rome.[29]

The division was organized as a divisione binaria (binary division) with two parachute regiments (the *1º* and *2º rgt. para.*) of three battalions each. Two *gruppo di artiglieria per divisione paracadutisti* (a parachute artillery group) was formed using

29 Puletti and Dell'Uomo *L'Esercito*, vol 2 book 1, p.95.

cadres from the two regimental companies of 47/32 c.c. to form the required gruppi with two batteries each. Included as part of the new division were the *VIII guastatori paracadutisti*, a *compagnia collegamenti* (signal company), and a *compagnia minatori-artieri* (mining and construction engineers).[30]

A division structure with only two regiments (divisione binaria) instead of the more common three regiments (divisione ternaria) was unique to the R.E. Born from experience during the Ethiopian War, the concept was to create a division that was easier to deploy into combat theaters. These divisions would have increased firepower but were smaller to reduce the logistical support needed to sustain the unit during combat. The key understanding was that the army corps, not the division, would be the important operational-level maneuver element on the battlefield. The role of the divisione binaria as a causal factor in the failures of the R.E. during the war has been assumed by many but never fully examined.[31]

On 4 October, the *3º reggimento paracadutisti* was organized.[32] Along with the *I btg. para. CC.RR.* already in A.S. plus the proposed Libyan parachute battalion, a *contro-carro* (anti-armor) parachute company would be provided from Italy to complete the regiment.[33] Yet the nascent Libyan battalion was being disbanded as the new regiment was formed, leaving one to wonder why a regiment was being placed in Africa. There is no information indicating that a third battalion for the regiment was ever planned.[34] *Superesercito* reported to the *Comando Supremo* on 11 November that the headquarters elements of the *3º reggimento paracadutisti* were ready to deploy to A.S. by the end of that month.[35]

It is difficult to understand the perceived need for a parachute regiment in A.S. by the *Comando Supremo*. The R.E. was building a division-size force at Tarquinia but now was dispersing scarce assets with no specific objective in mind. The lack of support systems required to maintain and successfully employ paratroopers in combat was completely lacking in that theater of operations. On 19 November at the start of Operation Crusader, there were only 24 transport aircraft in A.S., a mix of SM.75, SM.81s, and SM.82s. Four more SM.81s were available in the bomber squadron and six more SM.81s were supporting operations in the Sahara Desert region. Only 14–15 of these aircraft were listed as operational, a completely insufficient number for an

30 Di Giovanni, *I paracadutisti*, p.130; Giuseppe Lundari, *I paracadutisti italiani 1937/45* (Milan: Editrice Militare Italiana di Ivo Fossati, 1989), pp.13–14.

31 ANON, *L'esercito italiano tra la 1ª e 2ª guerra mondiale* (Rome: USSME, 1954), pp.122–129; Montanari, Mario, *L'esercito italiano alla vigilia della 2ª guerra mondiale,* (Rome: USSME, 1982), pp.268–269.

32 AUSSME, Comando Supremo *Oggetto: Comando 3º reggimento paracadutisti per A.S.*, M7 racc.405, cart.6.

33 It is unknown whether this company, identified as a *compagnia contrcarro* rather than a *compagnia cannoni*, would have eight 47/32 guns like the former or six guns like the latter.

34 Di Giovanni, *I paracadutisti*, p.90

35 Antonello Biagini and Fernando Frattolillo (eds) *Diario Storico del Comando Supremo*, vol V book 1 (Rome: USSME, 1995), pp.209.

airborne operation.[36] These 37 aircraft were all currently performing essential tasks and unlikely to be pulled from those tasks for the length of time necessary to train the crews for and then execute an airborne operation.

Without an operational requirement for employment as a parachute unit, the *paracadutisti carabinieri* that was already deployed to A.S. was employed in roles not well suited for their unique training and organization. The *paracadutisti carabinieri* were first employed as regular *carabinieri*, then as a regular infantry formation as discussed in the previous chapter. There is not any record of serious planning conducted by *Superasi* to employ the unit in an airborne role.

The impression one might form to explain the reasoning behind this decision of *Comando Supremo* is the understanding that until the reorganization of the *Stato Maggiore Generale* into *Comando Supremo* in May 1941, the *Comandi Superiori* of the various theaters were the highest warfighting headquarters. The *Stato Maggiore Generale* was only advisory and did not exercise any command functions, so the idea that *Comando Supremo* could control resources and direct their use was quite new. Once units were given to a theater, it was rare for any of them to be redeployed at a later date. This is in contrast to Germany where units were redeployed as needed throughout the war. The habit of giving resources to a theater and never exercising any further control of those resources likely proved difficult to break.[37]

One aspect of forming the new airborne speciality was creating the replacement system to maintain the strength of units deployed in combat zones. The R.E. used a system of unit replacement where each unit in a combat theater had a *reparto complemento* (replacement unit) at its home station in Italy. Units were recruited based on military districts, with units garrisoned in a specific military district only recruited/received conscripts from that district. The new soldiers would be equipped and trained by these units and then sent to the front as replacements when needed.

The men of the airborne units were not conscripts that supplied the manpower requirements for the R.E. but were all volunteers. The vast majority of these volunteers came from those already serving within the three services and not civilians that were newly enlisting to join the military. The exclusive use of volunteers significantly limited the manpower pool available to fill the ranks of the airborne forces. The rigorous assessment and training at Tarquinia further reduced the number of men available for the units. With the rapid expansion of the airborne force, the new volunteers were mainly needed to form the new units. The impact was there were few trained *paracadutisti* to form the *reparto complemento* that would be needed to support active operations. This was not a problem as long as none of the units were sent into

36 Mario Montanari, *Le operazioni in Africa settentrionale*, vol II (Rome: USSME, 1985); Tobruk, p.429.

37 Mario Montanari, *L'esercito italiano alla vigilia della 2ª guerra mondiale,* (Rome, USSME, 1982), pp.319–355; MacGregor Knox, *Hitler's Italian Allies* (Cambridge: Cambridge University Press, 2000), pp.69–70; Di Giovanni, *I paracadutisti*, p.90

combat, but the deployment of the *I btg. para. CC.RR.* to Africa brought this issue to the fore.

As the *Carabinieri Reali* was a separate service, it recruited its personnel separately from the R.E. Any new volunteers could be used to establish a replacement unit as the CC.RR. was not expanding its parachute force. A *compagnia complemento* for the *I btg. para. CC.RR.* was established in December 1941 and it was formally authorized on 4 January 1942. While enough enlisted *carabinieri* volunteered for the unit, the lack of officer volunteers remained a problem. No additional officers had volunteered since the establishment of the battalion, so the *cp. complementi* was organized with 13 NCOs and 101 *carabinieri*. The company was attached to the *Legione CC.RR. di Roma* and was administered by two officers from that unit. On 9 January the unit traveled to Tarquinia to begin training. After the destruction of the battalion and its formal disbandment in January by the S.M. of the CC.RR., the *cp. complementi* was also disbanded.[38]

The R.E. did not create a *reparto complemento* for the new *divisione paracadutisti* until March 1942. The unit was created as a *reparto misto complemento* (mixed replacement unit) that would train and maintain the replacements for all the different types of units in the division. Each regiment would be supported by a *battaglione complemento* with a total manning of 455 personnel. A *gruppo complemento* would support the *reggimento artiglieria paracadutisti*, and other smaller units would support the remainder of the division. It is unknown whether this replacement unit ever achieved its authorized strength as the demand for trained paratroops for the «*Nembo*» and «*Ciclone*», combined with the losses in the «*Folgore*» in the latter half of 1942 likely absorbed the bulk of the trainees.[39]

Officer volunteers were an issue for the speciality as a whole. As experienced when Balbo began recruiting officers for the first *reparti paracadutisti* in Libya, most officers were unwilling to risk their established career paths in their current corps for the uncertainty of the new airborne specialty. Officers in S.P.E. were very reluctant to change corps as promotion was based on seniority and moving to the new speciality meant giving up that seniority. The issue of seniority was one factor in sending the *I btg. para. CC.RR.* to Africa instead of one of the other army parachute battalions.[40]

Compounding the problem was that many of those officers who had volunteered were found to be unsuitable for the airborne speciality. The Regio Esercito had a very rigid societal structure that created a wide gap between officers and enlisted. Rations,

38 Enrico Cursi, *I Leoni del Deserto* (Rome: edizioni Chillemi, 2014), pp.80–81; Longo, *I «reparti speciali»*, pp.277–278.

39 AUSSME, Stato Maggiore R.E. memorandum 10 marzo 1942, *Oggetto: Complemento della divisione paracadutisti*, M7 racc.404, cart.9; AUSSME, Stato Maggiore R.E. marzo 1942, *Formazioni provvisorie di guerra del reparto complementi per div. paracadutisti*, M7 racc.404, cart.9

40 Cursi, *I Leoni*, p.52.

privileges, even the quality of the uniform material were significantly different.[41] The ethos that colonnello Baudion had instilled and fostered during training that officers and enlisted lived and worked together while sharing the same hardships was alien to the culture within the greater Italian Army. Baudion wrote in April 1942:

> 7) Recruitment of volunteers There are serious shortcomings especially in the officer branch. The best there are, however, do not come to the school. Officers who generally arrive who do not feel the spirit of their mission as educators, who do not understand the need to live with and like the soldier.
>
> They are individually excellent and valiant fighters, but they are neither the animators and amalgamators needed to organize soldiers from all [the different] corps.
>
> It appears that the regimental commanders at home and on the fronts are reluctant to deprive themselves of their best individuals and in various forms hinder their transfer to Tarquinia.
>
> This is an extreme character deficiency of the officers in S.P.E.
>
> The Duce categorically ordered Marshal Cavallero to set up a Paratrooper Officers School. Nothing more was known about it.[42]

One observable effect of this issue was that parachute units were often commanded by officers one or two grades below the authorized rank. *Generale* Sapienza was only a *generale di brigata* and not a *generale di divisione*. *Tenenti colonnelli* often commanded regiments and *capitani* commanded battalions. This was not uncommon in these units before they were involved in combat, where casualties seriously affected the number of officers available in the units.

The positive of this issue was that the results did justify Baudoin's focus on creating this ethos in the parachute units. The shared act of parachuting itself created a bond absence from other corps with the Regio Esercito. That bond was strengthened by the long periods of intense training that few other corps shared. Even when factors conspired to halt the parachute training, the *reparti paracadutisti* would enter into extended tactical training periods that few other Italian units would ever experience during the war. The two Libyan and the CC.RR. battalions all demonstrated a higher level of cohesiveness and tactic skill than similar units in the army as a whole during combat.

41 Macgregor Knox, 'The Italian Armed Forces, 1940-43' in Allan R. Millett and Williamson Murray (eds), *Military Effectiveness* vol III (Boston, Massachusetts: Allen & Unwin, 1988), p.164; Brian R. Sullivan, 'The Italian Armed Forces, 1918-40' in Allan R. Millett and Williamson Murray (eds.), *Military Effectiveness,* vol III (Boston, Massachusetts: Allen & Unwin, 1988), pp.200–201.

42 Di Giovanni, *I paracadutisti*, p.133.

An Airborne Corps once again?

The decision to exclude heavy weapons from the *divisione paracadutisti* and to once again study the formation of a *divisione aviotrasportabile* appeared to breathe new life into the idea of a *corpo d'armata aviotrasportabile*. As the new parachute division was taking shape, there was now additional discussion on the structure of an air transportable division.

In many ways, creating a *divisione aviotrasportabile* was a simpler challenge for *Supereserecito* than that of creating a *divisione paracadutisti*. Much of the R.E.'s basic equipment was developed for mountain warfare due to Italy's unique geographical setting. The equipment was designed to be transported by man or beast or could be quickly broken down into such portable loads. The 65/17 guns and 75/13 howitzers were easily transported in aircraft such as the SM.81 as demonstrated by *Operazione «Gefara»* and other various wartime transport missions. Water and food containers, cook stoves, and many other basic sustainment items were developed to be carried on a man's back to supply soldiers in difficult terrain. The challenge was using these elements to craft a combat formation that was transportable and sustainable by aircraft, yet effective in combat to achieve its assigned mission.

The basic design of the division was presented in an 8 May 1941 *Supereserecito* memorandum.[43] The design criteria included:

- the minimum number of aircraft to lift the unit;
- strong in anti-tank, anti-aircraft, and 81mm mortars;
- a reconnaissance battalion able to defend the debarkation airfield. The concept was that paratroopers would seize the airfield and then be replaced by this battalion. It is unclear from the memorandum whether the division would possess its own paratrooper unit or would they be provided by the parachute division.[44]

The division would consist of:

- a battaglione esplorante (reconnaissance battalion)
- two infantry regiments, each with two infantry battalions, a weapons and a mortar company (later a mixed weapons battalion replaced the two companies);
- an artillery regiment with two artillery groups of 75/18 mod.34 howitzers;
- two mixed weapons battalions of mortars, anti-tank, and anti-aircraft guns;
- a company of light tanks (sixteen L3 type tanks);

43 Cappellano and Pignato *Gli autoveicoli*, vol. 2, pp.733-734.
44 Cappellano and Pignato *Gli autoveicoli*, p.733. The phase in question was "destinato a sostituire le unità *paracadutisti* — costituenti, queste ultime, avanguardia della divisione, non considerata nel presente studio..." [intended to replace the paratroop unit — the latter constituting the vanguard of the division, is not considered in the present study]. Does vanguard imply it is part of the division or just the lead element of the assault?

- various engineer and service support units.

The memorandum stated that 260 sorties of SM.82 aircraft would be needed to transport this unit. Planning for an actual operation would require a minimum of 350 aircraft to account for losses and maintenance problems. The current number of transports available in Italy on this date was twelve SM.3, eight SM.75, and 60 SM.82s. The current production rate of SM.82 in 1941 was 10 aircraft a month. Using a 20 percent loss of aircraft due to various reasons, *Supereservito* estimated that the earliest date that required the number of aircraft would be available to deploy this unit was spring 1942.

Supereservito further refined the division design in a 15 June 1941 memorandum. Light artillery tractors were now included with the possibility of replacing them with carri L3. This would possibly increase the number of tanks companies from one to two in the design. Maximizing the number of 81mm mortars, 20/65 c.a., and 75/18 mod.34 guns was again stressed. The change now provided motorcycles and bicycles for the *btg. esplorante*, and *motocarrelli* (small trucks), *mototricicli* (motor tricycles), and hand carts for moving weapons, equipment, and supplies that cannot be easily transported by man-pack.[45]

Logistics were to be based on each unit landing with two days of rations, one unit of fire for weapons, and one day of fuel and lubricants. Resupply would be mainly through the use of aerorifornimenti (aerial resupply containers) if follow-on aircraft could not land at the secured airhead. Each infantry regiment would have twenty additional *motocarrelli* to move material from the airhead to the units.

Overall, this division's design was little different from that of a standard binary infantry division. The number of infantry battalions was reduced from six to four and a reconnaissance battalion was added. A second divisional mixed weapons battalion was included, along with the light tank company. The artillery regiment possessed only two instead of the normal three artillery groups, and all the guns were 75mm howitzers. All the equipment required for this division already existed in the army inventory and had been proven through use over the years.

The *80ª divisione fanteria aviotrasportabile «La Spezia»* was formed on 15 November, 1941. The two infantry regiments of the division was raised from the depots of existing infantry units; *125º regiment fanteria «La Spezia»* was raised from the regimental depot of the *88º reggimento fanteria*, while the *126º regiment fanteria «La Spezia»* was raised from the depot of the *22º reggimento fanteria*. The division was headquartered in Pisa.[46]

The two regiments were initially organized as outlined in the 8 May memorandum with two infantry battalions and one mixed weapons battalion in each regiment. The infantry battalions used the standard battalion structure with two large squads in

45 Cappellano and Pignato *Gli autoveicoli,* vol. 2, pp.735–736.

46 Giorgio Pirrone (ed) *L'Esercito e i suoi corpo – Sintesi storica* (Rome, USSME, 1979) vol 3, pp.167–168.

each platoon. This was changed in March 1942 with the conversion of the weapons battalion into an infantry battalion. The heavy weapons from that unit were placed in the three infantry battalions. The infantry platoons were also changed from the two 18-man infantry squads, each with two Breda 30 light machine guns, to three 9-man infantry squads with one Breda 30 each. This change provided greater firepower to the subordinate units, making them more capable for independent actions.[47]

The *80º reggimento artiglieria* was not authorized until 19 January 1942, but was not actually formed until 15 February. The men and equipment came from the depot of the *7º reggimento artiglieria da campagna* garrisoned at Pisa.[48] Instead of the planned 75/18 mod.34 mountain howitzers, the unit was organized with three gruppi of 65/17 guns (24 guns), along with the normal regimental complement of two batteries of 20/65mm c.a. The use of the 65/17 guns was likely due to the lack of the newer 75/18 howitzers. The army only had 178 of these howitzers in June 1940 and production was normally twenty howitzers a month. These were issued to those divisions that still retained animal transport. Seven-two 75/18 howitzers were needed to equip the *II Corpo d'Armata* that was preparing to deploy to Russia in spring 1942.[49] These guns were also used in the first series of the semoventi (self-propelled guns), the semoventi da 75/18.[50]

There was nothing remarkable about the equipment or training planned for the division. The main difference was the organization of the infantry regiments. The 81mm mortars and 47/32 c.c. guns normally found at the regimental level were now placed in the *compagnia armi accompagnamento* of the infantry battalions. The heavy machine guns and 45mm mortars usually assigned to the battalion were now part of the companies. Added at the regimental level were two *sezioni* of 20/65 c.a. guns. The *squadra fucile* (rifle squads) were only nine men with one f.m. instead of the 18 men with two f.m. of a regular infantry unit.[51] The placement of the heavier weapons in the lower echelons echoes the concept behind the divisone A.S. tipo 42 design but without the mixed companies of that organization.[52]

47 AUSSME, Stato Maggiore R.E. memorandum 11 marzo 1942, *Oggetto: Modifiche alle formazioni di guerra della 80º divisione "LA SPEZIA"*, M7 racc.430, cart.11.

48 Franco Dell'Uomo and Rodolfo Puletti *L'Esercito Italiano verso il 2000 — I corpo disciolti*, (Rome, USSME, 1998), vol 1, p.102; Franco Dell'Uomo, and Roberto di Rose *L'Esercito Italiano verso il 2000 — I corpo disciolti*, (Rome, USSME, 2001), vol 2, p.160.

49 Costantino De Franceschi (ed) *Le operazioni delle unità italiane al fronte russo (1941–1943)* (Rome: USSME, 1977), pp. 597–603; 629–631.

50 Filippo Cappellano *Le artiglierie del Regio Esercito nella seconda guerra mondiale* (Parma: Alberti Edizione Speciali s.r.l., 1998), pp.67–76, 282.

51 AUSSME, *Oggetto: Modifiche alle formazioni di guerra della 80º divisione "La Spezia", 11 marzo 1942*, M7 racc. 490, cart. 11.

52 The *divisione di fanteria A.S. tipo 42* was developed to increase firepower while reducing the size of the unit. Each infantry company consisted of four platoons: a rifle, a machine gun, a light anti-tank, and a 47/32 c.c. platoons. Jeffrey Leser, 'Divisional Organization

Discussion of forming an actual *comando corpo d'armata aviotrasportabile* would continue, but no corps headquarters would be formed. The *1ª d. para.* and the *80ª d. avoit.* would never operate together during the war as a corps.

With the destruction of the *I btg. para. CC.RR.* and the decision not to form a battalion in Africa, the order to transfer the *comando 3º rgt. para.* to A.S. was canceled on 1 January 1942. It was not until 15 March 1942 that the regiment was finally established in Italy. The regiment would consist of the *IX* and *X btg. para.* currently undergoing training and the *3ª cp. cannoni para.* The regiment was garrisoned at Viterbo along with the other two parachute regiments. A small staff of Italian *paracadutisti* remained in Libya to form a Libyan parachute company, but this too was eventually canceled.[53]

Specialized Equipment

Between the time the first unit was raised in 1938 throughout 1940, the *paracadutisti* were forced to use the existing equipment that was available in the Regio Esercito. Regia Aeronautica air crew parachutes, the current wool uniforms, ankle boots, First World War period weapons, leather helmets, etc., all generally unsuitable for parachute operations. It was not until 1941 that the men began to receive uniforms and equipment that was designed to better meet the needs of the airborne speciality.

The main equipment improvement for the units, the IP 41/SP parachute, was previously discussed. Another issue addressed by *tenente colonnello* Bettica is his January 1941 memorandum was the need for Discese Manovrate (maneuverable descents). He recognized that parachutists required an ability to guide their parachute to a specific point on the ground rather than rely on the serendipitous whim of the weather. Without tactical surprise and the likely enemy expectation of a possible airborne assault, such a parachute would allow the jumpers to avoid danger areas or obstacles on the ground. Bettica's concept was a combination of a smaller parachute and a flying suit that used the flow of air over the body surfaces to steer the parachutist to the selected point on the ground.

That concept was not pursued but work on a steerable parachute was undertaken. The result was the *parachute a velocità variabile* (variable speed parachute) mod. Lisi. The Lisi allowed the jumper to increase or decrease the speed of his descent by partially collapsing and reinflating the canopy through the use of control lines. These control lines were secured to the canopy to form an inner ring of suspension lines. When used by the jumper, the lines pulled the center section of the canopy down below the outer rim of the canopy, creating a smaller inflated canopy while the outer rim spilled air.

Tipo Africa Settentrionale (A.S.)', <https://comandosupremo.com/tipo-africa-settentrionale/> (accessed 11 May 2022).

53 Dell'Uomo and Puletti *L'Esercito Italiano*, vol 1, p.576; Di Giovanni, *I paracadutisti*, p.91.

The smaller canopy size increased the rate of descent. Once the jumper released the control lines, the center section would rise back up, reinflating the outer rim and once again reducing the rate of descent.

This capability allowed a parachutist to exit an aircraft at higher altitudes yet reduce the time the jumper was suspended in the air. The jumper would exit the aircraft and partially deflate the canopy, increasing his sink rate. As he neared the ground, he could inflate the entire canopy and reduce his sink rate to a safe landing speed. By manipulating the sink rate, a parachutist could aim for a specific point on the ground that was in general alignment with the direction of drift of the parachutist. While not suitable for mass parachute drops, the Lisi was used to insert agents behind enemy lines in Palestine and other eastern Mediterranean areas.[54]

The company of the *II btg. paracadutisti* that jumped onto Kefalonia were recently issued a new helmet, the *elmetto per paracadutisti mod.* 41. It retained the basic shape of the *elmetto mod. 33*, the standard helmet of the R.E., but the rim was removed creating a nearly symmetrical shape. A new liner was installed with padding that completely enclosed the paratrooper's head to absorb any shock upon landing. Y-chin straps were added to limit any shifting of the helmet on the wearer's head by the air stream during the jump. It was a significant improvement that better protected the jumper's head during the drop and in combat.[55]

Footwear was another improvement. The *scarpe per reparti paracadutisti mod.* 41 was officially adopted on 29 October 1941. This was a tall black leather boot with a rubber sole and heel. It is possible that an unofficial version of these boots was already in use. Pictures of the enlisted *paracadutisti* of the *II btg. paracadutisti* on Kefalonia appears to show two types of boots; the ankle boots with puttees and a taller boot with wool leggings.[56] The puttees and wool leggings were necessary as the pantaloni (pants) mod. 40 that were the standard issue uniform pants for the army ended just below the knee. The ankle boot was standard issue boot, but the source of the tall boots is unclear. The need for a tall boot that supported the ankle was known. The boots used by some of the *paracadutisti* at Kefalonia could be the scarponi mod. 35 issued during the Ethiopia War, or test versions of the boot that was later adopted as the mod. 41.

Individual equipment was undergoing a revision as well. The R.M. had designed the samurai vest for their parachutists that were issued the MAB 38A as their weapon. No similar equipment had been developed for those parachutists issued the M91 carbine. The M1909 leather equipment (and it's later modifications) was unsuitable for parachute operations. It lacked shoulder straps to fully secure the equipment on the man, it only held 36 rounds for the carbine, and the ammunition pouches themselves were bulky. An experimental set of equipment was issued for the army in 1939 but was

54 Arena, *Tarquinia*, p.47.
55 Di Martino, *Paracadutisti*, vol. 1, pp.84–91.
56 Anon, '30 aprile 1941 – La Folgore si lancia a Celefona' Congedati Folgore, <https://www.congedatifolgore.com/it/galleries/30-aprile-1941-la-folgore-si-lancia-a-cefalonia/> (accessed 29 April 2020 and 19 Feb. 2022).

The mod. Lisi parachute. Note how only the center section of the canopy is inflated as it has been pulled down below the outer rim of the parachute. (AUSSME)

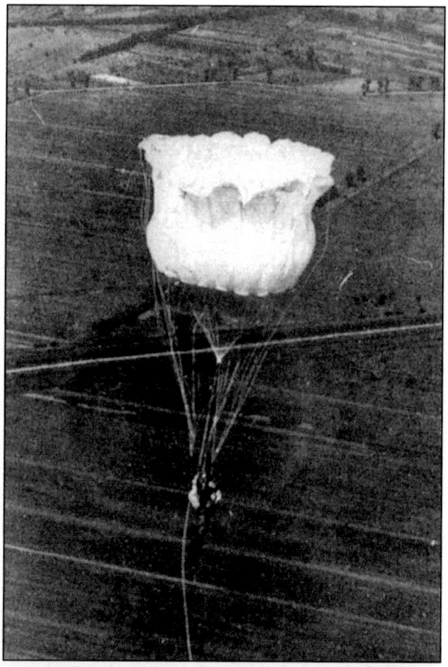

Paracadutisti boarding a Ca.133 for a training jumping with their weapons. Dummy weapons are being carried for the jump and the men are wearing the second style camouflaged patterned *combinazione di tela per reparti paracadutisti* and elmetti M42. (AUSSMA)

rescinded in 1940. This harness had a khaki color webbed belt and shoulder straps, with six individual leather ammunition pouches that each held one six-round Carcano clip. While the set still only carried 36 rounds, the pouches were narrow and laid flat against the wearer. A parachute harness could easily be worn over the set. The use of the simple white cloth bandoliers for the parachute drop on Cefalonia highlighted the lack of suitable individual equipment. That white bandoleer was still in use in the first part of 1942.[57]

Fleece lined leather gloves and padded cloth knee protectors were standard individual issue. A *tascapane per reparti paracadutisti* (haversack for parachute units) was produced to carry those individual items needed by the soldier (rations, extra ammunition, etc.). It was made with khaki canvas and either the mess kit or a canteen could be attached to the outside. A smaller spare parts and tool bag for the Breda mod. 30 f.m. was issued to replace the much larger backpack version carried by the infantry. These and other items were produced and issued in 1941 to better equip the *paracadutisti.*

The most visible change was the uniform. The wool giubba mod. 40 (tunic mod. 40) was replaced by a collarless version that was cut similar to the popular sahariana tunic used in A.S. The *pantaloni da paracadutisti mod. 41* were full-length pants that could be bloused into the top of boots and replaced the knee length mod. 40. A fabric gaiter was also authorized to better secure the pant cuff with the top of the boots. The R.A. *bustina mod.* 35 was the authorized head wear. Both a grigio-verde wool and khaki cloth version of this uniform were issued. The long pants were a popular uniform item and were adopted by the Italian ski units.

At the same time, all the necessary insignia were finalized. Hat fregi (hat badge), unit mostrini (unit collar insignia), and parachute qualification badge were now authorized for all qualified individuals. The *paracadutisti* now possessed a very distinct appearance and it visibly marked them as elite troops within the Italian military. Several other Italian elite units would later adopt many of these unique uniform items.

Specialized unit equipment was also developed. The standard company/battalion radio was the Stazione Radiotelegrafica e Radiotelefonica 1 (RF1). This was a man-pack radio that was fairly bulky in size and developed in the early 1930s. The parachute units needed a more robust system that could survive a parachute drop. The RF1/P was designed and produced starting in 1941. It was a very modern system with a range of 10/40km depending on the antenna used and the type of transmission. Its main drawback were the batteries, the battery box (consisting of three batteries) being heavier than the radio itself (12 kg for the radio, 14 kg for the battery box).[58]

57 A photograph of a demonstration during Generalmajor Ramcke's visit to Tarquinia in March 1942 shows the *paracadutisti* wearing these bandoleers. Di Martino, *Paracadutisti*, vol. 1, p.379.

58 Mario Galasso and Mario Gaticci *La radio in grigio-verde* (Faenza: Edizioni a cura della C&C, 1992), pp.109–111, 136–137; Di Martino, *Paracadutisti*, vol. 2, p.350. Arena,

The aerorifornimenti (aerial resupply containers) were redesigned to carry both more and a variety of different supplies (tipo Bordini) and 1,600 were ordered along with 600 equipment containers. Cargo parachutes were improved and a paper parachute was developed for ammunition resupply drops, saving scare canopy material. The planning for *Operazione «C3»* (Malta invasion) generated a requirement for a small parachute-deliverable vehicle that could be used to move supplies on the ground. The Officine Meccaniche Volugrafo began to develop the Aermoto aviolanciabile "Volugrafo", a minibike design that could be dropped using a standard supply container. The motorbike had a small cargo trailer that could be attached for transporting supplies. The vehicle was still under development when *«C3»* was cancelled and delivery would not begin until 1943.[59]

Individual weapons were still an issue. The parachute units of the R.E. were still issued the moschetto da cavalleria, although a very small number of the MAB 38A were authorized for officers and NCOs. The *rgt. «San Marco»* had completely equipped their *paracadutisti* with the MAB 38A, while the R.A. was doing the same. While the submachine gun authorization was only for officers and NCOs, this was similar with the authorizations of these weapons in other nations' armies. The R.E. would not begin to receive MABs from Beretta until the closing months of 1941, when the *btg. sciatori alpini «Monte Cervino»* obtained 40 MABs for its deployment to Russia.

Aircraft availability and capacity limitations had slowed the training. The Ca.133 was a poor aircraft to use for parachute training. It was slow and could only carry nine parachutists packed into its fuselage. While using the SM.82 for training would have been the best option, the demand for these aircraft for operational missions outweighed the needs of the school at Tarquinia. Even with prior notification as demanded by the R.A., sorties to support the school were canceled or reduced. The school only had one SM.82 that was mainly used for testing new parachutes and other equipment. Working with the Caproni factory, a parachutist version of the Ca.133 was developed. The Ca.148/P could carry 16 parachutists, four aerial resupply containers, and a crew of four including the jump master. The increased capability meant that more *paracadutisti* could be trained on those days when the weather allowed for jumping. 144 copies of the aircraft were ordered, but it would take time to deliver them to the school. Two would be delivered in 1942 and only sixteen more in 1943 before the armistice.[60]

Tarquinia, p.47 calls this radio a stazione radio SC.3 mod. De Paoli, but there is no such radio. His picture of the radio on p.57 is actually a RF1 and is the same picture in *La radio in grigio-verde*. p.110.

59 Nino Arena, Nino, *La Regia Aeronautica* (Rome: USSMA, 1981-1986), vol 2, p.597; Di Martino, *Paracadutisti*, vol. 2, p.351.

60 Arena, *Tarquinia,* p.46; Nino Arena, Nino, *La Regia Aeronautica* (Rome: USSMA, 1981-1986), vol 2, p.597, vol. 3, p.771,

An aerorifornimenti (aerial resupply container) tipo Bordini being loaded onto an aircraft. The tipo Bordini was a padded canvas design that could be used in multiple ways to package smaller items for airdrop. (AUSSMA)

Doctrine for the Airborne Force

By the end of the first quarter of 1942, *Superesercito* had created both a parachute and an air landing division. But *Superesercito* had yet to educate the army on how these units would be employed. Written doctrine had not kept up with the creation of these units, with only the battalion manual published in 1940 detailing the employment of the parachute units.

Impiego delle divisioni paracadutisti ed aviotrasportabili (Employment of the Parachute and Air Landing Divisions) was officially published in April 1942. In this manual the employment of both the *divisioni paracadutisti* and *aviotrasportabile* were addressed. The manual itself raised concerns on whether the R.E. was fully committed to the operational use of these units. Noting that this manual was released during the build-up for the invasion of Malta, the first paragraph of the manual stated:[61]

61 Stato Maggiore Regio Esercito, circolare N. 32000, *Impiego delle divisioni paracadutisti ed aviotrasportabili* (Rome, 21 April 1942), p.5.

> I – The following rules/dispositions sketch a summary outline on the use of the **paratrooper and air-landing divisions** as the most recent additions of special major units.
>
> Although the operations of the current war have already made it possible to ascertain their performance and recognize their success, we are still in the **experimental phase** of their use. [bold font in the original].

It is difficult to discern what the Italian leadership considered experimental about the use of airborne forces in the war. The R.E. had created both an airborne and air-landing division and was discussing the raising of a second airborne division. It had overcome the technical problems of the parachutes themselves, developed techniques for air dropping equipment, and tested various resupply systems. The R.A. possessed an excellent jump aircraft in the SM.82, while the SM.81 and other bomber aircraft were fully capable in the role. *Supercomando* was currently planning a military operation that placed the airborne capability as the critical element in the operation. As stated in the second sentence, the operational value of these units had been demonstrated in the first years of the war. What then remained to be tested?

If the concern was not technical, then what was unproven in the minds of the Italian leadership? The manual itself offers few clues. The discussion of the strategic and operational conditions, the advantages and disadvantages of their employment, and the need for their mission to be fully integrated into a scheme of maneuver reads as if written in a modern military manual. Only the section on the Coverage of a Land Approach appears to harken back to an outdated understanding for the employment of parachutists. The description of the unit roles and the statement that this mission is typical in colonial lands paints a picture of combat against tribes or raiders rather than against a modern military force.[62]

This statement could be read to imply that the senior military leadership still did not accept the airborne speciality as anything more than injecting arditi into an enemy's rear area or executing a coup d'main on a tactical objective. The consideration of the *reparti paracadutisti* as an operational maneuver element during planning was rare up to this time and such consideration was usually driven by an outside agency.

This hesitancy to fully embrace the employment of a divisional-sized parachute unit could also be examined in the light of the Italian military's inability to generate a successful offensive. As a mainly offensive tool, the inability to leverage any success gained by the *paracadutisti* would likely mean the total loss of the unit. The requirement for the R.E. to advance and link-up with the *paracadutisti*, the R.M. requirement to successfully land an amphibious force for the same purpose, or the R.A. requirement to resupply the unit would curtail any thought of employment if these services believed they were unable to fulfill their roles.

62 Circolare N. 32000, *Impiego delle divisioni paracadutisti ed aviotrasportabili*, pp.33–34.

None of this could be answered if *Supercomando* was unwilling to commit these units into an operation that was suited to their capabilities. Up until spring of 1942 one could argue that Italy never had a suitable objective for such an operation. However in late 1941 an objective had been selected, one that many would likely argue was the raison d'être for units such as the *paracadutisti*: the invasion of Malta.

9

Operazione «C3»

When one examines the strategic requirements facing the Italian military in 1939 and early 1940, the only operation that truly justified the creation of a sizable airborne force was the seizure of Malta. Yet an operation against that island was not seriously considered. All the prewar planning had anticipated that Italy would initially position itself on the defense and any offensive action would be based on the evolving situation as the war progressed. The one front where Italy saw the possibility of offensive action was against Yugoslavia. Any offensive action on that front was premised on the internal conditions within that nation creating the opportunity that Italy would attempt to leverage.[1]

Mussolini's secret memorandum of 31 March 1940, followed by *Maresciallo* Badoglio's reply on 6 April examined Italy's strategic situation and the operational priorities by individual theater. The Italian forces in Africa Orientale Italiana (A.O.I., Italian East Africa) were cut off from support and reinforcement from the home country by the UK control of the Suez Canal. That problem could not be solved as long as the Suez Canal was under British control and Italy lacked the ability to affect that situation. The other theaters were to maintain a defensive posture and await changes in the situation before any decision would be taken to move onto the offense.[2]

Within this framework of strategic defense was a problem that would require offensive action. The British control of the island of Malta impacted Italy's ability to maintain its forces in Libya. That island was 90 miles off the southern coast of Sicily and lay astride the maritime communications between Italy and its colony in Libya. Valletta, the largest harbor on the island, was the main base for the British Mediterranean Fleet which allowed the Britain to dominate the central Mediterranean. British submarines would be able to remain in the area for extended periods as their resupply base was close by. The airfields on the island were being expanded and improved. Aircraft based

1 Mario Montanari, *L'esercito italiano alla vigilia della 2ª guerra mondiale,* (Rome: USSME, 1982), p.138.
2 Montanari, *L'esercito italiano*, pp.135-137.

on the island would provide reconnaissance for British naval sorties, both detecting the Italian merchant ships while warning British warships of any approaching Italian naval threat. Those same aircraft could attack Italian shipping, creating a triple threat of air, sea, and undersea to be employed against the Italian merchant ships. Along with its control of Gibraltar in the west and the Suez Canal in the east, Malta allowed the British. to command the sea that Italy proclaimed as its own. This geographic positioning was such that British forces could disrupt or possibly completely cut off that flow of support to Libya.

Malta's strategic setting was enhanced by the Britain's alliance with the French. French naval forces stationed at Biserta in northeast Tunisia reinforced the British position in the central Mediterranean. French naval forces located at that port could join with those from Malta and intercept Italian ships sailing between Italy and Libya within hours.

R.M. Operational Assessment

The Regia Marina had recognized the problem during the years of planning prior to the war. The mission to support the Ethiopian War and the mobilization plan to reinforce and supply A.S. required free use of the Mediterranean Sea by Italian shipping. The R.M. had assumed the possibility of war against the Britain and France in its planning and assessed the required actions to meet its basic missions. The 1936 study of a hypothetical war saw that the seizure of the island would deprive the enemy of a base that would facilitate their passage through the Sicilian Channel. The problem of Malta was addressed by exploring two options, either occupation or suppression. One statement in this study discussing the occupation of the island is of interest. "The operation, however, [if] attempted during the war, may be delayed and may present strong elements of failure; it would therefore be necessary to carry out the invasion of the Maltese islands as an initial act of igniting the conflict." In many ways, prophetic words for the events of 1940-43.[3]

The next time the R.M. examined the Malta problem was in 1938. The Chief of the Regia Marina Naval Staff, *Ammiraglio* Cavagnari, signed a paper titled *Direttive Navali* (Di.Na.) N.0 (Naval Directive 0, often referred as Document Zero) on 25 May 1938. Document Zero was an appreciation of the strategic options as seen by the S.M.R.M. given the possible alignment of enemies against Italy and the missions the R.M. would be required to carry out. Document Zero identified that French naval and air forces operating out of Biserta would operate in conjunction with British efforts to cut Italian sea communications with its colonies. It was this document that first identified two courses of action, either occupation or suppression of the island. The final assessment was that suppression would not fully resolve the matter and that

3 Mariano Gabriele, *Operazione C3: Malta* (Rome: USMM, 1990), pp.11–12..

the occupation of Malta by Italy would be necessary. The document then directed a number of concepts to be developed for a range of missions, of which one was the protection of Italian lines of communications with the Aegean, Libya and Albania.[4]

Two documents were then written based on the guidance discussed in Document Zero; *Documento di Guerra* (D.G.) 10/A1 in June 1938 and D.G. 10/A2 that were released in December of that same year. The first addressed the requirement and the means to close the Sicilian Channel. The second, D.G. 10/A2 addressed the requirement to send an expeditionary force to reinforce Libya and to adequately maintain those forces. The two options from the previous studies were again addressed in D.G. 10/A2. The document concluded "it is necessary to foresee the occupation of Malta as an indispensable premise for any of our large scale operations in A.S.: the possession of Malta greatly increases the possibility of attaining the indispensable temporary dominion of the central Mediterranean."[5]

Given the decision to remain on the strategic defense, the R.M. had identified the need for an operational offense within that framework. In the years leading up to the war, the Regina Marina constantly identified the occupation of Malta as a requirement to support the defensive operations in Africa settentrionale. The question then is why did not Italy have a plan to secure Malta when a war broke out in Europe?

No definitive answer to that question can be provided within these pages. The prewar study that begot the Italian airborne force offers a clue.[6] What is important is not what the study did address but what the study did not include. In Part III (Outline of Application Cases) the section briefly touches upon the strategic setting of Fascist Italy. Subsection 1 of the study considered the use of paratroops on Italy's western, northern, and eastern borders, but omitted assessing the Mediterranean Sea and islands, as well as its African colonies. This apparent separation of war planning into two separate spheres created a void over the Mediterranean Sea that was seen as the Navy's problem to manage. The idea of combined operations to solve an operational problem likely felt alien to the *Stati Maggiori* of the three services. The *Stato Maggiore Generale* (S.M.G., *Comando Supremo/Supercomando* during the war) under *Maresciallo* Badoglio lacked any real power to formulate strategic plans and synchronize national power.[7] That central role was held by Mussolini alone until 1941.

Inter-service rivalry between the three services for funding and political power undermined the ability to develop a cohesive strategy that included joint planning to achieve operational objectives. Each service saw their part of the battlespace (air, sea, and ground) as distinctly separate. One example of this issue was the inability to form torpedo bomber squadrons prior to the war. Italy had developed an excellent aerial

4 Montanari, *L'esercito italiano*, pp.150–151; Gabriele, *Operazione C3*, pp.13–14.
5 Gabriele, *Operazione C3*, p.15–16.
6 AUSSME, no date, *Studio per l'impiego di unità paracadutisti,* I-4, b.17,fn.4.
7 Montanari, *L'esercito italiano*, pp.319–355 for a detailed discussion of the S.M.G. and the services' S.M. at the start of the war; John Gooch, *Mussolini's War* (London: Allen Lane 2020), pp.93–94.

torpedo and had employed torpedo bombers during the First World War. Rather than leveraging this lead and creating a formidable capability well suited to the operational requirements in the Mediterranean, its development was caught up in disagreements on which service would fund each part of the development of the new capability and operational fielding of the squadrons.[8]

What can be addressed is that the lack of any serious planning for an invasion of Malta left the development of the airborne speciality to laissez-faire rather than creating a military capability to solve a strategic problem. Issues of funding, control, and location were the points of debate rather than how this capability needed to be shaped to support wartime requirements. One can look towards Germany and Japan to see examples of how a strategic/operational requirement can drive the rapid development of new capabilities.

Germany was the first to deploy paratroopers as part of a significant offensive operation. The creation of the first Fallschirmjäger units in both the Luftwaffe and the Heer was initially championed by subordinate leaders who managed to gain a degree of approval from a key senior leader.[9] Where the development of the German airborne capability differed from the Italian experience was that German General Staff initiated a series of exercises to examine the range of capabilities such units offered. This examination was driven by the need to find tactical and operational solutions to create the ability to execute rapid advances. Balbo had intended to do the same with *Operation «Gefara»*, but resistance (or apathy) by the Italian S.M.G. stymied further work as previously discussed.

Based on guidance from Adolf Hitler in November 1937, Germany embarked on a series of offensive actions. Czechoslovakia was identified as the first target, but Hitler did not wish for a draw-out conflict with high casualties. The Fallschirmjägers were to be used to attack the weakest section of the Czech border defensives to open a line of advance for conventional forces. The diplomatic resolution to the crisis prevented the use of the German airborne troops at that time, but the concept of fully integrating their use to enable decisive ground maneuver was now embedded into German planning. The capture of the Alborg airfield in Denmark in April to enable operations in Norway, followed by the seizure of the Dutch Moerdijk and Dordrecht bridges and the capture of the Belgium Eben-Emael fort in May demonstrated the use of parachute forces at the operational level of war. The planning for an offensive war spurred the rapid development of the Fallschirmjäger, in contrast with the slow development of the *paracadutisti* under the Italian planning for a defensive war.[10]

The Japanese provide another example of how offensive planning enabled rapid development. Observing the German success of using airborne forces to achieve their

8 Giuseppe Santoro, *L'aeronautica italiana nella seconda guerra mondiale* (Rome: Edizioni ESSE di A. Silvestri, 1957), pp.50–51, 61–64.

9 Karl-Heinz Golla, *The German Fallschirmtruppe 1939–41* (Solihull: Association of the United States Army and Helion & Company, 2013), p.36.

10 Golla, *Fallschirmtruppe*, pp.39–40.

strategic objectives, the Japanese embarked on a similar rapid development based on their planning for an offensive war in Asia. The training of both the Imperial Japanese Army and Navy parachute units began in 1940 and 1941 respectively. German instructors assisted in preparing the schools and the training. In less than eighteen months, units from both services were employed during the initial Japanese offensives against the Dutch East Indies in January–February 1942.[11]

Strategic Defense

The outbreak of war in September 1939 saw Italy reexamining its strategic situation. The concerns expressed in D.G. 10/A2 drove a new discussion on Malta. An important aspect of this evaluation was a reassessment of Italy's amphibious warfare doctrine. Previously the R.M. and R.E. had anticipated using a small number of large vessels to land troops on hostile beaches. The R.M. had constructed five *cisterne per acqua* (water tankers) that were in fact large landing ships for this purpose. An event in 1939 forced a reassessment of this approach to amphibious warfare.

The Nationalist attempt to seize Cartagena from the Republicans during the Spanish Civil War was instructive. The Nationalists used a large merchant ship, the Castillo de Olite, as a landing ship in an attempt to capture Cartagena on 7 March 1939. The ship was sunk by Republican shore batteries resulting in 1,476 men killed and 242 men captured. The execution of the operation against Cartagena by the Nationalists was similar to the current R.M. doctrine and challenged whether such methods were valid. The R.M. and the R.E. now looked to numerous smaller vessels to land troops. *Generale* Pariani, then the current Chief of the S.M.R.E. in October 1939 requested that the R.M. initiate a construction program to build fifty 20-ton landing craft with bow ramps. These landing craft could carry up to 100 men or one M11/39 or M13/40 tank. Before this program could begin, Pariani was fired and the program canceled.[12]

With the move towards Italy's entry in the war, an exchange of memorandums and multiple meetings occurred in March–May 1940 between Mussolini, Badoglio, and the service chiefs to establish the strategic guidance that would shape Italy's operational plans. No changes were made to the policy of strategic defense. Parallel meetings were held with Germany during the same period to coordinate activities between the two allies but no coordination actions were developed. The German invasion of Norway and Denmark, followed by that of France and the low countries shifted the planning focus of the Italians away from the Mediterranean towards the

11 Willem Remmelink (ed), *The Invasion of the Dutch East Indies* (Leiden: Leiden University Press, 2015), p.5; Willem Remmelink (ed), *The Operations of the Navy in the Dutch East Indies and the Bay of Bengal* (Leiden: Leiden University Press, 2018), p.110.

12 Enrico Cernuschi, *Malta 1940-1943 La storia inconfessabile* (Vicenza: Edibus, 2016), p.79.

alpine frontier of France. In all of these discussions and meetings, the issue of Malta was not raised.[13]

Badoglio called a meeting of all the service chiefs on 5 June 1940 after Mussolini declared his intent to enter the war. The purpose of the meeting was to reinforce the previously issued instructions on Italy's planned conduct. No action was to be planned against France, already being defeated by Germany. Action against the United Kingdom was possible, but that action still remained unstated. For the first time in meeting with all the service chiefs the question of Malta arose. Graziani, now the Chief of the S.M.R.E. asked whether an amphibious assault against Malta was practical. *Ammiraglio* Domenico Cavagnari, the Chief of the S.M.R.M., expressed a lack of confidence in an invasion. Graziani and *generale* Ubaldo Soddu (the current Undersecretary of War) were in favor of an invasion after an intense period of aerial preparation. After a period of indecisive debate that led to no firm decision, Badoglio told Graziani 'All right, study it just in case'. No other guidance or timeline was offered[14]

During the meeting, Cavagnari did not share with the other chiefs that the R.M. had done still another study in the spring of 1940 on the practicability of an invasion of Malta.[15] Titled '*Progetto di sbarco a Malta della Primavera 1940*' (Landing Project on Malta in Spring 1940), it considered an invasion on the island against both the UK and France. In it, the naval staff recognized that the R.M. could only achieve and maintain local naval superiority for a limited time before the joint forces of the British and French navies intervened. The plan they outlined was a *coup de main* which was to land as many troops as possible in the shortest amount of time. Paratroopers were included in the plan with the caveat 'if they were available'. This was the first time the use of the *paracadutisti* was considered at the general staff level, although that staff considering their use was the Navy.[16] The study assumed that 600 paratroopers would be available, but the reality was that only the 320 men of the *I btg. para. libico* was an operational unit; the *I btg. para. nazionale* had only begun its training. The school at Tarquinia had yet to begin its first training cycle.

The result was that when Italy declared war on 10 June 1940, no plan for any action against Malta existed. Many Axis observers thought that Mussolini's insistence for entering the war no later than 10 June meant that the Italians had prepared a significant operation. They perceived that the deadline was due to the need to execute the operation before it could be compromised. In the Italian Navy's official history on Malta, *Operazione C3*, author Mariano Gabriele shared the following expectations expressed by Italy's allies.[17]

13 Montanari, *L'esercito italiano*, pp.135–142.
14 Gooch, *Mussolini's War*, p.94; Montanari, *L'esercito italiano*, p.167.
15 Gabriele was notable to identify an exact date for the study but places it in either April or May 1940. See Gabriele, *Operazione C3*, p.26.
16 Gabriele, *Operazione C3*, pp.26–31 and Appendix II.
17 Gabriele, *Operazione C3*, pp.36–37.

When Generalmajor Enno von Rintelen, the German military attaché in Rome, was asked by Admiral Wilhelm Canaris, the head of German military intelligence what Italy had planned, von Rintelen could only state he did not know and that he did not believe anything was planned. Canaris was surprised by that answer. Later when von Rintelen met with Mussolini before 10 June, Mussolini told him that he wanted to enter the war earlier but could not delay past 10 June. Von Rintelen then began to believe the Italians had something planned. On 11 June he was disappointed that nothing had happened. Afterwards...

> Italian officers of S.M. told me [von Rintelen] that the idea of a combined air-naval attack on Malta with a subsequent occupation had indeed been discussed between the three Armed Forces, but that it was not followed up as [it was] too difficult.

Naval Captain Mitunobu Tōyō, the Japanese naval attaché in Rome, also expected some plan to unfold once war was declared.

> From my point of view, for Italy to intervene in the current war, it had to be ready to conquer Malta and Tunisia, which are the key points for controlling the Mediterranean. Judging from the Italian internal propaganda, from the second half of May until the intervention in the war in June 1940, I thought that this would take place immediately after the intervention, but Italy declared, on the afternoon of June 10 [only] that it would be entering the war on the morning of 11 June. This surprised me. And then on 11, 12, 13 and 14 June, operations for the conquest of Malta and Tunisia had not yet begun. This was incomprehensible to me ...

After years of discussion and study, Fascist Italy entered the war without a concept or plan for dealing with Malta. The hope that the war would be short apparently was the excuse for delaying any decisions on the matter. Even if Italy had decided to invade Malta, the S.M.G. had procrastinated on creating the tools necessary to make such an invasion possible. The airborne capability that Balbo had initiated had languished and was only now slowly being rebuilt. The push to build the landing craft lasted for less than a month. The air transport fleet needed to fly the paratroopers to the island and to supply the forces once landed was nonexistent.[18]

The reality was that the best opportunity to capture the island had disappeared on 11 June 1940. Any attempt from this date forward would need to be developed amid the competing priorities of war. The British had been reinforcing the island over the past year and could be expected to continue to do so. The new strategic problem for the *STAMAGE* (the wartime identification of the S.M.G.) was that the longer the

18 Gabriele, *Operazione C3*, p.49.

war continued, the more materials/effort Italy would need to expend to suppress the island. There would come a point in time where the materials/effort used to suppress would exceed the materials/effort needed to take the island in 1940 if the required capabilities had been developed prior to the outbreak of war. The statement in the Navy's 1936 study was beginning to be validated.

Now that the war was a reality, the S.M.R.M. (now called *Supermarina*) again examined the Malta problem. The earlier '*Progetto di sbarco a Malta della Primavera 1940*' was followed by another study dated 18 June 1940. Titled '*Progetto del 18 Giugno 1940, Investimento di Malta*' (18 June 1940 Project, the Investment of Malta), the new study basically reversed the conclusions of all the previous studies. In the final section, Conclusive Considerations, it stated:

> Given the exceptional difficulties of the enterprise and the forces that would have to be employed, it would be only justified if Malta represented a decisive objective.
>
> But, England having abdicated for a long time its use as a main base of operations, the threat that Malta can exercise against our communications and against our naval bases is of secondary importance.
>
> It is sufficient that with aerial bombing, submarine ambushes, and (when it is necessary) the nighttime sorties of torpedo boats, to render impossible the permanent [stationing] at Valletta of important naval forces, to lay a trap for the movement of those few [units] that remain, and to prevent the resupply of the island.
>
> Malta will fall into our hands as a consequence of the final victory, obtained by concentrating all our energy on the fronts containing decisive objectives.[19]

It is difficult to avoid the conclusion that this study was written more to justify inaction by the navy against the island than a valid assessment of Malta's impact on future Italian operations.[20] It also transferred responsibility for Malta from *Supermarina* to *Superaereo,* allowing the navy to focus solely on the battle fleet and convoy operations. All the earlier studies clearly stated that a rapid resolution of the threat presented by Malta was the better course of action than trying to contain the problem. The key element in the study that justified investment, the fact that Malta was not a decisive objective in itself, would be challenged just two days later.

Italy's Offensive War

Mussolini informed *Comando Supremo* on 20 June to be ready to invade Egypt 'without bothering yourself about the possible future political considerations'.[21] This

19 Gabriele, *Operazione C3*, p.234;
20 Gabriele, *Operazione C3*, pp.44–45.
21 Gooch, *Mussolini's War*, p.105.

was followed by Badoglio issuing new orders on 25 June. By deciding on an offensive to capture Egypt, Africa settentrionale now became the principal front for the Italian military. *Superaereo* was charged with sterilizing (neutralizing) Malta through bombardment as part of the campaign. While the seizure of Malta was not seen as the endstate for this offensive, it now became a significant enabler to achieve success in Egypt. Balbo's eastward offensive would not only be affected by the limitations imposed by the ports, available shipping, and road transportation, but now would need to contend with the military threat generated by Malta. Regardless of the reasoning behind the decision, Mussolini's guidance ended any effective planning for an assault in 1940 and delayed any planning/preparation for an operation against the island in 1941.[22]

Germany was also examining the strategic situation in the Mediterranean Sea in late 1940. Grossadmiral Erich Raeder, the Commander in Chief of the German Navy, met with Hitler on 6 September 1940 and again on 26 September. Raeder discussed a Mediterranean strategy that focused on seizing both Gibraltar and Suez which appeared quite similar to what Italy had considered. No thought was given about Malta, as Malta was considered irrelevant if the two access points into the sea were under Axis control. Germany focused its diplomatic efforts to enable this strategy and did not comment on the Italian decision to suppress and not invade Malta.[23]

Before *STAMAGE* could settle into long-term planning based on the current guidance, the principal front for the Italian war effort changed in October. The initiation of the soon to fail Italian invasion of Greece on 29 October 1940 pushed Malta further into the backwaters of operational planning. By the third week of the attack, supplies and reinforcements originally destined for Libya were now being diverted to Albania. An amphibious assault against Corfù, part of the second phase of *Esigenza G* was canceled. In some respects this was an unfortunate change as such an attack likely would have yielded insights into the challenges of landing troops on Malta.

The initial failure in Greece was followed in early December by the British offensive in Libya, Operation Compass. Beginning on 9 December 1940, British forces would sweep the Italian out of Cirencia and destroy the Italian *10ª Armata*. What was originally a requirement to supply an army in Libya now became the requirement to rebuild an army in Libya. The danger posed by Malta had significantly increased.

There are many excellent accounts of the air and naval battles that involved the island and the Italian convoys in 1940 and 1941. Suffice it to say here that the attempts to suppress the island had a series of successes and failures but the island continued to resist. British leadership understood the value of the island and continued to supply and expand its offensive capabilities. The result was that Axis supplies only flowed with little hindrance to A.S. during those times when Italy and Germany maximized their effort to protect the convoys and suppress Malta. When that effort slackened,

22 Gooch, *Mussolini's War*, pp.105–106; Gabriele, *Operazione C3*, p.47.
23 Gabriele, *Operazione C3*, pp.55–56.

losses of men and material crossing the Mediterranean increased. The continual effort of safeguarding the supply routes was exacting a cost that one could argue exceeded the cost of invading the island.

The collapse of the talks between Germany and Spain to seize Gibraltar once again elevated the importance of Malta. The *Servizio Informazioni Militari* (S.I.M., Italian Military Intelligence) forwarded an information paper from the Italian military attaché in Berlin to *Comando Supremo* dated 24 January 1941. Titled (*Germania – Situazione militare e intendimenti operativi* (*Regio Addetto Militare a Berlino)* (Germany – Military situation and operational intentions (Royal Military Attaché in Berlin)), it stated that German intentions were being drawn toward an intervention in the Mediterranean. This intervention was along three lines of involvement: continuing the air-land contest, better operations against British naval and convoy activities, and to maintain an Axis presence in Libya. The paper states that there was support within the German General Staff, and especially within the Luftwaffe, for the occupation of Malta. A further report from Berlin dated 26 February informed Rome that the idea of occupying Malta was always alive within the circle around Reichsmarschall Göring.[24]

Raeder met with Hitler in February 1941 to press the necessity for that action. Hitler finally agreed to an assault against the island, but only after Russia was defeated. Regardless of that caveat, a German plan was developed in February–March that called for a solely German operation. The plan was similar to that used later against Crete but included an air-assault division along with an airborne division. An amphibious element was included as a secondary effort similar to the one adopted for Crete. None of this had been coordinated with their Italian counterparts and remained a theoretical study. As known today, the German attack against Crete (*Unternehmen Merkur*) was the German plan actually executed in May 1941.[25]

By April 1941 the attacks from Malta on Italian shipping had increased. On 14 April 1941, *Supermarina* requested that *Superaereo* increase its action against Malta to take pressure off the convoys. *Comando Supremo* (formerly *STAMAGE*) agreed and supported *Supermarina's* request on 19 May. All agreed that *Superaereo* needed to do more but the Air Force lacked the necessary means.[26]

Supermarina recognized that a direct attack to seize Malta was not currently under consideration. In an attempt to address the naval aspect of the Malta issue, the R.M. offered a proposal in April 1941 that Italy should secure the French ports in northern Tunisia. This would shorten the distance Italian convoys would need to travel and move the sea lanes further away from Malta. *Supermarina* again stated in a memorandum on 20 August 1941 that without an intent to occupy Malta, use of Tunisian

24 Antonello Biagini and Fernando Frattolillo (eds.) *Diario Storico del Comando Supremo* (Rome: USSME, 1989) vol III book 2, pp.113, 235.

25 Gabriele, *Operazione C3*, p.65.

26 Gooch, *Mussolini's War*, pp.207–208; Antonello Biagini and Fernando Frattolillo (eds.) *Diario Storico del Comando Supremo* (Rome, USSME, 1989) vol III book 1, pp.720, 764.

ports was the only way to increase supplies to Libya and decrease losses. Negotiations between Italy, Germany, and France to gain access to those ports would take place between April 1941 and February 1942 but little would come of these efforts.[27]

Generalmajor von Rintelen met with generale Guzzoni on 5 May 1941. Their discussion addressed multiple topics involving Africa settentrionale, Tunisia, and the Dodecanese Islands. During the meeting, Guzzoni highlighted the operational needs in A.S. and raised the issue that Malta might need to be occupied. The discussion was mainly informative and did not result in any agreements or understandings. This was followed by an order on 7 May from Comando *Supremo* to *Superesercito*, *Supermarina*, and *Superaereo* to resume their studies for the occupation of Malta. A small staff group operating between May and October 1941 began crafting a plan to invade Malta.[28]

By the fall of 1941 it had become clear to *Comando Supremo* that the suppression of Malta was not effective. The Axis convoy losses rose during the summer and a major British resupply effort for Malta, Operation Halbred, successfully reached the island in September. At the same time, *Superaereo* attacks had been decreasing, going from a high of over 400 attacks in June to only 221 attacks in September and October combined. An invasion of the island appeared to be the only satisfactory solution.[29]

The Germans had reached a similar conclusion about Italy's ability to suppress Malta. While not considering invasion at this time, they did decide to commit additional forces to the Mediterranean. With their apparent success in Russia, Germany decided they could transfer twenty-five submarines to the Mediterranean to operate against Malta, followed by the Luftflotte II to be based in Sicily. The latter would not begin to arrive until late November and would not begin their operations against Malta until 21 December 1941. The orders to Luftflotte II were to protect Axis communications with Libya and to interdict Allied efforts to supply Malta and Tobruk.[30]

On 21 August 1941, *Comando Supremo* sent a copy of a presentation that had been given to *generale di divisone* Antonio Scuero (now the deputy of *Comando Supremo*, having replaced Guzzoni May 1941) to *Superesercito*, *Supermarina*, and *Superaereo*. The presentation was written by two general staff officers that had spent much time on Malta before the war. The paper was passed to the three services as it 'contained some information that may be useful for any operations.' In the paper, the authors describe the geography of the island and its likely impact on military operations.[31]

27 Gabriele, *Operazione C3*, p.84.

28 Antonello Biagini and Fernando Frattolillo (eds) *Diario Storico del Comando Supremo* (Rome: USSME, 1992) vol IV book 1, pp.39, 53; Gabriele, *Operazione C3*, p.70, 92.

29 Gabriele, *Operazione C3*, p.88.

30 Gabriele, *Operazione C3*, pp.88–89. By 12 December the number of German submarines in the Mediterranean reached 36.

31 Antonello Biagini and Fernando Frattolillo (eds.) *Diario Storico*, vol IV book 1, p.636, book 2, pp.226–235. The names of the authors and the dates they were on the island are not given in any of the sources.

Operazione «C3» (Map 9.1)

Cavallero followed this action with a series of meetings discussing the practicality of invading Malta. He indicated in his diary that he spoke with Mussolini on 5 September and Mussolini supported the idea. He then met with Roatta on 13 September, with Roatta concurring that the best solution to Malta was invasion. Cavallero next met with *Ammiraglio di Divisione* Pellegrino Matteucci (*Comando Superiore Marina in Libia*) responsible for R.M. operations in support of Libya. The two discussed the current serious situation and options to improve the supply situation including action against Malta.[32]

Planning on *Esigenza «C3»*, the invasion of Malta, officially began on 14 October 1941. Given his belief that the Vichy government would not allow the Italians to use Biserta in Tunisia, Cavallero directed Roatta to begin planning on *«C3»* with the three services. This was the first time a coordinated planning effort for the capture of Malta had been initiated by *Comando Supremo.*[33] Only *Supermarina* had done more than writing an opinion paper on the matter during the previous four years. Even as late as October 11 *Ammiraglio di Divisione* Luigi Sansonetti, Deputy of *Supermarina*, stated that studies had not been abandoned by the navy. Three days after Cavallero, convinced of the inevitability of such action given the vanished hopes to use Biserta, wrote to Roatta:

> Regardless of the current situation in the Mediterranean, I consider it necessary to update and complete the studies already carried out concerning the possible operation for the occupation of the islands of Malta, also developing the parts relating to the preconditions, with particular regard to the indispensable special training of troops destined for the enterprise …[34]

An important point to note is that up to this date the creation of the Italian airborne force was not driven by any plan to invade Malta but was generated outside of any specified operational need. The reality was that in January 1942 none of the units that would participate in the invasion had been identified. While it had been assumed that the *1ª d. para.* and *«La Spezia»* would be used, no decisions had been made. Cavallero noted on 27 January 1942 that he was asked by generale Italo Gariboldi, currently attached to *Comando Supremo*, whether Gariboldi needed to prepare any special assault units/divisions for the attack. Cavallero replied yes, but no further information was offered.[35]

32 Antonello Biagini and Fernando Frattolillo (eds.) *Diario Storico del Comando Supremo* (Rome, USSME, 1995) vol V book 1, p.95, 103.
33 Biagini and Frattolillo (eds) *Diario Storico*, vol V book 1, p.308; Gabriele, *Operazione C3*, pp.87, 95.
34 Mario Montanari, *Le operazioni in Africa settentrionale* (Rome, USSME, 1985), vol II: Tobruk, p.340
35 Gabriele, *Operazione C3*, p.98.

Training for *Operazione «C3»*. The ability to carry 28 *paracadutisti*, eight resupply containers, operate two jump doors during parachute drops, and long range made the SM.82 an excellent aircraft for parachute operations. One can see two paratroopers simultaneously exiting from two of the aircraft in this photograph. (AUSSMA)

Concurrence and support for the invasion from Germany was essential. Details of the negotiations and meetings are not necessary for this account except to acknowledge that Hitler's support was always lukewarm at best and varied by whether Grossadmiral Raeder or Generalfeldmarschall Wilhelm Keitel (Chief of the Oberkommando der Wehrmacht) last spoke with him. The conventional thinking on the matter is that Hitler was shocked at the Fallschirmjäger losses on Crete and never again considered the use of massed airborne troops as a viable option. The heads of the two navies, Riccardi and Raeder met at Garmisch 14-15 January 1942 and agreed that Malta should be the primary focus for operations in the Mediterranean in 1942. Raeder and Kesselring were the two voices that consistently pushed for the Malta invasion to finally resolve the logistical problems in Libya.[36]

As part of the planning process for *«C3»*, the Italians convened a Military Commission under the provisions of the Tripartite Pact in February 1942. The meetings of the commission were between the Italian and Japanese militaries and focused on the materials and means required for an invasion of the scope and scale of Malta. General di divisione Antonio Gandin of *Comando Supremo* (Operations), *Ammiragli di Squadre* Vittorio Tur (*Forza Navale Speciale F.N.S.*) and Bruno Brivonesi (*Supermarina*) attended for Italy, while Rear Admiral Abe Katsuo and Captain Mitsunobu Tōyō

36 Gooch, *Mussolini's War*, p.299; Gabriele, *Operazione C3*, pp.103

(Navy) and Colonel Shimizu Moriakira (Army) headed the Japanese mission. It was decided that both the Italians and the Japanese would draw up concept plans to be compared to develop a definitive plan. The plan would then be used as a guide to create training exercises for the invasion.[37]

The comparison of the plans was done in a series of meetings held on 6–7 March. Added to the group was *Generale di Corpo d'Armata* Vittorio Sogno, the designated commander of the *XXX Cd'A* that would provide the main amphibious force. The resulting report compared the various viewpoints of the participants: *F.N.S.* (Tur), *XXX Cd'A* (Sogno), *Comando Supremo*, and the Japanese. There were several differences between the Italian and Japanese concepts, but the pertinent one for this discussion was in the employment of the airborne forces. The Italians saw the use of the paratroops to help set conditions prior to the amphibious landings and included the use of air landed units. The Japanese saw the use of the paratroopers after the initial landings and did not consider employing air landed units.[38]

While Luftflotte II and the R.A. were attacking Malta, the idea of attempting a *coup de main* against the island was being considered. First raised in a meeting by Kesselring to von Rintelen and Cavallero on 17 March 1942, Kesselring felt that any positive opportunity created by the aerial offensive should be immediately exploited. Cavallero was leery of attempting a *coup de main* as he felt that the minimum means necessarily were still lacking. While the Italians could rush the training for some of their units and other preparations, the Germans had yet to deliver the promised paratroops, gliders, and most importantly, fuel for the R.M. as their part of «*C3*».[39]

The grand aerial assault on Malta officially began on 20 March 1942 and increased in tempo and number of attacking aircraft over the following days. By 10 April Kesselring was asserting that the naval base on the island had been neutralized. The R.M. provided its assessment of the timeline for the various options on 17 April: between between 15 April-15 May, no invasion was possible, not even a *coup de main*; from 15-31 May, a *coup de main* was possible only if *Esigenza «C2»* (an invasion of Corsica) is not carried out; between 1 June–31 July only a *coup de main* but with increasing capabilities; only on 1 August and after could the full invasion plan be executed. During this period, the higher headquarters for *Operazione «C3»* was finally organized on 12 April.[40]

Overshadowing all the preparations for the invasion of the island was Russia. It was understood at the start that at some point the majority of Luftflotte II would be transferred back to Russia. When this happened, many felt the best chance to defeat the British on Malta would be gone.[41]

37 Gabriele, *Operazione C3*, pp.103–105. The *F.N.S.* was a dedicated amphibious command headquarters established in November 1940.
38 Gabriele, *Operazione C3*, pp.112-113, 243-245.
39 Gooch, *Mussolini's War*, pp.300-301.
40 Gabriele, *Operazione C3*, pp.131.
41 Gooch, *Mussolini's War*, p.301.

With the official creation of the *3º rgt. para.* just days away on 15 March, the *1º d. para.* was now organized as a ternary division on 10 March 1942 using the available units.[42] It was during this time that the commander of the *1º d. para.*, *Generale* Sapienza was replaced by *Generale di Brigata* Enrico Frattini on 1 March 1942. Sapienza had been replaced due to issues that had arisen during his regimental command in Greece. Frattini was familiar with the *paracadutisti*, having been the general officer from *Superesercito* that issued the orders to *maggiore* Zanninovitch for the jump on Kefalonia. On 18 April *Comando Supremo* instructed *generali* Gandin and Frattini, the latter now promoted to *generale di divisione* on 15 April, to finalize a parachute force that would be deployable by the end of May. That force would be identified in the 27 April memorandum that is discussed later in this chapter.[43]

It was in May that detailed plans for the invasion were finalized. The R.E. plan for the invasion had the airborne units dropping on Malta on X-Day to create a bridgehead that would clear any beach defenses and protect the amphibious landing along the southwest coast of the island (Famagusta coast). A simultaneous false airdrop with dummies would happen in the northern part of the island. Early morning of X+1 the first amphibious landings would happen along Famagusta and on Gozo Island to the north of Malta. Included were glider and *nuotatori* attacks on key installations during the night. Several diversionary attacks were planned around Malta. After the initial landings, two options were developed for the subsequent ground operations: "Hypothetical E.N." – which followed the guidance from *Comando Supremo* with a drive eastward to capture Bay of Marsa Scirocco; and "Hypothetical N." – a drive northward to split the island and turn the Vittoria Line (a line of British fortifications running east-west across the northern end of the island). In Hypothetical N., the landings on Gozo might be delayed to allow additional forces to be added to the amphibious assault force to support the advance. Hypothetical N. was seen as an option only if favorable conditions manifested during the battle.[44]

The parachute drop would be executed in two waves. The first wave would arrive in the mid-afternoon with four *battaglioni paracadutisti* and one company of 47/32 c.c. guns, and six fallschirmjäger battalions with four sections of infantry support guns. The second wave would arrive as quickly as possible and drop two more *btg. paracadutisti* and other Italian reinforcing elements, and the three remaining fallschirmjäger battalions with artillery and other heavy weapons. A third wave was planned to drop additional men and materials to help set the defensive perimeter around the planned beachhead. The short distance from Sicily to the island made the quick turn-around by the transport aircraft possible.[45]

42 Di Giovanni, *I paracadutisti*, p.130.
43 Biagini and Frattolillo (eds) *Diario Storico del Comando Supremo* (Rome: USSME, 1996), vol VI, book 1, p.1034; Di Giovanni, *I paracadutisti*, p.132.
44 Gabriele, *Operazione C3*, pp.153–168.
45 Gabriele, *Operazione C3*, pp.285–287; Antonello Biagini and Fernando Frattolillo (eds) *Diario Storico del Comando Supremo* (Rome, USSME, 1997), vol IV book 2, p.48.

One of the mass parachute training events in preparation for *Operazione «C3»*. (AUSSMA)

The need to capture Gozo went back and forth during the planning process. One concept saw the possible use of a battalion of *paracadutisti* as part of the landing force. Generalleutnant Kurt Student, the commander of the XI.Fliegerkorps, was against the idea, arguing that all the airborne units should be employed against the main objective. The decision was finally made to employ only seaborne forces,

The point that is often overlooked when discussing the possible success or failure of the Italian plan is the actual role of the airborne forces within the plan. The mission of the *paracadutisti* and the fallschirmjäger was to clear the beach defenses from the rear and set blocking positions against any UK counterattack. Mission success was to prevent any enemy direct fire against the landing sites. It was mainly defensive in nature and placed the onus for attacking in the first hours of the invasion on the British garrison. There are questions on whether the garrison had considered this situation and had adequate training to effectively attack the better trained paratroopers. Many of the defensive benefits of the terrain of the island subscribed to the garrison actually would belong to the Italo-German force during the first two days. It is only after the amphibious landing of the main force would the Italo-German force move onto the offensive to secure the island.[46]

One issue often raised about *Operazione «C3»* was the need for German aircraft to supplement the available Italian aircraft. The Italian planners established a

46 Gabriele, *Operazione C3*, pp.153–158.

requirement for two-hundred Ju 52 type aircraft, one-hundred DFS 230 gliders, and six of the Me. 323 Gigants. The DFS gliders were needed for their ability to deliver a combat group directly on or near specific defenses required in the plan. The Gigants would be used to bring in heavy equipment as part of the follow-on reinforcement of the parachute force. The R.A. had not begun development of a military glider until after the German success at Crete in 1941. Neither of their designs would fly until 1943.[47]

It is unclear how many of the Ju 52 aircraft were needed by the Italian force. The plan that was approved on 18 May 1942 lists 170 Italian and 216 German transports required for *Operazione «C3»*. The 27 April document from *Comando Supremo* stated that the Regia Aeronautica had a total of 130 transports available at that time. This number does not include the SM.81 type aircraft that could be quickly modified into a transport role as demonstrated in 1938. Calculations for the first lift of the *1° d. para.* (six battalions) was 172 aircraft, of which 126 were needed for the infantry and 46 for the artillery, mortars, and supplies. The Germans required twenty-four Ju 52s to transport a Fallschirmjäger battalion for a first lift requirement of 144 aircraft. The number of aircraft required likely reflected anticipated losses and moving the *«La Spezia»* if committed in an air landing role.[48]

Forces for «C3»

With the final details of the airborne part of the operation finalized, what was the current status of the Italian *aviotruppi* during this timeframe?

On 27 April 1942 *Comando Supremo* assessed the forces available to execute the coup de main if called upon. The Italian parachute forces were assessed at six battalions of paratroops, one battalion of *guastatori paracadutisti* (assault engineers), two parachute artillery groups of 47/32 c.c. guns, and one company from the *rgt. «San Marco»*; a total of 3,800 men and twenty-four guns. The Italian air landing force was assessed at six battalions of infantry and two artillery groups of 65/17 guns; a total of 5,000 men and twenty-four guns. Seventy SM.82 transports for the paratroopers were available, along with 60 other transport types giving a single lift troop capacity of approximately 3,300 men.[49] In a discussion on 23 April in Rome, it was stated that Germany could contribute two fallschirmjäger regiments for such an operation.[50]

47 Nino Arena, *La Regia Aeronautica* (Rome: USSMA, 1984), vol. 3, p.387.

48 Arena, *La Regia Aeronautica,* vol. 3, pp.392–393; AUSSME, Stato Maggiore di S.M. memorandum dated 23 febbraio 1942, *Oggetto: Aerei da trasporto*, L14, b.135 f.8; NARA, *Esigenza C.3 Progetto Operativo Sommario 31-5-XX*, T821, roll 251.

49 Biagini and Frattolillo (eds.) *Diario Storico,* vol VI, book 2, pp.113-114.

50 Biagini and Frattolillo (eds.) *Diario Storico,* vol VI, book 1, p.1069; book II, 113-115. There appears to be an error between the two books. The entry on p.1069 states two German

Paracadutisti unpack an aerorifornimenti carrying ammunition during training. (AUSSME)

The increasing demand for parachute training was stretching the capacity of the school. Training at Tarquinia in the first months of 1942 were the Regio Esercito's *3º rgt. para.* (*IX* and *X btg.* and *3º gruppo art. para.*) and the Regina Marina's *btg. NP «San Marco»*. To these training requirements were added several new units. It was beginning to become too much for the school to handle. During Mussolini's visit to Tarquinia on 14 April, *colonnello* Baudoin was able to speak with him about the issues he was facing at the school. Baudoin listed the concerns that have been previously mentioned: the location of the school and the facilities, lack of aircraft, living conditions, the lack of officers S.P.E. in the speciality, etc. He also gave Mussolini a six-page memorandum detailing these concerns.[51]

Baudoin's memorandum began with a paragraph addressing the lack of clear aims that would allow the school to successfully achieve an unstated goal. Instead he

battalions while p.113 states two German regiments. It is unlikely Kesselring would champion the coup de main with only two German fallschirm battalions.

51 Arena, *Tarquinia*, pp.54–56; Di Giovanni, *I paracadutisti*, p.131. Dante Pariset, *Storica del paracadutismo* (Roma-Milano, Vito Bianco Editore, 1962), pp.142–145, provides a copy of Baudoin's memorandum.

outlines the impulsive nature of the growth of the airborne forces where the authorized means are not matched to the changing goal:

> 1. – Aims and programs.
> It has never been possible to have a clear and precise program, which would allow the activity and potential [of the school] to be directed towards certain goals.
> Continuous increases are made outside of a logical plan; so that there is always a rush towards increasingly distant goals, changed before being reached; it is evident that this system is absurd.
> It began with the program of forming a single battalion, then two; within a few months, regiments were transformed into a binary division, now to a ternary division (120% of the manning), reinforced by supporting units. Between the initial and current program, there is a[n increase by a] ratio of 1:30. The potential of the School only increased from 1 to about 5. We are now talking about the establishment of a second division.
> The organization pursues [these] growing needs, and always remains behind.[52]

After the initial construction needed to begin parachute training at Tarquinia was completed in 1940, few of the desired upgrades had been accomplished. A concrete runway had not been built to replace the dirt/grass field, rendering it unusable for a period of time after heavy rains. Excessive winds were common as it was too dangerous to parachute in speeds greater than three meters per hour. Accommodations able to support both the units in training and the growing parachute division were lacking. The solution was to garrison the division at Viterbo, requiring those units to return to Tarquinia for any refresher or new equipment training.

The training problem that had the greatest impact and magnified the impact of the others was the lack of dedicated aircraft for the *reparti paracadutisti*. At the time when Germany began creating its airborne forces in the late 30s, it also created a transport group to support the Fallschirmjäger training and operational employment. The advantages were several. As the fallschirmjägers and the crews of the Ju 52s worked together over time, aircrews became qualified for parachute operations and maintained that skill by supporting the parachute school. Coordination and scheduling was simplified, allowing the fallschirmjäger to leverage good weather for training without requesting aircraft through various headquarters. As the aviation unit was part of the fallschirmjäger, the aircraft could not be tasked for other missions without first coordinating with the school or the Flieger Division.

As previously discussed, the R.A. did not create dedicated transport units until after Italy entered the war. Often these units were created with a mix of different aircraft types reflecting the lack of transport aircraft and the low production rates. As the Italian airborne specialty was being expanded in 1941, only 80 SM.82 transport

52 Pariset, *Storica del paracadutismo*, p.142.

Demonstrating the parachuting of a 47/32 c.c. gun during training. (AUSSMA)

aircraft were ordered by the R.A. in that year. This number was doubled to 160 aircraft for delivery in 1942. In those same years Germany built 502 and 503 Ju 52s respectively. The low production numbers would prevent the formation of a dedicated transport unit for the *paracadutisti* as competing demand for these aircraft would be high. The lack of a dedicated transport unit meant that anytime the weather allowed for training, requests for additional aircraft to maximize the number of student jumps or execute a unit mass jumping exercise would normally be too late or find that no suitable transports would be available that day. Visits by Mussolini to the school were welcome as the need to have a parachute demonstration meant that aircraft would be tasked to meet the requirement. These events were used to execute the mass drops needed to certify units.[53]

Besides the lack of aircraft to support both parachute training and airborne operation, there was a second shortfall: the lack of qualified *osservatori aerei per paracadutisti* (flight navigators for airborne operations) and *direttori di lancio* (aircraft jump masters). The former navigated the transport aircraft to the correct drop zones while the latter ensured the safe exit from the aircraft by the jumpers and timing it so they would land on the

53 Arena, *La Regia Aeronautica*, vol. 3, p.766–768; Di Giovanni, *I paracadutisti*, p.151; Pariset, *Storica del paracadutismo*, p.144.

drop zone. The air assault plan for *«C3»* required seventy-five *osservatori* and approximately two-hundred *direttori*. There were currently about sixty qualified *direttori* at Tarquinia, but those individuals were also the instructional staff at the school. The pilots in the school's flight detachment were the only currently qualified *osservatori*. Cavallero asked Rintelen on 10 May whether Germany could supply fifty *direttor*i to help meet the Italian requirement. No response to this request was found in the records.[54]

Normally the training to become a qualified *osservatori* was six months long, while the training for a *direttori* was two months. The original expectation was that Germany would provide the training for these men. It was not until 18 April that *Comando Supremo* issued the order to authorize the training, with the training to be completed by 30 May. Another expedient was to quickly train pilots who were no longer on flight status. These pilots, whether due to injuries or medical reasons, were no longer authorized to pilot aircraft but had the necessary navigational skills and experience.[55]

These and other factors outlined in the memorandum impacted the ability of the school to prepare the required units for *«C3»*. In closing, *colonnello* Baudion believed that if the R.A. did not wish to fully support the school, it should be turned over to the R.E. to operate. Baudoin's conversation and memorandum appeared to have some effect as *Comando Supremo* ordered a study on 18 April 1942 for establishing a new school at Viterbo.[56]

While Baudoin saw the solution to the problems as fully resourcing the school and accessing the larger and better facilities at Viterbo, *tenente colonnello* Bechi-Luserne saw a different answer to the problem. In a letter sent to the S.M.R.A. on 6 May 1942, Bechi-Luserna proposed that the *speciali paracadutisti* be completely moved under the Regia Aeronautica. His thoughts were clearly influenced by his discussions with Generalmajor Bernhard Ramcke and his proposal mirrored the German organization of responsibility of the parachute units. This proposal was not followed up and the three services continued to maintain their own units, while the R.A. maintained responsibility for the school.[57]

New training requirements were being identified as the planning for *Operazione «C3»* was further refined. The decision to include the *80ª divisione aivotraportabile «La Spezia»* into the force structure meant that the mission to quickly capture an airfield was now added to the operation.[58] The R.A. stated the new mission as:

54 Di Giovanni, *I paracadutisti*, pp.151–152; Arena, *La Regia Aeronautica* vol. 3, p.389; Nino Arena, *50ª di Tarquinia, 1939-1989, Scuole Militare paracadutismo* (Comitato Promotore ex Istruttori delle Scuole Militari di Paracadutismo, 1989), p.61; Antonello Biagini and Fernando Frattolillo (eds) *Diario Storico del Comando Supremo* (Rome, USSME, 1996) vol VI, book 1, p.73; Aldo Giorleo *Palestra Azzurra L'aeronautica militare e il paracadutismo cronistoria dalle origini ad oggi* (Roma, USSMA, 1975), p.51.

55 Di Giovanni, *I paracadutisti*, p.151; Arena, *Tarquinia*, p.61.

56 Biagini and Frattolillo (eds) *Diario Storico*, vol VI, book 1, p.1034.

57 Di Giovanni, *I paracadutisti*, p.152.

58 Giorleo *Palestra Azzurra*, p.47.

1. participate with paratrooper units in the conquest of the Malta's airports designated in the air-drop plan, guard them while retaining possession for subsequent use;
2. participate with its own specialized technical staff in putting airports and airport equipment back into operation, to maintain and ensure their technical-operational viability in the subsequent attack phase;
3. to contribute, if necessary, to the various attack phases on enemy positions by collaborating with the Italian and German paratrooper units engaged in the preliminary phase of Operation C.3.[59]

To execute the first part of this new mission statement, the R.A. stood up the *1º Reparto Paracadutisti Regia Aeronautica* on 12 May 1942. The mission of this unit was to capture and defend the Har Far airfield. The unit was organized at Tarquinia with an authorized strength of 365 men. The battalion had a headquarters section (29 men) and three companies. Each company had three patrols (squads), each with an authorized strength of the 28 *paracadutisti*. Weapons were the standard Carcano M91 moschetto per cavalleria for the men and MAB 38A submachine guns for the officers and NCOs. Their training focused on sabotage and the use of explosives. Shortly afterwards the unit was renamed the *1º battaglione paracadutisti Regia Aeronautica*. *Tenete colonnello* A.A.r.n. Edvino Dalmas commanded the battalion. [60]

The second part of the mission required the ability, if necessary, to quickly repair the airfield and place it back into operation. To do so would require an ability to repair any damage, install an airfield operations center to manage the flow of aircraft using the field, and provide an initial air defense capability to protect the field. The R.A. established the *Battaglione riattatori «Loreto»* on 10 June 1942 to execute this part of the mission.[61] Since the *«Loreto»* was not a parachute unit but a *reparto aviotrasportato* (air transportable unit), either the captured airfield had a usable runway or the unit would land using gliders. As parachute training was not a requirement, the battalion was organized at the airfield at Cameri northeast of Turin. The battalion would be

59 Nino Arena, *La Regia Aeronautica* (Rome: USSMA, 1981-1986), vol 3, p.719.

60 Aldo Giorleo *Palestra Azzurra L'aeronautica militare e il paracadutismo cronistoria dalle origini ad oggi* (Roma, USSMA, 1975), p.51; Luigi Emilio Longo, *I «reparti speciali» italiani nella seconda guerra mondiale* (Milan, Mursia 1991), p.160; Arena, *La Regia Aeronautica*, vol 3, pp.719–720; AUSSME, Relazione Edvino Dalmas, *Attività bellico svolta dal battaglione paracadutisti dell'aeronautica dal 16 novembre 1942 al'8 settembre 1943*, Cart.1160/C/11, p.1. The secondary sources state the battalion had three companies and a total of ten patrols which is a very odd organization. Dalmas states the battalion had 12 patrols when formed at Tarquinia and in Tunisia which makes the three company structure logical and is used here.

61 Some websites claim that the word riattatori was not part of the unit's official name. The Italian Air Force's official history volumes by Giorleo and Arena both identify the unit as the *Battaglione riattatori «Loreto»*.

flown into the captured airfield to establish the necessary operational infrastructure and local anti-aircraft defenses.[62]

The Regina Marina also placed new requirements for parachute training on the school. The R.M. had been planning to expand the *compagnia «P»* of the *rgt. «San Marco»* to a full battalion. This officially took place in March 1942 when the R.M. organized the 340 man *battaglione «P»*. The unit was created as a sabotage unit that would parachute into bodies of water near their objective and paddled ashore using the individual rubber boats developed in 1941. One hundred sailors had already completed their parachute training in 1941 and 200 were starting their training in 1942.[63]

At the same time, the R.M. decided to expand the small *reparto «G»* created in 1941 to a full battalion. This new unit was first called the *battaglione speciale «Mazzucchelli»*, then was renamed as the *battaglione N(uotatori)* (*btg. «N»*). The *btg. «N»* was developed as an assault diver unit and included personnel from the R.gt E. The *btg. paracadutisti* and the *btg. nuotatori* were similar in nature and yet very different. The men of the *btg. «P»* would parachute into the water and swim ashore to attack targets on the land. The men of the *btg. «N»* were equipped with dive equipment as well as their parachutes. Their objectives were normally shipping in ports and the port facilities itself. They could approach underwater using their dive equipment to reach the ships, docks, and harbor defensive barriers to clear and/or disable them. The unit would consist of 500 men.[64]

The Regio Esercito was also creating new units beyond the *battaglioni paracadutisti* needed for the *1ª d. para*. The origins of the Italian airborne speciality was rooted in sabotage and raids but had morphed into the traditional infantry role of gaining and holding terrain, albeit using a novel means of entering the fight. Now the R.E. decided that it needed to recreate a specialized force for operations behind enemy lines. On 10 May 1942 *Supereservito* authorized three companies of *Arditi*, the unit taking the name of the World War I special assault companies. Each company had a different speciality: the *101ª* (*paracadutis*ti), the *102ª* (*nuotatori,* swimmers), and the *103ª* (*camionette*, vehicles), respectively parachute, swimmers/landing, and motorized/ground. On 20 July 1942 the unit was renamed *Reggimento Arditi.* On 1 August the first three companies were grouped as the *I btg. arditi*, and the *II btg. arditi* was created on 20 August with the *111ª*, *112ª*, and *113ª compagnie*. Three new companies mirrored the same specialities as the first three companies but the *112ª cp.* was named *di sbarco* (sea landing) instead of *nuotatori*, and the *113ª cp.* was renamed *terrestre* (ground) instead of *camionette*. The regiment was renamed the *10º reggimento arditi* on 15 September.[65] Due to the number of units requiring parachute training and the

62 Giorleo *Palestra Azzurra*, p.52; Piero Crociani and Pier Battistelli, *Italian Navy & Air Force Elite Units & Special Forces 1940–45* (Oxford, Osprey, 2013), p.38.

63 Longo, *I «reparti speciali»*, pp.290–291.

64 Longo, *I «reparti speciali»*, pp.291–292.

65 Franco Dell'Uomo and Rodolfo Puletti, *L'Esercito Italiano verso il 2000 — I corpo disciolti*, (Rome: USSME, 1998) vol 1, book 1, p.564.

Tenente colonnello Bettica explaining the parachute rigging of the 47/32 c.c. gun to General Ramcke. (AUSSMA)

limitations of the school, the men of the *101ª cp.* would not begin their jump training until early December and not complete the course until the end of February 1943.[66]

One small unit created during 1942 was the *Centro Militare «I»*, the I standing for Indian. One of several foreign units created by the R.E. in this year, this unit was raised from captured enemy Indians soldiers held in Prisoner of War (P.O.W.) camps. Initially formed in late April, the unit was officially established on 15 July and renamed the *battaglione Azad Hindoustan* on 23 October. The battalion never exceeded 270 men and was organized with one infantry company and one machine gun company. Forty-four men were selected to form a *plotone paracadutisti* and were sent to Tarquinia for training in mid-September. While the platoon was at Tarquinia, the remainder of the battalion underwent a field training exercise between 21-30 October near Tivoli where the unit performed poorly. On 10 November the unit refused to form-up for roll call, and the unit was disbanded on 12 November, disarmed and returned to the P.O.W. camps.[67]

66 Massimo di Martino,, *Paracadutisti d'Italia – Uniformi distintivi equipaggiamenti.*, (Milan: Edizioni Libreria Militare, 2019), vol 1, p.278.

67 Piero Crociani and Pier Battistelli, *Italian Army Elite Units & Special Forces 1940–43* (Oxford: Osprey, 2011), pp.54–55; Romani H. Rainero, *I reparti arabi e indiani dell'esercito italiano nella Seconda Guerra Mondiale ("Le Frecce Rosse")* (Rome: USSME, 2007), pp.116, 132, 140; Arena, *Tarquinia,* pp.57–59.

Germany's role in «C3»

Often incorrectly called Unternehmen Herkules, the plan to seize Malta is properly called *Operazione «C3»*. *«C3»* was an Italian operation from its inception, with Germany deciding to support it in April 1942.[68] The operation was developed by the *Ufficio C3* (C3 Office), a joint planning office (R.E., R.A., and R.M.) within *Comando Supremo*.[69] Once Germany had committed to the operation, a German planning cell was added to the *Ufficio C3* in April 1942.

As Germany's experience in airborne operations vastly exceeded that of Italy's, *generale* Cavallero requested a German staff officer to assist in the planning. This was the start of a very unusual period of Italo-German cooperation during the war. The officer selected was Generalmajor Hermann-Bernhard Ramcke, a very experienced fallschirmjäger. Ramcke was one of the planners for Unternehmen Merkur (Operation Mercury, the assault on Crete) and finished the battle as the commander of a fallschirmjäger regiment. He was considered a leading expert on the planning and execution of large airborne operations. Ramcke arrived in Italy on 2 March and observed a tactical parachute drop at Tarquinia on 5 March. During that visit he met Mussolini who had also attended that exercise. For the next two weeks he observed the *paracadutisti*, their training and equipment. Once Hilter committed to *Operazione «C3»*, Ramcke was assigned to the planning staff.[70]

In a meeting with Cavallero and von Rintelen on 23 March, Ramcke provided his observations on the state of the Italian airborne force. Part of his mission was to determine any issues with the Italian paratroopers jumping from German aircraft. His main points were:

- That the Italian paratroopers are technically proficient in the skills needed for jumping from airplanes. They can jump from Italian aircraft as well as from the German aircraft (Ju 52). The length of the IF41/SP static line would need to be tested on the Ju 52 and possibly adjusted.
- The Italian weapons can be accommodated. As for the armament of our [Italian] troops, it is sufficient but we need to see how to arrange it on the German planes.
- He announced that it would also be advisable to try a type of small German parachute and he reserved the right to send some models.
- Soldier training is lacking in the coordination of fire and movement; Ramcke believed that the [heavier] armament to be insufficient and that it is necessary to use parachutes to drop the individual weapons. He believed that a greater supply

68 Biagini and Frattolillo (eds) *Diario Storico*, vol VI, book 1, p.1069. Hitler's approval was received by *Comando Supremo* on 23 April.

69 Alessandro Vivarelli, *The Axis and the Intended Invasion of Malta in 1942: A Combined Planning Endeavor* (Fort Leavenworth, Kansas: School of Advanced Military Studies Monograph, 2014), pp.26–27.

70 Biagini and Frattolillo (eds) *Diario Storico*, vol VI, book 1, p.1069.

of anti-tank and mountain artillery was necessary. He judged the 65/17 piece to be sufficient and thinks the 120mm mortar is too heavy.

- A single company of 81 mortars is insufficient and stated that a company was needed for each regiment. The same is true for the engineers. Engineer units of various types are needed, not just assault engineers. The communication systems (both equipment and training) was considered in the light of combat experience and judged insufficient.
- For supplies, the German division has specialized personnel with organized rates for each of the services. In addition, the Germans take a greater number of vehicles for supplies.
- The Italian parachute company was too small (only 100 men) and compared it to the German company size of 150 men.[71]

At the end of his observations, Cavallero asked how long would it take to ready the division for the invasion? Ramcke felt another two and one half months were needed, mainly ground tactical training. His estimate matched that of Cavallero's and *Comando Supremo* position that no attack could be executed in April.

General Ramcke closed with some additional comments. He had observed both the men from the *reggimenti paracadutisti* and from the *«San Marco»* and they presented a very good impression of the human material in both units. Ramcke felt that the more experienced men should be mixed with the newer trainees. The personnel of the first three battalions had trained together for over eighteen months and could be used to leaven the newer battalions in an exchange between units. When asked about the German instructors and technical experts, he informed everyone that they should be arriving in early April to assist the training programs and overcome any technical issues. Finally Ramcke added that he was giving a lecture on the lessons from Crete on 8 April to the Italian paratroopers.[72]

With Germany's participation in the invasion, its main contributions were the fallschirmjäger, landing craft, and the promise of transport aircraft and fuel for the R.M. It was also agreed that the headquarters of the airborne component of *«C3»* would now be the XI Fleigerkorps under Generalleutnant Student. The German airborne plan within *Operazione «C3»* was code named Unternehmen Herkules.

Tactical training by the units preparing for *«C3»* was also taking place during this period. The Germans trained with the Italians near Monte Romano and Cimini Mountains east of Tarquinia.[73] The two parachute regiments of the *1ª div para.* were

71 Biagini and Frattolillo (eds) *Diario Storico,* vol VI, book 1, pp.811-813.

72 Biagini and Frattolillo (eds.) *Diario Storico,* vol VI, book 1, p.813; Ramcke's full presentation on Crete is AUSSME, *Conferenza Tenuta al Comando Supremo l'11 aprile XX alla presenza del Duce e con la partecipazione dell'ecc. Cavallero e del Feldmaresciallo Kesselring ad ufficiali delle forze armata italiane e germaniche dal generale Ramcke*, I-3, b.1, f.1.

73 Arena, *La Regia Aeronautica*, vol 3, pp.386, 716. Arena does not provide a timeframe, but it likely happened whilst the *«Folgore»* was still at Viterbo.

sent to training areas north in the Tuscan Emilian Apennines region for tactical maneuvers. The *1° rgt. para.* then moved to the Bolzano-Merano area while *«La Spezia»* continued to train in the region around Pisa. In May Mussolini observed a battalion parachute drop which included a *compagnia da 47/32* in the Piana del Diavolo (Devil's Plain) near the town of Canino.[74] Afterwards the *1ª d. para.* was moved from the Alto Adige in northern Italy to the area near Ostuni in Puglia (south-eastern Italy) while the fallschirmjägers were moved further south to the area in Salento near Lecce. The area was selected due to its similarity to Malta, with stone walls and enclosed orchards and gardens that Malta is noted for. The *«La Spezia»* joined them in the area later that month.[75]

It is unclear which fallschirmjäger units were in Italy for training with the *paracadutisti* during the preparations for *Operazione «C3»*. Di Giovanni states that joint training had been conducted with a fallschirmjäger battalion at Viterbo at the beginning of 1942.[76] This could have been Fallschirm-Lehr Bataillon Burkhardt that was deployed to North Africa between January and March 1942, but none of the sources indicate that it had stopped in Italy for training.

Arena states that joint training was conducted with the 5.Fallschirmjäger Division under Ramcke in the Viterbo area, possibly in April. This is very unlikely as that division was not established until 1944. It is possible he was referring to Fallschirmjäger-Regiment 5, but that possibility is mere speculation. Arena also states that German FJ units trained in southern Italy in May and June. The only fallschirmjäger unit identified as being in Italy at this time was 1. Kompanie, Fallschirmjäger-Lehr Bataillon "Burckhardt". When the bataillon "Burckhardt" was withdrawn from North Africa and passed through Italy on its return to Germany in March 1942, the 1 Komp. was ordered to remain. The company was placed under the control of Ramcke and renamed the Fallschirmjäger Lehr Kompanie Herrmann. It was used to support the training of the *paracadutisti* in the *1ª d. para.* in preparation for *«C3»*.[77]

Another unknown is which German fallschirmjäger units would actually have participated in *«Operazione C3»*. Germany was rebuilding and expanding its airborne force after the losses sustained by the regiments in Russia. Most of the 7. Flieger-Division had returned from Russia to France in April–May 1942 for rebuilding and training. Two new regiments, Fallschirmjäger-Regiment 4 and 5 were being organized at this time. One source states that Fallschirmjäger-Regiment 2 was training for *«C3»* in July. The Mourmelon military training area south-east of Reims has been indicated

74 Arena, *La Regia Aeronautica*, vol 3, p.716.
75 Arena, *La Regia Aeronautica*, vol 3, pp.386, 389, 716; Paolo Morisi, *The Italian Folgore Parachute Division* (Solihul, Helion & Company, 2016), p.43; Antonello Biagini and Fernando Frattolillo (eds) *Diario Storico del Comando Supremo* (Rome: USSME, 1997) vol VII, book 1, p.161.
76 Di Giovanni, *I paracadutisti*, p.150.
77 Arena, *La Regia Aeronautica*, vol 3, pp.386, 716; Erich Busch, *Die Fallschirmjäger Chronik 1935–1945* (Dorheim: Podzun-Pallas Verlag, 1982), p.282.

as the training location for FJ preparing for Malta. Fallschirmjäger-Regiment 5 was also training at that location in July.[78]

Anlage 3 (gliederung, organizational diagram) in the German study for the operation found in the Italian records for *«C3»* showed the complete 7.Flieger-Division with three regiments, along with the attachment of the Fallschirmjäger-Regiment 4 under the XI.Fliegerkorps headquarters.[79] Anlage 1 of that study provided a timeline that placed the invasion date as 18 July. As indicated above, it was unlikely that the fallschirmjäger units would have been ready and available before July and August would have been a more realistic timeline.

What is known is that the Ramcke Brigade was not established as part of *«C3»*. Most of the sources state that the 1.Fallschirmjäger Brigade was authorized in July 1942 under General Ramcke for operations in North Africa. The brigade is not included in the forces diagrammed in the May study for the invasion. The brigade initially consisted of only the II Battalion, Fallschirmjäger Regiment 5 (II/FJR 5), but was joined by the I/FJR 2, I/FJR 3, and FJ-Lehr Bataillon "Burckhardt". There is no record of these units being in Italy at any time for training for *«C3»*.[80]

Cancellation of «C3»

As the preparations were nearing completion, the fate of *Operazione «C3»* was being decided by other events. The success of the Italo-German forces in A.S. in May and June placed pressure to retain the air units supporting ground operations in Libya rather than withdraw them for the assault on Malta. Those air units were withdrawn from attacking Malta to support the Italo-German attack on the Gazala Line on 26 May 1942. After nearly a month of fighting, the forces under Rommel by 15 June had successfully defeated the UK forces. Instead of returning the air assets to support the Malta invasion, permission was given for Rommel to continue the attack to capture Tobruk. Tobruk fell on 21 June and the way forward into Egypt was open. The Axis discussions were now focused on whether to stop at the Egyptian border and

78 Busch, *Die Fallschirmjäger Chronik*, 226; Anon, 'Infanterie-Einheiten der Luftwaffe' <https://www.lexikon-der-wehrmacht.de/Gliederungen/InfanterieLW.htm>, accessed 13 June 2022, Fallschirmjäger-Regiment 2, Fallschirmjäger-Regiment 5

79 NARA, Oberbefehlshaber Süd Study dated 31.5.1942, *Studie über die Vorbereitung und Durchführung des Unternehmens C3 ("Herkules')*, T821, roll 250. The 1., 2., and 3.Fallschirmjäger were the three regiments listed as part of the division.

80 Bruce Quarrie, *German Airborne Divisions: Mediterranean Theatre 1942–45* (Oxford: Osprey, 2005), p.26; Busch, *Die Fallschirmjäger Chronik*, 216; Anon, 'Infanterie-Einheiten der Luftwaffe', Fallschirmjäger-Brigade "Ramcke". Quarrie states the brigade was formed in April 1942 for *«C3»*. All the other sources place the formation of the brigade in July specifically for North Africa. The ad hoc nature of the brigade indicated a rapid formation using available units rather than the creation of a new unit separate from those already allocated for Malta.

reposition the air assets to assault Malta or continue into Egypt. The decision was to ride the wave of success and the Italo-German forces began their advance into Egypt.

At the same time that the air assets were retained in Libya, German aircraft were also being withdrawn and sent to Russia in support of the German summer offensive. The convoy battles in June depleted the R.M. fuel supply and the navy required an additional 40,000 tons of fuel from Germany to support the invasion. The request was denied by Germany on 15 June. With the final preparations being completed in June, the best invasion dates were 15 July and 10 August before the weather became too unpredictable.[81] The combination of these actions seriously compromised the ability to execute «*C3*».

Without the return of the Luftwaffe units to support the invasion, *Operazione «C3»* died a slow death. Germany began to recall their experts from Italy in early July. Cavallero instructed Gandin on 7 July to begin planning *Operazione «C4»*, the occupation of Tunisia. Cavallero's intent was to keep the Malta planning team together, along with all the resources collected for «*C3*» for possible employment in those operations. Meeting again with Gandin on 9 July, Cavallero was told by Gandin that Student did not believe «*C3*» could be executed after August. On 10 July Cavallero allowed some of the «*C3*» landing craft to be sent to A.S. to support the Italo-German supply lines to El Alamein. A second air offensive against the island was started on 1 July and lasted two weeks with negligible results. Spared from the heavy air bombardments since late May, Malta had begun to rebuild its offensive strength.[82]

The act that truly finalized the end of «*C3*» was the discussion on 12 July between Cavallero, Gandin, and *Generale di Brigata* Carlo Fassi about the future of the *reparti paracadutisti*. This meeting discussed transferring four battalions (three *btg. paracadutisti* and one *btg. guastatori*) to Africa. The next day (13 July) both *Superesercito* and *Superaereo* were ordered to transfer the complete *1ª d. para.* to A.S. with the utmost urgency. The assignment of the Italian, followed by the German paratrooper units to the Italo-German forces in Africa merely confirmed the expected decision. With the decision to transfer the division to Africa, any lingering possibility of executing *Operazione «C3»* in 1942 was now gone. The official order postponing the assault was issued on 27 July which finally acknowledged the reality.[83]

The words written in 1936 did in fact become prophetic: "The operation, however, [if] attempted during the war, may be delayed and may present strong elements of failure; it would therefore be necessary to carry out the invasion of the Maltese islands as an initial act of igniting the conflict."

81 NARA, Comando Supremo Ufficio Operazioni C3 memorandum 10 giugno 1942, *GIORNO X*, T821, Roll.251.

82 Gabriele, *Operazione C3*, pp.202–208; Biagini and Frattolillo (eds) *Diario Storico*, vol VII, book 1, pp.573.

83 Biagini and Frattolillo (eds) *Diario Storico*, vol VII, book 1, pp.547, 566, 603, 616; Arena, *La Regia Aeronautica*, vol 3, pp.423–425;

Final Thoughts on Operazione «C3»

A favorite discussion topic for many students of history is whether *Operazione «C3»* would have been successful. There are many positive indicators that the plan could have worked and have succeeded in capturing the island. The training of the Italian units was superior to what was normal for the R.E. during the war as demonstrated by the performance of those units in the campaigns that followed. The material preparation was also appropriate, with the necessary shipping, landing craft, air resupply containers, etc. produced in time for a July-August invasion.

The usual comments that are used to state the invasion might have failed include the strength of the garrison (especially the anti-aircraft defenses); the unsuitability of the types of landing craft; and the intervention of the Royal Navy. The condition of the garrison has become a point of discussion in the past years, focusing on whether they were physically fit for the type of close combat expected and whether their training was adequate to successfully counterattack the better trained Italo-German paratroops. The Axis air campaign itself was effective up until the time the aircraft began to be diverted to other tasks when the invasion date was repeatedly postponed. The lack of suitable landing craft, especially those with bow ramps ignores the reality that many of the landing sites were against rock faces where a ramp offered no advantage. The repurposed fishing vessels and other small craft, besides their improved seaworthiness, were better able to handle the challenges of discharging their cargo against the rocky face.

To address the impact of the Royal Navy, one must examine the operational plan. The RN had a limited time window to affect the invasion; limits imposed by the steaming time to reach Malta during the window of Italian landings and the length of time the RN could remain near Malta due to fuel limitations. During the time the RN was near the island, it would have been exposed to air and naval attacks that proved deadly in the summer during Operations Harpoon and Pedestal. The Allied reluctance to impose a naval blockade of Tunisia during the final months of the fighting in Africa was partially due to the effective threat of the Axis air and naval power in the central Mediterranean. The Italian plan was designed around these two critical time elements and the landing force likely could have avoided decisive defeat by the RN.

The plan also helped to neutralize the size of the garrison. The parachute drops were planned for the first day and they were defensive in nature. Their mission was to clear the beach defenses and block the garrison from covering the landing sites. Knowing that a seaborne invasion was to follow, the British commander would be faced with the decision on how large of a force he could commit against the paratroops. The enemy was the furthest away from the best beaches and the airborne landing could be seen as a feint. This tactical conundrum only needed to last for 12-16 hours, after which superior Italian numbers would decide the day.

Whether any of this would have worked is left to conjecture. Many things can go wrong in war, and there is no way to successfully determine the possibility of success or failure. Too often the impact of the Italian plan and the dilemmas created for

British decision-making are not considered in the discussions surrounding «*C3*». The chance of success or failure would likely have been determined by those decisions forced upon Britain's leadership.

Operazione «C3» was strategically a better option if executed in 1940. The level of committed resources required was vastly greater in 1942 and came after two years of losses attempting to neutralize the island. Taking the island in 1940 would have required fewer resources and the long term gain would have been significant. A successful 1940 invasion would have justified its initial cost, but that is using hindsight. Italy was not planning an offensive war and had decided that the possible threat did not justify that upfront cost in the years leading up to the war. By the time the decision was made to invade the island, too much time had been lost. Italy lacked the paratroops and the transport aircraft to attempt the invasion by itself in 1942, so required German assistance to mount the attack. This led to the ultimate cancellation of the operation as Germany had its own operational needs to satisfy.

Once *Comando Supremo* finally decided to implement a permanent solution to the operational problem of Malta, the three services were able to develop and prepare a plan with a good chance of success. The fatal flaw in the Italian plan was to be dependent on Germany for its execution. The strategic disconnect between Italy and Germany as displayed in Italy's concept of Parallel War illustrated the divergent nature of each of the two countries' strategic goals. The operational situation in the Mediterranean was a uniquely Italian problem and Italy should have prepared to overcome those issues solely within Italy's means. Germany was involved in the Mediterranean War only because Italy's failures created a German vulnerability; a vulnerability that would not have existed if Italy had remained neutral or had adequately planned and prepared for its Parallel War.

There is one final action that should be examined in the aftermath of «*C3*»; the decision to transfer the *1ª divisione paracadutisti* to Africa. The planning organization responsible for «*C3*» was transitioned to begin planning for *Esigenza «C4»*. Planning for *Esigenza «C2»*, the occupation of Corsica was also ongoing. Both of these were a force entry operation against a possible defending force. The employment of *1ª divisione paracadutisti* as a part of those plans would appear to be a natural requirement. It was fully trained and equipped and it could be quickly committed using the existing air transport capabilities. Given the contingency nature of the plans, retaining this unit in Italy for possible use would have created options if these plans were ordered into execution. This question again begs whether the Italian military truly possessed a vision or an understanding of need for this type of unit.

If the operational requirement for additional infantry in A.S. was so pressing that an infantry division needed to be quickly sent, there was the option of sending «*La Spezia*». While not as well trained as the *paracadutisti*, the division was completely deployable by aircraft. Its more traditional infantry structure, heavier weapons, and larger vehicle authorization was better suited to the type of combat expected in North Africa. Sending the *divisione aviotrasportabile* instead of the *divisione paracadutisti* would have retained the latter as a strategic asset available for use in either «*C3*» or «*C4*».

Instead the division was sent to North Africa to fight as a regular infantry unit. It is true that a new parachute division was in the process of being created, but when the historical situation to execute *«C4»* occurred, *Comando Supremo* had to scrape together an intervention force. One must ask how differently the campaign in Tunisia might have unfolded if the *1ª divisione paracadutisti* had been available for immediate employment in November 1942?

10

Divisione fanteria «*Folgore*»

It is difficult to reconcile the need for additional forces in Africa settentrionale with the decision to send an airborne unit to satisfy that need. The previous two years had conclusively demonstrated that mobility was the key to both the effectiveness and survivability of units fighting in the desert. Yet the *Comando Supremo* committed this strategic asset to a campaign that wasted its capabilities for the reason of expediency rather than providing the best units and materials to meet the need.

The problem facing the Italian and German leadership was how to reinforce the apparent success of the Italo-German forces in Africa under the newly promoted Generalfeldmarschall Rommel in his push to capture Alexandria. With the decision to delay *Operazione* «*C3*» in July, the transfer of resources to North Africa meant that the seizure of Malta would now be indefinitely postponed. Any attempt to revive the invasion would require taking back those resources and would effectively end Rommel's offensive effort. As Germany was unwilling to commit additional mechanized and motorized forces to North Africa, any units and material removed from Africa could not be replaced by Italy. Even if the island had been captured in July, the improved logistical situation would not have an impact at the front for one or two months as the supply system began to leverage the new situation.

Time was a critical element in the decision to send the division to A.S. For any reinforcements to affect the outcome of the campaign, they needed to be deployed to Egypt as quickly as possible. Units arriving months later would be unable to impact the operation that was currently unfolding as time favored the British. The time restriction limited the number of units available for deployment as any selected unit must already be fully equipped and trained. This was a serious limitation as most of the units available in Italy were short of equipment and training. All too often subordinate units and their equipment were stripped from those divisions in the *madrepatria* to fully outfit the divisions sent to active combat theaters. The units that had been assembled and trained for «*C3*» were now the obvious choices for immediate deployment to Africa to reinforce Panzerarmee Afrika (AOK, *Armata Corazzata Italo-Tedesca*). The regular infantry divisions prepared as part of the amphibious operations were the best choice given their heavy weapons, larger size, and vehicle authorization but would take several months to transfer to North Africa. As discussed in the previous chapter, even «*La Spezia*» could have been a better choice.[1]

Cavallero offered his logic and added a caveat to the decision to send the paratroops in his 22 July 1942 memorandum '*Direttive generali per le operazioni verso l'Egitto. Organizzazione trasporti. Difesa c.a. e costiera* (General Directive for Operations against Egypt. Organization of the Transportation, Air and Coastal Defense):

> Note: The paratrooper battalions have been assigned to the armored army to provide for the most urgent needs, but it is understood that once the front has stabilized, these battalions will have to be returned, subjected to determining the most appropriate location in relation to the use that the army command will make of the German paratroopers. Of the intention to recover the paratrooper battalions as soon as possible, it is agreed to notify the Command of the armored army … [2]

Cavallero saw the use of the division as a temporary measure and that the Panzerarmee would return the division to the control of *Comando Supremo* at some point. Also interesting was the statement that the use of the Italian paratroopers should be in a manner similar to the employment of the German paratroops. The implied concern appears to be that the Italian *paracadutisti* would be committed to combat while the German fallschirmjäger would be held in reserve.

One decision that might have enhanced the Italo-German effort in the July battles was to commit the airborne force to seize key locations in support of Rommel's advance. With the decision on 23 June that allowed Rommel to continue his advance, plans could have been made to use the assembled parachute units and transports in an airborne operation somewhere in the El Alamein area or further in the enemy's rear. Such an operation might have been considered infeasible if seriously studied, but initiating such a study would have indicated an attempt to use the *reparti paracadutisti* in some operationally decisive manner. Of interest was that the British intelligence

1 Paolo Morisi, *The Italian Folgore Parachute Division* (Solihull: Helion & Company, 2016), pp.62–63.

2 Anon, *Seconda offensiva italo-tedesca in Africa settentrionale da el Agheila a el Alamein (gennaio–settembre 1942)* (Rome: USSME, 1951), p.391. The author's translation differs from the one found in Morisi, *Folgore*, p.63. The original is "(Nota: I battaglioni *paracadutisti* sono stati assegnati all'armata corazzata per fronteggiare le necessità più urgenti, ma è inteso che, a schieramento assestato, questi battaglioni dovranno essere ricuperati, salva determinare la più appropriate dislocazione in relazione anche all'impiego che il Comando di armata farà dei *paracadutisti* germanici. Dell'intenzione di recuperare, appena possibile, i battaglioni *paracadutisti*, converrà preavvisare il Comando dell'armata corazzata)" and is found on p.391, not 390 as stated in Morisi.

noted the transfer as it was happening and did consider that such an operation was possible.[3]

On 8 July the *Comando Supremo* issued instructions that displaced soldiers in A.S. could volunteer for parachutist duty. This was an attempt to generate replacements for the division using existing personnel already present in A.S. It is unknown whether this gained any appreciable number of volunteers.[4]

Arrival of the *paracadutisti*

The formal order sending the division to A.S. was issued on 15 July.[5] The *3° reggimento paracadutisti* flew from Lecce and arrived at Derna during the middle of July. From Derna the units were flown directly to Fuka or trucked to El Adem and then flown to Fuka in Egypt. The *2° reggimento paracadutisti* was flown from the Tatoi airfield outside Athens to Tobruk beginning in the last week of July, then being flown directly to Fuka from Tatoi. The *1° rgt. art. para.* arrived at Derna beginning on 25 July and was trucked to El Adem and then airlifted to Fuka.[6] Flying transport aircraft into Fuka was dangerous at times with two SM.82 destroyed on the ground by strafing on 25 July.[7]

During this same time period the Italians and German were also transferring two additional divisions by air. The Germans were transferring the 164.Leichte Afrika Division and the Fallschirmjäger-Brigade "Ramcke". The German fallschirmjäger were transferred to A.S. between 4 and 20 August. Italy was transporting the *16° divisione motorizzata «Pistoia»*, an infantry division that was in the process of converting to a motorized division. The air movement of these units reflected a policy that no longer risked moving the personnel by sea. The men were moved by air and the equipment was sent by ship. The *S.A.S.* was able to transfer 500–700 men each day to A.S. using the available transports.[8]

3 I.S.O. Playfair, *The Mediterranean and Middle East* (London: HMSO, 1966) vol 3, p.373. The need to forward position German and Italian fighters close enough to cover the transport operation would likely be considered challenging during the month of July.

4 Biagini and Frattolillo (eds) *Diario Storico del Comando Supremo* (Rome, USSME, 1997), vol VII, book 1, p.555.

5 AUSSME, Stato Maggiore R.E. memorandum 15 luglio 1942, *Oggetto: Destinazione in A.S. della divisione paracadutisti*, M7 racc. 430, cart. 2

6 Nino Arena, *FOLGORE Storia del paracadutismo militare italiano* (Rome: Centro Editoriale Nazione, 1965), pp.147, 166; Nino Arena, *I PARACADUTISTI Cinquant'anni di storia, cronaca e immagini del paracadutisti italiano* (Modena, Società Tipografica Editrice Modenese Mucchi, 1972), p.115.;Antonello Biagini and Fernando Frattolillo (eds) *Diario Storico*, vol VII, book 1, p.602

7 Massimo Civoli, *S.A.S. I Servizi Aerei Speciali della Regia Aeronautica 1940-1943* (Cavallermaggiore: Gribaudo, 2000), p.65.

8 Nino Arena, *La Regia Aeronautica* (Rome, USSMA, 1984), vol 3, p.182.

A formation of a battalion of the «*Folgore*». The *paracadutisti* are equipped with the moschetto per cavalleria and the new web equipment designed for the carbine. Note the *folgorino* at the far right with a *fucile controcarro 35(P)*. (AUSSME)

This policy and the lack of capacity of the *S.A.S.* transport *gruppi* meant that these units would arrive in Africa in a very piecemeal manner. The units arrived with their basic equipment and small arms but needed to await their heavy equipment and vehicles arriving by ship. In several cases, companies and battalions were rushed forward to fill critical gaps before their equipment arrived, leaving these units dependent on other units for support.

In the case of the *1ª d. para.*, there was little heavy equipment to transport. Only the few vehicles assigned to the division and the equipment for the non-parachute capable elements needed to be shipped by sea. As the parachute battalions were smaller than the regular infantry battalions, each battalion could be flown in a single day with all their weapons and other equipment. Every man also carried their parachute as there was an expectation in the division that they would be employed as part of an airborne operation. This expectation would not last long as the *paracadutisti* would discover. The division's heavy equipment and the vehicles were sent to Brindisi for shipment to A.S. by sea. Some of this equipment would not reach the division until mid-September, complicating the support and supply of the unit as it participated in combat and then occupied its part of the El Alamein line. The special parachute equipment (the aerial resupply containers and the multi-parachute rigs for dropping heavier equipment) remained in Italy once the decision was made to employ the *divisione paracadutisti* as a regular infantry division.[9]

Prior to the regiments departing for A.S., the *1º* and *3º reggimenti* were reorganized. The *VIII btg. guastatori* that was part of the *3º rgt.* now became a separate unit under divisional command. The *XI btg.* was authorized on 22 June 1942 to replace the *VIII btg guastatori* in the *3º rgt.*[10] As the *XI btg.* was just beginning its training, it was transferred to the *1º rgt.* The *1º rgt.* gave the *II* and *IV btg.* to the *3º rgt.* and only kept the *III btg.* When the *3º rgt.* deployed to A.S., it had four battalions (*II, IV, IX* and *X btg.*) while the *1º rgt.* only had two (*III* and *XI btg.*). It is possible that the plan was for the regiments to reorganize once the *1º rgt.* arrived in A.S., but this transfer never happened. The *1º rgt.* would remain in Italy to form a new parachute division, the *184ª divisione fanteria «Nembo»*, but that event was still months in the future.[11]

The plan to deploy the *1ª divisione paracadutisti* to North Africa came with a name change. The division was briefly renamed the *divisione «Cacciatori di Africa»* as a cover to hide its deployment to North Africa from Allied intelligence.[12] In the records of the *Comando Supremo* during July 1942 it was referred to as the *divisione «Frattini»* after the name of the divisional commander. The division was officially named the *185ª divisione fanteria «Folgore»* on 27 July 1942.[13]

The renaming of the division was a little unexpected. *Generale* Sapienza had sent a memorandum on 9 January 1942 recommending the name *«Folgore»* along with a list of three mottos for consideration. *«Fologre»* translates as 'Lighting' and was considered a fitting name for the new unit, capturing the essence of striking from the sky. Also included was a sketch for a coat of arms for the division. The *Ispettorato della fanteria* (Infantry Inspectorate) responsible for this action on 6 February 1942 recommended approval of the name and the motto "COME FOLGORE DEL CIELO" (Like Lighting from the Sky), along with the sketch. The recommendations were then sent to the *Ministero della Guerra* for final approval.[14]

9 Mario Montanari, *Le operazioni in Africa settentrionale* (Rome: USSME, 1989), vol III, p.551;

10 AUSSME, Stato Maggiore R.E. memorandum 11 settembre 1942, *Oggetto: Costituzione e mobilitazione di reparti paracadutisti*, M7 racc.432 cart.3.

11 Lundari, *I paracadutisti italiani*, pp.14, 19.

12 Arena, *FOLGORE*, pp.146–147. Arena, *I PARACADUTISTI*, p.266. The name *«Cacciatori di Africa»* was never official. As previously noted, the British were aware of the transfers in July.

13 Giuseppe Lundari, *I paracadutisti italiani 1937/45* (Milan: Editrice Militare Italiana di Ivo Fossati, 1989), p.14; AUSSME, Stato Maggiore R.E. memorandum 17 luglio 1942, *Oggetto: Nuova denominazione dell'attuale divisione paracadutisti*, M7 racc.430, cart.2. Often the division is called the *185º divisione paracadutisti «Folgore»* in many works which is incorrect;

14 AUSSME Ministero della Guerra letter 9 gennaio 1942, *Oggetto: Nome e motto araldico divisione paracadutisti*, H1, cart.b36, fol.6; Ispettorato della Fanteria note 6 febbraio 1942,

The ministry responded on 12 April.[15] The motto was approved for use by the *1°* and *2° rgt. paracadutisti*. The name *«Folgore»* however was disapproved. The reason given was that the use of the word *paracadutisti* in the unit name was already sufficient as it worthily characterized these units. The coat of arms was also disapproved by Umberto, the Prince of Piedmont, who held the position as the commander of the infantry speciality in the R.E. A recommended coat of arms was attached to the letter but was not found in the archive file.

When the division and regiments were redesignated as *fanteria* and given the name *«Folgore»* on 27 July, the memorandum instructed that the title *paracadutisti* would not be used in any official or unofficial papers.

The regiments were renumbered as well under the same order. The *1° rgt. para.* became the *185° reggimento fanteria «Folgore»* (*colonnello* Giannetto Parodi). The *2° rgt. para.* became the *186° rgt. f. «Folgore»* (*col.* Pietro Tantillo), while the *3° rgt. para.* became the *187° rgt. f. «Folgore»* (*ten. col.* Luigi Camosso). The *I, II,* and *III gruppi artiglieria paracadutisti* were organized into the *185° reggimento artiglieria* (*colonnello* Ernesto Boffa) with three artillery groups of two batteries in each gruppo. The renaming of the units from *paracadutisti* to *fanteria* is a notable indicator that the role of the division had changed in the minds of the military leadership.[16]

The situation that existed in Egypt when the first parachute battalion arrived on 20 July was different from the expectation a mere month ago.[17] The much reduced Italo-German Army under Rommel had quickly resupplied from the captured enemy stocks at Tobruk and on 24 June pushed eastwards towards the Nile delta. The army reached Sid el Barrani that evening, while the British retreated further east and established a defensive position at Marsa Matruh. Continuing the advance on 25 June, the lead elements reached the western edge of the British defense on 27 June. A series of combats to cut the British retreat were partially successful and the Axis force entered Marsa Matruh on 29 June. Once again a number of prisoners and supplies were captured.

During that same week of fighting, the 8th Army was preparing the defense of the El Alamein position. The 8th Army brought new forces into position and was benefitting from the shortened supply line. If the Italo-German Army could break through that line before the British could fully secure it, Alexandria would be open to capture. Time was on Britain's side. and Rommel understood that the current advantage held by his army was both small and fleeting.

Oggetto: nome e motto araldico divisione paracadutisti, H1, cart.b36, fol.6.

15 AUSSME Ministero della Guerra letter 12 aprile 1942, *Oggetto: Nome e motto araldico divisione paracadutisti*, H1, cart.b36, fol.6;

16 Franco Dell'Uomo and Rodolfo Puletti *L'Esercito Italiano verso il 2000 — I corpo disciolti*, (Rome: USSME, 1998) vol 1, book 1, pp.561–578, book 2, p.147; Franco Dell'Uomo and Roberto di Rose *L'Esercito Italiano verso il 2000 — I corpi disciolti*, (Rome: USSME, 2001) vol 2, book 1, pp.356.

17 Biagini and Frattolillo (eds) *Diario Storico*, vol VII, book 1, p.678.

Sensing victory, Rommel again pushed his units eastwards towards the Nile delta, contacting the British defense near the railway station at El Alamein on 30 June. What followed was four weeks of attacks and counterattacks by both sides as each tried to defeat the other. Later named the 1st Battle of El Alamein, the fighting became confused and desperate at times during those 28 days. Both sides gained advantages and then missed the opportunities those advantages had created. By the time the fighting finally ended on 28 July, both sides were exhausted but the British held the position. The Italo-German Army had been stopped and now was forced to regroup and try to resupply. Rather than arriving to support a victorious advance, the *paracadutisti* would now be a part of the final push to the Nile River.

Italian accounts refer to the three Battles of El Alamein that occurred between July to November 1942. The first battle fought between 1-28 July was already lost. The Italo-German Army now began to prepare for the second. The need for troops at the front was pressing and the battalions of the «*Folgore*» were sent forward as they arrived in support of the other divisions at the front.

In the Desert (Map 10.1)

After arriving in A.S., the units of the division were moved through the Fuka airfield forward to a staging area at El Daba. El Daba would become the forward depot for the «*Folgore*» during its time in Africa. It was at El Daba that the *paracadutisti* were told to store their parachutes. Remembering that moment, *sottotenente* Lassalle Errani recalled:

> We left all hope in El Daba when they made us drop off the parachutes, which we had [been] individually carrying.[18]

Rommel's need for reinforcement was pressing. At a meeting at El Daba on 17 July, Rommel met with Cavallero and Kesselring. Rommel outlined that without reinforcement within a week, he would be forced to withdraw from Alamein. After Kesselring stated that a withdrawal would endanger the air forces, Rommel stated he first needed more 88mm guns and then the parachute battalions. The *paracadutisti* could not arrive soon enough to help solidify the Panzerarmee's forward position.[19]

First to arrive in A.S., the units of the *187° rgt.* were sent to various locations along the front. The *II btg.* occupied positions on the El Taga plateau, while the *IV btg.* occupied positions overlooking the El Qattara depression in the extreme south. The *IX* and *X btg.* deployed in the Bab el Qattara area as part of the Caposaldo

18 Marco Di Giovanni, *I paracadutisti italiani Volontari, miti e memoria della seconda guerra mondiale* (Gorizia: Editrice Goriziana, 1991), p.157.
19 Montanari, *Le operazioni*, p.484.

(Strongpoint) Menthon. The *186° rgt.* followed with the *V* and *VII btg.* reinforcing the *27ª d.f «Brescia»* positioned just north of the Bab el Qattara area, with the *VII btg.* reinforcing Kampfgruppe Menthon (288.Panzergrenadier regiment). The *VI btg.* was moved further south to cover the area just north of the El Taga Plateau. Because the *187° rgt.* was split, it was organized into two gruppi, *Gruppo Bechi* (*II* and *IV btg.*) and *Gruppo Camosso* (*IX* and *X btg.*).[20] The three artillery groups of the *185° regg, art.* were positioned in support of the entire sector, with the *II gruppo* supporting the northernmost battalions, the *III gruppo* in the center, and the *I gruppo* in the south.

Thus positioned, the division was spread over 28 kilometers The division's lack of vehicles required it to depend on trucks borrowed from other units to support its units with supplies and other material. Trucks from the army's *Intendenza Superiore A.S.* were only available to move the units from El Daba to their first positions; all other movement after that was by marching. Fifty-four supply trucks earmarked for the division arrived at Bengasi on 14 August but it would be another week before they would arrive at the front.[21] The *«Folgore»* found itself in the desert covering a vast frontage with little ability to rapidly move or support itself.

Along with the *«Folgore»*, Panzerarmee Afrika received the 164.Leichte Afrika Division and the Fallschirmjäger-Brigade "Ramcke". With these additional units Panzerarmee Afrika in August was reorganized:

> Deutsches Afrika Korps (DAK): 15. and 21.Panzerdivisionen.
> Italian *X Cd'A*: *d.f «Brescia»*, *d.f. «Folgore»*, and FJ Brigade Ramcke.
> Italian *XX Cd'A*: *d. cor. «Ariete»*, *d. cor. «Littorio»*, *and d. moto. «Trieste»*.
> Italian *XXI Cd'A*: *d.f «Trento»*, *d.f «Bologna»*, and 164.Leichte Afrika Division.
> 90.Afrika-Division (under army command).[22]

The situation at the end of July was a new experience for the armies in Africa. The El Alamein position was one of the few places during the North African Campaign where both flanks of a defensive line could be anchored on impassable terrain. The Mediterranean Sea secured the northern flank while the Qattara Depression (a deep depression with salt marshes and sand seas) fixed the southern end of the line. Once the 8th Army was reinforced with two additional armored divisions and two infantry divisions in late September, the Italo-German Army would lack the strength necessary to break through the position.

The time between the arrival of the various parachute battalions and the start of 2nd Alamein was spent in offensive combat patrols. Both sides were aggressively probing the other side to gain intelligence on the movements and dispositions of their

20 Arena, *FOLGORE*, pp.147,167.
21 Anon, *Seconda offensiva italo-tedesca*, p.413; Aldo Cocchia (ed), *La difesa del traffico con Africa settentrionale* (Rome: USMM, 1962), vol 7, pp.321–322.
22 Mario Montanari, *Le operazioni in Africa settentrionale* (Rome: USSME, 1989), vol 3, p.569.

A *paracadutisti* of the «*Folgore*» observing the Quattara Depression. This *folgorino* is armed with a MAB 38A, although the moschetto per cavalleria M91 was the main small arm of the division. (AUSSMA)

The Pista Whiskey (Whiskey Trail) by the Quattara Depression that was in the «*Folgore*» sector at El Alamein. The image depicts the desolation of this part of the Egyptian desert. It could be mislabeled as the author was unable to match the terrain in the photograph with a location of the road on a topographical map. (AUSSME)

units. The *V* and *VII btg.* were actively patrolling and attacking enemy patrols north in the Deir um Kawabir depression and south in the Rain Pool area. *Gruppo Camosso* was observing the Qattara Depression and the El Taga Plateau and attacking enemy raiding parties. This period gave the *paracadutisti* their first combat experience and validated the training they had undergone over the previous 18 months. The platoons and companies became grounded in their basic combat skills and further refined their tactics.[23]

Second Alamein (Battle of Alam el Halfa) (Maps 10.2, 10.3, 10.4)

Rommel's assessment of the shifting strength comparison between the Italo-German and the UK forced him to recognize that waiting until late September to attack would place his army at a great disadvantage. Based on the planned Axis reinforcements, the flow of supplies, and the moon cycle, the best time to attack was on or about 26 August. Rommel believed that the balance of forces would be in his favor and it was possible to trap and destroy the bulk of the British 8th Army.[24]

Rommel's plan was to attack the southern part of the El Alamein position before the British could hold it in strength. Attacking south of the Alam el Halfa Ridge, the armor forces (DAK and *XX Cd'A*) would strike eastward and once passed the ridge, turn north to trap the 8th Army. He expected that the Italo-German mobile forces would defeat those British mobile units placed in the southern sector of the Alamein to block such a move. The *XXI Cd'A* would attack the British defense in the north to pin those enemy units in place, while elements of the *X Cd'A* would advance in the center to secure key terrain to protect the northern flank of the Axis armor penetration. His plan was similar to that used during the Gazala battle in the previous May.

On 13 August *Superasi* (renamed *Superlibia* in August) sent a telegram to the *Comando Supremo* stating that Rommel was planning to employ two Italian parachute battalions and a group of parachute artillery from the *«Folgore»* in support of his upcoming offensive.[25] The request was for the special parachute equipment left in Italy and the necessary number of aircraft to execute an airborne operation be provided to the army. *Comando Supremo* sent a telegram to *Superesercito* ordering it to support the request.[26] As of the end of July the *S.A.S.* had 114 operational aircraft in the *Gruppi T* and 45 more in the various independent detachments.[27] All these transport groups had participated in the preparations for *«C3»* so had been trained in procedures for dropping parachutists. It is not known how Rommel intended to use the *paracadutisti* (capturing bridges over the Nile was one concept) and the request was likely a

23 Di Giovanni, *I paracadutisti*, p.159; Arena, *FOLGORE*, p.151.
24 Montanari, *Le operazioni*, vol 3, pp.552–553.
25 Biagini and Frattolillo (eds) *Diario Storico,* vol VII, book 1, p.924.
26 Biagini and Frattolillo (eds) *Diario Storico,* vol VII, book 1, p.937.
27 Civoli, *S.A.S.*, p.64.

reflection of the Generalfeldmarschall seeking ways to improve the success of the forthcoming attack. No planned use for the paratroops followed this request and the parachute equipment and aircraft remained in Italy.

The organization of the British 8th Army on the start of the offensive on 30 August was:[28]

13th Corps: 2nd New Zealand Div., 44th Inf. Div., 7th Arm. Div., 10th Arm. Div.
30th Corps: 1st South African Div., 4th Indian Div., 9th Australian Div., 23rd Arm. Bde.

The Axis defeat during the 2nd Battle of El Alamein (the Battle of Alam el Halfa, 30 August–5 September), was rooted in many areas. The main disadvantage was that ULTRA (the Allied signal intercept and code breaking operation) allowed Lieutenant General Bernard Montgomery (8th Army commander) to access Rommel's plan before the battle. With this information Montgomery could best position his forces to counter the Italo-German attack and avoid being deceived by enemy actions. The RN and the RAF were able to focus on key aspects of the Axis operation, especially logistics. Fuel tankers identified by ULTRA were the main targets at sea with several being sunk. The RAF had gained near total air superiority and attacked the Italian and German units both by day and night allowing little rest. Deceptions were employed including false minefields and other measures.

Rommel delayed the start of the offensive for various reasons from 26 to the night of 30 August. The Panzerarmee was unable to drive as deeply to the east on the first night (30–31 August) as required by the plan. The two main UK minefields, the western most minefield FEBRUARY and JANUARY further east, were denser and more complex than expected. This, combined with the soft sand, the night and day attacks by the RAF, and the 8th Army artillery slowed the advance. All together these problems limited the depth of the initial attack and caused higher fuel consumption than anticipated, limiting the Axis operational options. The impact was that the Panzerarmee was unable to continue to the east of Alam el Halfa Ridge. Unaware of the extent of the UK defense on the ridge, Rommel decided to turn north earlier than planned. The stubborn defense encountered on the western end of Alam el Halfa Ridge was now added to the other problems. Seeing no real success against the defense, short on fuel, and under the constant air attacks forced Rommel to stop the attack on 2 September and begin to withdraw.

The «*Folgore*» part of the battle was small yet important. The «*Folgore*» was organized into three mixed columns focused on securing several pieces of high ground that would protect the flanks of the Panzerarmee's attack. Only five *battaglioni paracadutisti*

28 Playfair, *The Mediterranean and Middle East*, vol 3, p.384.

were committed to the offensive as two battalions were to continue holding key positions.[29] The columns were organised as follows:

- Colonna Parris (*d.f «Brescia»*): *I, II/19º rgt. f., V, VII/186º rgt. f., II gruppo artiglieria/185ª d.f. Folgore, III/1º Articelere* : Its objective was to seize the ground overlooking the Deir Anqar depression. This column was commanded by *generale di brigata* Dino Parri, the deputy commander of the *«Brescia»*.[30]
- Colonna Ramcke: *IX, X/187º f. «Folgore» (Raggruppamento Camosso)*, FJ III/btn. (Hubner), FJ IV/Btn (Burkhardt), *III gruppo artiglieria/185ª d.f. Folgore, I/1º Articelere*: Its objective was to seize Quota 101 overlooking the Deir Alinda depression. This column was commanded by Generalmajor Bernard Ramcke.[31]
- *Raggruppamento Bechi*: *II and IV/187º f. and VI/186º f. «Folgore», I gruppo artiglieria/185ª d.f. Folgore*: The *IV/187º* would continue to hold the Naqb Abu Dweis position overlooking the Qattara Depression and secured the southern flank of the army. The *VI 186º* would replace the *II/187º* securing the El Taga Plateau so the latter could advance to secure Qaret el Himeimat. Himeimat was a commanding position that overlooked the entire southern area. The advance of the *II btg.* would follow the two German reconnaissance units covering the right flank of the army's attack.

Starting in the early morning of 31 August, all three columns were able to reach their assigned objectives by the end of the day. *Colonne Parris* and *Ramcke* had expected greater resistance but discovered that the New Zealand Division's defensive box did not extend as far south as the reconnaissance had reported. Both columns experienced harassing artillery fires and enemy patrols, but no substantial fighting occurred. In the far south the *II btg.* was able to occupy Qaret el Himeimat after some light combat to clear the summit. The greatest challenge all the columns faced was carrying all their heavy weapons, ammunition, rations and water, along with pulling their 47/32 c.c. guns through the deep sand in the desert heat for many kilometers.[32]

The night of 31 August/1 September was mainly quiet except for a raid executed by the 18th Battalion from the New Zealand 6th Brigade. The 14th Platoon with three Bren carriers and three Valentine tanks (A Squadron, 46/RTR) left at dusk to raid the

29 Montanari, *Le operazioni*, vol. 3, p.591; Arena, *FOLGORE*, pp.146–147

30 NARA, Comando divisione fanteria "Brescia", 29 agosto 1942, *Oggetto: Attacco posizioni Deir el Anqur – Deep Well*, T821, roll.488, p.2; Morisi, *Folgore*, p.68 lists the *XXVIII btg. bersaglieri* as advancing in the south with the *II btg.* but Montanari and *Seconda offensive Italo-tedesca* have the battalion further north with *«Brescia»*. Montanari does not include the *VII btg* in Parris. The Brescia attack order does include the *VII btg. para.* but also does not include the *XXVIII btg. bersaglieri.*

31 NARA, "Brescia", 29 agosto 1942, *Oggetto: Attacco posizioni Deir el Anqur*, p.2.

32 Morisi, *Folgore*, pp.68–71; Edger Alcidi, *Fallschirmjäger Brigade Racke in North Africa 1942–1943* (Atglen, Pennsylvania: Schiffer Military History, 2000), p.77;

Italian positions on Deir el Anqar. The raid hit the *V btg.* and the attack immediately fell apart. The tanks had raced ahead of the infantry and were able to overrun the forward positions. The New Zealand infantry was pinned by fire and was never able to reach the position. The tanks, fired on from all sides, were forced to retreat. The *paracadutisti* lack of heavy anti-tank guns likely saved the tanks from destruction.[33]

Little active fighting occurred on 1 and 2 September along the positions held by the units of the «*Folgore*» except for artillery shelling and the air attacks by the RAF Late in the morning on 2 September the division received word of the cancellation of the offensive and that the DAK and *XX Cd'A* had begun a staged withdrawal back to the west. Rather than returning to the original starting positions, Rommel decided to occupy the ground between the two British minefields that had caused so much trouble for the Panzerarmee. These minefields would now be incorporated in the Italo-German defense of the southern section of the El Alamein line.

Receiving word that the Italo-German army was retreating, Montgomery decided not to initiate a general counteroffensive. He ordered that 8th Army units should harass the enemy's retreat but authorized only one counterattack. This attack would be executed by the 2nd New Zealand Division with the aim of attacking south to block the withdrawal of the 21.Panzerdivision and 90.Afrika Division. The attack was planned to start the evening of 3 September.

Operation Beresford was a two-brigade attack designed to penetrate approximately ten kilometers south of the New Zealander box. The concept was to advance south to close the gaps in the JANUARY and FEBRUARY minefields made by the Panzerarmee, thereby trapping them in their penetration and creating targets for the artillery and the RAF. The 132nd Brigade (attached to the 2nd New Zealand) was the western arm of the attack with the northern edge of Deir Alinda as its objective. The 5th New Zealand Brigade was the eastern arm and its objective was the northern edge of Deir el Munassib. If initially successful, the two brigades would push an additional 4-5 kms south to close the minefields. The 6th New Zealand Brigade would launch raids further west against Deir Anqar to confuse the enemy while extending the western face of the N.Z. box further south using the 26th Battalion. That battalion would follow the 132nd Bde and set a defense facing west as the brigade moved south. One squadron each from the 46th and the 50/RTR would support the two brigades, with each squadron having about fifteen tanks.[34]

The Desert Air Force began a 90-minute continuous bombing effort of the Deir Munassib area at 2030 hrs on 3 September. The 6th N.Z. Bde raids started on time at 2300 with elements from the 18th and 25th N.Z. battalions against the two battalions of the *19º rgt.f.* on Deir el Anqar. This opening action alerted the Italian defense. The *21/VII btg.* launched some small counterattacks on the flank of the raid, but the New

33 Morisi, *Folgore,* p.72; Ronald Walker, *Alam Halfa and El Alamein* (Wellington: Historical Publications Branch, 1967), pp.101-102.

34 Playfair, *The Mediterranean and Middle East*, vol III, pp.388–389; Walker, *Alam Halfa*, p.124.

Zealanders were already withdrawing. No further action occurred in this area except for nightly patrols by both sides.

The 132nd Bde was an hour behind schedule as the 4th and 5th Battalions, Queen's Own Royal West Kent Regiment became lost in the dark and unable to find their passages through the minefields. As they finally got clear of the minefields and began to move south, they were caught by heavy fire from *ragg. Camosso* (*X btg.* in the west and *IX btg.* in the east) holding the ground north of Deir Alinda. The burning British vehicles helped to light up the area, silhouetting the advancing infantry. The attack was pressed into the *paracadutisti* positions with numerous incidents of bayonet and hand grenade combat. After three hours of fighting, the British attack was breaking down. The brigade commander of the 132nd Bde was wounded and the brigade commander of the 6th N.Z. Bde was captured. The left hand battalion of the 132nd, the 2nd Buffs, ran into the fallschirmjäger battalions to the right of *ragg. Camosso* and having lost communications with the 132nd Bde headquarters, halted in place.[35]

The delay of the 132nd Bde also delayed the movement of the 26th N.Z. battalion. A and B companies of the battalion were able to move into position, but C Company in the confusion moved further south than planned. It contacted the *X btg.* positioned at the eastern end of the Deir Anqar depression and was able to penetrate to the rear of the defense. At dawn on 4 September the company discovered it was isolated from the remainder of the brigade. Local counterattacks by the *X btg.* and the III F.J. Battalion occurred during the day and eventually forced the company to surrender. The company lost a total of fifty-three men killed, wounded, and captured.[36]

The 5th N.Z. Bde had better success. It had a little further to travel before reaching the enemy positions which were manned by the 90.Afrika-Division and the «*Trento*». As the 90.Division had been part of the main effort during the offensive, it had only just pulled back to its current location and it was still consolidating. «*Trento*» had been ordered to withdraw from the Deir el Muhafid position it had been holding and left only a company to cover its movement. Neither of these units had established strong defensive positions.

The 5th N.Z. Bde was able to push into the area but remained unsupported by the 132nd Bde. The plans for both sides fell into disarray and neither side fully understood the reality on the ground. The brigade's 28th (Maori) Battalion was able to penetrate deep into the positions of the two divisions and create confusion in the defense. The other two British battalions were unable to support the Maoris while the tank support was destroyed during the fighting.[37]

4 September found *ragg.* «*Camosso*» holding its positions. The 132nd Bde was still very disorganized and unable to continue the attack. The *IX* and *X btg.* executed several local counterattacks to clear up any enemy troops that remained within the

35 Walker, *Alam Halfa*, pp.130–131.
36 Frazer D. Norton, *Official History of New Zealand in the Second World War 1939–45*, 26 Battalion (Dunedin: Historical Publications Branch, 1952), p.178.
37 Walker, *Alam Halfa*, p.133–145.

defenses and consolidated its positions. The 132nd Bde retreated back to its original starting line. The 5th N.Z. Bde had created a salient in the German lines so the Axis counterattacks on 4 September were focused in that sector. Not much was gained by either side and the British decided to withdraw back to their lines, completing this action by dawn on 5 September.

Operation Beresford was a failure as the gaps in the minefields remained open. The 132 Bde losses were approximately 700 men, with over 200 of that number as prisoners. The New Zealanders lost about 380 men and sixty more captured. Approximately twenty-four British tanks were lost, mainly when they were separated from the infantry and charged into the enemy positions during the confusing night actions. The brigade commander of the 132nd was killed while the commander of the 6 N.Z. Bde was captured.[38]

The losses in the two *battaglione paracadutisti* were serious as well. *Ragg. «Camosso»* lost approximately one-hundred and ninety-eight men killed, and forty-five more were wounded. Both battalion commanders, *maggiore* Aurelio Rossi of the *IX btg.* and *capitano* Amleto Carugno of the *X btg.* were killed during the fighting, and col. Camosso was wounded.[39]

Near the end of the battle, the R.M. *guastatori* company of the *battaglione «N»* conducted an operation in support of the Panzerarmee. The target of the raid was the railway and water pipeline supporting 8th Army at Alamein. Thirteen *guastatori* divers were dropped off by torpedo boat on 3 September near Alexandria and swam ashore. Avoiding enemy patrols they marched several hours to their objective. An ammunition train was destroyed and the water pipeline damaged (it was quickly repaired). The exfiltration plan was for the Panzerarmee to conduct a raid through British lines and link-up with the *guastatori*, but it was completely unworkable. The men were all captured on 4 September. The insufficient planning demonstrated in this action will be repeated in all the future raids executed by these special units.[40]

Operational Pause

Once again both sides undertook an operational pause after the fighting. With the failure of the offensive, the Panzerarmee needed to rebuild its strength and its supplies to prepare for the likely enemy offensive. The 8th Army, having successfully stopped

38 Walker, *Alam Halfa*, p.165.

39 Arena, *FOLGORE*, p.167; Walker, *Alam Halfa*, p.165; Morisi, *Folgore*, p.87; AUSSME, *Relazione ten. col. Giovanni Verando*, pp.9, 1160 c, racc. 11, cart.2. Verando states the losses were only 38 killed and 45 wounded with no *paracadutisti* captured, but this was based on a wartime bulletin.

40 Luigi Emilio Longo, *I «reparti speciali» italiani nella seconda guerra mondiale* (Milan: Mursia 1991), pp.293–294; Nino Buttazzoni, *Solo per la Bandiera: I nuotatori Paracadutisti della Marina* (Milan: Gruppo Mursia Editore S.p.A., 2002), pp.60–61.

the Axis attack, now continued its preparation for a major offensive with the intent of completely destroying the Panzerarmee.

As previously stated, the Panzerarmee did not withdraw back to its previous positions. Instead it incorporated both JANUARY and FEBRUARY minefields that had been instrumental in the failure of its attack as part of a new defensive scheme. By 6 September the Panzerarmee had established a new defensive layout. The northern sector was held by the *XXI Cd'A*; the center by the *X Cd'A* to a line just south of the Deir Munassib; the *XX Cd'A* was given responsibility for the southern sector down to Qaret el Himeimat. It would take some days to move the divisions into their new positions. The mobile forces of the *XX Cd'A* assumed positions facing east, with the two Italian armoured divisions while the *«Trieste»* was removed from the corps and attached to the *X Cd'A*. The *«Folgore»* was attached to the *XXI Cd'A* and was responsible for the southern flank along the Qattara Depression. The division held a line from Naqb Abu Dweiss in the west to Qaret el Himeimat in the east.[41]

In the following week the *«Ariete»* and *«Littorio»* were pulled back from the frontline to refit and the *«Folgore»* assumed responsibility for the southern sector south of the *«Trieste»*. The *186º rgt.* (now with the *V* and *VI btg.*) moved from south of the Deir el Munassib to just north of Qaret el Himeimat. The *187º rgt* (now with the *II, IV battaglioni* and the *VIII guastatori*) covered the Qaret el Himeimat westward to the *Passo del Cammello*. The *VII btg.* was held as the divisional reserve and *ragg. «Camasso»* remained with the *«Trieste»*.[42]

One of the challenges faced by the Panzerarmee and *Comando Supremo* was how to better equip the *«Folgore»* for combat in the desert. The personnel and equipment authorizations were based on the needs of a parachute division that would only be in combat for three to four days. The unit staff and the services (supply, medical, transport, etc.) were provided only to meet the minimal needs during that time. After combat, the division would be withdrawn to refit and equip. Staying on the line and engaging in combat for months required a more robust manning and equipment authorization. Providing the *«Folgore»* with the means of prolonged combat was an immediate requirement.

Part of the solution was found within the army in Egypt. The Panzerarmee had disbanded the *d. f. «Sabratha»* on 25 July 1942 due to excessive losses and the lack of replacement personnel and equipment. The surviving *«Sabratha»* headquarters staff and its equipment, along with the 20/65 *c.a. sezione* from the artillery regiment, and the *20ª sezione sussistenza* (supply), were transferred to the *«Folgore»*. The *«Sabratha» 26ª sezione sanità* with its medical staff augmented the medical section of the division. This improved the situation but did not fully resolve the shortages in these areas.[43]

41 Montanari, *Le operazioni*, vol. 3, pp.607-609 and schizzo n.74;
42 AUSSME, *Relazione Verando*, pp.7–8; Arena, *I PARACADUTISTI*, p.123.
43 Pirrone, Giorgio (ed) *L'Esercito e i suoi corpo – Sintesi storica* (Rome: USSME, 1979) vol 3; Anon, *Seconda offensiva italo-tedesca*, pp.309–310; Anon, *Terza offensiva Britannica*,

What the division now needed was to create a logistical system that previously would have been managed by air drops. The divisional services section established a logistical base at El Daba. Here *capitano* Beltrani, the senior logistics officer, created a supply depot by finding abandoned drums and cans that could be filled with fuel and water. At the same time the *folgorini* were discovering abandoned vehicles in the desert that were collected and sent to El Dada. As these vehicles were delivered, Beltrani opened a workshop to repair and maintain this growing fleet using materials from the battlefields and *paracadutisti* with mechanical skills as mechanics. The men of the *«Folgore»* was beginning to earn a reputation in the Panzerarmee for finding materials and supplies that others would claim had not been abandoned.

In early September the *«Folgore»* was still technically a divisione ternaria (a three regiment division) with the third regiment of the division remaining in Italy. The decision to form a second parachute division had been made in July and the *185° rgt.* was held back in Italy as previously stated for that purpose. The reorganization order was finally issued on 4 September with an effective date of 15 September, officially transitioning the division from a ternary to a binary regimental structure. Only the *186°* and *187° rgt. ftr.* currently in Egypt would remain as part of the division. The *185° rgt. ftr.* would remain in Italy under the control of the *Comando Supremo*, first as a strategic reserve, then as part of the new division. Any units that had been sent to Africa but were not officially part of the new divisional organization would remain and were attached to the *«Folgore»*. This order codified the changes that had been made in July when the division was deployed to Africa.[44]

The artillery support in the division was designed such that each parachute regiment could be supported by an artillery *gruppo* in addition to their cannon company. As the *«Folgore»* was now reduced to two regiments, the order also reduced the *185° rgt. art.* from three *gruppi* to two. All three artillery *gruppi* had been deployed to Africa, so the division would retain the now excess batteries in accordance with paragraph II of the order. To adjust to the new organization and because it made tactical sense, the *II/185° artiglieria* was disbanded. The *3ª btr.* was transferred to the *187° cp. cannoni da 47* while the *4ª btr.* was transferred to the *186° cp. cannoni da 47.* This move increased the number of anti-tank guns to ten 47/32 c.c. in each of their regimental cannon companies.[45]

allegato 23; AUSSME, *Relazione La costituzione della Divisione Paracadutisti "Folgore"*, 10 febbraio. 1949. p.2.

44 AUSSME Stato Maggiore R.E. memorandum 4 settembre 1942, *Oggetto: 185° divisione «Folgore»*, M7 430/2: 0045380/3; Giuseppe Lundari, *I paracadutisti italiani 1937/45* (Milan: Editrice Militare Italiana di Ivo Fossati, 1989), p.19.

45 AUSSME, Commissione per l'interrogatorio degli Ufficiali R.E. reduci da prigionia di guerra, *Oggetto: Relazione Col. i.g.s. Fant. SP.E Bignami Riccardo, vice comandante della divisione Paracadutisti "Folgore"*, p.1; AUSSME, Commissione per l'interrogatorio degli Ufficiali R.E. reduci da prigionia di guerra, *Relazione La costituzione della Divisione Paracadutisti "Folgore"*, 10 febbraio. 1949. pp.1-2.

Most of September was used to move the battalions to their new defensive locations and begin to prepare for the expected UK offensive. The length of the front was too long for the forces available to the Italo-German Army to hold with great strength. As the northern sector of the line held by the *XXI Cd'A* was the section most likely to be attacked, those units held slightly shorter frontages than the units of the *X Cd'A* in the south. To increase the defensive power of the line in the north, the Italian battalions of the *«Trento»* and *«Bologna»* were interwoven together with German battalions of the 164.Leichte Afrika. The units established overlapping fields of fire with a mix of Italian and German weapons.

This corseting was not done to the same extent in the *X Cd'A* sector. The *«Brescia»* had two of the German fallschirmjäger battalions within its sector, but *«Folgore»* held its part of the line with only the *II/28° rgt. f.* from the *«Pavia»* and the German Aufklärungs-Abteilung 33 echeloned in reserve. These units were not under the command of *generale* Frattini but under control of the *X Cd'A*. Frattini was unable to maintain a divisional reserve as the length of the division's sector required all eight battalions to be in the main defensive line.

There was one event during September that directly affected the employment of the Italian airborne forces. On the night of 13–14 September the British executed a series of raids under the umbrella codename Operation Agreement. There were various objectives including occupying Gialo deep in southern Libya, and raids against various targets at Bengasi, Barce, and Tobruk. The operation had little success but it demonstrated the vulnerability of locations deep behind the Axis lines and the lack of maneuver units available to *Superlibia* to counter these threats. *Comando Supremo* took immediate steps to secure the Saharan Front.[46]

One step was to provide additional combat units to *Superlibia*. On 27 September *Comando Supremo* decided to send the *divisione fanteria «La Spezia»* to Libya. *Supereservito* issued their movement order to the division on 29 September. Before this decision had been finalized, the infantry regiments of the division had been reorganized. Previously each infantry battalion had a *guastatori* platoon. That structure better supported the use of each battalion as an independent maneuver element, a capability that is needed during an airborne operation. A 4 September 1942 order from *Supercomando* consolidated the three guastatori platoons into a single company within each regiment. A *plotone commando* was authorized to provide a command and control element and limited service support. This new structure centralized the engineer support which was better suited to support the regiment fighting together as a single unit in a traditional combat role.[47]

46 I.SO. Playfair, *The Mediterranean and Middle East* (London: HMSO, 1966) vol 4, pp.20-23; Montanari *Le Operazioni* vol 3, pp.644–646.

47 AUSSME, Stato Maggiore R.E. memorandum 4 settembre 1942, *Oggetto: Modifiche alle forazione di guerra dei rgt. di fanteria la 80° div. "La Spezia"*., M7 racc. 430, cart. 11.

Men of the «*La Spezia*» loading onto a SM.82 for transport to Africa. (AUSSMA)

The division would move its personnel and the listed equipment by air, the remaining equipment would be transported by sea. The equipment authorized for air transport were the individual small arms, the light and heavy machine-guns, the 20 mm anti-aircraft guns with their associated equipment, essential materials (kitchens and other items) for the health of the soldiers, and materials for medical support. The division began arriving in Libya on 1 October and took up positions near El Agheila. The only major airborne unit now remaining under *Comando Supremo* control in Italy was the *185º rgt.*, which was still incomplete due to the ongoing training of two of its battalions.[48] With the transfer of «*La Spezia*» to Africa, the airborne force that the R.E. had assembled for Malta was now fully committed to other efforts.

A significant change during this period was the departure of Rommel on 23 September 1942 for a prolonged rest and recuperation in Germany. He was replaced by General der Panzertruppe Georg Stumme, an experienced armored commander that had served in France, Greece and Russia. Under Stumme, the Panzerarmee continued to prepare the Alamein defenses in accordance with Rommel's basic concept.

48 Antonello Biagini and Fernando Frattolillo (eds), *Diario Storico del Comando Supremo* (Rome, USSME, 1984-2002), vol VIII, p.272; AUSSME, 29 settembre 1942, *Oggetto: Destinazione in Libia della div. ftr. "La Spezia" (80º)*, M-7 racc. 430, cart. 11.

Organizing the Defense

The defensive works implemented at Alamein were a further development of the concepts the R.E. had adopted given the realities of their equipment and limited manpower. The main disadvantages that the army faced while fighting in the desert was the lack of trucks and the lack of effective anti-tank weapons. To manage these problems, the R.E. implemented a new divisional organization and adopted new defensive tactics.

The new organization was called the *divisone fanteria tipo A.S. 42*. It was authorized in January 1942 after Operation Crusader and the Italian infantry units had implemented it over the next six months. All the infantry units had reorganized under this new structure by the time of 2nd Alamein, although to do so many units were short battalions due to the lack of personnel and equipment to both reorganize under *tipo A.S. 42* and replace losses.

The concept under *tipo A.S. 42* was to reduce the size of the unit while increasing its combat power. The *tipo A.S. 42* placed most of the heavy weapons at the company level, allowing these units to be self-supporting for a period of time. To do so, the *battaglione and compagnie armi di accompagnamento* (heavy weapons support battalions and companies) were disbanded and their weapons assigned to the infantry companies. An infantry company now had four platoons: an infantry platoon, a machine-gun platoon, a light anti-tank platoon (20mm-25mm), and a heavy anti-tank platoon (47/43 c.c.).

The structure required fewer soldiers to man while adding firepower. Fewer soldiers meant fewer trucks were needed to move the unit and fewer trucks were needed to supply the unit. The disadvantage of the structure was that the infantry component was significantly reduced. These units were basically defensive organizations and lacked significant offensive power. A company that previously had six infantry squads was now reduced to three. A fourth company was added to the battalion, but the result was still a one-third reduction in the battalion's infantry strength. The number of mortars in the regiment remained the same even as the number of companies to be supported increased from nine to twelve.

The new defensive concepts were born of necessity as the Regio Esercito proved unable to equip its *soldati* with anti-tank guns capable of stopping the newest enemy tanks. The Breda 47/32 was good in 1940, was marginal in 1941, and was now ineffective in 1942 against the Valentines, Grants, and Shermans that roamed the battlefield. It was unable to defeat the frontal armour of these tanks and needed to gain a flank or rear shot to have an effect. Even if it gained such a position, it still needed to be close to penetrate those weaker sides.

The new defensive tactics recognized that the enemy armour would likely penetrate the defense if not stopped by the artillery or minefields. Given the lack of infantry strength, a continuous defensive front was not possible. The strongpoints were therefore designed to offer a 360° defense against attacks from any direction.

A battalion and regimental front would consist of a series of individual company strongpoints holding key terrain while using firepower to control the empty ground between them. Normally one company would be forward to man the advance posts. An attacking enemy could maneuver through the gaps but would be under constant fire to prevent reinforcements and supply. Mobile forces placed in the rear of this defense would counterattack any enemy penetration that managed to move beyond the ground covered by the company strongpoints. The field artillery was placed closer to the front and was issued armour-piercing ammunition.[49] It became the main anti-tank system within the Italian infantry division. The division would also have a battery or two of either the German 88/55 or the Italian 90/53 anti-aircraft guns for use in the anti-tank role.

The company's strongpoints themselves were a series of interlocking positions. Each company built a main strongpoint consisting of a number of squad-sized infantry fighting positions holding several infantrymen with machine-guns and anti-tank weapons. The front of the position facing the direction of attack was solid, with the parapet/sangar wall providing protection from enemy direct fire. The firing positions were located at each end of the position such that the defending fire would cover/protect the front of the friendly positions to either side. Hence each position actually protected its neighbors while depending on its neighbors to protect it. Anti-tank and machine-gun positions would be built to provide fires over a complete 360° arc. An attacking enemy would be fired on from the flanks while it attempted to attack the defended position to its front. The company position would normally be covered by a mine belt and surrounded by barbed wire obstacles.[50]

Unlike the infantry divisions, the «*Folgore*» was not reorganized as a *tipo A.S. 42* division. The only anti-tank weapons in the company were the fucile controcarro 35(P), a weapon that was useless in 1942. This weapon would not be replaced by the 20mm fucile anticarro tipo S until 1943. There were not any additional anti-tank weapons at the battalion level, and the regiments only possessed the regimental cannon company with ten 47/32 c.c. The division could not depend on its artillery regiment to act as an anti-tank unit as it too was only issued the same ineffective 47/32 c.c. The *paracadutisti* did salvage a number of British 2 pdr guns, but these were also reaching their limit of effectiveness.[51]

Given these limitations, the *paracadutisti* further refined this defense scheme. In addition to the company strongpoint, they dug two/three man hidden fighting

49 The type of armor-piercing ammunition was Effetto Pronto (E.P.). This was a HEAT type of round but acted more like a HESH round.

50 Di Giovanni, *I paracadutisti*, p.171; Anon, *Terza offensiva Britannica*, p.91 and schizzo 6; Morisi, *Folgore*, p.91. This type of fighting position is called a front parapet or Dupuy foxhole in the US Army.

51 AUSSME *Formazioni provvisorie di guerra -Reggimento di fanteria paracadutisti, luglio 1941 – XIX*, Rep M-7 racc. 405, cart. 6, p.6; Filippo Cappellano *Le artiglierie del Regio Esercito nella seconda guerra mondiale* (Parma: Alberti Edizione Speciali s.r.l., 1998), p.242.

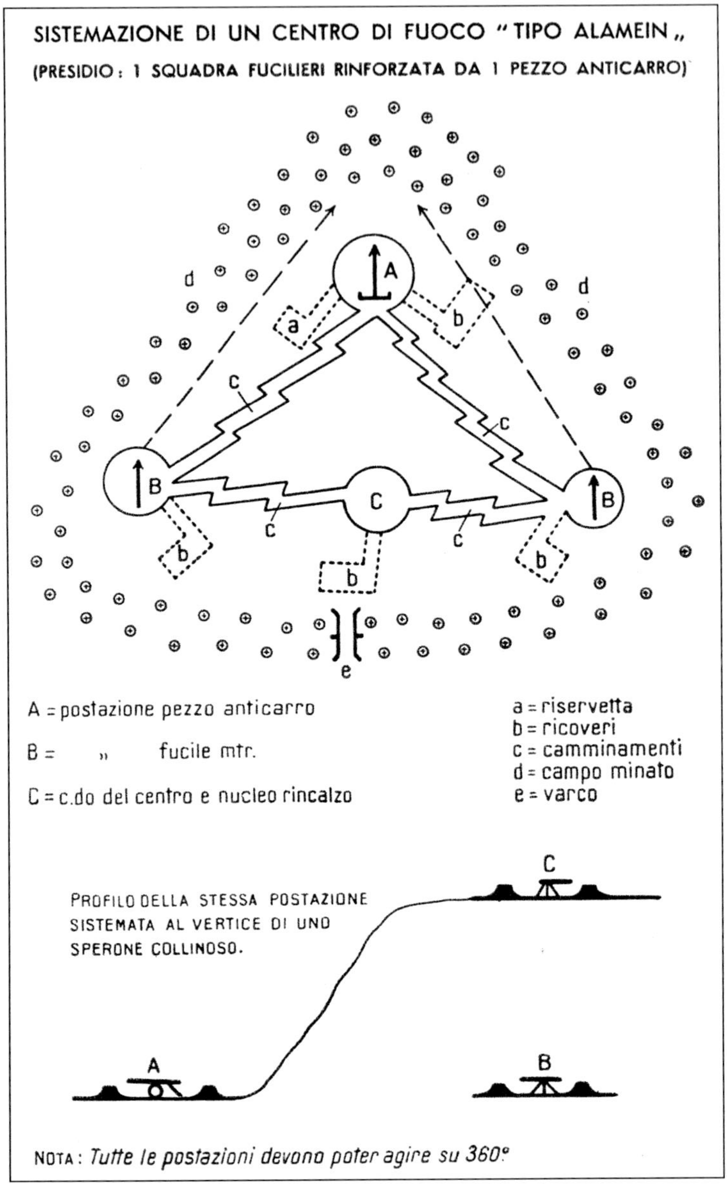

Diagram of a squad-sized fighting position *tipo «Alamein»*. Key: A – anti-tank gun, B – Light machine-gun (Breda 30), C – command post/reserve position, a – ammunition dump, b – personnel shelters, c – communication trenches, d – minefields, e – entry. The profile shows the command post/reserve position should overlook the fighting positions. All the positions should be constructed to provide 360° coverage with the weapons. (Comando 184° d. f. "Nembo", *Norme sull'addestramento formale e tattico dei minori reparti paracadutisti*, no date, diagram between pp.32 and 33)

positions outside the wire and usually near or in the mine belt. These positions would allow the enemy armor to pass and wait for the enemy infantry to get amongst them before firing upon them with automatic weapons and grenades. They would prevent the enemy infantry from supporting the tanks, allowing the main positions to destroy the latter with anti-tank weapons and infantry hunter-killer teams armed with grenades, mines, molotov cocktails and other makeshift devices. The *paracadutisti* also would use multiple small counter attacks within the defensive position to quickly break-down any enemy attempt to consolidate. This was different from a traditional defense which normally requires the defenders under attack to maintain their positions while a separate uncommitted unit would execute the counterattack. The *paracadutisti* had trained with these techniques in Italy but the British attack on 30 September would be their first opportunity to fully put them to the test.

Operation Braganza (Map 10.5)

The implementation of these new defensive schemes was ongoing when the UK initiated an attack against Deir el Munassib on 30 September. This position was one of the objectives for Operation Beresford back on 4 September. The attacking brigade had actually seized the position on 3-4 September but the general failure of the operation caused the New Zealand units to abandon it on 5 September. It was key terrain as the three hills in the area, Quotas 92, 94 and 101, provided excellent observation of the entire sector. The intent behind Operation Braganza was to deny these heights to the Panzerarmee and use the area around the depression for positioning of the artillery to better support the planned major offensive in October. A desired secondary effect was to let the Italian and German leadership believe that the main effort during the October offensive was in the south.[52]

The attacking force was the 131st Infantry Brigade from the 44th Division of the British 13th Corps. The brigade was supported by one medium and nine field artillery regiments (144 guns), as well as fighter and fighter-bomber support. The three infantry battalions would attack simultaneously from three directions: 1/6 Queen's Royal Regiment from the north, the 1/7 Queens from the northeast, and the 1/5 Queens from the east. The attack would begin at approximately 0400. At the time of the attack, the brigade believed that the deir was held by elements of the *d. moto. «Trieste»* and planned accordingly.[53]

52 I.S.O. Playfair, *The Mediterranean and Middle East* (London: HMSO, 1966), vol 4, pp.23-24.

53 AUSSME, *Relazione Verando*, pp.9–10; Anon, 'The Middle East, Prelude to Alamein Alam El Halfa and Deir El Munassib', The Queen's Royal Surrey Regiment The Regimental Association, <https://www.queensroyalsurreys.org.uk/ww2/middle_east/qme014.shtml> (accessed 25 July 2022).

They were partly correct in that assumption. The defending unit was actually the *IX/187º rgt.* of *raggruppamento «Camosso»*. The *raggruppamento* was still attached to the *«Trieste»* after the adjustment of the Panzerarmee defensive organization in mid-September. The three companies of the battalion were arranged in a triangle defense using the heights within the area of the deir. The *25ª cp.* held Quotas 92 and 94 forming the northeast side of the position, the *27ª cp.* held the northwest side on Quota 101, and the *26ª cp.* held the east around Quota 99. Each company had organized its position as an individual stronghold with 360º defense. The battalion had its ten Breda 37 machine-guns, three 81mm mortars and four 47/32 c.c. from the regiment cannon company. These weapons had been augmented by weapons captured from the earlier battles: eleven 2 inch and 3 inch mortars, ten 2 pdr anti-tank guns, twenty Bren machine-guns, and four Universal carriers. The *III gruppo/185º artiglieria* was in support with eight additional 47/32 c.c.[54]

The attack started off at approximately 0430 with the British artillery covering the forward movement of the three infantry battalions. The artillery preparation destroyed many fighting positions but Italian casualties were low. The 1/6 and 1/7 Queens easily reached the northern crest of the Deir el Munassib but then stopped at that location. Direct fires from the *25ª* and *27ª cp.*, combined with fires from the positions held by F.J. battalion Hubner to the west of the *IX btg.* held those two attacking battalions north of the depression.

The 1/5th Queens pressed forward against the eastern part of the *25ª cp.* on Quota 94 and the *26ª cp.* to the south on Quota 99. *Capitano* Chieppa, the battalion commander, decided to defend the position by allowing the enemy to approach at close range before opening fire. Approaching in the dark and not receiving any defensive fire, the British battalion pressed forward into the defensive positions of the two parachute companies. Once the enemy was about 200 meters inside the perimeter of the position, the *paracadutisti* launched flares and illuminated the battlefield, followed by rapid firing of all weapons. Anti-tank guns were used to immobilize the armoured vehicles which were then destroyed by *paracadutisti* using grenades. As the British troops attempted to work through the positions, they were caught in the crossfire from multiple sangars and foxholes. Local counterattacks by small groups of paratroopers isolated and eliminated any deep penetrations.

Daylight allowed a *gruppo* of 75/27 field guns to support the defense. By the afternoon the attack had been completely stopped. The brigade had suffered over 360 men lost, most of which were from the 1/5 Queens that had been decimated during the night. The brigade commander decided to hold the current positions during the day and resume the attack that evening. The preparations for renewing the attack did not go well and delay and confusion set in. No attack was launched that evening and on 1 October the 13th Corps commander, Lieutenant General B Horrocks, decided to

54 Montanari, *Le operazioni*, vol. 3, p.663; Morisi, *Folgore*, p.91.

end the attack. He instructed the brigade to consolidate the ground gained north of the Deir el Munassib until the 132nd Bde could move up and replace the 131st Bde.[55]

The *IX btg.* losses were significant, with the battalion losing twenty-four men killed and eighteen wounded. Most of the losses were from the *25ª cp.* The *paracadutisti* of the «*Folgore*» had once again proven themselves in combat and had validated their defensive concepts. The design of the company strongpoints and the manner in which the defense was executed would be the standard for the future battles.[56]

Finalizing the Defense

The defeat of Operation Braganza marked the end of any large-scale fighting for the next few weeks. Both sides settled into fighting patrolling to gain intelligence and disrupt the improvement of defensive positions. Panzerarmee instructed that the unit defenses would consist of:

- a line of advanced posts. These infantry posts were placed at the front edge of the first minefields. They were to provide early warning and interfere with mine clearing operations.
- a security zone. This was the mine belt and the pockets inside the belts.
- a resistance line. These were posts at the rear of the mine belt that overlooked the belt with fires and controlled the exits of the friendly maneuver corridors.
- the main resistance positions. Company and battalion strongpoints positioned to create a defended depth of 2-3 kilometers. It was normal that 2/3 of a unit's strength was placed in the 1st echelon within the main resistance position, while the remaining 1/3 was placed as a 2nd echelon in depth behind the 1st echelon.
- deployment area for artillery and reserves.[57]

Throughout October the newly renamed *Armata Corazzata Italo-Tedesca* (A.C.I.T.) adjusted its defensive plan. The final arrangement saw the *X Cd'A* responsibility adjusted northward to cover the Deir umm Khawabir. The «*Brescia*» held the line covering the Deir umm Khawabir to the Deir Alinda. The «*Folgore*» held from the Deir el Munassib to Qaret el Himeimat, then to the west to Naqb Abu Dweiss. The «*Pavia*» was behind the «*Folgore*» holding the line from Naqb Rala along the El Taga Plateau with the *27º rgt. f.* while the *28º rgt. f.* was behind the defense as the corps reserve.

55 Playfair, *The Mediterranean and Middle East*, vol 4 p.24; Montanari, *Le operazioni*, vol. 3, p.665; Di Giovanni, *I paracadutisti*, p.172.
56 Montanari, *Le operazioni*, vol. 3, p.665; AUSSME, *Relazione Verando*, p.11.
57 Anon, *Terza offensiva Britannica*, pp.90-91.

Examining the placement of each of the three divisions in the *X Cd'A*, one can see that the *«Folgore»* was holding the greatest frontage. In terms of the number of infantry battalions, the *«Folgore»* was the strongest of the three divisions; it had eight battalions (including the *guastatori*) while *«Brescia»* had five and *«Pavia»* only four. In terms of firepower, the situation was mixed. The regular infantry divisions had been reorganized as *divisione fanteria tipo A.S. 42* which significantly increased company level firepower at the expense of manpower. The *«Folgore»* had more infantry firepower mainly due to the number of Breda 30 light machine-guns and infantrymen, but the division was significantly weaker in anti-tank capability and lacked organic field artillery:

Divisione tipo A.S. 42:[58]
- Two *reggimenti fanteria* (three battalions) each with: 60 f.m., 36 Breda 37 machine-guns, 36 20mm or 25mm anti-tank guns, 36 47/32 c.c., nine 81mm mortars.
- *Reggimento artiglieria*: sixteen 100/17 howitzers, 16 75/27 field guns, eight 88/55 c.c/c.a.

Total of 432 infantrymen in the two regiments

«Folgore»:
- Two *reggimenti fanteria* (three battalions) each with: 18 anti-tank rifles, 164 f.m., 30 Breda 37 machine-guns, nine 81mm mortars, 10 47/32 c.c., 18 flame-throwers
- *Compagnia mortai divisionale*: nine 81mm mortars
- *Reggimento artiglieria*: 16 47/32 c.c.[59]

Total of 1,512 infantrymen in the two regiments.

Compared to a 1942 British infantry division:
- Three brigades (three battalions each). Each brigade with: sixty-three anti-tank rifles (Boys), 150 Bren light machine-guns, twenty-four 2"mortars, eighteen 3" mortars, twenty-four 2 pdr. anti-tank guns, and fifty-seven Universal carriers.
- Three artillery regiments with seventy-two 25 pdr guns.
- Anti-tank regiment with sixteen 2 pdr anti-tank guns.
- Machine-gun battalion with thirty-six Vickers machine-guns.

Total 3,456 infantrymen in three brigades.

The total number of infantrymen listed are those men actually assigned to infantry squads and does not include those manning the crew-served weapons except for the Breda 30 f.m. The numbers reflect authorized figures and not what the units actually

58 Jeffrey Leser, 'Divisional Organization Tipo Africa Settentrionale (A.S.)', <https://comandosupremo.com/tipo-africa-settentrionale/> (accessed 11 May 2022).

59 AUSSME, Oggetto: *Formazioni provvisorie di guerra – Reggimento di fanteria paracadutisti, luglio 1941 – XIX*. Rep M-7 racc. 405, cart. 6.

had assigned during September-October 1942. All the units in the A.C.I.T. were understrength and were slowly receiving replacements and equipment to replace those lost since the Battle of Gazala. As stated above, «*Pavia*» only had four infantry battalions while «*Brescia*» only had five. «*Folgore*» had not received any replacements and the fighting during 2nd Alamein and the smaller actions throughout September had slowly reduced the units, especially the two battalions in *ragg. Camosso*. In the first week of October the decision was made to disband the *X btg.* and merge the survivors with the reduced *IX btg.* to bring that battalion up to strength.[60]

With these instructions, *generale* Frattini finalized the defensive layout of his division. He reduced the number of tactical groups from four to three given the disbanding of the *X btg.* In the north was the *187° rgt. f.* with the *II* (minus the *6ª cp.*), *IV* and *IX btg.* and the *187° cp. cannoni da 47* (included the *3ª btr. da 47/32* from the disbanded *II/185° rgt. art.)*, supported by the *III/185° art.* In the center was *raggruppamento Ruspoli* with the *VII btg.* (plus the *6ª cp.*) and the *VIII btg. guastatori*, supported by two platoons of the *185° cp. mortai da 81* and the *I/185° rgt. art.* In the south was the *186° rgt. f.* with the *V* and *VI btg.* and the *186° cp. cannoni da 47/32* (including *4ª btr. da 47/32* from the disbanded *II/185° rgt. art*), supported by two platoons of the *185° cp. mortai da 81* and the anti-tank company from the *V/8° rgt. bersaglieri* from the «*Ariete*».[61] As both the *I* and *III gruppi* were attached to the regiments, the *185° reggimento artiglieria* was effectively without weapons.

One major deficiency of the division was the lack of field and heavy artillery. During the design discussions of the *divisione paracadutisti* in 1941, the solution selected was that the artillery of the *divisione aviotrasportabile* would be used to reinforce the parachute division. As the «*La Spezia*» had now been committed for a different mission A.S., that solution was no longer available (assuming that it was ever considered). Even if the *gruppi artiglieria* from that division had been sent, it would only have added the 65/17 guns as the 75/13 howitzers were never authorized.

The work-around solution was to take artillery from other units on the El Alamein line to equip the *paracadutisti* with something better than the anti-tank guns. Though the 47/32 c.c. had been attached to the battalions, the artillery regimental command company was not disbanded. Instead the A.C.I.T. created the *raggruppamento*

60 AUSSME, *Relazione Verando*, p.11; Arena, *FOLGORE*, p.168; Montanari, *Le operazioni*, vol. 3, p.663 fn.52; Anon, *Terza offensiva Britannica*, pp.425–428. Montanari stated the *X btg.* was disbanded in mid-September, but Verando's date was used.

61 Arena, *FOLGORE*, p.163; Arena, *I PARACADUTISTI*, p.131; Montanari, *Le operazioni*, vol. 3, p.736 and fn.4; Morisi, *Folgore*, pp.187–189; AUSSME, Commissione per l'interrogatorio degli Ufficiali R.E. reduci da prigionia di guerra, Oggetto: *Relazione Col. i.g.s. Fant. SP.E Bignami Riccardo, vice comandante della divisione Paracadutisti "Folgore"*, p.1; AUSSME, *Relazione Verando*, pp.12–13. Morsi states the division had seventy 47/32 c.c. on 23 October (p.100), but the author can only account for sixty-seven (including those with the *II/28° rgt. f.* and those provided by the «*Ariete*» and «*Littorio*»). In addition there were additional captured British A/T guns employed in the various positions, manned by two–three *paracadutisti*.

artiglieria «Folgore» and placed it under the command of col. Boffa and the *comando 185° rgt. art.* It was comprised of the following units:

> III *gruppo da 75/27/1° rgt. art. celere* from the «Brescia»,
> I *gruppo da 100/17/21° rgt. art.* from the «Trieste»,
> XXXI *gruppo da 88/55* from the «Ariete»,
> DI *gruppo da 90/53* from the «Ariete»,
> XLIX *gruppo* da 105/28 from X Cd'A,
> CXLVII *gruppo* da 149/28 from X Cd'A,
> Mixed German group with 105/32 and 210/36 guns[62]

Additionally positioned in the *«Folgore»* sector and able to support were the *II*, *III*, and *IV/26° rgt. art.* from the *«Pavia»* (all 75/27 guns). These batteries were not directly under the control of *colonnello* Boffa but a joint fire plan had been developed between the two artillery commanders to support the *«Folgore»* sector.

On 14 October *generale di divisone* Federico Ferrari Orsi, the commander of the *X Cd'A*, was seriously wounded by a land mine while inspecting the Deir el Munassib sector and died on 18 October. *Generale* Frattini was appointed to temporarily replace him as the corps commander with the *vice comandante* (deputy commander) of the *«Folgore»*, *colonnello* Riccardo Bignami now placed in command of the division.[63] Work continued on improving the defenses for the remainder of the month in expectation of the British offensive. All the *folgorini* knew was that the British offensive was approaching. What remained unknown was when it would start and where the main effort would be directed.

62 Arena, *I PARACADUTISTI*, pp.123–124; Anon, *Terza offensiva Britannica*, p.115 fn. 1 and allegato 23; Arena, *FOLGORE*, p.210.

63 Arena, *FOLGORE*, p.191; Montanari, *Le operazioni*, vol. 3, p.665.

11

Third Alamein

After the fighting in July and the appointment of General Montgomery to command 8th Army, 'Monty' and his staff began preparing an offensive on a scale not previously seen in the theater. As previously stated, the El Alamein position was one of the few in North Africa that could not be bypassed/turned in the south. The British planning had to focus on a breakthrough operation followed by a pursuit. Once the front had stabilized after the successful defense during Second Alamein, Montgomery issued his planning guidance on 14 September 1942.

Operation Lightfoot was conceived with two simultaneous attacks. The attack against the Italo-German northern sector was the main effort. A successful penetration here would completely unhinge the *Armata Corazzata Italo-Tedesca* (A.C.I.T.) defense and force a retreat. Any Italian or German forces that delayed their retreat would be trapped and destroyed. The attack in the south appeared to be only a supporting attack, but Montgomery decided it would be more. He wanted enough strength in the south to seriously threaten a breakthrough of its own. A successful penetration would force the A.C.I.T. to commit reserves to the south, weakening the northern sector. If unable to penetrate in the south, the strength of the attack would prevent any enemy forces moving north to reinforce the defense in that sector against the main attack. The number of reinforcements that were now flowing into the 8th Army made this concept possible.[1]

The Italo-German defense plan recognized the same overall situation. A penetration in the south, while breaking the defense, still allowed for an orderly retreat of the army if needed. A breakthrough in the north would threaten the retreat of every unit in the army. With this understanding, a valid defense would have the infantry dug in along the front and the mobile armoured reserve concentrated behind the northern sector. If the enemy threatened to break through in the north, the massed armoured force could immediately counter attack. If the enemy made a breakthrough in the

1 I.S.O. Playfair, *The Mediterranean and Middle East*, (London: HMSO, 1966), vol 4, p.5.

south, the time needed to travel the distance to cut the army's retreat was sufficient for the armoured reserve to move into a position to stop such an advance.

The Italian *XXI Cd'A* held the northern sector with the *«Bologna»* and *«Trento»* divisions along with the German 164.leichte Afrika-Division. The southern sector was held by the *X Cd'A* with the *«Folgore»*, *«Brescia»*, and *«Pavia»* divisions. The *102° d. moto. «Trieste»* and the German 90.Afrika-Division were further west along the coast to protect the rear of the Panzerarmnee. The challenge for Rommel was how to position the armored reserve.

The use of a central reserve can only work if the armored force has adequate fuel to move as needed during the battle. Fuel was the one commodity the A.C.I.T. lacked. The British use of ULTRA that successfully targeted tankers at sea during 2nd Alamein continued in September and October. Between 8 and 23 October the British sank 51 percent of the fuel sent from Italy. With the supply situation again becoming serious, another aerial assault to suppress Malta was planned. Commencing on 11 October, it was stopped by Kesselring on 16 October. There are conflicting accounts on whether the attacks were effective, but all efforts to subdue the island were now abandoned.[2]

In addition to the loss of fuel at sea, the length of the line of communication Tripoli–Bengasi–Tobruk forward to Alamein consumed a significant amount of the fuel that arrived safely. Rommel recognized that the A.C.I.T. could not afford to fight a mobile battle due to the fuel shortage. He therefore decided that the armoured counterattack force must be positioned near any possible breakthrough as the lack of fuel limited how far they could move.[3]

Rommel's solution was to split the armoured reserve into two groups. The northern group behind the *XXI Cd'A* consisted of the 15.Panzerdivision and the *133ª divisione corazzata «Littorio»*. The southern group behind the *X Cd'A* consisted of the 21.Panzerdivision and the *132ª divisione corazzata «Ariete»*. This disposition positioned a sizable counterattack force in the two sectors to challenge any initial breakthrough. He did recognize that at some point in the battle he would need to mass his tanks either in the north or in the south. Rommel believed he could make this decision once during the battle as the fuel shortage would prevent another such repositioning.

Operation Lightfoot placed the five infantry divisions of the 30th Army Corps (52nd (Lowland) Brit., 9th Aust., 2nd N.Z., 1st S.A., and 4th Indian), supported by the 9th and 23rd Armoured Bdes against the *XXI Cd'A*. Positioned to support the breakthrough and pursuit was the 10th Army Corps (1st and 10th Armoured Divisions). In the south was the 13th Army Corps (7th Armoured, 44th and 50th Infantry Divisions, with the 1st Greek Brigade and the 1ère and 2ème Brigade Française Combattante) against the *X Cd'A*.[4]

2 Mario Montanari, *Le operazioni in Africa settentrionale* (Rome: USSME, 1989), vol. 3, pp.657–659.
3 Montanari, *Le operazioni*, vol. 3, p.663.
4 Playfair, *The Mediterranean and Middle East*, vol 4, pp.7–8.

The total force under «*Folgore*» to repeal the attack consisted of as follows:

- *187º rgt. f.* (*II (-), IV, IX btg.*) to hold the Deir el Munaasbi area and the connection to the FJ Bde Ramcke to the northwest. The *187º* had a total of eight parachute companies, three 81mm mortar platoons (nine mortars), nine 47/32 c.c. platoons (18 guns), twenty-eight machine-guns, sixteen anti-tank rifles (f. c.c. 35(P)), and 18 flamethrowers.
- *Ragg. Ruspoli* (*VII, VIII btg.*) held Quota 105 position in the center. The ragg. had four parachute companies (one company from the *II btg.*) and two guastatori companies, three 45mm mortar platoons (18 mortars), four 81mm mortar platoons (twelve mortars), four 47/32 platoons (eight guns), 16 machine-guns, six anti-tank rifles (f. c.c. 35(P)), and twelve flamethrowers.
- The *186º rgt. f.* (*V, VI btg.*) held the Qaret el Himeimat area in the south. The rgt. had six parachute companies, three 81mm mortar platoons (nine mortars), nine 47/32 c.c. platoons (17 guns), three mortar platoons (nine mortars), 30 machine-guns, 12 anti-tank rifles (f. c.c. 35(P)), and 12 flame-throwers.

The fighting in August through the middle of October had cost the «*Folgore*» approximately 1,100 men. At this time the strength of a parachute company had been reduced to an average of 100 men. To improve their defensive firepower, the *folgorini* had collected captured weapons from the battlefield to strengthen the company positions. The 2 pdrs and Bren light machine-guns were especially popular, with their effectiveness limited by the amount of ammunition available. There are not any existing records of what each company possessed at the start of the battle except from what could be collected from survivor accounts.[5]

All of the battalions were placed in the main line of resistance or forward in the security of advance posts. Six companies occupied locations in the security zone while the remaining fourteen companies formed the main line of resistance. Behind the line of resistance was the attached *II/28º rgt. f.* «*Pavia*» which formed the sole reserve of the division. The «*Folgore*» had also been given the *XXXI btg. guastatori*, but this unit was there to assist in preparing the defense rather than as a combat element. It along with the *folgorini* and the *185ª cp. minatori*, worked to expand the minefield system and to increase their density.[6]

Before the UK attack, the Italo-German forces were able to lay nearly a million mines.[7] The majority of these mines were laid in the *XXI Cd'A* sector as the *X Cd'A*

5 Marco Di Giovanni, *I paracadutisti italiani Volontari, miti e memoria della seconda guerra mondiale* (Gorizia, Editrice Goriziana, 1991), p.173; Paolo Morisi, *The Italian Folgore Parachute Division* (Solihull, Helion & Company, 2016), p.108.

6 Morisi, *Folgore*, pp.187–189; Nino Arena, *FOLGORE Storia del paracadutismo militare italiano* (Rome, Centro Editoriale Nazione, 1965), p.131; Montanari, *Le operazioni*, vol. 3, p.668–669 and schizzo n.79.

7 Montanari, *Le operazioni*, vol. 3, pp.677 and 674.

was using the FEBRUARY and JANUARY minefields placed by the UK forces. For the *folgorini*, their effort was focused on thickening the existing minefields and creating what were called *Giardini del Diavolo* (Teufel-Garten or Devil's Gardens). This was a concept directed by Rommel that created boxes of interlocking minefields. Instead of simple linear rows of mines, the rows were connected by mines laid perpendicular to the rows to form boxes. When an enemy breached a row, rather than be able to maneuver left or right, the enemy would find itself in a box with mines on all sides. This limited any movement and created a kill box for friendly machine-guns, anti-tank weapons, and artillery. The devil part was created by placing booby traps and random mines inside the box limiting movement within the boxes themselves.[8]

The mine barriers were not as strong as they should have been. Only 10% of the available mines were antipersonnel mines, the majority being anti tank mines. A normal minefield would consist of both types with only a small majority of the type of mines needed to counter the main threat that the minefield was designed to protect against. In a minefield with fewer antipersonnel mines, the enemy infantry and engineers had greater freedom to move within the field to clear the mines. The *paracadutisti* compensated for this by placing there two-three man teams near the mine barriers to attack the engineers as they worked. The available manpower combined with the large extent of the frontage held by the division limited the area that could be covered in this manner.

The division also lacked an extensive battlefield communication system. The parachute units were not authorized field telephones, switchboards or the tens of kilometers of telephone wire needed to establish a robust telephone network. Each company did have a RF1(P) radio, a luxury that regular Italian infantry companies lacked. This radio was specifically developed for the airborne troops and was a reliable system but reflected the offensive nature of the airborne units. Its limited availability could not fully compensate for the lack of telephones in a defensive setting. The units from the disbanded *d. f. «Sabratha»* did bring some communication equipment to the division but it was not nearly enough. The *folgorini* instead scoured the desert battlefields for abandoned equipment and wire and were slowly able to create a basic communication system.[9]

23–24 October (Map 11.1)

The start of 8th Army's offensive was announced precisely at 2125 hours local time when the 13th Corps began its neutralization fires against the *X Cd'A*. The neutralization fires were targeted against the Italian artillery, headquarters, and rear services. The RAF added to this barrage with bombers operating over the battlefield, attacking

8 Arena, *FOLGORE*, p.184.
9 Arena, *FOLGORE*, pp.193-194.

rear areas and supply depots. 13th Corps initiated its neutralization fires against the *XXI Cd'A* at 2140, the different time likely to reinforce the idea that the main attack was in the south. The barrage in both areas ceased at 2155 hours.

The lull only lasted for five minutes. At 2200 hours the British artillery again resumed firing. Their targets were now the front line defenses. Simultaneously the attacking infantry rose front their attack positions and advanced toward the Italian and German defenses. The guns would continue to fire until 2107 hours when they would begin to shift fires deeper into the defenses as their infantry reached the first line of defense.[10]

Those Italians and Germans that had served in Russia might have previously experienced such an intensity of artillery fire. For those whose service had been limited to North Africa, the length and volume of the artillery fire was likely a shock. The Italian and German artillery response was mixed. Stumme had ordered that the artillery not respond to any British preparatory fires to conserve ammunition until targets could be defined. In the *XXI Cd'A* sector, the heavy barrage had disrupted communications and employed reporting, so little friendly counter fire was initiated.[11]

The British 13th Corps had planned two attacks against the positions of the *«Folgore»*. The heavier attack was directed against *ragg. «Ruspoli»* at the center of the division's sector. Here the 22nd Armoured Bde was to penetrate the JANUARY and FEBRUARY minefield, followed by the 4th Armoured Bde. The 131st Infantry Bde would protect the northern flank of the attack, while a heavy smoke screen laid by artillery and aircraft would screen the southern flank. The armoured brigade was to clear four lanes through the two minefields and secure the area around Quota 115 to the rear of the line of resistance. The 4th Armoured Brigade would follow the successful attack of the 22nd Armoured Bde to drive deep into the Italian position before turning north to completely unhinge the defense.[12]

Tenente colonnello Ruspoli had placed three of his six companies forward in the security zone. The JANUARY and FEBRUARY minefields had been connected by several east-west minefields to create boxes as previously discussed. The northern most of these connecting minefields formed the northern flank of *ragg. «Ruspoli»* sector. As JANUARY ended near that location, the connecting minefield was laid to the west to connect with FEBRUARY. This created an inverse L-shaped sector. The *19/VII* and *6/II para.* companies held the eastern face of the security zone along JANUARY, while the *22/VIII guastatori* covered the northern flank along the connecting minefield. Behind these companies was the FEBRUARY minefield and the remaining three companies of this section of the defense. These companies were positioned in a similar order, with the *20ª* and *21/VII* cp. *para.* facing eastward behind the FEBRUARY minefield. The *24/VIII guastatori* was also behind FEBRUARY but

10 Playfair, *The Mediterranean and Middle East*, vol 4, pp.35–37.
11 Montanari, *Le operazioni*, vol. 3, pp.689 and 721.
12 Playfair, *The Mediterranean and Middle East*, vol 4, pp.42–43.

facing north along the connecting minefield. The result was that the three companies in the security zone were inside a large minefield box (the southern part of the box was formed by another east-west connecting minefield), while the remaining three were positioned behind a linear minefield.

The 22nd Armoured Brigade attack started at 2200 hours.The minefield gaps were to be made by a force organized under the 44th Reconnaissance Regiment with attached engineers, a troop of the Royal Scots Greys (M3 Stuarts) and six Scorpion flail tanks to clear the mines. East of JANUARY the paratroops had randomly scattered mines and forced the Scorpions to start clearing earlier than planned. Bad terrain added to the delay and the force only reached the edge of JANUARY by 2300 hours. Here the advance posts began to engage the engineers with small arms and called for indirect fires to interdict the enemy's work. The *X Cd'A* artillery, ignoring the original orders, immediately answered the calls and began firing its artillery just as soon as the attack started. All the Scorpions were soon out of action either due to breakdowns or hit by the Italian fire. The British engineers finally got the two southern lanes open by 0230 hours, but they were still under fire from the surviving advance posts. Two companies of the 1st Rifle Brigade and the Scots Greys were now needed to eliminate those posts. The two northern lanes were clear within the next hour.

It was not until 0400 hrs that the breaching force could begin to penetrate FEBRUARY. Heavy casualties clearing JANUARY limited the new effort to creating only two gaps in FEBRUARY. The fire from the *VII/186º* in the line of resistance behind FEBRUARY and the continued flanking fires from the remains of *6/II*, *19/VII*, and the *22/VIII guastatori* continued to impede the attackers. At about 0430 hours the 7th Armoured Division commander, Major General John Harding ordered the 22nd Armoured Bde to push its tanks through the gaps in JANUARY to clear out the Italian forward companies. There was heavy fighting in and around the positions of the two parachute companies. The British tanks were finally able to break down the defense and the *6ª* and *19ª* companies were forced to retreat. While casualties were fairly light during the fighting, the retreat saw most of the survivors either killed or captured. By 0540 hours most of the Italian positions between JANUARY and FEBRUARY had been cleared, with the position of the *22/VIII guastatori* falling shortly afterwards. All three companies had been destroyed or rendered combat ineffective but had extracted a heavy cost on the attackers.

The fight to clear the Italian security zone resulted in more than just casualties for British forces; it had fatally delayed the attack towards FEBRUARY. The engineers were unable to push any cleared gaps through the minefield and with daylight the tanks inside the minefield box now found themselves taking direct fire from the Italian field artillery. With casualties mounting, Harding ordered the brigade to consolidate its bridgeheads on the west side of JANUARY and await orders. The two battalions of the 131st Bde that were to follow the armour through the gaps were never called forward.

The battle proved costly for both sides. The British brigade had lost approximately 200 men, thirty universal carriers, several tanks and all the Scorpions. The *6/II* and

A *folgorino* in a fighting position covering a minefield. (AUSSME)

the *19/VII* companies had been destroyed during the fight, mainly in their attempt to withdraw. Of the 220 *paracadutisti* in the two companies, only 50 made it back to the line of resistance.[13]

The supporting effort by the 131st Infantry Bde also was unsuccessful. The 1/7 Queens Royal Regiment's line of advance took it north of the connecting minefield. The Italian advance posts identified the enemy battalion near its starting line and called for artillery fire on its position. The battalion was thrown into confusion and took some time to sort itself out. Advancing westwards, it was caught by flanking fires from the *6/II para.* and the *22/VIII guastatori* companies. The battalion was forced to halt and finally retreated back out of range of the Italian positions. The British battalion had lost 180 men, including its commander, second-in-command, and all

13 Montanari, *Le operazioni*, vol. 3, pp.730–734; Morisi, *Folgore,* pp.119; Arena, *FOLGORE,* p.198; Playfair, *The Mediterranean and Middle East*, vol 4, pp.42–43; Ronald Walker, *Alam Halfa and El Alamein* (Wellington: Historical Publications Branch, 1967), pp.283–285. Morisi states that the British tanks penetrated the line of resistance, all the other sources state that FEBRUARY was never breached.

four company commanders. Most of the Italian losses were from the *6/II para.* that are included in the losses given above.[14]

The second attack planned for that night by the 13th Corps was a flanking attack against the southernmost point of the «*Folgore*» sector, the area of Naqb Rala. This attack was executed by the 1ère Brigade Française Combattante (1st Fighting French Brigade Group) under Général de brigade Marie Kœnig.[15] The 1st Fighting French Brigade Group consisted of three infantry battalions, two regiments of artillery, and supporting arms.[16] Kœnig's plan was to march around the south along the northern edge of the Qattara Depression and attack northward against Naqb Rala. The ground from Naqb Rala down to the depression was not steep and it was trafficable by tracked vehicles. The route was unfavorable for wheeled vehicles, so the artillery was placed east of Qaret el Himeimal to support the attack. Once the French had gained Naqb Rala, they would swing east to clear Qaret el Himiemat, then push northwest to seize Naqb el Khadim.

The *V/186° para.* was defending the southern end of the «*Folgore*» sector. The battalion sector was six kilometers long, much too long to hold everything. The battalion commander, *tenente colonnello* Izzo had three companies (400 men), seventeen 47/32 c.c., nine machine-guns, and three 81mm mortars. He positioned the *14/V para.* forward holding Qaret el Himiemat in the security zone, behind which he placed the *13ª* and *15/V* on the line of resistance. He recognized the possible threat from the south to Naqb Rala, so placed several 47/32 c.c. at the southern end of the *13ª cp.* position that could cover the approach from the south. Izzo also took a parachute platoon from each of the companies to form a reserve that could move into prepared positions to block that avenue of attack.

The French began their approach march at 1915 hours on the evening of 24 October. At 2125 hours the neutralization artillery fires began to impact in the *V btg.* sector. The lead French units reached the minefield south of Qaret el Himiemat at about 2300 hours. Here the French radio operators began to experience transmission problems and the radio network broke down, impacting Kœnig's ability to synchronize the actions of his force. Clearing the minefield, they arrived at their line of departure by 0100 hours. After deploying the two bataillons de Légion Etrangère (1re and 2e BLE) into their attack formations (the 1re BLE leading, the 2e BLE following), the French began to advance north towards the *paracadutisti* defense.

14 Playfair, *The Mediterranean and Middle East*, vol 4, p.43; Walker, *Alam Halfa*, p.286.

15 Marie-Anne Corvisier-de Villèle, *Inventaire des Archives de la Guerre, série p 1940–1946* (Château de Vincennes : Ministère de la Défense, 1998), tome II Grandes Unités, p.214. The Française Libre (Free French) units had been renamed as the Française Combattante (Fighting French) in October 1942, but reverted back to Free French in December 1942.

16 1re, 2e Bataillon/13e Demi-Brigade de Légion Etrangère, Bataillon d'Infanterie de Marine et du Pacifique, 22e compagnie nord-africaine, 1re régiment d'artillerie, 2e compagnie anti-char, and the 3rd Field Artillery, R.A. Attached was the 1ère compagnie de char (Crusaders).

The Italian advance posts near Qaret el Himiemat could hear vehicle nosies south of them at about 0200 hours and alerted the defense. It was now that the Italian began to experience a breakdown of communications similar to that of the French. In all, the fire support plan of the *V btg* failed. The *gruppo da 75/27* that was in general support of the battalion had just moved into position the day before and direct communications had yet to be established. Radio and telephone communications with the 75/27 battery in direct support of the battalion failed during the British artillery barrage and had not been repaired, delaying their initial fires. The mortars experienced difficulties as well and did not fire at this time. Izzo discovered that a German 88/53 battery that was placed to support his battalion had been ordered to move north earlier that day. The one part of the plan that did work was the three reserve platoons rapidly moved into the positions covering Naqb Rala. Deprived of indirect fire support, the *folgorini* manned the two strongpoints that had been built and prepared to meet such an attack. One hundred *paracadutisti* without supporting arms prepared to stop thirteen hundred French legionnaires.[17]

The French share of problems continued to increase as the attack developed that night. The lead elements discovered a previously unidentified minefield that had been placed to block this line of approach. Clearing gaps in the field took additional time. Then the radio problems again prevented contacting their supporting artillery, resulting in the legionnaires advancing without their planned second round of preparatory fires. Battlefield friction had caused both sides to enter into combat with only the weapons within their units.[18]

The 1re BLE led the attack as the narrow access to Nab Rala plateau did not allow both French battalions to advance abreast. The lead French company made contact at about 0300 hours in the morning. The Italian defenses were placed to the sides of approach to allow the attack to move forward into a kill zone. The 81mm mortars had by now corrected the communication issue and the Legionaries were caught in a machine-gun crossfire supported by mortar rounds impacting throughout the area. The Legionnaires pressed on and overran one position, killing or capturing twenty-eight parachutists. This success threatened to break the defense. Pressing their attack, the French were now too close to the defending *paracadutisti* and the mortars had to cease fire. Gaining the open plateau, the French were preparing to overwhelm the small number of remaining *folgoini*.

Sensing the moment, Izzo collected about 30 *paracadutisti* and ordered them to gather as many grenades as they could carry. Using the night, the *folgorini* would rush in onto the flanks for the French advance, throwing their grenades and then dash back into the darkness. These rushes were alternated with heavy machine-gun fire. By use

17 Montanari, *Le operazioni*, vol. 3, pp.736–737;
18 Montanari, *Le operazioni*, vol. 3, pp.736–737; Playfair, *The Mediterranean and Middle East*, vol 4, p.43; Morisi, *Folgore*, pp.127.

of these hit and run tactics, they were able to throw the French into confusion and stop the advance.

The French too were also using the night to maneuver onto the flank of the Italians. A small French detachment had managed to maneuver around behind the Italian position by overrunning two small advance positions. Moving into a position to attack the rear of the *paracadutisti*, the detachment was detected by *tenente* Marco Gola, the commander of the mortar platoon. As his mortars could not fire, he gathered up his mortar men and charged the flank of the French, driving them back. This and the other counterattacks initially halted the French advance and then began to push them back.

It was apparent to the French commander that the infantry attack had failed by 0500 hours. The 1re BLE was too disorganized to continue, so he ordered the battalion to withdraw and replaced it with the 2e BLE. Daylight allowed the Italian artillery and mortars to fire with great effectiveness, resulting in the disorganization of the 2e BLE. By 0700 hours the *paracadutisti* had cleared the upper part of Naqb Rala of the French and had been joined by six armoured cars from the German Aufklärungs-Abteilung 33. A coordinated attack by the *folgorini* and the armoured cars at 0730 hours continued to push the French back until the 2e BLE found itself back at the bottom of the escarpment. Threatened by more counterattacks and his units still in considerable disarray, Kœnig ordered his units to retreat back to their side of the minefield at 1000.

The combat against the French cost the battalion 62 dead and wounded, and 20 missing (the latter were likely captured). Amongst the wounded was the battalion commander, *tenente colonnello* Izzo who had been in the center of the fighting. French losses were 123 killed and wounded, including 12 officers. Two tanks, eight armoured cars, and thirty-three Universal carriers were lost to mines and artillery.[19]

The morning of 24 October found that none of the British objectives along the front had been achieved. Hard fighting by the *XXI Cd'A* in the north had stopped the main British attack, but many positions had been overrun and several Italian and German battalions had been destroyed. The British and Commonwealth forces occupied the security zone and had gained some positions inside the Italo-German line of resistance. The situation in the *X Cd'A* sector was better with all the attacks stopped without any significant penetration of the line of resistance. Losses had been high but limited to only a few units. During the day the British withdrew the majority of the forces from the captured security zone to the east side of the JANUARY minefield but retained some forces west of JANUARY in the mine box between the opposing forces.

19 Montanari, *Le operazioni*, vol. 3, p.738; Renato Migliavacca, 'Gli artiglieria della «Folgore» nel combattimento di Naqb Raga (Alamein) 24 ottobre 1942', *Memorie Storiche Militari 1979*, (1980), pp.290–291; Franck Ségretain, 'October 1942: Qaret el Himeimat', *Qattara*, p.17.

24-25 October (Map 11.2)

In the north the British were looking to press forward while the Italo-German army was trying to shore-up the defense by building a stop-gap line behind the line of resistance. In the south both sides were planning counterattacks to secure the security zone in-front of the *«Folgore» VII btg.*

Frattini decided that a significant counterattack was needed to reclaim the security zone. The *XXXI guastatori* was recalled from mine laying work and placed in the weakened *«Folgore»* defense along with the *II/28° «Pavia»* between the *187° rgt.* and *ragg. «Ruspoli»*. He also released the *1/28° «Pavia»*, a small detachment from the *«Ariete»*, and a German panzerjäger detachment for the counterattack. While the counterattack was being organized, the Italian observation post atop Qaret el Himiemat was directing artillery fire on the British formations along the *«Folgore»* sector. That height gave the division an excellent field of view as any movement was quickly spotted. In return, the RAF and the Allied artillery were hitting the Italian positions all day. The RAF would keep the Italian and German forces under attack both day and night throughout the entire battle, providing little rest for the soldiers of the A.C.I.T.

The RAF bombing helped to disrupt the Italian counterattack by delaying the movement of the Italian forces. The *I/28°* took too long to reach the front as the battalion commander only arrived at the sector headquarters for his orders at 1600 hrs. By then the counterattack was already underway. Two companies of the *II/28°* were used instead, and because the panzerjägers were delayed after accidentally running over several Italian engineers, the infantry advanced without them. Seeing that the entire attack was becoming disjointed, the sector headquarters tried to recall the infantry. Unlike the paratroop companies, the regular infantry lacked radios and could not be recalled. The companies managed to clear the zone and set a defensive position on the west side of JANUARY. The Panzerjägers engaged a few tanks, but the British artillery forced them to retreat.[20]

While the Italian counterattack was unfolding, the 13th Corps was also planning another attack. The 131 Infantry Bde, followed by the 22 Ar. Bde, would again attack *ragg. «Ruspoli»*. The 4 Ar. Bde would screen the left (south) flank of the attack while massed anti-tank guns screened the right (north) side. The movements of the *II/28°* and the *XXXI guastatori* were just in time.

Launching their attack at 2100 hours, the two lead infantry battalions, the 1/5 and 1/6 Queens, first came up against the two companies of the *II/28°* in their hasty defense. This was not much of a fight as the two companies had little time to dig positions and were overwhelmed. The fight to breach FEBRUARY was hard fought, as two hundred and fifty *paracadutisti* defended against the 1,500 men of the two attacking battalions. *Tenente colonnello* Ruspoli was killed while leading a counterattack. After several hours the British had established a small bridgehead west of FEBRUARY at

20 Montanari, *Le operazioni*, vol. 3, pp.745-746.

a cost of 350 men. The *folgorini* had lost over 100 and had been pushed back, but still held a continuous line. Now was the time for the 22 Ar. Bde to push through and break the defense.

The infantrymen of the Queens waited for the tanks to arrive but they never did. During the delay between the infantry breaching FEBRUARY and the arrival of the armoured brigade, *generale* Frattini had ordered several batteries of 75mm and 105mm guns pushed forward into the gaps between the parachute companies to provide effective anti-tank fires. As the men of the Queens waited, they heard gunfire to the south of their position. One account states that the sappers had moved in the wrong direction and their gaps for the tanks did not lead to the infantry bridgehead but instead led into open ground between the Italian strongpoints. Another account states the gaps were correctly made, but the tanks got lost and missed the cleared lanes. In either case, the 4th County of London Yeomanry (CLY) and the 1/RTR pushed forward under a very bright moon. There the «*Folgore*» artillery and elements from the «*Ariete*» and 21st Panzer that had moved forward caught them in the open and quickly destroyed 31 Crusaders and Grants, stopping the attack. At 0400 hours Harding decided to suspend the attack and reassess the situation at daylight. Once he was able to see the battlefield, Harding recognized that nothing further could be done. The 4 CLY was withdrawn back east of JANUARY while the 1/ and 5/RTR were pulled back into the old security zone between the minefields. The infantry were ordered to hold the bridgehead they had gained west of JANUARY.[21]

25–26 October (Map 11.3)

Montgomery assessed the situation during the early morning of 25 October. A ten kilometer wide breach had been created in the north that he planned to expand with the 30th Corps. The Italo-German armoured reserve in the north had been worn down and the 10th Corps could likely handle any enemy counterattack. The 13th Corps had no real success in the south and the Italo-German armour reserve in the south was basically intact. The RAF continued its attacks both night and day against any moving Italian or German units, as well as supporting the British attacks against the Axis positions.

Montgomery planned to keep pressing with the bulk of the 8th Army in the north while the 13th Corps continued to threaten a breakthrough to keep the Italian *X Cd'A* and the two Axis armoured divisions focused on the south. General Horrocks proposed another attack against Deir el Munassib to accomplish that goal. Part of the reason for shifting the corps attack northwards was to avoid observation from Qaret

21 Playfair, *The Mediterranean and Middle East*, vol 4, pp.46–47; Montanari, *Le operazioni*, vol. 3, pp.750–751; Walker, *Alam Halfa*, pp.317–318.

Conditions in the desert. These *folgorini* are all equipped with the moschetto per cavalleria. Note the bunker is barely above ground level making it difficult for the enemy to see. (AUSSME)

el Himiemat; the failure to seize the height on the night of 24–25 October was now having an impact.[22]

The 13th Corps plan was to feint with the 4th Ar. Bde south of Deir el Munassib, followed by an infantry attack against the position itself using the 69th Infantry Bde. The armor feint was moving in the same area in which the 1/7 Queens had attacked on the night of 23–24 October. A unit of dummy tanks was moved to the northeast of Deir el Munasssib to distract the Italian defenders. Once the initial positions were overrun, the infantry would press northwest to unhinge the defensive line.

The position was now held by the *IV/187° rgt.* Its three companies held the same strongpoints built by the *IX/187° rgt.* during the fighting on 30 September. The position had been strengthened to include the completion of two minefields that extended JANUARY and FEBRUARY further north. The actual Deir el Munassib position was now in the security zone, with the *IX btg.* directly to the west in the line of resistance. The *10ª cp.* had about 120 men and was the western most company facing north. East of it was the *11ª cp.* with approximately 100 men and three 47/32 c.c. that faced in

22 Playfair, *The Mediterranean and Middle East*, vol 4, p.47; Walker, *Alam Halfa*, pp.327–328.

an arc towards the north, northeast and east. South of the *11ª cp.* was the *12ª cp.* with approximately one hundred twenty men and three 47/32 c.c. This company covered the east face of the position.[23]

The 4/8 Hussar Regiment of the 4th Ar. Bde began their feint/attack at 1500 hrs from the east. The engineers leading the way to clear the minefield were caught by heavy fire and the mine clearing was incomplete. The tanks pushed forward and while they penetrated the minefield, no breach had been made. Splitting, they moved both north towards *11ª cp.* and south towards *12ª cp.* Fired on by the 47/32 c.c. and the larger guns of the *ragg. art. «Folgore»*, the Hussars were forced back after losing fifteen tanks. During this time to the south of Deir el Munassib, the two battalions of the Queens that held the small bridgehead west of FEBRUARY were withdrawn to the east side of that minefield.[24]

The next attack was by the infantry of the 69th Bde. The 6 Bn Green Howards Regiment was the north (right) of the attack and was directed against the *11ª cp.* The 5th Bn East Yorkshire Regiment was the southern (left) of the attack and went against the *12ª cp.* Both battalions approach the minefields at 2100 hours. The Howards were able to effectively use the smoke screen and the artillery barrage and broke into the *11ª cp.* strongpoint where a number of firing positions were overruned. Fires from flanking firing positions and local counterattacks by small groups of *paracadutisti* finally wore down the attackers and stopped the Howards just short of the company command post. The close-in fighting created time for a small group of reinforcements from the *10ª cp.* to reinforce the *11ª cp.*, while elements from the *IX btg.* covered the flanks and helped secure the position. The *11ª cp.* was basically destroyed, losing sixty killed and wounded and forty-five prisoners. The Howards lost one hundred and forty-four men and only gained part of the position.[25]

The attack of the 5 East Yorkshire never got beyond the advance posts. Effective indirect artillery and automatic weapons fires caused 106 casualties by 0100 hours. Unable to breach the minefield, the battalion abandoned the attempt and fell back. With the partial failure in the north and the complete failure in the south, the second phase of attack was canceled.

26 October-2 November (Map 11.4)

The morning of 26 October found that the *«Folgore»* defensive line was still intact. Horrocks planned another brigade attack against Deir el Munassib in the afternoon, but then received Montgomery's order not to endanger his armor and to conserve

23 Montanari, *Le operazioni*, vol. 3, p.754.

24 Walker, *Alam Halfa*, p.329; Montanari, *Le operazioni*, vol. 3, p.754; Morisi, *Folgore*, pp.146–149.

25 Walker, *Alam Halfa*, p.329; Montanari, *Le operazioni*, vol. 3, p.754; Morisi, *Folgore*, pp.149–153.

ammunition. Instead a scaled down attack was substituted using a company from the 6 Bn Green Howards and the Bataillon de Marche nº5 from the 2ème Brigade Française Combattante, while simultaneously executing a feint by the movement of the dummy tanks towards the depression at dusk to simulate another armoured attack.[26]

The French began advancing at 1430 hours behind an artillery barrage and smoke. The attack was aimed at the positions of the *10ª cp.* which was now holding an extended line in the security zone due to the losses of the *11º cp* the previous night. The fighting was hard but the French were able to seize two of the advance fighting positions. It was only when they attempted to storm the main strongpoint that their attack was stopped. A counterattack by elements of the *10ª cp.* and supported by the 81mm mortars broke the French effort and forced them to retreat. Losses were again heavy in the *10ª cp.*, including the death of the company commander *capitano* Gastone Simoni as he led the counter attack against the French forces.[27]

The company from the Howards also advanced at 1430 hours and moved to seize The Moor (Quota 94) between the *II* and *IV btg*. Their advance initially only met light opposition given the actions of the French to their east. The remaining *paracadutisti* of the *11ª cp.* were exhausted and 18 men were captured before the company reacted. Supported by heavy artillery fire, the *11ª cp.* was able to maneuver against the enemy and forced them to retreat.[28]

This was the last major attack against the «*Folgore*» during Alamein. General Montgomery's assessment of the success and failures of Lightfoot informed him that the offensive was slowing down. While the 30th Corps was able to break into the Italo-German line of resistance in the north, the armoured divisions of the 10th Corps had not succeeded in breaking out into the open. The possible turning movement by the 13th Corps in the south had been completely stopped. Montgomery decided that he needed to reposition his forces and recreate a reserve. To do the latter, he abandoned all attempts to penetrate the *X Cd'A* in the south and focused his army for a breakthrough in the north.[29]

The impact of General Montgomery's order to the 13th Corps to conserve the 7th Armoured and ammunition that arrived on 26 October changed the 13th Corps plans. Now 7th Armoured Division was given an order to be prepared to move north

26 Morisi, *Folgore,* p.154; Arena, *FOLGORE,* p.200; Walker, *Alam Halfa*, p.334; Anon., *Terza offensiva Britannica in Africa settentrionale La battaglia di El Alamein e il ripiegamento in Tunisia (6 settembre 1942–4 febbraio 1943)* (Rome: USSME, 1961), p.128; Arena, *FOLGORE,* p.200; Anon, 'Bataillon de Marche nº5', Mémoire de la 1ère DFL <https://1dfl.fr/category/les-unites/decouvrez-les-unites/les-bataillons-de-marche/bataillon-de-marche-n5/> (accessed 21 September 2022). Morisi states only the French attacked, Arena and *Terza offensive* claim both the Howards and French attacked, and Walker states only the Howards. 'Bataillon de marche' states that the French only conducted deception movies and feints during this time.

27 Morisi, *Folgore,* p.154.

28 Walker, *Alam Halfa*, p.334; Arena, *FOLGORE,* p.201.

29 Playfair, *The Mediterranean and Middle East*, vol 4, p.52.

while the infantry divisions in the corps were to continue active patrolling. The 7th Ar. Div. was actually ordered north on 27 October without the 4th Ar. Bde but taking the 131st and 151st Infantry Bdes with it. The 13th Corps zone was extended further northwards to now include the 4th Indian Division in its order of battle to release additional forces for the attack in the north.[30]

Generale Frattini returned to the command of the «*Folgore*» on 26 October. Although he was commanding the entire *X Cd'A* during these first days of the battle, he was never far from his «*folgorini*». The enemy's focus on attacking the «*Folgore*» allowed him to use the resources of the corps to support their defense. On this day *generale di divisione* Eduardo Nebbia arrived at the front and assumed command of the corps and Frattini returned to his divisional command post.

Like Montgomery, Rommel was also assessing the battle and ordering changes. The 90.Afrika Division was ordered to move from El Daba to the northern sector, while the 21.Panzerdivision and a *raggruppamento* from the «*Ariete*» was ordered to move from the southern to the northern sector. The successful defense by the «*Folgore*» not only prevented an enemy penetration in the south, it enabled the release of these armored formations for the critical battle up north in the *XXI Cd'A* sector.[31]

The French and the Greek brigades continued to make harassing attacks and feints, but none of these seriously threatened the «*Folgore*» defense. As the fighting in the south subsided, the RAF aerial offensive continued unabated. Both Italian and German troops were worn down by the near ceaseless attacks as 8th Army continued its attacks in the north. These attacks against the *XXI Cd'A* were initially to reposition forces and secure starting points for the planned offensive. While none of these efforts were able to break through the Italo-German defense, they did continue the erosion of the A.C.I.T.'s combat power. By 1 November, Montgomery was ready to launch Operation Supercharge, the new offensive to smash the Axis forces.

2–6 November (Map 11.5)

Operation Supercharge began at 2115 hours on 1 November with the RAF striking command and logistical centers in the A.C.I.T.'s rear. Another massive artillery barrage similar to that seen on 23 October prepared the way for the start of the ground offensive at 0105 hours on 2 November. The New Zealand Division reached its initial objectives on time and with light casualties. The follow-on attack by the 9th Ar. Bde met heavy resistance and the brigade was almost destroyed, but it gained the ground needed to pass through the 1st Armoured Division. The Italo-German line in the north was barely holding, but the cost was too great.[32]

30 Playfair, *The Mediterranean and Middle East*, vol 4, p.57.
31 Montanari, *Le operazioni*, vol. 3, p.754
32 Playfair, *The Mediterranean and Middle East*, vol 4, pp.63–69;

Rommel recognized that the battle was lost on 2 November. Receiving reports from the major subordinate commanders, he understood the A.C.I.T. was worn down and lacked the strength to maintain the current positions. The A.C.I.T. headquarters issued the initial instructions for the retreat from the Alamein position at 1600 hours. At 1730 hours detailed orders for each corps were issued. For the *X Cd'A*, the initial move was to withdraw back to the positions held before the start of the 2nd Battle of Alamein during the morning of 3 November. The other corps would occupy similar positions north of the *X Cd'A*, which would array the army on a continuous north-south line. This would position the divisions for the next phase of the retreat.[33]

The main problem for the A.C.I.T. was the lack of vehicles to transport the Italian and German infantry. The army requested on 1 November for at least 1,500 trucks from the rear areas and the line of communications units to move the five infantry divisions. One hundred and fifty trucks with fifty trailers were all that was available but were inadequate for all the infantry and their heavy weapons. These trucks were still being collected on 3 November so the initial moves would be by foot. The mobile units (armoured and motorized infantry) would stay in place to cover the movement of the infantry, then fall back to rejoin those units in the new positions. The plan was to have the infantry begin that night and if undetected by the British Army, make the move back without being disturbed.[34]

The artillery and heavy weapon companies in the regular infantry divisions were motorized, so those units had the means to move their artillery, mortars, and machine-guns by truck even if the infantry themselves had to walk. Nothing in the «*Folgore*» was motorized. Any heavy weapons that the «*Folgore*» needed to take with them on the march had to be pulled or carried by the *paracadutisti*.

The detailed order was received by the *X Cd'A* at 1730 hours and issued to the divisions. The «*Brescia*» and the «*Pavia*» only needed to move about fifteen kilometers. This was a short enough distance that they could employ their remaining trucks as a shuttle service to transport their men and equipment. These two divisions reached the initial retreat line by 1200 hours on 3 November.[35]

Up until this date, the «*Folgore*» had lost 1,500 casualties (1,000 dead and wounded, and about 500 captured) in the fighting since 23 October.[36] The loss of leaders was especially heavy, with the majority of platoon, company, and battalion commanders among those numbers. It was a much reduced division that began its trek into the desert.

The «*Folgore*» received the detailed order at 2100 hours on 2 November. The division would occupy a line between the two Quotas 112 just north of the Gebel Kalakh, a march of nine to twelve kilometers. The mortars and machine-guns had pack frames designed to allow soldiers to carry these weapons on their backs, but the 47/32 c.c. had

33 Montanari, *Le operazioni*, vol. 3, pp.796–797.
34 Montanari, *Le operazioni*, vol. 3, p.788. These trucks could move 3,000 troops with all their equipment.
35 Montanari, *Le operazioni*, vol. 3, pp.800-801.
36 Morisi, *Folgore*, p.155.

to be hand towed through the sand. All the heavier weapons were destroyed. Only a limited amount of ammunition could be carried along with the rations and water, a critical problem if the *folgorini* were forced to fight. The main body of the subordinate units began movement by midnight while small detachments were left in defense to cover the retreat. The main body arrived at the two quotas by noon and set some hasty positions. The retreat went unnoticed by the British and the covering detachments were able to withdraw at 1000 hours on 3 November. The first phase of the retreat had gone well.[37]

Rommel received the no retreat, hold at all cost order from Hitler at approximately 1200 hours on 3 November. Wrestling with the decision to either obey or not, he compromised. New orders were issued at 1510 hours to the corps to hold their current positions. Some units were ordered to move to create a contiguous defensive line but none were able to act on them until late into the night or the next day. After marching most of the night and part of the following day, «*Folgore*» held its current positions through that night and into 4 November.

The 8th Army had finally achieved their breakthrough in the northern sector on 4 November. With the initial withdrawal of the A.C.I.T. on the night of 2-3 November, the attacks planned for the morning of 4 November met little resistance. The 8th Army now had to reorganize itself for pursuit as the battle had forced the premature commitment of the forces Montgomery had hoped to use once this moment arrived.

Units of the British 13th Corps did not begin to notice that the «*Folgore*» was missing until about 1000 hours on 3 November. Patrols sent out during the day had penetrated about four kilometers into the former defensive area by nightfall. The 13th Corps needed some time to organize a pursuit having lost the 4th Ar. Bde to the 10th Corps that morning. Much of the corps transport had been sent to the other corps to replace their losses over the twelve days of the battle. It was not until the morning of 4 November that an operation designed to sweep the area could be mounted. Contacting the «*Folgore*» defense in the afternoon, General Horrocks decided not to order an attack. Instead he used artillery to shell the positions while asking if the *paracadutisti* wished to surrender. The offer was declined by the *folgorini*.[38]

Planning to attack the morning of 5 November, the British were surprised to find the «*Folgore*» was gone. *Generale* Frattini had received orders to continue the retreat at 1900 hours the previous evening. The corps commander, *generale* Nebbia ordered the retreat to be accomplished in three night stages, each about 25 kilometers long. This plan would place the *X Cd'A* on the Fuka line by the morning of 7 November. The ability of the men of the «*Folgore*» to accomplish this feat was unlikely. No food or water had been issued since the division left its lines on 3 November except for what was available at the supply points they passed on that first day.[39]

37 Montanari, *Le operazioni*, vol. 3, p.801; Arena, *FOLGORE*, pp.220–221.
38 Playfair, *The Mediterranean and Middle East*, vol 4, pp.72 and 92; Arena, *FOLGORE*, p.221.
39 Montanari, *Le operazioni*, vol. 3, p.816.

Frattini organized the division into a box formation to provide all-round security. The strength of the division was badly depleted by the two marches since the start of the retreat. Most battalions now averaged the strength of a strong company. The *VIII guastatori* led the march to the west, supported by the *II/28° art. «Pavia»*; *II/187°* on the left (southern) flank; the *V/186°* on the right (northern) flank; the *IV* and *IX/187°* were combined to form the rearguard as the *IX btg.* was down to a strength of about one hundred men, along with the *II/185° art. Folgore»*. The *VI* and *VII/186°*, along with the division command and the artillery (*I/185° art. Folgore»*, *I/21° art. «Trieste»*, and an 88mm battery from the *«Ariete»*) were in the center of the formation. Marching during the night, the division reached kilometer marker 144 on the *Pista Rossa* (Red Trail, the Rahman Track) at 0100 hours on 5 November and stopped for a rest.[40]

The *paracadutisti* resumed their march at dawn on 5 November. To the north of them marched the *«Pavia»* column. Taking up the chase, the Household Cavalry Regiment and the 44th Reconnaissance Regiment were dispatched in the direction of the *«Folgore»*. To the north was the 69th Infantry Bde searching for the *«Brescia»* and *«Pavia»*. The 1ère Brigade Française Combattante was advancing in the south. These movements were boxing in the retreating *X Cd'A*, leaving marching west into the desert as the only option for escape.[41]

The British armored cars found the *folgorini* by mid-morning on 5 November and the long-ranged harassment started again. Reaching Allam Gaballa at 1400 hours, the artillery repelled an attack while the weary men caught some rest. Surprisingly, three supply trucks carrying a half-day's worth of rations and one-half liter of water per man reached the *«Folgore»*.[42] Setting off at 1730 hours, the division resumed the march while leaving the *IV btg.* as a rear guard, joined by the *VII btg.* Marching through the night, the division stopped during the early morning for another pause.

Sunrise on 6 November found the *«Folgore»* now north of the *«Pavia»*. During the night the two columns had crossed each other's line of march and changed relative positions. That was not the only surprise as the *IV btg.* had also become separated from the main body. The British armoured units were able to surround the isolated battalion and overwhelm it, the survivors surrendering to the enemy.[43]

The remaining battalions started their march at 0730 hrs, but it was clear that 6 November would be the last day for the *«Folgore»*. The *II btg.*, with only forty-six men was next to fall. By 1030 hours, armored vehicles appear in-front of the march columns, closing off the last open route to Fuka. All the ammunition for the heavy weapons was exhausted by noon; only small arms remained to resist the enemy. Pinned by the enemy fire and without rations or water, the *folgorini* held for another few hours. At 1500 hours the remaining ammunition was fired off; it was the end as there was

40 Arena, *FOLGORE*, p.222; Anon, *Terza offensiva Britannica*, pp.209-210.
41 Playfair, *The Mediterranean and Middle East*, vol 4, p.92, Map 12.
42 Morisi, *Folgore*, p.160; Arena, *FOLGORE*, pp.222–224.
43 Anon, *Terza offensiva Britannica*, p.211.

nothing left to fight with. The order was given to destroy the remaining weapons and surrender. The *folgorini* were unhappy with this order, but they knew there was no longer any choice. The number of *paracadutisti* surrendering on this final day varied between three hundred and four hundred men. The division had previously lost 1,500 men during the three months of combat, but the harshness of the retreat and the enemy actions reduced the remaining *folgorini* from 2,500 to the mere 400 men that remained to the division on 6 November. Beaten but not broken, the *folgorini* formed up in ranks and saluted their commanders as the British soldiers approached to take their surrender.[44]

Lessons of the Desert War

The men of the «*Folgore*» demonstrated that the failures of the *Regio Esercito* were not due to the failings of the Italians as soldiers. Given adequate training and solid leadership, the *folgorini* had stood up to the best its enemies had to offer and won. Their ultimate failure was created when the decision was made to commit them into a role that was unsuitable for their organization and equipment. They were sent to Africa in an attempt to make good on a bad decision. The mirage of Alexandria lured the Italian leadership away from the reality of Malta. The disjoined nature of the Axis strategic planning (if such planning even existed) and the lack of its own national resources forced Fascist Italy to follow wherever Germany led.

The lessons learned from the Libya parachute battalions and the *I btg. CC.RR.* were once again reinforced by the «*Folgore*». Excellent training can only take a unit so far in combat. Units need to have the right equipment and organization for the conditions under which the unit would fight. Men become the replacement for the lack of weapons and the leadership pays a heavy price for success. The «*Folgore*» lost one regimental commander dead and one wounded; six battalion and six company commanders were killed, while three other battalion and five company commanders were wounded in the fighting before the start of the retreat. The division suffered a loss of fifty percent of the senior leadership, along with an overall loss of 40% of all ranks within a period of three months.[45]

Of the several theaters where the R.E. fought during the war, the army possessed the least capability for successful operations in Africa settentrionale. North Africa was a war fought by tanks, anti-tank guns, and trucks; fuel was the horsepower that made all the activity happen. Fascist Italy lacked all of those elements and the Italian soldiers found themselves fighting an enemy they had little chance of defeating.

44 Morisi, *Folgore*, p.160; Arena, *FOLGORE*, p.225.
45 Arena, Nino, *I PARACADUTISTI Cinquant'anni di storia, cronaca e immagini del paracadutismo italiano* (Modena, Società Tipografica Editrice Modenese Mucchi, 1972), pp.134–135.

Within this environment the «*Folgore*» was the poorest pauper amongst all paupers that were the regular Italian infantry divisions. The division lacked mobility, heavy weapons, and a logistical system to sustain itself. Yet for a few months the division found itself fighting on a static front where these shortages could be off-set by fortifications, combat skills, and most importantly the bravery of the *paracadutisti*. The *folgorini* made the most of the situation and established a tradition that marked them among the best combat troops of the war. The cost to establish that tradition was high: once forced from that static role and into a mobile battle, the «*Folgore*» was chased, cornered, and finally destroyed without any ability to change the outcome.

12

Tunisia

Four days after the British 8th Army broke through the Italo-German defense at El Alamein, the Anglo-American forces began landing in French Morocco and Algeria on 8 November 1942. The success of Operation Torch completely transformed the military situation in North Africa. The landings codified the Allied success in North Africa; even if Rommel had successfully defeated Operation Lightfoot/Supercharge, Operation Torch ended any hope of lasting Axis victory in North Africa.

The new situation placed the A.C.I.T. in an untenable position. The Italo-German forces lacked the strength to defeat the 8th Army and now would also need to defend against what would later become the Allied 1st Army. Any attempt to defend along the Libyan-Egyptian border or anywhere in Cirenaica was now forgotten. The discussion of whether the Axis should (or could) hold Libya and Tunisia is outside the scope of this book. The final decision to hold both created the operational problem of how to rapidly move adequate forces into Tunisia to prevent an Allied dash to occupy Biserta and Tunis. Simultaneously there was the problem of whether the A.C.I.T. could be reinforced to a point where it could successfully protect Tripolitania.

Steps had already been taken to protect Tripolitania. As previously stated, «*La Spezia*» had been deployed to Libya and placed under the command of *Superlibia*. The division had been moved forward to El Agheila and had begun to prepare a defense position in that area. Once the results of 3rd Alamein were known, the *136ª d. corazzata «Giovani Fascisti»* had been ordered to join «*La Spezia*» and would arrive in the area between 16–18 November. The *131ª d. corazzata «Centauro»* had also been ordered to Libya and elements were deployed forward as they arrived and added to the defense.[1]

The decision to occupy Tunisia was made a few days after the Torch landings. Two days before the landings (6 November 1942), *Supercomando* issued a warning order to the three services that the execution of *Esigenza «C2»* (the occupation of Corsica) was

1 Mario Montanari, *Le operazioni in Africa settentrionale* (Rome : USSME,1993), vol IV: Enfidaville, pp.51–53. The «*Giovani Fascisti*» was an armoured division in name only as it never received the planned armoured regiment. It was a small infantry division.

likely.[2] After the invasion on 8 November, discussions were held with Germany on the evolving strategic situation and how to treat Vichy France. *Supercomando* issued the order for the execution of *«C2»* on 10 November, with the landing to happen on 11 November. Hitler finally gave his consent on 11 November for the occupation of Tunisia. *Supercomando* issued the order to execute *Esigenza «C4»* on 12 November.[3]

Planning for *Esigenza «C4»* had actually begun in July 1942 when the planning staff for *«C3»* was instructed to start development of *«C4»*. The forces in the initial draft comprised nine divisions, including one paratrooper and one armoured. Now in November, neither of these types of divisions were available. *«Folgore»* had been destroyed and the new *184ª d. fanteria «Nembo»* was only officially authorized on 1 November 1942. Both the *132ª «Ariete»* and the *133ª «Littorio»* armoured divisions had been destroyed at El Alamein and the *131ª «Centauro»* was committed to the defense of Tripolitania. The *«La Spezia»* was also committed to the defense of Tripolitania, but there was some discussion on 4 November on sending this division to Tunisia.[4]

The problem of how to execute both *«C2»* and *«C4»* was noted by Cavallero on 8 November. *Supercomando* calculated that the worst case situation was that the Allies could have two divisions in northern Tunisia by the morning of 21 November, with two more by 23 November. The R.M. lacked fuel for its ships so were unable to support an amphibious landing in Tunisia. The R.E. lacked tanks and the 20–30 merchant ships needed to transport the army divisions to Biserta and Tunis. Of the few Italian divisions fully equipped and combat ready, the *44ª d.f. «Cremona»* and the *20ª d.f. «Friuli»* were already identified for *«C2»* under the command of the *VII Cd'A.*

Responsibility for occupying Tunisia was given to the *XXX Cd'A*. This corps was originally the designated headquarters for the landing forces programmed for *Operazione «C3»*. Of its three assigned divisions, only the *1ª d.f. «Superga»* remained under its command. Upon notification of the order to execute the mission, *generale di corpo d'armata* Vittorio Sogno was given a brief memorandum outlining the terrain, the possible lines of operations, and the assessed logistical capacity of the theater. Sogno would later state that the memorandum did not provide any real planning guidance and failed to even specify the forces that would be available to execute the mission. The corps as it was eventually constituted was a heterogeneous mixture of elements taken from multiple units and assigned to the corps. Many of the major subordinate units were in themselves a heterogeneous collection of units thrown together for this task. The lack of a strategic reserve that could be rapidly committed in support of contingencies was starkly displayed in *Supercomando's* response to the Torch landings.[5]

2 Antonello Biagini and Fernando Frattolillo (eds), *Diario Storico del Comando Supremo* (Rome: USSME, 1984-2002), vol 8, book 1 p.634.
3 Biagini and Frattolillo (eds) *Diario Storico,* vol VIII, book 2, pp.96–101.
4 Montanari, *Le operazioni*, vol IV, pp.92, 94.
5 Vittorio Sogno, *Il XXX Corpo d'Armata Italiano in Tunisia* (Rome: USSME, 1952), p.49 and Allegato 1; Montanari, *Le operazioni*, vol IV, p.108.

Given the urgency that was called for in order to secure Tunisia, it is appropriate to examine the decisions *Supercomando* had previously made on the employment of the airborne units. If the *«Folgore»* and/or the *«La Spezia»* had been maintained as a strategic reserve, what options would have been available to execute *«C4»*? The *S.A.S.* had over three hundred transport aircraft available in November 1942 (over two-hundred and seventy were SM.82s). These numbers do not include those transports assigned to the various fighter and bomber groups that could be used if needed. If two hundred of these aircraft had been dedicated to moving the airborne units, *«Folgore»* likely could have been transported to Tunisia in one to two days, while *«La Spezia»* likely would have required no more than three to four days.[6]

Securing an airhead is a classic airborne mission and is discussed in the various R.E. military manuals.[7] If *«Folgore»* had been employed to secure Biserta and Tunis, the follow-on force would have been free to immediately deploy to the west to expand the Tunisian bridgehead. The number of Allied units that were currently moving into Tunisia were limited by logistical issues. When the German commander, General der Panzertruppe Walter Nerhing decided on 16 November that offensive action was better than remaining on the defense, only a small number of Italian and Germans were available. If *«Folgore»* or *«La Spezia»* had been available to secure the bridgehead on 9–10 November, Nerhing's decision would have been simpler to implement with larger forces and with considerably less risk.[8]

Nor was the *«Folgore»* available to execute the types of missions the Allies paratrooper units were performing in the early stages of the campaign. At this stage of what would become the Tunisian Campaign, the situation on the ground was fluid, neither side had air superiority, and both sides were trying to quickly gain dominant positions. The Italo-German forces were using trucks to move forces forward to seize terrain. The Allies were employing their British and American airborne units to do the same ahead of the Allied ground force advance. This option could have been available to the Italians if the *«Folgore»* had been maintained as an army strategic reserve.

Paracadutisti to Tunisia (Maps 12.1, 12.2)

Whilst the overarching strategic direction of the war in the Mediterranean was evolving, the simultaneous execution of *Esigenza «C2"* and *«C4»* was underway. The transportation of men and equipment to Corsica was mainly by sea and would last

6 Nino Arena, *La Regia Aeronautica* (Rome: USSMA, 1981-1986), vol 2, pp.610; AUSSME 'General Frattini's notes on the number of aircraft needed to airdrop *«Folgore»*', These estimates are based on a 60 percent operational rate and the increased aircraft capacity as the units would be air landed and not parachuted.

7 Anon, Circolare n.32000, *Impiego delle divisione paracadutisti ed aviotrasportabili* (Rome: Stato Maggiore Regio Esercito, 1942), pp.9 and 22–36.

8 Montanari, *Le operazioni*, vol IV, pp.106–107.

fourteen days (11–22 November). During the same period, men, equipment, and supplies were being sent to Biserta by air and sea. The Germans moved nearly all of their personnel by air, mobilizing eleven transport groups with over six-hundred aircraft. The R.A. was able to field twelve transport squadrons with approximately one hundred aircraft. The limited R.A. effort as compared to the Luftwaffe must be seen within the ongoing requirement to supply the retreating A.C.I.T., an effort that was mainly Italian and consumed significant resources.[9]

The movement of Italian troops to Tunisia was slow. The Germans transported two parachute companies from the 5.Fallschirmjäger Regiment and one company of the 104.Panzergrenadier Regiment on 12 November. On 14 November the 11.Fallschirmjäger Pioneer bataillon, a reconnaissance group and a tank company landed in Tunisia. The first Italian units, the *10º rgt. bersaglieri*, the *III/92º «Superga»* and three semoventi groups landed on 14-15 November. These Italian units were originally meant for the A.C.I.T. but were now diverted to Tunisia.[10] All this was happening at the time when discussions at *Comando Supremo* on 15 November raised the question of whether Libya could be held. General von Rintelen stated that the Panzeramree should retreat to Gabès in Tunisia. Cavallero stated that a retreat to Gabès would not only abandon Tripolitani but meant that Tunisia was also lost.[11]

The first Italian parachute unit to be deployed to Tunisia was the *1º battaglione d'assalto paracadutisti R.A.* Both it and the *Battaglione riattatori «Loreto»* were moved to Sicily in November and were officially formed into the *Reggimento d'assalto «Duca d'Aosta»*. A third unit, the *Battaglione Arditi Distruttori Regia Aeronautica* (A.D.R.A.) was planned as part of the regiment, but instead became an independent unit. The *1º btg. para. R.A.* would become known as the *parà azzurri* (the blue paratroopers) during the fighting because of the blue color of their R.A. uniforms.[12]

Organized and equipped as a raid force to attack lightly defended objectives such as airfields using surprise, the battalion lacked heavy weapons, helmets, and its training focused more on small unit combat actions associated with raid and sabotage than company and battalion level operations. Some sources state that the battalion was authorized a number of heavy machine guns, but the commander, *tenente colonnello* Edvino Dalmas wrote that the unit lacked automatic weapons when it arrived in

9 Nino Arena, *La Regia Aeronautica* (Rome: USSMA, 1984), vol.3, pp.329–330, 334.
10 Montanari, *Le operazioni*, vol IV, p.101; Sogno, *XXX Corpo*, pp.240–241.
11 Montanari, *Le operazioni*, vol IV, p.44.
12 Aldo Giorleo, *Palestra Azzurra L'aeronautica militare e il paracadutismo cronistoria dalle origini ad oggi* (Rome: USSMA, 1975), pp.52–53; Luigi Emilio Longo, *I «reparti speciali» italiani nella seconda guerra mondiale* (Milan: Mursia 1991), pp.160–161. The official name of the regiment is unclear as both Giorleo and Longo use *«Duca d'Aosta»* and *«Amedeo d'Aosta»* interchangeably.

Tunisia. The total strength of the battalion when it arrived in Tunisia was 306 men with the patrols averaging 22–25 men.[13]

The *1º btg. para. R.A.* moved from Arezzo where it was stationed to Trapani, Sicily by train, then was sent across the Strait of Sicily to Biserta on two old barges on the morning of 16 November. After a welcome speech at Biserta, the commander of the battalion, *tenente colonnello pilota* Edvino Dalmas, was ordered to immediately move his unit to the road junction at Menzel Djemil several kilometers south of Biserta to block the expected Allied advance. Leaving three patrols in Biserta, it arrived that evening at Menzel Djemil without encountering any opposition. The battalion remained there until the next day when the *parà azzurri* received new instructions and trucks to move them west to link-up with Kampfgruppe (KG) Witzig. Departing on 18 November, the battalion traveled westward until they linked up with KG Witzig just east of Djebel Abiod on 19 November.[14]

The Kampfgruppe had previously been ordered to block any Allied advance towards Biserta in the northern sector of Tunisia. The KG advanced along the road passing through Mateur to occupy Tabarka before that town could be secured by the Allies. As the Kampfgruppe reached the road junction at Djebel Abiod on the afternoon of 17 November, it was ambushed by Hartforce, a battlegroup that had been pushed forward by the British 36th Infantry Brigade to secure this important road junction. Arriving before dawn on 17 November, Hartforce had established a defensive position manned by the 6th Battalion Queen's Own Royal West Kent (QORWK) Regiment supported by two troops of 25 pdr field guns. Warned of the approaching KG by its attached reconnaissance unit, Hartford was able to surprise the German force. Heavy fighting followed for several hours with KG Witzig losing several tanks and other vehicles before being forced to retreat. The KG occupied a line of hills about five kilometers northeast of Djebel Abiod where it established a defensive position to block any further British advance. It was there that the nine patrols of the *1º btg. para RA* linked up with the Kampfgruppe Witzig on 19 November.[15]

While enduring air and artillery strikes, KG Witzig continued to hold this position until 21 November. Due to the length of the position that needed to be defended, the *paracadutisti* were spread out using 2–3 man fighting positions placed every 15 to 20 meters. The Italian paratroopers lacked entrenching tools, so simple fighting positions

13 Giorleo *Palestra Azzurra*, p.53; Longo, *I «reparti speciali»*, pp.160–161; AUSSME, Relazione Edvino Dalmas, *Attività bellico svolta dal battaglione paracadutisti dell'aeronautica dal 16 novembre 1942 al'8 settembre 1943*, Cart.1160/C/11, p.1.

14 Montanari, *Le operazioni*, vol IV, p.44 and fn.50; Nino Arena, *FOLGORE Storia del paracadutismo militare italiano* (Rome: Centro Editoriale Nazione, 1965), p.334; Sogno, *XXX Corpo*, p.25. Witzig commanded the fallschirmjägers that captured Eben Emael. KG Witzig consisted of the 1. and 4. companies/11.Fallschirmjäger Pioneer Battalion, 4/190th Panzer battalion, 5/190 Artillery regiment, the *2ª cp./CXXXVI btg. semoventi da 47*, and the *DLVII gruppo semoventi da 75/18.*

15 Howard D. Chaplin, *The Queen's Own Royal West Kent Regiment, 1920-1950* (London: Michael Joseph, 1954), pp.228–229;

were dug using hands and fighting knives. A German detachment of 20 fallschirmjägers and two armoured vehicles supported the battalion on its right (western) flank. The inability to construct proper defensive positions once again made the *paracadutisti* vulnerable to enemy fire, resulting in the battalion taking casualties.[16]

On 21 November, there was a discussion on what the KG should do. Here the sources differ in their accounts. Dalmas stated that he and Witzig discussed options and decided to attack the British positions around Djebel Abiod.[17] German sources state that Witizig decided to send out a combat patrol and does not mention any Italian coordination or involvement.[18] British sources call the events of 22 November a raid and nothing more. The size of the forces committed by the Italians and Germans indicate that it was a spoiling attack, although Dalmas implies that the plan was to seize the hills above Djebel Abiod and the town itself.

The movement forward would start at 2100 hours without any preparatory artillery fire with the assault itself launched just prior to dawn breaking. The plan was for the *1º btg. para* to seize Djebel Souif which overlooked the town, while the 1.kompanie of the Fallschirmjäger would capture the town itself. The *paracadutisti,* who were without heavy weapons, would have to rely on surprise to overcome any resistance using only small arms, hand grenades, bayonets, and combat knives.[19]

Dalmas decided to use three patrols (about 78 men) for the assault, one patrol from each of the three companies. The patrols were led by the respective company commanders. The Germans committed one company, making the total assault force approximately 200 men strong. The British forces in the area were the 8/Argyll & Sutherland Highland Battalion, D Coy, 6/QORWK, and two companies of the 5/ Royal East Kents (The Buffs). This force of over 1,200 men was supported by two batteries from the 138 Royal Artillery (25 pdr) and a battery from the 64 Anti-Tank Regiment (Glasgow Yeomanry)(6 pdr).[20]

The British routinely dispatched security patrols each night, and the night of 21 November was no different. Because the 8 A&SH were still moving to occupy their positions, the only patrol sent was towards the north towards the Nefza Station. Without any patrols to the northeast, the Italian's five kilometer approach march went

16 Dalmas, *Attività bellico svolta dal battaglione paracadutisti*, pp.1–2. The armoured vehicles were likely semoventi da 47s.

17 Dalmas, *Attività bellico svolta dal battaglione paracadutisti*, p.2.

18 Gilberto Vilhermosa, *Hitler's Paratrooper: The Life and Battles of Rudolf Witzig* (Barnsley: Frontline Books, 2010), p.133.

19 There are few accounts of the following action and what is available is contradictory and lacking detail. Sources used are Dalmas, *Attività bellico svolta dal battaglione paracadutisti*; TNA WO 175/491: 8 Argyll & Sutherland Highlanders War Diary, Nov. 1942–Jun. 1943; Longo, *I «reparti speciali»*, pp.164–166; Giorleo, *Palestra Azzurra*, pp.53–54; Gilberto Vilhermosa, *Hitler's Paratrooper: The Life and Battles of Rudolf Witzig* (Barnsley, Frontline Books, 2010), pp.133–134; A.D. Malcolm, *History of the Argyll and Sutherland Highlanders: 8th Battalion* (London: Thomas Nelson and Sons Ltd., 1949), pp.84–88.

20 Malcolm, *History of the Argyll and Sutherland Highlanders*, p.86.

undetected by the British. As the *paracadutisti* moved steadily towards their objective, fighting was heard to their right at about 0340 hours as the 1/11.Fallschirmjäger Pioneer Battalion began their attack, providing another indicator that the movements of the two forces were not coordinated. Dalmas decided to continue forward as planned to attack shortly before dawn.

As the sky began to lighten the *parà azzurri* rushed forward. It was fortuitous for the attackers that the 8th Argyll and Sutherland Highlanders had just relieved the West Kents on the night of 20–21 November. Only D Company of the 6/QOWK remained in the area after the bulk of the battalion had moved back to Tabarka. Due to the German raid, the movement of the 7 Platoon, B/8 A&SH and a platoon from the Buffs to Quota 149 had been delayed until 30 minutes before dawn. Wearing Greatcoats and carrying all their equipment to establish a defensive position, the two platoons were heavily burdened and moving slowly. They were moving up the slope of Quota 149 when Dalmas launched his attack. The *parà azzurri* were able to surprise and surround the 7 Platoon and the unit had no choice but surrender.

There was some initial confusion on the part of the British units observing the action on the hill as the blue uniforms of the *parà azzurri* appeared to be French. The 8/A&SH battalion commander, Lieutenant Colonel Mackellar, quickly deduced what was happening and directed suppression fire on the *paracadutisti*. The British artillery and machine guns opened fire and prevented the Italian paratroopers from continuing the attack. Stopped, the *paracadutisti* immediately began to organize a defense against the expected counterattack. With the sun now up in the sky, the British artillery pounded the Italian positions while the Argyll and Sutherland infantry moved to counterattack. Supported by D/6 West Kents, the Highlanders worked around the Italian positions and launched several counterattacks. Within hours heavy losses finally forced the surviving *paracadutisti* to retreat and the captured enemy were freed.

Rejoining the remainder of the battalion, the losses to the attacking force were severe. The *paracadutisti* had lost 24 dead and eight wounded. Thirty-nine *paracadutisti*, most of whom were wounded, were captured by the British. Combined with the losses that had occurred over the previous two days from air and artillery attacks, the battalion had lost over 100 men. *Tenente colonnello* Dalmas had been wounded during the attack and *capitano* Aldo Molino took command of the battalion. British losses were light with only six dead and 11 wounded, with all the men of 7 platoon captured by the Italians freed. Eleven additional men in the patrol that had gone north during the night had also been captured when they encountered the German 1.kompanie in the dark.

Without a clear purpose and the lack of coordination between the Italian and the German forces, this operation did not achieve a positive result. The Italian sources claim that the Germans were to take the town of Djebel Abiod while the Italians attempted to seize the high ground, but the Germans limited their actions to harassing fire and placing mines at the western entrance to the town. Lacking heavy weapons and with their supporting units more than five kilometers to the north, the attempt by the *paracadutisti* to capture the high ground and move into the town could not be sustained.

Assessing the outcome of the action on the evening of 22 November, it was clear to Dalmas and Witzig that the kampfgruppe lacked the strength to retake the town and crossroads. Using a feint against the Nefza Station by a German platoon, the Italians and the Germans retreated twenty kilometers to the crossroad at Sedjenane on 23-24 November. When the 36th Brigade initiated its offensive on 25 November towards Biserte, it only encountered small rear guards but did capture 12 more *paracadutisti*. The kampfgruppe held the position at Sedjenane until 26 November when, after the British advance neared that town, it again retreated to a stronger position at the Djebel el-Azag/Djebel el-Ajred gap along the road to Mateur. Using the hills on both sides of the gap and the nearby village of Jefna, Witzig established a new defensive position blocking the northern road.[21]

The *1º btg. para R.A.* was not present when the next battle was fought on 28 November. It had been ordered to withdraw on 25 November, and the battalion moved back to Mateur that night. Two days later the *parà azzurri* were again ordered to withdraw, now back to Tunis and began to do so either that evening or early on 29 November. The R.A. battalion arrived at the airfield in La Goulette in Tunis on 1 December where it would remain while its future assignment was determined. Now with less than 180 effectives, it had lost all offensive capability. Originally raised to secure and defend airfields, possible assignments to Tripoli or Gabès were considered before the decision was made to move the battalion to Sfax in early January 1943.[22]

The assessment of the performance of the *1º btg. para. R.A.* during its first combat from the various sources is decidedly mixed. The Italians generally saw the battalion as aggressive and well trained, quite capable of accomplishing all of its assigned tasks. An interview with a German veteran of the battles stated that the battalion was poorly-armed, ill-equipped, and weakly trained.[23] Given the well documented issue of Germans downplaying the abilities of their allies, the truth likely resides somewhere in-between. The battalion's equipment and training was unsuitable for the type of combat it was engaged in during November 1942, lacking light and heavy machine guns and the mortars found in the R.E. parachute battalions. When compared to its German counterparts, the battalion could easily be seen as poorly armed and the lack of steel helmets possibly added to that impression. The battalion had taken significant losses and would not return to the front lines until the desperate days of April 1943.

The mission to protect the airfields was a high priority for *Supercomando*. The airfields were needed to both quickly move units and supplies into Tunisia and to deny

21 Giorleo *Palestra Azzurra*, p.54; Longo, *I «reparti speciali»*, p.164; Sogno, *XXX Corpo*, carte 1; Arena, *La Regia Aeronautica*, vol.3, p.331.

22 Sogno, *XXX Corpo*,, p.33 and carte 2; Longo, *I «reparti speciali»*, p.166; Dalmas, *Attività bellico svolta dal battaglione paracadutisti*, p.3.

23 Vilhermosa, *Hitler's Paratrooper*, p.134. The interviewee was Matthias Scheurer, a member of Witzig's battalion.

A unit of the *btg. Riattatori «Loreto»* in Tunisia. The picture was likely taken near the airfield at Enfidaville. (AUSSMA)

their use to the Allies. The latter was a concern as the Americans and British both possessed significant airborne capability. *Supercomando* decided in December 1942 to transfer the *Battaglione riattatori «Loreto»* to Tunisia to reinforce the security at several airfields. Only the *1ª* and *2ª compagnie* were eventually transferred. It was planned that once an assessment of the airfields in Tunisia was completed, the *3ª* and *4ª compagnie* would be sent to execute any necessary repair work. By the time the assessments were completed, transport priorities and Allied interdiction efforts delayed sending the *3ª* and *4ª compagnie* and the move was finally cancelled. Those two companies would remain at Marsala, Sicily performing airfield security and repairs from Allied bombing missions. Arriving in January 1943, the *1ª cp.* was stationed at the airfield near Enfidaville while the *2ª cp.* was stationed at La Marsa, with detachments at the Gammarth and Biserta airfields.[24]

Retreat of the A.C.I.T. (Map 12.3)

With the destruction of the *«Folgore»* on 6 November, no organized Italian parachute units remained in Egypt and Libya. The much reduced A.C.I.T. had established a defensive position around Fuka, but Rommel knew the army could not remain there. He lacked an armoured force strong enough to counter any enemy movement using the open desert flank to the south with the intent to get between his army and the

24 Giorleo, *Palestra Azzurra*, p.55; Longo, *I «reparti speciali»*, p.167; Arena, *La Regia Aeronautica*, vol. 3, p.336.

safety of Libya. In fact, this problem would prevent holding any position short of El Agheila and require abandoning all of Cirenaica.

From Fuka the army retreated to Marsa Matruh and then onto the border of Libya, establishing a defensive cordon on 10 November. Fortunately the British 8th Army was also having its share of problems and the A.C.I.T. was able to prevent any turning movement that endangered the army. The retreat continued on 11 November to the old positions at Gazala. Early in the morning of 14 November the A.C.I.T. was again on the move, abandoning Bengasi and arriving at El Agheila by 19 November. Here the A.C.I.T. linked up with the forces dispatched from Tripoli to hold Marsa el Brega. The *«Giovani Fascisti»* had already joined the *«La Spezia»* at that location a few days prior to the arrival of the army.

The *80ª d. f. «La Spezia»* had moved advanced elements to El Agheila in October, but then established a defensive position further west near Marsa el Brega. Like the *«Folgore»*, the *«La Spezia»* required reinforcement to better enable it to fight in Africa. The air landing division was initially better off than the parachute division when it first arrived in Africa due to the wide-spread authorization of two and three-wheeled motorcycles. These motorcycles were issued to move heavy weapons and supplies, giving the division a degree of mobility that the *«Folgore»* lacked. A fourth artillery gruppo, the *CCCXLIII* was assigned to the *80º rgt. art.* equipped with 100/17 howitzers. The division had also been reinforced with the *III btg. «Tobruk»* from the *reggimento «San Marco»*, the *VI btg. CC.NN.*, the *CCCXXXI gruppo art.* with 75/27 guns, and three batteries of 75/46 c.a. There was an attempt by *Superlibia* to motorize the division but the limited number of vehicles to support all the needs of the A.C.I.T. never existed in the A.S.[25]

As the remainder of the A.C.I.T. arrived and strengthened the position, Rommel knew that the position could not hold against a determined attack. Only 8,000 anti-tank mines had been laid with a promise of 11,000 more anti-tank mines and 3,000 anti-personnel mines from Tripoli. These numbers were insignificant compared to the nearly one million mines used at Alamein. Barbed wire and other barrier material was non-existent and fuel was still too limited to allow major maneuvering. The A.C.I.T. lacked heavy artillery and the ammunition stocks needed to support an active defense. The issue was whether the army could be reinforced with enough men and material to withstand such an attack before the British could launch that attack.[26]

In Rommel's mind, the answer to that question was no. After various high-level meetings and a trip to Germany, the A.C.I.T. began its retreat on the evening of 6 December. The army would retreat to Bureat while the question of whether to defend

25 AUSSME, *Oggetto: Derrata, materiali e munizioni per la div. "La Spezia"*, 7 ottobre 1942, M7, racc. 430 cart. 11; Anon, *Terza offensiva Britannica in Africa settentrionale La battaglia di El Alamein e il ripiegamento in Tunisia (6 settembre 1942–4 febbraio 1943)* (Rome: USSME, 1961), pp.463, 466. For example, the *XXXIX btg. esplorante* was never able to replace issue bicycles with motor vehicles.

26 Montanari, *Le operazioni*, vol IV, pp.59–61 and fn. 76.

A battery of 65/17 guns from the *80º reggimento artiglieria «La Spezia»* retreating to Mareth along the via Balbia. The *mototricicli* (tricycle motorcycle) was the main prime mover for the division. (AUSSME)

A 65/17 gun of the *«La Spezia»* takes up a temporary position during the retreat. (AUSSME)

Tripoli was decided. On 26 November it was recognized that holding Tripoli was not an achievable endstate for the A.C.I.T.; the final act of defending Libya would be the retreat into Tunisia. The Italian and German infantry began retreating from the Bureat position the night of 3 January 1943 to occupy another position at Homs. However the 8th Army offensive which began on 15 January made any long-term delay at Homs and Tripoli unlikely. The A.C.I.T. retreat continued and the lead elements of the 8th Army entered Tripoli on 23 January. On 31 January the last of the Italo-German forces entered Tunisia and *Superlibia* was deactivated.

Reborn «Folgore»

During the retreat, the army had been reorganizing survivors and detachments from the units destroyed during the fighting at Alamein. Those *paracadutisti* that had been working in the rear of the army, recovering in the hospitals, or temporarily assigned to other units had been collected at the *Centro Istruzione di Fanteria* at Breviglieri southeast of Tripoli. Six hundred men had been assembled and on 7 December the *285º battaglione paracadutisti «Folgore»* was authorized. After a week of training, the battalion moved to Bureat and was assigned to the *66º reggimento motorizzata «Trieste»*.[27]

While calling itself a *battaglione paracadutisti*, the unit was actually rebuilt as a *battaglione fanteria tipo A.S. 42*. Each company would be equipped with 47/32 c.c., 20 mm c.a., 20 mm Solothurn, and Breda heavy machine-guns. Quite a different suite of armament than the *paracadutisti* normally had been issued. Gone was any consideration of being employed as a parachute unit. There were enough *folgorini* to form five rifle companies in the battalion (*compagnia comando di battaglione, 107ª, 108ª, 109ª, 110ª*, and *111ª*).[28]

Personnel available to rebuild units destroyed in October were scarce, so men were moved to other units to even out the strength of battalions within various regiments. In the case of the *285º*, one company (the *108ª*) was assigned to the *IV battaglione controcarro Granatieri di Sardegna* that was also being rebuilt. The grenadiers were originally an anti-tank battalion assigned to the *102º d. f. «Trento»* during the Battle of Alamein. Like the *folgorini*, the surviving *granatieri* were now organized as an infantry battalion. As the *tipo A.S. 42* battalion only had four rifle companies, the *285º btg.* was able to send the *108ª cp.* to the *Granatieri* to complete that battalion. The *folgorini* assigned to the *Granatieri* kept their individual identification and were

27 Arena, *FOLGORE,* p.247.
28 Arena, *FOLGORE,* p.248; Nino Arena, *I PARACADUTISTI Cinquant'anni di storia, cronaca e immagini del paracadutisti italiano* (Modena: Società Tipografica Editrice Modenese Mucchi, 1972), p.140. Arena is inconsistent in listing the company numbers. He later lists the 112º cp.

referred to as the *compagnia «Folgore»* within the battalion. The company was transferred to the *Granatieri* on 15 December.[29]

The survivors of the *185º sezione CC.RR.* were initially reorganized as the *315º sezione CC.RR.* The commanding general of the *Carabinieri Reali*, *generale* Remo Gamballi requested on 2 December that the remaining *carabinieri paracadutisti* be returned to Italy. This request was denied by *Superlibia* as all the other surviving *paracadutisti* were being retained in Africa. *Superlibia* reasoning was that it did not wish to create a double standard with regard to the future employment of the *folgorini*.[30]

The two new battalions were formally assigned to the *101º d.f. «Trieste»* as the *II/66º reggimento fanteria «Granatieri»* and the *III/66º reggimento fanteria «Folgore»* on 29 November. The carabinieri were incorporated into the *22º sezione carabinieri* assigned to the *«Trieste»*, reuniting all the remaining *folgorini* within that division.[31]

During the retreat from Tripolitania, the *«Trieste»* was often used as part of the rearguard. The *III/66 «Folgore»* on 19 January 1943 found itself moving to occupy positions to protect the airfield at Castel Benito, the birthplace of the first *reparti paracadutisti*. The battalion remained until 21 January, then withdrew back to the Mareth Line in Tunisia as the British Army again attempted to encircle and trap the Italo-German Force.

Unternehmen Capri (Maps 12.4, 12.5)

The major organizational change at this time was the creation of the *1ª Armata Italiana* and 5. Panzerarmee on 5 February 1943. *Generale d'armata* Giovanni Messe, recently returned from Russia, was appointed commander of the *1ª Armata* and Generaloberst Jürgen von Armin was given the 5.Panzerarmee. Both armies would serve under *Gruppo d'Armate Africa*/Heeresgruppe Afrika commanded by Generalfeldmarschall Rommel.

There were several discussions over where best to defend Tunisia against the advancing British 8th Army in January–February 1943. Route n.1 was the main road that generally followed the coast similar to the via Balbia in Libya and was the line of advance the British must follow. The first location considered for the defense was the area around the town of Mareth. It was there that the French had built a system of fortifications and as it was further east, it provided more operational depth for retreat.

29 Anon., *Il IV battaglione controcarro autocarro Granatieri di Sardegna in Africa settentrionale (dicembre 1941 maggio 1943) «Diario di Guerra»* (Rome: Comando Brigata Granatieri di Sardegna Museo Storico, 1991), p.94; Arena, *I PARACADUTISTI*, p.140.

30 Cursi, Enrico, *Carabinieri Paracadutisti 1940–1946* (edizioni Chillemi, 2020), p.28. Arena states that the carabinieri were incorporated into the *285º*, but Cursi's newer research in the Carabinieri archives is considered more accurate.

31 Arena, *FOLGORE*, p.248; Anon., *Il IV battaglione controcarro*, p.92; Cursi, *Carabinieri Paracadutisti*, p.28.

Its disadvantages were that many of the French works had been destroyed after the armistice (work had since started in January 1943 to repair/improve the system) and it had a large, open western flank that would need to be protected. The second position was the Chott-Wadi Akarit Line sixty kilometers further to the rear of the Mareth line. Its advantage was a much shorter front to defend and the right (western) flank was anchored on difficult terrain. Its disadvantage was the lack of any prepared defenses and that it offered less operational depth for any retreat.[32]

Generale Messe strongly favored the Chott-Wadi Akarit Line. He felt that the limited mobile forces available to the *1ª Armata*, combined with the fuel shortage would make defending the long open flank of the Mareth Line difficult, if not impossible. Rommel too preferred the second, but did not strongly advocate for it. *Supercomando* had favored Mareth since December and had directed resources to improve the position, hence the decision that the *1ª Armata* would defend Mareth.

When Messe formally took command of the army on 20 February, some work had been done to improve the line. Sixty-eight kilometers of barbed wire had been installed of the 118 kilometers planned for the defense, while 18,000 of 35,000 mines had been laid. An advanced position about 4-6 km kilometers to the front of the main line had been laid-out along the Wadis Zeuss and Negheb which formed a good tactical position. Although initially planned as a security zone, Messe felt that the advance line should be held in strength to add defensive depth and positioned additional forces in it.[33]

Both *101º d. «Trieste»* and *80º d. «La Spezia»* were placed in the main line of defense. The organization of the Mareth Line placed the *XX Cd'A* on the *1ª Armata* left with the *«Giovani Fascisti»* on the coast, then the *«Trieste»*, and then the 90.Afrika-Division. On the right of the *XXI Cd'A* was the *XX Cd'A* with the *«La Spezia»* and then the *«Pistoia»* holding the right flank of the line. The 164.leicht Afrika-Division was echeloned forward from the *«Pistoia»* towards Medenine, covering the open flank. The DAK was held in reserve behind the line.

Rommel decided on 28 February to launch a spoiling attack named Unternehmen Capri (Operation Capri). The purpose of the attack was to disrupt the preparations of the 8th Army and delay any offensive plans. The objective was the town of Medenine approximately 35 kilometers southeast of Mareth along Route n.1. Originally the operation was planned as a pincer movement with an attack from along the coast and one south from the desert. Further study indicated that an attack in the north would be unable to penetrate the enemy's defense in the planned time frame, so the plan was modified to be a traditional desert hook from the south. The DAK (10., 15., and 21.Panzerdivisionen) was the main effort and would hook around the British flank to attack Medenine from the southwest.[34] The role of

32 Montanari, *Le operazioni*, vol IV, pp.347–348.
33 Montanari, *Le operazioni*, vol IV, p.348.
34 The 21. Panzer Division had been attached to the 5.Panzerarmee when it retreated into Tunisia. It and the 10.Panzer Division had been moved south after the offensive against the 1st Allied Army in central Tunisia in February to support Capri.

«Trieste», *«La Spezia»* and 90.Afrika during the offensive was limited, designed to be a holding attack to fix the British defense in-place. Each division would form a column consisting of two battalions to attack the enemy units forward of the security zone. As the attack would take place outside the range of the artillery placed in the Mareth Line, each column would be supported by two artillery groups. The assault was planned for 6 March 1943.

Unternehmen Capri was a complete failure. Forewarned by Ultra intercepts, Montgomery had prepared a defensive plan that used air attacks, artillery, and anti-tank guns to stop the *1ª Armata* attack. While the weather on 6 March prevented the Allied use of air, the artillery and anti-tank gun screens were effective. The panzer divisions were never able to breach the 8th Army's defense and all three divisions took serious losses before both Messe and Rommel decided to end the attack that same afternoon. The operation had no impact on the 8th Army's upcoming offensive against the Mareth Line.[35]

It remains unknown which two battalions formed *Colonna Spezia*. *Colonna «Trieste»* consisted of the *III/65º «Trento»* and the *III/66º «Folgore»* battalions, supported by the *IV/21º art.* (twelve 75/27 field guns). As these attacks were not meant to seriously penetrate the enemy defense, the paratroopers were able to reach their objectives and hold them until ordered to retreat that evening. The battalions only suffered light casualties.[36]

Battle of Mareth (Maps 12.6, 12.7)

Following the return to the *1ª Armata* lines, improvements to the Mareth Line continued. The 10. Panzerdivison was returned to the 5.Panzerarmee while the 21.Panzerdivison was retained by the *1ª Armata*. The *XXI* and *XXI Cd'A* occupied the same sectors, but the 164. was pulled back from its forward position and was now echeloned back to cover the flank. If Montgomery's plan was to turn the western flank, his forces would need to execute a much wider turning movement which would allow time for the *1ª Armata* to react. This wider area was covered by the *raggruppamento «Sahariano»* with the task to report and delay any such turning movement. The 15.Panzerdivison was held in reserve, while the 21.Panzerdivison was moved back to Gabès.

«Trieste» with the *paracadutisti* was positioned in front of the town of Mareth controlling Route n.1 as it entered the position. The *I/66º* was placed in three company strongpoints across the front of the security zone, with the *II/65º* in a battalion strongpoint near the rear of the security zone. The *III/66º «Folgore»* occupied a strongpoint in the middle of the *«Trieste»* position astride the road itself.

35 Montanari, *Le operazioni*, vol IV, p.360.
36 Anon, *Il IV battaglione controcarro*, p.108; Arena, *FOLGORE*, p.248

Members of the *«La Spezia»* in the Mareth Line defensive position. This type of trench construction was very difficult to see from a distance. (AUSME)

The previous position from a different angle. One can see how the position for a Breda 37 machine-gun is constructed to provide 360° firing. (AUSSME)

The *«La Spezia»* occupied a section of the defense near the southern end of the French fortifications. The *XXXIX btg. esplorante* held the security zone, reinforced with two platoons each from the *I/125° and I/126° reggimenti*. The two regiments were on-line in the main line of resistance, each with two battalions forward and one battalion to the rear. The *126°* was in the northern part of the divisional sector with the *III btg. Tobruk* in support. The *125°* was in the southern part of the sector with the *VI btg. CC.NN.* in support.[37]

Montgomery did indeed plan to turn the *1ª Armata* western flank in a wide arc to avoid detection. The New Zealand Corps would begin a move around the inland flank of the Mareth Line on 11 March. Once the corps was in position, it would strike at the Tebaga Gap well to the rear of the Mareth Line as the 30th Corps (Operation Pugilist) attacked the northern part of the line near the coast. This coordinated assault would commence at 2145 hours on 20 March. The 30th Corps was the main effort while the N.Z. Corps was supporting.[38]

All appeared well until 19 March when the N.Z. Corps was spotted by Italian reconnaissance. The *1ª Armata* immediately ordered the 164.Afrika-Division to move into that sector and reinforce the *ragg. «Sahariana»* defending the Tebaga Gap. Informed that it had been detected, the N.Z. Corps sped up its movement to arrive twelve hours earlier than planned. The corps initially had some success but then hesitated, allowing the 164.leicht to establish a strong defensive position.[39]

The 30th Corps attack created a bridgehead in the *«Giovani Fascisti»* position, but local counterattacks, followed by attacks by the 15. Panzerdivision stabilized the position. Fighting continued through 22 March without change. The N.Z. Corps was pressing at the Tebaga Gap and was making some headway against the dangerously weak flank, but Messe had few reinforcements available. It was clear to him that the flank could not hold, and any reinforcements would need to be drawn from the Mareth position. Given the seriousness of any Allied success if they broke through the Tebaga Gap and reached El Hamma, Messe decided on 23 March to take the *125° rgt.* with the *I* and *II btg.* out of the Mareth Line and moved it back as a reserve. The *III/125° rgt.* would remain in the division's sector while the *VI btg. CC.NN.* was moved forward into the positions being vacated.[40]

There was no significant change in the situation on 23 March but lacking decisive success, Montgomery changed his plan by reinforcing the N.Z. Corps and making it the main effort. Now called Operation Supercharge II, Montgomery committed the 1st Armoured Division to the flanking movement under the N.Z. Corps. Seeing the signs of a change in the British offense on 24 March, Messe discussed the situation with von Armin. Not believing that the flank could be held for more than 24 hours, both generals agreed to initiate a withdrawal to the Chott-Wadi Akarit Line. At the

37 Messe, Giovanni, *La I° armata italiana in Tunisia* (Rome: USSME, 1950), tavola n. 4.
38 I.S.O. Playfair, *The Mediterranean and Middle East* (London: HMSO, 1966) vol IV, p.320.
39 Montanari, *Le operazioni*, vol IV, p.387; Playfair, *The Mediterranean and Middle East*, vol 4, p.343.
40 Montanari, *Le operazioni*, vol IV, pp.37–398;

same time those elements of the *125° rgt* that had been pulled from the Mareth Line as a reserve were now committed to the threatened flank.

The *1ª Armata* began the initial moves on the evening of 25 March. Half of the *«Trieste»* and 90.Afrika withdrew to the heights behind the Mareth Line to cover the later movement of other units. Simultaneously two-thirds of the *«La Spezia»* that remained on the Mareth Line moved back to Gabès. These moves were executed just in time and created some tactical depth in the *1ª Armata* position.

Supercharge II opened at 1600 hours on 26 March with heavy air attacks by the Allied air forces. Shortly afterwards the assault began with tanks and infantry and met with quick success. Several German units were destroyed or bypassed and the N.Z. Corps finally achieved the desired breakthrough. Some command indecision on the part of the British and quick actions by the remaining units of the 15. and 21.Panzerdivisionen, joined by the *gruppo «Novara»*, the *350° reggimento fanteria A.S.*, and the two battalions of the *125° rgt.* created enough time for the bulk of the army to retreat. Trucks were sent to the non-motorized units to support their withdrawal, but only the *350° rgt.f.* from the *ragg. Sahariana* was able to retreat. Without trucks and stating that he had not received orders to withdraw, the commander of the *125° rgt.* opted to stay in place and defend. The defense did not last long and the regiment surrendered on 28 March.[41]

During the fighting, neither the *«Trieste»* or the *«La Spezia»* were heavily engaged and losses were light. The loss of the majority of the *125° rgt.* was during the retreat and caused by the lack of vehicles, a common fate that this regiment now shared with the other airborne units sent to North Africa.

Special Operations[42] (Map 12.8)

During the first months of 1943, the *10° reggimento arditi* began to be employed in North Africa in support of the *1ª Armata*. The *103ª cp.* was flown to Tunisia in January while its vehicles were transported by sea. By the time the unit was ready for employment, the fighting had moved from the open desert areas of Libya to the broken and confined terrain of Tunisia. This theater was unsuitable for the type of operations the *103ª cp.* had prepared for and the unit was broken up into three patrols and used for reconnaissance and security missions.[43]

41 Montanari, *Le operazioni*, vol IV, pp.409; Messe, *La I° armata italiana*, pp.146–147, 154.

42 The information on the operations of the RE and RA arditi is gleaned from Crociani and Battistelli, *Italian Army Elite Units*, pp.48–50; Longo, *I «reparti speciali»*, pp.116–149; Arena, *FOLGORE,* pp.308–354; Arena, *I PARACADUTISTI,* pp.143–149; Giorleo, *Palestra Azzurra; Piero* Crociani and Pier Battistelli, *Italian Navy & Air Force Elite Units & Special Forces 1940–45* (Oxford, Osprey, 2013), pp.40–41; Arena, Nino, *Aquile senza Ali: I paracadutisti italiani nella seconda guerra mondiale* (Milan: Mursia 1970), pp.177–188.

43 Piero Crociani and Pier Battistelli, *Italian Army Elite Units & Special Forces 1940–43* (Oxford: Osprey, 2011) p.49.

A planned attack using two patrols from the *101ª cp.* and two from the *102º cp.* on an airfield on Cyprus in January was canceled due to the lack of aircraft to transport the patrols to their staging airfield on Rhodes. The regiment was then ordered to target the Allied lines of communications in Algeria. The first operational missions were planned against assumed strategic bridges and airfields.

The first actual mission executed by the *101ª cp.* was on 14–17 January. The *6ª pattuglia* patrol, consisting of two officers, two non-commissioned officers, and seven *arditi* under the command of *sottotenente* Leo Zoli flew from the Elmas airfield near Cagliari, Sardinia, and jumped behind the Allied lines in Algeria on the night of 14-15 January. Their objective was a railroad bridge across the Eddous River at Bouira. Attacking on the evening of 16 January, they successfully destroyed the bridge. Afterwards they were engaged by a unit of French soldiers and eventually forced to surrender on 17 January.

The next raid by the *paracadutisti arditi* of the *101ª cp.* was on 11–16 February. The *2ª pattuglia Fede* under *tenente* Nino De Totto flew from the airfield at Decimomannu on Sardinia. Their target was the railroad bridge near Beni-Mansoor in Algeria. Weather and navigational error saw the patrol dropped about thirty kilometers as the crow flies from their objective. Exiting the aircraft at an altitude of 300 meters, the men were scattered over a large area. It was not until the morning of 15 February that they arrived in sight of the bridge. They observed it during the day and waited until 2100 hours before they began their approach. The *arditi* were discovered a half hour before their time of attack at 0130 hours and a fight broke out. Some damage was done to the bridge, but all the *arditi* were either killed or captured.

The next actions were not executed until April 1943. Three patrols of the *101ª cp.* were sent out on the night of 10–11 April to attack once again the Allied lines of communication in Algeria. The 4ª *pattuglia Elettrica* under *tenente* Pietro Graff was to destroy the Duvivier bridge; the target for the *8ª pattuglia Pantano* under *capitano* Emanuale Bosco was the airfield at Biskrà; the *9ª pattuglia Inafferrabile* under *sottotenente* Arduino Varutti was to destroy the bridge at Le Kroub. All three patrols were detected shortly after landing and captured without reaching their objectives.[44]

These operations resulted in the loss of half of the *101º cp.* with little success to show for the effort. Insufficient planning and intelligence work, inadequate training for the aircrews, and poor weather all played a role in the negative results. The *10º reggimento arditi* would not execute any additional missions until the forthcoming summer.

44 Arena, *FOLGORE*, pp.318, states four patrols were launched, the fourth under *tenente* Mario Betti. None of the other sources list a fourth patrol and Longo, *I «reparti speciali»*, p.143 lists Betti as a member of the *102ª cp.*

Chott-Wadi Akarit Line (Maps 12.9, 12.10)

The *1ª Armata* was able to establish a new defense on the Chott-Wadi Akarit Line on 30 March. The new line was significantly shorter than the Mareth Line and offered good defensible terrain. The main disadvantages were that little work had been accomplished on building defensive works/strongpoints and barrier materials (mines, barbed wire, construction material for bunkers, etc.) were lacking. Even if adequate amounts of barrier material was available, there would not be enough time to make significant use of it. Montgomery was not planning to allow the *1ª Armata* time to prepare as the 8th Army was preparing its new attack within six days. Nor was the shorter line a significant improvement as the *1º Armata* now had few troops available for the defense. The army had lost the equivalent of sixteen battalions and thirty-one batteries at Mareth and was still hobbled by the meager reserves of fuel and ammunition.

The new line arrayed the *XX Cd'A* from the coastline westward barring Route n.1. The *«Giovani Fascisti»* was in the east, with the 90.Afrika on its right, then the *«Trieste»*, and finally the *«La Spezia»* on the western flank of the corps. The corps defense in the east and center was anchored mainly behind the Wadi Akarit which provided a good anti-tank obstacle. The *«Trieste»* was set on the eastern portion of the Djebel el Roumana while the *«La Spezia»* occupied the western end and then continued onto the eastern side of the Djebel Tebaga-Fatnassa. There the *«Pistoia»* of the *XXI Cd'A* was placed, with that corps (164.leicht and *ragg, Sahariana*) continuing westward along a series of djebels to the Chott el Djerid, a salt marsh that was generally impassable.

One difficulty that would plague the defense during the upcoming battle was the lack of communications between units and their headquarters. Much of the field telephone wire had been lost at El Alamein and never fully replaced. The retreat back to Tunisia saw more field telephone wire abandoned and the army remained critically short. The Mareth Line offered some relief as the existing French system built into the line could be used, but the heavy British barrages and the hasty withdrawal meant most of the wire was damaged and could not be recovered. Radios were in short supply and not always reliable. As the few supplies being shipped to Tunisia consisted mainly of ammunition and fuel, the lost communication wire was not replaced.[45]

Montgomery's plan of attack, Operation Scipio, was scheduled to begin the evening of 5 April. By necessity it was a frontal assault against the *XXI Cd'A* by the 30th Corps as neither of the enemy's flanks could be turned. The Allied air force would begin nearly round the clock attacks on the *1ª Armata* positions in the week prior to the attack. During the night of 5–6 April, the 7th Indian Bde, followed by the 5th Indian Bde of the 4th Indian Division, would execute a surprise attack against the junction of the *«La Spezia»* and *«Pistoia»* to seize the Djebel Tebaga-Fatnassa prior to

45 Montanari, *Le operazioni*, vol IV, p.453.

0800 hours on 6 April. At 0415 hours on 6 April the 201st Guard Bde would attack the *«Giovani Fascisti»*, the 154th Bde of the 51st Division would attack the *«Trieste»*, while the 152nd Bde (51st Division) and the 69th Brigade of the 50th Division would attack *«La Spezia»*. After its successful night attack, the plan had the 5th Indian Bde to simultaneously turn and attack *«La Spezia»* from the flank. Once the 30th Corps had created a breach, the 10th Corps with its divisions would pass through and force the Italo-German forces away from the coast and deny them the best route of retreat. The offensive was synchronized with an attack by the Allied 1st Army in western Tunisia to attack eastwards behind the *1ª Armata* to trap and destroy the army before it could retreat to the north.[46]

The two brigades of the 4th Indian Division began to move forward after dark on 5 April. To achieve surprise, no artillery barrage was planned to support the attack. Instead an artillery bombardment program was timed to the attack of the 50th and 51st Divisions. The 7th Indian Bde's attack first hit the *I/36º rgt.* of the *«Pistoia»*. The Italian battalion fought hard, but by midnight it had been pushed off the high ground. As the 7th Ind. Bde pressed forward, the 5th Ind. Bde passed to the right the 7th and attacked the *III/125º rgt.* of the *«La Spezia»* on the Djebel Tebaga-Fatnassa. The battalion completely collapsed creating a hole in the Italo-German line into which the entire 4th Indian Division pushed through.

The attacks of the two British Divisions east of the 4th Indian, supported by the heavy artillery bombardment hit both the *«Trieste»* and *«La Spezia»*. The 154th Bde's attack was focused on the positions held by the *II/65º rgt.* of the *«Trieste»*. The battalion resisted for a few hours but was finally overcome and the brigade was able to advance onto its objective. The 152nd Bde to its left of the 154th was able to smash through the *I* and *II/126º* battalions in the center and open lanes for the tanks to pass through. The intervention of the *III/126º* managed to stop further penetration, but the high ground remained in Scottish hands.

The 69th Brigade of the 50th Division was west of the 152nd Bde and attacked the *«Tobruk»* and the *XXXIX bersaglieri* battalions. These battalions held until early morning, but were finally overwhelmed and destroyed. Due to the complete breakdown of communications in the *«La Spezia»* sector, no word of the loss of these two battalions reached army headquarters during the morning.

Messe began to receive reports of the attack at 0300 hours on 6 April. He learned of the attack on the *I/36º* from the headquarters of the *«Pistoia»* and was told it was being contained. There was no word from the *«La Spezia»* and the actions of the *III/125º*. Messe's assessment of the current situation was that the *«Trieste»* had some penetrations and that a gap was opening between the *«Pistoia»* and the *«La Spezia»*. Based on threat information, the reserves of the *1ª Armata* were directed to these locations. Counterattacks by *I/66º* and the *III/66º «Folgore»* had at first blunted, then stopped the 154th from expanding the penetration to the west. Follow-on counterattacks were

46 Playfair, *The Mediterranean and Middle East*, vol. 4, pp.365–367.

able to push the brigade off the high ground it had captured and forced the 154th to reorganize. There was no activity in-front of the other divisions of the *XX Cd'A*, so Messe waited for more reports to clarify the situation.

Actions and counterattacks to restore the left flank of the *«Pistoia»* were being executed. Attacks by the *III/36° rgt.* and the 361.Panzergrenadier were launched but only achieved partial success against the Indians. Messe decided he needed to pull the 164.leichte, currently positioned further to the west, out of the defensive line to launch a counterattack on the morning of 7 April. While he felt the situation was stabilizing, he remained unaware of the collapse of the center of the *«La Spezia»* position. The British artillery barrage that started early in the morning had destroyed the telephone and radio network, preventing any complete reports from units within that sector. Most of the information on the status of the division was being provided by the flank units who were unable to discern the conditions in the center of the division's sector.

It was not until 1600 hours that the true situation became known to Messe. Not only did he learn that the *«Tobruk»* and the *XXXIX bersaglieri* battalions had been destroyed, but that the *III/126°* which had earlier been containing the breakthrough had been overwhelmed. Both the 21.Panzerdivision and the I/382.Panzergrenadier were committed against the gap, but the Allied air force and the 8th Army artillery stopped the attack before it could achieve any results. The Allied counter attacks that had been executed throughout the day had worn down the Italian and German units. By 2000 hours Messe had decided to retreat to the next defensible line, which was at Enfidaville, two-hundred and fifty kilometers to the north.

Moving in stages, the battered infantry units moved north as quickly as possible given the limited number of transport vehicles. The mobile units, with the few remaining tanks and motorized infantry companies, fought a series of delaying actions to slow the 8th Army's pursuit. An attempt by the British 9th Corps from the 18th Army Group reserve to cut the line of retreat at Kairouan was stopped at Fondouk, allowing the *1ª Armata* to reach the new position at Enfidaville.

The losses to the airborne troops had been heavy. The *«La Spezia»* had been destroyed. Only one and one-half companies of infantry remained in the division from the sixteen companies present at 0400 hours that morning. Most of the artillery had either been overrun by the British and Indian troops or abandoned during the retreat. The *III/66° «Folgore»* lost two companies during their attacks to seal the enemy penetrations. Most of the heavy equipment in the infantry battalions was lost or abandoned. The surviving infantry units could not be used in combat until they had been rebuilt and re-equipped.[47]

Despite their best efforts and planning the Allied 1st Army had failed to cut the *1ª Armata* retreat and by 13 April all its remaining units of the *1ª Armata* were safely on the Enfidaville Line. The Allied 1st and 8th Armies were finally able to link together

47 Montanari, *Le operazioni*, vol IV, p.495; Messe, *La I° armata italiana*, p.234.

on 11 April and the *1ª Armata* and the 5.Panzerarmee were now confined to the northeast corner of Tunisia. It was there that the survivors of the «*Folgore*» and «*La Spezia*» would make their final stand.

Enfidaville (Map 12.11)

Once back into the new defensive line, the main effort was to rebuild and re-equip units. The wounded were returned to units once they had recovered and the stragglers gathered up as they reached the Enfidaville position. The remaining *paracadutisti* of the *cp.* «*Folgore*» that were with the *II/66° granatieri* was reassigned to the *III/66°* «*Folgore*» to bring that battalion back to a strength of two companies.[48] The surviving infantry of the «*La Spezia*» were consolidated into the *III/125°* and the *III/126° battaglioni*. The *LXXXIV btg. di complemento* (replacement battalion) was renamed the *I/126°* and the *CCCL btg. Guardia alla Frontiera* (Frontier Guards) was renamed the *II/126°*. The *CVI bis btg. controcarro* was formed but was still awaiting its anti-tank guns.[49]

It had been decided back in March to reform the *reggimento R.A.* «*Duca d'Aosta*» as a ground combat unit for use by the *1ª Armata*. The *1° btg. para. RA.* and the «*Loreto*» were being used as anti-parachutist units and airfield security. The *1ª* and *2ª* companies of the *1° btg. para. R.A.* were formed using the remaining personnel of the battalion. A *3ª cp.* mitraglieri was formed from disbanded ground crew and airfield support personnel and a fourth company was planned but never organized. The *Battaglione riattatori* «*Loreto*» was similar, with the two companies that had been transferred from Sicily remaining as the *1ª* and *2ª cp.*, and the *3ª* and *4ª compagnie mitraglieri* formed using excess R.A. personnel as done with the *1° btg. para. R.A.* Officers and non-commissioned officers from disbanded *bersaglieri* units were assigned to provide experienced leadership for the two battalions. The intent was that the regiment was to be given time to be trained as infantrymen, but the rapid pace of the Allied operations precluded this luxury. The *reggimento* «*Duca d'Aosta*» was put into the line on 11 April.[50]

The Enfidaville position marked the transition of the open rolling plain in the central part of Tunisia to the broken, craggy, and steep systems of hills and djebels in the north. Movement was channelized by the complex terrain and fields of fire and observation was limited. The main line of resistance was along this transition from flat to broken terrain that restricted movement and offered excellent defensive positions. Forward of this line were two points of terrain that jutted south as pillars,

48 Anon, *Il IV battaglione controcarro*, p.111.
49 Montanari, *Le operazioni*, vol IV, p.500; Messe, *La I° armata italiana*, pp.235–236, 437.
50 Montanari, *Le operazioni*, vol IV, p.496; Messe, *La I° armata italiana*, p.236; Giorleo, *Palestra Azzurra*, p.55.

A picture of Takrouna taken during the battle. (AUSSME)

breaking the line into three sectors. Takrouna to the east was a precipitous rocky outcrop approximately one-hundred and sixty meters in height. The Djebel Garci to the west was a large, complex terrain feature generally over three-hundred meters in height. These two points dominate any approach to the main line of resistance and would flank any Allied advance against the line.

Generale Messe had organized the defensive of the Enfidaville Line by intermixing the Italian and German units and creating strongpoints on the two key positions of Takrouna and Djebel Graci. The eastern section of the line was held by the *XX Cd'A*. It had the 90.Afrika in the east anchored on the coast. Next on its right was the *136ª d. «Giovanni Fascisti»*, then the *101ª d. «Trieste»*. The *XXI Cd'A* was holding the western end of the line. The *16ª d. f. «Pistoia»* was next to the *«Trieste»*, then was the 164.leicht, and finally the *80ª d. «La Spezia»*. The DAK (part of the 5.Panzerarmee) was on the right (west) of the *«La Spezia»*. The 15.Panzerdivision was in reserve with four operational tanks and twenty-one more under repair, and a single panzer grenadier battalion. The *«Duca d'Aosta»* and the *5º reggimento bersaglieri* were in reserve as well, but neither were fully ready for combat.[51]

«Trieste» was responsible for the strongpoint on Takrouna. The task was given to the *I/66º rgt.*, reinforced by a platoon from the German III/47.Grenadiere Regiment and a *sezione* (two pieces) of 65/17 guns. *«Pistoia»* was responsible for the Djebel Garci and it

51 Montanari, *Le operazioni*, vol IV, pp.502–503; Messe, *La Iº armata italiana*, p.246.

was held by the *gruppo mitraglieri «Novara»*, the *CCCXL btg. mitraglieri*, and a platoon from the *raggruppamento esplorante corazzato (RECO) «Lodi»*.[52]

The Allied plan for what is now called the 1st Battle of Enfidaville was a coordinated attack by both the 1st and 8th Armies. The 8th Army would attack on 20 April with three divisions across the front of the *1ª Armata*. The 1st Army would attack on 22 April, while the US II Corps would attack on 23 April against the 5.Panzerarmee.

The 8th Army plan was to use the 50th Division to hold in front of the eastern and central sections of the *XX Cd'A* positions. The 2nd N.Z. Division was to attack and seize Takrouna while the 4th Indian Division would attack the Djebel Garci. Once these two forward positions were captured, the 8th Army would continue to penetrate into the *1ª Armata* defense.

Operation Oration began with the 5th Indian Brigade moving forward at 2130 hours on 19 April to get into position for their assault. The artillery barrage started at 2300 hours against both Takrouna and Djebel Garci. The Italian patrols had identified the enemy brigades moving forward, but the extreme shortage of ammunition kept the gun silenced until the enemy began their attacks. The fighting was hard, but the Indians slowly gained ground. By dawn on 20 April the 5th Ind. Bde firmly held part of the Djebel Garci but had not seized all of it. They had beaten back several Italian counterattacks but lacked the strength to go further.

The 5th and 6th N.Z. brigades attacked at 2300 hours on 19 April. Both brigades seized their initial objectives and were able to isolate Takrouna from the remainder of the *1ª Armata* positions, but the 5th Brigade failed to capture the rocky outcrop. Both sides took losses and the fighting appeared to be a stalemate. At daybreak, a small party of Maori's from the 28th Battalion, reinforced by a few other New Zealanders from different units, managed to climb the outcrop and secure the highest point. The *I/66º* commander, *capitano* Politi, had defended the outcrop from various locations around the ridge and garrisoned the town, but few troops were placed on the summit. From this position, the Maoris' could fire down onto the defending units of the *«Trieste»*.

Generale di brigata Francesco La Ferla, commander of the *«Trieste»*, quickly understood the seriousness of the situation. He decided to commit his reserve, the *II/66º «Granatieri»* (consisting of one company) and the *III/66º «Folgore»* (consisting of two companies) to reinforce the *I/66º btg*. The three companies launched their counterattack in the afternoon of 20 April and by 2100 hours had cleared the summit, but the Maoris still held positions on the southern ridge that they had first scaled. The situation had settled into a stalemate, but the New Zealanders had fully surrounded Takrouna and cut the *folgorini* off from any support. At daybreak on 21 April, the 5th N.Z. Bde began an attack to finally clear Takrouna of all its Italian defenders. The British artillery and mortars supported the attacks and the assaults broke down into many close combat/hand to hand situations. The fighting lasted most of the day,

52 Montanari, *Le operazioni*, vol IV, pp.504, 509; Messe, *La Iº armata italiana*, pp.245–246.

but by the afternoon the *folgorini* were taking too many casualties and running out of ammunition. By 1800 hrs the fighting was over with the surviving *folgorini* captured.[53]

The combat at Takrouna had destroyed the *III/66º «Folgore»*. Of the approximately 170 *paracadutisti* available on the morning of 20 April, only 20 managed to rejoin the *1ª Armata* after the fighting had ended. Only the *paracadutisti* of the *reggimento «Duca d'Aosta»* remained to fight in Tunisia as a complete unit.[54] The New Zealand casualties were heavy as well, with 408 men killed or wounded in the 5th N.Z. Brigade.[55]

Although Takrouna had fallen, the remainder of the 8th Army offensive had stalled. The New Zealanders could not advance any further and the 4th Indian Division failed to gain full control of the Djebel Garci. The 90.Afrika and the «*Giovani Fascisti*» had not been seriously challenged in the east and the 7th Armoured Division attack was never intended to press the 164.leicht in the west.

The End in Tunisia (Map 12.12)

Following the failure of Operation Oration, the Allies decided that the best route to Tunis and Biserte was from the west and southwest where the 1st Army was operating. The 8th Army now would only have a supporting role in the final destruction of Heeresgruppe Afrika. Several of its best formations, including the 2nd New Zealand and 4th Indian Divisions, were transferred to the 1st Army to support the main effort.

Operation Vulcan, the hopeful final offensive, was initiated on 22 April. The 1st Army executed a series of attacks along the western flank of the Tunisia bridgehead which targeted various parts of the Axis defense and stretched thin the available Italo-German resources. The Allied advantage was simply too great and the 5.Panzerarmee was unable to hold. The American 9th Infantry Division entered Biserta on 7 May and the American 1st Infantry Division entered Tunis on 8 May. Between 8-9 May, the northern front of the Tunisian bridgehead collapsed and the 5. Panzerarmee surrendered on 9 May.

Up until 9 May the *1ª Armata* defending the southern portion of the line had not been seriously threatened by the British 8th Army and continued to hold their current positions. Messe had planned for an orderly retreat into the Cape Bon Peninsula and had issued the necessary orders. With the surrender of the 5.Panzerarmee, the northern part of the Axis defense had evaporated. The question now was whether the German units under the *1ª Armata* would continue to respond to Messe's orders or surrender to the Allies.

53 Montanari, *Le operazioni*, vol IV, pp.509–510; Arena, *FOLGORE,* pp.262–272; Paolo Morisi, *The Italian Folgore Parachute Division* (Solihull: Helion & Company, 2016), pp.171–182.

54 Arena, *FOLGORE,* pp.253; Morsi, *Folgore*, p.182.

55 W.G. Stevens, *Bardia to Enfidaville* (Wellington: Historical Publications Branch, 1962), p.339.

The *1ª Armata* established a line across the base of the Cape Bon Peninsula. Initially the DAK continued to fight and attempted to hold the western and northern face of the defense.[56] However the lack of fuel impacted the retreat and the remaining combat power was inadequate for a successful defense of the peninsula. On 10 May the British 5th Corps broke through along the northern coast of the peninsula and drove across the rear of the army. Reaching the southern coast, the move preempted any possible retreat deeper in the peninsula by the *1ª Armata*. Holding the Enfidaville line in the south, Messe attempted to create a new line of defense to the north, forming a pocket against the Mediterranean Sea. He organized the *raggruppamento «Meggio»* composed of the *rgt. R.A. «Duca d'Aosta»*, the *II/35º rgt. f.*, and the III/361.Panzergrenadier on 10 May. This *raggruppamento*, along with the remains of the *reggimento corazzato «Lodi»* created a new defense line to form the northern face of the pocket. *«La Spezia»* pivoted its front so it now faced west, completing the third side of the pocket.[57]

This line held until 12 May. On that day the morale of the remaining Germans troops collapsed and the German commanders began surrendering their units to the Allies. The men of *«La Spezia»* watched in surprise as the officers and soldiers of the 47.Panzergrenadier marched in formation into the British lines to surrender. Heeresgruppe Afrika also surrendered in the afternoon of that day. The Italian units continued to obey orders and resist, but Messe understood there was nothing left to be done. He sent a message to the Allies that he was willing to surrender his army under honorable conditions. The British responded that it must be unconditional, which Messe rejected. A message from Mussolini that evening gave Messe permission for surrender and promoted him to *Maresciallo d'Italia*. A further message received from the 8th Army that evening was an offer to negotiate terms, to which Messe accepted. On 13 May the *1ª Armata* formally surrendered.[58]

The end of the campaign in Africa settentrionale also marked the end of any major combat operations by the *reparti paracadutisti*. By May 1942, Italy had created an airborne capability that was only matched by Germany: a parachute division and an air landing division fully trained and equipped. By May 1943 this force had been completely destroyed without executing a single mission using its unique capabilities. During this same period the first attempts to implement the small-scale commando doctrine which had originally spawned the *reparti paracadutisti* had also resulted in failure. Used against objectives that had little operational value, the five patrols committed during the Tunisian campaign were too few to achieve any operational effect.

The events in Tunisia and Russia in late 1942 and early 1943 firmly placed Italy and Germany on the strategic defense. With this shift, the ability to employ airborne

56 DAK was under the command of Heeresgruppe Afrika and not the 5. Panzerarmee.
57 Montanari, *Le operazioni*, vol IV, pp.547–548;
58 The nature of the surrender is unclear and disputed. See Montanari, *Le operazioni*, vol IV, pp.548–550; Playfair, *The Mediterranean and Middle East*, vol. IV, pp.458–459.

forces for any great operational effect was also gone. Without an offensive drive to link-up with any deep parachute operation, any airborne units committed to such an operation would be isolated and invariably be lost. With the «*Nembo*» completing its training and the prospect of forming another parachute division in the offing, what role could airborne forces play in the defense of Italy that could not be better performed by conventional infantry units?

13

Sicily & Calabria 1943

When the *1ª divisione paracadutisti* was deployed to Africa in July 1942, the *1º reggimento paracadutisti* remained in Italy. It had retained the *III btg. para.*, a fully trained battalion while accepting the untrained *XI btg. para.* from the *3º rgt.* that was exchanged for its *II* and *IV btg.* This left the now renamed *185º rgt.* with only two battalions. Along with the *185º*, the *23ª compagnia* of the *VIII btg. guastatori*, and the *185º compagnia motociclisti* also remained in Italy. These units would comprise the cadre for a second parachute division.[1]

It is unclear when the actual decision was made to form a second *divisione paracadutisti*. Di Giovanni has offered that the division was part of Mussolini's grand plan to expand and strengthen the army that was formulated in the spring of 1941.[2] This plan led to the creation of more divisions than Italy could afford to properly train and equip. Many of the divisions in Italy raised during 1941-42 lacked much of their authorized equipment and were mainly used as replacement resources for maintaining divisions in the active theaters of combat. Discussions had started in the spring of 1942 on forming a second parachute division but focused more on the how rather than the why. Was the new division merely a sop to Mussolini's megalomania and lacked any real strategic function?

Nor are there any real discussions of the operational role for a new parachute division in 1942. Given the reclassification of the «*Folgore*» as an infantry division and its transfer to North Africa, was the new division only meant to be a replacement and Italy would continue to maintain only one airborne division? Or if one remembers Cavallero's statement on 22 July 1942 that the units of the «*Folgore*» should be recovered as soon as possible, was there an intent to have two parachute divisions available to *Supercomando*? Were two divisions part of an idea to invade Malta in 1943 using

1 AUSSME, Stato Maggiore Esercito memorandum,10 febbraio 1949, Relazione ten. col. Giovanni Verando, *La costituzione della Divisione Paracadutisti "Folgore"*, 1160/C/11/2.

2 Marco Di Giovanni, *I paracadutisti italiani Volontari, miti e memoria della seconda guerra mondiale* (Gorizia: Editrice Goriziana, 1991), pp.191–192.

only Italian resources? All this is speculation as discussions addressing the strategic requirements, what capabilities were needed to satisfy those requirements, and the actual resources available did not happen in Fascist Italy.

The formal proposal for a new division began on 24 July when Cavallero held a meeting with the chief of the S.M.R.E. Operations Section, *generale di divisione* Gandin on 24 July to discuss forming the first units of a second division.[3] The delay in transporting the *1° rgt. para.* to Africa to join the remainder of the division presented an opportunity to create a cadre for the new unit. The mobilization of the *XII btg. paracadutisti* had been authorized on 14 July and would be the first battalion of a new regiment.[4] The *XIII btg. paracadutisti* was mobilized on 21 August and the new regiment, the *184° reggimento fanteria*, was authorized on 24 August.[5]

The *comando 184ª divisione fanteria «Nembo»* was formally mobilized on 1 November 1942.[6] A memorandum dated on 18 November completed the mobilization of the unit as a *divisione binaria*. The division would consist of the existing *185° rgt. ftr.* and the newly authorized *184° rgt. ftr*, with the *XIV btg.* mobilized on 16 September to complete the latter regiment. The *184° rgt. artiglieria* with two gruppi of 47/32 c.c. was established at the same time, along with other divisional level assets. A new *X btg.* was mobilized on 14 November to complete the *185° rgt.* with three battalions. *Generale di brigata* Ercole Ronco was appointed as the commander of the new division.[7]

The reasoning behind the decision to rebuild the *X btg.* would require further research in the Italian Army archives. The R.E. created new units as it expanded the specialty and none of the other parachute battalions lost in A.S. were replaced. Within that fact might offer a possible reason for the decision. Unlike the other battalions, the *X btg.* was not destroyed but disbanded on orders from the division. Rebuilding the *X btg.* was likely seen as reactivating an inactive unit rather than replacing a lost unit and remained the sole example.

3 Antonello Biagini and Fernando Frattolillo (eds) *Diario Storico,* vol VII, book 1, p.717; Di Giovanni, *I paracadutisti,* p.192.

4 AUSSME, Stato Maggiore R.E. memorandum 11 settembre 1942, *Oggetto: Costituzione e mobilitazione di reparti paracadutisti*, M7 racc.432 cart.3.

5 AUSSME, Stato Maggiore R.E. memorandum 9 ottobre 1942, *Oggetto: Costituzione e mobilitazione di reparti paracadutisti*, M7 racc.432 cart.3.

6 Rodolfo Puletti (ed), *L'Esercito e i suoi corpo – Sintesi storica* (Rome: USSME, 1973) vol 1, book 1, p.63; AUSSME, Stato Maggiore R.E. memorandum 23 ottobre 1942, *Oggetto: Costituzione e mobilitazione del comando 184° div. ftr. "Nembo"*, M7 racc.432 cart.3

7 AUSSME, Stato Maggiore R.E. memorandum 9 ottobre 1942, *Oggetto: Costituzione e mobilitazione di comandi e reparti per la 184° div. ftr. "Nembo"*, M7 racc.432 cart.3; AUSSME, Stato Maggiore R.E. memorandum 2 novembre 1942, *Oggetto: Costituzione e mobilitazione di reparti paracadutisti*, M7 racc.432 cart.3; AUSSME, Stato Maggiore R.E. memorandum 14 novembre 1942, *Oggetto: Costituzione e mobilitazione X btg. ftr. per il 185° rgt. ftr. "Nembo".*, M7 racc.432 cart.3; AUSSME, Stato Maggiore R.E. memorandum 18 novembre 1942, *Oggetto: Costituzione e mobilitazione di comandi e reparti per la 184° div. ftr. "Nembo"*, M7 racc.432 cart.3

The division did benefit from the experiences of the «*Folgore*» in terms of equipment. The standard small-arms weapon for all the parachute battalions was the MAB 38A, replacing the bolt action M91/38 moschetto di cavalleria. The division possessed over five thousand of these submachine guns and had three hundred and eighty-four Mauser 98K rifles for use as sniper weapons and grenade launchers. An armoured unit, the *184º reparto corazzato* equipped with a mix of sixteen L6/40 light tanks and M15/42 medium tanks, was part of the division. The service units supporting the division were more robust with additional vehicles, but still inadequate for mobile operations. In the spring of 1943 the «*Nembo*» replaced its 7.92 *fucile controcarro* with the 20mm Solothurn. Artillery and anti-tank guns available to the division remained weak with only the 47/32 c.c. guns authorized in those units.[8]

The division was assigned to the *5ª Armata* on 27 November 1942 instead of being kept under the direct authority of *Supercomando* as a strategic reserve.[9] This army was responsible for the defense of Tuscany and the units of the division were stationed at various locations in the region once they completed their parachute training. Units were garrisoned at Pisa, Livorno, Pistoia, and Prato in the northern part of the country. The units began their tactical training and exercises in these new locations throughout the winter and into the spring of 1943.

The «*Nembo*» was formally transitioned from a *divisione binaria* to a *divisione ternaria* on 11 January 1943.[10] The order authorized the creation of the *183º reggimento fanteria* (*VIII, XV, XVI btg.*); the *III gruppo, 184º rgt. artiglieria*; and the additional sections needed to make the existing units capable of supporting three regiments. As the *battaglione guastatori* was now numbered separately from the *battaglioni paracadutisti*, the new *VIII btg. para.* was used to complete the parachute battalion numbering sequence that was interrupted by the original *VIII btg. guastatori*. Replacing the *VIII btg.* was different from the *X btg.* previously discussed as the original battalion was a *guastatori* (assault engineer) battalion and not a *paracadutisti* battalion. The authorization was formally followed up by the mobilization order on 22 February 1943 in which the *comando 183º rgt.* was mobilized on 1 February and the *VIII btg.* on 15 February.[11]

8 Nino Arena, *Nembo!* (Rome, IBN Editore, 2013), pp.26–27; AUSSME, Stato Maggiore R.E. memorandum 9 ottobre 1942, *Oggetto: Costituzione e mobilitazione di comandi e reparti per la 184º div. ftr. "Nembo"*, M7 racc.432 cart.3; Filippo Cappellano *Le artiglierie del Regio Esercito nella seconda guerra mondiale* (Parma: Alberti Edizione Speciali s.r.l., 1998), p.242.

9 Di Giovanni, *I paracadutisti*, pp.192–193 and fn.20.

10 AUSSME, Stato maggiore R.E. memorandum 11 gennaio 1943, *Oggetto: Trasformazione della 184º div. for. "Nembo" in div. ternaria*, M7 racc. 432, cir. 3.

11 AUSSME, Stato Generale R.E. memorandum 22 febbraio 1943, *Oggetto: Costituzione e mobilitazione unità paracadutisti*, M7 racc. 432, cir. 3. The new *VIII btg.* is sometimes listed as the *VIIIbis btg.*

The M1934 Beretta pistol. This was the standard sidearm of the Regio Esercito. The grigs-verde leather holster carried a second 7-round magazine. (John Arends Collection, Photography by Joshua Arends)

The M91/38 moschetto per cavalleria (cavalry carbine). This was the standard individual weapon of the paracadutisti in 1940–1942. The six round clip was loaded from the top and the clip was dropped through an opening in the bottom once empty. The fixed bayonet is in the carry position and was rotated forward for use. (John Arends Collection, Photography by Joshua Arends)

The fucile mitragliatore Breda M1930. This was the standard light machine-gun of the Italian military during the war. The fixed magazine swung forward and was reloaded using the 20-round stripper clips shown in the picture. (John Arends Collection, Photography by Joshua Arends)

The MAB 38A with the 40-round magazine. The web/canvas jump bag in the picture was commonly called the fodero chiatarra (guitar case) and was exclusively used by the R.A. units. Once the MAB was removed from the case, the case itself was designed to be worn around the waist as an ammunition pouch. The case in the picture is a reproduction. (John Arends Collection, Photography by Joshua Arends)

The Moschetto Automatica Beretta (MAB) 38A with the 10-round magazine. This sub-machine gun replaced the moschetto per cavalleria as the standard individual weapon in 1943. The web/canvas carry bag was employed as a jump bag and carried spare magazines. The bag in the picture is a reproduction. (John Arends Collection, Photography by Joshua Arends)

The scarpe per reparti paracadutisti M41. This high boot replaced the R.E. standard ankle boots for paratroopers. (John Arends Collection, Photography by Joshua Arends)

A pair of ginocchieri (knee pads). (John Arends Collection, Photography by Joshua Arends)

A fully equipped *folgorino* in 1942. The display is wearing the first camouflage version of the jump smock, the combinazione di tela grigia per reparti paracadutisti. and the cintura porta lastrine e bomba (belt for clips and grenades) developed specifically for the paracadutisti. The belt carries ten Carcano ammunition boxes and six grenades. (John Arends Collection, Photography by Joshua Arends)

The desert version of the M41 parachutist uniform. The uniform and ammunition belt ares reproductions, but the other items are original. (John Arends Collection, Photography by Joshua Arends)

The display wearing the chitarra jump bag as an ammunition belt. (John Arends Collection, Photography by Joshua Arends)

A New School (Map 3.1)

To handle the increasing requirement for parachute training, the study that was initiated on 18 April 1942 resulted in affirming the decision to establish a new school at the airfield at Viterbo. The S.M.R.A. confirmed that the airfield had sufficient barrack space on 23 April and further requested on 9 May that the field only be used for two months to support the training required for «*C3*». A parachute demonstration was held at Viterbo on 13 May and again on 23 May attended by various dignitaries including the Crown Prince on 13 May.

At the 9 May event the chief of *Supercomando*, *generale di armata* Vittorio Ambrosio met with *generale di corpo d'armata Aerea* Rino Fougier, the chief of the S.M.R.A. The issue they discussed was how to train 4,000 men in preparation for «*C3*». To resolve this, Ambrosio asked whether Tarquinia could train 1,100 men every forty days and whether Viterbo could be outfitted to train up to an additional fifteen hundred. Fougier agreed not to transfer the *2° stormo* to Viterbo to free up the facilities at Viterbo for parachute training.[12]

Viterbo had been one of the airfields considered in the original study that selected Tarquinia in 1939. The location offered much of what Tarquinia lacked. It was a major air base for the R.A. with concrete runways, modern buildings and barracks, gymnasiums,a swimming pool, and other amenities. Stationed at the airfield at the end of 1942 was part of the *18° Stormo Trasporto* which augmented the school aircraft detachment. Viterbo was also better defended than Tarquinia, with anti-aircraft batteries protecting the area. *Colonnello pilota* Luigi Gori Savellini was appointed as the commander and began work to establish the new school.

The training at Tarquinia had not slowed down. On the days that the weather cooperated and aircraft were available in 1943, the school was able to execute 6,700 student jumps. The school was operating forty aircraft to support training, the majority being the Ca.133s. To achieve this, the main change was the tactical training had been reduced and made the responsibility of the units after the students qualified as parachutists. Access to SM.82 aircraft remained a challenge and limited the number of students that could complete their qualification jumps on a single day. Overall the school averaged 3,000 to 3,500 students billeted at Tarquinia each month, stressing the physical infrastructure of the airfield. During 1942, there were only seven deaths due to parachute accidents at Tarquinia, but twenty-three died when two Ca.133s collided in mid-air on 16 March.[13]

It took many months to prepare the training staff and organize the facilities to support the parachute training. It was not until 10 November 1942 that the first parachute class began training at the new school. The aircraft detachment consisted of nine Ca.133/P, one SM.81, two SM.82s, and one Cant.1007, with several lighter

12 Biagini and Frattolillo (eds.) *Diario Storico,* vol VII, book 1, pp.96, 178–179
13 Nino Arena, *La Regia Aeronautica* (Rome, USSMA, 1984), vol. 3 pp.716–717.

Students from the newly authorized *divisione fanteria «Nembo»* board an SM.82 at the new parachute school at Viterbo. (AUSSME)

Student *ripiegatori* (riggers) learn to repair and pack parachutes at Viterbo. Unlike the fallschirmjägers, the *paracadutisti* did not pack their own parachutes. (AUSSMA)

aircraft to support the training in administrative roles. Each school took responsibility for training specific categories of units. Viterbo became the school for training the parachute battalions, the artillery groups, and the combat patrols of the various *arditi* units. Tarquinia trained all the engineers (*guastatori, artieri, collegamenti*, and *zappatori*), the service units (*sanità, sussistenza*, etc.) and the replacement units from the *rgt. San Marco*, the *A.D.R.A.*, and the *10° rgt. arditi*.[14]

On 17 December 1942, *colonnello* Baudoin was informed that he was being replaced as the commander of the parachute school. No reason was given and the move literally came out of the blue. He traveled to Rome the next day and met with Mussolini and informed him of his new assignment. Mussolini was unaware of the change, but acquiesced to the decisions of the S.M.R.A. His new assignment was to command the R.A. forces on Corsica, the *Comando Aviazione Corsica*. The occupation of the island by the Italian military was to begin on 14 November. He left the school on 10 November to take up his new command. Baudoin is considered the most influential individual in shaping the character and esprit de corps of the *paracadutisti italiani*. His instance that the officers live and work with the enlisted soldiers was shared only by the alpini, who also created a similar tradition of combat skill and unit cohesiveness. Initially *Colonnello pilota* Renato Di Jorio was to command at Tarquinia, but in December *colonnello* Gori Savellini was moved from Viterbo to take command, while Di Jorio then was assigned to Viterbo.[15]

Experienced observers noted a difference in quality between the units of the *«Folgore»* and the new *«Nembo»*. Recruiting challenges created by the realities of war meant broader selection criteria with the associated lessening of standards. Testing and selection of the personnel for the new parachute units in late 1942 and early 1943 was less rigorous than that previously seen when the R.E. was building the *«Folgore»*. Fewer officers in S.P.E. had volunteered to form the new division, forcing the use of an increasing number of reserve officers to fill the leadership positions. Numerous disciplinary problems in the garrison towns of the *«Nembo»* were documented by the local newspapers in late 1942 and continuing into 1943. The ethos manifested by col. Baudoin and embedded in the training and the daily lives of the *paracadutisti* seemed lessened or not present. Certainly part of this was a reflection of the disastrous direction the war had taken for Italy. Losses and hardships had not been compensated by military success, but instead justified by valorous acts by individuals and units in the face of defeat. The result was that these new units were more fragile in terms of morale, mental and physical staying power.[16]

Supercomando decided in June to replace the *«Folgore»* with a new parachute division. Tentatively named the *183ª divisione fanteria «Ciclone»*, the first battalions were

14 Nino Arena, *50ª di Tarquinia, 1939–1989, Scuole Militare paracadutismo* (Comitato Promotore ex Istruttori delle Scuole Militari di Paracadutismo, 1989), pp.74, 106; Arena, *La Regia Aeronautica*, vol. 3 p.718; Di Giovanni, *I paracadutisti*, pp.191.

15 Nino Arena, *Tarquinia*, p.66; Arena, *La Regia Aeronautica*, vol. 3 p.718.

16 Di Giovanni, *I paracadutisti*, pp.193, 195–206.

organized in March 1943 (*XVII* and *XVIII*).[17] This was followed by the mobilization of the *XIX btg.* on 1 June and the *XX btg.* on 15 June. Along with the *XIX btg.*, the same order authorized the first divisional elements including a *gruppo artiglieria*, engineers and *guastatori* companies, and support units. *Generale di brigata* Giorgio Morigi was designated as the new commander.[18]

The *d. f.* «*Ciclone*» would never be officially authorized or formed. Only the *XIX btg.* would become fully operational, the other three battalions and the artillery group were still in their advanced training in September. The *XVII* and *XVIII btg.* would become *btg. complementi* (replacement battalions) for the «*Nembo*» and the *XIX* and *XX btg.* would be organized as the *raggruppamento* «*Cicilone*» under *generale* Morigi during the events in August and September 1943.[19]

Fighting Partisans

The first combat operation for the «*Nembo*» was not on a battlefield against a similar enemy, but was in the Venezia-Giulia region of north-eastern Italy. Here the Slovenian partisans were disrupting Italian control in the Gorizia area. This region was subject to centuries-old ethnic tensions and the border decisions that followed the First World War. The activities of the Yugoslavian partisans fighting each other and their German and Italian occupiers was spilling over into Italy proper. Attacks on small garrisons and public transportation in the cities, along with those against the railways in the countryside were increasing. Minority conscripts and recruits in the R.E. were beginning to desert and join the guerrillas. Like all the countries at the time, Italy lacked a counter insurgency doctrine and the specialized units with the organization, training, and weapons best suited for this style of fighting.[20]

The *III btg.* was selected to be sent to the region by the division in March 1943. It was the oldest, best trained battalion in the «*Nembo*» and was considered the most reliable. The battalion, along with the regimental *compagnia servizi* (service company) was first sent to the border region between Caporetto and Postumia to assist the local forces in combating the partisan actions. At this time the common tactic employed was to garrison key population and transportation centers while conducting occasional large scale sweeps to capture or kill partisans. On the whole, this approach was not working and new tactics were being considered at the time of the *III btg.* arrival in the region.

17 AUSSME, Stato Maggiore R.E. memorandum 2 giugno 1943, *Oggetto: Unità aggiuntive paracadutisti*, M7 racc.432, cart.3;
18 AUSSME, Stato Maggiore R.E. memorandum 17 giugno 1943, *Oggetto: Unità aggiuntive paracadutisti*, M7 racc.432, cart.3; AUSSME, Stato Maggiore R.E. memorandum 30 giugno 1943, *Oggetto: Unità aggiuntive paracadutisti*, M7 racc.432, cart.3; Di Giovanni, *I paracadutisti*, p.195.
19 Arena, *Tarquinia*, pp.77–78; Arena, *Nembo!*, p.29
20 Arena, *Nembo!*, pp.19–20;

The new tactic was one of continuous small unit observation and attacks, combined with a large intelligence effort to map out the area to better understand the population and the terrain. A radio and telephone communication system was put into place for rapid response to partisan activity. Under this program, the *paracadutisti* were the best unit available for those types of actions. Their training had focused on operating as small, independent units which was nearly ideal for this approach.[21]

The *Ministero dell'Interno* (Ministry of the Interior) created the *Ispettorato Speciale di Pubblica Sicurezza per la Venezia Giulia* (Special Inspectorate of Public Security for Venezia Giulia) to oversee the operations against anti fascist movements. This was a repressive organization that used torture to gather intelligence. It had its own military force consisting of elements from *Carabinieri*, *Guardia di Finanza, Guardia alla Frontiera*, and legionaries of the *Milizia Volontaria per la Sicurezza Nazionale* (M.V.S.N.), in total about 1800 men. The *Ispettorato* synchronized the movements of the military forces in the area, including the *III btg.*

With the implementation of this concept, the *III btg.* was sent to the area between Gorizia and Lublijana in April. Assigned to the *159ª divisione fanteria «Veneto»*, the battalion was stationed in Montenero d'Idria. After arriving in that town and establishing their base, the battalion immediately began to execute surveillance patrols to gauge the locations where the partisans were operating. They were especially seeking those areas in which the partisans dominated and felt safe, as those areas would be the first targets of the *paracadutisti*. After a few failures, the *III btg.* refined its small-unit tactics and began to gain military success. The use of the RF1/P radios was an important factor in the ability of the unit to react quickly to the changing situations created by guerrilla warfare.[22]

Because of the small unit military successes of the *III btg.*, the *XI btg.* was dispatched from Florence in May to join the other battalion. Rather than send the regimental headquarters with the *XI btg.*, the two battalions were organized as a *raggruppamento* with limited staff under the regimental commander, *tenente colonnello* Carmelo Giangreco. The *XI btg.* was garrisoned at Aidussina, which was near Montenero d'Idria. The two battalions were successful in reestablishing Italian control of this area in Slovenia. However the *paracadutisti* were frustrated at the role they were ordered to play in the war and still longed for an actual airborne operation. These were the two best trained and disciplined battalions in the *«Nembo»* and the experience would be invaluable if given an opportunity to leverage it. The reverse impact of the experience was that the two battalions accumulated significant wear and tear on the men and the equipment, and the *paracadutisti* saw the uglier side of war which impacted morale of the units. The battalions would remain operating in the region until early June.[23]

21 Di Giovanni, *I paracadutisti*, pp.193–194; Arena, *Nembo!*, p.20
22 Di Giovanni, *I paracadutisti*, pp.193-194.
23 Nino Arena, *I PARACADUTISTI Cinquant'anni di storia, cronaca e immagini del paracadutisti italiano* (Modena: Società Tipografica Editrice Modenese Mucchi, 1972), p.151.

Corsica or Sardinia?

Supercomando was considering their options to prepare for the next Allied invasion. Sicily, Sardinia, and Corsica were all possible objectives and the three services discussed means to reinforce the defenses of the three islands. On 21 March *generale* Ambrosio addressed the possible use of the «*Nembo*» in Sardinia with *generale di armata* Mario Caracciolo, the commander of the *5ª Armata*. One issue was the commitment of the two battalions in the Venezia-Giulia; another issue was the transportation of the division through Italy and onto the island.[24]

It was in April that the decision was made to send the «*Nembo*» to Sardinia. Both *Supereserciito* and *Superaereo* were informed on 8 April to begin planning for transporting the division to the island. The problems facing *Supercomando* in redeploying large units were the Allied naval and air superiority, limited shipping, and competing priorities. During this same time period, *Supercomando* began considering on 13 April whether to create a *raggruppamento artiglieria* for the «*Nembo*». Like the «*Folgore*», the «*Nembo*» lacked a field and medium artillery element to support the traditional types of combat now expected of the division. The *156º rgt. art.* had been temporarily assigned to the «*Nembo*» after the *156ª divisione fanteria* «*Vicenza*» was transferred to Russia as a security division. In the role of a security division, it did not need an artillery regiment which reduced its transportation requirement. While discussed, nothing came of the proposal and the «*Nembo*» still retained the *156º rgt. art.* as an attached unit until June 1943.[25]

While the fate of the division was awaiting resolution, the *XV* and *XVI btg.* battalions of the *183º rgt.* completed their parachute training in May. The battalions of this regiment had been sent to Viterbo for training in February when the new school was not yet fully functional. Besides the parachute regiment, the school was training the new artillery group and the other support units. As the *VIII btg.* had been mobilized on a later date, it was still in training at the school.

The order to transfer the «*Nembo*» to Sardinia was issued on 30 May 1943. Like the «*Folgore*» before it, only two of its regiments would initially deploy to the island. As the *VIII btg.* was still in training, it would remain behind and be temporarily assigned to the *185º rgt.* The *X btg.* from the *185º rgt.* would be used to replace it in the *183º rgt.* Only the *I* and *II gruppi artiglieria* of the *184º rgt. art.* would deploy, the *III gruppo* would remain with the *185º* along with the *156º rgt. art.* All the other divisional assets were transferred with the division. The units remaining in Italy would be under the command of the *vice comandante* of the division, [26]

24 Antonello Biagini and Fernando Frattolillo, (eds) *Diario Storico del Comando Supremo* (Rome: USSME, 2002), vol IX, book 1, pp.718–720.

25 Biagini and Frattolillo, (eds) *Diario Storico*, vol IX, pp.895, 945; Franco Dell'Uomo and Roberto di Rosa, *L'Esercito Italiano verso il 2000 — I corpi disciolti*, (Rome: USSME, 2001) vol 2, book 2 p.178. At the time the artillery regiment had the *I* and *II gruppi da 75/27 T.A.*

26 AUSSME, Stato Maggiore R.E. memorandum 30 maggio 1943, *Oggetto: Trasferimento divisione "Nembo"*, M7 racc.432, cart.3; Di Giovanni, *I paracadutisti*, p.207.

Like the *folgorini* before them, the *nemboini* were frustrated that they had yet to be employed as paratroops. The order sending them to Sardinia did not improve matters. The mission that the division was given could be seen as being 180° opposite of the type of missions a paratrooper was trained for: that of guarding airfields and possible airborne landing areas against enemy paratroopers. The division was required to establish *reparti anti-paracadutisti* (anti-parachute units) at multiple locations across the island and form several mobile rapid reaction units to respond to any such enemy landings.

While the «*Nembo*» was transported to Sardinia, a role for part of the «*Nembo*» on Corsica had not completely disappeared. The two battalions of the *185° rgt.* had been released from their anti-partisan mission in Venezia-Giulia and returned to Florence in late June. Here the units were joined by the *VIII btg.* that had just completed parachute training. On 22 June *Supereservito* ordered the transfer of the regiment to the command of the *VII Cd'A* on Corsica. Attached to the regiment was the *VIII* and *XIX btg.*, along with the *III gr. art.* from the *184° rgt. art.* The *XIX btg.* was only recently mobilized on 17 June and still being formed and awaiting training. The «*Nembo*» was fated to never command its three regiments in combat.[27]

With these moves, *Supercomando* had dispersed the only unit that could rapidly respond to changes in the operational situation. The mission given to the «*Nembo*» was one that could have been done by almost any other division in the R.E. The «*Folgore*» had demonstrated that given a fixed location to defend, the *paracadutisti* could stop even armoured forces. Instead they were spread out over the island in small groups that were not mutually supporting. If *Supercomando* suddenly needed the «*Nembo*» elsewhere, it would take days to collect the units and assemble the aircraft.

It also brings into question why the Italian leadership was forming these specialized units at a time in the war when they offered little operational value. The time and resources used for parachute training would have been better spent on preparing the conventional infantry for the upcoming fight.

Sardinia (Map 13.1)

The «*Nembo*» was transported to Sardinia in June by six convoys with R.M. escorts. The convoys left from La Spezia and Genoa and arrived at Palau and Olbia transporting the bulk of the division. The tactical headquarters of the division was moved by air from Pisa to Cagliari. None of the ships or aircraft were lost during the transit.[28]

Once on the island, *generale* Ronco established his headquarters at Villanova Forru just outside of Cagliari. The «*Nembo*» was responsible for the airfields located at

27 AUSSME, Stato Maggiore R.E. memorandum 22 giugno 1943, *Oggetto: Unità divisione "Nembo" destinate in Corsica*, M7 racc.432, cart.3;

28 Arena, *Nembo!*, p.29.

Fertile, Venafiorita, Villacidro, Serramanna, Decimomannu, Oristano, Milis, Elmas, Monserrato, and Chilivani. These airfields were located in the north, center and the southern part of the island, forcing Ronco to distribute his units all over Sardinia. He decided to organize the division into five *raggruppamenti tattici autonomi* (independent tactical groups) and position them where they could rapidly react to any Allied actions. These were as follows:

Gruppo di manovra «Quaroni» (*col.* Giuseppe Quaroni) at Assemini: *XV, XVI btg., II/184° rgt. art.*
Raggruppamento tattico «Renzoni» (*ten. col.* Bruno Renzoni) at Serramanna: *XII, XIV btg., I/184° rgt. art.*
Gruppo di manovra «Tantillo» (*col.* Pietro Tantillo) at Sanluri: *184ª cp. motociclisti, 284ª cp. ciclisti, 184ª cp. minatori-artieri, 184ª cp. mortai da 81(-), 186ª cp. mista genio.*
Raggruppamento tattico «Invrea» (*ten. col.* Ademaro Invrea) at Marrubbiu: *XIII btg., 3° gr. Corazzato Carri L6/40, 184° rgt. cp. cannoni da 47/32*
Gruppo tattico «Valletti» (*magg.* Felice Valletti-Borgnimi) at Alghero-Fertilia: *X btg., 183° rgt. cp. cannoni da 47/32, one plt. mortai da 8* [29]

The division conducted training exercises and rehearsals with the German 90. Panzergrenadier Division now stationed on the island. This division was the reconstituted 90.Afrika-Division that was originally part of the Afrika Korps.

Morale and discipline continued to be a problem. The *nemboini* were initially unhappy about their deployment to Sardinia. Training helped to improve both for a while, but after the Allied invasion of Sicily, more incidents of indiscipline occurred. The men, eager to fight, now saw themselves as trapped on an island that was becoming a side-show as the war passed them by. Allied air attacks caused some casualties, but the greatest danger was the malaria present in many places on the island. Over time the division suffered 30 percent of its personnel sick with the disease. The fall of Mussolini on 25 July was another factor as many were now believing the war was lost. The question now was whether the *nemboini* still had the will to fight.[30]

The *«Nembo»* was not the only unit from the airborne force that was moved during this time. Previously in May the two companies of the *btg. «Loreto»* that had remained in Sicily were transferred to Sardinia. The *3ª* and *4ª cp.* would continue their main mission of airfield repair and maintenance in the face of the Allied aerial bombardment.[31]

29 Arena, *Nembo!*, p.27.
30 Di Giovanni, *I paracadutisti*, pp.208–209.
31 Piero Crociani and Pier Battistelli, *Italian Navy & Air Force Elite Units & Special Forces 1940-45* (Oxford: Osprey, 2013), p.40.

More Arditi Raids

The surrender of the Italo-German forces in Tunisia now opened Italian territory to invasion. Sicily, Sardinia, and even occupied Corsica were considered possible objectives for the next Allied move. Efforts were made by *Supercomando* and Germany to strengthen those locations. For Italy, this was a major challenge as the effort was beset by shortages of equipment. The remains of the *8ª Armata* had returned from Russia after being destroyed during the Soviet Little Uranus and Little Saturn operations. Some of those returning divisions were simply disbanded while others were ordered to be rebuilt. Most of the mechanized and motorized units of the R.E. were lost in Africa and also needed to be replaced. What was needed was time and Italy had few offensive options available to create additional time.

The only readily available offensive tools were the various *arditi* units that had been created in 1942.[32] Along with the two battalions of the R.E. *10º rgt. arditi* that had been organized in that year, the R.A. had raised the *Battaglione Arditi Distruttori Regia Aeronautica* (*A.D.R.A.*). Authorized on 28 July 1942, recruiting and other problems delayed assembling the volunteers for training until December. *Superaereo* defined the unit's mission in an order published on 31 December, and finalized its organization in one published on 25 January 1943. The unit was intended to be the third battalion in the R.A.'s *reggimento d'assalto «Duca d'Aosta»*, but shortfalls in equipment and delays in training prevented the battalion from being ready before the regiment was lost in Tunisia. The battalion was officially made an independent unit on 10 April 1943.[33]

The *btg. A.R.D.A.* was organized in three companies, with each company having nine patrols consisting of nine personnel. Equipment was similar to the other parachute units in the Italian military but with a specific mission of sabotage. The *arditi* were issued the MAB 38A as their main weapon. One unusual item of equipment was a cargo container with its own small parachute. The *A.D.R.A.* sabotage mission required a quantity of explosives that could exceed the capacity of the IP41/SP parachute when combined with the weight of the *arditi*'s normal equipment. The explosives were packed in the separate container that was connected to the jumper by a short line. Once the jumper's main parachute had inflated, he would release the cargo container triggering the small cargo parachute to open. Both the man and the explosives descended together under their own parachutes connected by the short line to the jumper.[34]

The first commander of the battalion was *capitano* Araldo De Angelis. He led the unit during its outfitting and training until April 1943. In that month, *tenente colonnello* Dalmas

32 Luigi Emilio Longo, *I «reparti speciali» italiani nella seconda guerra mondiale* (Milan: Mursia 1991), p.169.

33 Aldo Giorleo, *Palestra Azzurra L'aeronautica militare e il paracadutismo cronistoria dalle origini ad oggi* (Rome: USSMA, 1975), p.52; Arena, *La Regia Aeronautica*, vol. 3, p.721.

34 Nino Arena, *FOLGORE Storia del paracadutismo militare italiano* (Rome: Centro Editoriale Nazione, 1965), p.308.

assumed command of the battalion. Dalmas had been badly wounded while commanding the *I btg. d'assalto* in Tunisia and had been recently released from the hospital. As his former command was now destroyed, he was given command of the new battalion.

The battalion was ready for employment in April 1943. At that time, the battalion had 301 men assigned and had completed general training. Of those men, 60 were fully trained for sabotage operations. Because of the worsening situation in Tunisia, there were rumors that the battalion could be sent in a desperate attempt to prolong the fighting. Fortunately calmer thinking prevailed and planning was initiated for a major sabotage operation against Allied airfields in North Africa.

Operazione «Campi Africani» (Maps 13.2, 13.3)

The plan coordinated between *Supersercito* and *Superaereo* was a massive raid that would strike multiple targets over a two-to-three day period. Patrols from the *10° rgt. Arditi* and the *A.D.R.A.* would participate. A total of fourteen patrols were committed for the raids, flying in eleven SM.82 transport aircraft for the parachute insertions. The patrols would take off on the night of 13 June over a period of two hours between 1930 to 2130 hrs. Once dropped over their respective drop zones, the patrols would move to their targets and prepare for their attack. The attacks by the four patrols on the two airfields in the Bengasi area were synchronized for execution on the evening of 18 June. This was planned so the assault by one patrol would not alert the defense before the other patrols could launch their attacks. It is unclear whether all fourteen of the raids were timed for that date or whether dates were synchronized only between patrols operating near each other.[35]

The recovery plans for the patrols likely varied. Those patrols departing Iraklion would move to an emergency landing ground at Aisilan located to the south-east of Bengasi. An SM.75 would fly to that location ten days after the parachute drop (23 June) and circle while looking for a signal. If the signal was given, the plane would land and retrieve the *arditi*. If there was not a signal, the plane would depart without landing. The same procedure would be followed three days later (26 June) in case more time was needed for the patrols to reach the pick-up point. It is likely that similar recovery plans were in-place for the other patrols, but the details are lacking.[36]

The *A.D.R.A.* patrols assembled at the Miramare airfield near Rimini between 6 and 8 June 1943. Here those patrols undertook refresher training on up-date techniques and procedures that would be used during the operation. The *101ª cp.* and the *111ª cp.* of the *10° rgt. Arditi* arrived at the Miramare airport on 9 June to make their final preparations for the mission. On 11 June, officers from *Supercomando* and the S.I.M. arrived to provide the latest intelligence briefings and the materials they would

35 Aldo Giorleo, *Palestra Azzurra*, pp.61, 67; Longo, *I «reparti speciali»*, pp.146–147, 171.
36 Giorleo, *Palestra Azzurra*, p.69. It is called a *campo di fortuna* in the text.

Members of the A.D.R.A. training at Tarquinia in February 1943. Note the distinctive jump bag for the MAB 38A that was unique to the A.R.D.A. (AUSSME)

need for the operation including French and American money, photographs of their targets, etc.). The senior officers of the *10° rgt, arditi* and the *A.D.R.A.* worked together to finalize the plan that was briefed to the patrols only on 11 June. On 12 June, the patrols departed Rimini by SM.82 and flew to the four airfields that were to be used as their launch points for the raids: Salon en Provence, France; Decimomannu, Sardinia; Gerbini, Sicily; and Iraklion, Crete.[37]

During the entire time the patrols were at Rimini, strict security procedures were enforced. However the latest routes, times, and updated sensitive mission data was being radioed to the patrols at Rimini. This information was likely intercepted by the Allies and decoded, providing detailed information on all aspects of the missions. The impact of this possible breach of security cannot be understated.[38]

The mission was executed on 13 June 1943. The patrols, their departure points and departure times, their actual jump times, and their targets were as follows:

- *Ten.* Renato Giuliattini, *111ª cp.* – Salon en Provence, France, take-off at 2005 hrs – Jump time 0210 hrs 14 June, – La Senia airfield, Algeria
- *Ten.* Marvulli, *A.D.R.A.* – Salon en Provence, France, take-off at 2010 hrs – Jump time 0210 hrs 14 June, – Tafaraui airfield, Algeria

37 Giorleo, *Palestra Azzurra*, p.60; Nino Arena, *La Regia Aeronautica* (Rome: USSMA, 1986), vol. 4, p.593.

38 Arena, *La Regia Aeronautica*, vol. 4, p.595. The role of ULTRA in this operation requires further research.

- *S. ten.* Confetto, *A.D.R.A.* – Salon en Provence, take-off at 2015 hrs – Jump time 0205 hrs 14 June, Blida airfield, Algeria
- *Serg. magg.* Stramaccioni, *A.D.R.A.* – Decimomannu, Sardinia, take-off at 2040 hrs – Jump time 0015 hrs 14 June, – Biskra, Algeria
- *Serg. magg.* Pennacchiotti, *A.D.R.A.* – Decimomannu, Sardinia, take-off at 2100 hrs – Jump time 0015 hrs 14 June, – Biskra, Algeria
- *S. ten.* Antonino Rizzo, *111ª cp.* – Decimomannu, Sardinia, take-off at 2130 hrs – Jump time 0005 hrs 14 June, – Oulmene, Algeria
- Serg. Di Giusto, *A.D.R.A.* – Gerbini, Sicily, take-off at 2015 hrs – Jump time 0030 hrs 14 June, El Diem airfield, Libya
- *S. ten.* Pizzianico, *101ª cp.* – Gerbini, Sicily – Castel Benito, Libya. Mission canceled
- *S.ten.* Degli Effetti, *A.D.R.A.* – Gerbini, Sicily – Castel Benito, Libya. Mission canceled
- *Serg.* Carraretto, *A.D.R.A.* – Gerbini, Sicily – Castel Benito, Libya. Mission canceled
- *Ten.* Luigi Di Tommaso, *101º cp.* – Iraklion, Crete, take-off at 1930 hrs – Jump time 2315 hrs 13 June, – Bengasi airfields, Libya
- *Ten.* Baccaro, *A.D.R.A.* Iraklion, Crete, take-off at 1930 hrs – Jump time 0010 14 June, Bengasi airfields, Libya.
- *S. ten.* Balmas, *A.D.R.A.* – Iraklion, Crete, take-off at 2000 hrs – Jump time 2315 hrs 13 June, – Benina airfield, Libya
- *S. ten.* Comis, *A.D.R.A.* – Iraklion, Crete, take-off at 2000 hrs – Jump time 2315 hrs 13 June, – Benina airfield, Libya[39]

R.A. maggiore Beltramo with R.E. *sergente* Capponi as his radio operator accompanied *ten.* Baccaro's patrol and would parachute with them. Baltramo was to maintain radio contact with Italy to report on the patrols' actions and successes.

The plan began to unravel at once.[40] Three of the four patrols launching from Gerbini did not fly because their two SM.82s were destroyed on the ground by a bombing attack during the daylight hours of 13 June. All the remaining nine aircraft wandered off their flight plan and were unable to correctly identify the designated drop zones for the patrols. The navigational error for *sottotenente* Confetto's patrol was so great that the patrol discovered they were over 70 kms away from their intended target. Inexperienced aircrews released the aerial supply containers at the wrong times, with the result that the patrols were often three to five kilometers away from their supplies and equipment. Gusty winds were encountered at all the drop zones, increasing the

39 Giorleo, *Palestra Azzurra*, pp.60–61; Longo, *I «reparti speciali»*, pp.146–147, 171.
40 The account of the raids are from Arena, *FOLGORE!*, pp.343–354; Giorleo, *Palestra Azzurra*, pp.61–69; Longo, *I «reparti speciali»*, pp.146–149; Nino Arena, *Aquile senza Ali: I paracadutisti italiani nella seconda guerra mondiale* (Milano, Mursia 1970), pp.183–188; Arena, *La Regia Aeronautica*, vol. 4, pp.593–600.

dispersion of men and equipment. The cargo parachute supporting Capponi's long range radio separated from its container and the radio smashed into the ground.

All these problems had a secondary effect – they forced the patrols to consume time. The *arditi* had to walk back along the flight path to try and find their supply containers. Some patrols were successful and others were not. Most patrols had to wait until daylight just to determine their location. After landing, the few terrain features they could see in the dark informed them that they were not at the correct locations. They needed the morning sun to see enough terrain to determine their actual locations. This required more time and delayed their movement towards their objectives.

By remaining near their drop zones for a longer period of time searching for the containers, they became vulnerable to Allied detection. The Italian sources speculate whether there was a security breach and the Allied forces were alerted to the raids. A British radio station at Apollonia began transmitting a warning on the morning of 15 June. The message stated that about one-hundred Italian paratroopers had landed in the area and they must be captured or killed. The message was sent to all stations 'in the clear' (uncoded) to prevent misunderstanding and delays in acting on the information. Bounties were offered to the Arab population for information and for capturing or killing the *arditi*.

Tenente Giuliattini's and *sergente* Di Giusto's patrols were captured within hours of landing. The patrols of *sottotenente*. Rizzo and *sergente maggiore* Stramaccioni and Pennacchiotti could not get near their objective and as they were being hunted, they split up to try to cause as much havoc as possible. The *arditi* were able to avoid their searchers for several days, but the men were all finally captured by 19 June. *Sottotenente* Marvulli's patrol had landed in and around a farm and were quickly surrounded by Arabs. An attempt to bribe the Arabs was followed by a short firefight ending in the patrol being captured.

In the case of Confetto's patrol, once they realized they were too far away from their planned objective, they decided to try and attack a secondary objective: the airfield at Affreville. Approaching that target in the morning, they realized the airfield was no longer in active use. The only decision left was to walk to the primary objective at Blida and they set off on the evening of 14 June. Walking all night, they covered about twenty kilometers and stopped to rest during the day. After a few hours the *arditi* who was on guard saw a column of French vehicles moving up. It became clear that the French had intelligence on the location of the patrol and were attempting to surround it. After changing their position and exchanging fire with the French, the *arditi* finally surrendered that evening.

Two of the patrols that departed Iraklion for the airfields near Bengasi also found themselves far from their objectives. The patrols of *s. ten.* Baccaro and *ten.* Di Tommaso landed about forty kilometers from their planned drop zone. They encountered groups of Arabs in the desert which were not friendly towards the Italians and several small actions were fought. After walking over thirty kilometers, they reached the railway line running between Bengasi and Solluch. There was a motor road running alongside the line, so they decided to ambush a vehicle and use it to drive near their objective.

Instead of some unarmed trucks, a motorized infantry column with armoured cars approached their location. It was evident that the enemy knew they were in the area and had set out to search for them. After destroying their papers and equipment and a brief exchange of fire, the two patrols surrendered.

The last two patrols, those under the command of *sottotenenti* Balmas and Comis, actually landed on the correct drop zone. This was due more to serendipity than planning. On board the SM.82 with the *arditi* was an artillery officer, *capitano* Pasquale Varone. Not only was Pasquale a trained *osservatori aerei*, but he had considerable experience flying over Cirenaica on reconnaissance missions. He navigated the aircraft to the correct location and also controlled the drop of the *arditi* and their supplies. While the patrols did lose some explosives and water due the gusty winds blowing the containers away, most of the containers landed with the *arditi*. Quickly collecting their materials, the two patrols were able to leave the area and reach the jebel before dawn. Hiding in the ravines and broken ground, they observed enemy aircraft searching the area. On 15 June a small party was able to sneak down to a well and refill all the canteens. In the afternoon they discovered an enemy patrol too close to avoid. A fire fight erupted and the *arditi* split into small groups to evade the enemy. The British sealed off the area and in a deliberate search, managed to capture all but two of the *arditi*.

The two remaining *arditi*, *primo aviere* (senior airman) Vito Procida and *aviere* (airman) Franco Cargnel, had been sent on a reconnaissance mission towards Benina and had yet to return. Hearing the firing, the two decided to march to their objective and try to complete the mission. They were able to avoid detection and reach a point overlooking the Benina north airfield on the evening of 17 June. Here they observed the security protecting the base while waiting until the planned time of 18 June to launch the attack. At sunset on 18 June, they quietly moved to the perimeter wire and cut an opening in the fence. They were able to plant bombs on twenty of the aircraft that were present and then managed to leave the airfield without being spotted. While walking back to the jebel they heard the detonation of the explosives. Hiding during the day, they continued to their retrieval point at Aisilin. Short of water and out of food, they encountered an armed Arab on 20 June. At first acting as a friend and feeding them, the Arab then turned them over to the British for the announced bounty.

The final act of the operation happened on 23 June when a SM.75 arrived over the airfield at Aisilan looking for the signal. Not seeing or receiving anything, the pilot decided to land in hope that some had made the rendezvous. The aircraft waited most of the day in the open at great risk, but there was not any sign of the *paracadutisti* or the British. In the evening the aircraft took off and returned to Crete. It would repeat the journal once more on 26 June, but only circled looking for a signal. Again not seeing anything, it departed never to return.

Thus ended this major sabotage effort. Of the fourteen patrols dedicated to *Operazione «Campi africani»*, three were unable to depart, ten were unable to attack their objectives, and only two *arditi* from one patrol succeeded in reaching their airfield and destroying some aircraft. There is debate on how many aircraft were destroyed at

Benina. The likely result was two American B24s, two British Wellington's and two Hurricanes were destroyed. American sources stated that some of the bombs were discovered and removed before they detonated.[41] All the *arditi* in the eleven patrols that actually parachuted into North Africa were either killed or captured. At the cost of 101 men killed or captured, the results were six aircraft destroyed and some consternation of the Allies to improve their rear area security.

The problems that occurred during the previous sets of sabotage attacks in Algeria were repeated in the operation in June. The patrols were only given a day to study their objectives and plan their operation. Little intelligence was available on the targets and the lack of current weather conditions in North Africa made the raids more of an 'execution on the run' rather than following a well-planned and rehearsed action. The aircrews of the eleven SM.82s were not trained in parachute operations and lacked trained *osservatori aerei* who had time to study the route and the drop zones to guide the aircraft to their correct locations. The mission required the patrols to operate for ten or more days based on the recovery plans, forcing the patrols to carry excessive supplies. There were multiple indicators that the operation had been compromised before the first aircraft took off on 13–14 June. The fact that two *arditi* managed to carry out their mission reflects more on the training and strength of the individuals than the preparations leading up to the raids.

The *arditi* efforts in Tunisia and Libya demonstrated the failure of the Italian doctrine of raid and sabotage at the operational level of war. The means selected (small patrols) were unable to achieve the desired operational effect (delaying the Allies' next operation). How many Allied aircraft would need to be destroyed to set-back the enemy's timeline? How long would a bridge need to be out of operation to do the same? To have an operational effect, the target must be critical to the enemy's war effort and difficult to replace. The *Xª MAS* attacks against the British battleships in Alexandria harbor is an example of a raid with an operational impact. None of the *arditi* raids between January–June 1943 were directed against this type of target.

War comes to the Schools (Map 3.1)

In addition to training the units of the «*Nembo*» and «*Ciclone*», the two schools were training the personnel needed for the expanding *arditi* forces. The *10º rgt. Arditi* added the *III btg.* in February 1943 and reorganized the first two battalions. The *III btg.* had the *121ª cp. paracadutisti*, the *122ª cp. da sbarco*, and the *123ª cp. terrestre*. In May the *IV btg.* was organized with the *110ª*, *120ª*, *130ª cp. speciali* and the *133ª cp. terrestre.*

41 Bjunior, 'The June1943 Italian Arditi attack on B24 US Bombers' <https://bjuniornewblog.blogspot.com/2019/04/the-june1943-italian-arditi-attack-on_22.html> (accessed 15 July, 2022).

In June the battalions were reorganized, placing the three *cp. paracadutisti* in the *IV btg.* and the other battalions were a mix of the *terrestre, sbarco* and *speciale* companies.[42]

The R.A. authorized the formation of the *II btg. A.D.R.A.* in August 1943. This battalion was still forming at Viterbo in September. The commander was *maggiore a.a.* Renato Trepiedi and it was structured the same as the *I btg.*[43]

Colonnello Gori Savellini received word in mid-June that the school at Tarquinia would be closed. The reason given was the airfield was needed to base the *5º stormo d'assalto* at the airfield. Nothing was officially transmitted at that time, but the school rushed to complete the training of the students currently present and then move all training equipment to Viterbo. The official order to close the school came in July. The staff at Tarquinia were able to complete the qualification jumps of 147 officers, 249 non-commissioned officers, and 2239 soldiers by 10 July. Once the school closed those personnel that were not needed at the Viterbo school requested assignments to various combat units.[44]

Up until 1943 Italy had been spared the heavy bombing that Germany was experiencing. Now that all of North Africa was under the control of the Allies and bases were available, the level of bombing began to increase. Tarquinia and Rome would share the same fate on 19 July 1943, for on that day Allied bombers attacked both locations. The Allies had initiated a bombing campaign against airfields in preparation for their invasion of Sicily. By 15 July all the airfields on Sicily had been rendered inoperable and the Allied air forces now turned its attention to mainland Italy.[45]

The first bombing raid against Tarquinia was one of opportunity. A group of Allied bombers returning from an anti-shipping mission with ordinance still on-board chose to expend it over Tarquinia in the late afternoon. The bombers were flying at a high altitude so some accuracy was lost but damage was done to the facilities at the base. This was followed by a planned raid at 2300 hours that night that caused much damage, destroying aircraft and starting fires. Another raid of opportunity followed at 0044 hours on 20 July but inflicted little additional damage.[46]

Next it was the turn of Viterbo to experience the Allied bombing campaign. The bombers arrived at 1410 hours on 29 July and destroyed hangers, workshops, barracks and other buildings. Fifteen aircraft were destroyed on the ground. This raid forced the school to disperse the instructor department, vehicles, and supplies into the nearby woods. Tactical training continued in the Cimini Mountains region as the school was completing the instruction of the *XX btg.* Qualification jumps were executed

42 Massimo Di Martino, *Paracadutisti d'Italia – Uniformi distintivi equipaggiamenti, 1938–1969* (Milan: Edizioni Libreria Militare, 2019), vol. 1, p.277–278; Piero Crociani, and Pier Battistelli, *Italian Army Elite Units & Special Forces 1940–43* (Oxford: Osprey, 2011), p.45.

43 Giorleo, *Palestra Azzurra*, pp.71; Longo, *I «reparti speciali»*, p.180. Little is known about this battalion

44 Arena, *Tarquinia*, p.78.

45 C.J.C. Molony, *The Mediterranean and Middle East* (London: HMSO, 1973), vol. 5, p.127.

46 Arena, *Tarquinia*, p.79.

in-between the bombing raids. School operations continued in this manner until 5 September when a massive raid by one-hundred and thirty American B-17 bombers permanently put the airfield out of operation.[47]

Operation Husky (Map 13.4)

The Allies had decided that Sicily would be their next target and on 10 July 1943 they initiated Operation Husky. This was an amphibious landing along the southern coast of the island, supported by an airborne operation using two airborne divisions. The Italo-German forces, technically under the command of the *6ª Armata*, planned to delay the Allies force on or near the beaches until a sizable counterattack could be organized. Weather and friendly fire from the ships off the beaches scattered the allied airborne operation, but the amphibious landings were successful. Several counter attacks were launched by both Italian and German units, but a lack of synchronization of the Axis effort and Allied firepower (both naval and air) defeated those attempts.

Part of the defense plan for Sicily was establishing caches of weapons and supplies for use by the *arditi* operating behind the enemy's lines. The concept was that the *arditi* patrols would gain the enemy's rear using their trained means (parachuting, swimming, or infiltration), then use the caches to sustain their operations as long as possible. The caches, combined with the support expected from the Sicilian population, should allow the patrols to avoid detection for an extended period of time.[48]

The *112ª* and *113ª cp.* of the *II/10° rgt. Arditi* were deployed to Sicily shortly after the landings, while the *111ª cp.* remained in Italy. While the two companies on the island executed several raids, none had any significant impact on the Allied advance. They discovered that the caches had been emptied by the local population and that the Sicilians had no desire to help the Italians. It was not unusual for an *arditi* patrol to be reported by the locals to the Allied military, leading to its quick capture.[49]

Only two parachute operations were executed during the battle for Sicily. During the night of 21/22 July, four patrols from the *111ª cp.* parachuted into Sicily to attack various targets. The patrol under *sottotenente* Vincenza Belletti was to attack the airfield at Lentini. They were unable to reach the airfield but did manage to do some other damage over the next few days before managing to cross over into friendly territory. The patrol under *sottotenente.* Rodolfo Felici parachuted into the area of Lentini but did no damage. *Tenente* Gino Apostolo's patrol was to attack targets in the Augusta area but was quickly captured after a short firefight. *Sottotenente* Salvatore Pizziamico's patrol's target was the airfield at San Pietro di Caltagirone but also failed

47 Arena, *Tarquinia*, p.81.
48 Longo, *I «reparti speciali»*, p.140.
49 Di Giovanni, *I paracadutisti*, p.191; Alberto Santoni, *Le operazioni in Sicilia e in Calabria* (Rome, USSME, 1983) pp.327, 331.

to reach the airfield. The patrol wandered the area for fifteen days and destroyed a bridge before being captured. Overall the patrols did little damage and most of the *arditi* were captured.[50]

The second operation was a single patrol under *capitano* Gabriele Bussoli which parachuted onto Sicily during the night of 24/25 July to attack an ammunition storage site near Catania. The patrol was able to destroy the ammunition dump and then successfully crossed back through enemy lines into friendly territory. This was the last combat parachute jump of the *reparti paracadutisti* until after the armistice.[51]

Again there is speculation by the Italians that the missions of the patrols had been compromised by the enemy. *Sottotenente* Apostolo claimed that during his interrogation after he was captured, he gave false information about his name and unit. The interrogator interrupted him and then stated Apostolo's true name, unit, and unit commanders. The interrogator then added that *tenente* Apostolo's patrol was late as they had been awaiting its arrival for four days. The belief that the *arditi* patrols had been compromised prior to their missions in Africa and Sicily is a common thread in many of the Italian accounts. Research is needed in the Allied sources to verify whether this was actually the case.[52]

As previously seen, these patrols again achieved little military effect. Even if all these objectives had been successfully attacked, there would have been little to no impact on Allied operations. None of the targets were critical to the ongoing Allied efforts in Sicily, nor were the targets connected to any Italian or German actions to help achieve a positive outcome.

The Nembo in Sicily (Map 13.4)

The *185º rgt.* was in Florence awaiting transportation to Corsica when word arrived of the Allied landings in Sicily on 10 July. Rather than being sent to Corsica as planned, these orders were canceled and the regiment was ordered south to the Salento region of Puglia. Here the regiment was used for anti-parachute tasks while arrangements were made to transfer the regiment to Sicily. The regiment had its three battalions (*III*, *VIII*, and *XI*) and the *III gr. art.* from the *184º rgt. art.*[53]

The regiment began its movement by rail to Calabria on 14 July. Allied bombing against roads, railways and tunnels slowed the movement across southern Italy. The

50 Arena, *FOLGORE,* p.318; Longo, *I «reparti speciali»*, p.153; Arena, *Aquile senza Ali*, p.190; Crociani, and Battistelli, *Italian Army Elite Units*, p.52..

51 Arena, *FOLGORE,* p.318; Longo, *I «reparti speciali»*, pp.146–149; Crociani, and Battistelli, *Italian Army Elite Units*, p.52.

52 Longo, *I «reparti speciali»*, pp.153.

53 Arena, *Aquile senza Ali*, p.194; Arena, *Nembo!*, p.23; Di Giovanni, *I paracadutisti*, p.207. It is unclear whether the regiment was sent to Salento before or after 10 July. A move south before the invasion is counter to the orders for the regiment to move to Corsica.

regiment was forced off the trains by these attacks and continued its movement by vehicle. The marching columns had to be observant to avoid being surprised by Allied fighters. As the unit arrived in the area around Reggio Calabria, the *nemboini* encountered the dispirited troops that had been withdrawn from Sicily and the disorganization of the ferry operation across the Straits of Messina. The regiment currently had 2,000 men and eighteen 47/32 c.c. as it prepared to cross over to Sicily.[54]

The *185º rgt.* began to ferry over to Messina starting on 25 June. That evening the word began to spread that Mussolini had been ousted by the Fascist Grand Council and his request to remain in power was rejected by the King. It was not until 29 July that the entire regiment was on Sicily where more dispirited Italian troops were encountered and the destruction of towns could be seen.[55]

The regiment traveled along the northern coastal road and then south to Castroreale. Here the *nemboini* would link-up with the remains of the *4ª d.f «Livorno»* that had been withdrawn from the combat due to losses reaching 60 percent of its strength. The *6ª Armata* had been requesting replacements and equipment to refit the division on the island. The *185º rgt.* was attached to the division and would operate with it once it finished reorganizing. While at Castroreale, two *paracadutisti* were killed and eighteen wounded when the motorized column of the regiment was strafed by Allied fighter aircraft.[56]

It quickly became apparent that the *«Livorno»* would not be rebuilt on Sicily. The operational situation deteriorated during the first week of August. On the evening of 5 August, *generale* Guzzoni sent a message to *Superesercito* on the current situation and recommendations for future actions. Included in this was the recommendation that the *d.f. «Livorno»* be rebuilt using the *185º rgt.* and an additional regiment provided by Rome. The proposal was not acted upon and the *185º rgt.* and the *«Livorno»* were ordered to retreat towards Messina.[57]

With the Allies pressing forward, *Superesercito* approved the withdrawal of the *6ª Armata* headquarters from Sicily on the night of 9 August. This was quickly followed later that evening with the approval to withdraw all Italian troops from the island except the garrison of Messina which was placed under German command.[58]

For the *paracadutisti*, the withdrawal from Sicily occurred during the nights between 11 and 13 August without having fought in Sicily. The Germans operating the ferry service informed the *paracadutisti* that they must leave their vehicles behind at Messina due to the need to evacuate as many men as possible. The Germans had imposed a ban against bringing any Italian vehicles into the port area. While in the port area, the regiment experienced more casualties. Four *paracadutisti* were killed and twelve injured in the *33ª cp.* when a cargo of bombs on the quay accidentally exploded. Later

54 Arena, *Nembo!*, p.23; Santoni, *Le operazioni in Sicilia,* pp.324, 327–328.
55 Santoni, *Le operazioni in Sicilia,* p.327; Arena, *Aquile senza Ali*, p.194.
56 Arena, *Aquile senza Ali*, pp.194–195;
57 Santoni, *Le operazioni in Sicilia*, p.364.
58 Santoni, *Le operazioni in* Sicilia, p.382.

when boarding the ferries, another explosion killed another five *nemboini* and wounded twenty more. Among the wounded was *colonnello* Parodi, the regimental commander. *Maggiore* Angelo Massimino assumed temporary command of the regiment.[59]

Calabria (Maps 13.5, 13.6)

Once back across the straits, the regiment was initially concentrated at Melito Porto Salvo on the southernmost point of mainland Italy. While in the town, the *nemboini* began to notice the Germans were operating trucks with Italian military license plates, some with numbers belonging to the regiment. The *32ª cp.* of the *XI btg.* organized a raid and seized thirty of their trucks from the Germans. This provoked a confrontation between the Germans and Italians, but it ended peacefully when the Germans agreed to provide a ferry to retrieve the remaining trucks from Sicily.[60]

The «*Livorno*» had been ferried over to Calabria during the withdrawal and moved into the mountainous Aspromonte massif area to rest and refit. While the regiment remained attached to the division, a reorganization was underway. The *XVI Cd'A* was transferred north to La Spezia and the remaining units assigned to the *XXXI Cd'A*. The new corps commander, *generale di corpo d'armata* Camillo Mercalli, considered the «*Livorno*» as unfit for combat in his assessment on 24 August. The *185º rgt.* was then reassigned to the *211ª d. costiera* which was defending the southern coast of Calabria from Reggio Calabria to the vicinity of Soverato.[61]

With the *185º rgt.* now attached to the *XXXI Cd'A* in Calabria, it was unlikely that the regiment would rejoin the *d. f.* «*Nembo*» in Sardinia. *Supereservito* decided to make the exchange of the *VIII* and *X btg.* between the two regiments permanent. The order issued on 17 August 1943 now authorized the *183º rgt.* to have the *X*, *XV*, and *XVI* while the *185º* would have the *III*, *VIII*, *XI*. This only codified the reality that had existed since June.[62]

Rather than keeping the regiment together, its three battalions were spread out across the toe of Italy's boot. The *III btg.* was placed close to the northern shore at Piani Milea, while the *XI btg.* was in the center at Santa Cristina d'Aspromonte. The *VIII btg.* was attached to the *143º rgt. f. costiera* in the area of Melito Porto on the southern coast. The *comando 185ª rgt.* was at Cittanova. This disposition had the non-motorized regiment spread over twenty kilometers in an area of broken terrain

59 Arena, *I PARACADUTISTI*, p.152.

60 Santoni, *Le operazioni in* Sicilia, p.386; Arena, *Aquile senza Ali*, pp.195–196. The story of the trucks might be apocryphal, but similar German actions are well documented.

61 Arena, *FOLGORE!*, p.361; Santoni, p.389–390

62 AUSSME, Stato Generale R.E. memorandum 17 Agosto 1943, *Oggetto: Dipendenze VIII e X btg. paracadutisti*, M7 racc.432, cart.3.

and few roads. In the area were the II and III/15.Panzergrenadier Regiment from the 29.Panzergrenadier Division.[63]

The British 8th Army executed Operation Baytown (the invasion of Calabria) on the early morning of 3 September. There was little resistance on the shore as the Germans had decided not to commit their forces. Kesselring had sent an order on 3 September for the German divisions located in Calabria not to move forward and engage the landing, but instead begin to pull back and use demolitions in the broken and mountainous terrain to retard the Allied advance.[64] The only resistance, little as it was, was from the Italian coastal units which lacked sufficient means to offer an effective defense.

The *XI btg. para.*, with the *534ª cp. mortai* from the *211° d. cost.*, was ordered on 3 September from its position at Santa Cristina d'Aspromonte forward to Gambarie. *Capitano* Luciano Della Valle, the commander of the battalion, decided to move a few kilometers forward to Santo Stefano to establish his defense. Here the unit came into contact with the 1/48th Highlanders of Canada from the 1st Canadian Infantry Brigade of the 1st Canadian Division on 4 September.[65] Skirmishing lasted most of the day, but at the end of the day the battalion had been pushed back from Santo Stefano and Gambarie. Rather than support the *paracadutisti*, the German II/15. Panzergrenadier Regiment that was in the area followed its orders and retreated, destroying parts of the roads behind it. Recognizing that to stay in place would result in being surrounded, *capitano* Delle Valle decided to order his battalion to retreat to rejoin the remainder of the regiment. The destruction created by the German battalion to the roads during its withdrawal hindered the retreat of the Italians.[66]

On the same day (4 September) the *VIII btg.* commanded by *capitano* Gianfranco Conati was in an assembly area at the town of Bagaladi awaiting orders. The *148° rgt. costiero* was defending the road along the southern coast, but its defense rapidly collapsed against the lead elements of the 3rd Canadian Brigade. After entering Melito Porto late on 3 September, a detachment of 1/The Carleton and York Regiment continued to push north towards Bagaladi on 4 September and ran into the *VIII btg.* The *paracadutisti* surprised the Canadians and held their positions until Conati received orders to withdraw. The problem for the *VIII btg.* was that the Canadians controlled both the main road along the coast and the roads north of them through the Aspromonte region. The only option was to use the mountain tracks to escape the advancing allies.[67]

63 Arena, *FOLGORE!*, p.361; G.W. Nicholson, *The Canadians in Italy 1943-1945* (Ottawa, Edmond Cloutier, 1956), pp.193–194.
64 Santoni, *Le operazioni in Sicilia*, p.431; Molony, *The Mediterranean and Middle East*, vol. 5, p.239.
65 Nicholson, *The Canadians in Italy*, p.207.
66 Arena, *I PARACADUTISTI*, p.160; Nicholson, *The Canadians in Italy*, p.207.
67 Arena, *I PARACADUTISTI*, pp.160–162; Nicholson, *The Canadians in Italy*, p.207. Nicholson writes "this enterprising detachment ran into unexpectedly spirited groups of Italian paratroopers of the Nembo Division, who strongly contested the tangle of ravines

The *btg.* moved throughout 5-6 September and finally came within sight of Plati on a road connecting the two coasts of Calabria on 7 September. However the Canadians, using the roads had beaten the *paracadutisti* to the town and the area was full of Allied vehicles. The battalion was effectively cut-off from the rest of the regiment. Conati discussed the situation with his company commanders and decided to attack with the *22ª cp.*, combined with a flanking movement by the *23ª cp.* The remainder of the battalion would try to slip past the enemy during the fighting. During the night, a detachment from the Loyal Edmonton Regiment contacted the elements of the *VIII btg.* and a small, short skirmish broke out with the *nemboin*i retreating into the darkness.

Early in the morning of 8 September the two companies attacked units of the 1/ West Nova Scotia Regiment. An intense battle broke out that lasted approximately an hour. The Canadians were able to quickly reinforce their units in contact and defeat the attack. The *VIII btg.* lost seven killed, 16 wounded, and 57 *paracadutisti* were captured. The remainder of the battalion was scattered and escaped into the mountains, but the *VIII btg.* was broken as a combat unit.[68]

During the time that the *VIII btg.* was attempting to escape, the *185º rgt.* with the other two battalions continuing to retreat. The *III* and *XI btg.* had joined together at Plati and then set out for Cardinale. Arriving at that location, the regiment joined the column consisting of the *210º d. cost.*, the *gruppo tattico «Carbone»* and elements of the 29. Panzergrenadier Division. The withdrawal of the units then continued to Soveria Mannelli under strafing attacks from Allied aircraft. The regiment was just short of reaching that town when the *paracadutisti* were informed of the Italian surrender on the evening of 8 September. For the Italian units, the questions that needed answering were what did it mean and what were they supposed to do now?[69]

and barren peaks about the villages of San Lorenzo and Bagaladi before withdrawing eastward into the mountains".

68 Arena, *I PARACADUTISTI*, pp.164–165; Nicholson, *The Canadians in Italy*, p.211.

69 Arena, *I PARACADUTISTI*, p.165.

14

Nord, Sud o Casa?

The announcement on Radio Rome at 2000 hrs on the evening of 8 September 1943 took all of Italy by surprise. After the fall of Mussolini on 25 July, the Badoglio government that had replaced the fascist régime agreed that the war was lost. The government spent the next weeks attempting negotiations with the Allies in order to gain favorable terms for Italy's surrender. The Allies, wary of Italian motivation and disdainful of Italian military capabilities, offered little except surrender. The Italian side of the negotiations were poorly handled, with several different initiatives simultaneously pursued, leading to miscommunications and misunderstandings. The reality was that Italy was attempting to bargain without having anything to bargain with, a position which the Allies fully understood. The tragic events that followed 8 September were solely due to the Italian leadership failing to accept and plan for that reality.[1]

Much of the problem experienced by the Badoglio government was rooted in its fear of German actions in retaliation once the armistice with the Allies was announced. The fear was so excessive that the government took extreme steps to keep the planning and negotiations secret which included keeping all knowledge of the contingency planning for the execution of the armistice from the senior Italian military leadership. The result was many of the army commanders and their main subordinates had no knowledge of how the government intended for them to act when confronted by the Germans.

Planning commenced on 18 August with the objective of creating a defense against German aggression that would protect the government and the naval bases of La Spezia and Gaeta. The concept was to transfer the most capable units of the

1 A good introduction to these events is Elena Agarossi, *A Nation Collapses* (Cambridge: Cambridge University Press, 2000). Melton S. Davis's *Who Defends Rome?* (London, George Allen & Unwin Ltd. 1972) focuses on the defense of Rome but addresses in detail the military negotiations and planning of the Italian leadership. F.W. Deakin's *The Brutal Friendship* (New York: Harper & Row, Publishers, 1962) focuses on the political aspects of the crisis and places the events in their broader political/strategic setting.

R.E. to a central location north of Rome best positioned to achieve that objective. By 22 August this objective was scrapped as the Germans continued to move fresh units into Italy to counter the likely Allied invasion. The objective of the plan was now changed to simply provide guidance to the commanders as to how the Italian forces should react to the expected German aggression. This plan would be modified based on the evolving military situation on the peninsula and the negotiations with the Allies. The plan was finalized on 2 September after the terms of the armistice were agreed upon.[2]

The result was *Memoria 44*, a document issued by *Superesercito* that provided guidance in the case of German aggression against Italian forces. The *memoria* was approved for limited distribution (only twelve copies were made) and hand delivered to a very select group of senior leaders. Once read by the senior officer, it was to be destroyed (burning was specified) with only the signed receipt page maintained and returned to *Superesercito*. This was deemed necessary to prevent the Germans from discovering a copy. The original of *Memoria 44* maintained by *Superesercito* was burned on 9 September. Because of this provision, no copy of *Memoria 44* survived and maintained in the archives. What is known about the *memoria* was reconstructed from the officers that had read the document.[3] The order specified:

> General Tasks, confirming the previous orders: avoiding surprises, supervising, reinforcing the protection of the commands, communication routes, plants, supervising the movements of the German forces, arranging coup de main strikes on their depots, bases and warehouses, guarding the points militarily more important.
>
> Specified Tasks:
> - 2ª Armata: take out the 71st German Division and interrupt communications to the Germans from Tarvisio to the sea;
> - 4ª Armata: gather the remaining forces in the Roia and Vermenagna Valleys and, acting on the flanks of the German units, interrupt communications with the Cornice (Liguria); with the XX raggruppamento sciatori [skiers] to block the passes of Mont Cenis and Montgenèvre, and interrupt the Fréjus railway;
> - 5ª Armata: to hold La Spezia firmly and focus on German forces and vehicles located between Lake Bolsena and the Sienese;
> - 7ª Armata: firmly hold Taranto and possibly Brindisi too;

2 Mario Torsiello, *Le operazioni delle unità italiane nel settembre-ottobre 1943* (Rome, USSME, 1975), pp.41–42.

3 Torsiello, *Le operazioni delle unità italiane*, pp.42–43; Davis, *Who Defends Rome?*, pp.331–332. Memoria 44 is also referred to as the Memoria Roatta.

- 8ª Armata: cut communications between Germany and the South Tyrol, act against German forces on the move or positioned in Trentino and South Tyrol, interrupt, in support of the 2ª Armata, communications from Tarvisio to the sea;
- Forza Armata Sardegna: take out the 90th German Division;
- Forza Armata Corsica: take out the German SS. Armoured Brigade.

The subordinate commands would implement *Memoria 44* either when directed by a further communication or by the individual commanders if they felt the situation was warranted.[4]

Memoria 44 did not provide much in the way of specific guidance. A major omission was any information about the signed armistice. Because of this, it did not clearly indicate whether Germany or the Allies were the subject of the document. Many of the army commanders in fact understood the *memoria* to apply to the Allies. Further instructions were provided in *Promemoria* n.1 and n.2, and in *Memoria 45*, all issued on 6 September. These documents clarified what actions should be taken against German offensive actions but did little to clarify how the Germans were to be treated without a clear initiation of hostilities. Again there was no mention of the armistice and its provisions. This omission would leave commanders unclear as to the status of Italian relations with both Germany and the Allies once the armistice was announced.[5]

Without defining the relationship between the nations affected by the armistice, commanders could not prepare their soldiers, airmen, and sailors for the impending change. The servicemen of the three services had been fighting alongside their German counterparts for three years. While there had been much friction between the two along the way, the Germans were still seen as comrades-in-arms. It was desirable to mentally prepare the men by giving them time to rationally assess the change without the pressure of the need for an immediate decision on their part.

Germany had also been preparing for a possible Italian defection from the Axis cause. Hitler was concerned that Italy would abandon the Axis so directed planning for what would become Fall Achse after the fall of Tunisia in May 1943. The Germans began a build-up of forces in Italy, presented as preparation against an Allied invasion but positioned with an eye towards Fall Achse. Germans commanders and headquarters that worked closely with their Italian counterparts noticed an increasing resistance to their requests which heightened concerns of Italian reliability.

By the time of the surrender on 8 September, there were seventeen German divisions and two brigades in Italy, concentrated mostly in northern and central Italy. The R.E. only had twenty-six divisions, many of which were in various states of rebuilding.[6] *Supercomando* had been protesting the increase of German units in Italy, but it was

4 Torsiello, *Le operazioni delle unità italiane*, pp.43–44.
5 Torsiello, *Le operazioni delle unità italiane*, pp.63–72.
6 Alberto Santoni, *Le operazioni in Sicilia e in Calabria* (Rome: USSME, 1983), p.422.

torn between preparing for a possible surrender and trying to improve Italy's defense against an Allied invasion. Generalfeldmarschall Kesselring was able to smooth over these issues as they arose, allowing the German military build-up to continue. To counter this increase of German forces, *Supercomando* began ordering units in occupied France and the Balkans back to Italy. These actions were initiated too late, and on 8 September many units were still in the process of moving back to Italy.

The announcement of the armistice by the Allies at 1745 hrs on 8 September caught everyone by surprise. The Italian government had expected the announcement would be days later, but the Allies had never made such a statement and kept the invasion date a secret. Rumors of a possible armistice had been circulating all day, but at 1600 hrs Reuters began to announce the news. Apparently the word had been leaked to the press in New York, but the Allies did not do anything to contain the information once it was out. Several Italian army headquarters queried *Supercomando*, but *Supercomando* denied the story. The next hours were filled with confusion as more and more radio stations carried the story. Many Italian commanders were wondering whether any Allied landings should be contested or whether to allow them to proceed without interference. What was the relationship between the Allied armed forces and the Italian military, and conversely that with the Germans? The Italian government continued to believe that the Allies had decided to announce the armistice four days early instead of dealing with the current reality. No new guidance was issued to the three services.[7]

Two hours after denying that Italy had requested an armistice, *Maresciallo d'Italia* Badoglio announced at 1945 hrs that an armistice had in fact been signed. More confusion followed as *Supercomando* did little to clarify what was happening. The broadcast also lacked any guidance for the Italian service men and people, leaving most to believe that the war was over for Italy.

The rapid, decisive decision-making and communications of the German leadership must be contrasted with the ineffectual and hesitant decision-making of the Italians. No new instructions were sent by *Supercomando* detailing the new relationship to be established with the Germans on the evening of 8 September. Learning of the announcement, Hitler immediately ordered the implementation of Fall Achse. This order was communicated to the German units in Italy for immediate execution. These units began disarming Italian units and replacing them at key locations throughout Italy during the night of 8–9 September. Italian units either passively accepted disarming and imprisonment, or the soldiers simply decided the war was over and abandoned their units to return home.

It was not until 0020 on 9 September that *Supercomando* issued a clarifying order that again stressed that Italian units were not to initiate combat unless the German units acted first. The effect of this clarification meant that Italians units were hesitant to take firm action in fear of violating an assumed agreement between Italy

7 Davis, *Who Defends Rome?*, pp.371–377.

and Germany, the conditions of which they remained unaware. *Superesercito* pressed *Supercomando* for authorization to implement *Memoria 44*, but *generale* Ambrosio refused.[8]

This lack of unambiguous instructions led to orders and counter orders as the commanders in the units tried to understand the unfolding events and adjust to the rapidly changing situation. Many units were ordered to stay in the barracks as officers awaited orders and tried to maintain discipline, only to be easily captured there by the Germans.[9] For those servicemen who only wished that the war was over, the lack of firm leadership was apparent. As one man later recounted:

> And then they would not even give us any clear orders. There was a flood of orders, but each one was different or the opposite of the others. Resist the Germans; don't fire on the Germans; don't let the Germans disarm you; kill the Germans; lay down your weapons; don't give up your weapons.[10]

It was not until 11 September that *Supercomando* finally issued instructions that German units were to be treated as enemies. It was too late as any attempt for coordinated military action in response to Fall Achse was gone. Too many units had been lost or disintegrated in the days immediately following 8 September. Only the *Regia Marina* remained as a coherent military force by ordering the fleet to sail to Allied controlled harbors.[11]

Mussolini would be freed from captivity on 12 September by German fallschirmjägers in a daring raid on the Campo Imperatore Hotel on Gran Sasso. Eleven days later on 23 September Germany and Mussolini announced the creation of the Repubblica Sociale Italiana (R.S.I., Italian Social Republic), often called the Republic of Salò. The R.S.I. would nominally govern the northern part of Italy that was occupied by Germany. With the continuation of the Badoglio government in the south in the area occupied by the Allies, the country was now split into two.

For the men of the three services, and the *reparti paracadutisti* in particular, the radio announcement would force a decision in the coming days. Nord, Sud, o Casa? (North, South, or Home?).

185° Reggimento Paracadutisti

The *paracadutisti* of the *185° reggimento* heard the announcement as they were retreating out of Calabria as part of a column that included elements of the German

8 Torsiello, *Le operazioni delle unità italiane*, p.51; Agarossi, *A Nation Collapses*, p.96.
9 Agarossi, *A Nation Collapses*, pp.104-112.
10 Agarossi, *A Nation Collapses*, p.105.
11 Torsiello, *Le operazioni delle unità italiane*, pp.50-51.

29.Panzergrenadier Division. The German division had received orders to rapidly move to Salerno to counter-attack the Allied landing on 9 September. With no clear orders or guidance from *Supercomando*, the regiment continued its northward march with the German unit. The movement on 9 September was only marred by a violent Allied air attack on the column which destroyed many vehicles. On 10 September the Panzergrenadiers were instructed to hurry their movement as they were vitally needed at Salerno. To do that meant separating from the slower moving Italian units.[12]

Major Ziegler, the commander of the Panzer-Aufklärungs-Abteilung 129, was instructed to disarm the Italian so they could not interfere with the German withdrawal. The German commander instead offered that the *paracadutisti* join the Germans in their movement to Salerno to continue to fight.[13] Nord, Sud, o Casa? – this would be the question all the *paracadutisti* would have to answer in the coming days

The Italian commanders conferred amongst themselves and their men, and the decisions were made. For the *III btg. fanteria* under *capitano* Edoardo Sala, the decision was to join with the Germans and continue to fight against the Allies. The *XI btg*, under *capitano* Luciano Della Valle opted instead to stay true to their oath to the King and remain where they were to await further orders from *Supercomando*. With that, the Germans with their remaining Italian allies and those Italians that decided to honor the armistice parted ways.

It was not long before many of the soldiers that had decided to join with the Germans began to rethink their decision. *Capitano* Sala had been quite persuasive in extolling the soldierly virtues of the Germans and the need to honor their commitment to the Axis, but the passion of the moment had now passed. The bulk of the *9ª cp.* under *capitano* Francesco Guy separated from the battalion and marched to join the forces that remained loyal to the King. A little later, part of the *7ª cp.* under *capitano* Giustino Romano separated as well and then disbanded, the men deciding to return to their homes. Sala now found himself leading a battalion of approximately 100 men when the *III btg.* reached the Salerno area. With these acts, the *185º reggimento fanteria* had ceased to exist.[14]

Sardinia (Map 14.1)

Generale di corpo d'armata Antonio Basso was in command of the *Comando Forze Armate Sardegna*. Under his command were all the R.E., R.A., and R.M. assets, as well as any German forces on the island. The reality was that while the German units

12 Nino Arena, *Nembo!* (Rome, IBN Editore, 2013), p. 46.
13 Nino Arena, *FOLGORE! Storia del paracadutismo militare italiano* (Rome: Centro Editoriale Nazione, 1965), p.375–376.
14 Arena, *Nembo!*, p.46; Marco Di Giovanni, *I paracadutisti italiani Volontari, miti e memoria della seconda guerra mondiale* (Gorizia, Editrice Goriziana, 1991), p.221.

would collaborate with the Italians, the real senior commander for those units was Generalfeldmarschall Kesselring in mainland Italy.

Basso faced a challenging defensive problem. The island was 24,090 square kilometers with a coastline of over 1,500 km long. To defend the island he had a total of approximately 130,000 Italians and 30,000 Germans. Of the Italians, 56,000 men were in the coastal divisions of limited combat power, 9,000 men were in the *Camicie Nere* (CC.NN.) Legions (Blackshirts) also with limited training and equipment, and 12,000 men were in support units operating the logistical and medical systems on the island.[15]

The primary combat power available to the *FF.AA. Sardegna* were the four Italian infantry divisions and the German 90.Panzergrenadier Division. Basso lacked an effective Italian armoured formation and planned to rely on the German armoured units assigned to the 90.Panzergrenadier for any attacks against Allied landings. Two of the Italian regular divisions, the *30ª d.f. «Sabauda»* and the *31ª d.f. «Calabria»* were assigned to the *XIII* and *XXX corpo d'armata* respectively. The remaining two divisions, *47ª divisione fanteria «Bari»* and the *184ª divisione fanteria «Nembo»* were assigned as the army reserve, along with the 90.Panzergrenadier Division.[16]

Of the four regular Italian divisions on the island, only the *«Nembo»* was considered fully mobile. The Italian parachute division had rehearsed multiple rapid reaction deployments in close coordination with the 90.Panzergrenadier in preparation for an Anglo-American landing. Over time, a strong bond had developed between the two units and there was some concern about the reliability of the *paracadutisti* should a rupture occur between Italy and Germany.

Gen. Basso received his copy of *Memoria 44* on 3 September. In it the *FF.AA Sardegna* was charged with neutralizing the 90.Panzergrenadier Division and preventing it from joining other German forces on the mainland. The challenge for Basso was how to tackle the most powerful unit on the island. On the morning of 6 September he gathered his major subordinate commanders and informed them of the instructions contained in *Memoria 44* and issued his own directive, *Memoria Azione «Emergenza T»* (Emergency Plan «T»). Present at the meeting were *generali di divisione* Gustavo Reisoli (*XIII Cd'A*), Giangiacomo Castagna (*XXX Cd'A*), Ismaele Di Nisio (*«Bari»*), and Carlo Petra (*Comando difesa Territoriale*); *ammiraglio di divisione* Bruno Brivonesi (*Marina militare*); *generale di divisione aerea* Umberto Cappa (*Aeronautica militare*); and *gen.* Ronco (*«Nembo»*).[17]

Memoria Azione «Emergenza T» provided two possible scenarios that could generate conflict between the German and Italian units. The first scenario was if the Italians initiated hostilities against the German units; the second was if the Germans were

15 Torsiello, *Le operazioni delle unità italiane*, pp.271–274.

16 Filippo Cappellano and Nicola Pignato, *Gli autoveicoli da combattimento dell'Esercito Italiano* (Rome: USSME, 2002), volume secondo, p.104. The *raggruppamento corazzato* had a mix of M14/42, L6/40, and semoventi da 75/18.

17 Torsiello, *Le operazioni delle unità italiane*, p.295.

the ones to initiate hostilities between the two sides. The instructions given in the *memoria* were general in nature and lacked any priorities, timelines, or sequence of actions. The document gave enough guidance for the subordinate units to begin generalized planning, but the prohibition against the issuance of written orders would needlessly complicate and delay the process. The desire to prevent any knowledge of the approaching armistice leaking to the Germans precluded the use of the most rapid systems to transmit instructions to subordinates.[18]

What Basso did not know was when the armistice would be announced and the details of the agreement between Italy and the Allies. All the discussions between the leadership on Sardinia were framed by the lack of guidance with little more than to be prepared for something changing. Were German units to be treated as friendly, enemy, or something in-between? What German actions could be allowed? What level of confrontation/conflict was the government prepared to authorize to achieve the unstated outcome of the armistice? This pattern of planning in the face of uncertainty was repeated in all the senior headquarters of the Italian military.

The «*Nembo*» participation in the upcoming confrontation was limited under «*Emergenza T*». Deployed mainly in an anti-parachutist role, the units of the division had been broken down into small detachments and scattered at the various airfields and large open areas across the island. *Generale* Ronco would require time to assemble his two regiments and prepare for large-scale combat. As the division lacked heavy weapons and having concerns on the reliability of the *paracadutisti*, *generale* Basso decided to place the division under the control of the *XIII Cd'A* rather than give it an independent role. The only specified order in the *memoria* for the division was to move the battalion currently at Fertilia (outside Alghero) to Stazione Tirso to act as a mobile reaction force protecting the nearby airfields.[19]

That evening (6 Sep) *comando FF.AA. Sardegna* received a new order from *Supercomando. Gen.* Basso was to reinforce the garrison at La Maddalena with a 'first-rate' (*ottimo*) *raggruppamento* consisting of three battalions and an artillery group. Basso formed the raggruppamento under the *comando 59° rgt. fanteria «Calabria»* with one battalion from that regiment, a battalion from the «*Bari*», and the *XXI btg. volontari sardi* (Sardinian Volunteer battalion). Attached was the *gruppo da 75/27 T.M.* from the *raggruppamento motocorazzato*. With orders to assemble this force issued the morning of 7 September, the unit would not be fully assembled until 11 September. Unknown to the *comando FF.AA. Sardegna* was that this force was meant to secure La Maddalena as an anchorage for the Italian battle fleet after it left La Spezia in accordance with the armistice.[20]

What the leadership did not realize is that after the meeting ended on the morning of 6 September, the announcement of the armistice was less than sixty hours away.

18 Torsiello, *Le operazioni delle unità italiane*, p.293-295.
19 Torsiello, *Le operazioni delle unità italiane*, pp.293-295.
20 Torsiello, *Le operazioni delle unità italiane*, p.270.

Unable to issue written orders, the staff of the two corps and the divisions had to develop a complex plan that must account for multiple variations and then distribute it to the units. None of this was achieved in the remaining time. The end result was that none of the units below the divisional level had any orders or guidance when the time for action had arrived.

Due to this, little was accomplished to prepare the Italian military units for any confrontation with Germans. In accordance with Basso's guidance contained in «*Emergenza T*», the *X btg.* began its move from Fertilia to Stazione Tirso outside of Bolotana on 7 September. That same evening, *FF.AA. Sardegna* was informed by *Supercomando* of the sailing of several large allied convoys from North Africa with their destination unknown. Sent along with that intelligence was the order to resist any landings by Allied forces. No further guidance was received that evening by *FF.AA. Sardegna*. Basso's first knowledge of the armistice was similar to that of everyone else, the announcement on the radio on the evening of 8 September.[21]

The announcement was not as great a surprise to Generalleutnant Carl-Hans Lungerhausen, commander of the 90.Panzergrenadier Division and all the German forces on Sardinia. Lungerhausen had been in communication with Kesselring's headquarters throughout the day of 8 September and was aware changes were happening. In response to the announcement, Lungerhausen forwarded a message from Kesselring to Basso at 2130 hours stating that the armistice was a betrayal to the agreements between the two countries. Kesselring encouraged that the armistice be ignored and that the Italian forces on the island join with the Germans and continue the fight against the Allies. Basso immediately rejected the proposal and informed Lungerhausen that the Italians had orders to get the Germans off the island. Lungerhausen replied that he had orders to evacuate the island and hoped that this could be achieved without conflict.[22]

Generale Basso considered what Lungerhausen had stated. Basso felt that allowing the Germans to retreat off the island unmolested did not conflict with his understanding of *Memoria 44* or the subsequent instructions. He therefore announced that the Germans were to be allowed to withdraw from the island without interference as long as the German did not initiate any hostile actions, or damaged/destroyed any defensive works. He provided the Germans a basic route to follow to the ports in the north for their evacuation. He communicated this decision to *Comando Supremo* to confirm the correctness of this course of action. The general would not receive a reply to his message until 12 September.[23]

On 9 September *generale* Basso ordered *generale* Ronco to assemble his division (minus the *X btg.*) and moved it north to the area near Tempio. Basso was trying to increase the strength of the Italian forces in the northern part of the island should any

21 Torsiello, *Le operazioni delle unità italiane*, p.270.
22 Torsiello, *Le operazioni delle unità italiane*, pp.277–278.
23 Arena, *Nembo!*, pp.46–47;Torsiello, *Le operazioni delle unità italiane*, pp.277–278.

issues arise with the German withdrawal. The division would then come under the command of the *XXX Cd'A*. However this order would never be carried out.[24]

German encouragement of Italian units to disobey the armistice was not limited to senior Italian command. The call to disobey was repeated throughout the island as German and Italian soldiers came into contact. The lack of preparation of the Italian leadership and soldiers for this situation resulted in that individual units were forced to make spur of the moment decisions in response to German demands. These decisions were taken without an understanding of the larger picture and in the absence of any overarching intent or plan from *Supercomando* to guide them. As recollected by *generale* Basso at the end of September:

> The group of young officers, born and raised in the fascist climate, who had received no other education outside of that given by the regime, blindly believing in the infallibility of the fascist institutions, had acknowledged the change of government with much malice [...] and with a partisan spirit it [the fascist government] circulated among the subordinates a hollow, devious propaganda, which somehow caught the minds and souls of the most hesitant and indecisive.[25]

The fate of the «*Nembo*» would now be determined by individual acts and decisions by junior leaders and soldiers.

Faced with the need to decide without any orders, each unit of the «*Nembo*» made its choice. The *XII btg.* (minus the 35ª cp.) under *maggiore* Mario Rizzatti at Decimomannu decided to join the Germans in their retreat. Joining them was the *1ª batteria* of the *II/184ª rgt. art.* and a mortar platoon. Parts of the *XIII* and *XIV btg.* also opted to join their German allies. Other battalions were favorable to the Germans, but their leadership was able to maintain a level of discipline. While not openly joining the Germans, these officers were able to keep their units together and avoid mass desertions. This did not prevent small acts of support from happening, like allowing Germans units to pass freely through roadblocks.[26]

Generale Ronco found himself operating in a vacuum of guidance. With elements of the division stationed at multiple locations, he was unable to personally intervene in every crisis. The result was that the battalion commanders were forced to immediately deal with the evolving situation. When informed of the actions of *maggiore* Rizzatti, Basso contacted Lungerhausen to attempt to have the German general intervene. Lungerhausen demurred and told Basso he should speak personally to the officer. The meeting between the two officers achieved nothing as the rebellious unit arrested Ronco for a brief period of time before releasing him. Rizzatti was determined to

24 Torsiello, *Le operazioni delle unità italiane*, pp.279.
25 Di Giovanni, *I paracadutisti*, p.211.
26 Arena, *Nembo!*, p.46; Arena, *FOLGORE!*, p.386; Torsiello, *Le operazioni delle unità italiane*, p.279 and fn. 22; Nino Arena, *R.S.I., Forze Armate della Repubblica Sociale, la guerra in Italia 1943* (Parma: Ermanno Albertelli Editore, 1999), p.87.

maintain his honor and to continue the fight. "General, let me die for my homeland!" has been quoted as *maggiore* Rizzatti's parting words to the general. The *XII btg.* marched north with the Germans to escape the island.[27]

The *X btg.* under *maggiore* Felice Valletti-Borgnini on 9 September continued to move from Nurra to Bolòtana in accordance with the order contained in «*Emergenza T*». Marching south, the *nemboini* passed German columns moving north. Many of the men desired to join that march and return to the mainland to continue the fight. At Bolòtana Valletti managed to keep the battalion together when many of the men again expressed a wish to join the Germans. Under orders from *generale* Ronco, the battalion was put under guard and the officers separated from the men. Ronco spoke with the officers but it became apparent that the battalion was too fractured for operational use. At the end of five days, the decision was made to disband the *X btg.*, as well the *184ª cp. ciclisti*. The members of those units considered unreliable were retained under guard while the remainder were sent to other units.[28]

Other arrests happened during this time. The *vice comandante* of the division, *colonnello* Pietro Tantillo and *tenente colonnello* Ademaro Invrea, both veterans of El Alamein, along with other officers and *paracadutisti* were arrested and held based on their expressed desire to continue the war. Many *nemboini* attempted to escape to the mainland to join the Germans. It was quickly becoming apparent that the morale and discipline of the division was breaking down and the units could not be relied upon to follow orders.[29]

The most serious incident occurred on 10 September when the division chief of Staff, *tenente colonnello* Alberto Bechi-Luserna attempted to dissuade the *XII btg.* from joining the Germans. Luserna was famous in the *paracadutisti* community, having commanded the *IV btg.* when it was first formed and then commanded that battalion and the *187º rgt.* at El Alamein. After *generale* Ronco's failed attempt, Luserna drove out to the battalion to speak to *maggiore* Rizzatti and the other officers. He was stopped at a roadblock established by the rebellious battalion near Macomer. An altercation erupted between *capitano* Corradino Alvino and Luserna when the latter attempted to assert his authority. Most accounts state that a *paracadutist*i thought Luserna had attacked Alvino and opened fire, killing Bechi-Luserna. Luserna's death was a shock to most of the *paracadutisti* as his writings extolling the feats of the specialty had been widely read.[30]

After the death of Luserna, *generale* Ronco canceled all the operational orders for the division and ordered it to stand down and assemble in the southern part of the island. The «*Nembo*» was placed under the command of the *d.f* «*Bari*» and that division was ordered to reassert discipline and control. The *132º rgt. costiero* was charged with

27 Arena, *FOLGORE!*, p.387.
28 Arena, *FOLGORE!*, pp.388–391; Di Giovanni, *I paracadutisti*, p.219.
29 Di Giovanni, *I paracadutisti*, pp.215-217.
30 Arena, *FOLGORE!*, p.386; Torsiello, *Le operazioni delle unità italiane*, p.279 and fn. 22.

disarming the *paracadutisti* and guarding its personnel. As stated by *Generale di corpo d'armata* Paolo Berardi, the *capo* (chief) of the reconstituted S.M.R.E. under the new government in the south:

> ... during the operations conducted against the Germans from 8 to 20 September, the «Nembo» had represented a nuisance for the Italian command; not only was it unusable but it had to be watched over in its turn."[31]

The division was broken up after the German departure from Sardinia. Sixteen hundred men of the division's service support units, generally not being trained *paracadutisti*, were transferred to other divisions and corps. Six hundred men were deemed politically unreliable and were imprisoned. Four hundred and ten *paracadutisti* were expelled from the specialty and sent to other infantry units, while 300 more were transferred to various other units. Elements of the *«Nembo»* would be reformed under both the militaries of northern and southern Italy in the following year.[32]

Viterbo, Tarquinia, and Florence (Map 14.2)

As per the Fall Achse plan, the 3.Panzergrenadier Division had orders to occupy both Tarquinia and Viterbo during its movement towards Rome. Kampfgruppe Borchert would move through Viterbo to Tarquinia and then south along the coast to Civitavecchia, forming the western prong of the advance. Kampfgruppe Busing would also pass through Viterbo, but then turn south towards Rome as the center prong. Kampfgruppe Grosse would advance from Civita Castellana through Nepi to Rome in the east.[33]

Training at Viterbo in September were the *XVII*, *XVIII* and *XX btg. paracadutisti* and the *I gruppo artiglieria*. The *XIX* and *XX btg.* and the *I gruppo artiglieria* had been organized into the *raggruppamento «Ciclone»*. The *XIX btg.* had already completed all its training and had moved to Florence. The *XX btg.* had completed its parachute training on 13 July and was undergoing tactical training in the area. The artillery, along with the *XVII* and *XVIII btg.*, were still being formed and undergoing parachute training. The city itself was in the middle of the staging area of the 3.Panzergrenadier Division, with German units deployed in the surrounding countryside.[34]

On the morning of 9 September the commander of the *XX btg.*, *capitano* Manlio D'Abundio, received orders to occupy the national telephone exchange located in

31 Arena, *Nembo!*, pp.47–48;
32 Arena, *Nembo!*, p.52;
33 Torsiello, *Le operazioni delle unità italiane*, p.184; Nino Arena, *50ª di Tarquinia, 1939-1989, Scuole Militare paracadutismo* (Comitato Promotore ex Istruttori delle Scuole Militari di Paracadutismo, 1989), p.86.
34 Arena, *FOLGORE!*, p.392; Arena, *Nembo!*, p.29.

the city to maintain the military communications for the *5a Armata*. Shortly afterwards, the 149.Panzergrenadier Regiment of the German 3.Panzergrenadier Division attempted to secure the building but were stopped by the *paracadutisti*. Negotiations followed, but after the Germans sent reinforcements, the exchange was attacked and the defending *paracadutisti* were forced to retreat. The *5a Armata* was organizing an attempt to retake the exchange when the order arrived to cease all resistance to the Germans. The *paracadutisti* units still in training were disbanded to avoid capture.[35]

Once through Viterbo, Kampfgruppe Borchert sent an armoured reconnaissance detachment, supported by two companies of the I/29.Panzergrenadier Regiment forward to Tarquinia. A company of the *battaglione «P»* under the command of *tenente di vascello* Rodolfo Ceccacci was at Tarquinia on 8 September. Without orders to guide him, Ceccacci and the German commander came to an agreement that their units would not fight each other and that the *paracadutisti* would move the hills outside the airfield. Once in the hills, the unit hid their weapons and waited for orders. After a day without orders, Ceccacci decided to disband the unit.[36]

In the area west of the airfield were elements of the *7a divisione fanteria «Lupi di Toscana»*. That division belonged to the *XII Cd'A* of the *4a Armata* and was one of the units being repositioned from France to Rome. The unit was moving by train and was scattered from Tarquinia south to Civitavecchia. The units of the division were completely unprepared for any combat and unable to offer any real resistance.[37]

The Fight for the Apennine Passes (Maps 14.3, 14.4)

Farther north, German units were moving to occupy Bologna and Livorno on the northern side of the Apennine mountains with the aim to then move to secure the mountain passes leading to Florence and the Tuscan plains to the south. The area south of the mountains was under the control of the *II Corpo d'armata* commanded by *generale di corpo d'armata* Gervasio Bittossi. Florence was also the garrison city of the *comando Difesa territoriale di Firenze* which had received word during the evening of 8 September of the German movements. Seeing there was little it could do at that time to intervene north of the mountains, its focus was set on defending the mountain passes and the city of Florence.

The forces available to defend the city were limited. The city was nominally the home garrison of the nascent *183a divisione fanteria «Ciclone»*, but only the *XIX btg.*

35 Arena, *FOLGORE!*, pp.392–394; Nino Arena, *I PARACADUTISTI Cinquant'anni di storia, cronaca e immagini del paracadutisti italiano* (Modena: Società Tipografica Editrice Modenese Mucchi, 1972), p.169; Torsiello, *Le operazioni delle unità italiane*, p.184; Arena, *Tarquinia*, p.77.

36 Aldo Bertucci, *Guerre segrete oltre le linee* (Milan: Gruppo Ugo Mursia Editore S.p.A., 1995), pp.12–13.

37 Torsiello, *Le operazioni delle unità italiane*, p.114; Arena, *Tarquinia*, p.86.

was present. Along with the *XIX btg.* were units available from the *18° Reggimento Esplorante Corazzato (R.E.Co) bersaglieri*, two *sezioni carabinieri*, and various depot units in the city. The *18° R.E.Co.* was being transferred to Rome as part of the build-up of Italian forces near the capital. The armistice found part of the unit already in Rome and the remaining part still in Florence loaded on trains ready to continue its journey before being ordered to remain in Florence. The regiment unloaded its equipment and it came under the control of the *comando Difesa territoriale di Firenze.*[38] The defense of the city was complicated by the fact that several small German units and detachments were stationed within the city and were now arranging to coordinate their actions with the main German forces located north and south of the city.

The defense of the northern and eastern approaches to the city through the passes of the Apennines Mountains was given to *maggiore* Giovanni Taffiorelli. Called *Settore E*, the former commander of the *VI btg.* was responsible for defending three passes through the mountains: the Futa, Giogo, and the Casaglia (also called the Marradi). The *XIX btg.*, commanded by *maggiore* Giuseppe Blotto was placed under his command. When *Generale* Bittossi asked Taffiorelli whether the battalion could be depended upon to carry out its orders. Taffiorelli stated that it could be relied upon to do so.[39]

A section of artillery with two 100/17 howitzers was initially sent to the Futa Pass earlier on 9 September, but it was surprised and captured by a group of Germans as it was moving to occupy the area.[40] *Maggiore* Blotto had already ordered the *56ª cp.* to move to the pass to reinforce the artillery and there was a concern that it too would be surprised. Blotto was able to notify the *paracadutisti* about the changed situation at the pass and the company changed its movement into an attack. A fight broke out at about 1730 hrs in which the *paracadutisti* quickly gained the upper hand. When it was over, the *56ª cp.* had recaptured the pass, freed the artillery men, and killed or wounded fifty of the German soldiers. One 100/17 howitzer was recovered while the second had been pushed into a ravine. The company itself had only a few wounded during the fight and set about to establish a defense of the pass.

While the *56ª cp.* was securing the pass, *maggiore* Taffiorelli established his headquarters in Scarperia, a town northeast of Florence that was near the three passes.

38 Torsiello, *Le operazioni delle unità italiane*, p.181 and fn.15.There is some question whether the *XVII* and *XVIII* would be part of the «*Ciclone*». Arena, *Tarquinia*, p.77, 81, states that these two battalions were transformed into *battaglione complementi* (replacement battalions) for the «*Nembo*». Di Giovanni, *I paracadutisti*, p.195, states that the nucleus of the «*Ciclone*» was the *raggruppamento* «*Ciclone*» that all sources list as only the *XIX, XX btg.* and the *I gruppo art.*

39 The account of the *XIX btg.* was based on Arena, *FOLGORE!*, pp.394–418; Torsiello, *Le operazioni delle unità italiane*, pp.181, 183–185; Dante Pariset, *Storica del paracadutismo* (Rome-Milan: Vito Bianco Editore, 1962), p.340; NARA, *K.T.B der 24.Pz.Div. 8/9/1943 bis 30/9/1943*, T-315 Roll 850. Pariset miss-identifies the *56ª cp.* as the *59ª*.

40 NARA *K.T.B der 24.Pz.Div.* Anlage 26. These Germans were likely a detachment manning a Luftwaffe communications station located at the pass. Several German columns were moving through the area as well and reported combat with Italian units.

Here he attempted to set-up a functional headquarters but lacked basic communications equipment. He only had four radios and two motorcycle couriers to maintain communications with the three widely separated passes. Two of the radios were with the units at the Futa and Giogo passes. Taffiorelli could use the private telephone line in the villa he occupied in Scarperia to talk with the *comando Difesa territoriale* in Florence.[41]

His first challenge was to discover what forces currently protected the other passes. The Giogo Pass was unguarded, so Taffiorelli ordered a paratroop platoon and a machine gun section to secure the pass. There was a force at the Casaglia Pass that had been sent by the *comando Difesa territoriale di Firenze*, but Taffiorelli did not have any communication with that element. He dispatched a motorcycle courier with the third radio to discover the strength of the garrison and its supply status. The *XXX battaglione avieri* (airmen), a R.A. training and replacement unit located in Scarperia, was placed under his command. Only a small part of that battalion had weapons and they lacked ammunition, so the *maggiore* did his best to arm and supply the unit.

Along with all the Italian activity on 9 September, a German unit stationed in Florence tried to enter Scarperia from the south but was captured and disarmed. The Germans were placed under guard by the *XXX btg. avieri*. A few hours later at 2400 hrs that same evening the *comando Difesa territoriale di Firenze* authorized free passage for any German units going to Bologna. The captured Germans were then released, but their weapons were not returned.

While this was happening, automatic weapon's fire could be heard in the evening of 9 September coming from the Futa Pass. A German column from Bologna had tried to push through the pass at 2330 hrs and was defeated. Unknown to Taffiorelli, the *Difesa territoriale di Firenze* had dispatched the *7ª cp., III/127º rgt. fanteria* under *capitano* Ciolli to defend the pass. This company was part of the depot of the *127º rgt. f.* in Pistoia northwest of Florence and joined the *paracadutisti* shortly after they had regained the position.[42] Both companies were able to stop the German column. Then another German column, this one now from Florence, came up behind the Italian position at 0100 hrs and attacked the two companies. After an hour of combat in which the original column from Bologna rejoined the fight, the Italian positions were in danger of being overrun from the front and rear. Opting to retreat, the *paracadutisti* and *fanti* found several mountain trails that allowed them to escape the deteriorating situation, surrendering the pass. One platoon from the *56ª cp.* was missing after the action, likely separated and lost in the darkness somewhere on the mountain paths.[43]

41 Arena, *FOLGORE!*, p.400.

42 The *127º rgt. fanteria* was part of the *41º divisione fanteria «Firenza»*. That division was currently stationed in Albania, but its depot was in Pistoia. It is unclear why this company was in Pistoia. The copy of the message sent by *maggiore* Taffiorelli found in Arena, *FOLGORE!*, p.411 clearly states the *127º rgt.* so further research is needed.

43 There is no mention of these actions in the German records that were accessed. The German accounts only mention that the pass was lost by 1830 on 9 September. The fact

Fresh forces were arriving to reinforce *Settore E* during the events on the evening of 9–10 September. A detachment from the *18º R.E.Co.* under *capitano* Alfonso Quaranta arrived at Scarperia at approximately 0100 on 10 September. The detachment consisted of the *4ª cp. motociclisti* from the *LXVIII btg. bersaglieri* and two platoons of *semoventi da 47/32* from the *5ª cp./LXIX btg. bersaglieri. Maggiore* Taffiorelli ordered *capitano* Quaranta to immediately dispatch a motorcycle platoon from the *4ª cp.* to reinforce the garrison at the Futa Pass. Taffiorelli also sent a 47/32 c.c. gun that he had received from Florence to reinforce the garrison at the Giogo Pass.[44]

The *56ª* and *7ª cp.* returned to Scarperia in the early morning of 10 September, along with the motorcycle platoon that had not been involved in the action. Informed by *gen.* Morigi of the urgent need, Taffiorelli organized a force to retake the pass. The *56ª cp. paracadutisti* and the *4ª cp. motociclisti bersaglieri* (two platoons), along with the *7ª cp. III/127º* were the main force. It was supported by a platoon of *semoventi da 47/32* and the one 100/17 howitzer that had been recaptured from the Germans. The howitzer crew did not have any ammunition for the gun, but it was sent in the hope that ammunition would arrive. This force was placed under the command of *cap.* Quaranta for the attack against the pass.

As the force was being organized, *maggiore* Taffiorelli positioned the remaining elements of the *18º R.E.Co.* (one motorcycle and one *semoventi* platoon) from Scarperia south to the bivio di Novoli (Novoli crossroad). This position would block any German units moving up from Florence and was a central point from where he could reinforce any of the three passes. The *Carabinieri* station just south of the position at Vaglia provided telephone communication with the *comando Difesa territoriale* in Florence. *Generale* Morigi arrived at the crossroad at 0900 hrs to gain situational awareness of the developing fight.

The Germans had not attempted any action against the Giogo or Casaglia Passes on 9 September. The headquarters of 24.Panzerdivision organized three kampfgruppen in the early morning of 10 September to clear the various passes. Two of the kampfgruppen, KG Herff moving through the Porretta Pass, and KG Heyking moving through the Futa pass, were directed against Florence. These units had moved out of Bologna by 0730 on 10 September.[45]

Capitano Quaranta's forces were already in contact with the German defenders by 1000. The Germans were supported by several tanks, some armoured cars, and a few

that the pass was blocked by Italian troops was reported by several unidentified German columns and it is possible that these elements did fight at the pass. See NARA, *K.T.B der 24.Pz.Div*, 10 September 1943, 0200 hrs.

44 Anon., *18º R.E.Co – Reggimento Esplorante Corazzato* <https://digilander.libero.it/lacorsainfinita/guerra2/42/67corazzato18reco.htm> (accessed 18 August 2022); Arena, *FOLGORE!*, pp.402. The Novoli crossroad is not marked on any of the period maps examined. It is likely just south of S. Piero a Sieve where the roads from the Futa and Giogo Passes connect, given the descriptions in the accounts.

45 NARA, *K.T.B der 24.Pz.Div*, 10 September 1943, Anlage 28.

artillery pieces covering the road. Quaranta had the *paracadutisti* use the terrain on the west side of the pass to work close into the German positions, while the *semoventi* and motorcycles advanced along the road. After some hard fighting, the two companies had cleared the enemy from the pass by 1200 hrs.[46]

The *XIX btg.* again held all three passes by the afternoon of 10 September. An artillery section with one 75/13 mountain howitzer arrived at the crossroad that morning. After coordinating with *maggiore* Taffiorelli, the section continued on to the Casaglia Pass. Taffiorelli then called the *comando Difesa territoriale di Firenze* urgently requesting fuel, ammunition and food for his units. All was promised by *generale di corpo d'armata* Armellini Chiappi, commander of the *Difesa territoriale di Firenze.*

Several drums of fuel were delivered by 1600 hrs that day, but still no food or ammunition. Shortly afterwards, *maggiore* Taffiorelli received a call from the *comando Difesa territoriale.* His orders were now to abandon the passes and withdraw his units south to Monte Rinaldi, which was just on the northern side of Florence. He would receive new orders from *generale* Morigi once he arrived at that location. The retreat was to begin immediately. In just a few hours the hold at all costs order had now changed into an unforced retreat.

This change began earlier that day. *Generale* Chiappi had asked *generale* Morigi that morning for his assessment of the situation. *Generale* Morigi explained that the forces were too spread out, therefore too weak to hold the passes against a determined attack. It was likely that word was received during this time that the Italian forces holding the Porretta Pass had surrendered, allowing the Futa Pass to be outflanked from the west. Morigi believed that a defense using the hills north of Fiesole provided a shorter and better position to defend Florence. Both Chiappi and *generale* Caracciolo, commander of the *5ª Armata* agreed with the recommendation.

By 2100 hrs the majority of the force under *maggiore* Taffiorelli had reached Monte Rinaldo. However at 1800 hrs Morigi received new orders to move his units to Bagno a Ripoli, south of the Arno River on the south-east side of Florence. The reason is not given, but it is apparent that the Italian command wanted to declare Florence an open city in order to avoid unnecessary destruction of the city and its cultural treasures. On the morning of 11 September the *XIX btg.* moved to Bagno a Ripoli and assembled in the town square to await orders. Unknown to Morigi, Taffiorelli, and Blotto was that the Germans had entered Florence that same morning under the pretext to negotiate the open city status of Florence. At 1000 hrs *generale* Morigi received a telephone call and was told to disband the battalion.[47]

The men stored their weapons and began to go their separate ways. *Maggiore* Blotto and some of the *paracadutisti* of the *XIX btg.* decided to join the Germans. Unlike the

46 Again this action is not mentioned in the German sources. This could be the light reconnaissance elements sent by the 24.Pz.Div. early on 10 September. NARA, *K.T.B der 24.Pz.Div*, 10 September 1943, 0830 hours.

47 Nino Arena, *Aquile senza Ali: I paracadutisti italiani nella seconda guerra mondiale* (Milan: Mursia 1970), p.212.

officers in other units who made the same decision, Blotto had carried out his orders to the very end and only decided to change sides after he had been released from his military obligations. Some of the men stayed in the area and were arrested by the Germans – others simply chose to go home.[48]

The *Arditi, R.A.* and *R.M. paracadutisti* (Maps 14.2, 14.5)

Shortly after the coup that toppled Mussolini from power (25 July 1943), the *10° rgt. arditi* was ordered to provide a detachment to protect the headquarters of the *Servizio Informazioni Militari* (S.I.M., the Military Intelligence Service). Two companies, the *111ª cp. paracadutisti* and the *122ª cp. da sbarco* were moved to Rome and began their new duties. The companies were garrisoned in the barracks at Viale Giulio Cesare when the armistice announcement was aired.

The morning of 8 September found the four battalions of the *10° rgt. arditi* stationed at various locations throughout Italy. The *I btg.* was on Sardinia and the *II btg.* was at Santa Marinella after returning from Sicily. The *III btg.* had the *122ª cp.* at the barracks in the Prati district of Rome and the *133ª cp.* was completing its training at Santa Severa on the coast outside of Rome. Two of the *cp. paracadutisti* of the *IV btg.*, the *101ª* and *121ª cp.*, were also at Santa Severa, while as previously stated the *111ª cp.* had been transferred to Rome with the *122ª cp.*[49]

The initial reaction of the Romans was euphoric, celebrating what they believed was the end of the war. Some of the military garrison of the city joined in, believing that they would soon be going home. The *paracadutisti* of the *111ª cp.* were ordered to the Forte Braschi to guard the S.I.M. headquarters, keeping firm discipline as they marched through the streets and took up their post around the building.[50]

When the company was relieved and returned to the barracks, they discovered most of the regular army units were gone. The buildings were silent, with equipment scattered and abandoned, and papers strewn around the offices. The telephones still worked, but there was not an answer when the *paracadutisti* attempted to contact the various headquarters in Rome.

Finally orders arrived from the *comando Corpo d'Armata di Roma* on the afternoon of 9 September. The *111ª* and *122ª cp.* were ordered to secure the Porta S. Paolo, one of the main gates to the city, to block any German attempt to occupy the city. As the units began to move to their new position, one officer told his company commander that he could not fight against the Germans. The officer was dismissed from the unit and the companies then drove to the city gate.

48 Di Giovanni, *I paracadutisti*, p.214.
49 Luigi Emilio Longo, *I «reparti speciali» italiani nella seconda guerra mondiale* (Milan: Mursia 1991), p.157.
50 Arena, *FOLGORE!*, p.423. Arena incorrectly identifies the S.I.M. headquarters in Rome as the Palazzo Puccinelli, a location that does not exist in the city.

Arriving at the *Basilica di S. Paolo, capitano* Carlo Bonicani (commander of the *111° cp.*) received his orders. His company was responsible to watch the area from the via Ostiense (road SS 8) east to the Tre Fontane Hill. This was an area covering about two kilometers, over which Bonicani only had about fifty *paracadutisti* to deploy. The *1° reggimento «Granatieri di Sardegna»* was occupying Strongpoints 5, 6, and 7 south of the city, while the *2° reggimento «Granatieri di Sardegna»* occupied Strongpoint 8, 9, 10, and 11 south-east and east. The *Lancieri di Montebello (R.E.Co.)* was moving into positions to support the southern part of the defense.[51]

Some fighting had broken out during the day, but the situation had settled down by nightfall. Units of the German 2.Fallschirmjäger Division had been leveraging the confusion and the lack of clear orders for the Italians units and had pushed the *Granatieri* back from several locations. Bonicani's earlier orders were now out of date and the company attached itself to the *Lancieri*. The *paracadutisti* were instructed to occupy a position just north of the Ponte della Magliana between the Tiber River and the via Laurentina.[52]

Needing to understand the current situation, *capitano* Bonicani dispatched three patrols during the night of 9 September. These patrols were sent in the direction of Magliana to the south-west and south towards the Esposizione Universale Roma (E42 as it was called), the site for the planned 1942 World Fair. The patrol that *capitano* Bonicani personally led made contact with a German patrol in the E42. Small detachments of the 2.Fallschirmjäger Division had been pushing north towards the city and had captured a few locations. The Germans were still leveraging the confusion and did not wish to unnecessarily alarm the Italians, so both sides decided not to fight each other. Paratroopers from both sides began talking to one other while sharing cigarettes. The two patrols soon parted peacefully, each going their own way. The next day would be very different.[53]

Fighting started at 0500 on 10 September with a heavy bombardment by the German artillery and advancing fallschirmjägers but the Italian defense was soon compromised by orders announcing an agreement with Germans. The Italian units were ordered to withdraw and began to move back towards the city. But shortly afterwards new orders arrived instructing the Italian units to now recapture the locations they had just abandoned. The better German training and equipment, combined with the steady erosion of the Italian morale from the conflicting orders prevented the *paracadutisti* from regaining what had been given up. The *111ª cp.* then reinforced the defense of the Montagnola, joining the *granatieri* defending the area. The Italian forces were slowly pressed back towards the Porta S. Paolo with desertions weakening

51 Arena, *FOLGORE!*, p.423; Mario Buscemi (ed.), *La difesa di Roma e i Granatieri di Sardegna nel settembre 1943* (Rome: USSME, 1993), p.105; Bruno Mei, *I Lancieri di Montebello alla difesa di Roma* (Rome, Corporazione Arti Grafiche, 1981), pp.50–51.

52 Arena's timeline in *Folgore!* is very unclear. Mei, *I Lancieri di Montebello*, p.55, places the arrival of the company in the defense at 2200 hrs on 9 September.

53 Arena, *FOLGORE!*, p.424.

the outnumbered Italian units. With civilians now joining the soldiers, the resistance stiffened as the Germans attempted to press through the city gate. Fighting at the Porta S. Paolo and the nearby Piramide Cestia was intense with the Germans slowly moving forward. Everything changed at 1600 hours as the news arrived that the Italian forces in the city had surrendered. The document of surrender had been signed by *tenente colonnello* Leandro Giaccone, the chief of staff of the *136ª divisione corazzata Centauro*, as none of the Italian generals present who had taken part in the negotiations would put their name on the document.[54]

The ultimate cause of the collapse of the city's defense was due to the senior leadership not understanding the real situation on the ground and the lack of any overarching idea of what needed to be achieved. No one appeared to be in command, nor did anyone wish to be in command. The bulk of the army was ordered east to Tivoli in a hope that the Germans would honor their agreements, yet the agreements did not promise anything to the Italians. The soldiers sensed this and the army continued to disintegrate during the fighting.[55]

Capitano Bonicani disbanded the survivors of his company and urged them to disappear or try to reach the battalion at Santa Severa. What he did not know was that Kampfgruppe Borchert had already occupied that town and the regiment had been disbanded. Most of the *paracadutisti* would hide and join the Italian resistance while others journeyed south to join the new parachute unit being formed by the Badoglio government.

The *Xª MAS* and the *battaglione «N»* of the *Reggimento San Marco* were at La Spezia when the armistice was announced. The two units remained at their post awaiting orders. The Battle Fleet sailed from the port on 9 September on its way to Malta. Still without orders, the commanders of the two units negotiated with the Germans. An agreement was made allowing the two units to join with the Germans, with the provision that those individuals who did not wish to continue the fight were released on unlimited leave. Many of the men in both units chose to remain and formed a new *btg. «NP»* which became part of the new *Xª MAS* under the fascist government established in northern Italy.[56]

At Tarquinia a number of men from the company disbanded by *tenente* Ceccacci remained in the area. Ceccacci himself was seeking to contact the naval headquarters for orders. On 12 September Ceccacci met with *capitano* Buttazzoni, vice commander of the *battaglione «NP»*. Buttazzoni had been in Rome planning the next series of attacks involving the battalion when the armistice was announced. Buttazzoni on the previous day had met with *tenente* Moloino who commanded a squadron of the *battaglione «G»* stationed at Minturno just north of Naples. He and Buttazzoni had agreed to move north to join the Germans and continue the fight. Buttazzoni soon convinced

54 Davis, *Who Defends Rome?*, pp.442–443, 451, Buscemi, *La difesa di Roma*, pp.156–157; Mei, *I Lancieri*, pp.61–64.
55 Davis, *Who Defends Rome?*, p.451.
56 Arena, *FOLGORE!*, pp.418–420; Longo, *I «reparti speciali»*, pp.302-303.

Ceccacci and those *paracadutisti* still in the area to do the same. The remaining personnel of both of these units were transported to La Spezia in the following days.[57]

The *I battaglione A.D.R.A.* under *tenente colonnello* Dalmas with approximately 200 *arditi* was stationed at the Centocelle airfield just east of Rome on 8 September. The Allies had planned to drop the 82nd Airborne at Centocelle to support the Italian military against the Germans as the armistice was announced. This mission was canceled at the last movement due to the Allied distrust of *Supercomando* and the lack of any assurances that the R.E. could execute its part of the plan. On 10 September units of the 2.Fallschirmjäger Division occupied the airfield, disarming and arresting the *arditi*. General Ramcke commanded the division and remembered Dalmas from the time he spent at Tarquinia planning «*C3*». Upon being informed that Dalmas and his men were being held, Ramcke ordered their release. Dalmas and most of his unit will join the new government in northern Italy.[58]

The *II btg. A.D.R.A.* under *maggiore a.a.* Trepiedi was at Viterbo. The unit was still in training and along with the R.E. *paracadutisti,* could only offer limited resistance. After being captured, many of these *arditi* opted to continue the fight against the Allies. The battalion was moved to Tradate where the R.S.I. had created a new parachute school to complete its instruction.

The *3ª* and *4ª cp.* of the *btg.* «*Loreto*» stationed on Sardinia for airfield repair were able to avoid actions against the Germans. The leadership was able to maintain discipline and control of the units through the chaotic days of the armistice. Both companies returned to the peninsula and would later be used to form the *battaglione* «*Azzurro*» in the south in 1944.[59]

The events of September 1943 rent the Regio Esercito and the Regia Aeronautica apart. The majority of the army units voluntarily disbanded believing that the war was over. Only those units with firm leadership managed to maintain their organization and continued to function as an effective military unit. After the surrender to the Germans, all the remaining units in the German area of occupation were disbanded and the soldiers held as prisoners. Many of these soldiers would later be sent to Germany as forced labor.

Several of the specialized/elite units such as the *paracadutisti* managed to navigate these times and remain intact. Germany valued these units and made some effort to recruit them to remain loyal to the Axis. The Allies had less need for additional units so the status of those units that remained in the south was uncertain. It required several months before the Badoglio government finalized the conditions under which Italy would actively participate with the Allies in the war. The continuation of the war after 8 September would see *paracadutisti* fighting on both sides of the frontlines.

57 Nino Buttazzoni, *Solo per la Bandiera: I nuotatori Paracadutisti della Marina* (Milan: Gruppo Mursia Editore S.p.A., 2002), p.86; Bertucci, *Guerre segrete*, p.13.

58 Longo, *I «reparti speciali»*, pp.180-181.

59 Piero Crociani and Pier Battistelli, *Italian Navy & Air Force Elite Units & Special Forces 1940-45* (Oxford: Osprey, 2013), p.40; Aldo Giorleo, *Palestra Azzurra L'aeronautica militare e il paracadutismo cronistoria dalle origini ad oggi* (Rome: USSMA, 1975), p.71.

Conclusion

Of the six nations that developed a significant airborne capability during the interwar years and throughout the course of the war, only Italy did so without an identified operational requirement. Germany and Russia conceived the use of large airborne formations as a solution to preventing a First World War style stalemate from occurring. Imperial Japan viewed their employment to overcome time and distance to gain critical strategic resources. Great Britain and the United States adopted the use of paratrooper units to set the conditions for successful invasions. In these cases, airborne units were identified as an offensive means to achieve an operational end and their development of benefited from the clear articulation of those requirements.

The Italian development of its *Fanti dell'aria* was an outlier from these other countries. Italy had followed Russia and Germany in the late 1930s in creating its *reparti paracadutisti* but lacked an offensive component to its strategic planning. Whilst Mussolini talked about creating a *Mare Nostrum* (Italian Mediterranean) or achieving *Irredentismo italiano* (recovering the lost lands), neither of these aims were embedded into the Italian strategic planning during this period. There were a few indicators towards transitioning to the offense if the opportunity arose, but the planning never discussed how to achieve the goals addressed in Mussolini's speeches. This lack of planning in support of strategic goals was vividly demonstrated when Italy entered the war in June 1940. Of the three offensive operations initiated in 1940 by Italy, one was purely political (France) to place Italy at the table for the peace talks. The other two assaults (Egypt and Greece) were more to fill the operational void to do something, and their hasty planning and lack of the necessary resources did little to move Italy closer to any identified Fascist objectives.

The one offensive move that would support either goal of *Mare Nostrum* or *Irredentismo italiano* was the capture of Malta. The *Regia Marina* repeatedly identified neutralizing the island as a necessary operational act to achieve the strategic goal of maintaining Italy's colonies. The use of vertical envelopment to seize the island was a viable operational means, but the need to take Malta was never embedded into Italian planning. As the requirement to secure the island was never agreed upon by the three services, no serious planning was undertaken to tackle the technical problems of capturing Malta until 1941. It is only after Malta occupied the dominant role in the Mediterranean Sea that the *Regia Marina* had predicted in the late 1930s that the island became a focus of Italian operational level planning.

Due to this lack of focus, the R.E. development of its airborne force remained mired in hypotheticals rather than shaped to solve specific challenges. Decisions on the structure and equipment appeared to have been made based on what was the easiest to implement rather than what was required based on a likely mission, with the debate over artillery offering one example. While the prewar studies stated that the *paracadutisti* could be used in a defensive setting, none of the war planning provided them with that role. The push to form the units that became the *«Folgore»* and the *arditi* forces of the other services only took shape once serious planning against Malta was initiated. Actual planning to solve real challenges led to the creation of the *I btg. R.A.* and the *«Loreto»* and gave purpose to the development of the *«Folgore»*.

Without any intent to execute a massed airborne operation in 1940, why weren't these units employed in the traditional tactical role of raid and sabotage? That was the focus of their creation, yet the R.E. failed to execute any of these types of missions in the first two and one-half years of the war. *Comando Superiore FF.AA. dell'A.S.* had no plans to use the Libyan battalions in 1940, nor did *Superalba* have any for Greece. Although these units were requested, there were apparently no plans for their use in an airborne role during 1941-42.

When Italy finally committed to implement the original concept of sabotage and raids, the results were generally a failure. The early organization and training of the first parachute battalions was focused on independent small-unit actions against priority targets using speed and surprise. Once the original battalions had transitioned away from those missions, new *arditi* units were raised to replace them. So why did these raids fail?

Italian doctrine stated that these units should be placed under the control of the theater commander, yet these missions were planned and executed from Rome. The strategic level headquarters was now planning tactical missions, believing that these missions would have an operational effect. None of the *arditi* missions executed by parachute during the war were connected to an operational scheme of maneuver or a plan that could leverage any of their success. The missions were completely separate from what was transpiring along the front lines and offered nothing more than harassment of the enemy. The raids themselves focused on destruction but lacked the ability to destroy enough material to make an impact. The means selected didn't match the operational effects desired by *Supercomando*. It is only proper to highlight that Germany also attempted several similar raids in North Africa in late 1942 and those raids achieved the same poor results.[1]

With the minimal employment as paratroops and subsequent lack of success during those deployments, it is difficult to determine whether the resources Italy expended to create the airborne force were justified. One can argue that too little was expended

1 The German executed a parachute raid in early December and two glider raids on 26 and 30 December 1942 respectively. All were failures.

and that was the reason for its lack of employment and success during the war. Or it can be argued that given the lack of any operational need, too much was expended on a force that was only employed as a traditional ground force.

Did the Italian strategic goals create an operational capability gap that the creation of an airborne force would satisfy? Yes, but only if achieving those goals would draw Italy into direct conflict with the United Kingdom. Without solving the operational problem that Malta presented, significant naval and air assets would be needed to contain that threat. Like a fleet-in-being or a fortress, the island would consume Italian resources that could be better used elsewhere. The *reparti paracadutisti* provided a means to eliminate that threat but necessitated that their employment be crafted into an operational plan that was fully resourced. This was never achieved during the war as the 1942 invasion depended on additional German resources.

If Italy's long-term strategic aim was to avoid such a conflict, Italy had little need for the airborne specialty. The concept of sabotage and raid could have been achieved by employing the ground and sea based forces as was demonstrated during the war. Given the Mediterranean basin was Italy's operational theater, assets such as the *X MAS* proved to be better tools for achieving operational-level effects.

It is clear that the senior Italian military leadership lacked any understanding or intent to employ these units leveraging their primary advantage. Without a plan for rapid offensive action, the large parachute units became little more than lightly armed fire brigades. Besides the brief statement by Cavallero in July 1942, *Comando Supremo* made no plans to maintain or preserve the *reparti paracadutisti* as an operational-level asset. Unlike the Allied use of airborne forces in times of crisis, the «*Folgore*» was thrown into North Africa with no real intent to replace it once the situation was stabilized. The fact that elements of the «*Nembo*» weren't immediately committed to Tunisia to secure critical locations must be contrasted against the Allied and German use of parachute forces in the opening maneuvers of that campaign. Committed as regular infantry divisions, the parachute units would either need to be extensively reinforced or they would be lost. The former never happened so the latter was the fate of all the *reparti paracadutisti* committed to combat in 1941–1943.

Despite the failures and shortsightedness of the political leadership and Military High Command, the *paracadutisti Italiani* were acknowledged by all as skilled, brave soldiers and achieved a degree of fame and the respect of its enemies during the war. The «*Folgore*» at El Alamein prevented the UK forces from achieving a breakthrough, thereby preserving the «*Ariete*» and 21.Panzerdivision for action when they were finally called up to the north. The *I btg. libici paracadutisti* and *I btg. carabinieri paracadutisti* successfully held significantly larger forces at bay until ordered to withdraw. Lieutenant General Brian Horrocks, the commander of the British 10th Corps in Tunisia, stated that the fight for Takrouna was the most gallant feat of arms he witnessed in the course of the war, honoring both the *folgorini* and the New Zealanders that took part. These events easily rank alongside those of the German 1.Fallschirmjäger Division at Cassino or American 101st Airborne Division at Bastogne.[2] This fame was earned however, without executing their *raison d'être*: conducting a mass airborne operation. While the *5ª cp.* jump onto Kefalonia is known as the *Regio Esercito's* only mass parachute mission, the operation itself was essentially an uncontested operation.

With or without a valid requirement, the *paracadutisti italiani* demonstrated that Italy could create an elite fighting force that could provide military options for operational needs. Deployed only on missions that were better suited for the traditional infantry forces, their training, skill, and *esprit de'corps* allowed them to overcome many of their organizational limitations and were able to execute those missions to a high standard.

Today there are few visible signs of the infrastructure created during the war for the establishment of the *paracadutisti*. Libya gained its independence in 1951 and the military airfield at Castel Benito became the Tripoli International Airport. At the time of publication, it remains closed due to the civil unrest in Libya and is in need of repairs and upgrades.

Little remains of the school at Tarquinia which is still controlled by the military but is largely abandoned. A fence still surrounds the perimeter with one of its gates sporting the *paracadutisti* emblem woven into the iron work. The original brick administration building is still standing while the abandoned runway is slowly broken up by grass and weeds.

The school at Viterbo is also gone, although the airfield itself is still a major military and civilian airport. The *Centro Addestramento Paracadutisti* (CAPAR, the Italian Military Parachute School) is now located at Pisa, a garrison town with connections to various *reparti paracadutisti* during the war.

The traditions of the *paracadutisti* today are carried on by the units of *brigata paracadutisti «Folgore»*. The celebration day of the *186º* and *187º reggimenti paracadutisti «Folgore»* is 23 October, the first day of the Third Battle of El Alamein. The celebration day of the *183º reggimento paracadutisti «Nembo»* is 27 April, the anniversary of the Battle of Grizzano in 1945.[3] These days honor the fighting qualities displayed by the *paracadutisti* during the war. It is this tradition as an elite fighting force that is carried today by the *paracadutisti italiani*.

2 W.G. Stevens, *Bardia to Enfidaville* (Wellington: Historical Publications Branch, 1962), p.341

3 This battle was fought by the *reggimento paracadutisti «Nembo»* against units of the 1.Fallschirmjäger Division. Anon, *I gruppi combattimento* (Rome: USSME, 1951), pp.292–303.

Appendix I

List of the Italian Paracadutisti e Aviotrasportabile units

The following is a list of all the airborne units raised by the Italian military up to September 1943. It is generally in chronological order and reflects the units when first organized. Units that were part of a parachute unit but not trained as parachutists are not included. The list doesn't reflect the changes in unit organization or assignment over time. Refer to the chapters or the other appendices for those changes on specific dates. Units in bold are the higher headquarters for the indented units listed below that entry.

Regio Esercito

Paracadutisti

Reggimento «Fanti dell'aria»
- I battaglioni *paracadutisti* libici
- II battaglione *paracadutisti* libici

I battaglione *paracadutisti* nazionale
I battaglione *paracadutisti* carabinieri

1° reggimento paracadutisti (later the 185° reggimento fanteria)
- II battaglione *paracadutisti*
- III battaglione *paracadutisti*
- IV battaglione *paracadutisti*
- 1° compagnia cannoni *paracadutisti* (later the 185° compagnia cannoni)

2° reggimento paracadutisti (later the 186° reggimento fanteria)
- V battaglione *paracadutisti*
- VI battaglione *paracadutisti*
- VII battaglione *paracadutisti*
- 2° compagnia cannoni *paracadutisti* (later the 186° compagnia cannoni)

3° reggimento paracadutisti (later the 187° reggimento fanteria)
- VIII battaglione *paracadutisti* guastatori
- IX battaglione *paracadutisti*
- X battaglione *paracadutisti*

3° compagnia cannoni *paracadutisti* (later the 187° compagnia cannoni)

1° reggimento artiglieria paracadutisti (later the 185° reggimento artiglieria)

I gruppo artiglieria *paracadutisti* (1ª, 2ª batteria da 47/32 c.c.)
II gruppo artiglieria *paracadutisti* (3ª, 4ª batteria da 47/32 c.c.)
III gruppo artiglieria *paracadutisti* (5ª, 6ª batteria da 47/32 c.c.)

Comando 1° divisione paracadutisti (later Comando 185° divisione fanteria «Folgore»)

185ª sezione CC.RR.
260° ufficio postale (post office).
260° nucleo CC.RR. per ufficio postale (carabinieri detachment for the post office).
Compagnia comando

Compagnia mortai *paracadutisti* da 81 (later renamed 185° cp. mortai *paracadutisti* da 81)
Compagnia collegamento *paracadutisti* (later renamed 185° cp. collegamento *paracadutisti*)
Compagnia minori-artieri *paracadutisti* (later renamed 185° cp. minori-artieri *paracadutisti*)
Sezione sanità *paracadutisti* (later renamed 185° sez. sanità *paracadutisti*)
Compagnia autonoma *paracadutisti* (ex. PoW)

184° reggimento fanteria

XII battaglione *paracadutisti*
XIII battaglione *paracadutisti*
XIV battaglione *paracadutisti*
184° compagnia cannoni *paracadutisti*

Comando 184° divisione fanteria «Nembo»

184ª sezione CC.RR.
CLXXXIV battaglione guastatori
284ª compagnia ciclisti
184ª compagnia mortai
184ª compagnia collegamenti
184ª compagnia minatori-artieri
184° sezione sanità
Compagnia servizi/184ª d.f.

183° reggimento fanteria

VIII battaglione *paracadutisti*
XV battaglione *paracadutisti*
XVI battaglione *paracadutisti*
183° compagnia cannoni *paracadutisti*

184° reggimento artiglieria

I gruppo artiglieria *paracadutisti* (1ª, 2ª batteria da 47/32 c.c.)
II gruppo artiglieria *paracadutisti* (3ª, 4ª batteria da 47/32 c.c.)
III gruppo artiglieria *paracadutisti* (5ª, 6ª batteria da 47/32 c.c.)

101ª compagnia arditi *paracadutisti* (10° reggimento arditi)

111° compagnia arditi *paracadutisti* (10° reggimento arditi)
121° compagnia arditi *paracadutisti* (10° reggimento arditi)
Elements of the proposed 183° divisione fanteria «Ciclone»
XVII battaglione *paracadutisti*
XVIII battaglione *paracadutisti*
XIX battaglione *paracadutisti*
XX battaglione *paracadutisti*
I gruppo artiglieria *paracadutisti* (1ª, 2ª batteria da 47/32 c.c.)

Aviotrasportabile

Compagnia carri L lanciafiamme aviotrasportabile
185ª compagnia motociclisti (later renamed 184ª compagnia motociclisti)
Comando 80° Divisione Aviotrasportabile
80° squadra Carabinieri Reale (CC.RR.) motociclisti
80° squadra topocartografico
115° ufficio postale
115° nucleo CC.RR. per ufficiavo postale
XXXIX battaglione esplorante bersaglieri
125° reggimento fanteria
I battaglione fanteria
II battaglione fanteria
III battaglione fanteria
126° reggimento fanteria
I battaglione fanteria
II battaglione fanteria
III battaglione fanteria
80° reggimento artiglieria
I gruppo (1ª, 2ª batteria da 65/17)
II gruppo (3ª, 4ª batteria da 65/17)
III gruppo (5ª, 6ª batteria da 65/17)
7ª, 8ª batteria da 20/65 contraerei
80° battaglione controcarro
1ª compagnia controcarro da 47/32
2ª compagnia controcarro da 47/32
3ª compagnia controcarro da 47/32
LXXX battaglione misto del genio
80° sezione sanità
80° sezione sussistenza
80° posto di distruzione carburanti

Regia Aeronautica

Paracadutisti

Reggimento «Duca d'Aosta»

I battaglione *paracadutisti* d'assalto
I Battaglione Arditi Distruttori della Regia Aeronautica
II Battaglione Arditi Distruttori della Regia Aeronautica

Aviotrasportabile

Battaglione ricattatori «Loreto»

Regia Marina

Paracadutisti

Sezione «P»
Reparto «G» (guastatori)
Battaglione «P» (paracadutisti)
Battalions «N» (nuotatori)

Appendix II

Organization of the Libyan parachute Units

Battaglione Paracadutisti libici

24 March 1938[1]

Battaglione paracadutisti:
Comando
Three compagnie

Comando di battaglione
- 1 Tenente colonnello or maggiore commanding

Three compagnie *paracadutisti*
  Comando
  - 1 Capitano commanding

  Four squadre fucilieri (each with)
  - 1 Tenente commanding
  - 1 Sergente libico
  - 1 Caporale libico
  - 5 Soldato libico

Total strength of the battalion was 16 officers, 12 NCO, and 72 Libyans. The battalion was armed with 16 Beretta M34 pistols, and 84 moschetti per cavalleria M38.

1 Nino Arena, *I Fanti dell'Aria da Castel Benito ad Azizia (libia) (1938-1941)* (Bologna : Edition Eurographis, 1989), pp.149–150.

Battaglione Paracadutisti Libici

March 1939[2]

Battaglione paracadutisti:
Compagnai comando
Three compagnie *paracadutisti*

Comando di battaglione
- 1 Tenente colonnello or maggiore commanding
- 1 Capitano or tenente adjutant

Plotone comando
Comando
- 1 Tenente commanding
- 1 Sergente or sergente maggiore staff

Squadra collegamenti
- 2 Caporali/soldati libico signalman (signal panels)
- 4 Caporali/soldati libico signalman (aerial signal panels)
- 3 Caporali/soldati libico courier cyclists (three bicycles)

Squadra servizi
- 1 Caporale/soldato libico trumpeter (acts as a signaler and runner)
- 2 Caporali/soldati libico drivers (one staff car, one light truck)
- 1 Soldato libico office clerk
- 3 Soldato libico batmen
- 5 Soldato libico assigned to various services (two Breda 30 f.m.)

Three compagnie *paracadutisti*
Comando
- 1 Capitano commanding
- 1 Soldato libico batman/courier

Squadra guastatori
- 1 Tenente commanding
- 1 Sergente libico (36 capsules of mercury fulminant)
- 1 Caporale libico (50 meters of detonating cord)
- 3 Soldato libico (1 kilo of TNT each)
- 1 Soldato libico (30 meters of slow-burning fuse)
- 1 Soldato libico (Demolition Kit/tools)

Five squadre fucilieri (each with)
- 1 Tenente commanding
- 1 Sergente libico (spare parts)

2 Stefano Ales, Piero Crociani, & Andrea Viotti, Andrea, *Struttura, uniformi, distintivi, ed insegne delle truppe libiche 1912-1943* (Rome: USSME, 2012), pp.66–67.

- 1 Caporale libico gunner (one Breda 30 f.m.)
- 5 Soldato libico ammunition bearers (one soldato libico also acted as a batman)

Total strength of the battalion was 24 officers, 1 NCO, and 150 Libyans. 17 light machine guns, 134 carbines, a car, 1 truck, and 2 bicycles.

The actual organization of the two Libyan parachute battalion requires further research. Neither battalion was organized in accordance to the documents above. Both battalions always had four parachute companies and their manning was greater than the 100 or 175 men authorized by these documents.[3] The following is a possible reconstruction of their wartime organization:

Battaglione Paracadutisti Libici

June 1940[4]

This reconstruction is an attempt to reconcile the authorized organization of the two battalions with the reported manning and weapons during the combat in early 1941. The final manning document of the *3ª cp.*, *I btg. paracadutisti libico* shows a company organization of three platoons which doesn't include a *guastatori* squad. The document doesn't reflect any support personnel at the company level. The photographic evidence supports the use of an eight man squad with two f.m. which mirrors the squad organization found in the June 1940 *battaglione paarcadutisti* authorization. This organization shouldn't be considered definitive but only as a starting point for further research.

Battaglione paracadutisti:
Compagnai comando
Four compagnia *paracadutisti*

Nucleo controcarro
Comando di battaglione
- 1 Tenente colonnello or maggiore commanding
- 1 Capitano or tenente adjutant

3 Arena, *I Fanti*, pp.18, 66.

4 This reconstruction is using information from: Stefano Ales, Piero Crociani & Andrea Viotti, Andrea, *Struttura, uniformi, distintivi, ed insegne delle truppe libiche 1912-1943* (Rome: USSME, 2012), pp.66–67; Arena, *I Fanti*, pp.92, 145 and the various photographs of Libyan squads; AUSSME *Formazioni provvisorie di guerra del battaglione paracadutisti*, 12 giugno 1940.

Plotone comando
Comando
- 1 Tenente commanding
- 1 Sergente or sergente maggiore staff
Squadra collegamenti
- 2 Caporali/soldati libico signalman (signal panels)
- 4 Caporali/soldati libico signalman (aerial signal panels)
- 3 Caporali/soldati libico courier cyclists (three bicycles)
Squadra servizi
- 1 Caporale/soldato libico trumpeter (acts as a signaler and runner)
- 2 Caporali/soldati libico drivers (one staff car, one light truck)
- 1 Soldato libico office clerk
- 3 Soldato libico batmen
- 5 Soldato libico assigned to various services (two Breda 30 f.m.)
Four compagnie fucilieri (each with)
- 1 Capitano commanding
- 1 Tenente deputy commander
- 1 Soldato libico batman/courier
Squadra comando
- 1 Sergente commanding
- 6 staff and resupply *paracadutisti*
Three Plotoni fucilieri (each with)
- 1 Tenente commanding
Three squadre fucilieri (each with)
- 1 Sergente commanding
- 1 Caporale vice commander
- 2 Machine-gunners (two Breda 30 light machine guns)
- 5 *paracadutisti* ammunition bearers
Nucleo controcarri
- 1 Tenente commanding
Four squadra cannoni (each with)
- 1 Sergente or sergente maggiore commanding
- 3 Paracadutisti gun crew (one 47/32 c.c.)
- 4 Paracadutisti ammunition bearers

Total strength of the battalion was 24 officers, 45 NCO, and 365 Libyans. 98 pistols, 336 carbines, 74 light machine guns, four 47/32 c.c. guns, 1 car, 1 truck, and 2 bicycles.

Appendix III

Organization of the Italian Parachute Units

Battaglione Paracadutisti

12 June 1940[1]

Battaglione Paracadutisti
Comando
Three compagnia fucilieri

Comando di battaglione
- 1 Tenente colonnello or maggiore commanding
- 1 Maggiore vice commander (Aiutante)
- 1 Tenente Medical Officer

Squadra comando
- 1 Sergente or sergente maggiore commanding
- 1 Caporale maggiore Medical staff
- 3 Radio/Signalmen (one R.F.1 and one R.A.1 radios)
- 3 Signalmen (30 aerial signal panels)
- 2 Litter bearers

Plotone minatori (Demolition Platoon)
- 1 Tenente commanding
- 2 signalmen (1 set signaling panels)
  Three squadre minatori (each with)
  - 1 Sergente commanding
  - 6 Paracadutisti minatori

Three compagnie fucilieri (each with)
- 1 Capitano commanding
- 1 Tenente vice commander

1 AUSSME *Formazioni provvisorie di guerra del battaglione paracadutisti*, 12 giugno 1940.

Squadra comando
- 1 Sergente commanding
- 6 Staff and resupply *paracadutisti*
- 2 Radio men/signalmen (one R.F.1 radio and one set signaling panels)

Three Plotoni fucilieri (each with)
- 1 Tenente commanding
- 2 Staff/signalmen (1 set of signaling panels)

  Three squadre fucilieri (each with)
  - 1 Sergente commanding
  - 2 Machine-gunners (two Breda 30 light machine guns)
  - 5 Paracadutisti ammunition bearers

Total strength of the battalion was 19 officers, 34 NCOs, and 260 men. The battalion was armed with 313 combat knives, 313 Beretta M34 pistols, 52 Revelli semi-automatic rifles, 203 moschetti per cavalleria M38, and 54 fucili mitragliatori Breda 30. The Revelli would be replaced by the M38 carbines until they were available. No MAB 38As were authorized in this document.

Battaglione Paracadutisti

20 November 1940[2]

The following changes were made to the *battaglione paracadutisti*:

Battaglione Paracadutisti
Comando
Three compagnie fucilieri

Comando di battaglione
- 1 Tenente colonnello or maggiore commanding
- 1 Maggiore vice commander (Aiutante)
- 1 Tenente Medical Officer

Squadra Comando
- 1 Sergente or sergente maggiore commanding
- 2 Caporali or caporali maggiori Medical staff
- 3 Radio/Signalmen (one R.F.1 and one R.A.1 radios)
- 3 Signalmen (30 aerial signal panels)
- 4 Litter bearers

2 AUSSME *Formazioni provvisorie di guerra del battaglione paracadutisti*, 12 giugno 1940, with change Circolare 7720 dated 20 November 1940.

- 1 Trumpeter (acts as a signaler and runner)
- 2 Cooks
- 2 Drivers
- 2 Officer batmen (ordinanza d'ufficiali)

Plotone minatori (Demolition Platoon)
- 1 Tenente commanding
- 2 Signalmen (1 set signaling panels)
  Three Squadra Minatori (each with)
  - 1 Sergente commanding
  - 6 Paracadutisti minatori

Three Compagnie fucilieri (each with)
- 1 Capitano commanding
- 1 Tenente vice commander
  Squadra comando
  - 1 Sergente commanding
  - 6 Staff and resupply *paracadutisti*
  - 2 Radio men/signalmen (one R.F.1 radio and one set signaling panels)
  - 1 Trumpeter (acts as a signaler and runner)
  - 2 Cooks
  Three Plotone fucilieri (each with)
  - 1 Tenente commanding
  - 1 Tenente vice commander
  - 2 Staff/signalmen (1 set of signaling panels)
    Three Squadra fucilieri (each with)
    - 1 Sergente commanding
    - 2 Machine-gunners (two Breda 30 light machine guns)
    - 5 Paracadutisti ammunition bearers

Total strength of the battalion increased to 24 officers, 34 NCOs, and 280 men. The battalion was now armed with 343 combat knives, 343 Beretta M34 pistols, 62 Revelli semi-automatic rifles (planned increase to 343 Revelli), 220 moschetti per cavalleria M38, and 54 fucili mitragliatori Breda 30.

Further changes to the battalion were contained in the organization of the *reggimento paracadutisti*.

Reggimento Paracadutisti

February 1941[3]

This organization wasn't adopted

Reggimento paracadutisti:
 1 comando di reggimento
 3 battaglione *paracadutisti*
 1 compagnia armi d'impiego eventuale (*paracadutisti*)
 1 deposito (depot)

Comando di Reggimento
- 1 Colonnello commanding
- 1 Aiutante maggiore in 1° (not parachute qualified)
- 1 Tenente colonnello or maggiore vice commander (training officer)
- 2 Capitani/tenenti aerial observer
- 1 Capitano engineer
- 1 Capitano aerial logistics (not parachute qualified)
- 1 Tenente various assignments (not parachute qualified)
- 1 Capitano/tenente Medical Officer (not parachute qualified)
- 1 Tenente administration (not parachute qualified)
- 1 Chaplain

Reparti Comando
-1 Capitano commanding
 Plotone Comando
 - 1 Tenente commanding
 Staff Squadra
 - 1 Sergeant staff NCO
 - 1 Sergente or sergente maggiore administration
 - 1 Sergente or sergente maggiore engineer
 - 1 Sergente or sergente maggiore aerial photograph
 - 2 Sergenti administrative assistants
 - 1 Caporale or caporale administrative staff
 - 1 Caporale or caporale maggiore engineer
 - 1 Caporale or caporale maggiore medical
 - 5 Paracadutisti typist and draftsmen
 - 5 Paracadutisti batmen
 - 2 Litter bearers
 Squadra collegamenti (Communications squad)

3 AUSSME *Formazioni ed organici del reggimento paracadutisti*, febbraio 1941

- 1 Sergente commanding
- 3 Caporali or caporali maggiori
- 6 Paracadutisti radiomen (two R.F.1/P and one R.A.1 radios)
- 1 Caporale or caporale maggiore
- 3 Paracadutisti signalmen (48 aerial signal panels)

Plotone servizi (Service Platoon)
- 1 Tenente commanding

Squadra Servizi
- 1 Sergente commanding (armorer)
- 3 Paracadutisti apprentice armorers)
- 4 Trumpeters (acts as a signalers and runners)
- 6 Officer cooks
- 14 Unit cooks
- 9 Personal maintenance *paracadutisti* (3 tailors, 3 cobblers, and 3 barbers)

Reparto autocarreggio (vehicle park)(not parachute capable)
- Sergente commanding
- 4 Caporali or caporali maggiori
- 20 Paracadutisti (drivers) (4 staff cars, 16 light trucks, 3 buses)
- 4 Motorcyclists (4 motorcycles)

Plotone Attendenti (Attendent Platoon)
- Tenente commanding

Three squadre attendenti (one per battalion, each with)
- 1 Caporale or caporale maggiore
- 8 attendenti

Total strength of the regimental headquarters was 15 officers, 12 NCOs, and 174 men. The headquarters had 2 R.F.1/P radios, 1 R.A.1 Radio, 48 aerial signal panels. 4 staff cars, 16 light trucks, and 3 Buses.

Battaglione di paracadutisti

Squadra comando

3 compagnie fucilieri

Comando di battaglione
- 1 Tenente colonnello or maggiore commanding
- 1 Capitano adjutant
- 1 Tenente Medical Officer

Squadra Comando
- 1 Sergente or sergente maggiore commanding
- 2 Caporali (caporali or caporali maggiori) Medical staff
- 6 Radio/Signalmen (one R.T. speciale, R.F.1, and one R.A.1 radios)
- 3 Signalmen (30 aerial signal panels)
- 4 Litter bearers

Plotone minatori (Demolition Platoon)
- 1 Tenente commanding
- 1 Tenente vice commander
- 2 Signalmen (1 set signaling panels)
    Three Squadra Minatori (each with)
    - 1 Sergente commanding
    - 6 Paracadutisti minatori

Three Compagnie fucilieri (each with)
    Comando
    - 1 Capitano commanding
    - 1 Tenente vice commander
    Squadra comando
    - 1 Sergente commanding
    - 6 Staff and resupply *paracadutisti*
    - 2 Radio men/signalmen (one R.F.1 radio and one set signaling panels)
    Three Plotone fucilieri (each with)
    - 1 Tenente commanding
    - 1 Tenente vice commander
    - 2 Staff/signalmen (1 set of signaling panels)
        Three Squadra fucilieri (each with)
        - 1 Sergente commanding
        - 2 Machine-gunners (two Breda 30 light machine guns)
        - 5 Paracadutisti ammunition bearers

Total strength of the battalion was 29 officers, 34 NCOs, and 266 men. The battalion was armed with 329 combat knives, 329 Beretta M34 pistols, 268 moschetti per cavalleria M38, and 54 fucili mitragliatori Breda 30.

Compagnia armi d'impiego eventuale (paracadutisti)
Comando
Three plotoni eventuale

Comando
- 1 Capitano commanding
- 1 Tenente vice commander

Squadra comando
- 1 Sergente commanding
- 8 Staff and resupply *paracadutisti*

Three Plotone armi (each with)
- 1 Tenente commanding
- 1 Tenente vice commander
- 2 Staff/signalmen (1 set of signaling panels)
    Three Squadra armi d'impiego (each with)

- 1 Sergente commanding
- 1 Caporale or caporale maggiore
- 6 Paracadutisti

The weapons in the squads had not been finalized. A squad was either one Breda 37 machine gun, one 81mm mortar, two 45mm Brixia mortars, one 47/32 cannoni controcarro, or a variable number of flame throwers. The men in this company were to be trained on all the different weapons.

Total strength of the company was 8 officers, 10 NCOs, and 77 men. The battalion was armed with 95 combat knives, 95 Beretta M34 pistols, 95 moschetti per cavalleria M38.

This company was never established and most of the listed weapons were added to the battalions.

Deposito del reggimento paracadutisti
Squadra comando
Ufficio material (Materials Office)
Ufficio mobilitazione (Mobilization Office)
Ufficio amministrazione (Administration Office: direttore conti – pagatore – matricola – ragazzine materiale gruppi A & B)(account manager – paymaster- registration – material warehouse for A & B groups)

Total strength of the depot was 7 officers, 10 NCOs, and 52 men.

Total strength of the regiment was 117 officers, 135 NCOs, and 1101 men. The battalion was armed with 1088 combat knives, 1087 Beretta M34 pistols, 1088 moschetti per cavalleria M38, and 162 fucili mitragliatori Breda 30.[4] 4 staff cars, 16 light trucks, and 3 Buses.

Reggimento Paracadutisti[5]

July 1941

Reggimento paracadutisti:

4 There is an addition error in the number of Breda 30 f.m. in this document. The unit breakdowns lists 54 per battalion (162), but the total recap states 172.

5 Information from AUSSME Stato maggiore R.E. memorandum 18 luglio 1941, *Formazioni provvisorie di guerra dei reparti di ftr. paracadutisti, luglio 1941* unless otherwise noted..

Comando di reggimento
3 battaglione *paracadutisti*
Compagnia cannoni da 47/32 a.c.
Compagnia servizio (non *paracadutisti*)

Comando di Reggimento
- 1 Colonnello commanding
- 1 Tenente colonnello or maggiore vice commander
- 1 Maggiore or capitano aiutante maggiore
- 1 Capitano aerial observer
- 2 Lieutenants staff
- 1 Capitano aerial logistics (not parachute qualified)
- 1 Capitano/tenente Medical Officer
- 1 Tenente administration (not parachute qualified)

Plotone Comando
- One of the two staff lieutenants above command this platoon.
  - Squadra Comando
    - 2 Sergente
    - 2 Clerks
    - 2 Litter bearers
    - 4 Bicyclists (four bicycles)
  - Squadra collegamenti (Communications Squad)
    - 1 Sergente commanding
    - 10 Paracadutisti radiomen (four R.F.1/P and one R.A.1 radios)
    - 4 Paracadutisti signalmen (48 aerial signal panels)
  - Squadra Servizi (Service Squad)
    - 1 Sergente commanding
    - 3 Caporali or caporali maggiori
    - 18 Paracadutisti (18 hand carts)

Total strength of the regimental headquarters was 10 officers, 4 NCOs, and 44 men. The headquarters had four R.F.1/P radios, one R.A.1 Radio, 48 aerial signal panels. 4 staff cars, 16 light trucks, 3 Buses, 4 bicycles, and 18 hand carts.

Battaglione paracadutisti:
Compagnia comando
Three compagnie

Comando di battaglione
- 1 Tenente colonnello or maggiore commanding
- 1 Capitano vice commander
- 1 Capitano Aiutante
- 2 Tenente Medical Officer

Compagnia Comando
- 1 (Vice comandante above commands this company)
  Plotone misto (Mixed platoon)
  - 1 Tenente commanding
  Squadra comando e collegamenti (command and communications)
  - 1 Sergente
  - 1 Caporale or caporale maggiore
  - 1 Caporale medical staff
  - 6 Paracadutisti radiomen (three RF1/P radios)
  - 3 Paracadutisti staff and signalmen
  - 4 Litter bearers
  - 1 Student gunsmith
  Squadra lanciafiamme (Flame Thrower Squad)
  - 1 Sergente or sergente maggiore commanding
  - 6 Flame Thrower gunners
  - 6 Flame Thrower assistants
  Plotone mitraglieri (Machine Gun Platoon)
  - 1 Tenente commanding
  - 1 Tenente vice commander
    Four squadra mitraglieri (each with)
    - 1 Sergente or sergente maggiore commanding
    - 1 Paracadutisti gunner (Breda 37)
    - 1 Paracadutisti tripod
    - 1 Paracadutisti Spare parts
    - 4 Paracadutisti ammunition bearers
  Plotone mortai da 81 (Mortar Platoon)
  - 1 Tenente commanding
  - 1 Tenente vice commander
  - 1 Paracadutisti Plotter/calculator
  - 1 Paracadutisti signalman with signaling panels
  - 1 Paracadutisti Staff
    Three squadra mortai da 81 (each with)
    - 1 Sergente or sergente maggiore commanding
    - 1 Paracadutisti gunner carrying the base plate
    - 1 Paracadutisti carrying the bipod
    - 1 Paracadutisti carrying the tube (81mm)
    - 1 Paracadutisti loader
    - 6 Paracadutisti ammunition bearers (two hand carts)

Three Compagnie fucilieri (each with)
Comando
- 1 Capitano commanding
- 1 Tenente vice commander
  Plotone comando

- 1 Tenente commanding
    - Squadra commando
    - 1 Sergente or sergente maggiore commanding
    - 4 Staff and resupply *paracadutisti*
    - 2 Radio men/signalmen (one R.F.1 radio and one set signaling panels)
    - 1 Student gunsmith
    - 2 Caporali nucleo fucili anticarro (anti-tank rifle detachment)
    - 2 Paracadutisti fucili anticarro (anti-tank rifle detachment)
    - Two squadra mitraglieri (each with)
    - 1 Sergente or sergente maggiore commanding
    - 1 Paracadutisti gunner (Breda 37)
    - 1 Paracadutisti tripod
    - 1 Paracadutisti Spare parts
    - 4 Paracadutisti ammunition bearers

Three Plotone fucilieri (each with)
- 1 Tenente commanding
- 1 Tenente vice commander
- 2 Staff/signalmen (1 set of signaling panels)
    - Three Squadra fucilieri (each with)
    - 1 Sergente commanding
    - 2 Machine-gunners (two Breda 30 light machine guns)
    - 5 Paracadutisti ammunition bearers

Total strength of the battalion was 37 officers, 45 NCOs, and 374 men. The battalion was armed with 419 Beretta M34 pistols, 419 moschetti per cavalleria M38, 54 fucili mitragliatori Breda 30, 6 anti-tank rifles, 10 Breda 37, three 81mm mortars, and 6 flame throwers. The battalion had 6 hand carts.

Compagnia cannoni da 47/32 a.c.
Comando
Three plotoni cannoni da 47/32

Comando
- 1 Capitano commanding
- 1 Tenente vice commander

Squadra comando
- 1 Sergente or sergente maggiore commanding
- 2 Staff/signalmen (1 set of signaling panels)
- 2 Radio men/signalmen (one R.F.1 radio and one set signaling panels)

Three plotoni cannoni da 47/32 (each with)
- 1 Tenente commanding
- 1 Tenente vice commander
- 2 Paracadutisti Plotter/calculator

- 2 Paracadutisti signalman with signaling panels
  Two squadra cannoni (each with)
  - 1 Sergente or sergente maggiore commanding
  - 3 Paracadutisti gun crew (one 47/32 c.c.)
  - 8 *paracadutisti* ammunition bearers (two hand carts)

Total strength of the company was 8 officers, 7 NCOs, and 82 men. The company was armed with 97 Beretta M34 pistols, 97 moschetti per cavalleria M38, 6 Breda 47/32 anti-tank guns, and 12 hand carts).

Compagnia servizio (non paracadutisti)
Plotone servizio misto (Mixed Service Platoon supporting all the regimental assets)
Three Plotoni servizi (Service Platoons, one for each battaglione *paracadutisti*)

Total strength of the company was 5 officers, 14 NCOs, and 282 soldati. The company had 4 staff cars, 15 light trucks, 6 motorcycles, 3 Buses, and 9 bicycles.

Total strength of the regiment was 134 officers, 160 NCOs, and 1530 men. The regiment was armed with 162 fucili mitragliatori Breda 30, 18 anti-tank rifles, 30 Breda 37, nine 81mm mortars, 6 Breda 47/32 anti-tank guns, and 18 flame throwers. The regiment had 4 staff cars, 15 light trucks, 3 Buses, 6 motorcycles, 13 bicycles, and 48 hand carts.

Reparti Divisionale Paracadutisti[6]

July 1941

Reggimento Artiglieria Per Divisione Paracadutisti
Compagnia comando
Three gruppi artiglieria
Batteria servizi

Three gruppi artiglieria (each with)
Nucleo comando
Two batteria da 47/32 con traino a mano (pulled by men)

6 Information from AUSSME Stato maggiore R.E. memorandum 18 luglio 1941, *Formazioni provvisorie di guerra dei reparti di ftr. paracadutisti, luglio 1941* unless otherwise noted..

Comando
- 1 Tenente colonnello or maggiore commanding
- 1 Capitano or tenente adjutant

Nucleo comando
- 1 Sergente or sergente maggiore commanding
- 2 Paracadutisti fire calculators
- 3 Paracadutisti staff (three motorcycles)
- 4 Cooks
- 2 Paracadutisti clerk/typists
- 6 Radiomen (three RF.1 or RF.1P radios)
- 1 Paracadutisti office administration
- 3 Paracadutisti (tailor, cobbler, barber)
- 14 Batmen
- 2 Drivers (two light trucks)
- 1 Motorcyclist (one motorcycle w/ sidecar)

Two batterie artiglieria (each with)
- 1 Capitano commanding
- 1 Tenente vice commander
- 1 Sergente or sergente maggiore
- 2 Radiomen (one RF.1 radio)

    Two plotoni cannoni da 47/32 (each with)
    - 1 Tenente commanding
    - 1 Tenente vice commander

        Two squadra cannoni (each with)
        - 1 Sergente or sergente maggiore commanding
        - 3 Paracadutisti gun crew (one 47/32 c.c.)
        - 8 *paracadutisti* ammunition bearers (two hand carts)

Total strength of the gruppo was 20 officers, 19 NCOs, and 173 soldati. Four 47/32 c.c. The gruppo had 1 motorcycle, 1 motorcycle with sidecar, 2 light trucks, 3 bicycles, 16 hand carts.

Compagnia Motociclisti Per Divisione Paracadutisti

Squadra comando
Three plotoni motociclisti
Squadra servizio (non *paracadutisti*)

Comando
- 1 Capitano commanding (1 motorcycle)
- 1 One tenente vice commander (1 motorcycle)

    Squadra comando
    - 1 Sergente or sergente maggiore commanding (1 motorcycle)
    - 1 Caporale or caporale maggiore staff (1 motorcycle)

- 1 Motorcycle courier/staff (1 motorcycle)
- 6 Radio operators (three R.F.1/P radios, six motorcycles)

Three plotoni motociclisti
Comando
- 1 Tenente commanding (1 motorcycle)
- 1 Tenente vice commander (1 motorcycle)
- 1 Motorcycle courier/staff (1 motorcycle)

Three squadre motociclisti
- 1 Sergente or sergente maggiore commanding (1 motorcycle)
- 2 Caporali or caporali maggiori machine-gunners (two Breda 30 machine guns, two motorcycles)
- 4 Paracadutisti ammunition bearers (four motorcycles)
- 2 Paracadutisti scouts/ammunition bearers (two motorcycles)

Squadra servizio (non *paracadutisti*)
- 1 Tenente commanding
- 1 Clerk soldier
- 1 Supply soldier
- 1 Bicycles courier (one bicycle)
- 2 Cooks
- 1 Driver (one light truck)
- 1 Motorcyclist
- 1 Motorcycle mechanic (one tricycle motorcycle)
- 5 Batmen
- 9 Personal maintenance soldiers (3 tailors, 3 cobblers, and 3 barbers)

Total strength of the company was 8 officers, 11 NCOs, and 105 men. The compagnia was armed with 101 Beretta M34 pistols, 1124 moschetti per cavalleria M38, 18 fucili mitragliatori Breda 30. The company had 1 light truck, 101 motorcycles, 1 tricycle motorcycle, and 1 bicycle.

Compagnia Mortai Per Divisione Paracadutisti
Squadra comando
Four plotoni morati
Squadra servizio (non *paracadutisti*)

Comando
- 1 Capitano commanding
- 1 Tenente vice commander

Squadra comando
- 1 Sergente or sergente maggiore commanding
- 1 Caporale medical staff
- 4 Staff *paracadutisti*
- 6 Litter bearers

- 4 Radio operators/signalers (one R.F.1/P radios, one set signal panels)

Three Plotone mortai da 81 (Mortar Platoon)
- 1 Tenente commanding
- 1 Tenente vice commander
- 1 Paracadutisti Plotter/calculator
- 1 Paracadutisti signalman with signaling panels
- 1 Paracadutisti Staff

  Three squadre mortai da 81 (each with)
  - 1 Sergente or sergente maggiore commanding
  - 1 Paracadutisti gunner w/ base plate
  - 1 Paracadutisti w/ bipod
  - 1 Paracadutisti w/ tube (81mm)
  - 1 Paracadutisti loader
  - 6 Paracadutisti ammunition bearers (two hand carts)

Squadra servizio (non *paracadutisti*)
- 1 Tenente commanding
- 1 Clerk soldier
- 1 Supply soldier
- 2 Staff soldiers (one motorcycle, one bicycle)
- 1 Driver (one light truck)
- 2 Cooks
- 6 Batmen
- 9 Personal maintenance soldiers (3 tailors, 3 cobblers, and 3 barbers)

Total strength of the company was 10 officers, 14 NCOs, and 170 men. The compagnia was armed with 194 Beretta M34 pistols, 194 moschetti per cavalleria M38, twelve 81mm mortars The company had 1 light truck, 1 motorcycle, and 1 bicycle.

Battaglione Guastatori Per Divisione Paracadutisti

Comando di battaglione

Three compagnie guastatori

Plotone servizio (non *paracadutisti*)

Comando di battaglione
- 1 Tenente colonnello or maggiore commanding
- 1 Capitano vice commander
- 1 Capitano Aiutante
- 2 Tenente Medical Officer

Compagnia Comando
- 1 (Vice comandante above commands this company)

  Squadra comando e collegamenti (command and communications)
  - 1 Sergente commanding
  - 1 Caporale or caporale maggiore

- 2 Caporali medical staff
- 6 Paracadutisti radiomen and signalmen
- 4 Litter bearers
- 1 Student gunsmith
- 3 Staff *paracadutisti*/signalmen (aerial signal panels)

Plotone mitraglieri (Machine Gun Platoon)
- 1 Tenente commanding
- 1 Tenente vice commander

Four squadre mitraglieri (each with)
- 1 Sergente or sergente maggiore commanding
- 1 Paracadutisti gunner (Breda 37)
- 1 Paracadutisti tripod
- 1 Paracadutisti Spare parts
- 4 Paracadutisti ammunition bearers

Plotone mortai da 81 (Mortar Platoon)
- 1 Tenente commanding
- 1 Tenente vice commander
- 1 Paracadutisti Plotter/calculator
- 1 Paracadutisti signalman with signaling panels
- 1 Paracadutisti Staff

Three squadre mortai da 81 (each with)
- 1 Sergente or sergente maggiore commanding
- 1 Paracadutisti gunner/base plate
- 1 Paracadutisti bipod
- 1 Paracadutisti tube (81mm)
- 1 Paracadutisti loader
- 6 Paracadutisti ammunition bearers (two hand carts)

Three Compagnie guastatori *paracadutisti*

Comando
- 1 Capitano commanding
- 1 Tenente vice commander

Squadra comando
- 1 Sergente or sergente maggiore commanding
- 4 Staff and resupply *paracadutisti*
- 2 Radio men/signalmen (one R.F.1 radio and one set signaling panels)
- 2 Caporali nucleo fucili anticarro (anti-tank rifle detachment)
- 2 Paracadutisti fucili anticarro (anti-tank rifle detachment)
- 2 Paracadutisti ammunition bearers
- 1 Student gunsmith

Three plotone guastatori
- 1 Tenente commanding
- 1 Tenente vice commander
- 1 Staff *paracadutisti*

Gruppo distruzione (Destruction Group)
- 1 Sergente or sergente maggiore commanding
- 3 Guastatori with elongated (Bangalore) charges
- 4 Guastatori with block charges
- 1 Guastatori with smoke bombs
- 1 Flame Thrower gunner
- 1 Flame Thrower assistant

Gruppo sostegno (Support Group)
- 1 Sergente or sergente maggiore commanding
- 3 Mortar gunners (Three 45mm Brixia mortars)
- 6 Paracadutisti ammunition bearers
- 1 Machine-gunners (one Breda 30 light machine gun)
- 2 Paracadutisti ammunition bearers

Plotone servizio (non *paracadutisti*)

Comando
- 1 Tenente commanding

Squadra comando
- 1 Sergente or sergente maggiore commanding
- 4 Accountants/clerk
- 1 Clerk
- 2 Bicycle courier/staff (two bicycles)
- 2 Postal clerk/batmen
- 2 Trumpeters (acts as a signalers and runners)

Squadra servizio e attendenti
- 1 Sergente or sergente maggiore commanding
- 1 Caporale or caporale maggiore
- 4 Quartermasters
- 8 Cooks
- 20 Batmen
- 20 Personal maintenance soldiers (3 tailors, 3 cobblers, and 3 barbers)
- 3 Drivers (three light trucks)

Total strength of the battalion was 34 officers, 31 NCOs, and 394 men. The battalion was armed with 389 Beretta M34 pistols, 258 moschetti per cavalleria M38, 51 MAB 38A, 9 fucili mitragliatori Breda 30, 4 Breda 37, 27 Brixia 45mm mortars, three 81mm mortars, 6 anti-tank rifles, and 9 flame throwers. The battalion had 3 light trucks, 2 bicycles, and 6 hand carts.

285º Battaglione Paracadutisti

Battaglione fanteria tipo A.S.42[7]

Comando di battaglione
Four compagnie fucilieri

Comando di battaglione
- 1 Tenente colonnello or maggiore commanding
- 1 Maggiore or capitano adjutant
- 1 Tenente chemical/engineer officer
- 1 Tenente Medical Officer

Plotone comando
- 1 Tenente commanding
    Squadra Comando
    - 1 Sergente or sergente maggiore commanding
    - 1 Caporale or caporale maggiore staff
    - 1 Caporale or caporale maggiore) Medical staff
    - 1 Trumpeter (acts as a signaler and runner)
    - 2 Clerks
    - 2 Litter bearers
    Squadra collegamenti
    - 1 Sergente commanding
    - 6 Radio/Signalmen (three radios)
    - 10 Telephone operators
    - 6 Observers/batmen
    - 4 motorcycle couriers (four motorcycles)
    Squadra servizio
    - 1 Sergente or sergente maggiore commanding
    - 1 Sergente quartermaster
    - 1 Student gunsmith
    - 12 Personal maintenance soldiers (4 tailors, 4 cobblers, and 4 barbers)
    - 4 Drivers (three light trucks)
    - 1 Mechanic

Four Compagnie fucilieri (each with)
    Comando
    - 1 Capitano commanding
    Squadra comando
    - 1 Sergente commanding
    - 2 Couriers

7 NARA T-821, roll.21

- 2 Batmen
- 2 Litter bearers
- 1 Orderly
- 4 Drivers (three heavy trucks)

Plotone fucilieri
- 1 Tenente commanding
- 1 Courier
  Three squadre fucilieri (each with)
  - 1 Sergente commanding
  - 2 Machine-gunners (two Breda 30 light machine guns)
  - 8 Soldiers ammunition bearers

Plotone mitraglieri
- 1 Tenente commanding
- 1 Courier
  Three squadre mitraglieri (each with)
  - 1 Sergente or sergente maggiore commanding
  - 1 Caporale or caporale maggiore gunner (Breda 37)
  - 1 Paracadutisti tripod
  - 1 Paracadutisti Spare parts
  - 3 Paracadutisti ammunition bearers

Plotone controcarro 20mm or 25mm
- 1 Tenente commanding
- 1 Batman
- 1 Courier
  Three squadra controcarro (each with)
  - 1 Sergente or sergente maggiore commanding
  - 3 Paracadutisti gun crew (20mm Solothurn or French 25mm)
  - 3 Paracadutisti ammunition bearers

Plotone controcarro da 47/32 c.c
- 1 Tenente commanding
- 1 Batman
- 1 Courier
  Three squadra controcarro (each with)
  - 1 Sergente or sergente maggiore commanding
  - 4 Paracadutisti gun crew (one 47/32 c.c.)
  - 6 Paracadutisti ammunition bearers

Total strength of the battalion was 29 officers, 34 NCOs, and 256 men. The battalion was armed with 329 combat knives, 329 Beretta M34 pistols, 268 moschetti per cavalleria M38, and 54 fucili mitragliatori Breda 30.

Appendix IV

Organization of the Italian Air Landing Units

Compagnia carri L3 lanciafiamme aviotrasportabile

This company was designed to be transported by the SM.82 transport and air-landed on a captured airfield. The L3 lf were carried using a special connecting mechanism that was installed in the bomb bay of the SM.82. Once the transport landed, it was only a few minutes to lower and detach the vehicle from the aircraft. The vehicle crews were parachute qualified and would jump prior to the transports arriving so to be ready to quickly uncouple the L3s from the SM.82s. This unit was operational between January 1941 and October 1941 but remained in Rome. The vehicles were returned to their original configuration in October 1941.

Compagnia carri L3 lanciafiamme aviotrasportabile
Comando
- 1 Capitano or Tenente commanding
- 1 Vehicle driver (one L3 lf)

Two plotoni L3 lanciafiamme (each with)
- 1 Tenente commanding
- 3 Sergenti vehicle commanders
- 4 Vehicle drivers (four L3 lf)

Compagnia reserve
- 1 Tenente company vice commander
- 2 Tenentes plotone vice commanders
- 4 Sergenti vehicle commanders
- 6 Vehicle drivers (one L3 lf)

Company total: 6 officers (3 in reserve), 10 NCOs (3 in reserve), and 15 carristi (5 in reserve). 10 L3 lanciafiamme (1 in reserve).

Divisione Aviotrasportabile

March 1942

***Divisone aviotrasportabile*:**[1]
Comando di divisione
Battaglione esplorante bersaglieri
3 Reggimenti fanteria
Reggimento artiglieria
Battaglione controcarri
Battaglione misto del genio
Reparto servizio

Comando di divisione
Comando
Stato maggiore (General Staff)
Compagnia comando

Battaglione esplorante bersaglieri
Compagnia comando
Two compagnie ciclisti (bicycle)
One compagnia motociclisti (motorcycle)

Compagnia Comando – 3 officers, 2 NCOs, 19 bersaglieri. 3 motorcycles, 2 two-seat motorcycles, 1 motor tricycle, 2 hand carts.

Two Compagnie ciclisti (each with) – 4 officers, 10 NCOs, 125 bersaglieri. 3 motorcycles, 3 two-seat motorcycles, 12 motor tricycle, 114 bicycles, 8 hand carts. 9 Breda 30 f.m.

Compagnia motociclisti – 4 officer, 10 NCOs, 83 bersaglieri. 27 motorcycles, thirty 2-seat motorcycles, 22 motor tricycles, 4 hand carts. 6 Breda 30, 3 Breda 37 machine guns.

Battalion total: 15 officers, 32 NCOs, 352 bersaglieri. Forty-six 1-seat motorcycles, 30 two-seat motorcycles, 22 motor tricycles, 228 bicycles, 14 hand carts. 24 Breda 30, 3 Breda 37 machine guns.

1 Information from AUSSME, Stato Maggiore R.E. memorandum 11 marzo 1942, *Oggetto: Modifiche alle formazioni di guerra della 80° divisone"LA SPEZIA" (aviotrasportabile)*, M7 racc.490, cart.11.

Reggimento fanteria
Compagnia comando e collegamenti
Three battaglione fanteria

Comando di reggimenti
- 1 Colonnello commanding
- 1 Maggiore or capitano adjutant
- 1 Capitano information
- 2 Capitani or tenenti staff
- 1 Capitano medical officer
- 1 Tenente administration
- 1 Chaplain

Compagnia comando
-1 Capitano commanding

Plotone comando (headquarters platoon)
- 1 Tenente commanding
- 1 Sergente or sergente maggiore clerk
- 1 Sergente or sergente maggiore information
- 1 Caporale or caporale maggiore medical staff
- 2 Couriers (two motorcycles)
- 2 Couriers (two bicycles)
- 7 Motorcyclists (one 2-seat motorcycle, 6 motor tricycles)
- 6 Soldiers staff (6 hand carts)
- 11 Batmen

Plotone collegamenti (communications platoon)
- 1 Tenente commanding
- 4 Caporali or caporali maggiori radiomen (four 2-seat motorcycles)
- 4 Soldiers radiomen (three stazioni R.F. 2 and one posto R.A.2 radios, one motor tricycle, two hand carts)
- 10 Telephone operators (five telephone stations, one 10-line telephone exchange, 10km of wire, two hand carts)
- 3 Soldier observers
- 2 Pigeon handlers

Two sezioni da 20/65 contraerei (each with)
- 1 Tenente commanding
- 1 Sergente or sergente maggiore
- 2 Sergenti or sergenti maggiori gun capitano (two 20/65 c.a. guns)
- 6 Gun crewmen
- 2 soldiers aerial calculators
- 4 Ammunition bearers (4 hand carts)
- 2 motorcyclists (4 motor tricycles)
- 2 Gun crewmen with various duties

Total: 14 officers, 5 NCOs, 96 personnel. Two motorcycles, five 2-seat motorcycles, 11 motor tricycles, 2 bicycles, 18 hand carts. 3 radio stations R.F. 2 and 1 radio post R.A. 2. 5 telephones, one 10-line telephone exchange, 10 km of wire. Four 20/65 c.a. guns.

Battaglione fanteria
Comando
Three compagnia fucilieri
One compagnia armi d'accompagnamento

Comando
- 1 Tenente colonnello or maggiore commanding
- 1 Maggiore adjutant
- 1 Tenente medical officer

Plotone comando
- 1 Tenente commanding

Squadra comando
- 1 Sergente or sergente maggiore commanding
- 1 Caporale or caporale maggiore medical staff
- 1 Caporale or caporale maggiore student armored
- 4 Batmen
- 4 Soldiers staff (two hand carts)
- 2 Couriers (two bicycles)
- 2 Couriers (one motorcycle, one 2-seat motorcycle)
- 3 Motorcyclists (three motor tricycles)

Squadra telefonisti e guardafili (linesmen)
- 2 Sergenti or sergenti maggiori
- 8 Telephone operators (four telephone stations and 4km of wire)

Squadra osservatori e segnalatori
- 1 Caporale maggiore observer
- 3 Signal observers
- 4 Signalers (two photoelectric 45mm stations and four set of signaling panels)

Three compagnie fucilieri
Comando
-1 Capitano commanding

Plotone comando
- 1 Sergente or sergente maggiore
- 1 Solider staff (one bicycle)
- 2 Signalers
- 8 Soldiers for patrols (one caporale or caporale maggiore)
- 4 Litter bearers
- 2 Staff/Batmen
- 1 Apprentice armorer

- 1 Motorcyclist (one motor tricycle)
    Squadra mortai da 45
    - 1 Sergente or sergente maggiore commanding
    - 3 Caporali maggiori
    - 3 Soldiers gunners (three Brixia 45mm mortars)
    - 1 Caporale ammunition leader
    - 6 Soldier ammunition bearers
    Squadra rifornitori (supply)
    - 1 Caporale or caporale maggiore commanding
    - 8 Soldier supply (four hand carts)

Three Plotoni fucilieri
- 1 Tenente commanding
- 1 Staff/batman
    Three squadra fucilieri (each with)
    - 1 Sergente or caporale commanding
    - 1 Soldier gunner (one Breda 30 f.m.)
    - 2 Soldiers ammunition bearers
    - 5 Soldiers

Plotone mitraglieri
- 1 Tenente commanding
- 1 Staff/batman
    Four squadra mitraglieri (each with)
    - 1 Sergente or sergente maggiore commanding
    - 1 Caporale gunner (one Breda 37)
    - 1 Soldier tripod
    - 1 Soldier Spare parts
    - 4 Soldiers ammunition bearers

One compagnia armi d'accompagnamento
Comando
- 1 Capitano commanding

Plotone comando
- 1 Tenente commanding
    Squadra comando
    - 1 Sergente or sergente maggiore commanding
    - 1 Caporale medical staff
    - 1 Gunnery specialist
    - 1 Craftsman
    - 1 Apprentice armorer
    - 4 Litter bearers
    - 3 Motorcyclists (one 2-seat motorcycle, two motor tricycles)
    - 2 Orderlies/staff
    Squadra collegamenti

- 1 Caporale or caporale maggiore commanding
- 4 Telephone operators (three telephone stations and 3 km of wire)
- 4 Signalers (two photo-electric 45mm stations and one set of signaling panels)

Squadra rifornitori (supply)
- 1 Caporale or caporale maggiore commanding (one bicycle)

Two Plotoni mortai da 81 (Mortar Platoon) (each with)
- 1 Tenente commanding
- 1 Soldier Plotter/calculator
- 1 Soldier orderly/staff
- 1 Motorcyclist (one motor tricycle)

Three squadre mortai da 81 (each with)
- 1 Sergente or sergente maggiore commanding carrying the tube
- 1 Caporale gunner carrying the base plate
- 1 Soldier carrying the bipod
- 1 Paracadutisti loader
- 5 Paracadutisti ammunition bearers (one hand cart)

Two plotoni cannoni da 47/32 (each with)
- 1 Tenente commanding
- 1 Soldier orderly/staff
- 2 Motorcyclists (two motor tricycles)

Two squadre cannoni (each with)
- 1 Sergente or sergente maggiore commanding (one 47/32 c.c. gun)
- 5 Soldiers gun crew
- 4 Soldiers ammunition bearers (one hand cart)

Battalion Total: 29/40/613 personnel. One 1-seat motorcycle, Two 2-seat motorcycles, 14 motor tricycles, six bicycles, twenty-seven hand carts. 27 Breda 30, 12 Breda 37, six 81mm mortars, nine 45mm Brixia mortars, four 47/32 anti-tank guns.

Regimental total: 101/125/1935 personnel. 5 motorcycles, eleven 2-seat motorcycles, 53 motor tricycles, 20 bicycles, 91 hand carts. 81 Breda 30, 36 Breda 37, Twenty-seven 45mm mortars, eighteen 81mm mortars, four 20/65 c.a., twelve 47/32 c.c.

The 9° reparto mototricicli was added to the division on 25 April 1942.

Reparto mototricicli[2]
Comando
Four sezione mototriciclili

Comando
- 1 Capitano or tenete commanding (1 motorcycle)
- 1 Sergente or sergente maggiore administration
- 1 Caporale or caporale maggiore administration
- 1 Staff soldier (one 2-seat motorcycle)
- 5 Soldier for various tasks
- 1 Batman
- 10 Motorcycle drivers (6 are reserve drivers, 4 motor tricycles))
- 2 Mechanics

Four sezioni motocicli
- 1 Tenente commanding (1 motorcycle)
- 1 Staff soldier (1 motorcycle)
- 1 Sergente or sergente maggiore motorcycle driver (1 motor tricycle)
- 23 Motorcycle drivers (23 motor tricycles)

Unit Total: 5 officers, 6 NCOs, 115 soldiers. 9 motorcycles, One 2-seat motorcycle, 100 motor tricycles.

A guastatori platoon was added to each infantry battalion on 21 July 1942. This platoon replaced a rifle platoon in the *1ª cp.* of each battalion.

Plotone guastatori
Comando plotone
- 1 Tenente commanding (1 MAB, 1 Beretta 34)
- 1 Staff/batman (1moschetto 38)
- 1 Motorcyclist (1 motorcycle, 1 moschetto 38))
- 4 Supply soldiers (1 MAB, 4 Beretta 34)

Gruppo distruzione (Destruction group)
- 1 Sergente or sergente maggiore (1 MAB, 1 Beretta 34)
- 2 Soldiers (smoke pots or grenades, 12 signal panels, 1 flare pistol, 2 MABs)
- 4 Soldier (Bangalore or tube explosives, 4 MABs)
- 2 Soldiers (2 picks, 2 shovels, explosives, 2 MABs)
- 1 Flame thrower (lanciafiamme 41, 1 Beretta 34)
- 1 Assault flame thrower (lanciafiamme assalto, 1 Beretta 34)

Gruppo sostegno (support group)

2 AUSSME, Stato Maggiore R.E. memorandum 25 aprile 1942, *Oggetto: Costituzione e mobilitazione del 9º reparto mototricicli per divisone "La Spezia"*, M7 racc.490, cart.11

- 1 Sergente or sergente maggiore (1 MAB, 1 Beretta 34)
- 1 Machine gunner (1 Breda 30 f.m., 1 Beretta 34)
- 2 Ammo bearers (2 Beretta 34)
- 1 Morar gunner (1 Mortai da 45, 1 Beretta 34)
- 2 Ammo bearers (2 Beretta 34)

Platoon Total: 1 officer, 2 NCOs, 24 soldiers. 1 motor tricycle, 1 bicycle. 15 Beretta 34, 2 moschetti 38, 14 MAB 38A, 1 Breda 30 f.m., one Brixia 45mm mortar, one flame thrower, one assault flamethrower.

In September The *plotoni guastatori* were removed from the *1ª cp.* of each battalion and grouped to together to form a regimental *compagnia guastatori*. Six new rifle platoons were authorized to replace the *plotoni guastatori* in the *1ª cp.* Each regiment now consisted of:

Reggimento fanteria
Compagnia comando e collegamenti (command and communications company)
Three battaglioni fanteria
One compagnia guastatori

The regimental command and the three infantry battalions

Compagnia guastatori di fanteria[3]
Plotone comando
Three plotoni guastatori

Comando
- 1 Capitano commanding

Plotone comando
- 1 Tenente commanding
- 1 Sergente or sergente maggiore administration
- 1 Sergente or sergente maggiore signalman
- 3 Caporali or caporali maggiori various tasks
- 1 Trumpeter (acts as a signaler and runner)
- 1 Draftsman
- 4 Litter bearers
- 2 Batmen
- 3 Signalmen
- 3 Soldiers various tasks

3 AUSSME Stato Maggiore R.E. memorandum 4 settembre 1942, *Oggetto: Modiche alle formazioni di guerra dei rgt. di fanteria della 80^ div. "La Spezia"*, M7 racc.490, cart.11.

- 5 Supply soldiers
- 2 Staff soldiers
- 3 Motorcyclists (3 motor tricycles)

Three Plotoni guastatori (each with)

Comando plotone
- 1 Tenente commanding (1 MAB, 1 Beretta 34)
- 1 Staff/batman (1moschetto 38)
- 1 Motorcyclist (1 motorcycle, 1 moschetto 38))
- 4 Supply soldiers (1 MAB, 4 Beretta 34)

Gruppo distruzione (Destruction group)
- 1 Sergente or sergente maggiore (1 MAB, 1 Beretta 34)
- 2 Soldiers (smoke pots or grenades, 12 signal panels, 1 flare pistol, 2 MABs)
- 4 Soldier (Bangalore or tube explosives, 4 MABs)
- 2 Soldiers (2 picks, 2 shovels, explosives, 2 MABs)
- 1 Flame thrower (lanciafiamme 41, 1 Beretta 34)
- 1 Assault flame thrower (lanciafiamme assalto, 1 Beretta 34)

Gruppo sostegno (support group)
- 1 Sergente or sergente maggiore (1 MAB, 1 Beretta 34)
- 1 Machine gunner (1 Breda 30 f.m., 1 Beretta 34)
- 2 Ammo bearers (2 Beretta 34)
- 1 Morar gunner (1 Mortai da 45, 1 Beretta 34)
- 2 Ammo bearers (2 Beretta 34)

Company Total: 5 officers, 8 NCOs, 99 soldiers. One 2-seat motorcycle, 1 motor tricycle, 5 bicycles, 5 hand carts. 54 Beretta 34, 26 moschetti 38, 42 MAB 38A, 3 Breda 30 f.m., 3 Brixia 45mm mortars, 3 flamethrowers, 3 assault flamethrowers.

La Spezia had the following breakdown of personnel, vehicles, and weapons on 7 October 1942.[4]

1 *Comando di divisione*

25/18/103 personnel. 30 motorcycles, eight 2-seat motorcycles, 2 motor tricycles, 3 bicycles

1 *battaglione esplorante bersaglieri (XXXIX btg. esplorante bersaglieri)*

16/32/358 personnel. 48 motorcycles, forty 2-seat motorcycles, 28 motor tricycles, 256 bicycles. 24 Breda 30 f.m., 3 Breda 37 mtr.

4 AUSSME, Stato maggiore R.E. memorandum 7 ottobre 1942, *Oggetto: Derrate, materiali e munizioni per la div. La Spezia"*, M7 racc.490, cart.11.

2 *reggimenti fanteria (125° and 126° rgt. fanteria)*
214/272/4096 personnel. 10 motorcycles, thirty 2-seat motorcycles, 118 motor tricycles, 50 bicycles, 108 hand carts. 168 Breda 30 f.m., 72 Breda 37 mtr., 60 Brixia 45mm mortars, thirty-six 81mm mortars, 12 lanciafiamme, eight 20mm a.c., twenty-four 47/32 c.c.

1 *reggimento artiglieria (80° rgt. artiglieria)*
63/42/889 personnel. 3 motorcycles, fourteen 2-seat motorcycles, 79 motor tricycles, 35 bicycles, 70 hand carts. 6 Breda 37 mtr., six 20mm a.c., twenty-four 65/17 guns.

1 *battaglione controcarri divisionale (80° battaglione c.c.)*
23/29/249 personnel. 1 motorcycle, one 2-seat motorcycle, 16 motor tricycles, 1 bicycle, 16 hand carts. Twenty-four 47/32 c.c.

1 *battaglione misto del genio (LXXX battaglione misto del genio)*
17/25/370 personnel. 2 motorcycles, four 2-seat motorcycles, 33 motor tricycles, 7 bicycles, 17 hand carts. 6 Breda 30 f.m., 6 Brixia 45mm mortars, 6 lanciafiamme.

1 *sezione sanità (80° sezione sanit*à)
8/4/100 personnel. One 2-seat motorcycles, 8 motor tricycles, 1 bicycle.

1 *sezione sussistenza (80° sezione sussistenza)*
3/2/38 personnel. 7 motor tricycles, 2 bicycles.

1 *reparto mototricicli (9° reparto motocicli)*
5/6/115 personnel. 9 motorcycles, One 2-seat motorcycle, 100 motor tricycles.

1 *reparto distribuzione carburanti (80° posto di distruzione carburanti)*
1/1/16 personnel. 3 motor tricycles, 1 bicycle.

1 *reparto rifornitori (resupply unit)*
6/9/165 personnel. 8 staff cars, 4 light/medium trucks, 1 heavy truck, four 2-seat motorcycles, 12 motor tricycles, 8 bicycles.

Appendix V

Organization of the Parachute Units

Regia Aeronautica

Information on the organization of the R.A. parachute units is a challenge to find. The secondary sources disagree on many details and the author has not been able to visit the appropriate archives. Those sources that cite archive documents do not always agree on the numbers or structure. It is possible that some units were committed to combat before they had achieved their authorized structure. What follows are reconstructions that attempt to deconflict the available information and provide a fairly accurate organization for the various units. It is not definitive and uses several assumptions by applying standard R.E. organizations that might not be applicable to R.A. units.

The parachute units raised by the R.A. tend to lack the command and support services found in the R.E. units. This is mainly due to their roles: as either a sabotage/raid unit or as an assault unit that would specially target airfields, these units were not planned for use in extended independent combat. If used for extended operations, they would be located at airfields where the command and logistical functions would be provided through normal R.A. channels.

I Battaglione d'assalto paracadutisti R.A.
Plotone Comando
Plotone servizi
3 compagnie fucili

Comando
- 1 Capitano commanding
- 1 Capitano vice commander
Plotone comando
Plotone servizi

3 compagnie fucili (each with)[1]
- 1 Tenente commanding
    4 Squadre *paracadutisti* (each with)[2]
    - 1 Tenente
    - 2 Sergenti or sergenti maggiori
    - 25 Paracadutisti

Information on strength and equipment vary and is generally based on what the unit actually had rather than what was authorized. Dalmas reported that he had 17 officers, 19 NCOs, and 272 *paracadutisti* when the battalion arrived in Tunisia. Di Martino gives 9 officers, 28 NCOs, and 308 *paracadutisti*. As it is likely that the battalion was not at fully authorized strength, the possible authorized strength is: 17 officers, 28 NCOs, and 317 *paracadutisti*.

Both Longo and di Martino state that the battalion had both Breda 30 f.m.s and Fiat M14/35 heavy machine-guns, with di Martino giving that the unit had twelve of each type of weapon. Dalmas stated that the battalion did not have automatic weapons when it arrived in Tunisia. Given that the battalion was moved by train and then by ship to Biserta, there was no reason that these weapons would have been left behind if the battalion had possessed them.[3] Based on di Martino, the unit was authorized 362 Beretta M34, 196 moschetti per cavalleria, 12 Breda 30 f.m., 12 Fiat M14/35. Based on Dalmas, the battalion in Tunisia only had the Beretta pistols, the moschetti per cavalleria, and the MAB 38A for officers and NCOs.

Battaglione ricattatori «Loreto»

Plotone comando
1ª Compagnia contraerei
2ª Compagnia fuciliere
3ª Compagnia servizi tecnici
4ª Compagnia servizi logistici

1 Most sources give ten squads in the battalion. The commander of the battalion, tenente colonnello Edvino Dalmas wrote in his report on the battalion's operations in Tunisia as having twelve squads, so that number was used here. AUSSME, Relazione Edvino Dalmas, *Attività bellico svolta dal battaglione paracadutisti dell'aeronautica dal 16 novembre 1942 al'8 settembre 1943*, Cart.1160/C/11, p.1.

2 Piero Crociani and Pier Battistelli, *Italian Navy & Air Force Elite Units & Special Forces 1940–45* (Oxford, Osprey, 2013), p.36. This squad organization is used as the numbers closely match the strength of the three squads in AUSSME, Dalmas, *Attività bellico svolta dal battaglione paracadutisti*, p.2.

3 Massimo Di Martino, *Paracadutisti d'Italia – Uniformi distintivi equipaggiamenti 1938–1943*, (Milan, Edizioni Libreria Militare, 2019), pp.239–240; Luigi Emilio Longo, *I «reparti speciali» italiani nella seconda guerra mondiale* (Milano, Mursia 1991), pp.160–161.

Plotone comando

1ª cp. contraerei
- 1 Capitano commanding
- 1 Tenente vice commander
    Squadra comando
    - 1 Sergente or sergente maggiore
    - 2 Staff/batmen

Plotone contraerei
- 1 Tenente commanding
- 1 Staff/batman
    3 sezioni da 20/65 (each with)
    - 2 Sergenti or sergenti maggiori gun capitano (two 20/65 c.a. guns)
    - 6 Gun crewmen
    - 2 soldiers aerial calculators
    - 4 Ammunition bearers (4 hand carts)
    - 2 motorcyclists (4 motor tricycles)
    - 2 Gun crewmen with various duties
    Sezione munizioni
    - 1 Sergente or sergente maggiore
    - 13 Airmen

3 plotoni fucili mitragliatori (each with)
- 1 Tenente commanding
- 1 Staff/batman
    3 Squadra fucili mitragliatori (each with)
    - 1 Sergente or sergente maggiore (one Breda 30 f.m.)
    - 12 Airmen

2ª cp. fucilieri

Squadra comando
- 1 Capitano commanding
- 1 Tenente vice commander
- 3 Sergenti or sergenti maggiori
- 2 Staff/batman
    3 plotoni fucilieri (each with)
    - 1 Tenente commanding
    - 1 Staff/batman
    3 squadre fucilieri (each with)
    - 1 Sergente or sergente maggiore (one Breda 30 f.m.)
    - 21 Airmen

3ª cp. servizi tecnici – 8 officer, 9 NCOs, 199 airmen.

4ª cp. servizi logistici – 8 officers, 14 NCOs, 185 airmen.

This is a major reconstruction and likely the least accurate of the R.A. organizations presented. The baseline employed for the reconstructions are the company personnel strengths given in Crociani and Battistelli.[4] All the sources list the same armament for the battalion, 18 Breda 30 f.m. and six 20/65 c.a. The only source that provides any organizational detail below company is Crociani and Battistelli. That source states that the 1ª cp. had three light machine-gun platoons. This is a very unique unit that one does not find anywhere else in the Italian military and raises the challenge of how the Breda 30 f.m. were divided between the 1ª and 2ª cp. The organization diagrammed above is based on the few photograph of the men of the «Loreto», which show that the Breda 30 f.m. was part of an infantry style squad and not a machine gun style squad that massed the weapons.

Battaglione Arditi Distruttori della Regia Aeronautica (A.D.R.A.)[5]

Battaglione A.D.R.A
Plotone comando
3 compagnia arditi

Comando
- 1 Tenente colonnello commanding
- 1 Capitano vice commander
- 1 Tenente chaplain
- 3 Airmen batman

Plotone comando
- 1 Tenente commanding
- 1 Airmen batman
- 6 Airmen staff

3 compagnia arditi (each with)
Comando
- 1 Tenente commanding
    - 3 plotoni arditi (each with)
    - 1 Tenente commanding
    - 2 Airmen batman
    - 3 squadre (each with)
    - 1 Graduato commanding
    - 8 arditi

4 Crociani and Battistelli, *Italian Navy & Air Force Elite Units*, p.38.
5 Longo, I «reparti speciali» italiani, pp.170–171; di Martino, *Paracadutisti d'Italia – 1938–1943*, pp.265–266; Aldo Giorleo, *Palestra Azzurra L'aeronautica militare e il paracadutismo cronistoria dalle origini ad oggi* (Rome: USSMA, 1975), p.95; Crociani and Battistelli, *Italian Navy & Air Force Elite Units*, p.40.

The organization above reflects the likely planned authorized strength. The unit above should have 15 officers, 24 NCOs, and 270 airmen. The reality was that this unit, like many of the *reparti paracadutisti*, was understrength in officers and NCOs. The sources provide a mix of different information on the organization of this battalion. All the sources state the battalion had 270 enlisted (non-NCO) airmen and 24 NCOs. This meant that the 27 squads were led by a mixture of NCOs and graduati. The number of officers varies between the sources, with 7, 11, 14, and 15 are listed. Six officers and four NCOs led the ten patrols used in June 1943, which brings into question whether graduati would have led any of the squads. Crociani and Battistelli stated that each platoon would have two officers and three NCOs, creating a requirement for at least 18 officers and 27 NCOs. This does not include the officers and NCOs needed for battalion and company command.

This battalion was completely armed with Beretta M1934 pistols and MAB 38A submachine guns.

Reggimento Regia Aeronautica «Duca d'Aosta»

April–May 1943

This regiment was rebuilt using the displaced airmen that had been operating the numerous airfields in Tunisia that were no longer in service. The decision to use these unemployed airmen was made in March with the plan to provide infantry training before being employed in combat. Leadership in the units would be augmented by assigning Bersaglieri officers and NCOs from disbanded units. Support artillery and 47/32 c.c. guns were authorized for the regiment.

In the end, little of this occurred as time had run out. Sources vary on whether training was complete or not. None of the guns were available, so the regiment's firepower was limited to machine guns, hand grenades, and any field expedient weapons they could procure. Neither unit had an adequate number of officers and NCOs assigned.

Reggimento Regia Aeronautica «Duca d'Aosta»
Compagnia comando
Battaglione d'assalto *paracadutisti* R.A.
Battaglione ricattatori «Loreto»
Two batteries 20/65 c.a.

Battaglione d'assalto paracadutisti R.A.
Platone Comando
2 compagnie fucili
1 compagnia mitraglieri

Plotone comando
- 1 Capitano commanding
2 Compagnie (1ª e 2ª) fuciliere (each with)
Squadra comando
- 1 Tenente commanding
    3 Squadre *paracadutisti* (each with)[6]
    - 1 Tenente
    - 2 Sergenti or sergenti maggiori
    - 25 *paracadutisti*
1 Compagnia (3ª) mitraglieri
Squadra comando
    3 Plotoni mitraglieri (each with)
    2 Squadre mitraglieri (each with two SAFAT 12.7 machine guns)

The two compagnie fucilieri were formed from the surviving R.A. *paracadutisti*, the third compagnia mitraglieri was formed using the excess personnel from the *5ª Squadra Aerea*. The assumption used here was the structure of the *squadra paracadutisti* was maintained from the earlier battalion organization.

Battaglione ricattatori «Loreto»
Compagnia comando
2 Compagnie fucilieri
2 Compagnie mitraglieri

Compagnia comando
2 Compagnie (1ª e 2ª) fucilieri (each with)
    Squadra comando
    3 Plotoni fucilieri (each with)
    3 Squadre fucilieri (each with 21 airmen with one Breda 30 f.m.)
2 Compagnie (3ª e 4ª) mitraglieri (each with)
    Squadra comando
    4 Squadre mitraglieri (each with two SAFAT 12.7 machine guns)

The first two companies were the two original companies of the battalion. It is unclear whether the 1ª cp. was reorganized or retained its current structure of one plotone c.a. and three plotoni fucilieri. Arena stated four batteries, so the assumption here is

6 Piero Crociani and Pier Battistelli, *Italian Navy & Air Force Elite Units & Special Forces 1940–45* (Oxford: Osprey, 2013), p.36. This squad organization is used as the numbers closely match the strength of the three squads in AUSSME, Dalmas, *Attività bellico svolta dal battaglione paracadutisti*, p.2.

that the heavy weapons were removed from the company and formed into separate batteries.[7]

Sources vary on what weapons were actually on hand. Arena states that the 20/65 c.a. were still assigned to the «Loreto» while they are not mentioned in the other sources. SAFAT 12.7 machine guns are also mentioned.

Batterie 20/65 c.a.[8]
2 Batterie da 20/65 c.a. (each with eight 20/65 c.a. guns)

7 Nino Arena, *La Regia Aeronautica* (Rome: USSMA, 1986), vol. 4, pp.125–126.
8 Both Arena and Longo state that the regiment had the Breda 20/65 c.a. guns. Arena states four batteries of Breda 20/65 c.a. and 12.7 mm guns but fails to provide any breakdown by type or weapons. Nino Arena, *La Regia* Aeronautica, vol. 4, p.125.

Appendix VI

Libyan Units Orders of Battle

Libyan Units

Derna

18–31 January 1941

Gruppo mobile «Tonini»[1]

1ª compagnia libici
2ª compagnia libici
3ª compagnia libici
4ª compagnia libici
nucleo controcarro (four 47/32 c.c. guns)

Two bersaglieri anti-tank platoons (four 47/32 c.c. guns, 83 men)
60° bersaglieri motociclisti (two platoons), 129 infantry and bersaglieri.
14ª batteria contraerea (six 20/65 c.a. guns)
Formazione carri M (four M11/39 tanks, one captured Herrington armored car)
One btr. da 75/27 from the *II/10° rgt. art. «Bologna»*.
Formazione fanteria (175 men, six 20/65 c.a. guns, three 47/32 c.c. guns.

1 Both Anon, *La prima offensiva britannica*, p.209 and Arena, *I Fanti*, p.92 give the *gruppo* a total of eleven 47/32. cc. The actual breakdown of sub-units only lists seven of these guns. It is likely that the *btg. paracadutisti* itself had four guns (two platoons) assigned to it while at Barce.

Beda Fomm

5–6 February 1941

I battaglioni *paracadutisti* libici ***«fanti dell'aria»***

- 2ª compagnia libici
- 3ª compagnia libici
- 4ª compagnia libici
- nucleo controcarro (three 47/32 c.c. guns)
- nucleo contraerei (four 20/65 c.a guns)

Strength of the three companies was only ~50 men each.

I battaglione nazionale

- 1ª compagnia *paracadutisti*
- 2ª compagnia *paracadutisti*
- 3ª compagnia *paracadutisti*
- 4ª compagnia *paracadutisti*

Strength of the four companies was only ~60 men each.

Appendix VII

Folgore Orders of Battle

Italian Parachutists/Folgore

November 1940

I battaglione *paracadutisti* Carabinieri Reali (cdo., 1^a, 2^a, 3^a compagnie).
II battaglione *paracadutisti* (cdo., 4^a, 5^a, 6^a compagnie).
III battaglione *paracadutisti* (cdo., 7^a, 8^a, 9^a compagnie)

March 1941

1° reggimento *paracadutisti*
    compagnia comando
    I battaglione *paracadutisti* Carabinieri Reali (cdo., 1^a, 2^a, 3^a compagnie).
    II battaglione *paracadutisti* (cdo., 4^a, 5^a, 6^a compagnie).
    III battaglione *paracadutisti* (cdo., 7^a, 8^a, 9^a compagnie)
    1° compagnia cannoni *paracadutisti* da 47/32 c.c.

Compagnia carri L3 lanciafiamme aviotrasportabile

September 1941

I battaglione *paracadutisti* Carabinieri Reali (cdo., 1^a, 2^a, 3^a compagnie) (In Africa settentrionale)

1° Divisione paracadutisti
Comando
1° reggimento *paracadutisti*
    compagnia comando

- II battaglione *paracadutisti* (cdo., 4ª, 5ª, 6ª compagnie).
- III battaglione *paracadutisti* (cdo., 7ª, 8ª, 9ª compagnie)
- IV battaglione *paracadutisti* (cdo., 10ª, 11ª, 12ª compagnie).
- 1º compagnia cannoni *paracadutisti* da 47/32 c.c.
- compagnia servizi/1º reggimento *paracadutisti*.

2º reggimento *paracadutisti*
- compagnia comando
- V battaglione *paracadutisti* (cdo., 13ª, 14ª, 15ª compagnie).
- VI battaglione *paracadutisti* (cdo., 16ª, 17ª, 18ª compagnie). (November 1942)
- VII battaglione *paracadutisti* (cdo., 19ª, 20ª, 21ª compagnie).
- 2º compagnia cannoni *paracadutisti* da 47/32 c.c.
- compagnia servizi/2º reggimento *paracadutisti*.

1º reggimento artiglieria *paracadutisti*
- compagnia comando
- I gruppo (1ª, 2ª batteria da 47/32 c.c.)
- II gruppo (3ª, 4ª batteria da 47/32 c.c.)
- compagnia servizi/185º reggimento artiglieria *paracadutisti*.

VIII battaglione guastatori *paracadutisti* (cdo., 22ª, 23ª, 24ª compagnie).
1ª compagnia collegamenti *paracadutisti*
1ª compagnia minatori-artieri *paracadutisti*

Compagnia carri L3 lanciafiamme aviotrasportabile

19 November 1941

Battle of Eluet el Asel

I Battaglione carabinieri *paracadutisti*
Comando
1ª compagnia carabinieri
- Comando
- Nucleo fucili controcarro (two anti-tank rifles)
- 1ª plotone fucilieri
- 2ª plotone fucilieri
- 3ª plotone fucilieri
- Plotone mitraglieri (four Fiat 14/35 machine guns)
- Plotone *paracadutisti* libici
- Plotone guastatori
- Plotone c.c./8º rgt. Bersaglieri (two 47/32 c.c. guns)

2ª compagnia carabinieri
- Comando
- Nucleo fucili controcarro (two anti-tank rifles)

1ª plotone fucilieri
2ª plotone fucilieri
3ª plotone fucilieri
Plotone mitraglieri (four Fiat 14/35 machine guns)
Plotone c.c./8º rgt. Bersaglieri (two 47/32 c.c. guns)
3ª compagnia carabinieri
Comando
Nucleo fucili controcarro (two anti-tank rifles)
1ª plotone fucilieri
2ª plotone fucilieri
3ª plotone fucilieri
Plotone mitraglieri (four Fiat 14/35 machine guns)
Plotone c.c./8º rgt. Bersaglieri (two 47/32 c.c. guns)

1ª Divisione *paracadutisti*

March 1942

Comando
Stato maggiore.
315ª Sezione mista CC.RR.
260° ufficio postale (post office).
260° nucleo CC.RR. per ufficio postale (carabinieri detachment for the post office).
Compagnia comando
1º reggimento *paracadutisti*
compagnia comando
II battaglione *paracadutisti* (cdo., 4ª, 5ª, 6ª compagnie).
III battaglione *paracadutisti* (cdo., 7ª, 8ª, 9ª compagnie)
IV battaglione *paracadutisti* (cdo., 10ª, 11ª, 12ª compagnie).
1º compagnia cannoni *paracadutisti* da 47/32 c.c.
compagnia servizi/1º reggimento *paracadutisti*.
2º reggimento *paracadutisti*
compagnia comando
V battaglione *paracadutisti* (cdo., 13ª, 14ª, 15ª compagnie).
VI battaglione *paracadutisti* (cdo., 16ª, 17ª, 18ª compagnie). (November 1942)
VII battaglione *paracadutisti* (cdo., 19ª, 20ª, 21ª compagnie).
2º compagnia cannoni *paracadutisti* da 47/32 c.c.
compagnia servizi/2º reggimento *paracadutisti*.
3º reggimento *paracadutisti*
compagnia comando
IX battaglione *paracadutisti* (cdo., 25ª, 26ª, 27ª compagnie)

X battaglione *paracadutisti* (cdo., 28ª, 29ª, 30ª compagnie).
XI battaglione *paracadutisti* (cdo., 31ª, 32ª, 33ª compagnie).
3º compagnia cannoni *paracadutisti* da 47/32 c.c.
compagnia servizi/3º reggimento *paracadutisti*.

1º reggimento artiglieria *paracadutisti*
compagnia comando
I gruppo (1ª, 2ª batteria da 47/32 c.c.)
II gruppo (3ª, 4ª batteria da 47/32 c.c.)
III gruppo (5ª, 6ª batteria da 47/32 c.c.)
compagnia servizi/185º reggimento artiglieria *paracadutisti*.

VIII battaglione guastatori *paracadutisti* (cdo., 22ª, 23ª, 24ª compagnie).
Compagnia mortai *paracadutisti* da 81
Compagnia collegamenti *paracadutisti*
Compagnia minatori-artieri *paracadutisti*
Sezione sanità (medical section) *paracadutisti*
Reparto trasporti (transportation unit)

185ª Divisione Fanteria «Folgore»

July 1942

Comando
Stato maggiore.
315ª Sezione mista CC.RR.
9a squadra pilotaggio per zone desertiche (liaison and pathfinder squadron).
260° ufficio postale (post office).
260° nucleo CC.RR. per ufficio postale (carabinieri detachment for the post office).
Compagnia comando

186º reggimento fanteria
compagnia comando
V battaglione fanteria (cdo., 13ª, 14ª, 15ª compagnie)
VI battaglione fanteria (cdo., 16ª, 17ª, 18ª compagnie)
VII battaglione fanteria (cdo., 19ª, 20ª, 21ª compagnie)
186º compagnia cannoni *paracadutisti* da 47/32 c.c.
compagnia servizi/186º reggimento fanteria

187º reggimento fanteria
compagnia comando
II battaglione fanteria (cdo., 4ª, 5ª, 6ª compagnie)
IV battaglione fanteria (cdo., 10ª, 11ª, 12ª compagnie)
IX battaglione fanteria. (cdo., 25ª, 26ª, 27ª compagnie)
X battaglione fanteria (cdo., 28ª, 29ª, 30ª compagnie)

187º compagnia cannoni *paracadutisti* da 47/32 c.c.
compagnia servizi/187º reggimento fanteria
185º reggimento artiglieria
compagnia comando
I gruppo (1ª, 2ª batteria da 47/32 c.c.)
II gruppo (3ª, 4ª batteria da 47/32 c.c.)
III gruppo (5ª, 6ª batteria da 47/32 c.c.)
compagnia servizi/185º rgt. reggimento artiglieria.
VIII battaglione guastatori (cdo., 22ª, 24ª compagnie)
185ª compagnia mortai da 81
185ª compagnia collegamenti
185ª compagnia minatori-artieri.
185° sezione sanità (medical section)
185° reparto trasporti (transportation unit)

185ª divisione fanteria «Folgore»

August 1942

Comando
Stato maggiore
315ª Sezione mista CC.RR.
9a squadra pilotaggio per zone desertiche (liaison and pathfinder squadron).
260° ufficio postale (post office).
260° nucleo CC.RR. per ufficio postale (carabinieri detachment for the post office).
Compagnia comando
186º reggimento fanteria
compagnia comando
V battaglione fanteria (cdo., 13ª, 14ª, 15ª compagnie)
VI battaglione fanteria (cdo., 16ª, 17ª, 18ª compagnie)
VII battaglione fanteria (cdo., 19ª, 20ª, 21ª compagnie)
186º compagnia cannoni *paracadutisti* da 47/32 c.c.
compagnia servizi/186º reggimento fanteria.
Raggruppamento Bechi
II battaglione fanteria (cdo., 4ª, 5ª, 6ª compagnie)
IV battaglione fanteria (cdo., 10ª, 11ª, 12ª compagnie)
187º compagnia cannoni *paracadutisti* da 47/32 c.c.
Raggruppamento Camosso
compagnia comando/187º reggimento fanteria
IX battaglione fanteria. (cdo., 25a, 26a, 27a compagnie)
X battaglione fanteria (cdo., 28a, 29a, 30a compagnie) 1

- compagnia servizi/187º reggimento fanteria
- 185º reggimento artiglieria
    - compagnia comando
    - I gruppo (1ª, 2ª batteria da 47/32 c.c.)
    - II gruppo (3ª, 4ª batteria da 47/32 c.c.)
    - III gruppo (5ª, 6ª batteria da 47/32 c.c.)
    - compagnia servizi/185º reggimento artiglieria
- VIII battaglione guastatori (cdo., 22ª, 24ª compagnie)
- 185ª compagnia mortai
- 185ª compagnia collegamenti
- 185ª compagnia minatori-artieri
- 20ª sezione intendenza
- 185°sezione sanità (medical section)
- 185°reparto trasporti (transportation unit)
- 20° sezione sussistenza (quartermaster section)

185ª divisione fanteria «Folgore»

October 1942

- Comando
    - Stato maggiore.
    - 315ª Sezione mista CC.RR.
    - 9a squadra pilotaggio per zone desertiche (liaison and pathfinder squadron).
    - 260° ufficio postale (post office).
    - 260° nucleo CC.RR. per ufficio postale (carabinieri detachment for the post office).
    - Compagnia comando
- 187º reggimento fanteria
    - compagnia comando
    - II battaglione fanteria (cdo., 4ª, 5ª compagnie)
    - IV battaglione fanteria (cdo., 10ª, 11ª, 12ª compagnie)
    - IX battaglione fanteria. (cdo., 25ª, 26ª, 27ª compagnie)
    - 187º compagnia cannoni *paracadutisti* da 47/32 c.c.
    - 3ª batteria, II gruppo/185º artiglieria
    - III gruppo/185º artiglieria (5ª, 6ª batteria da 47/32 c.c.)
    - compagnia servizi/187º reggimento fanteria
- Raggruppamento tattico «Ruspoli»
    - VII battaglione fanteria (cdo., 6ª, 19ª, 20ª, 21ª compagnie).
    - VIII battaglione guastatori (cdo., 22ª, 24ª compagnie)
    - Two platoons/185ª compagnia mortai da 81
    - I gruppo/185º artiglieria (1ª, 2ª batteria da 47/32 c.c.)

186° reggimento fanteria
compagnia comando
V battaglione fanteria (cdo., 13ª, 14ª, 15ª compagnie)
VI battaglione fanteria (cdo., 16ª, 17ª, 18ª compagnie)
Two platoons/185ª compagnia mortai da 81
186° compagnia cannoni *paracadutisti* da 47/32 c.c.
compagnia accampamento V/8° reggimento bersaglieri
4ª batteria, II gruppo/185° artiglieria
compagnia servizi/186° reggimento fanteria
Raggruppamento artiglieria «Folgore»
compagnia comando/185° reggimento artiglieria
III gruppo da 75/27/1° rgt. art. celere from the «*Brescia*»
I gruppo da 100/17/21° rgt. art. from the «*Trieste*»
XXXI gruppo da 88/55 from the «*Ariete*»
DI gruppo da 90/53 from the «*Ariete*»
XLIX gruppo da 105/28 from *X Cd'A.*
CXLVII gruppo da 149/28 from *X Cd'A.*
Mixed German group with 105/32 and 210/36 guns
compagnia servizi/185° reggimento artiglieria.
II/28° reggimento fanteria «Pavia» (cdo., 1ª, 2ª, 3ª, 4ª compagnie)

III «Folgore» 66° reggimento fanteria

March 1943

Comando
107ª, 109ª, 110ª, 111ª compagnie

Appendix VIII

La Spezia Orders of Battle

80ª divisione fanteria (aviotrasportabile) «La Spezia»

Listed below are the aviotrasportabile units that were in existence in the month indicated and their organization at that time.

October 1941

80ª Divisione Aviotrasportabile[1]
Reparto comando
    Comando
    Stato maggiore
    80º squadra Carabinieri Reale (CC.RR.) motociclisti
    80º squadra topocartografico
    115º ufficio postale
    115º nucleo CC.RR. per ufficiavo postale
XXXIX esplorante bersaglieri
    compagnia comando
    1ª compagnia ciclisti
    2ª compagnia motociclisti
125º reggimento fanteria
    compagnia comando
    I battaglione (cdo., 1ª, 2ª, 3ª compagnie fucilieri)
    II battaglione (cdo., 4ª, 5ª, 6ª compagnie fucilieri)
    III battaglione d'accompagnamento

1 AUSSME, Stato Maggiore R.E. memorandum 19 ottobre 1941, *Oggetto: Costituzione della 80º divisone di fanteria "Spezia" (aviotrasportabile)*, M7 racc.490, cart.11.

126º reggimento fanteria
compagnia comando
I battaglione (cdo., 1ª, 2ª, 3ª compagnie fucilieri)
II battaglione (cdo., 4ª, 5ª, 6ª compagnie fucilieri)
III battaglione d'accompagnamento
80º reggimento artiglieria fanteria
compagnia comando
I gruppo (1ª, 2ª batteria da 65/17)
II gruppo (3ª, 4ª batteria da 65/17)
III gruppo (5ª, 6ª batteria da 65/17)
7ª, 8ª batteria da 20/65 contraerei
compagnia servizi/80º reggimento artiglieria fanteria.
80º battaglione controcarro
comando
1ª compagnia controcarro da 47/32
2ª compagnia controcarro da 47/32
3ª compagnia controcarro da 47/32
LXXX battaglione misto del genio
comando
102º compagnia artieri
118º compagnia marconisti
Servizi
80º sezione sanità
80º nucleo sussistenza
80º posto di distruzione carburanti

March 1942

80ª Divisione Aviotrasportabile[2]
Reparto comando
Comando
Stato maggiore
80º squadra Carabinieri Reale (CC.RR.) motociclisti
80º squadra topocartografico
115º ufficio postale
115º nucleo CC.RR. per ufficiavo postale

2 AUSSME, Stato Maggiore R.E. memorandum 11 marzo 1942, *Oggetto: Modifiche alle formazioni di guerra della 80º divisone"LA SPEZIA" (aviotrasportabile)*, M7 racc.490, cart.11.

XXXIX battaglione esplorante bersaglieri
- compagnia comando
- 1ª compagnia ciclisti
- 2ª compagnia ciclisti
- 3ª compagnia motociclisti

125º reggimento fanteria
- compagnia comando
- I battaglione (cdo., 1ª, 2ª, 3ª compagnie fucilieri, compagnia d'accompagnamento)
- II battaglione (cdo., 4ª, 5ª, 6ª compagnie fucilieri, compagnia d'accompagnamento)
- III battaglione (cdo., 7ª, 8ª, 9ª compagnie fucilieri, compagnia d'accompagnamento)

126º reggimento fanteria
- compagnia comando
- I battaglione (cdo., 1ª, 2ª, 3ª compagnie fucilieri, compagnia d'accompagnamento)
- II battaglione (cdo., 4ª, 5ª, 6ª compagnie fucilieri, compagnia d'accompagnamento)
- III battaglione (cdo., 7ª, 8ª, 9ª compagnie fucilieri, compagnia d'accompagnamento)

80º reggimento artiglieria fanteria
- compagnia comando
- I gruppo (1ª, 2ª batteria da 65/17)
- II gruppo (3ª, 4ª batteria da 65/17)
- III gruppo (5ª, 6ª batteria da 65/17)
- 7ª, 8ª batteria da 20/65 contraerei
- compagnia servizi/80º reggimento artiglieria fanteria.

80º battaglione controcarro
- comando
- 1ª compagnia controcarro da 47/32
- 2ª compagnia controcarro da 47/32
- 3ª compagnia controcarro da 47/32

LXXX battaglione misto del genio

Servizi
- 80º sezione sanità
- 80º sezione sussistenza
- 80º posto di distruzione carburanti

April 1942

80ª Divisione Aviotrasportabile[3]

Reparto comando

3 AUSSME, Stato Maggiore R.E. memorandum 11 marzo 1942, *Oggetto: Modifiche alle formazioni di guerra della 80º divisone"LA SPEZIA" (aviotrasportabile)*, M7 racc.490, cart.11.

XXXIX battaglione esplorante bersaglieri
125° reggimento fanteria
126° reggimento fanteria
80° reggimento artiglieria fanteria
80° battaglione controcarro
LXXX battaglione misto del genio
9° reparto mototricicli[4]
    comando
    1° sezione mototricicili
    2° sezione mototricicili
    3° sezione mototricicili
    4° sezione mototricicili
Servizi

15 March 1943

Battle of Mareth

80ª Divisione Aviotrasportabile[5]
Reparto comando
XXXIX battaglione esplorante bersaglieri
125° reggimento fanteria
    compagnia comando
    I battaglione (cdo., 1ª, 2ª, 3ª compagnie fucilieri, compagnia d'accompagnamento)
    II battaglione (cdo., 4ª, 5ª, 6ª compagnie fucilieri, compagnia d'accompagnamento)
    III battaglione (cdo., 7ª, 8ª, 9ª compagnie fucilieri, compagnia d'accompagnamento)
126° reggimento fanteria
    compagnia comando
    I battaglione (cdo., 1ª, 2ª, 3ª compagnie fucilieri, compagnia d'accompagnamento)
    II battaglione (cdo., 4ª, 5ª, 6ª compagnie fucilieri, compagnia d'accompagnamento)
    III battaglione (cdo., 7ª, 8ª, 9ª compagnie fucilieri, compagnia d'accompagnamento)
80° reggimento artiglieria fanteria
    compagnia comando
    I gruppo (1ª, 2ª batteria da 65/17)
    II gruppo (3ª, 4ª batteria da 65/17)
    III gruppo (5ª, 6ª batteria da 65/17)

4 AUSSME, Stato Maggiore R.E. memorandum 25 aprile 1942, *Oggetto: Costituzione e mobilitazione del 9° reparto mototricicli per divisone "La Spezia"*, M7 racc.490, cart.11
5 Giovanni Messe, *La I° armata italiana in Tunisia* (Rome: USSME, 1950), Tavola 4, 8; Mario Montanari, *Le operazioni in Africa settentrionale* (Rome: USSME,1993), vol IV: Enfidaville, p.370.

IV gruppo (3 batterie da 75/27)(formerly the CCXII gruppo)
V gruppo (3 batterie da 100/17)(formerly the CCXIII gruppo)
7ª, 8ª batteria da 20/65 contraerei
compagnia servizi/80° reggimento artiglieria fanteria.
80° battaglione controcarro
LXXX battaglione misto del genio
9° reparto mototricicli

Reinforcements
VI btg. CC.NN.
Btg «Tobruk»
E/1ª gruppo (three batteries 77/28)
CCCXXXI gruppo (three batteries 77/28)
43ª/2ª contraerei (three batteries 75/50 c.a.)
6ª batteria da 65/17

6–7 April 1943

Battle of Chotts el Djerid

80ª Divisione Aviotrasportabile[6]
Reparto comando
XXXIX battaglione esplorante bersaglieri
125° reggimento fanteria
compagnia comando
III battaglione (cdo., 7ª, 8ª, 9ª compagnie fucilieri, compagnia d'accompagnamento)
126° reggimento fanteria
compagnia comando
I battaglione (cdo., 1ª, 2ª, 3ª compagnie fucilieri, compagnia d'accompagnamento)
II battaglione (cdo., 4ª, 5ª, 6ª compagnie fucilieri, compagnia d'accompagnamento)
III battaglione (cdo., 7ª, 8ª, 9ª compagnie fucilieri, compagnia d'accompagnamento)
80° reggimento artiglieria fanteria
compagnia comando
I gruppo (2 batterie da 100/17)
II gruppo (3ª, 4ª batteria da 65/17)
III gruppo (5ª, 6ª batteria da 65/17)
CCXII gruppo (batteria 75/27)
7ª, 8ª batteria da 20/65 contraerei
compagnia servizi/80° reggimento artiglieria fanteria.

6 Giovanni Messe, *La I° armata italiana*, Tavola 9.

80º battaglione controcarro
LXXX battaglione misto del genio
9º reparto mototricicli

Reinforcements
- VI btg. CC.NN.
- Btg «Tobruk»
- Gruppo E/1ª (three batteries 77/28)
- Gruppo CCCXXXI (three batteries 77/28)
- 43/2ª contraerei (three batteries 75/50 c.a.)
- 6ª batteria da 65/17

April 1943

Enfidaville

80ª Divisione Aviotrasportabile[7]
Reparto comando
125º reggimento fanteria
- compagnia comando
- III battaglione

126º reggimento fanteria
- compagnia comando
- I battaglione (formed from the 84º btg. complemento)
- II battaglione (formed from the 350ª btg. Guardia Frontiera)
- III battaglione

I/47.Grenadier
CVI btg. controcarro
252º btg. mortai da 81
281º btg. mitraglieri guardia frontiera
213º gruppo da 100/17 (2 guns)
209º gruppo da 77/28 (6 guns)
III/3º gruppo da 75/27 (8 guns)
IV/3º bis gruppo da 75/27 (8 guns)
43º gruppo da 75/50 c.a. (8 guns)

7 Giovanni Messe, *La Iº armata italiana*, p.438; Montanari, *Le operazioni*, vol IV: Enfidaville, p.501.

Appendix IX

Nembo Orders of Battle

184ª Divisione Fanteria «Nembo»

April 1943

- Comando
  - Stato maggiore.
  - 314ª Sezione CC.RR.
  - Compagnia comando
- 185º reggimento fanteria
  - compagnia comando
  - III battaglione fanteria (cdo., 7ª, 8ª, 9ª compagnie)
  - X battaglione fanteria (cdo., 28ª, 29ª, 30ª compagnie)
  - XI battaglione fanteria (cdo., 31ª, 32ª, 33ª compagnie)
  - 185º compagnia cannoni da 47/32 c.c.
  - compagnia servizi/185º rgt.
- 184º reggimento fanteria
  - compagnia comando
  - XII battaglione fanteria (cdo., 34ª, 35ª, 36ª compagnie)
  - XIII battaglione fanteria. (cdo., 37ª, 38ª, 39ª compagnie)
  - XIV battaglione fanteria (cdo., 40ª, 41ª, 42ª compagnie)
  - 184º compagnia cannoni da 47/32 c.c.
  - compagnia servizi/184º rgt.
- 183º reggimento fanteria
  - compagnia comando
  - VIII battaglione fanteria (cdo., 22ª, 23ª, 24ª compagnie)
  - XV battaglione fanteria (cdo., 43ª, 44ª, 45ª compagnie)
  - XVI battaglione fanteria (cdo., 46ª, 47ª, 48ª compagnie)
  - 183º compagnia cannoni da 47/32 c.c.
  - compagnia servizi/183º rgt.

184º reggimento artiglieria
compagnia comando
I gruppo (1ª, 2ª batteria da 47/32 c.c.)
II gruppo (3ª, 4ª batteria da 47/32 c.c.)
III gruppo (5ª, 6ª batteria da 47/32 c.c.)
compagnia servizi/184º rgt. art.
CLXXXIV battaglione guastatori (cdo., 1ª, 2ª, 3ª compagnie).
184ª compagnia motociclisti.
284ª compagnia ciclisti.
184º reparto carristi.
184ª compagnia mortai
184ª compagnia collegamenti
184ª compagnia minatori-artieri.
186ª compagnia misto genio.
184º reparto trasporti.
184º sezione sanità
Compagnia servizi/184ª d.f.

185º reggimento fanteria «Nembo»

June 1943

185º reggimento fanteria
compagnia comando
III battaglione fanteria (cdo., 7ª, 8ª, 9ª compagnie)
VIII battaglione fanteria (cdo., 22ª, 23ª, 24ª compagnie)
XI battaglione fanteria (cdo., 31ª, 32ª, 33ª compagnie)
185º compagnia cannoni da 47/32 c.c.
compagnia servizi/185º rgt.
III gruppo/184º rgt. art. (5ª, 6ª batteria da 47/32 c.c.)

184ª Divisione Fanteria «Nembo»

June 1943

Comando
Stato maggiore
314ª Sezione CC.RR.
Compagnia comando
184º reggimento fanteria
compagnia comando

  - XII battaglione fanteria (cdo., 34ª, 35ª, 36ª compagnie)
  - XIII battaglione fanteria. (cdo., 37ª, 38ª, 39ª compagnie)
  - XIV battaglione fanteria (cdo., 40ª, 41ª, 42ª compagnie)
  - 184º compagnia cannoni da 47/32 c.c.
  - compagnia servizi/184º rgt.
- 183º reggimento fanteria
  - compagnia comando
  - X battaglione fanteria (cdo., 28ª, 29ª, 30ª compagnie)
  - XV battaglione fanteria (cdo., 43ª, 44ª, 45ª compagnie)
  - XVI battaglione fanteria (cdo., 46ª, 47ª, 48ª compagnie)
  - 183º compagnia cannoni da 47/32 c.c.
  - compagnia servizi/183º rgt.
- 184º reggimento artiglieria
  - compagnia comando
  - I gruppo (1ª, 2ª batteria da 47/32 c.c.)
  - II gruppo (3ª, 4ª batteria da 47/32 c.c.)
  - compagnia servizi/184º rgt. art.
- 184° battaglione guastatori (cdo., 1ª, 2ª, 3ª compagnie)
- 184ª compagnia motociclisti.
- 284ª compagnia ciclisti.
- 184º reparto carristi
  - Comando (one L6 comando, one L6/40, one M14/41)
  - 1º e 2º plotone carri L (each with four L6/40)
  - 3º plotone carri L (five M14/41)
- 184ª compagnia mortai
- 184ª compagnia collegamenti
- 184ª compagnia minatori-artieri
- 186ª compagnia misto genio
- 184º reparto trasporti
- 184º sezione sanità
- Compagnia servizi/184ª d.f.

Attached:
3rd gruppo squadroni Cavalleggeri di Sardegna.
II/3º reggimento carristi.

The «Nembo» in Sardinia

The main sources of information on the tactical organization and locations of the units under the command of the «*Nembo*» on Sardinia are the books written by Nino Arena. The same information is repeated in the three books consulted, but there are differences and errors between these sources. What is presented below is the best reconstruction using those sources[1]

Generale di brigata Ercole Ronco initially created five tactical groups to cover the division's area of responsibilities. He also dispersed the division's support elements to avoid creating a significant concentration that could be targeted by the Allied forces. Each group was garrisoned in one area for command and control purposes.

Division Command in the area of Villanova Forru (gen. Ercole Ronco), S.M. (ten. col. Alberto Bechi-Lusema): cp. comando (cap. Mainetto), 314ª sec. CC.RR. (cap. Max Ambrosi), 184º d.f. cp. services (cap. Giuseppe Messina), 184º d.f. cp. command (cap. Vittorio Dogliani).

> *Gruppo di manovra Quaroni* at Assemini (col. Giuseppe Quaroni): Comando 183° rgt. with the XV btg. (magg. Umberto Lusena), XVI btg. (cap. Vittorio Pelagatti), 184° reparto trasporti (ten. Vincenzo Costa), Comando 184° rgt. artiglieria (ten. col. Mario Accili), 184° Guastatori (cap. Giuseppe Conte) rinforzato dal II/184° Artiglieria (ten. col. Luigi Cigersa) su due batterie.
>
> *Raggruppamento tattico Renzoni* at Serramanna (ten. col. Bruno Renzoni): Comando 184° Rgt. with the XII btg. (magg. Mario Rizzatti), XIV btg. (cap. Salvatore Corrias), and I/184° artiglieria (ten. col. Alfonso Madia).
>
> *Raggruppamento tattico Invrea* at Marrubbiu (ten. col. Ademaro Invrea): XIII btg. (cap. Costanzo), 3° Gruppo Squadroni cavalleggeri di Sardegna with L/6 light tanks (magg. Cadeddu Efisio), 184º rgt. cp. cannoni da 47/32 (ten. Arnaldo Manciocchi), and 184º rgt. cp. servizi (cap. Nicola Colizzo).
>
> *Gruppo di manovra Tantillo* at Sanluri (col. Pietro Tantillo): II btg. corazzato del 3° Rgt. Carristi with M14/41 tanks, 184ª cp. mortai da 81 (cap. Giuseppe Fabbri), 184ª cp. motociclisti (cap. Vittorio Nicoletti-Altimari), 284ª cp. ciclisti (ten. Mario Sussarello), btr. servizio/184º rgt. art. (ten. Carlo Ludovici), 184ª cp. collegamenti (ten. Mario Cervellini), 184ª cp. minatori-artieri, (cap. Luigi Fabrizzi), 186ª Cp. mista del genio (ten. Vinicio Centonze), 184° sez. sanità (Magg. Medico Vincenzo Iacono).
>
> *Gruppo tattico Valletti* at Alghero-Fertilia - (magg. Felice Valletti-Borgnimi): X bis btg., 183º rgt. cp. cannoni da 47/32 (Ten. Spagnolo), cp. servizi /183º rgt. (cap. G. Battista Brunetti), and a plotone mortai da 81.

1 Nino Arena, *Nembo!* (Rome: IBN Editore, 2013), pp.27-28; Nino Arena, *I PARACADUTISTI Cinquant'anni di storia, cronaca e immagini del paracadutisti italiano* (Modena: Società Tipografica Editrice Modenese Mucchi, 1972), pp.154-156; Nino Arena, *FOLGORE Storia del paracadutismo militare italiano* (Rome: Centro Editoriale Nazione, 1965), p.359.

The units of the «Nembo» were repositioned at the end of June due to a greater focus on airport defense, lessons learned from the rehearsals, and trying to reduce the problems created by malaria in various parts of the island.

Segariu: Comando 184ª divisione, 314ª Section CC.RR., 184ª Cp. Cannoni, 4/II gr. art., 184th reparto trasporto
Assemini: Comando 183° rgt.
Alghero: X bis btg.
Capoterra: XV btg., 183ª Cp. Cannoni 47/32
Decimomannu: XII btg., XVI Btg., 3/II gr. art.
Serramanna: Comando 184° rgt., XIII btg., XIV btg., 1/I gr. art.
Villacidro: 2/I gr. art.
Lunamatrona: servizio btr./184° rgt. art.
Sanluri: 184° btg. guastatori, 184ª cp. mortai, II btg. carri L.6 and M.15/42
Turri: 184ª cp. motorcyclists, 184° reparto carristi
Villamar: 284ª cp. ciclisti, 184th sez. sanità
Furtei: 184ª cp. collegamenti
Villanova Forru: 184ª cp. minatori-artieri, 186 ° Cp. misto genio
Sili: 3ª gr. squadroni carri L

Reinforcing: 236° reggimento fanteria

Appendix X

Airborne Operations

There are many different issues that must be successfully resolved for the employment of an airborne assault capability. The following is a brief discussion of these issues/considerations focused on the operational use of massed airborne forces.

The key elements in the tactical employment of airborne forces to achieve an operational objective are surprise and time. Surprise is usually achieved by selecting objectives that are operationally important but unlikely to be attacked by conventional forces. These objectives are considered protected by their distance from any threats or by challenging terrain, both of which provide the defender time to react and counter any threat. Because their locations on the battlefield provide an inherent degree of security, these objectives are normally lightly defended.

Time is a major component in achieving surprise. Airborne operations depend on placing sufficient (ideally overwhelming) force against the objective so it is rapidly destroyed and/or captured before the enemy can react. The time window airborne units plan to leverage is the time span between the dropping of the parachutists on the selected drop zone to the arrival of enemy reinforcements. During that window the parachutists need to either destroy the objective or secure it with sufficient forces to defend against the enemy reactions.

The time window is further leveraged by the use of aircraft to fly the attacking airborne force as close as practical to the objective, thereby reducing the time requirement imposed by distance and/or barriers that would confront a conventional ground based attack. The airborne force must be delivered quickly to the drop zone, land, organize, and seize their objective before the defense can react with significant forces. Even if the aircraft are detected as they cross the front line, the enemy would not always be able to quickly predict the objective/target of the attack. By the time the defender has discerned the objective, the aircraft are likely to have already dropped the paratroopers. It then becomes a race between the paratroopers reaching and securing the objective and the defender moving additional forces to protect the objective.

Objective

Due to the risks involved in using large airborne forces, the selected objective must be one that provides a significant operational advantage for the friendly force. The desired operational effect must be achievable with what are basically light infantry forces, ideally supported by major aviation assets. The aviation assets must be able to both safely transport to the objective and then support that force both logistically and with adequate firepower. This requires, as a minimum, local air superiority. Because of the fragility of the airborne force, the operational advantage must manifest itself quickly before the airborne force loses effectiveness due to attrition.

The attrition of airborne forces is serious as the replacement of losses or providing additional reinforcement is significantly more difficult due to the isolation of the parachute units once the initial element of surprise has been lost. The types of missions that justify the use of paratroopers require those units to be on the offensive, increasing their vulnerability to enemy fire. Casualties tend to remain high even if the paratroops transition to a defensive posture due to the lack of time, equipment, and materials to fortify their positions. In twelve of the 16 major airborne operations executed during the Second World War, the airborne forces suffered over 25 percent casualties in the first 24 hours.[1]

Selecting the Drop Zones

The selection of drop zones (DZ) evolved into three different approaches. The first was placing the DZ directly on the objective. This worked only if the objective could be taken with a small force, that full surprise was achieved, and the unit was successfully dropped on the DZ. This approach worked best using gliders instead of parachutes, with the assault on Fort Eben Emael and the raid on Gran Sasso as successful examples. When used by parachutists against larger enemy forces without surprise as on Crete, it failed with significant losses.

The second approach was to place the DZ near the objective. Here the DZ was placed outside the reach of immediate enemy reaction but still within rapid striking range of the objective. The intent was that surprise and the support of friendly airpower would allow the paratroops to rapidly land and organize before any effective enemy counter action could be taken against the DZ. The paratroops would then seize their objective before any local enemy counter attacks could be initiated. The successful German actions on Crete were those fights where the German fallschirmjägers landed

1 Marc DeVore, 'The Airborne Illusion: Institutions and the Evolution of Postwar Airborne Forces', (Cambridge: Massachusetts Institute of Technology Security Studies Program paper, 2004), p.6. Three of those operations with less than 25 percent losses were first-use cases in 1940 and the fourth was a limited raid to steal technology in 1942.

and organized outside of direct enemy fire and then maneuver towards their objectives as a complete unit in a short period of time.

The third approach was to place the DZ completely outside any rapid enemy reaction. The intent with this approach was to land a very large force that could be organized and then move towards the objective similar to a conventional ground force. The key requirement was that the landed force was strong enough to take the objective without surprise and before any sizable enemy reaction force could reinforce the defense. The British plan to seize Arnhem used this approach, but failed because sizable German reaction forces were already much closer than planned/expected.

The drop zone itself should meet several parameters. It should be fairly flat and free of obstacles. Trees, fences, ditches, rocks, etc. all create additional hazards for the parachutists during landing. Drop zones with softer soil such as recently plowed fields or sand are better than hardpack soil. The areas that meet these conditions need to be large enough to allow the aircraft to drop all of its men and equipment in a single pass. It will be rare to find suitable drop zones that meet all these requirements, so compromises must be made. The Italian parachute jump onto the rocky field with stone walls on Kefalonia saw a 20 percent injury rate, of which half of those were serious.

Getting to the Drop Zone

The size of the operation will determine the number of required transport aircraft. The number of available transport aircraft will determine how many echelons (lifts) will be needed. When the number of paratroops and their supply containers to be dropped exceeds the capacity of the available aircraft flying one sortie each, then the transport aircraft will need to fly more than one sortie in an additional echelon to support the operation.[2] The number, size, and distance of the supporting airfields from the DZs will further modify the flow of aircraft during the operation.

Fast transport aircraft were an advantage as speed reduced the transit time to the DZ and exposure to enemy reactions. However, faster aircraft could also be a disadvantage if their design also required a higher minimum cruise speed resulting in a possibly higher than desirable jump speeds. If the aircraft is required to fly multiple sorties, a faster aircraft is able to fly more sorties in a single day.

Using a direct route to the drop zone (DZ) minimized flight time but allowed the defender a better chance to identify the possible objective before the aircraft arrived. The direct route could take the transports through heavily defended areas increasing the chance of losses to enemy anti-aircraft fire.

Routes can be developed that threaten multiple possible objectives and avoid heavily defended areas, but the price is usually more flight time. That gives the enemy additional time to direct fighters against the transports before they reach the drop zone.

2 A sortie is one aircraft flying one mission. An aircraft can fly multiple sorties in a single day.

Likewise the further the objective is located behind enemy lines, the more time the enemy has to detect and counter the operation before the paratroopers arrive at the drop zone. One counter to this is to delay the enemy's ability to detect the aircraft. This was usually attempted by routing the transports over areas with less enemy observation, flying below the radar coverage, and/or to fly at night. The airborne assault prior to D-Day had the Allied transports flying at night below 150 meters in altitude to avoid radar detection as long as possible, then climb to the jump altitude of between 150 to 250 meters as the aircraft approached the DZ.

Finding the designated drop zone was a challenge in itself. The pilot or the aircraft flight navigator had to successfully direct the transports to their designated DZs. Each country was a little different in how these important individuals were provided and trained. Italy provided a dedicated *osservatori aerei per paracadutisti* (aerial navigator for parachute operations) to direct the fight of each group of aircraft. This individual was in addition to the regular aircraft flight crew. Along with mastering the normal tools of in-flight navigation, he was trained in terrain recognition, meteorology, and parachute operations. He would guide his group of aircraft to their drop zone and then determine the actual line-of-flight for the drop based on the weather to successfully drop the paratroopers so they would land on the DZ.

Planners tried to select easily spotted landmarks along the routes for the pilots and *osservatori* to use to navigate to the correct location. The Italians did not develop any electronic systems during the war to guide the pilots and they never adopted the use of pathfinders to mark the DZ prior to the arrival of the main force. It could be difficult to identify the DZ during daylight, and at night it could be (and often was) a nightmare. Every parachute operation during the war saw a degree of missed drop zones, in some cases spreading the actual parachute drops up to a distance of 40 kilometers from the correct location.

Drop Zone: Success or Failure

When examining historical airborne operations, what happened at the drop zone was causal to success or failure. While the senior leaders were envisioning battalions and regiments maneuvering off of the drop zone and into combat, paratroopers of all nations understood that the actual fighting would be done by LGOPS (Little Groups of Paratroopers). Read any detailed history of airborne operations and it will be a story of LGOPS either overcoming or succumbing to the odds. One must remember that for the most part the dispersion of the units was predetermined by several factors before a single paratrooper exited his aircraft as detailed below.

In the case of the *paracadutisti* each aircraft had a *direttori di lancio* (jump master) on board. His duties began before the *paracadutisti* boarded the aircraft, ensuring that the men and their equipment were correctly prepared and ready for the jump. He then ensured that the aircraft was correctly loaded and the *paracadutisti* ready for the flight. When informed by the *osservatori aerei per paracadutisti*, he prepared the interior of the aircraft and the *paracadutisti* for the actual jump, static lines connected and supply containers readied. Once the signal to jump was given, he could adjust the actual timing of the jumps to a limited degree based on his actual observation of the DZ and the other aircraft in the group. If the *paracadutisti* were jumping out of a SM.82 using both doors, he controlled the timing by alternating the exit of the parachutists on each side to avoid collisions under the aircraft. Usually the jump master would remain in the aircraft during training but would jump with the unit in combat.

The load plan for each aircraft is an important decision affecting the events on the DZ. It is ideal that each aircraft carried a complete unit which can then drop together on the DZ. The challenge is that aircraft capacity and unit size do not often match, requiring compromise on how the units are assigned and loaded onto each aircraft. One does not want a unit to land in two different locations and their ammunition landing in a third location. Thought must also be given to the possible loss of aircraft prior to reaching the DZ, leading to the consideration of splitting important assets over several aircraft. In the end, the decision must address how best to manage the risk to ensure that combat capable units land on the DZ given the many factors that can impact the plan.

Modern terms (US) for aircraft load are "chalk" and "stick". A chalk is everything (men and equipment) carried by one aircraft. A stick is a group of paratroopers that will exit a single door during a single pass over the DZ. It was unusual during the war that an aircraft would not drop everything during one pass over the DZ, hence Italy only used aircraft numbers (chalks) to designate aircraft loads as there was no difference between a chalk and a stick. Occasionally the paratroopers and supply containers were dropped separately in two passes, mainly due to the small size of a DZ. Often a supply container was positioned at the jump door and was the first item dropped, followed by the parachutists, then by any additional containers. The Italian aircraft, having been designed with bomb bays, could drop supply containers without loading them in the troop carrying space. Normal practice for the *paracadutisti* was to drop the containers first, followed by the *paracadutisti* during the same pass.

Once approaching the (hopefully) correct drop zone, multiple factors impacted whether the paratroopers would land on the DZ in a compact, ready to fight posture or scattered in the general area and needing time to orient themselves (where am I?), gather, collect equipment, and then execute their mission.

Formation flying during a drop was at a premium. If using a three-aircraft wedge with wedges in trail (a series of wedges one behind the other) the ability to maintain the correct relative position, distance and altitude was important for the safe delivery of the paratroopers. A loose formation will spread the jumpers over a wider area. The wrong altitude could have transports flying into paratroopers already floating down under their canopies. Too tight and the aircraft turbulence can create hazardous conditions for the jumpers.

Gauging the wind was a critical task for the *osservatori* and the *direttori di lancio*. Drifting once the parachutes open can cause the jumpers to miss the DZ if the aircraft line-of-flight was not adjusted to account for the wind. The aircraft needed to fly upwind of the DZ by a calculated distance based on wind speed so the *paracadutisti* would drift towards and onto the DZ.

Time now becomes a factor during the actual drop. Time has both a horizontal and vertical impact on the success or failure of the jump. The horizontal factor is the speed of the aircraft and the wind speed. Both will act to string-out and scatter the paratroops while they are in the air. The impact of aircraft speed is modified by the number of paratroopers carried and the rate they can exit the aircraft. Most armies trained to achieve a paratrooper exiting the jump door no slower than one man a second. The Fallschirmjäger trained to exit 13 jumpers in seven-seconds from a JU 52. The *paracadutisti* trained for eight jumpers to exit in 4.5 seconds from a SM.81/82. At an aircraft speed of 150 kph, the paratroopers will land 20.5 meters apart given no other variables. A 13-man German chalk will be dispersed over 266 meters on the ground, while a 28-man Italian chalk will be dispersed over 285 meters if using both doors on the SM.82. That does not include the distance of any supply containers if not simultaneously dropped. A slower aircraft speed will reduce the spread of the jumpers, but increase the aircraft's vulnerability to defensive ground fire.

The drop altitude adds a vertical time component. The higher the drop altitude, the longer it takes the jumpers to reach the ground. This in turn determines the amount of time that the wind can affect the fall of the parachutist and induce scatter. A lower altitude increased the chance of the paratroopers landing in the drop zone and reduced (but not eliminate) the effect of any wind. A parachute with a descent rate of 5 m/s takes 50 seconds to reach the ground from an altitude of 250 meters Above Ground Level (AGL).[3] A three m/s cross-wind will move the parachute 150 meters horizontally in that same amount of time. As wind speed and direction are not consistent over time, there could be considerable differences in its effect on individual paratroopers.

It was this factor of jump altitude where the differences between the types of parachutes was important. The Italian and German designs allowed for lower jump altitudes minimizing time aloft and improving the chances to land successfully on the DZ. The Italian D.40 could be safely jumped from 70 meters AGL, and the IF41/SP was used at altitudes of 90–100 meters AGL.[4] Full canopy inflation was normally achieved in the first 30 meters of the jump. The American T-5 parachute was also a fast opening parachute with the reputation that the shock of the opening could render the jumper unconscious. American airborne troops carried a reserve parachute that required a higher jump altitude in order for it to be useful. For these and various other reasons, the Allies normally jumped at altitudes between 150–250 meters (the planned D-Day drop height was 214 meters/700 feet). An Allied paratrooper was in the air an average of 15 seconds longer than his Italian or German counterpart.

Tests conducted by the German Fallschirm-Lehr Bataillon (parachute instruction battalion) during the war illustrate the impact of using a higher jump altitude. A

3 AGL is the actual distance the aircraft is flying above the ground at that location. This is different from aircraft altitude which is the distance the aircraft is flying above sea level.

4 Anon., 'Italian Parachute Artillery Equipment' *Tactical and Technical Trends*, n.18, 11 February 1943. The parachute training for *Operazione «C3»* was conducted at 90–100 m AGL.

chalk of 13 fallschirmjäger jumping at 100 meters AGL with an aircraft speed of 150 kph resulted in a spread of about 275 meters long and 90 meters wide. The same unit jumping at 200 meters covered an area of 820 meters long and 180 meters wide. During the same tests, jumping from as low as 60 meters resulted in 20 percent greater number of injuries.[5]

Once on the ground, the paratroopers must get out of their harnesses and organize. Here the Allied harness design was better as it was fitted with a single quick-release system. The Italian harness on the IF41/SP was a little slower to remove as it had two quick release buckles. The German RZ-16 system was poor, with multiple regular style buckles to unfasten, but the RZ-20 developed in 1940 did use a quick-release.

The German and Italian parachute design is often faulted due to their suspension line/riser connection to a waist belt rather than to the shoulders, preventing them from being steered while in the air. The reality was that none of the World War 2 troop parachutes could be steered. While one could 'climb the risers' on the Allied parachute harnesses, this had little effect on the direction of travel.[6] Without canopies designed to provide forward drive, the parachutist was carried by the wind. Even if such canopies were used, the altitudes employed for mass tactical jumps did not allow time for any practical effect. Jumping at night meant the parachutist had nothing to orient upon to steer the parachute in a desired direction. The sky was already crowded during mass parachute jumps and steering likely would only add to collisions.

It has been often cited that the Italian and German parachutes which used a forward roll were more dangerous for landing than other types. While possibly true to a point, this is mainly anecdotal and the degree to which one was safer has never been studied. Once the IF41/SP parachutes were adopted by the Italian parachute schools at Tarquinia and Viterbo, there did not appear to be a significant difference in the injury rate when compared to the American parachute school.[7] The actual terrain of the DZ, the weather at the time of the paratroop drop, and the accuracy of the drop likely had a greater causal effect for injuries than the difference in the chutes and harnesses.

While it was true that the Germans and Italians initially parachuted with only pistols and collected their rifles from supply containers, this was a safety concern and not a limitation of their equipment. The American paratroopers that jumped during

5 Hellmuth Reinhardt, ed., *Airborne Operations A German Appraisal,* Washington D.C., CMH Pub 104-13, 1951), p.50.

6 A paratrooper could grab one riser and attempt to climb up it like a rope.This would pull that side of the canopy down, spilling air from the opposite side to create thrust. Without a canopy designed to create the forward thrust when level, the best this did was to rotate the jumper in the air but did little to change the direction of fall. A parachutist could not grab the risers when using the Italian or German parachutes as the risers were behind him.

7 The US Army injury rate in 1940–41 was 2.7 percent. See JJ. Knapik 'United States Military Parachute Injuries. Part 1: Early Airborne History and Secular Trends in Injury Incidence'. J Spec Oper Med. 2019 Fall;19(3):110-115. doi: 10.55460/Z8WL-VMS6. PMID: 31539444., abstract. The Italian rate was below 3 percent.

Torch and subsequent parachute operations in North Africa also jumped with only their pistols for the same reason.[8] There has been debate on whether some fallschirmjäger units actually jumped with their weapons on Crete. The Italians understood by the end of 1940 that the battlefield had changed and were parachuting with their rifles and submachine guns in 1941 with no change to the parachute system itself.[9] Heavy weapons and additional supplies still required the use of resupply containers, so the need to find and collect these containers was a limitation affecting all armies.

Parachutes verses Gliders

Gliders had many advantages over parachutes when delivering combat-ready units to a location. These advantages are evident when one recognizes that helicopters have replaced gliders in the post-1945 period. They delivered complete combat ready units to a landing zone (LZ). The soldiers were not scattered by the weather, not encumbered by parachutes after they landed, and had all their heavy weapons and other supplies with them. As they are flown, gliders can deliver their men with a higher degree of accuracy to a LZ than transports can accurately drop parachutists on a DZ. Gliders were quiet and because they were released kilometers away from their LZs, there was not any engine noise to alert or alarm the enemy which better enabled surprise. It was for these advantages that gliders were used against Fort Eben-Emael and Gran Sasso as previously stated. Gliders were planned for use against key locations on Malta as part of *Operazione «C3»* but these needed to be supplied by Germany.

After the DZ

Once the airborne units are on the ground and moving off the DZ, the battle is now a conventional fight. The enemy will fight using the means and methods they would normally have available. For the airborne force, fire support must come from the air as parachute units lack any means of delivering massed fires. They are also fighting under significant logistical restraints as their supplies and munitions are limited to what they initially carried and what their air assets can deliver. The battle becomes a race between friendly ground forces trying to achieve a link-up or maneuvering the enemy away from the paratroopers, or the enemy overwhelming the paratroopers before assistance arrives.

8 Timothy M. Clauss, *The U.S. Army Airborne Division, 1942 To 1945 Concept, Combat, And Evolution* (Fort Leavenworth, Kansas: US Army Command and General Staff College Master's Thesis, 2011), pp.17–18, 22–23

9 Alberto Bettica, Report to the S.M.R.E. dated 22 January 1941, *Attività e Lavori presso la Scuola Paracadutisti*, found in Antonello Biagini, and Fernando Frattolillo, (eds), *Diario Storico del Comando Supremo* (Rome: USSME, 1989), vol. 3, book 2, pp.136–142.

Appendix XI

Transport Aircraft, Weapons and Parachutes

Transport aircraft[1]

Caproni Ca.133
Mainly used for training.
Maximum speed: 230 km/h (140 mph, 120 kn)
Cruise speed: 200 km/h (120 mph, 110 kn)
Range: 1,350 km (840 mi, 730 nmi)
Service ceiling: 5,500 m (18,000 ft)
Capacity – 8 paratroopers and 2 resupply canisters OR 12 soldiers

Caproni Ca.148/P
Modification for paratroop training.
Max. speed 241 km/h at 3900 m (150 mph, 130 kn)
Cruising speed 200 km/h (124 mph, 107 kn)
Range 900 km,
Service ceiling 3900 m
Capacity – 16 paratroops and 4 resupply conisters

Savoia-Marchetti SM.81 T Pipistrello
Transport configuration of the S.81 bomber.
Maximum speed: 340 km/h (210 mph, 180 kn) at 4,000 m (13,123 ft)
Cruise speed: 260 km/h (160 mph, 140 kn)
Parachute drop speed – 180 kph (112 kn)
Range: 1,500 km (930 mi, 810 nmi)
Service ceiling: 7,000 m (23,000 ft)
Capacity – 12 paratroops and 2 resupply canisters OR 18 soldiers

1 Aircraft capacities are from AUSSME collection of various transport calculations by *generale* Frattini and the «*Folgore*» staff February–July 1942, M7 racc.430, cart.2.

Savoia-Marchetti SM.82/P Marsupiale
Version of the SM.82 fitted out for parachute operations.
Maximum speed: 347 km/h (216 mph, 187 kn)
Cruise speed: 250 km/h (160 mph, 130 kn) at 3,000 m (9,843 ft)
Parachute drop speed – 180 kph (112 kn)
Range: 2,100 km (1,300 mi, 1,100 nmi)
Service ceiling: 6,000 m (20,000 ft)
Capacity – 28 paratroopers and 6 resupply canisters OR 35 soldiers

Savoia-Marchetti SM.82/T Marsupiale
Standard SM.82 for transport.
Maximum speed: 347 km/h (216 mph, 187 kn)
Cruise speed: 250 km/h (160 mph, 130 kn) at 3,000 m (9,843 ft)
Parachute drop speed – 180 kph (112 kn)
Range: 2,100 km (1,300 mi, 1,100 nmi)
Service ceiling: 6,000 m (20,000 ft)
Capacity – 35 soldiers

Fiat G.12/P
Version of the G.12 fitted out for parachute operations
Maximum speed: 390 km/h (240 mph, 210 kn) at 5,000 m (16,404 ft)
Cruise speed: 303 km/h (188 mph, 164 kn) [6]
Parachute drop speed – 180 kph (112 kn)
Range: 2,300 km (1,400 mi, 1,200 nmi)
Service ceiling: 8,500 m (27,900 ft)
Capacity – 24 paratroopers and 6 resupply canisters OR 30 soldiers

Fiat G.12/T
Standard transport version.
Maximum speed: 390 km/h (240 mph, 210 kn) at 5,000 m (16,404 ft)
Cruise speed: 303 km/h (188 mph, 164 kn) [6]
Range: 2,300 km (1,400 mi, 1,200 nmi)
Service ceiling: 8,500 m (27,900 ft)
Capacity – 30 soldiers

SM.74, SM.75, SM.85 Civilian transports
Not equipped for parachute operations.
Capacity – 20 soldiers

Weapons

Combat knife

Pugnale da combattimento (fighting knife) in the WW2 Italian military were a mark of elite units that specialized in close assault/combat. *Arditi*, *guastatori*, *sciatori*, and *paracadutisti* were among the type of units authorized to carry these knives as part of the uniform. The knife issued to the *paracadutisti* was the *pugnale per paracadutisti e assaltatore M1939.*

Semi-Automatic Pistols & Revolvers

The Beretta M1934 semi-automatic pistol was slowly replacing the Bodero 1889 revolver in the R.E. There is no information indicating that any Bodero pistols were issued/used by the *paracadutisti.*

Beretta modello 1934

A simple, reliable, and well-made firearm, the Beretta M34 was a popular pistol during the war. Criticism of the weapon focused on the 9 mm corto (380 APC) ammunition, believing it to be underpowered for a military hand gun. The 7-round magazine was also singled out, forgetting that the American Colt M1911 and the German Walther P38 and Luger P.08 also used a 7 or 8-round magazine. Its compact size and light weight made it a good weapon for the *paracadutisti.*

Cartridge – 9mm corto (short)/380 APC
Action – Semi-automatic Blowback
Muzzle velocity – 229 m/s (750 ft/s)
Feed System – Magazine, 7 rounds
Sights – fixed front blade/rear notch

Rifles and Submachine Guns

The original intent was that the *paracadutisti* were to be armed with the Armaguerra mod.39 semi-automatic rifle. Until the Armaguerra was available, the moschetto per cavalleria M38 was issued. Its short length, light weight, and ease of use made it a decent weapon for the airborne units. Attempts to replace the moschetto with the Beretta submachine were limited until 1943.

Carcano M1891 Moschetto da Cavalleria (Cavalry Carbine)
Cartridge – 6.5x52 Carcano
Action – manual bolt
Muzzle velocity – 700 m/s (2,300 ft/s)
Feed System – Mannlicher feed clip, 6 rounds
Sights – fixed front blade/rear notch
Bayonet – folding-fixed spike

Carcano M1891TS Moschetto per Truppe Speciali (Special Troop Carbine)
Cartridge – 6.5x52mm Carcano
Action – manual bolt
Muzzle velocity – 700 m/s (2,300 ft/s)
Feed System – Mannlicher feed clip, 6 rounds
Sights – fixed front blade/rear notch
Bayonet – Detachable M91 knife bayonet

Moschetto Automatica Beretta (MAB) 1938A
Considered one of the best submachine guns during the war, versions of the MAB would continue in service until the 1980s. Like the Beretta M34 pistol, the MAB was simple, reliable, and well-made firearm. The MAB 38A was only available to the *paracadutisti* in small numbers until 1943.

Cartridge – 9x19mm Luger
Action – automatic and semi-automatic blowback, open bolt.
Rate of fire – 600 rpm
Muzzle velocity – 420 m/s (1,378 ft/s)
Feed System – Detachable staggered box, 10, 20, and 40 rounds.
Sights – fixed front blade/adjustable rear notch
Bayonet – No (early versions had a bayonet, but those were only issued to the P.A.I.

Grenades
Italian grenades were exclusively designed as an offensive type of grenade. These grenades used concussion more than fragmentation to incapacitate the enemy. This lighter design, along with a percussion detonator rather than a time fuse, made these grenades less reliable and effective than the heavier type of defensive grenades used by other countries. Painted red, they were widely known as Red Devils.

Società Romana Costruzioni Meccaniche (S.R.C.M.) Modello 35 Grenade
Type – Offensive fragmentation
Weight – 240 gr (8.5 ounces)
Explosive – 36 gr of TNT.
Trigger – Percussion

Odero Terni Orlando (O.T.O.) Modello 35 Grenade
Type – Offensive fragmentation
Weight – 150 gr (5.3 ounces)
Explosive – 43 gr of TNT.
Trigger – Percussion

Breda Modello 35 Grenade
Type – Offensive fragmentation

Weight – 200 gr (7 ounces)
Explosive – 63 gr of TNT.
Trigger – Percussion

Passaglia or P Grenade
A field-made grenade using ration tins and engineer explosives to provide an anti-tank capability to the Italian infantry. Its weight made it difficult to throw any great distance and employment usually required the user to be quite close to the target.

Type – Anti-Tank
Weight – varied
Explosive – 1kg or 2 kg TNT or Romite.
Trigger – OTO M35 Grenade

Flame Throwers
Lanciafiamme Spalleggiato (Backpack) Modello 41
Rate of fire – 20-25 seconds
Range – 20 m

Lanciafiamme Modello 41 d'assalto
Rate of fire – 3-5 seconds
Range – 20 m

Machine guns
Fucile Mitragliatore Breda modello 30
The Breda 30 fucile mitragliatore (rifle machine gun) was the authorized squad machine-gun for all the various units in the Italian military. There is no denying that the Breda 30 possessed several features that impacted its usefulness in combat compared to similar weapons, but it was a serviceable weapon that fulfilled its intended role. No research of the impact of the Breda 30 on the effectiveness of the R.E. units has been undertaken, especially to establish the causality of success and failure against the totality of the Italian tactical combat system.[2] The Breda 30 was used in all active Italian theaters and many of the problems recorded were also documented for similar weapons of other nations.

Cartridge – 6.5x52mm Carcano
Action – closed-bolt, short recoil automatic
Rate of Fire – 150 rpm practical
Muzzle velocity – 620 m/s (2,000 ft/s)

2 A comprehensive examination of the military's weapons, communications, training, organization, leadership, and doctrine to obtain tactical battlefield success.

Range – 2,800 m (3,100 yd)
Feed System – Fixed 20 magazine, 20 round reload stripper clip
Sights – fixed front blade/adjustable rear notch

Mitragliatrice Breda calibro 8 modello 37

Unlike the Breda 30, the Breda 37 earn a positive reputation during the war as an effective machine gun. Its lower rate of fire and heavier 8 mm round were seen as advantageous. Its feed system is considered complex but proved to be reliable.

Cartridge – 8x59mm BR Breda
Action – open-bolt, gas automatic
Rate of Fire – 200 rpm practical
Muzzle velocity – 800 m/s (2,600 ft/s)
Range – 5,400 m (5,900 yd)
Feed System – 20 round feed strips
Sights – fixed front blade/adjustable rear notch

Mortars

Brixia Model 35

Round – Fragmentation 465 gr (1 lb)
Action – Breech loaded, trigger fired. 15 round ignition cartridge magazine
Rate of fire – 8-10 rpm
Muzzle velocity – 83 m/s (270 ft/s)
Max range – 530 m (580 yd)

Mortaio da 81 Mod. 35

Round – Heavy HE or smoke bomb 6.8 kg (15 lb), Light HE round 3.2 kg (7 lb. 1 oz)
Action – Breech loaded, trigger fired. 15 round ignition cartridge magazine
Rate of fire – 8-10 rpm
Muzzle velocity – 83 m/s (270 ft/s)
Max range – Heavy round 1.5 km (.92 mi), Light round 4 km (2.5 mi)

Anti-tank weapons

Note: Obtaining accurate data on the effectiveness of Italian anti-tank weapons (range/penetration) is difficult. The information provided here is taken from multiple sources and those sources don't often agree.

Model 35 antitank rifle

Polish anti-tank rifle that was purchased by Italy from Germany. Relied on spalling instead of penetration to obtain a vehicle kill. Marginal effectiveness in 1939, ineffective by 1941.

Cartridge – 7.92x107mm DS
Action – manual bolt
Muzzle velocity – 1,275 m/s (4,180 ft/s)
Range/penetration – 100 m (110 yd) 33 mm of armor, 300 m (330 yd), 15mm of armor
Feed System – Detachable box 4 rounds
Sight – Fixed front blade/rear notch

Fucile controcarro S da 20mm
Issued to the Nembo in 1943 to improve its anti-armor capability as a regular infantry unit, there isn't a source that states this weapon would be air-dropped during airborne operations.

Cartridge – 20x138mmB (Solothurn Long)
Action – Semi-automatic recoil
Muzzle velocity – 850 m/s (2,800 ft/s)
Range; penetration – Max 1,500 m; 100 m/0° 38 mm; 400 m/15° – 20 mm of armor, 500 m/0° – 30mm of armor
Feed System – Detachable box 5 rounds
Sight – Telescopic

Cannone-Mitragliera da 20/65
The 20/65 c.a. was developed as light dual anti-aircraft/anti-tank gun of the Regio Esercito. Considered heavier than most of its contemporaries, it was considered a good weapon and captured guns were used by the British. It was widely authorized throughout the R.E. in both towed and truck-mount versions.

Cartridge – 20x138mmB
Action – Gas automatic
Rate of fire – 240 rpm
Muzzle velocity – 840 m/s (2,800 ft/s)
Range – 5.5 km (3.4 mi)
Feed System – 12 round feed strip
Sight – Telescopic

Cannone da 47/32 mod. 1935
The 47/32 mod. 1935 was adopted by the R.E. to replace the 65/17 gun in all the regimental *compagnia armi d'accompagnamento* as the standard infantry support weapon. Mainly designed as an anti-tank gun, the 47/32 also had a useful HE round. While competitive in 1940 against tanks, by 1942 it was unable to penetrate the frontal armour of many main battle tank. Man-portable and simple to conceal, it could be air-dropped by parachute or transported by aircraft. It could be disassemble into five loads for animal transport. It remained the standard artillery piece of the *divisione paracadutisti* throughout the war.

Round – 47x195R HE, 47x227R APHE
Action – Semi-automatic breech
Rate of fire – 7-8 rpm
Muzzle velocity – HE 250 m/s; AP 630 m/s (2,800 ft/s)
Range; penetration – Max 7 km; 100 m/0° 64mm; 650 m/30° 40 mm; 1,600 m/30° – 30 mm
Sight – Telescopic

To improve performance, the Italians developed the *effetto pronto* (E.P.) anti-tank round for the 47/32 in late 1941. This was a HEAT-type of munition that was widely available by the summer of 1942. Problems with the base fuzing often meant the round performed more as a HESH ammunition. The round did improve the effectiveness of the 47/32, but not enough to make it a first class anti-tank weapon.

E.P. range; penetration – 100 m/0° – 112 mm.

Cannone da 65/17 modello 13
Developed right before the beginning of the First World War as a mountain gun, it was replaced by the 75/13 mod. 15 in the 1920s in all the *divisione alpina*. Finding new service as an infantry support gun, it replaced the older 37F used during the earlier war. Planned to be replaced by the 47/32 mod. 35, production was never able to completely removed the 65/17 for service. It gained a new life as an anti-gun, mostly due to its larger caliber. It was only effective in that role at close range due to low muzzle velocity.

Round – 65x172 HE
Action – Interrupted screw breech
Rate of fire – 7-8 rpm
Muzzle velocity – HE 348 m/s; AP 345 m/s (1,130 ft/s)
Range/penetration – Max 6.8 km; 100 m/0° 37 mm.
Sight – Telescopic

Like the 47/32 c.c., the 65/17 was also issued an E.P. anti-tank round in 1942. This provided better penetration, but still required the gun to be fired at close range.

E.P. range; penetration – 100 m/0° – 120 mm.

Parachutes[3]

There are two common misconceptions about the Italian and German parachutes. The first is that Allied parachutes could be steered and the Italian/German parachutes could not. The reality is that neither the Allied or Axis parachutes could be steered. Without a built-in forward drive in the canopy, all the WW2 parachutes would only go to where the winds took them.[4]

The second misconception is that parachutists using Italian or German parachutes couldn't jump with weapons. The reality was that jumping with weapons was seen as a general safety issue (less equipment on the body meant less chance of injury) by all nations. Once the tactical conditions required that parachutists jumping with issue weapons (Crete is viewed as the tipping point), the Italians and Germans began jumping with weapons with no changes to their equipment.[5]

Salvator D.37.[6]
Canopy – 45 sq/m (57 sq/yd), 16 suspension lines
Weight – 8 kg
Rate of decent – 6 m/s (19.5 ft/s)
Deployment – Pack tray/pilot chute
Activation – Static line and manual
Notes – Only one leg and shoulder strap. Risers attached to the back of the waist belt.

Salvator D.39.[7]
Canopy – 45 sq/m (sq/yd), 16 suspension lines
Weight – 12 kg
Rate of decent – 6 m/s (19.5 ft/s)
Deployment – Pack tray/pilot chute
Activation – Static line and manual
Notes – Two leg and shoulder straps. Risers attached to the back of the waist belt.

3 Guy Richards, *World War II Troop Type Parachutes: Axis,* (Atglen, Pennsylvania: Schiffer Military History, 2000); Anon., *Addestramento e impiego dei reparti paracadutisti* (Rome, Ministero dell'Aeronautica, 1939).

4 Air from a descending parachute normally escapes the canopy through the apex vent which also helps stabilize the canopy. Forward drive is created by openings in the rear of the canopy that directed some of the escaping air and creates horizontal thrust. Without a thrust vector great enough to counter-act the air current, a parachute is like a free balloon and can't be steered.

5 The Italians had already identified the need to jump with weapons in late 1940. They only awaited the new IF41/SP parachute to being testing and training.

6 Anon., *Descrizione ed istruzioni per l'impiego del paracadute "Salvator D 30" e Salvator D 37* (Rome: Ministero dell'Aeronautica, 1936)

7 Anon., *Descrizione ed istruzioni per l'impiego del paracadute "Salvator D 39"* (Rome: Ministero dell'Aeronautica, 1939);

Salvator D.40
Canopy – 54 sq/m (54 sq/yd), 16 suspension lines
Weight – 12 kg
Rate of decent – 6 m/s (19.5 ft/s)
Deployment – Pack tray/pilot chute
Activation – Static line and manual
Notes – Improved harness from the D.39. Risers attached to the shoulders.

Imbracatura da Fanteria 41/Scuola Paracadutisti (IF41/SP)
Canopy – 59 sq/m (70 sq/yd), 18 suspension lines
Weight – 9.95 kg
Rate of decent – 5 m/s (16.5 ft/s)
Deployment – Deployment bag
Activation – Static line
Notes – Improved harness from the D.40. Risers attached to the back of the waist belt.

Appendix XII

Servizi Aerei Speciali (S.A.S.) Regia Aeronautica Transport Units

Organization[1]

The basic aircraft unit employed by the Regia Aeronautica transport formations was the *squadriglia* (squadron). Each squadriglia consisted of three *sezioni* (sections) of three aircraft each for a total of nine aircraft.

Squadriglie were normally organized into *gruppi* (groups) with each *gruppo* consisting of two *squadriglie* for a total of 18 aircraft.

Gruppi could be organized into a *stormo*. A *stormo* normally consisted of one type of aircraft. Each *stormo* could consist of two or three gruppi. Transport *stormi* were normally organized in two *gruppi* (36 aircraft) plus four additional aircraft to support *stormo* operations (supply, transport spare parts, move personnel, etc.).

A *gruppo* or *squadriglia* could be *autonomo* (independent). These were generally assigned to a theater command and the number of aircraft could vary based on the theater requirements. By 1943 all *gruppi* were assigned to a *stormo* and the *gruppi autonomi* were eliminated.

The reality was different in many cases. The initial *squadriglie* were formed in 1940 using existing civilian transports from the national airlines. The airlines possessed a small number of a mixed of aircraft types that limited the size of these first units. Production of new transport types such as the SM.82 could not keep up with the expanding requirement for transports and the operation losses of airframes. The transfer of bomber aircraft such as the SM.81 from frontline combat units to transport formations helped, but never fully satisfied the demand for transports. Transport *squadriglie* were normally short of aircraft and maintenance further reduced the number of aircraft available for operations.

1 Nino Arena, *La Regia Aeronautica* vol 1 (Rome: USSMA, 1981), pp.95–107; Chris Dunning, *Courage Alone: The Italian Air Force 1940-1943* (London: Hikoki Publication Ltd.,1998), pp.13-14.

Transport Units

The Regia Aeronautica operated two transport commands. The *Servizi Aerei Speciali* (Special Air Service, S.A.S.) was the military command responsible for supporting the transport requirements of the three services (Army, Navy, and Air Force). The other command was the *Nuclei Comunicazione Aerei* (Aerial Communication Detachments, N.C.A.) responsible for operating and maintaining the civilian transportation system. The N.C.A. operated the three Italian civilian airlines, Ala Littoria, Aviolinee Italiane, and Linee Aeree Transcontinental Italiane (LATI) during the war. Whilst some of the airlines' aircraft were mobilized to form the first S.A.S. units, they retained a number of aircraft to continue many of their peacetime commercial routes. As their aircraft became worn out or loss through combat or accidents, military production was used to maintain the N.C.A. operating strength. N.C.A. crews and aircraft did occasionally augmented the S.A.S. operations as needed.

The following is a list of the transport units operated by the S.A.S. during the war. The type and number of aircraft is based on the date they were formed. As more and newer aircraft became available, the composition of the *squadriglie* often changed. Several *squadriglie* were subsequently disbanded during the war and their aircraft transferred to other *squadriglie* to bring those up to strength.

Note that this information is incomplete and does not fully captured the many changes during the war. The sources used (Arena's four volume history and Dunning's *Courage Alone*) are not consistent in their presentation of information on the transport units.

Squadriglia				
47ª	Jul 1941	SM.82	4	Formed from a bomber unit
48ª	Jul 1941	SM.82	4	Formed from a bomber unit
222ª	Nov 1941	SM.81	6	Formed from a bomber unit
223ª	Nov 1941	SM.81	6	Formed from a bomber unit
224ª	Oct 1941	SM.81	?	
225ª	Oct 1941	SM.81	?	
245ª	Sep 1941	SM.81	?	Formed to support units in Russia
246ª	Nov 1941	SM.81	6	Formed to support units in Russia
247ª	May 1942	SM.75	4	Formed to support units in Russia
248ª	Apr 1943	P108T	1-3 (sources vary)	
600ª	Sep 1940	Ca.133S	3	
		SM.81S	2	
		Ca.309	1	
601ª	Jun 1940	SM.75	4	
602ª	Jun 1940	SM.75	4	
603ª	Jun 1940	SM.75	5	

604ª	Jun 1940	SM.74	6	
605ª	Jun 1940	SM.73	8	
606ª	Jun 1940	SM.73	5	
607ª	Jun 1940	SM.82	4	
608ª	Jun 1940	SM.82	4	
609ª	Jun 1940	SM.82	4	
610ª	Jun 1940	SM.75	8	
611ª	Jun 1940	Ba.44	5	
615ª	Jun 1940	SM.83	8	
616ª	Jun 1940	SM.74	3	Jul 40 Disbanded and aircraft transferred to *604ª Squadriglia*
617ª	Mar 1942	SM.82	4	
618ª	Mar 1942	SM.82	4	

Gruppi
37º Gruppo T – Formed July 1941 from a bomber unit with 47ª and 48ª Squadriglie.
56º Gruppo T – Formed November 1941 from a bomber unit with 222ª and 223ª Squadriglie
144º Gruppo T – Formed March 1942 with 617ª and 618ª Squadriglie.
145º Gruppo T – Formed June 1940 with 604ª and 610ª Squadriglie.
146º Gruppo T – Formed March 1941 with 603ª Squadriglia from 147º Gruppo and 609ª Squadriglia from 149º Gruppo.
147º Gruppo T – Formed June 1940 with 601ª, 602ª and, 603ª Squadriglie.
148º Gruppo T – Formed June 1940 with 605ª and 606ª Squadriglie.
149º Gruppo T – Formed June 1940 with 607ª, 608ª and, 609ª Squadriglie.
245ª, 246ª, 247ª, and 248ª squadriglia were autonomo.

Stormi
18º Stormo T
39º Stormo T
44º Stormo T
45º Stormo T
48º Stormo T

Strength

June 1940
145º Gruppo T Base Bengasi (604ª, 610ª): 11 SM.75.
147º Gruppo T Base Napoli/Capodichino (601ª, 602ª, 603ª): 13 SM.75.
148º Gruppo T Base Littoria (605ª, 606ª): 13 SM.73.
149º Gruppo T Vase Catania (607ª, 608ª, 609ª): 12 SM.82.

615ª Squadriglia T Autonomo Base Guidonia: 8 SM.83.
616ª Squadriglia T Autonomo Base Rome/Littorio: 1 SM.79, and 3 SM.74.

December 1940
145º Gruppo T (604ª, 610ª) Base Bengasi: 11 SM.75.
147º Gruppo T (601ª, 602ª, 603ª) Base Napoli/Capodichino: 13 SM.75.
148º Gruppo T (Autonomo) Base Ciampino (605ª and 606ª): 16 SM.73
149º Gruppo T (Autonomo) Base Rome/Urbe (607ª, 608ª, and 609ª): 12 SM.82 and 2 SM.83
615ª Squadriglia T (Autonomo) Base Guidonia: 8 SM.83.

December 1941
18º Stormo T – Base Castelvetrano.
- 56º Gruppo T (222ª, 223ª): 8 SM.82
- 57º Gruppo T (224ª, 225ª): 22 SM.81.
- 245ª Squadriglia – Base Krivoi Rog: 6 SM.81
- 246ª Squadriglia – Base Stalino: 6 SM.81
37 Gruppo BT (47ª, 48ª) Base Viterbo: 10 SM.82.
145º Gruppo T (604ª and 610ª) Base Bengasi: 10 SM.82 and 3 SM.75.
146º Gruppo T (603ª and 609ª) Base Castelvetrano: 21 SM.82.
147º Gruppo T (Autonomo) Base Ciampino (601ª and 602ª) : 17 SM.82.
148º Gruppo T (Autonomo) Base Ciampino (605ª and 606ª): 7 SM.82 and 4 G.12 T.
149º Gruppo T (607ª and 608ª): 15 SM.82.
616ª Squadriglia T (Autonomo) Base Guidonia: 8 SM.83.

At the end of December, the R.A. had 120 SM.82 aircraft on hand (both transport and bomber types) and had lost and additional 27 SM.82 due to combat or accidents. The R.A. had begun to transfer the 165 remaining SM81 aircraft from bomber units and then reconfigured them as transports. This conversion work was supplemented by new construction of SM.81T.[2]

December 1942[3]
18º Stormo T. Base Orvieto Italy
- 56º Gruppo T (222ª, 223ª): 18 SM.82 and 26 SM.81
- 245ª Sqd. Autonomo (Russia): 12 SM.81
- 246ª Sqd. Autonomo. (Russia):10 SM.81
- 247ª Sqd. Autonomo (Russia): 8 SM.73

2 Nino Arena, *La Regia Aeronautica* vol 2 (Rome: USSMA, 1982), p.537.
3 Nino Arena, *La Regia Aeronautica* vol 3 (Rome: USSMA, 1984), pp.597–599.

44º Stormo T. Base: Rome/Littorio
- 146ª Gruppo T. (603ª, 609ª): 16 SM.82
- 149º Gruppo T. (607ª, 608ª): 16 SM.82

45º Stormo T. Base Rome/Campino Sud
- 37º Gruppo T. (47ª, 48ª): 16 SM.82
- 147º Gruppo T. (601ª, 602ª): 16 SM.82 and 3 G.12

48º Stormo T. Base Rome/South Centocelle
- 144º Gruppo T. (forming 617ª, 618ª): 8 SM.82
- 148º Gruppo T. (605ª, 606ª): 16 G.12/T

145º Group Aut. T. (600ª, 604ª, 610ª) Base Castel Benito/Tripoli: 14 SM.82, 4 SM.81, and 6 Ca.133.

Autonomo Section T. Base Rome/Littorio, then Casale Marcigliana: 8 SM.82 and 4 SM.75

Complementary Group T. Base Rome/Littorio then Casale Marcigliana: 14 SM.82, 4 SM.81, and 2 SM.75.

August 1943
18º Stormo T. Bases Orvieto, Viterbo, Foligno
- 56º Gruppo T (222ª, 223ª): 1 SM.73, 5 SM.75, 6 SM.82
- 57º Gruppo T (224ª, 225ª): 1 SM.73, 10 SM.82

44º Stormo T. Bases Ferrara, Rimini, Poggia Renatico
- 146ª Gruppo T. (603ª, 609ª): 19 SM.82
- 149º Gruppo T. (607ª, 608ª): 20 SM.82, 1 SM.75

45º Stormo T. Bases Rome/Littorio, Tarquinia, Foligno
- 37º Gruppo T. (47ª, 48ª): 16 SM.82[4]
- 147º Gruppo T. (601ª, 602ª): 41 SM.82

48º Stormo T. Bases Jesi, Fano
- 144º Gruppo T. (610ª, 618ª): 25 SM.82
- 145º Gruppo (605ª, 606ª): 9 SM.82, 2 SM.81, and 5 Ca.133S.
- 148º Gruppo T. (604ª, 617ª): 28 G.12/T

4 Arena, *La Regia Aeronautica* vol 4 (Rome: USSMA, 1989), p.590 lists the 37º Gruppo. Dunning, *Courage*, p.67 is unsure, while it is omitted on p.195.

Autonomo Section T. Base Guidonia.[5]
Complementary Group T. Bases Rome/Littorio, Casale Marcigliana, Rimini.[6]

Production of Transport Aircraft[7]

1940:
Ca.133T – 0 ordered, 0 delivered.
SM.75 – 32 ordered, 32 delivered.
SM.81T – 27 ordered, 15 delivered.
SM.82T – 70 ordered, delivered.

1941
Ca.133T – 6 ordered, 6 delivered.
Ca.148P – 0 ordered, 2 delivered.
G.12T – 61 ordered, 24 delivered.
SM.75 – 12 ordered, 16 delivered.
SM.81T – 70 ordered, 15 delivered.
SM.82T – 80 ordered, 162 delivered.

1942
Ca.133T – 20 ordered, 20 delivered.
Ca.148P – ordered, 2 delivered.
G.12T – 30 ordered, 24 delivered.
P.108T – 12 ordered, 2 delivered.
SM.75 – 14 ordered, 16 delivered.
SM.81T – 70 ordered, 15 delivered.
SM.82T – 160 ordered, 162 delivered.

1943
Ca.133T – 18 ordered, 14 delivered.
Ca.148P – 100 ordered, 16 delivered.

5 Arena, *La Regia Aeronautica* vol 4 (Rome: USSMA, 1989), p.590. No strength information was found.
6 Arena, *La Regia Aeronautica* vol 4 (Rome: USSMA, 1989), p.590. No strength information was found.
7 Numbers taken from Arena, *La Regia Aeronautica* 4 volumes (Rome: USSMA, 1981–1989), Dunning, *Courage Alone*; Emily Brotzu and Gherardo Cosolo, *Dimensione Cielo, Aerei Italiani nella 2ª Guerra Mondiale Trasporto 7* (Rome: Edizioni Bizzarri, 1975); *Dimensione Cielo, Aerei Italiani nella 2ª Guerra Mondiale Trasporto 8* (Rome: Edizioni Bizzarri, 1975); *Dimensione Cielo, Aerei Italiani nella 2ª Guerra Mondiale Trasporto 9* (Rome: Edizioni Bizzarri, 1976).

G.12T – 36 ordered, 22 delivered.
P.108T – 15 ordered, 5 delivered.
SM.75 – 30 ordered, 21 delivered.
SM.81T – 80 ordered, 26 delivered.
SM.82T – 310 ordered, 154 delivered.

Bibliography

AWM — Australian War Memorial
FAA — French Army Archives
HAGS — Hellenic Army General Staff
NARA — National Archives and Records Administration (United States)
TNA — The National Archives (Kew UK)
USSMA — Ufficio Storico Stato Maggiore Aeronautica
USMM — Ufficio Storico della Marina Militare
USSME — Ufficio Storico Stato Maggiore dell'Esercito

Archival Sources

AUSSME, F-4: Studi, Carteggio, Circolari dell'Ufficio Ordinamento e Mobilitazione
AUSSME, H 1: Ministero Guerra – Gabinetto
AUSSME, I 3: Carteggio Versato dallo Stato Maggiore Difesa
AUSSME, I 4: Carteggio Stato Maggiore Generale – Comando Supremo – Stato maggiore Difesa
AUSSME, L 14: Carteggio Sussidiario S.M.R.E.
AUSSME, M 3: Documenti IT
AUSSME, M 7: Cicolari Vari Uffici
AUSSME Consiglio dell'esercito, 8 maggio 1939 I: Nuovo ordinamento dell'esercito e principali provvedimenti nel campo organico, pp.5-7. Rep F-9 racc. 6/f.3
AUSMM Governor Generale della Libia, Comando Superiore Forze Armata Africa Settentrionale, Esercitazione anno XVI in libra (XI-XXIV maggio 1938) (Cartelle Numerate b.2726/f.2)
AWM, War Diary of the 19 Australian Infantry Brigade – January 1941, AWM52 8/2/19/3
AWM, War Diary of the 2/4 Australian Infantry Battalion – January 1941, AWM52 8/3/4/7
AWM, War Diary of the 2/8 Australian Infantry Battalion – January 1941, AWM52 8/3/8/6
AWM, War Diary of the 2/11 Australian Infantry Battalion – January 1941, AWM52 8/3/11/7

AWM, War Diary 6 Australian Division Cavalry Regiment – January 1941, AWM52 2/2/7/10

AWM, War Diary 6 Australian Division Cavalry Regiment February-March 1941, AWM52 2/2/7/11

NARA, Record Group 242 National Archives Collection of Foreign Records Seized, 1675–1958, T821 Collection of Italian Military Records

TNA Operations – 4th Ind. Div. 18 Nov. 41 – 28 Feb. 42, WO221/559

TNA Secret War Diary of the 5th Indian Brigade – May–December 1941, WO169/3342 PAIF Box 15

TNA War Diary The Central Indian Horse, March–December 1941, WO169/3409

TNA War Diary 3rd South African Armored Reconnaissance Battalion, WD Box 384

TNA War Diary of the 3-1 Punjab 41, WO169-3423

TNA War Diary 1/6 Rajputana Rifles I.A., Dec. 1941, WO169/3432

TNA War Diary 4/6 Rajputana Rifles I.A., Dec. 1941, WO 169/3434

TNA War Diary 4/16 Punjab I.A., 18-20 Dec. 1941,WO169-3344

TNA Numerous British War diaries cited in the text.

Primary Sources

Anon., *Addestramento e impiego dei reparti paracadutisti* (Rome: Ministero dell'Aeronautica, 1939)

Anon., *L'addestramento tattico dei minori reparti di fanteria* (Rome: Ispettorato dell'Arma di fanteria, 1937)

Albertazzi, Amleto, *Esercitazioni Tattiche 1942-XX fanteria – Camicie Nere – unità paracadutisti – celere – corazzata* (Bologna: Soc. An. Poligrafici il Resto del Carlino, 1942-XX)

Badoglio, Pietro, *Italy in the Second World War* (Westport: Greenwood Press, 1976)

Battistelli, Pier Paolo, *Mussolini's Army at War* (Milan: Agrafe, 2021)

Bedeschi, Giulio, *Fronte d'Africa: c'ero anch'io* (Milan: Mursia, 1979)

Bertucci, Aldo, *Guerre segrete oltre le linee* (Milan: Gruppo Ugo Mursia Editore S.p.A., 1995)

Biagini, Antonello and Frattolillo, Fernando (eds.), *Diario Storico del Comando Supremo* (Rome: USSME, 1984-2002) 9 vols

Biagini, Antonello and Mazzaccara, Carlo (eds.), *Verbali delle riunioni tenute dal Capo di SM Generale,* (Rome: USSME, 1984) vol. 1

Biagini, Antonello and Frattolillo, Fernando (eds), *Verbali delle riunioni tenute dal Capo di SM Generale,* (Rome: USSME, 1983-1985), vol 2-4.

Buttazzoni, Nino, *Solo per la Bandiera: I nuotatori Paracadutisti della Marina* (Milan: Gruppo Mursia Editore S.p.A., 2002)

Caccia-Dominioni, Paolo, *Alamein 1933-1962 An Italian Story* (London: George Allen & Unwin Ltd., 1966)

Caccia-Dominioni, Paolo, *Takfir cronaca dell'ultima battaglia di Alamein* (Milan: Mursia, 2001)
G.H.Q. Middle East Force, *Brief Notes on the Italian Army August 1942* (Military Library Research Service Ltd., 2006)
Anon, Circolare n.32000, *Impiego delle divisione paracadutisti ed aviotrasportabili* (Rome: Stato Maggiore Regio Esercito, 1942)
Anon., *Descrizione ed istruzioni per l'impiego del paracadute "Salvator D 30" e Salvator D 37* (Rome: Ministero dell'Aeronautica, 1936)
Anon., *Descrizione ed istruzioni per l'impiego del paracadute "Salvator D 39"* (Rome: Ministero dell'Aeronautica, 1939)
Anon., *Manuale di Regolamenti per i corso allievi ufficiali di complemento* (Rome: Comando di Stato Maggiore, 1940)
Anon. *Manuale per l'ufficiale frequentatore dell'I.S. di G. booklet IV Servizio di Stato Maggiore*
(Istituto Superiore di Guerra, 1935)
Iezzi, ten. col. Emilio, *V° battaglione Carri M.13/40 costituito il 5-11-1940* (Associazione Nazionale Carristi d'Italia, no date)
Marini, Eligio, *Un indifferente e la guerra* (San Silvestro: Tipolitografia SIGRAF, 1995)
Messe, Giovanni, *La I° armata italiana in Tunisia* (Rome: USSME, 1950)
Messe, Giovanni, *La guerra al fronte russo* (Rome: Rizzoli Editore, 1947)
Magliavacca, Renato, 'Gli artiglieri della «Folgore» nel combattimento di Naqb Raga (Alamein) 24 ottobre 1942', *Memorie storiche-militare 1979* (Rome: USSME, 1980)
Naldi, Adolfo, *I servizi della fanteria* (Rome: Istituto Poligrafico dello Stato, 1931)
Anon., *Norme sull'addestramento formale e tattico dei minori reparti paracadutisti* (Comando 184ª div. ftr. "Nembo",)
Anon, *Nozioni armi, tiro, e materiali vari* (Rome: Stato Maggiore Regio Esercito, September 1942)
Anon, *Nozioni di organica per i corsi allievi ufficiali di complemento* (Rome: Stato Maggiore Regio Esercito, July 1942), Parts I & II
Anon, *Organizzazione e impiego tattico dei reparti paracadutisti* (Rome: Ministero di Guerra Stato Maggiore Regio Esercito, 1940)
Anon, *Il IV battaglione controcarro autocarro Granatieri di Sardegna in Africa settentrionale (dicembre 1941 maggio 1943) «Diario di Guerra»* (Rome: Comando Brigata Granatieri di Sardegna Museo Storico, 1991)
Reinhardt, Hellmuth ed., *Airborne Operations A German Appraisal* Washington D.C., CMH Pub 104-13, 1951)
Santoro, Giuseppe, *L'aeronautica italiana nella seconda guerra mondiale* (Rome: Edizioni ESSE di A. Silvestri, 1957)
Sogno, Vittorio, *Il XXX corpo d'Armata italiano in Tunisia* (Rome: USSME, 1952)
Anon., *La Squadra della fanteria* (Parma: Scuola di Applicazione di Fanteria, 1943)
Trovero, Battista G., *Ritorna a el Alamein* (Milan: Mursia, 1999)

US Military Intelligence Service, *Handbook on the Italian Armed Forces 2 August 1943* (Nashville, Battery Press, 2004)
US War Department *TM 30-259 Military Dictionary English-Italian Italian English* (Washington DC, 1943.

Secondary Sources

Agarossi, Elena, *A Nation Collapses* (Cambridge: Cambridge University Press, 2000)
Alcidi, Edger, *Fallschirmj*äger Brigade Racke in North Africa 1942-*1943* (Atglen, Pennsylvania: Schiffer Military History, 2000)
Ales, Stefano & Crociani, Piero & Viotti, Andrea, *Struttura, uniformi, distintivi, ed insegne delle truppe libiche 1912-1943* (Rome: USSME, 2012)
Arena, Nino, *50ª di Tarquinia, 1939-1989, Scuole Militare paracadutismo* (Comitato Promotore ex Istruttori delle Scuole Militari di Paracadutismo, 1989)
Arena, Nino, *Aquile senza Ali: I paracadutisti italiani nella seconda guerra mondiale* (Milan: Mursia 1970)
Arena, Nino, *FOLGORE Storia del paracadutismo militare italiano* (Rome: Centro Editoriale Nazione, 1965)
Arena, Nino, *I Fanti dell'Aria da Castel Benito ad Azizia (libia) (1938-1941)* (Bologna : Edition Eurographis, 1989)
Arena, Nino, *Nembo!* (Rome: IBN Editore, 2013)
Arena, Nino, *I PARACADUTISTI Cinquant'anni di storia, cronaca e immagini del paracadutisti italiano* (Modena: Società Tipografica Editrice Modenese Mucchi, 1972)
Arena, Nino, *La Regia Aeronautica* (Rome: USSMA, 1981-1986) 4 vols
Arena, Nino, *R.S.I., Forze Armate della Repubblica Sociale, la guerra in Italia 1943* (Parma: Ermanno Albertelli Editore, 1999)
Arendell, Russ & Balducci, Luca & Leser, Jeff *Italy at War: Uniforms, Weapons, Photographs, Equipment & Ephemera* (Arditi Books, 2014)
Arendell, Russ & Wooddrum, Steve, *Italy's Battle Rifle The Story of the Mannlicher-Carcano Series of Rifles*, (Arditi Press, 2012)
Atkinson, Rick, *An Army at Dawn* (New York: Henry Holt and Company LLC, 2002)
Ball, Simon, *The Bitter Sea* (London: Harper Press, 2009)
Bragadin, Marc' Antonio, *The Italian Navy in World War II* (Annapolis: US Naval Institute, 1957)
Bharucha, P.C., *The North African Campaign 1940–43* (Delhi: Ministry of Defence Government of India, 2012)
Brotzu, Emilio and Cosolo, Gherardo, *Dimensione Cielo, Aerei Italiani nella 2ª Guerra Mondiale Trasporto 7* (Rome: Edizioni Bizzarri, 1975)
Brotzu, Emilio and Cosolo, Gherardo, *Dimensione Cielo, Aerei Italiani nella 2ª Guerra Mondiale Trasporto 8* (Rome: Edizioni Bizzarri, 1975)

Brotzu, Emilio and Cosolo, Gherardo, *Dimensione Cielo, Aerei Italiani nella 2ª Guerra Mondiale Trasporto 9* (Rome: Edizioni Bizzarri, 1976)

Busch, Erich, *Die Fallschirmjäger Chronik 1935–1945* (Dorheim: Podzun-Pallas Verlag, 1982)

Cannistraro, Philip V. (ed.), *Historical Dictionary of Fascist Italy* (Westport: Greenwood Press, 1982)

Cappellano, Filippo *Le artiglierie del Regio Esercito nella seconda guerra mondiale* (Parma: Alberti Edizione Speciali s.r.l., 1998)

Cappellano, Filippo and Pignato, Nicola *Gli autoveicoli da combattimento dell'Esercito Italiano* (Rome: USSME, 2002) volume secondo

Carrier, Richard, *Mussolini's Army against Greece October 1940-April 1941* (New York: Routledge, 2021)

Campbell, David, *Soviet Airborne Forces, 1930-91* (Oxford: Osprey Publishing, 2020)

Cernuschi, Enrico, *Malta 1940-1943 La storia inconfessabile* (Vicenza: Edibus, 2016)

Ceva, Lucio *La condotta italiana della guerra Cavallero e il Comando Supremo 1941/1942* (Milan: Feltrinelli, 1973)

Chaplin, Howard D., *The Queen's Own Royal West Kent Regiment, 1920-1950* (London: Michael Joseph, 1954)

Chiusano, Amedeo and Saporiti, Maurizio, *Immagini della Seconda Guerra Mondiale – Le Alpi Occidentali* (Rome: USSME, 1995)

Civoli, Massimo, *S.A.S. I Servizi Aerei Speciali della Regia Aeronautica 1940-1943* (Cavallermaggiore: Gribaudo, 2000)

Cocchia, Aldo (ed.), *La difesa del traffico con Africa settentrionale* vols VI-VII (Rome: USMM, 1958–1964).

Corvisier-de Villèle, Marie-Anne, *Inventaire des Archives de la Guerre, série p 1940-1946*, (Château de Vincennes : Ministère de la Défense, 1998), tome II Grandes Unités

Crociani, Piero and Battistelli, Pier, *Italian Army Elite Units & Special Forces 1940-43* (Oxford: Osprey, 2011)

Crociani, Piero and Battistelli, Pier, *Italian Blackshirts 1940-45* (Oxford: Osprey, 2010)

Crociani, Piero and Battistelli, Pier, *Italian Navy & Air Force Elite Units & Special Forces 1940-45* (Oxford: Osprey, 2013)

Cursi, Enrico, *I Leoni del Deserto* (Rome: edizioni Chillemi, 2014)

Cursi, Enrico, *Carabinieri Paracadutisti 1940-1946* (Rome: edizioni Chillemi, 2020)

Dancy, Peter and Vajda, Fernec A., *German Aircraft Industry and Production 1933-45* (Bath : SAE International, 1998)

Davis, Melton S. *Who Defends Rome?* (London: George Allen & Unwin Ltd., 1972)

De Franceschi, Costantino (ed) *Le operazioni dell unità italiane al fronte russo (1941–1943)* (Rome: USSME, 1977)

Dell'Uomo, Franco and Puletti, Rodolfo *L'Esercito Italiano verso il 2000 — I corpo disciolti*, (Rome: USSME, 1998) vol 1

Dell'Uomo, Franco and Rosa, Roberto di *L'Esercito Italiano verso il 2000 — I corpo disciolti*, (Rome: USSME, 2001) vol 2

Di Giovanni, Marco, *I paracadutisti italiani Volontari, miti e memoria della seconda guerra mondiale* (Gorizia: Editrice Goriziana, 1991)

Di Martino, Massimo, *Paracadutisti d'Italia – Uniformi distintivi equipaggiamenti 1938–1969*, (Milan: Edizioni Libreria Militare, 2019)

Dunning, Chris, *Courage Alone The Italian Air Force 1940-1943* (London: Hikoki Publication Ltd.,1998)

Fabbri, Manuela, 'Un paracadutista: Luigi Fabbri' in *Studi Storico-Militare 2008* (Rome: USSME, 2010)

Ferrara, Arnoldo, *I carabinieri dell'Aria* (Rome: Ente Editoriale per l'Arma dei Carabinieri, 1983)

Ferrari, Dorello, 'Il piano segreto di Balbo', *Studi Storica-Militari 1984* (Rome: USSME, 1985)

Fioravanzo, Giuseppe, *L'Organizzazione della Marina Durante il Conflitto*, vol. XXI, book 1 (Rome: USMM, 1972)

Gabriele, Mariano, 'L'Operazione C3 (1942)', in A. Biagini and R.H. Rainero (eds) *L'Italia in Guerra: il terzo anno – 1942* part 2 (Rome: Stabilimento Grafico Militare GAETA, 1993)

Gabriele, Mariano, *Operazione C3: Malta* (Rome: USMM, 1990)

Galasso, Mario and Gaticci, Mario *La Radio in Grigio-verde* (Faenza: Edizioni a cura della C&C, 1992)

Gallinari, Vincenzo, *Le operazioni del giugno 1940 sulle alpi occidentali* (Rome: USSME, 1981)

Giorleo, Aldo *Palestra Azzurra L'aeronautica militare e il paracadutismo cronistoria dalle origini ad oggi* (Rome: USSMA, 1975)

Girlando, Rafaele, *I Paracadutisti Libici* (Foggia: Italia Editrice new di Giancarlo Arcano, 2006)

Golla, Karl-Heinz, *The German Fallschirmtruppe 1939–41* (Solihull: Association of the United States Army and Helion & Company, 2013)

Gooch, John, *Mussolini and His Generals* (New York: Cambridge University Press, 2007)

Gooch, John, *Mussolini's War* (London: Allen Lane 2020)

Green, Jack and Massignani, Alessandro *The Naval War in the Mediterranean 1940-1943* (London, Chatham Publishing, 1998)

Anon, *I gruppi combattimento* (Rome: USSME, 1951)

Isserson, Georgii, tr. by Brice Menning, *The Evolution of Operational Art* (Fort Leavenworth, Kansas: Combat Studies Institute Press, 2013)

Jowett, Philip *The Italian Army 1940–45 (1) Europe 1940–43* (Oxford: Osprey, 2000)

Jowett, Philip *The Italian Army 1940–45 (2) Africa 1940–43* (Oxford: Osprey, 2001)

Jowett, Philip *The Italian Army 1940–45 (3) Italy 1943–45* (Oxford: Osprey, 2001)

Knox, Macgregor, *Hitler's Italian Allies Royal Armed Forces, Fascist Regime and the War of 1940-1943* (Cambridge: Cambridge University Press, 2000)

Knox, Macgregor, 'The Italian Armed Forces, 1940-43' in Allan R. Millett and Williamson Murray (eds), *Military Effectiveness* vol III (Boston, Massachusetts: Allen & Unwin, 1988)

Knox, Macgregor, *Mussolini Unleashed 1939-1941* (New York, Cambridge University Press, 1982)

Latimer, John, *Operation Compass 1940* (London: Praeger, 2004)

Long, Gavin, *To Benghazi* (Canberra: Australian War Memorial, 1961)

Longo, Luigi Emilio, *La campagna italo-etiopica (1935-1936)* (Rome: USSME, 2005)

Longo, Luigi Emilio, *Immagini della Seconda Guerra Mondiale – La campagna di Tunisia* (Rome: USSME, 2007)

Longo, Luigi Emilio, *Immagini della Seconda Guerra Mondiale – La campagna italo-greca* (Rome: USSME, 2001)

Longo, Luigi Emilio, *I «reparti speciali» italiani nella seconda guerra mondiale* (Milan: Mursia 1991)

Longo, Luigi Emilio, 'La sopravvivenza occulta in un plotone di carabinieri *paracadutisti* in una zona occupate dal nemico (Africa settentrionale, dicembre 1941-febbraio 1942)', in *Studi storico-militare 1991* (Rome: USSME, 1993)

Lundari, Giuseppe, *I paracadutisti italiani 1937/45* (Milan: Editrice Militare Italiana di Ivo Fossati, 1989)

Manzari, Giulliano and Pagano, Marina, *La Regina Marina nelle Isole Ionie aprile 1941-settembre 1943* (Rome: SMDUS, 2020)

Maughan, Barton, *Tobruk and El Alamein* (Canberra: Australian War Memorial, 1966)

Malcolm, A.D. *History of the Argyll and Sutherland Highlanders: 8th Battalion* (London: Thomas Nelson and Sons Ltd., 1949)

Anon, *I mezzi d'assalto* (Rome: USMM, 2001)

Mencarelli, Igino, *Prospero Freri, Apostolo del paracadutismo italiano* (Rome: Ufficio Storico Aeronautica Militare, 1971)

Migliavacca, Renato, *Cannoni nel Deserto* (Milan: Auriga, 2012)

Minniti, Fortunato, 'Gli obiettivi di guerra nella pianificazione operativa (1938-1939)', in A. Biagini and R.H. Rainero (eds) *L'Italia in Guerra: il primo anno – 1940* (Rome: Publisher Unknown, 1991)

Molony, C.J.C., *The Mediterranean and Middle East* (London: HMSO, 1973) vol 5

Montanari, Mario, *La campagna di Grecia* (Rome: USSME, 1980) 3 vol.

Montanari, Mario, *L'esercito italiano alla vigilia della 2ª guerra mondiale,* (Rome: USSME, 1982)

Montanari, Mario, *Le operazioni in Africa settentrionale* (Rome: USSME, 1985), vol I, Sid el Barrani

Montanari, Mario, *Le operazioni in Africa settentrionale* (Rome: USSME, 1985), vol II: Tobruk

Montanari, Mario, *Le operazioni in Africa settentrionale* (Rome: USSME, 1989), vol III: El Alamein

Montanari, Mario, *Le operazioni in Africa settentrionale* (Rome: USSME,1993), vol IV: Enfidaville

Morisi, Paolo, *The Italian Folgore Parachute Division* (Solihull: Helion & Company, 2016)

Nicholson, G.W., *The Canadians in Italy 1943-1945* (Ottawa: Edmond Cloutier, 1956)

Norton, Frazer D., *Official History of New Zealand in the Second World War 1939–45*, 26 Battalion (Dunedin: Historical Publications Branch, 1952)

Pariset, Dante, *Storica del paracadutismo* (Rome-Milan: Vito Bianco Editore, 1962)

Playfair, I.S.O., *The Mediterranean and Middle East* (London: HMSO, 1954-1968) vol 1-4

Anon, *L'Esercito e i suoi corpo – Sintesi storica* (Rome: USSME, 1971) vol 1

Puletti, Rodolfo (ed) *L'Esercito e i suoi corpo – Sintesi storica* (Rome: USSME, 1973) vol 2

Prekatsounakis, Yannis, *Crete The Battle of Heraklion 1941* (Solihull, Helion & Company, 2016)

Quarrie, Bruce *German Airborne Divisions: Mediterranean Theatre 1942-45* (Oxford: Osprey, 2005)

Rainero, Romani H., *I reparti arabi e indiani dell'esercito italiano nella Seconda Guerra Mondiale ("Le Frecce Rosse")* (Rome: USSME, 2007)

Remmelink, Willem (ed.) *The Invasion of the Dutch East Indies* (Leiden: University Press, 2015)

Remmelink, Willem (ed.) *The Operations of the Navy in the Dutch East Indies and the Bay of Bengal* (Leiden: University Press, 2018)

Ricco, Ralph and Afiero Massimiliano, *'Luck Was Lacking, But Valor Was Not'* (Solihull: Helion & Company, 2021)

Richards, Guy, *World War II Troop Type Parachutes: Allies* (Atglen, Pennsylvania: Schiffer Military History, 2003)

Richards, Guy, *World War II Troop Type Parachutes: Axis* (Atglen, Pennsylvania: Schiffer Military History, 2000)

Rovighi, Alberto and Stefani, Filippo, *La partecipazione italiana alla guerra civile spagnola (1936-1939)* (Rome: USSME, 1992)

Sadkovich, James J., *The Italian Navy in World War II* (Westport, Connecticut: Greenwood Press, 1994)

Santoni, Alberto, *Le operazioni in Sicilia e in Calabria* (Rome: USSME, 1983)

Scala, Edoardo, *Storia delle Fanteria Italiane* (Rome: USSME, 2020) vol. XIV

Stefani, Filippo, *La Storia della Dottrina e degli Ordinamenti dell'Esercito Italiano* vol II (Rome: USSME, 1895)

Stevens, W.G., *Bardia to Enfidaville* (Wellington: Historical Publications Branch, 1962)

Sullivan, Brian R., 'The Italian Armed Forces, 1918-40' in Allan R. Millett and Williamson Murray (eds.), *Military Effectiveness,* vol III (Boston, Allen & Unwin, 1988)

Sweet, John J.T., *Iron Arm: The Mechanization of Mussolini's Army 1920-1940* (Westport, Connecticut: Greenwood Press, 1980)
Torsiello, Mario, *Le operazioni delle unità italiane nel settembre-ottobre 1943* (Rome: USSME, 1975)
Anon, *In Africa settentrionale: La preparazione al conflitto l'avanzata su Sidi Barrani* (Rome: USSME, 1955)
Anon, *La prima offensiva britannica in Africa settentrionale (ottobre 1940–febbraio 1941)* (Rome: USSME, 1964)
Anon, *La prima controffensiva italo-tedesca in Africa settentrionale* (15 febbraio–19 novembre 1941) (Rome: USSME, 1974)
Anon., *Seconda offensiva Britannica in Africa settentrionale e ripiegamento italo-tedesco nella Sirtica orientale (18 novembre 1941–17 gennaio 1942)* (Rome: USSME, 1949)
Anon, *Seconda offensiva italo-tedesca in Africa settentrionale da el Agheila a el Alamein (gennaio–settembre 1942)* (Rome: USSME, 1951)
Anon, *Terza offensiva Britannica in Africa settentrionale La battaglia di El Alamein e il ripiegamento in Tunisia (6 settembre 1942–4 febbraio 1943)* (Rome: USSME, 1961)
Anon, *L'esercito italiano tra la 1ª e la 2ª guerra mondiale* (Rome: USSME, 1954)
Walker, Ronald, *Alam Halfa and El Alamein* (Wellington: Historical Publications Branch, 1967)
Vilhermosa, Gilberto, *Hitler's Paratrooper: The Life and Battles of Rudolf Witzig* (Barnsley, Frontline Books, 2010)
Viotti, Andrea, *Uniformi e distinctive dell'Esercito italiano nella seconda guerra mondiale 1940-1945* (Rome: USSME, 1988)

Journals

Andreski, Stanislav, 'Italian Military Efficiency: A Debate', *The Journal of Strategic Studies*, 5:2 (1982), pp.248-256
Biani, Vincenza, 'Operazioni aeree di sbarco', *Rivista Aeronautica*, XIII (1935), pp.1–6
Biffi, Giuseppe, 'Il parachute', *Rivista Aeronautica*, XII, 2 (1936), pp.153–162
Bordini, Gianni 'Sbarchi aerei', *Rivista Aeronautica*, XIII:4 (1937), pp.15–24
Braneschi, Francesco, '"Come Nembo di Tempesta" Storica ed analisi della divisione *paracadutisti* "NEMBO"', Dissertation, *Libera Università Internazionale degli Studi Sociali "Guido Carli"* (2016)
b.s.c., 'Aerorifornimenti', *Rivista Aeronautica*, XIII:7 (1937), pp.1–10
Burtt, John D. and Pastore, Davide, 'Planning for the Invasion of Malta, 1942', *World at War,* 16 (2011), pp.4–16
Caruana, Joseph, 'Le tre previste invasioni di Malta' part 1, *Storia Militare,* 244 (2014), pp.4–15
Caruana, Joseph, 'Le tre previste invasioni di Malta' part 2, *Storia Militare,* 245 (2014), pp.18–28

Cambosu, Sebastiano, 'Aerorifornimenti', Publisher Unknown (Milan, 1942), pp.976–981

Cappellano, Filippo and Formiconi, Paolo, 'Italo Balbo e le grandi manovre del 1938 in Libia', *Storia Militare*, 218 (2011), pp.4–16.

Anon, 'Le fanterie dell'aria', *Rivista Aeronautica*, XV:3 (1939), pp.380–385

Ceva, Lucio, 'Balbo e la preparazione della guerra in Africa Settentrionale', *Italia Contemporanea,* 243 (2006), pp.213–226.

Ceva, Lucio, 'The North African Campaign 1940-43: A Reconsideration', *The Journal of Strategic Studies*, vol 13 n.1 (1990).

Curami, Andrea and Rastelle, Achille, 'La Forza Navale Speciale',Storia Militare, n.3 dicembre 1993, pp.23–29; n.4 gennaio 1994, pp.29–38

Davies, Christis, 'Itala Sunt Imbelles', *The Journal of Strategic Studies*, 5:2 (1982), 266–269

DeVore, Marc, 'The Airborne Illusion: Institutions and the Evolution of Postwar Airborne Forces', (Cambridge, Massachusetts Institute of Technology Security Studies Program paper, 2004)

Di Martino, Basilio 'Balbo e le aviotruppe. L'esperimento di aviosbarco delle grandi manovre in Libia', *Rivista Aeronautica*, 6 (2013), pp.104–111

Di Martino, Basilio 'Il controllo a lungo raggio del deserto. Le esperienze italiane in Libia negli anni Trenta' *Antologia Militare* 1:4 (2020), pp.3–60

Ferrando, Pier G., 'I Fanti dell'aria', *Rivista militare*, 4/2008, pp. 122–127.

Freri, Prospero, 'Arditismo aereo', *Rivista Aeronautica*, XIII:7 (1937), pp.18–24

Freri, Prospero, 'Bilancio di salvataggi con paracadute', *Rivista Aeronautica*, XIV:1 (1938), pp.580–586

Gobbi, Luigi, 'Reparti Speciali d'Assalto', *Rivista Aeronautica*, XI:5 (1935), pp.284–286

Gooch, John, 'Italian Military Competence', *The Journal of Strategic Studies*, 5:2 (1982), 257–265

Lopasic, Alexander, 'Italian Military Performance in the Second World War: Some considerations', *The Journal of Strategic Studies*, 5:2 (1982), 270–275

Marcon, T. 'Testimonianze: Gambut, 17 dicembre 1940', *Storia Militare*, 51 (1997) pp.35–38

Migliavacca, Renato, 'Gli artiglieri della «Folgore» nel combattimento di Naqb Raga (Alamein) 24 ottobre 1942', *Memorie Storiche Militari 1979*, (1980), pp.273–292.

Sadkovich, James, 'Some Considerations Regarding Italian Armored Doctrine prior to June 1940', *Global War Studies*, 9:1 (2012), pp.40–74

Sadkovich, James, 'Understanding Defeat: Reappraising Italy's Role in World War II', *Journal of Contemporary History*, 24:1 (1989), pp.27–61

Anon, 'La Scuola di *paracadutisti* di Stendal', *Rivista Aeronautica*, XV:5 (1939), pp.335–337

Ségretain, Franck, 'October 1942: Qaret el Himeimat', *Qattara*, pp.8–18

Zurlo, Teodoro, 'Emergenza «E». Studi e Predisposizioni Militare alla Frontiera Giulia nel periodo Luglio-Ottobre 1940', *Memorie Storiche Militari 1979* (Rome: USSME, 1980), pp.369–426.

Electronic Sources

Anon., *30 aprile 1941 – La Folgore si lancia a Celefona' Congedati Folgore* <https://www.congedatifolgore.com/it/galleries/30-aprile-1941-la-folgore-si-lancia-a-cefalonia/>

Anon, 2nd Battle of El Alamein, 4th/8th Hussars, 23-29 October 1942, <https://www.qrhmuseum.com/2nd-battle-of-el-alamein-4th-8th-hussars-23-29-october-1942>

Anon., *Bataillon de Marche n°5',* Mémoire de la 1*ère DF* <https://1dfl.fr/category/les-unites/decouvrez-les-unites/les-bataillons-de-marche/bataillon-de-marche-n5/>

Bertozzi, Gianluca, 'Il piano di invasione di Malta del 1940: lo studio finale', *Ocean 4 Futures* (2011) <http://www.ocean4future.org/savetheocean/archives/48699>

Biermann, Andreas, 'The Crusader Project' <https://rommelsriposte.com/> accessed December 2022

Bjunior, *The June 1943 Italian Arditi attack on B24 US Bombers* <https://bjuniornew-blog.blogspot.com/2019/04/the-june1943-italian-arditi-attack-on_22.html>

Cattarossi, Emanuele, 'Delusione nel deserto' Dall'entrata in guerra (10-6-1940) alla vigilia del contrattacco inglese (9-12-1940)' Società di Cultura e Storia Militare (n.d.) <https://www.arsmilitaris.org/pubblicazioni/deserto.pdf>

Comando Supremo: Italy in WW2 <https://comandosuptemo.com>

Anon., 'I Bersaglieri ne la Seconda Guerra Mondiale <https://digilander.libero.it/lacorsainfinita/guerra2/42/67corazzato18reco.htm

Anon, *Infanterie-Einheiten der Luftwaffe* <https://www.lexikon-der-wehrmacht.de/Gliederungen/InfanterieLW.htm>

Leser, Jeffrey, *Divisional Organization Tipo Africa Settentrionale (A.S.)* <https://comandosupremo.com/tipo-africa-settentrionale/>, accessed 11 May 2022

Lexikon der Wehrmacht <https://www.lexikon-der-wehrmacht.de/>

Anon, *Lo sbarco italiano a Crete – Maggio 1941* <https://www.dodecaneso.org/content/lo-sbarco-italinao-a-crete-maggio-1941/>

Anon, *IL PAPA' DEI PARA': GIUSEPPE BAUDOIN* <https://digilander.libero.it/trombealvento/indicecuriosi/temerari2.htm>, accessed 10 Mar. 2021

The Perry-Castañeda Library (PCL) Map Collection <https://maps.lib.utexas.edu/maps/index.html>

Anon., *'Reggimento paracadutisti "Fanti dell"aria* <https://it.wikipedia.org/wiki/Reggimento_*paracadutisti*_%22Fanti_dell%27aria%22cite_ref-10>

Anon., *Settant'anni fa ci lanciavamo così: Le prime esperienze, gli errori, le vittime, i progressi del paracadutismo italiano, Castelbenito* <https://folgore.it/storia_e_tecnica/castelbenito.htm> accessed 10 Mar. 2021

Anon., *Settant'anni fa ci lanciavamo così: Scuola militare di Paracadutismo, Aeroporto di Tarquinia* <https://folgore.it/storia_e_tecnica/tarquinia.htm>

Anon., *Storia del paracadutismo Militare Italiano Sezione di Monza dell'Associazione nazionale paracadutisti d'Italia* (2019) <http://www.*paracadutisti*monza.it/storia-del-paracadutismo-militare-italiano/>

Tomaszewski, Maciej, *Libijscy spadochroniarze marszałka Italo Balbo, "Ascari del Cielo" Army 1914-1945* <https://army1914-1945.org.pl/wlochy2/bitwy-kampanie-dowodcy-italia/215-libijscy-spadochroniarze-marszalka-italo-balbo-ascari-del-cielo> accessed 2 Mar. 2021

Anon, 'The Middle East, Prelude to Alamein Alam El Halfa and Deir El Munassib', *The Queen's Royal Surrey Regiment The Regimental Association* <https://www.queensroyalsurreys.org.uk/ww2/middle_east/qme014.shtml>

Anon., 'La Regie Scuole Paracadutisti: Tarquinia e Viterbo', *Associazione Nazionale "Nembo"*, <http://www.nembo.info/Paracadutismo/le_regie_scuole.htm>

Anon., *30 aprile 1941 – La Folgore si lancia a Cefalonia' Congedati Folgore* <https://www.congedatifolgore.com/it/galleries/30-aprile-1941-la-folgore-si-lancia-a-cefalonia/>

Index

PEOPLE AND PLACES

MILITARY UNITS